Brigadoon of the Sixties

Revelry & Kerfuffles
at the Oregon Country Fair

Suzi Prozanski

Coincidental Communications, LLC
Eugene, Oregon

Brigadoon of the Sixties: Revelry & Kerfuffles at the Oregon Country Fair
Copyright © 2019 by Suzi Prozanski
All rights reserved

ISBN: 978-1-935516-08-8

Library of Congress Control Number: 2019905087

Published by
Coincidental Communications, LLC
P.O. Box 11511
Eugene, OR 97440

Book design by Niki Harris
Cover custom tie-dye design by
Maggie Quinlan of Maggie's Farm Tie Dye

Photo permissions: Many individual photographers generously shared their photographs for this project. Photo credits name the person who took a photo, or the person who shared it from their personal collection. Every effort was made to find the photographers of the photos found herein.

"Art, freedom, and creativity will change society faster than politics."
—Victor Pinchuk, Ukrainian businessman, philanthropist, and founder of the Future Generation Art Prize

"Written history is, in fact, nothing of the kind: It is the fragmentary record of the often inexplicable actions of innumerable bewildered human beings, set down and interpreted according to their own limitations by other human beings, equally bewildered."
—Cicely Veronica Wedgwood, English historian

Contents

	11	Preface
Introduction	15	Barry "Plunkr" Adams, the Rainbow Family, and the Beginnings of the Oregon Country Fair
Chapter 1	28	Tom Noddy and the W.C. Fields Memorial Stage
Chapter 2	39	Oregon Energy Horizons aka Energy Park
Chapter 3	47	The Flying Karamazov Brothers
Chapter 4	60	Starflower and Community Village
Chapter 5	72	A Wild Fair
Chapter 6	88	Anita Sweeten and Phoenix Rising
Chapter 7	97	A Fair Honeymoon for Bud and Jana Chase
Chapter 8	104	The Old Time New Age Chautauqua aka The New Old Time Chautauqua
Chapter 9	114	Jill Heiman and Freedom of Assembly
Chapter 10	123	Ibrahim Hamide and Casablanca Middle Eastern Cafe
Chapter 11	131	Celebration
Chapter 12	139	Folksinger Faith Petric
Chapter 13	147	The Second Decadenal Field Trip
Chapter 14	155	Robert DeSpain and Main Camp

Chapter 15	**167**	Who'll Stop the Rain?
Chapter 16	**175**	Leo de Flambeaux and Gypsy Caravan Stage
Chapter 17	**187**	Paul and Judy Fuller, Divine Balance Fruit Salad
Chapter 18	**198**	Archaeology Rocks
Chapter 19	**211**	Richard and Debbie Bloom, Obsidian Wind Chimes
Chapter 20	**223**	Alpha Farm and Community Village
Chapter 21	**235**	The Pride of Ownership
Chapter 22	**245**	Toby's Tofu Palace
Chapter 23	**253**	Silk-screen artist Diane McWhorter
Chapter 24	**261**	Happy Zones
Chapter 25	**271**	Jay Hogan and Risk of Change
Chapter 26	**285**	Consensus, Cooperation, and Community Village
Chapter 27	**302**	Stephen Cole aka Admiral Kohl of the Oregon Country Fair Navy
Chapter 28	**313**	Mark Miller and the University of Oregon Drug Information Center
Chapter 29	**322**	Option F: Psychospiritual Rejuvenation
Chapter 30	**335**	Royal Famille Du Caniveaux and Daredevil Vaudeville Palace Stage aka Du Caniveaux Vaudeville Palace Stage

Contents

Chapter 31	**347**	Troubled Waters
Chapter 32	**356**	Twentieth Anniversary Fair
Chapter 33	**371**	The Radar Angels
Chapter 34	**385**	Dahinda Meda and the VegManECs
Chapter 35	**395**	The Left Bank
Chapter 36	**406**	State of the Peach: Bruised
Chapter 37	**422**	Fair Family News
Chapter 38	**430**	Leslie Scott and the Fair's Neighbors
Chapter 39	**442**	Stage Left and the Fighting Instruments of Karma Marching Chamber Band/Orchestra
Chapter 40	**456**	The Line in the Sand
	470	Epilogue
	483	Fair Thee Well
	493	Notes & Sources
	529	Index

Preface

Welcome to my second venture into describing the indescribable Oregon Country Fair and its history. This book (*Brigadoon of the Sixties*) starts where the first book (*Fruit of the Sixties*) ended, in 1980. Together, these two volumes tell the story of the fair from its founding as a Renaissance Faire in 1969 through the mid-1990s. During that span, many Oregon Country Fair traditions took root.

Parents held the first fair in November 1969 as a fund-raiser for an alternative school. People enjoyed the gathering of kindred spirits at the first fairs so much that the event would take on a life of its own and continue for five more decades. Born amid the turbulence and strife of the 1960s cultural wars, the fair would provide for thousands a three-day positive affirmation of alternative values such as feisty fun, earth awareness, world peace, human kindness, group cooperation, and individual respect.

The first two fairs were held at different locations near Eugene, Oregon. Every fair since October 1970 has taken place on several hundred acres of wooded pastures and forested floodplains along the Long Tom River outside of Veneta, Oregon. The location was first rented for the October 1970 fair by Bill and Cindy Wooten, proprietors of the Odyssey Coffee House in Eugene, who coordinated the fair through the 1970s. The Wootens would help create a consensus-driven organization based on volunteer crews helmed by crew coordinators. That unique volunteer system would serve the fair well for many decades to come.

Dozens of those volunteer crews create a small village that pops up like a living Brigadoon. The original *Brigadoon* musical depicted a mystical Scottish village that protected its culture from the outside world by magically reappearing one day every hundred years. The Country Fair makes its cultural magic three days once a year.

The fair's sinuous pathways are lined by hundreds of rustic booths with artisans displaying their finest handmade crafts and cooks serving tasty delights. The paths lead to dozens of stages vibrant with live bands and unusual, original performances. The Oregon Country Fair in 2018 served up a raucous symphony of sights, sounds, and scents:

Cooks preparing salmon burgers, falafels, strawberry lemonade, and fresh-baked cookies. Pedestrian pathways overflowing with parades, mime art, eye-catching outfits, and spontaneous music. Artisans selling stained-glass mandalas, silkscreened prayer flags, handmade guitars, and tie-dye T-shirts. Workshops in Community Village offering open heart meditation, cannabis sustainable agriculture, and tools for the everyday activist; and classes in Energy Park teaching about solar design, wind power, and biodiesel vehicles. Signs along the way declaring: "Om Sweet Home," "Yes! Yes! Yes!" and "Thank You for Being Us."

From a small fund-raiser for a children's school, the fair would blossom into a raucous three-day arts and culture extravaganza that would give away thousands of dollars annually to other nonprofits. Across the decades, the fair would donate more than a million dollars to nonprofit charity and arts organizations in the surrounding neighborhoods of Veneta and Elmira as well as throughout Lane County, Oregon.

This second book differs from the first in that I personally witnessed some of the events described in the following pages. This is my insider's affectionate account of Country Fair history. Many of the people featured in these pages are friends who I've met through the fair. That makes this project a personal tribute to many everyday people I count as community heroes and fair treasures.

I first stepped on the Eight-shaped pathways of the Oregon Country Fair in 1984 after moving to Eugene from Houston, Texas. With the election of Ronald Reagan as U.S. President in 1981, the fair remained in 1984 firmly at odds with the mainstream culture, similar to when the fair was founded during the Nixon era in 1969. Reagan's war on drugs and saber-rattling international strategy contrasted vividly with the fair values favoring marijuana legalization and peaceful relations among peoples.

My first fair in 1984 opened my eyes to the number of people in my newly adopted community who shared my dreams and values. My husband, Floyd, and I returned for a second day that first year to catch the Flying Karamazov Brothers juggling at the Not-Chumleighland Stage. At the time, I wondered who in tarnation was this guy Chumleigh? And where did he go? Delightfully, this project has given me answers to those and many other questions.

Preface

Floyd and I would attend the fair as paying public for at least two days a year until 1990, when we were invited to help out with the booth of a friend, pottery artist Gil Harrison. Floyd and I have camped out overnight at the fair ever since. In 1991, he joined the fair's Info Crew and brought me along with a Significant Other Pass. In 1993, I also became an Info Crew volunteer where I learned much about the fair "on the job."

In 1997, Floyd would leave the Info Crew to join the fair's volunteer management team, which helped fair General Manager Leslie Scott. Floyd first was a trainee, and later became a Back Up Manager, or BUM. The nickname is intended to remind the BUMs of their true "place" at the fair: Nobody rises above anyone else; we're all in this together.

Before the days of cell phones, I would find myself sitting in Main Camp, where the BUMs would gather for meetings before and during the fair, waiting for another long meeting to end. As I sat out on the couches under the trees visiting with longtime Main Camp folks, I heard fabulous fair stories that captured my imagination. That sparked my desire to write a book on fair history.

In 2002, financial circumstances allowed me to quit my copy editing job at the daily newspaper in Eugene, the *Register-Guard*. I soon joined the *Fair Family News* Crew, giving me a creative outlet for editing and writing, and I began researching fair history by interviewing key people. Little did I realize then that fifteen years later, I would finally be completing a second book on the fair's long and quirky history while contemplating a third.

None of this would have been possible without the cooperation, advice, and help from hundreds of people who graciously agreed to be interviewed for this project. I am deeply grateful to everyone who shared their stories and photos and agreed to be quoted, and to everyone who shared old fair records so that I could learn more about the 1980s behind the scenes. What an amazingly eclectic group of people make up the fair! It has been quite an honor to get to know fair folks who contributed to this project. Thank you from the bottom of my heart.

Particular thanks go to Hal Hartzell, who interviewed dozens of people at the fair's History booth in 2004; and to the people who shared extensive collections of their old documents from the fair: Brian and Chris Bauske, Jana and Bud Chase, Robert DeSpain,

Marshall Landman via Chelsea Landman, Brian Livingston, Kathryn Madden, Tom Noddy, Palmer Parker, Ron Saylor, Wally Slocum via Rebecca Bradvica, Indi Stern, and Janet Tarver.

A few folks who helped me put this project into book form deserve particular praise: my editor, Mike Thoele; layout artist Niki Harris, proofreader Norma Sax, and transcriber Sally Reidy. You all rock!

I am keenly aware that these stories represent only a small fraction of fair participants. Hundreds more stories could be told about volunteer crews, longtime fair crafters, musicians, and performers. In this book, I stitched together as many interviews and great fair stories as possible. It is my hope that the resulting crazy-quilt of chapters will entertain, enlighten, and intrigue readers with the magical mystique of the Oregon Country Fair.

Just like the first book, the most painful part of ending this volume was leaving wonderful fair stories on the cutting room floor. Many of the untold stories intertwine with the ones that appear here. There simply wasn't enough room for them all. I apologize to those who have told me their stories and have yet to see them in print. Please don't lose hope. I plan to keep writing.

The fair's original Eight-shaped path that matches the mathematical symbol for infinity should have been my first clue: Once you start writing about the Country Fair, the stories will never end. I remain grateful for the chance to travel this amazingly amusing Infinity Path. Thanks for joining me on this part of the journey. May there always be a good ol' Oregon Country Fair.

Introduction

1969

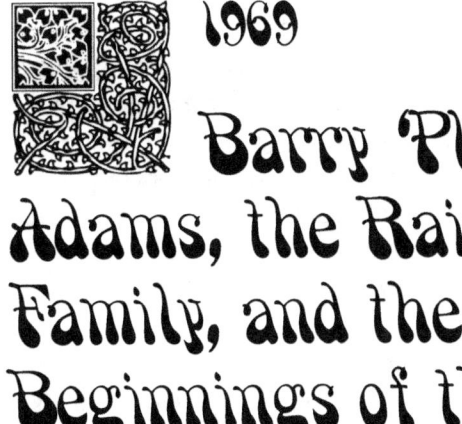

Barry 'Plunkr' Adams, the Rainbow Family, and the Beginnings of the Oregon Country Fair

"Now everyone has their own story. My story might be slightly different than other people's versions. So the vibration for me is, collect all the versions and then people can take up whatever story they happen to like."
—Brother Barry "Plunkr," interview at the Oregon Country Fair, July 2018

Thousands of alternative-minded people split the California scene after things got too wild and weird in the streets following the 1967 Summer of Love. The Bay Area was overrun by footloose souls and runaways seeking a better, freer life. Several articles in the counterculture newspaper, the San Francisco *Oracle*, exhorted readers to leave the city and go back to the land to live in tune with nature.

Many of those who took heed of the *Oracle's* advice would flee north in Volkswagen vans or caravans of funky cars, joining hundreds of young people from around the nation who gravitated to the greener pastures of Oregon. Some would set up communes and farms in Oregon's fertile valleys, where they were mostly tolerated by locals who were often eccentric in their own right. Young men with low draft numbers sought ways to drop out of society so they couldn't be found, or else travelled farther north to Canada to avoid getting sucked into the killing fields of the Vietnam War.

The fact that Oregon's U.S. Senator Wayne Morse opposed the Vietnam War from the beginning made the state more attractive to the people of the peace movement. With its mild climate and tolerant attitudes, Eugene became a favorite spot for counterculture migrants to land. The new mix of people in Eugene would give rise to numerous communes, cooperative businesses, natural food stores, and new services like White Bird Sociomedical Aid Station and Switchboard call center.

Another key attraction in the area for many carefree young folks in the early 1970s was famed author Ken Kesey, who made his home in Pleasant Hill, Oregon, near Eugene. Kesey wrote *One Flew Over the Cuckoo's Nest*, and *Sometimes a Great Notion*. But more importantly, Kesey's wild lifestyle had captured the imagination of many young people who had read *The Electric Kool-Aid Acid Test* by Tom Wolfe, documenting Kesey's LSD-fueled cross-country bus trip with the Merry Pranksters and Kesey's connection to the Grateful Dead band.

Meanwhile, the University of Oregon campus bristled with protests against the war and against racial prejudice. Local coffeehouses attracted people interested in having deep conversations and hearing interesting new music. Young parents looked for ways to raise their children with more freedoms than they had experienced growing up.

In the midst of those turbulent times, a group of parents in Eugene held the first Renaissance Faire in Oregon on November 1 and 2, 1969, as a fund-raiser for a free-style alternative school called Children's House. The school's philosophy centered on a child's right to play.

Parents Ron and Robin Ulrich had proposed the fund-raiser after they returned from a Renaissance Faire in California. They envisioned creating a smaller version of the fair with an emphasis on crafters. They invited people to potluck meetings at their home to plan the event. Barry "Plunkr" Adams, a friend who had been staying at their house, volunteered to be one of the janitors doing cleanup for the proposed event. Age twenty-three and a military veteran, Barry worked as a tree planter with his friend Wally Jones.

One of the Children's House teachers volunteered to host the Renaissance Faire on the farm where she lived. Parents from the school hammered together rudimentary booths with wood recycled from old sheds on the property. Several dozen crafters displayed their handmade candles, clothing, leatherwork, pottery and other crafts. Food vendors served simple fare like soups, barbecue chicken, and baked breads.

Fairgoers entered through a pasture gate. The suggested donation was one dollar; children got in free. As the fair began on Saturday, the morning fog lifted into sunshine and fairgoers enjoyed a beautiful fall afternoon.

Barry brought his two-stringed "plunker," an ancient instrument known as the dutar (also spelled dotar or duttar).

"It's a drone instrument," Barry would explain to anyone who asked. "This was invented by the women. Everybody knows and it's been historically proven that women discovered weaving. So after people got done howling on the caves and stomping on the floor of the caves, in those days called Rock 'n' Roll, they'd quiet way down and then in the night, you would hear this," Barry started plucking his dutar, "which is the women and the old people pulling at the weavings. …

"It's the grandmother instrument," he added. "These are known all over the world and by various places and names."

Barry was hanging out at the fair, plunking away when a guy named Garrick Beck walked up and started singing a song in rhythm. Afterward they sat and chatted a while and discovered they were both storytellers. Thus began a long friendship.

"Listen, I'm gonna do a Punch and Judy show," Garrick told Barry at that first encounter, "and I need somebody. Would you come over and help me keep track of the kids while I get prepared?"

Barry agreed and rounded up a "sister" nearby to pitch in. When a bunch of kids started milling around in front of the puppet show booth near starting time, the two adults tried to get the kids to be patient for just a little longer while Garrick got everything ready.

Suddenly the tiny curtains parted on a window in the booth and a puppet popped up. "Garrick got up and did the entire Punch and Judy show," Barry said, "which is totally amazing. He made these puppets, and he did the whole rap. The kids started jumping up and we were getting them to settle down."

As the fair continued, Barry enjoyed playing his plunker, with his friend Wally Jones on guitar and other musicians joining the impromptu jam. When the fair was over and people left, Barry pitched in on cleanup as promised. Organizers enjoyed the fair's vibes so much that they pledged to put on another fair soon.

The Memorial Day weekend of 1970 was targeted for the next Renaissance Faire. Ron and Robin Ulrich had divorced, but Robin helped with the second fair, along with several other people who had organized the first event. One of them knew a member of the Breeden family, who built homes locally. Organizers got permission to stage the fair on forty-five acres of land that Breeden Brothers owned along Crow Road.

Barry came down early from Portland, where he was staying with the Family of Man commune, with others from the group. They helped prepare the fair site, spreading straw around to create a path with two loops. One loop traversed a pasture close to Crow Road and the other circled through an oak grove by a pond. Where one trail crossed a creek, volunteers built a temporary wooden bridge. The two loops created an infinity symbol, and fairgoers would walk the Infinity Path.

The second fair was bigger than the first and attracted a wider spectrum of humanity. Turnout was much higher than anyone expected, snarling traffic. The *Augur*, a counterculture newspaper in Eugene, printed a euphoric account under the headline, "Gathering of the Tribes." "The woods become enchanted," the story said, "and beautiful people begin to blossom like flowers."

In the evenings, campfires lit enclaves where people gathered. The fire at the Family of Man campsite became a center of energy. "Brother Barry keeps everything moving, and drumming and dancing lasts far into the night," the *Augur* reported.

When the fair ended on Monday afternoon, Barry and his brothers and sisters in the Family of Man stayed behind to clean up.

In August of 1970, Garrick Beck and his cohorts at the Alder House in Portland joined a loose collective of Portland activists to help organize Vortex I, the biodegradable festival of life held at McIver State Park south of Portland. The festival grew out of a desire of those

Portland peace groups, who called themselves The Family, to provide a positive alternative not only to the negativity of the U.S. government but also to the confrontational tactics of some groups on the radical left.

Specifically, the People's Army Jamboree in Portland had been planning a whole weekend of anti-war activities—from demonstrations to workshops—for Labor Day weekend to try to disrupt an American Legion national convention scheduled at the same time. The Legion had invited President Richard Nixon to speak.

It was only a few months after the nation had been shocked by Ohio National Guardsman opening fire on students at Kent State University, killing four students. In June and July, anti-war riots had erupted in downtown Portland's Park Blocks and at Portland State University. The Family hoped that by planning a rock concert, they could offer a peaceful alternative. Organizers saw the event as a vortex for peace.

Members of The Family found an unusual ally in Oregon's Governor Tom McCall. He not only endorsed the concert, he directed state resources toward staging it and told law enforcement officers to ignore nudity and marijuana smoking during the event. He believed the concert could effectively draw young people away from confrontations in Portland. In a speech broadcast on television and radio, Governor McCall presented the concert to Oregonians as an innovative "safety valve" that would help prevent violence.

With no entry fee, the number of attendees could only be estimated. Anywhere from 30,000 to a 100,000 people arrived over three days. As Governor McCall had anticipated, the concert-goers went naked, swam in the Willamette River, and smoked pot. Portland-area bands kept the beat going as the crowds danced and twirled.

Concert-goers by all accounts enjoyed a very groovy time. Natural food restaurants and communes set up kitchens at McIver Park's bathhouses, where there was plumbing and water, to cook food that was served for free.

Garrick Beck had invited Barry Plunkr to assist with the concert effort. They were among the volunteers erecting thirteen tipis donated by an Explorer Scout troop. Each tipi had a designated use: volunteer coordination, childcare, lost and found including lost parents and children, medical aid, and firewood storage. Two tents called "Rainbow Tipis" were designated as safe places for tripsters overwhelmed by their drug experience to rest and find calm guidance. The "Shanti Sena Tipi" (Sanskrit for Peace Scene) became the central hub for the volunteer peacekeepers of Vortex I. Several tipis simply provided a quiet place to rest.

"This community of people, everybody, there were so many colors," Barry said. "Seventy-five thousand people standing and going, 'Peace and love,' right? It was very amazing. It was 1970 when most people were either pro-war or anti-war. We were trying to do a new thing—not a new thing on the earth, but a thing called peace."

At the concert, Garrick and Barry talked at length about dreams they shared of creating a huge group to bring together all of the communes, cooperatives, and wandering hippies. Late at night in a drumming circle around a central campfire, a name emerged that would reflect the essence of their visions. As the drumming kept up a steady rhythm, someone yelled "We are …!" Another person hollered, "the Rainbow!" More people shouted, "Family! …" And a clear voice chimed in, "of Living Light!" Everyone erupted in cheers.

After all the crowds had gone home, Barry and Garrick joined the other post-event volunteers cleaning up. They replaced sod in the campfires they had dug and picked up trash.

"So then we did the cleanup," Barry said. "We got word that they were going to send in the National Guard to chase people out, so we sent out word: 'Hey, we're the janitors! We're the cleanup! Please, let us be!' And Tom McCall flew in in a helicopter to let us know it was okay to stay." Barry would cherish the memory of the governor and the governor's aides, all dressed in business suits, holding hands in a circle with the scruffy, smiling free spirits.

The concert had entertained thousands of blissful young people for a few days, and Governor McCall met his goals of keeping Portland mostly mellow despite the tensions of the times. It helped greatly that Richard Nixon had canceled his visit at the last minute. Only two vocal but peaceful anti-war demonstrations took place in downtown Portland during the American Legion Conference that weekend. Peace had prevailed.

Afterward, Barry returned to Eugene, still buoyed by the energy of Vortex. "I was hanging out around the Odyssey Coffee House, which was run by Bill and Cindy Wooten," Barry said. "A brother named Mitchell and a bunch of family hung out there and they played music. Cindy Wooten came over to me and asked me, 'Listen, we have this land out here by Veneta and we don't really have anyone to help us, so would you?'" So Barry and the new-born Rainbow Family helped the Wootens and other volunteers put together the third Renaissance Faire set for October 16-18, 1970, just five months after the Crow Road fair in May 1970.

It would be the first fair to be held at the site along the Long Tom River. The property the Wootens had rented stretched across 400 wooded acres. The Long Tom River predictably flooded parts of the land during Oregon's rainy winters. The clay soil would get sticky and slick whenever it rained.

"I hitchhiked out here, and I had farmer's jeans on at the time," Barry said. "I came out and I met the farmer up on the hill there, by his house."

The farmer stood next to Barry, looked toward the fair site and said, "Yup, it's a swamp."

"Yep," Barry agreed. "It's a swamp." They walked around to explore the land. "We come up on this kind of a flat, open field, and I go, 'Oh, wow, we can do it here! You have a parking lot!'"

"Really?" the farmer commented in surprise. "I thought you'd probably want to put the cars down there somewhere and put the fair up there in the dry ground."

"Oh, no, no," Barry said. "We want to put the fair down there in the swamp and we're going to put the parking lot up here. We're gonna park them just like downtown in nice, neat rows. We can get more in that way."

Grass grew waist- or chest-high on the land along the Long Tom River. Cows had not been allowed to graze in the parts that flooded every year. Barry invited several groups to help prepare the site for the fair. He asked half a dozen friends from the cleanup crew for the Sky River Rock Festival in Washington State, who had three years of festivals under their belts already. He also invited a crew from the People's Army Jamboree, who came down from Portland to assist.

Barry said key individuals included his friend Harold Williams, who taught meditation in Eugene and helped coordinate the setup; and Reggie DeSoto, a member of the Family of Mystic Arts, who directed traffic for parking for the event while riding horseback.

They set up a kitchen and brought out street people from Eugene to help. "What we did was ship people out there who lived in the streets and had nowhere to go," Barry said. "We brought them out there and we fed them. They lived there and they didn't have to work because anybody that lives ought to be able to eat and be sheltered. But we did ask them in the mornings to get up and go with us."

The street people's "job" was to walk on the tall grass to make it lay down flat. Barry and the Rainbow Family paced out another infinity path like they created the previous spring for the fair along Crow Road, only much larger.

"We used the street people to push down the grass," Barry said. "We cut through all the thorny bushes. Then we came out at little places and we cleared out some of the bushes so there was overhang. People could go and hang their candles and such.

"We got to the lower end of the circle and came back," Barry said, "Then we went back and we started doing infinity, which was the other side. And we were cutting, cutting, cutting, cutting through. We were like, 'Oh, my god this is never gonna end.' But finally we came all the way around, so that you can always turn back to yourself when you walk the Infinity Path."

Barry said the Rainbow Family pulled together a nominal security crew. "We formed what we called the Shanti Sena, which means, some people say 'Peace Army' but to me it always meant, 'Peace Scenes.' It was a way to keep the scene peaceful," he said.

Meanwhile, Cindy and Bill Wooten held coordinator potlucks in town to figure out other logistics of the event. A week or two before the fair was set to open, about a dozen people camped out at the site to finish preparations. When fair time came, the opening was uneven. Not all booths had finished setting up and Main Stage wasn't completed until Friday night.

When the public came the next day, Barry Plunkr and Garrick Beck presented the play "Pied Together" from Main Stage. Riffing on "The Pied Piper of Hamlin," Barry told the story of the Rainbow Family. "It's about freedom and 'rat-icles.'" Barry said. "Garrick played all the rats. ...It ends in everyone holding hands and singing 'America the Beautiful.'"

Saturday hummed along in high spirits until a steady rain put a damper on everything Saturday night. The rainfall turned the fair's paths into slick, mucky mud that went knee-deep in some places. The mud would trap larger vehicles in the parking lot for several days until the soil dried out.

Despite the problems, the third Renaissance Faire netted a small profit. Organizers donated $200 to a community Thanksgiving Dinner in the Whitaker neighborhood of Eugene, and loaned $250 to the Wood and Fuel Co-Op to purchase a truck. The balance became seed money for the spring 1971 fair.

In 1971, Garrick Beck and friends established the Rainbow Farm cooperative in the Coast Range west of Eugene while Barry Plunkr and other Rainbow members established the loosely associated Rainbow House near downtown Eugene. Rainbow House stood next to the WOW Hall, owned by the Eugene branch of the Woodmen of the World fraternal organization. The police started bringing by runaways who had no other place to go and would drop them off at the Rainbow House, Barry said. "We were doing potlucks and feeding street people," Barry said. Soon they were using the kitchen in the basement of the WOW Hall to feed people every week.

The Rainbow Family helped with both the spring and fall Renaissance Faires held in 1971. "During the fair, we helped out with everything," Barry said. "We did Shanti Sena, we did the parking. We kind of helped out every way possible. At night, people would sleep at the bottom end of the circle. The top circle, that's where we partied because in the dark, in no way, shape or form would the police ever come that far down in there. And anybody who was a tourist, anybody who felt uncomfortable being in the woods with a bunch of freaks, would leave. So what you have now they call a Sweep but we didn't have to do that. People just left in the dark and other people who were brave stayed."

Barry said the Rainbow Family camp had always brought street people to the fairs. "We hauled in street people out there and brought them to our camp and then they would come in to the fair," he said. But after 1971, the fair organizers put a stop to that practice.

"They asked me—they kind of told me—that they were going to basically close the Rainbow door, which was for the street people" Barry said. "They were moving toward a tighter operation. And I said, 'Okay,' and then I moved on and did other things."

Bill and Cindy Wooten would implement a more organized approach to setting up the fair. Instead of establishing a kitchen to feed street people, they recruited friends to be crew coordinators.

Each crew of hand-picked volunteers would work together in cooperation to get the jobs done. Only a dozen or so volunteers would camp out on the site a month before each fair to prepare the land for the event. That dozen would be fed by a cook in Main Camp Kitchen.

Barry moved on to concentrate on Rainbow Family events. The Rainbow Family planned its first Rainbow Gathering to pray for peace on July 4, 1972, in the Roosevelt National Forest near Granby, Colorado. Nobody claimed to be the main organizer of any Rainbow Gathering; everyone simply showed up and contributed in cooperation with each other.

"It was peaceable assembly," Barry said. "Open to all. New Jerusalem. Come in peace, be in peace. Share common ground. How does a family work? Regard each other with equality. Respect for all. Consensus process. …No authoritarian trip. We are presenting a way to be and to do. Give your consensus. It's not perfect. It's not ideal. But it does do this: It empowers the individual."

That was the same weekend that the 1972 Renaissance Faire was held along the Long Tom River. The scheduling marked the first major schism between the fair and its early allies from the Rainbow Family.

In 1975, the fair would change its name under pressure from the Renaissance Faire in Marin County, California, which claimed copyright to the name "Renaissance Faire." At a meeting at Bill and Cindy Wooten's home, coordinators and volunteers kicked around ideas and finally agreed to name the event the Oregon Country Fair.

Organizers implemented the name change with a transition year; the fair was known as the Oregon Country Renaissance Fair in 1975. To help introduce the new name, organizers commissioned a new logo—a peach adapted from a woodcut of a Japanese family crest. From 1976 on, the event would be known as the Oregon Country Fair and the peach would become its symbol.

The schism between the Country Fair and the Rainbow Family would widen in 1978, when the Rainbow Family planned a Gathering just a week before the fair in the national forests near Roseburg, a hundred miles southeast of Eugene. Fair organizers worried that the fair would be overrun by Rainbow Family members wanting to crash the party. They sent an emissary, a friend of Barry's named Mitch, who appeared before the main circle of the Rainbow Family gathering to ask everyone not to come to the Country Fair.

"That was the beginning of the days of the two halves," Barry said. "People would come to the fair, and they would be fair people. And then they would come home to the Gathering and they'd be Rainbow. When they were at the fair, they wouldn't cop to being Rainbow."

The Oregon Country Fair would become a recognized Oregon nonprofit agency in 1977 when attorney Jill Heiman, a friend of Cindy Wooten's, filed the paperwork. The fair also expanded its entertainment offerings beyond music when Cindy and Bill Wooten asked the Flaming Zucchini, aka Reverend Chumleigh, aka Michael Mielnik, to present a show at the fair. They had seen his performance that combined offbeat humor with old vaudeville tricks at the Saturday Market in Eugene.

Michael Mielnik would pull together a stage show for the fair in the style of New Vaudeville, a movement that was emerging from the burgeoning ranks of street performers in the 1970s. He invited musicians from Evergreen State College in Washington to form a marching band. He also invited several performer friends: two jugglers known as the Flying Karamazov Brothers, and tap-dancer Michael "Toes" Tiranoff.

From those humble beginnings, the fair would help launch a revival of the New Vaudeville movement by providing an annual gathering place where creative entertainers could try new material, learn from each other, and enjoy each other's company as they all camped together in a wooded meadow near the Long Tom River.

In the late 1970s, fair organizers had their hands full just keeping the event afloat. Conservative members of the Lane County Board of Commissioners would support efforts of the Lane County Sheriff's Office to make it as difficult as possible for the fair to take place each year. Commissioners kept ratcheting up the requirements the fair had to meet to secure the all-important outdoor assembly permit.

In 1979, the Lane County Commissioners would approve a bond requirement for the fair that applied to no other event. Fair attorney Jill Heiman sued the county over the new requirement, based on the constitutional guarantee of freedom of assembly. That case would take years to wind through the courts and would eventually be decided in the fair's favor in the 1980s.

Barry would remain deeply involved with Rainbow Family Gatherings for decades, but he wouldn't return to the Oregon Country Fair until 2018. Much had changed in the intervening years. The map showed that the original Eight-shaped Infinity Path had been transformed into an Infinity of Pathways after organizers expanded the fair's internal footprint three times between 1991 and 2018.

Barry "Plunkr" Adams brought his dutar to the 2018 Oregon Country Fair.

Barry noted how much taller the trees had grown since 1971, and how the craft booths all displayed much nicer, more polished handiwork. And of course, the event had grown enormously.

He also noted striking similarities. "Some of the things I see are still here" he said in 2018. "Some of the elements, like the straight-on parking. I knew right away, I wasn't in California because this is so Oregonized. It's very highly efficient, the people have got a lot of spirit. …

"To my mind, there's various ways in which people are trying to present the Peace Culture—the Culture of Now and the Culture of the Future, which is to live on the Earth in peace with other people in peace," he said. "Now, we have Rainbow Gatherings all around the world and there's thousands of other peace gatherings, all of which have little communities around them." His examples included the Kerrville Folk Festival in Texas, the Okanongan Family Fair in Washington, Burning Man in Nevada, and the Seattle Hempfest.

"We are Humanly Interested People, with friendly eyes," Barry said. "You're a hip-eye, I'm a hip-eye; we're not necessarily hippies. … At the first fairs we wanted to bring a renaissance of the spirit. … We wanted to help people, sponsor their crafts, and help elevate what's going on. That was their vibes. That was the blessing.

"So for me, that's what this fair is really about," Barry said. "The fact that it runs really efficiently, I think is awesome. A lot of the young brothers and sisters have a lot of good spirit. They're really into it. They're very polite, nice humans. This has become a collective. I'm sure it's a 501(c)(3) nonprofit." He paused and looked out at the people starting to gather at Main Stage meadow on Saturday morning of the 2018 Oregon Country Fair and said, "This is excellent."

1980
Tom Noddy and the W.C. Fields Memorial Stage

"It ain't what they call you, it's what you answer to."
—W. C. Fields

The annual Oregon Country Fair had always offered fertile ground for the entertainers who had popped up on the West Coast street scene during the "happenings" of the 1960s and 1970s. From the campuses of California to Seattle's Pike Place Market, performers entertained the masses at peace vigils, Human Be-ins, protests, and campus hangouts.

A prime example was Tom Noddy, who took to the streets with a puppet act and soap bubble tricks. By 1977 Tom, age twenty-seven, was living in a large van with a puppet stage built into the curbside window. "I came to Santa Cruz and ended up in the company of several other people living in a way that is now referred to as homeless," he said. "But actually, we were for a short time, a community living together at one campground."

Tom's act became part of the grassroots revival of old vaudeville arts—served with a twist of hip humor—that arose spontaneously among young activists around the country.

He kept an eye out for opportunities to perform inside, where his bubble tricks could shine. One night he signed up for a talent competition at a Santa Cruz bar. "Called 'The Bong Show,' it was a takeoff on the television talent show popular at the time, *The Gong Show*," Tom recalled. The bar charged the performers an entry fee and offered a large cash prize for first place.

When he performed inside, Tom could pull off his magical bubble tricks without worrying about the wind blowing his artistry away. He had perfected some complicated tricks he wanted to show off. But his bubble tricks found tough competition at the Bong Show: a sword-swallower named Moz Wright.

The "Bong Show" judges, three reviewers from local newspapers, sat at a long table with microphones, drinking from free pitchers of beer. "It was awful, actually," Tom said. "They joked around with each other and as they got drunker, the jokes became less funny to anyone but them. Meanwhile, some poor poet took the stage late in the evening and the judges were banging on the gong before he got started. In the end, Moz won second place and I won first place with bubbles. When I got on stage to accept the money, I used the time to berate the judges and I offered back the entry fee to all entrants."

Tom ended up visiting late into the night with Moz, sharing stories and discovering they had mutual friends who also were street performers. At the time, Tom performed in the streets of California's Bay Area. "I was a regular on the Wharf and over at Powell and Market, as well as Berkeley and San Francisco State University campuses," Tom said. Moz traveled up and down the West Coast to perform between his regular gigs in Portland at the Storefront Theatre and the Medieval Inn. The Medieval Inn had "heavy wooden benches, the whole thing," Moz said. "It looked medieval except the ceiling was so low that I couldn't stand up and swallow swords. I had to stand on my knees."

Their mutual friends included the Flying Karamazov Brothers, Avner the Eccentric, and Magical Mystical Michael. Moz told Tom about an incredible place called the Oregon Country Fair, where these friends came together, performed during the daytime, then camped, visited, and partied together long into the night. Tom had heard of the fair, but had no special plan to go until he heard of this gathering of vaudevillians. His political puppet satire might well fit in, but the bubble portion of his show needed indoor venues. Dust would pop fragile bubble orbs, after all, and an outside fair with dirt paths was bound to kick up lots of dust. But now Moz's stories piqued his interest.

Tom's slippery path to bubble artistry started with a long strange trip from home. He was born Tom McAllister to a large family in Northern New Jersey. His father worked in a factory, but periodic layoffs kept times lean. When Tom was ten, his father moved the whole family to California to seek better opportunities. They moved back two years later when nothing panned out, and his dad came back to the same factory job he had left. For Tom, California memories were compelling.

"I was in junior high school when we moved back," Tom said, "and I finished high school in Paterson, New Jersey. But I always knew that there was another way that people lived."

Tom went away in 1967 to Memphis State University in Tennessee during the turmoil of civil rights demonstrations calling for integration reforms in the South. Like many college students then, he participated in those demonstrations and civil actions. "I was a student in Memphis and involved with the local anti-war and civil rights movements when Martin Luther King came to town to support striking sanitation workers and was assassinated," Tom said.

Devastated and discouraged, he quit school in 1969. "I left college in Memphis and simply put my thumb out to let the winds and the countercultural waves carry me across North America," he said. In college, he had let his kinky red hair grow out to a soft Afro, and he sported a red goatee and mustache. "In many of the places that I traveled through, I was, for a lot of people, the first actual hippie that they'd ever seen live and not on TV," he said. "The big fluffy head of hair seemed to add to the experience for them and brought out the smiles."

Along the way, he watched the moon landing on an outside screen. "I had only made it to Toronto," he said. "I tripped with some students from a university there, then we all went down to Nathan Phillips Square where they had a large screen set up. People without TVs—most hippies didn't have them in those days—came out to watch the moon landing. It was … um … far-out, man."

A few weeks later he joined thousands of "those wet and happy hippies" in Bethel, New York, for the soon-to-be legendary Woodstock Music Festival. After that psychedelic experience, he hitchhiked through the South and across the country to the West Coast.

He decided to go to Europe, but first had to save money. He moved back to New Jersey and took a factory job, like his dad. The day he took the job he set a quitting date, giving himself ten months. "I flipped pages on the calendar. I circled that one and I said, 'Okay, September fifteenth I'm out of here.' When I came home at night from the factory, I had to find a way to keep myself busy," he said. His friends would call to ask him to go out on the town. But Tom wanted to save his money. He knew he'd enjoy spending the cash once he got to Crete much more than he would spending it on drinks at the local bars of New Jersey, so he stayed home.

He took up the yo-yo, because he had never been good at it as a kid. "Some kids could take a yo-yo and make a loop-de-loop and rock the cradle and round the world," Tom said. "When I was nine, I wasn't one of those kids. But I figured, I'm twenty-one now, I can figure out a yo-yo." His father made a similar observation in a different tone of voice: "You're twenty-one years old and you've got a damned yo-yo?" Tom went home every night and spent hours practicing the yo-yo. It became an obsession. But once he got good at it, he "got bored because it was a yo-yo," he said.

Next he tried the paddle ball, the wooden paddle toy with an elastic-attached red ball. "Babba-de-babba-de-babba-de-babba-de-babba-de-babba-de-babba-de ... six hundred was my record," Tom said. "My father said, 'Go back to the yo-yo! This thing's really stupid!' But I got really good with it. Then I got bored." But his plan was working—these obsessive hobbies kept him at home, saving money.

"And then I thought, okay, what's another? Uh, bubbles, what do you do with bubbles? You make a big bubble and then I guess you make a bigger bubble. So I got bubbles and I never got bored," Tom said with a broad smile. "I started seeing things in them, the colors, the angles, the rhythm, and I started finding tricks. I was a cigarette smoker, so I put smoke into some of the bubbles and I found shapes and structures. I can do a bubble cube now, a dodecahedron, a truncated octahedron and shapes without names. Every night for the rest of that ten months I was playing with bubbles. I got really good at bubbles. Then I quit the job and went to Europe."

In 1972 he took a cheap flight from New York to Luxembourg, with $200 in his pocket. He hitchhiked across Europe and landed on the Greek island of Crete for eight months, then moved on to the United Kingdom for six months more. To earn money for living expenses, he picked olives in Greece and apples and potatoes in England.

After another New Jersey factory job and another set quitting date, Tom moved to San Francisco in 1975 and started earning a living with street performance. He drew inspiration for his *nom de theatre* from *The Hobbit*, by J.R.R. Tolkien. "When Bilbo worked to free the dwarves from the spiders in Mirkwood Forest," Tom said, "he hollered out and called them names: Attercop and Tomnoddy. Tolkien then explained 'No spider has ever liked being called Attercop, and Tomnoddy of course, is insulting to anybody.' I took my stage name from that line."

At first Tom's show featured puppets; he'd use his bubble tricks only when the wind wasn't blowing and he needed to attract a crowd. "My show was focused on 'Political, Social, and Spiritual Satire with Puppets,'" Tom said. "I used no puppet stage and no scrim to hide the puppeteer. It was mainly because I was broke, but I put the best face on it and referred to what I did as 'honest puppetry.'" He developed a hippie puppet that wore patched jeans and a backpack, naming him "John Peter Zenger" after a printer arrested in pre-Revolutionary America for the crime of libel for criticizing the Royal Governor.

"John Peter Zenger was critical of the Royal Governor of New York," Tom said. "He admitted saying the bad things, but he pled not guilty with the defense that what he said was true. But truth was not a defense against a charge of libel at that time. In fact, the prosecutor argued that if what he said was true then it was all the more libelous! That rebellious American jury nonetheless found him not guilty ... and three 'Huzzahs' were heard in the courtroom."

Tom began organizing street performers into variety shows at Bay Area cafés or rented halls, calling it San Francisco Cabaret. He initially produced the shows so he could bring his bubble act inside. Outdoors, his bubble tricks were at the mercy of the weather. The shimmering orbs would pop into oblivion when breezes blew in from San Francisco's Bay.

"I asked a couple of jugglers I met to be in one of my shows, two street jugglers who called themselves the Flying Karamazov Brothers," Tom said. "They said they couldn't make that date." But Howard Patterson (aka Ivan Karamazov) and Paul Magid (aka Dmitri Karamazov) told Tom about a performer named Michael Mielnik (aka Reverend Chumleigh) who also had been organizing variety shows for street performers along the West Coast.

"I was calling mine cabaret," Tom said. "He was calling his

vaudeville. And he was right! It's vaudeville! I went to the library and I read everything I could about the vaudeville era. These kinds of skill sets ... are older than vaudeville. They go back to the fairs of Babylon! But there was this fifty-year period in America where they called it 'vaudeville.' It was organized into shows, they traveled by trains together, they had the same lingo, the kids learned from the older ones, and it was called vaudeville."

Tom Noddy realized he was part of a new vaudeville revival. Young performers who earned their living on the streets borrowed tricks of the trade from old-style vaudeville comedians, but deleted sexism and racism from the jokes. "That was new," Tom said. "Before the seventies, there was no movement calling us to drop sexism, it was always a natural subject of jokes. You could punch a joke up by making it about your wife. ... You get old joke books and they're almost all sexist or based on ethnic stereotypes."

Street performing gave birth to a new kind of comedy. "I saw this on college campuses," Tom said. "With the women's movement in the seventies, young women would often hiss if something was said that they thought was sexist, just a little 'sssss.' ... And if you played the college campuses often enough, you would notice with that one joke, you heard that hiss. It interrupted the flow of the show. Even if you debated your right to say that joke, after a while you took it out just because they were always interrupting you."

Tom said that was similar to what happened in the old vaudeville days. If the material didn't work, the audiences didn't laugh or they booed. It provided an instant feedback loop for the performers, who could quickly figure out what audiences found funny.

"Street performing just blossomed in the late sixties and early seventies across America spontaneously, it seemed," Tom said. "Avner the Eccentric was a street performer in Atlanta. He didn't know others. He was just doing this thing. The Karamazovs, Chumleigh, Moz, and Artis the Spoonman were up in the Northwest. ... I was on the streets in San Francisco and then Santa Cruz all the time in those days, doing my shows periodically and living off of the coins that I earned that way. It was beautiful time."

In 1979 organizers of the Oregon Country Fair asked Moz Wright to help pull together the fair's entertainment lineup. Moz invited Tom to join the entertainers, and provided him with the requisite, good-as-gold, overnight pass: a round piece of construction paper stamped with the fair's peach logo.

By the time Tom arrived at the fair, the annual village had already taken shape at the hands of crafters and volunteer carpenters. Rustic booths full of artistic wares lined both sides of a meandering pathway that on the map looked like a figure 8. Every so often, the scent of cooking food enticed fairgoers to one of the many booths serving creative delights from primitive but clean, county-inspected camp kitchens in the forest.

A few wide spots in the paths and gaps between booths provided places for entertainers to set out a hat and reach a small crowd. "That first fair I was run really ragged," Tom said. "I was a street performer, essentially. At that time they didn't really have people organizing where vaudeville performers played. There were street performers. We played the streets of the fair."

One stage with three scheduled performances a day had been built a few years earlier by the entertainers themselves. The OCF official map designated the spot as Circus Stage, but the performers called it Chumleighland in honor of the guy who loosely organized the stage: Reverend Chumleigh, aka Michael Mielnik.

Tom took a break to catch a show at Chumleighland. The variety-style show featured the comical wacky antics of Reverend Chumleigh, the wildly rhythmic juggling of the Flying Karamazov Brothers, and the tumbling finesse of the Daring Deviante Sisters. Tom loved the show and picked up a few tips on timing and delivery as he watched them peak the show at the moment it was time to pass the hat.

"They'd rush into the crowd," Tom said. "People were baffled. They didn't have time to reach for coins; they couldn't look at how big the bill was. They reached in and grabbed something and gave it, worried they'd be passed by. But when I passed the hat, I'd say 'If you have coins, bills, joints, a place to crash tonight, a ride north in the morning, that's okay. If you don't have anything, that's okay too. Neither do I, ha, ha, ha, have a nice day!' And so I got that kind of money."

After the fair, Tom, Moz, singer Jan Luby, and Deni Schadegg formed a partnership called Westwind Travelin' Vaudeville. They wanted to re-establish a West Coast vaudeville circuit like the old days. "Big-time vaudeville died long ago," Tom said. "Efforts to bring it back have failed many times. But the real heartbeat of the vaudeville circuit always was small-time vaudeville, all these little towns throughout America. ... Small-time vaudeville—we figured we could do that with counterculture-style vaudeville."

Westwind invited various performers to join them at different venues. "We'd travel along the West Coast from Vancouver to Seattle to Portland to Eugene and all the way south to Santa Cruz. I would travel up in the summertime, essentially on the way to the Oregon Country Fair, and the route would carry me back home," Tom said.

Westwind Travelin' Vaudeville partnered with nonprofit groups to raise funds for the causes the groups espoused. For each show, members of the nonprofit group would take care of putting up posters, selling tickets, and publicizing the event. Westwind provided an incentive for the local group to sell the show out ahead of time: The nonprofit earned a percentage from all tickets sold in advance. All proceeds from tickets sold on the day of the show went to the performers.

Tom brought out his puppets and blew bubbles, Jan sang, and Moz swallowed swords. As their "Coordinator of Anarchy," Deni handled the stage sets and worked with the locals. Moz enjoyed the group's camaraderie. "Avner [the Eccentric] came with us one year," Moz recalled. "We had Jan Luby and Rebo [Flordigan aka Rebecca Hanson]. David the Minstrel and Liv were with us quite a few years. Magical Mystical Michael came with us. It was always a good cast." Champion juggler Roberto Morganti also often joined them.

Moz especially enjoyed the variety shows at schools where students wrote and performed. Often, family and friends of the young performers would be sitting in the audience. It resembled a scene from "The Music Man"—parents beaming with pride and exclaiming "That's my boy!" as they watched their children sing in the spotlight. Ticket sales were always successful at those shows, and the performers loved watching the kids ham it up almost as much as the parents did.

In 1980 Moz became co-coordinator of Entertainment at the Oregon Country Fair. He and his sweetie, Deni Schadegg, arrived early on site to tackle the workload. Tom also showed up a little early to scout out the fair's eight-shaped path and get a better idea of the best places to perform. Serendipitously, Tom came across a large, flat wooden box—a small stage—sitting in the path outside the area that was informally known then as Keseyland. (So-called because Oregon author Ken Kesey would hang out there behind the Springfield Creamery booth run by his brother Chuck and Chuck's wife, Sue. That area would be renamed Energy Park two years later.)

Tom asked around and learned that the small stage had been set out to be recycled. "I got some friends of mine to help me drag it around the fair," Tom said. "We found a wide spot on the trail, right across from what is now the Youth Stage. We put it there, found some driftwood, and roped it all together as a backdrop. Presto! We had created a new vaudeville stage."

Tom Noddy built the first W.C. Fields Memorial Stage in 1980. In 1981, he attached hand-made panels to each side to reduce the wind.

Tom Noddy created bubble magic at the W.C. Fields Memorial Stage for years.

He quickly encountered objections from fair organizers. The stage faced the backside of Main Camp, the key gathering area for fair organizers and coordinators. Unbeknownst to Tom, the "wide spot" in the path actually functioned as an access road used by heavy trucks every night after the fair closed and every morning before the fair opened the gates to the public. The Water Crew drove lumbering semi-tanker trucks through to bring fresh water to food booths and to refill water barrels morning and night. The Recycling Crew also clattered through early every morning in a ragtag assortment of old trucks carrying empty barrels for trash and recycled bottles and cans. Recycling Crew would then haul the previous day's full barrels out before the public arrived.

Fortunately, Tom and other vaudeville folks had a new ally at Main Camp. Deni Schadegg had been recruited by fair President Sandra Bauer to assist in Main Camp. Deni quickly became a key liaison between Main Camp and the vaudeville performers at the fair. Organizers started to realize that the new stages built by the entertainers could help solve a problem.

"We entertainers were clogging up the aisles," Tom said. "That's what we did. On crowded trails, if we could stop a few people, that would stop many people. And if many people would stop, then other people thought, 'Oh there's a crowd watching something.' And they joined the throng. We know how to do it. We do it on college campuses. We do it on sidewalks and at street fairs. We attract an audience by clogging foot traffic." Fair organizers had been responding by sending out volunteer staffers to break up the show and urge the crowd to move on. Now Tom—like the Karamazovs and Chumleigh before him—offered another alternative: Book street performers on stages.

"Deni helped to calm down some resistance in Main Camp to the unruly vaude performers," Tom recalled. "They had finally stopped trying to fight us and, instead started helping." Deni procured straw bales for audience seats. They broke apart a few bales and spread straw to define the audience area. Deni made Tom promise to remove the bale seats at the end of the day and refresh the straw floor each day after the water trucks and other vehicles had trundled through.

"Deni found a parachute for us to use to cover the goofy driftwood structure that we'd improvised," Tom said. Because of the parachute used that first year, Tom wanted to call it the Amelia

Earhart Memorial Stage. But the friends helping him build the stage—Jan Luby and Gary Deloe—suggested that naming it after W.C. Fields would be more appropriate for a vaudeville venue, and Tom agreed. Deni asked Main Camp sign-painters to make a sign, and the W.C. Fields Memorial Stage was born.

A couple of years later, the fair would build vault toilets near the stage and Tom gleefully pointed out to audiences that the stage had been aptly named. In England, toilets are marked "W.C" for water closet. With the toilets nearby, the stage most certainly stood in the W.C. field.

Tom Noddy often performed at the Circus Stage (aka Not Chumleighland).

1981 Oregon Energy Horizons aka Energy Park

"In our concern for the future of life—for ourselves and our children in this region and on this planet—we have assembled to share with one another about how best to deal with the dangers now facing us."
—Bill Wooten, 1981 *Peach Pit*

Advertising ahead of the 1981 Oregon Country Fair trumpeted the creation of an alternative energy park called Oregon Energy Horizons.

"In the fair's Community Village, there has always been an Alternative Technology booth but never enough space to give it the exposure it deserves," Sallie Edmunds, who coordinated the new area, told a newspaper reporter that year.

Sallie had participated in Community Village since 1979 with the Willamette Valley Solar Energy Association. "I was still working for the same organization," Sallie recalled, "and I got a phone call at work one day from Sandra Bauer. ... They were looking for somebody to coordinate a new area at the fair that was focused on alternative technology, energy-related issues. Somebody had referred her to me. I got together with her and we just hit it off from the very beginning. We had a wonderful time and laughed, and I was on board right away."

The fair's focus on ecology was not new. Even the first fair in

1969 emphasized living lightly on the Earth. In 1976, fair coordinators had decided to demonstrate what "living lightly on the Earth" means by opening an Appropriate Technology park. Several organizations set up exhibits in the park to show the benefits of composting, beekeeping, urban gardening, and passive solar water heaters.

The Appropriate Technology park transformed into Community Village in 1977, expanding to embrace a wider range of social issue groups with messages to share with the public. In 1980 Community Village renewed its commitment to highlight appropriate technology by building Integral House, a model sustainable home. "We demonstrated composting toilets," said Craig Patterson, who helped coordinate the project. "We demonstrated solar water heating in both flat plate collectors as well as batch collectors. We did work with the Lorena mud stove. We held [workshops] about building with bamboo. We extended the envelope about what's possible."

While Integral House successfully displayed useful ideas, it also made clear how little space was left in the Village to showcase alternative energy technology.

In the aftermath of the energy crisis in the late 1970s and the Three Mile Island nuclear accident in 1979, many activists put their hopes for future energy in the development of alternative and renewable energy sources, especially solar and wind energy. Decades before the concept of carbon limits, fair President Sandra Bauer, fair co-founder Bill Wooten, and fair attorney Jill Heiman advocated for a new area to highlight steps people could take as individuals to lessen their dependence on oil and nuclear power. They convinced the board to change fair rules to allow high-tech businesses specializing in renewable energy to present information.

In 1981 Oregon Energy Horizons debuted in the meadow behind the Springfield Creamery booth, an area that had previously been known as Kesey Park since it sat right behind the Springfield Creamery booth run by Chuck and Sue Kesey and their family.

Coincidentally, Kesey Park had been the site of the very first solar energy demonstrations at the fair. In the mid-1970s, Oregon author and icon Ken Kesey, and brother of Chuck Kesey, joined his Merry Prankster friend Michael Hagan to bring in a passive solar oven. Joyce Theios, who had helped staff Ken Kesey's 1973 Bend in the River conference, said he asked her to help cook corn on the solar oven at

Oregon Energy Horizons aka Energy Park

Ken Kesey jammed on harmonica with a guitarist (name unknown) at the 1975 fair.

Volunteers, including Gary Newman (left), built new structures in 1981 for the debut of Oregon Energy Horizons, aka Energy Park.

the fair a year or so after the conference.

Unfortunately, the solar oven technology wasn't up to the task of cooking corn for a crowd. Its passive reflector system could not generate enough heat in Oregon's summer sun. They came up with a solution typical of Ken Kesey's band of Merry Pranksters. "We called it 'solar corn,' but we were really cooking it in the back," Joyce confessed.

By the 1980s solar technology had advanced much further. Solar energy groups had sprouted up all over Oregon, recalled Sue Jakabosky, who worked then as an officer with Solar Energy Resources Group in Roseburg. "Most every little community had a small solar group because it was the heyday of solar," Sue said. "The federal government had put money in to encourage the formation of those groups. There was Willamette Valley Solar Energy Association, Portland Sun, Sunergi down in Ashland."

At the fair, Portland Sun and Sunergi set up small greenhouses, while students in Lane Community College's Energy Research Group brought in a thermo-siphon water heater and window box solar collectors. Sue's Solar Energy Resources Group lugged in a demonstration batch water heater, basically a big black tank in an insulated box with a glass lid positioned to catch sunlight.

"It must've weighed a gazillion tons," Sue said. "We built it in the back of a pickup, hauled it up here, unloaded it, and propped it up against the back wall of the Nancy's Yogurt booth" (the Springfield Creamery).

Willamette Valley Solar Energy Association conducted a solar collector construction workshop each day. The group also set up an array of photovoltaic cells to power a slideshow examining the history and environmental impact of different energy producing technologies. Representatives from various organizations sat in rustic wood booths and offered information on alternative energy ideas ranging from geothermal heat to electric cars.

The exhibits and information services at Oregon Energy Horizons became an instant hit, although the groups putting it on experienced two disappointments. First, the slideshow in a dark yurt "was a bust," observed Anthony Stoppiello, an architect who had brought information on passive solar design that year. "Who wanted to come inside on a sunny day at the Country Fair to look at slides under a dark canvas?"

Second, the thermosyphon hot water system set up for solar-heated showers didn't work. The shower water came out cold. Tom Scott, a solar business owner who taught in the Energy Management program at Lane Community College, diagnosed the problem in one quick glance. The student builders "had taken big barrels and laid them on a rack, painted them black, and then spun them so that the fittings on the bottom came off and made a showerhead so you could take showers," Tom said. "Only trouble was, when you keep water in a black barrel, all the hot water goes to the top and all the cold water goes to the bottom. So when you turned the showers on, all you got was freezing-ass cold showers. When they tried to tear it down when it was over, they almost scalded themselves with the hot water from the top."

For the 1982 fair, Sallie Edmunds asked Tom to take charge of the solar showers. "I took one of the barrels and put it up." Tom said,

"Then I brought the water into it so it was higher than the others. It pushed the hot water over the top of the barrels, and we had the solar showers going." They hooked up a small water pump—powered by a bicycle rider cranking the foot pedals—to push the water up into the top barrel. Sue Jakabosky said: "If you wanted to shower, you had to ride the bicycle for a while."

In 1982, the area was renamed Energy Park because Oregon Energy Horizons was too similar to the name of an existing Oregon business. That same year, an information desk was added with "a variety of informative literature on solar, wind, geothermal and hydro power, and most importantly on energy conservation," the fair's *Peach Pit* program guide noted. "Energy experts will also be on hand to answer any questions you may have."

Even though owners of alternative energy companies were among those experts, early on the Energy Park group decided the area would remain a commercial-free zone. "So if you are a business," Anthony Stoppiello said, "and now there's a fair number of booths that come that are businesses—they can make contacts and they can talk to people about prices and that kind of stuff, but they can't sign anybody up. We won't allow people to sell T-shirts. Now if somebody wants to throw down a five dollar bill as a donation, that's fine. We don't even allow performers to sell CDs inside the park either, and that has been a real pain in the neck for some of them if they don't get it. We've been a commercial-free zone for a long time."

Many of the same groups from 1981 returned in 1982 to hand out literature and visit with fairgoers about how to live more sustainably. "There were all these little groups that were doing something like that, and it was a ball," Sue Jakabosky said. "We were young, we were idealistic, and everything was happening. Solar was just taking off like crazy. We were sure we were saving the world. Had they listened to us then, oh my gosh, think where we would be now!"

In the 1990s, Energy Park gave birth to the "Energy Park Electric Company" at the fair. EPEC consisted then of two solar energy electricians—"Bob-O" Schultz and "Bob-1" Maynard—who helped set up and run the solar power at the fair's acoustic stages. "We would bring some of our own batteries and some of our own solar panels to show people how to make a little bit of electricity," Bob-1 said. They first powered Kesey Stage in the back of Energy Park to amplify the

A banner across the path at East Thirteenth marked the entrance to Energy Park.

acoustic music enough to be heard over the passing crowds. Fair volunteers who ran other acoustic stages took note and requested solar power for their area, as well.

"We started scrounging a little bit deeper into our personal batteries and solar panels so we could start powering these stages," Bob-1 said.

The Energy Park Electric Company also helped food booths set up safer nighttime lighting than the standard propane-fueled Coleman lanterns that they used for years. "So many people had these Coleman lanterns," said Energy Park member George Patterson. "They were such a serious fire safety hazard, but also—if you've ever seen one of those at night—they're blinding. Replacing them with more mellow sorts of lighting was a real treat to the fair family."

EPEC secured financing for the project in the 2000s from the fair board through its liaison, board member Anna Scott. The volunteers went to each food booth, offering lights powered by solar electric batteries. "Using a 12-volt deep-cycle battery with a small inverter and several 13-watt or 15-watt compact fluorescent light bulbs, suddenly we could go to electric lighting for the booth," Bob-1 said. "Then we'd pick up their battery each morning and take it out and charge on the sun for a few hours and bring it back. It made a huge difference."

Anna also carried the ball to get the board to back the Peach Power fund, where people who purchased tickets to the fair could opt to donate money to support use of alternative power sources.

Over the next few decades, the hard work of Energy Park advocates would bear some fruit in the solar energy field. "First we were community activists," Sue said. "Then a lot of us ended up working for utility companies or governments. All of a sudden, everything we were promoting started to get mainstreamed." It took a long time for building codes to reflect the new technologies, but once that happened, everyone knew that the solar industry had finally come into its own.

During the many years of activism, a core group would reunite annually to run Energy Park at the Oregon Country Fair. Every morning of the fair, Energy Park participants would gather in a morning circle to greet each other and make announcements. Some of the participants each year were new to the group, but many would participate year after year, forming close friendships. "This is a family," Anthony Stoppiello said. "I don't get to see some of these people except at the fair. Some of them live thousands of miles away. ... That whole family reunion part, that to me is very important because I get to hug some of my best friends I only see once a year.

"One of the traditions of Energy Park is we like to have a good time," Anthony added. "Work hard, honor your commitment and have a good time. Or, have a good time, honor your commitment and work hard. However you want to do it."

Bob-O Schultz had lived completely off the grid since 1970 and would go on to run Electron Connection, a renewable electricity outfitter from 1988 until he retired in 2014. The company designed, sold, and installed renewable power systems based on clients' needs. Some systems were designed completely off the grid, others tied in to the grid to exchange power.

Bob-1 Maynard would found Energy Outfitters in 1991 to consult, sell, and install solar energy systems. He ultimately sold Energy Outfitters in 2006 to groSolar and became vice president for Northwest sales in that company, where he specialized in site-specific integration of renewable solar energy.

In 1999, Bob-O and "Bob-1" would successfully lobby the Oregon Legislature to pass a bill permitting net-metering in Oregon. The law allowed utility customers to offset some or all of their energy use with onsite renewable energy generation.

In 2001, they would lobby for the Renewable Energy Technician license for electricians, which also became law. "That allowed us to

Banners welcomed visitors to the booths and displays at Energy Park.

no longer be outlaws in solar power," Bob-1 said. "It created a legal pathway for us to do our work. ... When Bob-O and I started doing solar electric, it was thought of as absolutely never going to be feasible or practical. And now here we are, fifteen or twenty years later with some legislative changes, and we have a real industry in Oregon."

In July 2007, the work of Bob-O and Bob-1 at the legislature to literally empower utility customers to give back to the grid would come full circle to the Oregon Country Fair. The two Bobs and colleague George Patterson completed installing a panel of solar photovoltaic cells—paid for by the fair's Peach Power fund—that would generate energy all year. The project's photovoltaic cells started flowing energy into the grid at 10:00 a.m. on the Fourth of July, 2007. It marked the first step in the fair's long-term goal of becoming a net alternative energy exporter.

1981
The Flying Karamazov Brothers

"Time is what keeps everything from happening at once."
—Flying Karamazov Brothers souvenir T-shirt

The Flying Karamazov Brothers, a juggling quartet, burst onto the international scene in March 1981, taking their quirky humor and gravity-defying routine to London's Mayfair Theatre. In typical madcap fashion, they not only played their theater run, they also joined the Grateful Dead twice in Europe to entertain between the band's sets.

By then, the Karamazov Brothers had performed several times at the Grateful Dead's legendary New Year's Eve concerts at the Oakland Coliseum. In London they noticed a poster advertising the band playing at the Rainbow Club. When they got in touch, the band invited the Karamazovs to perform a half-hour comedy act between music sets at the club.

Tim Furst, aka Fyodor Karamazov, remembered they tried something new during the Rainbow Club sets. "We worked out some percussion things with Mickey Hart and Billy Kreutzmann," Tim said. "So we ended up not only doing something in between their sets, but then coming back out during their stretch when they went into their long percussion piece, and we did some percussion juggling along with them."

The audience loved it. After the show, the band persuaded the Karamazovs to join them for their upcoming concert with the Who in Essen, Germany, that would be televised throughout Europe. The Karamazov Brothers figured it would make great publicity for their London gig. "So we flew down to Essen with the Dead," Tim said. But it didn't go as expected.

The audience turned out to be filled with Who fans, who had snapped up most of the tickets for the concert. "It was not our crowd," Tim said. To make matters worse, the Grateful Dead performed first, followed by the Flying Karamazov Brothers. But the audience wanted to see the Who, and that was the last act to take the stage. "It was a semi-disaster," Tim observed. "They were not interested in seeing people juggling and did not understand the jokes."

But that concert was just a small blip during the Flying Karamazov Brothers' flying leap to fame that year. Their run in London went well; the Goodman Theatre in Chicago had already booked them for later that spring; and the Arena Theatre in Washington, D.C., had them slated for the fall of 1981.

Yet the Karamazovs still made room in their busy schedule to perform at the 1981 Oregon Country Fair. For the sixth year, they would camp in tents with a bunch of their vaudeville friends amid the lush emerald hues of Oregon's rolling countryside at the Oregon Country Fair site. The entertainers would pull together an improvised show and then rehearse it once before the fair. They would stage the show several times a day during the fair's three-day run.

Each year in early July, a Brigadoon-like village rose up along the forested banks of the Long Tom River like magic. Long-haired carpenters in faded blue jeans could be seen hammering together peeled-wood posts to reinforce leaning craft booths. Fair volunteers climbed stepladders to hang colorful cloth banners in trees while others cobbled temporary stages into place. Out in the fields in front of the fair grounds, volunteers rode tractors to cut and bale hay to create parking lots for the public. The Main Camp Kitchen crew washed and chopped vegetables for salads and prepared hearty meals to feed the hungry pre-fair crews. Soon, the 300 acres along the Long Tom River would explode in the annual riot of color, sound, and celebration.

Each year, the Flying Karamazov Brothers looked forward to camping at the fair with other performers in the meadows and forests hugging the Long Tom River. They would reconnect with their West

Coast friends who still performed in the streets and at festivals. It had become tradition for the entertainers to gather around a campfire late each night to catch up and reminisce, swapping jokes and stories.

Their old partner Randy Nelson would rejoin them at the 1981 fair, making a quintet of jugglers on stage. The newest Karamazov brother, Sam "Smerdyakov" Williams, would enjoy visiting with his old partner in comedy Bliss Kolb, who performed at this fair as the Magnificent Mazuba. Moz Wright would again coordinate fair Entertainment with help from his partner, Deni Schadegg. Also expected were Tom Noddy the Bubble Guy, Artis the Spoonman, mime clown Avner "the Eccentric" Eisenberg, singer Jan Luby, and juggler Roberto Morganti.

Missing, though, would be ringleader of the Circus/Chumleighland Stage: Reverend Chumleigh himself, aka Michael Mielnick, along with his partner, Spike Wilder, aka Peggy Wendel. Reverend Chumleigh accepted a well-paying gig in Chicago for the summer and missed the fair.

Back in 1975, Michael, aka Chumleigh, had started a major trend when he invited a collection of vaudeville entertainers to perform at the fair in the first place, including the Flying Karamazov Brothers during those college days when the troupe was simply a duo—Paul and Howard.

Michael had accepted the task of coordinating the Circus stage at the request of Bill and Cindy Wooten, the fair's top coordinators in 1975. Michael had previous experience creating a circus in the neo-vaudeville style, when he started Major Chumleigh's Amazing Traveling Circus in 1971 in California.

Chumleigh, as his friends and fans called him, had pulled together the 1975 fair show with a miniscule budget of $500 supplemented by vigorous sweat equity. Besides the two Flying Karamazov Brothers, Chumleigh invited tap dancer Toes Tiranoff, and musicians from Washington's Evergreen State College to play in a band. Trombonist Thaddeus Spae (aka Carl Spaeth) became their nominal bandleader.

Chumleighland at the Oregon Country Fair was by far not the first gig for college comrades Howard and Paul. They had been juggling and performing together for two years by then—mainly around the campus of the University of California in Santa Cruz, and at Renaissance Faires in California. They had met their freshman year at UCSC, where they lived across the hall from each other in the dorm. Even living so close, it took a mutual friend to bring them together.

"Paul liked to test people with his personality to see if they could look past his obstreperous surface," Howard recalled. "I didn't at first." But their friend Laurie Riven persuaded Howard to reconsider. Howard and Laurie sang in a madrigral quartet that often performed at Renaissance Faires. Laurie noted that Paul, an English major, had talent. He could sing, play clarinet, juggle, and recite Shakespeare. Howard, a biology major, also sang, played trombone and baritone horn (aka euphonium), and had been juggling since he was twelve years old. Howard was eager to practice tricks he had recently picked up from three jugglers he also met through Laurie. That trio called themselves "Cock & Feathers" as they traveled the Renaissance Faire circuit.

Once Howard and Paul started juggling together, any early tension between them melted away in laughter. They cracked jokes and poked fun at each other as they practiced. They would taunt each other mercilessly as the cafeteria chair legs they were juggling inevitably clattered to the ground after a miss. Later, they would add the funniest insults and jokes to their act.

The pair tried on various names as they started out on the Renaissance Faire circuit: Tuck & Roll, Snout & Glybb, Moeck & Meier. They came up with the Flying Karamazov Brothers in 1974 when Howard was reading *The Brothers Karamazov*. Paul said that they "thought 'The Flying Karamazov Brothers' was a funny literal mix of the dark passionate characters of the book and the silliness of the circus." Howard adopted the stage name Ivan Karamazov; Paul became Dmitri Karamazov.

In 1974 Laurie introduced Howard to Michael Mielnik (aka Chumleigh). Her Cock & Feathers buddies had once performed with Major Chumleigh's Amazing Traveling Circus. One day when Michael dropped in to visit his Santa Cruz friends, Laurie brought him by to meet Howard. "We talked awhile and seemed to be kindred spirits," Howard said.

That impression held true with the stupendous show the Chumleighland troupe pulled off in the rough conditions of the 1975 Oregon Country Renaissance Fair. Chumleigh brought to the fair the first marching band, the first parade through the throngs, and the very first Saturday night Midnight Show.

Everyone had enjoyed their time performing together at the fair so much that the jugglers agreed to Chumleigh's invitation to take a sailing trip "around the world." The troupe planned to stop frequently at ports-of-call to perform and pass the hat. Chumleigh envisioned their combined acts would draw huge audiences that would stuff their hats with cash at every stop. He proposed they start with a shakedown trip to Alaska.

After the 1975 fair, Howard and Paul hitched a ride home to Santa Cruz to pack. They asked Howard's girlfriend, Seiza de Tarr, to join them, and the trio hitchhiked their way back to Eugene to meet Chumleigh. To attract potential rides, Howard and Paul juggled by the side of the road—taking turns sticking out their thumbs between tosses—while Seiza danced about waving a hand-lettered sign proclaiming "EUGENE" as their destination.

Somewhere along a lonely stretch of Highway 101, the main route that traces Oregon's dunes and cliffs along the edge of the Pacific Ocean, their hitching luck ran out. Stranded near nightfall in a grove of towering Douglas fir overlooking a cliff edge, they could barely see ocean waves foaming in thin lines in the dusky distance. After a very long while, a young woman sailed by in an aqua convertible. Giving a cheerful wave, she motored around the bend.

Paul shouted "That's our ride," and took off running. Howard and Seiza watched him leave in astonishment, musing "What's he doing?" Howard remarked that Paul had raced cross-country in high school, but the idea of catching a speeding car was beyond belief. They waited as they wondered how far the notoriously determined Paul would chase the car before giving up.

"After a much longer dramatic pause than made any kind of sense at all," Howard said, "the car came sailing back around the bend, Paul smirking triumphantly in the passenger's seat. The woman—whose name is, sadly, lost in the mists of time—drove us, after a refreshing sleep break in the verdant woods, all the way to our Eugene rendezvous."

Once they met up, Chumleigh had arranged transportation—of sorts—for the rest of the trip, starting with a Volkswagon Beetle driven by their musician friend Thaddeus Spae. Seven people and Chumleigh's Labrador retriever Birdalone—plus a bed of nails, juggling props, a clarinet, a baritone horn, and everyone's gear—had to fit into the tiny car for the long trip to Anacortes, Washington, to catch a ferry to the San Juan Islands.

Fortunately, Thaddeus used the vehicle as a camping rig. He had removed the passenger seat to make room to sleep in the car. The group stuffed most of their gear in the small trunk, but Chumleigh's bed of nails wouldn't fit. So they folded it up, nails sandwiched in, and laid it on the passenger-side floor where the seat had been removed. Four passengers lined up toboggan-style on top of the bed of nails. Two others squeezed in with the dog behind Thaddeus, who took the driver's seat.

Packed like clowns in a tiny circus car, they traveled for hours north on Interstate 5 until they navigated Seattle's tangled spaghetti web of interchanges to arrive at the ferry terminal. There the entertainers emerged stiffly from the tight space, one by one, stretched their legs and unloaded the gear. Thaddeus drove off waving.

The ferry ride should have been smooth sailing, but a couple got separated from the group when they stayed on the ferry instead of getting off at the right stop. After much scrambling about (rumored to be complicated by some green plant material), everyone serendipitously found each other and made their way to Friday Harbor, where they boarded the unmistakable Lion's Roar, a gaff-rigged twenty-two-foot wooden sailboat with a brightly tie-dyed mainsail.

Captain Myron greeted them from the helm wearing an engineer's cap and a woman's skirt. The first mate impressed them with "a bushy red beard, a bandana on his head, and a paratroop tattoo on his bum," Howard recalled. Chumleigh had booked the troupe at a festival in Point Roberts, a geographic anomaly south of Vancouver, Canada. The tiny piece of Washington state sits at the southern tip of a Canadian peninsula that has no land connection to Washington. It became part of the United States because it falls below the U.S.-Canadian borderline drawn in the nineteenth century.

"The voyage was not without its problems," Howard reminisced. "My favorite was when we became stuck in a whirlpool between islands, rotating about once every minute and a half. If the boat had been equipped with an engine, an outboard, or even a decent set of oars we could have escaped easily. But the Lion's Roar only had a pair of poles with boards nailed to them, and after several minutes of fruitless splashing we resigned ourselves to waiting six hours for the tide to change and the whirlpool to disappear. As we sat, we played music that attracted a small group of porpoises, who sang to us as we slowly rotated."

They arrived at Point Roberts barely in time for the show, which became the first and last show of the around-the-world tour. Captain Myron made clear that he would not take the troupe any further. Howard surmised that the three couples' "rampant rutting" in the sailboat's close quarters had gotten on the good captain's nerves.

With the rest of summer 1975 stretching ahead of them, Howard, Seiza, and Paul retreated to one of the dilapidated Gray Houses in Anacortes known as crash pads for like-minded travelers back in the day. Paul and Howard hopped on the ferry each morning to perform, plying the waters among the scenic San Juan Islands. As passengers boarded, the two Karamazovs announced their presence from an upper deck by playing nautical medleys on clarinet and euphonium. The gig, while lucrative, lasted only a week. Word finally filtered back from ferry headquarters to ban the pair from boarding. Busking wasn't allowed.

By the next summer, 1976, Paul and Howard had graduated as co-valedictorians from University of California-Santa Cruz. During their speech at the commencement ceremony, the pair juggled flaming torches as they chastised students for hiding away in college while the world was burning around them. They kept juggling the torches as a third student stepped up to the podium.

"We juggled around him while he stood in the middle reading a book," Howard said. "We'd never juggled torches around somebody before, but we didn't tell him that! We then dashed into town to the Convention Center to perform Paul's senior project, our first big multi-vaudevillian play, 'Everything You Are About to See is Actually Happening.' He wrote it for Chumleigh, who hated the script, and Randy Nelson ended up playing the lead instead."

By then, the Flying Karamazov Brothers had become a quartet, with Randy Nelson and Tim Furst joining Paul and Howard. Fresh out of college, they all were in their early twenties. Tim worked mainly as technical director, running the lights and sound for their shows, and building props. "But he was a better juggler than we were," Howard said, "and we'd have him come up and do specialty numbers." Tim adopted Fyodor Karamazov as his nom de théâtre.

Tim had learned to juggle from his father, a chemist who had been an Olympic-class gymnast. Starting with three oranges from a tree in their backyard in Palo Alto, California, Tim practiced until he worked his way up to swinging multiple clubs with aplomb. He entered Stanford University in 1969 to study architecture and philosophy. On ethical grounds, he refused a student deferment to the draft for the Vietnam War, and sought conscientious objector status. Drafted at age nineteen, he was assigned two years of alternate service working in the Stanford Medical Library. Afterward, running the stage lights for his friends and juggling once in a while looked a heck of a lot more appealing than going back to college.

Randy Nelson had been good friends with Paul Magid since childhood and had performed with the troupe off and on since 1974, although he considered it a drawback that he did not know how to juggle. Randy took on the stage name Alyosha Karamazov and did tricks with a rope and with magic linking rings, which became his signature contribution. He also chimed in on the jokes and made funny faces while standing still as Paul and Howard hurled flying sharp objects around him. Eventually Randy learned to juggle well enough to join in.

After Paul and Howard graduated, the foursome took off for San Francisco to seek fame and fortune. They shared digs in the Haight-Ashbury district, performed along the streets and the wharf, and booked gigs at local clubs.

During a show at the Magic Cellar in San Francisco, they decided on the spur of the moment to include Tim in the juggling set even though he was also working the lights. "I set the lights for a certain level, ran up to the stage, did the juggling pattern, came back, and continued running lights," Tim said. With no rehearsal and no time to craft new lines, Tim remained silent as he juggled. "After the show, we got feedback that it worked really well to have three people talking consistently and one person as a silent character," Tim said. That made it easy for Tim to join the juggling set without rehearsing lines.

They also opened six shows for Robin Williams at the Boardinghouse in San Francisco. "That was on his return to San Francisco after 'Mork and Mindy' became a hit" on television, Howard said. As they watched Robin Williams work the crowd night after night, they picked up tips, especially the way he'd use humor to squelch the hecklers. "When someone in the audience yells at you during the show," Howard said, "the idea is to get the audience to laugh at that person and get them to stop. ... 'You remind me of my brother, only he has a human head.' That was one of the more surreal ones I really liked."

By the late 1970s, the Flying Karamazov Brothers had started playing large enough venues that it became impossible for Tim to run between the stage and the lighting booth; he had to choose. Tim ended up onstage full-time as the silent Karamazov, Fyodor, and they recruited techies to run the lights and sound.

On Dec. 31, 1979, the Flying Karamazov Brothers performed with the Grateful Dead during their New Year's Eve concert at the Oakland Coliseum. The foursome—Paul Magid, Howard Patterson, Randy Nelson, and Tim Furst going by their respective noms de théâtre—Dmitri Karamazov, Ivan Karamazov, Alyosha Karamazov, and Fyodor Karamazov—had been honing their juggling routines for four years, whirling flying objects at one another in intricate rhythms while fishing for laughs with their puns, sly insults, and silly jokes. They had busked in the streets of cities up and down the West Coast, and had performed at renaissance festivals, the Oregon Country Fair, school auditoriums, and the occasional Bay Area club. Yet they aimed for a bigger audience and the bright lights of show biz success.

The Grateful Dead started the first set of the 1979 New Year's Eve show with a rockin' "Jack Straw" and kept it up through "Franklin's Tower," and "Mexicali Blues" before they took their first break. Just before midnight a truck wheeled on stage as the tune of "Truckin'" was piped through the public address system. Suddenly the music switched to the main theme from "Star Wars" and concert promoter Bill Graham—attached to rope and harness Peter-Pan style—"flew" out of the truck dressed as a butterfly. As butterfly Bill floated off stage and the truck wheeled away, the crowd began the Midnight Countdown.

The Dead followed up with two more sets. Deep into the last set, the Flying Karamazov Brothers juggled in the spotlight as the band played "Sunshine Daydream." The Brothers K began the wee hours of the year 1980 juggling clubs like crazy in front of thousands of wildly happy Deadheads who were cheering themselves hoarse as the concert came to a close. It made a fitting start to the 1980s, when the brothers' careers would take wing and fly higher than Bill Graham's butterfly.

In the spring of 1980 the Karamazovs booked their first stage show, "Juggling and Cheap Theatrics," at Chicago's Goodman Theatre. A brief run afterward at the Bitter End Theatre (aka the Other End) in New York won the Flying Karamazov Brothers a special Obie Award in 1980 for the off-off-Broadway production. "It's kind of silly we got an award out of those one- and two-night runs," Paul Magid told a newspaper reporter at the time, to which Howard Patterson added: "But it's a prestigious award. And we like it."

In October 1980 they brought "Juggling and Cheap Theatrics," to the Arena Theatre in Washington, D.C. In November the Flying Karamazov Brothers got their break on television—appearing on "The Tom and Dick Smothers Brothers Special" on NBC, a gig that merited coverage in *People* magazine, which placed the Flying Karamazov Brothers "on the cutting edge of comedy."

People magazine described parts of the act: "'Anarchy is the only way,' one proclaims, as the foursome storms onto the stage amid an explosion of tuba blowing, wild shrieking, and dervish-like dancing. Immediately the air is full of whirling blades, flaming torches, and noxious puns. They're called the Flying Karamazov Brothers, but they don't fly, they're not Russian and they aren't brothers. ... The group calls its finale 'Nine Objects of Terror.' For thirty seconds the Brothers fling around a cleaver, a peace pipe, a bottle of champagne, a ukulele, a sickle, a rubber fish, a flaming torch, an egg, and a skillet. At one point the egg flips into the pan just as the torch passes underneath to 'fry' it. And at the very end, of course, the champagne blows its cork so the frantic Karamazovs can be toasted."

Even as the frenetic stage show propelled the four juggling jokesters into a new phase of fame, there was a catch. Randy Nelson wanted to take a break from life on the road to start a family. "We were figuring out what was going to happen next with my wife and I and our burgeoning family, and it wasn't exactly clear what we were going to do and how it was going to happen," Randy said.

He thought of his friend Sam Williams and the balloon juggling routine he watched Sam perform at the Oregon Country Fair's Midnight Show. "The routine was just wonderful," Randy said. "Sam had this terrific rapport with the audience and it was just funny as hell. So I told the other guys that I thought Sam would be a good person to take my slot in the show. He'd be a different sensibility. ... The guys were open to it."

At the time, Sam performed in a comedy duo called Laughing Moon Theater with Bliss Kolb. Sam had started out staging skits in 1978 in the streets of Seattle and at the Oregon Country Fair, and he was a regular in Reverend Chumleigh's Alligator Palace vaudeville revues in La Conner, Washington. So Sam had already joined the entertainer "family" that camped together every year at the Country Fair, which included the Karamazovs, whom he greatly admired.

"It certainly was a surprise to me that I became a Karamazov," Sam recalled in later years. "Though I was aware of the ever so vague pie-in-the-sky possibility of it, I never thought it would actually happen. They were basically my heroes as well as my friends. Seeing them doing the street stuff was what inspired me to start doing street performing. ... So it was very exciting for me when they asked me to join." He adopted the nom de théâtre Smerdyakov Karamazov and started practicing with the troupe in December of 1980.

Despite the failure of Reverend Chumleigh's round-the-world tour, the Flying Karamazov Brothers and other fair entertainers kept looking for ways to perform together beyond the fair.

"Each year we would come together with all of our best friends and throw this show together," Howard said. "On Friday it would suck and by Sunday it was this totally hot show. We had a band, we had cues, all the timing, things were just ripping through. And we'd say, 'That was such a great show. I loved it. If only we could do this show somewhere else now that it works, tour it someplace.'" Starting in 1976, they performed at free charity shows for prisoners and shut-ins sponsored by California's Bread and Roses nonprofit. In the late 1970s, they often entertained at the Douglas County Fair near Roseburg, Oregon, caravanning south together after the Oregon Country Fair ended.

In 1977, Michael Mielnick and his partner, Peggy Wendel, had opened The Alligator Palace in La Conner, Washington, where they frequently booked their fair friends. When the Alligator Palace closed in 1979, Tom Noddy the Bubble Guy and sword-swallower Moz Wright joined forces to create Westwind Travelin' Vaudeville, a traveling show that also featured fair entertainers.

In spring 1981 over a dinner, Paul Magid and Patch Adams (nearly two decades before Patch was immortalized in the self-titled movie) hatched a plan to resurrect the Chautauqua movement, the cultural enrichment program that became hugely popular in rural America and Canada at the turn of the twentieth century.

"Chautauquas were, and are, this sort of self-betterment movement that's very American," Paul said. "It started from the Lyceum movement, which was a self-betterment movement before that, and it had a religious, Christian, tone to it initially. Basically the idea was to go to communities and bring professors and scientists in to give out new information about all the latest things that were happening, and include great performances—vaudeville performances and orchestras—and politicians. ... It became the most popular form of entertainment in America up until the end of the 1920s. Over thirty million Americans a year would come to them. There were about a thousand traveling Chautauquas going to little towns by the end of it.

"And I thought, wow, this sounds like something we could use," Paul added. "We'd take out the religious element to it, put in the vaudeville element with our marching band, and get people who are educators to do workshops. And I started talking about this with Patch Adams, who's also a healer and a doctor and a clown."

The Flying Karamazov Brothers displayed their banner at the Chumleighland entrance.

Paul and Patch envisioned an entertainment and education extravaganza that would travel to small communities in the summertime. Their "Old Time New Age Chautauqua" would start after the 1981 Oregon Country Fair ended, taking the fair acts on the road. Patch would bring volunteers from the Gesundheit Health Collective to offer workshops on health care, alternative energy, and alternative agriculture. Entertainers from the Country Fair would attract the audience with a parade and show, then give workshops on performance arts. Paul wanted to play "under the noses of the presidents at Mount Rushmore" and across from the White House in a grand, cross-country tour.

But then the Flying Karamazovs flew off to Ireland for a series of gigs and left Tom Noddy the Bubble Guy and his friend Jan Luby to house-sit the Karamazov home in Santa Cruz. With Tom's experience on Westwind Travelin' Vaudeville, Paul and Howard figured Tom would be a natural to coordinate the logistics of the Chautauqua tour in their absence.

But as he tried to arrange the tour, Tom kept hitting roadblocks. "It started falling apart," he said. "I didn't have any authority. I couldn't answer questions about insurance or anything. The Karamazovs were going to keep in touch, but they didn't. Zero."

When the Brothers K finally returned in June 1981, a discouraged Tom handed a stack of paperwork to Paul, saying, "I think maybe we could salvage a tour in the Northwest."

1981 Starflower and Community Village

> "Growers Market was the nuts who sold the fruit and Starflower was the fruits who sold the nuts."
> — Hayfield aka Sally Sheklow

When the Oregon Country Fair's focus on alternative energy switched from Community Village to the larger Oregon Energy Horizons area in 1981, the Village Coordinating Council cast a wide net to diversify the village's mission and outreach. In the spring of 1981, the council mailed out 400 invitation letters to nonprofits and collectives around the region. A flurry of responses poured in.

New nonprofits that would participate in the 1981 Community Village included Chicano Affairs, Citizens for Safe Energy, Gay Hotline, Head Start, Starflower, and People for Prison Alternatives. In the village setup, each booth was shared by groups of similar interests. For example, Chicano Affairs and Gay Hotline became part of the Human Services booth that also hosted previous fair participants such as Switchboard, the Single Men's Support Group, and Family Shelter House.

As the volunteers from different organizations staffed the booths together, they would find ample opportunity to share views and develop friendships. The arrangement helped build lasting connections among the groups, extending the spirit of Community Village well beyond the three days of the fair. In 1981, the village's eighteen booths hosted nearly a hundred different groups that assembled under banners including Art, Local Self-Reliance, Spirit, Life-Long Learning, Health, Environmental Awareness, and Economic Cooperation. The system fostered plenty of personal connections that would last beyond the fair.

Starflower, a feminist collective that distributed natural foods around the region, joined the Local Self-Reliance booth that year. "I worked at a mostly women's natural foods wholesaler called Starflower," said Jain Elliott, who was thirty-two in 1981. "We got a letter from Community Village saying 'We're broadening our outreach. We'd like to have some representation from groups that haven't been in the village before. We've heard Starflower is one of the cooperative businesses in Eugene and we wonder if anybody would like to come to our meeting.' And as soon as whoever got the mail that day got that letter, she said, 'Jain, this one's for you. It's the hippies calling.'"

The meeting was held on the second floor of Growers Market, where several small rental offices share a common area with a large table, lots of chairs and a couple of benches. On a hot spring day, Skeeter Duke facilitated a meeting attended by several dozen village participants. "He wore no shirt," Jain recalled. "He's a very skinny guy and was very peaceful. I was entranced." After the meeting, Jain joined others for social time at Skeeter's house, and visited a while with Robert DeSpain, who served on the Village Council. "Robert told me he was glad that Starflower was going to be in the Fair," Jain

Hayfield, aka Sally Sheklow (left), and Jain Elliott represented Starflower in Community Village in the early 1980s.

said. "We felt so very, very welcomed.

"So I went to all of the Community Village meetings" where decisions were made by consensus, Jain said. "We sang loving songs to each other at the end of every meeting. I got one other hippie at Starflower to agree to come with me. Her name at that time was Hayfield. And now she's Sally Sheklow. We shared her little tent. That first year, we were in the cooperative food booth."

Sally had changed her name to Hayfield in 1973 when she came out as a lesbian. "Lesbian consciousness was really rising and I didn't want to have a patriarchal name," Sally said. "I wanted to have a name of my own choice." She was living south of Eugene on a ranch in Lorane at the time. There she had learned how to mow, bale, and buck hay. She felt so at peace in the hayfield that when she experienced her first guided meditation and was instructed to visualize herself in a completely safe place, she saw herself in a hayfield. Shortly thereafter, she took Hayfield as her name.

Her family never got used to it. "They couldn't stand it," she said with a laugh. "I was Hayfield for eleven years. My poor family!"

Starflower joined the booth shared by Growers Market, Willamette People's Co-op, and Mollalla Co-op. "The other organizations were all retail co-ops," Jain said. "They were all more or less on shaky financial ground. All but the Growers Market went out of business in the next few years. I was the accounts receivable person at Starflower. So their relationship to us at that time, was 'Please let us have our order. I promise the check won't bounce.' My answer to them was 'Well, I guess so.'"

But the roles reversed a bit in the village, with the two newbies from Starflower asking the others what needed doing next. "I cut watermelon all day," Jain said.

Sally Sheklow, who was thirty years old then, remembered trying to educate people about natural foods. "It wasn't like this common knowledge, about pesticides and herbicides and preservatives," she said. "People weren't reading labels. Buying in bulk was this big radical thing. Now you can buy in bulk anywhere, but at the time that was radical."

Starflower started as a home-based, feminist business in 1972, delivering herbs to stores around Eugene/Springfield and Portland. The six original members lived together in a house. They would sit around a table in their basement to measure and weigh the herbs. Then they slapped on labels and sealed the cellophane bags with a household iron. Eventually Starflower added rennet-free cheese, brown rice, and fruit juice to the lineup.

Christine Frazer, then age thirty-two, was offered a job at Starflower in 1981 after she helped one of the workers fix the smashed top of a Starflower truck at a welding shop. "That is when I met Jain Elliot," Christine said. "We're both Geminis and we were the twelfth and thirteenth addition to the Starflower family. From there Starflower grew into a collective worker-owned business. It was never a co-op."

Starflower members used the worker-owned model to frame a business committed to feminist ideals, making all decisions by consensus. Nobody was boss. They developed two kinds of stock to make it affordable for women to join. If worker-owners couldn't pay cash for stock, they could work to earn stock equity.

Members took turns working the jobs: loading fifty-pound bags of rice, operating forklifts, repacking the food, driving semi-tractor trucks to make deliveries, purchasing the inventory, and keeping the books.

"When I first started, we still were rotating to all the jobs," Christine said. "But it quickly became apparent that some of us were no good at books and some of us were no good at driving trucks. We started specializing and forming teams. Charlie Glass took me on one trucking run and then I was lead driver. It was an International Tilt Cab—flat nose front and you sit above the engine—tractor with a forty-foot trailer. We were insane!"

Starflower moved operations to a warehouse by the railroad tracks in the Whiteaker area of Eugene in 1974 and expanded its line of products to include nuts, oils, pastas, cereals, sweeteners, and more types of cheese. The collective had trouble at first securing bank loans to purchase food upfront. But a local bank came through.

Pacific Continental Bank supplied loans to Starflower that helped keep the warehouse full of stock. "We'd buy 40,000 pounds of buckwheat and 40,000 pounds of wheat," Christine said. "I'd go to Idaho to pick it up and then I'd drop off half of it in Seattle. Then [in Seattle] I'd pick up cashews from China in five-gallon tins" and shuttle the load of cashews, buckwheat, and wheat down Interstate 5 to Eugene.

In Eugene, Starflower would warehouse the food briefly before distributing it among natural food grocers up and down the I-5 corridor. "Starflower visited many co-ops throughout the Northwest," Jain Elliott said. Palmer Parker, who was the fair's publicity coordinator, would bring a batch of fair posters to Starflower. "We'd take them out to the co-ops," Jain said. "They would put in a Starflower order and then they'd say 'Is our Country Fair poster coming yet?' It was such a thrill to us to see their eyes light up when we walked in."

Hayfield joined Starflower in 1976 after she had graduated from the University of Oregon with a degree in broadcast communications. "I had auditioned at KVAL and KEZI, was looking for a job," Sally Sheklow said. One day she was eating lunch at Mama's Homefried Truckstop, a collective-run restaurant near the UO campus that served as a gathering spot for student activists. "There was a collective meeting of Starflower happening," Sally said. "I had recently come out (as lesbian) in '73, and I noticed the amazing power of the women of Starflower."

Someone suggested to Sally that she drop by the Starflower warehouse. "They were unloading a truck and needed volunteers," she said. "I went and helped unload fifty-pound bags of rice. You could not get brown rice at Safeway in those days. Brown rice was radical. Same with rice cakes, same with Nancy's Yogurt—you couldn't get any of that stuff at a mainstream store. I helped unload that truck and it was such an empowering, awesome thing that when they had an opening, I applied."

By 1979 Starflower had become the largest distributor of bulk natural foods in the Northwest. Of the thirty-two worker-owners, three were men.

"It was such a challenge to be a socialist enterprise in a capitalist system," Sally said. "Starflower was mostly women, but ... there were men. They were gay men. I'd kind of been in Lesbo Land. So working with men—Whoa, there's men in the gay community? Who knew?"

Hayfield felt empowered at Starflower. "It was just so founded on feminist principles," she said. "That was really the core of it and women were doing everything: Driving trucks and getting strong, lifting heavy stuff, using pallet jacks, and stacking those fifty-pound bags over your head. ...

"Being around strong women, being where women were honored, working together, coming to consensus. I had never heard of consensus. We had consensus training." They even put on talent shows to entertain each other. The women grew so close that their menstrual cycles came at the same time.

"All that affirming, positive energy about who we were, coming out of a super-sexist system. I personally felt really supported and encouraged to be myself and express myself in ways I'd never had a chance to do before," Sally said. She was inspired to celebrate their work with songs and poetry.

STARFLOWER NATURAL ANTHEM
(Please rise)

Oh, sesame seed
Pinto beans and brown rice
What so proudly we stacked
'Til the six o'clock mee-ting

Invoices and phone calls
Handled by the desk-ies
While the truckers on runs
Were so gallantly driving

And the purchies be-ware
Bookies say cash ain't there
Still margins must rise
While the prices stay fair

Oh, say does that Starflowered
Banner yet wa-ave
O'er the land of the cheese
And the home of the grain

(Alternate ending:
O'er the land of the cheese
And the hope of a raise.)

Outside of Community Village, Sally felt the fair was not

particularly welcoming to lesbians and gays in 1981. "There wasn't much of a lesbian presence," she said. "Starflower wasn't all lesbians, but it was a lot. Other than us, there wasn't really much visibility. There was a band then called the Fabulous Dyketones. They sang parody covers of early rock-n-roll songs. I had a Dyketones tank top that I wore to the fair that first time, kind of trying to advertise, like, any other lesbians out here? And there weren't so much.

"Even though everybody was really loving, there was still a noticeable lack of consciousness," Sally said. "Even around disability, there was no accessibility then. Starflower members had educated ourselves and pushed for accessible outhouses and ramps and water. … It was jarring for me to realize that just because people were good on one thing, like natural foods, didn't mean they were conscious of feminism or accessibility or racism or class issues or anything, so we all had a lot of educating ourselves to do."

Still, Hayfield enjoyed the incubator feeling of Community Village enough to sign up to serve on the Village Council in 1982. That's when she introduced "The Hokey Pokey" to the village meetings. Dancing "The Hokey Pokey" at village meetings would remain a tradition for decades. Hayfield also landed a coveted spot in the fair's Saturday night Midnight Show, reciting her poem about a Starflower truck driver in front of 3,000 blissed out fair folks, her biggest talent show yet.

ODE TO PAULA JO
The Truckers Epic Poem
(Dedicated to the memory of Sharon Janeschild)
By Sally Sheklow aka Hayfield

You don't know how good I feel
When I see you at the wheel
Of the semi heading out to do a run
I see you checking out your mirrors
As you shift her through the gears
Squinting in the early morning sun

I like the way you take control
When those big wheels start to roll

And you set that rig to moving down the line
And you know you look so sweet
Just a-bouncing in that seat
Racking up your hours of overtime

You've already been to Hoot's
In your high-top lace-up boots
Got your thermos full of coffee for the trip
Now you're heading down I-5
Feeling glad to be alive
You've got your travel sub, your toothbrush, and your clip

Four wheelers hit the brakes
And the folks do double takes
When they see that there's a WOMAN at the wheel
Kids signal for your horn
While their mom looks on with scorn
And poor dad goes swerving off into some field

You turn your C.B. on
And you start ratchet jawin'
With some guy with eighteen wheels at your back door
You say "I'm hauling natural foods"
He replies with something crude
So you push your hammer closer to the floor

Paula Jo Vaden at the wheel of a Starflower truck.

"Uh, wait up girl," you hear him say
"I ain't had a chick all day
And that's hard on a fella, don't you know"
You say "Your rudeness makes me sick
I'm a driver, not a chick
Get your filthy mouth off my ra-did-io"

"Break 1-7" someone calls
"This here's Suzy from Sioux Falls,
Is that an angry woman's voice I read?"

Brigadoon of the Sixties

"Yeah, that's a big 10-4
I'd like to talk to you some more
Some sisterly support's just what I need"

Well, you check your 10-36
You see it's time for a coffee fix
So you arrange with Suzy for a rendezvous
At the truck stop you shake hands
And you start making plans
And talk about just what you're gonna do

You say I'd like to show that boy
A feminist convoy
With big mean women drivers and their rigs
Sue says "I'll give some friends a shout
And see if they'll come out
And help us teach a lesson to that pig

Well, Sue heads off to her C.B.
And it's not long before you see
A purple Diamond Reo pulling in
"You must be Pea" the driver says
"They call me Irate Inez"
And I can't wait to see the fun begin

You hear an air horn sound
And you quickly turn around
To feast your eyes on a pink cab-over Pete
And when you turn around again
Three more semis have pulled in
That makes seven women drivers in the fleet

"How we doing, Pea?" calls Sue
"You think that ought to do?"
"Yeah, I think that's plenty" you reply
"Then come on girls let's go" says Sue
"That guy won't know what to do
When he sees seven women driven diesels cruising by"

Starflower and Community Village

One by one the rigs pull out
And you can see without a doubt
You've got strong courageous women on your side
Sisters out to lend a hand
And you know they understand
What it's like to feel a woman trucker's pride

You feel like you're in some dream
And then up ahead you see 'im
Having trouble hauling doubles up the hill
"You see what I see, Pea?" calls Sue
"Yes, my friend, I surely do"
"Come on girls let's move in for the kill"

John checks his fish-eye mirror
Then he finds he's lost a gear
And every time he tries to shift his tranny grinds
He's losing power steady
And he knows he isn't ready
For that female fleet that's roaring up behind

Well, he turns his C.B. on
And he says "This here's Jake Brake John"
And I'm looking for a brother for a 10-33
"You got Sioux Falls Sue here, John
You got some trouble, boy? Come on"
But John just changes channels on his C.B.

But every channel that he tries
Some angry woman's voice replies
And poor Jake Brake John just don't know where to turn
"This here's Pea" you finally say
"And you offended me today
And there's a couple things you ought to learn

We drive the same big rigs as you
Got just as much hard work to do
But we believe in workers' cooperation"
Then every woman gives her rap

About taking sexist crap
And Jake Brake John gets himself an education

They tell him how it is
To have to hear remarks like his
In the middle of a long hard working day
Men's jokes and crude flirtation
Are unwanted aggravation
That make a woman feel like blowing men away

John listens and he learns
About the women's true concerns
And he agrees to clean his act up then and there
So, remember Jake Brake John
Respect your sisters, and from now on
Support women truckers everywhere!

Starflower would close its doors in 1987, after fourteen years. Changes in the natural food industry, the loss of skilled workers, and a lack of capital available to the worker-owned business would lead to its decline.

After Starflower folded, Sally would work odd jobs and become

In 1984, Starflower announced its presence in the Cooperative Fruit Booth with a banner.

a humor writer. Later she would work as a local organizer for a peace and justice nonprofit Community Alliance of Lane County and as an instructor of Women's Studies and Queer Studies at Portland State University.

For fun, Sally would help create a comedy improvisation group called WYMPROV! All four of the performers were lesbians. WYMPROV! would become her ticket to return to the fair in the 2000s.

"Going back to the fair as a performer was really great," Sally said. "Having a place to camp, having a certain number of gigs but not being tied to a booth having to work all day—that was really fun. And the fair crowd is just so awesome. You can do any silly little thing and they'll crack up and go along with you."

Tom Noddy would invite WYMPROV! to perform in the Midnight Show several times. "I adored Tom Noddy," Sally said. "He's such a delightful guy. To find myself being able to really appreciate a man instead of resenting men? That was big for me. He's my groovy guy."

Sally noted that the fair had gotten its act together a little more. "Accessibility really improved," she said. "That was a very visible, conscious effort they made." She also connected with people at the fair who shared her Jewish faith. "I discovered that people in the hat booth do a Friday night Shabbat," she said. "We did that with them several years. That was very cool, a magical time."

Fairgoers enjoyed a circle dance in Community Village in the early 1980s.

5 1981
A Wild Fair

> "The Oregon Country Fair is a festival of life in its unashamed exuberance and bubbling vitality."
> —Bill Wooten, 1981 *Peach Pit*

After thirteen years of experience, the volunteer organizers of the Oregon Country Fair had gotten their act together enough that fair preparations had smoothed into a routine of only minor frenzy. The cooperative system of autonomous, volunteer crews played out almost like clockwork by this time. Crew coordinators needed few instructions to get started. Volunteers knew their jobs and simply set-to. As usual, crews constantly strived to improve their "piece of the fair."

The new Oregon Energy Horizons area was the most advertised of three big changes at the fair in 1981.

A second change emerged from the Information Crew, which proposed giving each booth a unique number—an actual numbered address—and compiling a database to make it easier to find food and craft booths and give directions to them. Surprisingly, the idea generated controversy and stiff resistance at first.

Info Crew coordinator Jack Delay said he talked to crafters who were apprehensive about putting their names down. "I had to assure them that we only used this for the event, and we destroyed the information right after the fair," he said.

"It was very difficult to get that database done because of privacy issues," agreed Chris "Ruby" Bauske, who volunteered then for Info Crew. "People did not want to be found at the Fair. A lot of them used aliases. ... There was a lot of paranoia because a number of people there were still draft-dodgers [from the Vietnam War] and they had not been part of the general culture for many years. Or they were people who supported draft-dodgers. And we had to respect people's need for that."

For many years, Info Crew volunteers had struggled with how to describe "where" something is at the fair. A rudimentary numbering system existed. Numbers were written on stakes pounded in the ground at the start of the fair, but the stakes would fall sideways into the brush or disappear into the background by the time the fair started. Info Crew members were stuck with giving cryptic directions: "... go around that large tree on the left. ..."

Not being able to help customers find a certain craft or food booth was inconvenient and frustrating. But not being able to tell the White Bird medical team where to find someone experiencing a medical emergency loomed as a larger problem. Still, the plan to create a fair database was met with intense debate when Info Crew coordinator Jack Delay presented it at the May 31 planning meeting. After much discussion, fair organizers approved the database on the condition that the lists would be destroyed after the fair.

Info Crew volunteer Brian Bauske—who worked in Eugene for Datanex Incorporated, an early software company in Eugene—agreed to help create and print the database. Two decades before the advent of personal laptops, Datanex owned one of the huge, room-sized computers needed then for basic computing. After work hours, the crew could use Datanex's computer to build the database and print it out.

Info Crew members also reached out to fair cartographer Peter Eberhardt to work on the booth numbering system. Peter had drawn the fair's first accurate map in 1980 at the request of Main Camp. The Info Crew wanted to work with Peter to add the new booth numbering system to the official 1981 fair map.

Chris Bauske, who worked for the city of Eugene, borrowed one of the city's measuring wheels so they could more precisely determine booth locations. Peter, Chris, and Brian spent a pleasant spring Saturday walking the figure-eight pathway of the fair, measuring the distances for each booth as they went. They devised a three-digit numbering system for booth addresses. "Odd numbers on the outside, even numbers on the inside," Peter said, "starting at Odyssey (the Info booth at the entrance) and going all the way around."

In the weeks running up to the fair, Info Crew members worked hours into the night furiously typing data entry form information from the fair's Registration Crew into six categories: products, booth address, booth name, booth representative name, people, and hometown. Late Thursday night before the Fair opened to the public, Brian Bauske stood vigil in his office in town as a long length of computer printout paper—old-style blue and white striped, fifteen inches wide with holes punched down both sides—came sputtering out of the computer's massive printer, line by line.

Brian had just entered the final batch of names and booth numbers that the Registration Crew had gathered Thursday from last-minute booths as well as corrections. He folded the long printouts accordion-style and clipped them into five giant plastic binders: one for each Info booth, and one for Main Camp. Then he drove back to the fair site to sleep a few winks in his tent before the fair began the next morning.

During the fair, the Info Crew would find the databases very useful for answering fairgoers' questions. The addresses on the map made it much easier to point out locations. Many crafters made an extra sale because their booth could more easily be found. In fact, having fixed addresses on a map made it easier for the entire fair to operate more efficiently, from Recycling and Security to Main Camp and Fair Central.

The third change made by organizers would enhance the public's fair-going experience for years to come. Organizers agreed to a suggestion from Barbara Stern, who handled the fair's public relations, to print the fair's first-ever event guide. Barbara had advocated for the guide for several years because she had heard frequent requests for an entertainment calendar prior to the fair.

Named the *Peach Pit* to honor the fair's peach logo, the 1981 issue contained one newsprint page folded in half to make four tabloid-size pages. Sprinkled with old-fashioned and psychedelic clip art, the inside pages listed schedules for the stages and events at Community Village and Oregon Energy Horizons. The cover included a stylized peach and a welcome essay written by Bill Wooten, one of the earliest organizers of the fair. Peter Eberhardt's map on the back would help fairgoers navigate the pathway known as the Eight, an endless loop that mirrors the symbol for Infinity.

Fair organizers sighed in relief when the county assembly permit came through without the usual big hassle. Things had gotten so onerous in previous years that the fair's attorney, Jill Heiman, had sued the county commissioners for impeding fair participants' right to free assembly. The lawsuit cited a Lane County ordinance that required only the fair (and no other group) to post a huge bond—in addition to purchasing event insurance. With the lawsuit wending its way through the courts, Lane County commissioners in May 1981 rescinded the ordinance requiring the bond and quickly approved the fair's permit.

In June, the hub of all fair operations—Main Camp—clicked into pre-fair preparations. Nancy Albro, one of the original Main Camp volunteers, again served as Main Camp coordinator. Fair cofounder Bill Wooten was still on the scene, although he had become more of an honorary spokesman than an active participant. After he and Cindy Wooten divorced in 1979, Cindy had remained "on call" to Main Camp, but she mostly distanced herself from the fair to keep the peace with Bill.

The Main Camp regulars who spent a month together on site before the fair included Sandra Bauer and her sister Marcia O'Dell, Reese Prouty, Terry Patrick, Michael Killgallon, Mike Martin, Ron Chase, and Main Camp cook Jesse Bolton. Closer to fair time, they were joined by banner-hanger Wally Slocum and a few others.

"Every night at 6:00 or 7:00, 9:00, we'd close the gate and everybody was gone except us," Reese Prouty recalled. "It was mandatory [to leave]. There was nobody from crews staying the night, just the twelve of us left in Main Camp. Even if you had main jobs, like Traffic Coordinator, you couldn't come out there and stay. You could come out during the day, but just the Main Camp people could stay."

One time a local television station came out to film the pre-fair preparations. "We were all thrilled," Reese said. "I can't remember which channel was coming out. We were going to do a walk-through, and we were going to be on TV!" It was especially exciting because they had just purchased a generator and had brought a TV in to camp for the first time. "When Michael bought that generator," Reese said, "all of a sudden light bulbs went off in the boys' heads. Generators! Oh! Electricity! … We used it for TV for quite a while."

Before the day the show was to be aired, the women of Main

Reese Prouty was a Main Camp regular in the late 1970s and early 1980s

Main Camp stalwarts Marcia O'Dell, Sandra Bauer, Nancy Albro, and Jill Heiman in 1981.

Camp went shopping in town. They were planning a "dress-up" night, and asked Jesse to cook up a fancy dinner for the evening newscast. In town they bought white T-shirts and fabric paint. "We knew the boys wouldn't dress up," Reese said, "so we painted their dress-up outfit on these white T-shirts. Ron was an accountant, so he had a little bow tie and the pocket-saver with all the pencils in it that we painted on. Then Wally had this really beat-up tie, his tie clip was a wheelbarrow, and he had a bad hammer attached to his pocket. … Michael was always talking about Farrah Fawcett so he had Farrah Fawcett painted on his tie."

The day the TV show was going to be aired, Main Camp folks went around the Eight path and told everyone working on booths and crew projects that the gates would be shut early that evening. As dinnertime neared, they went around again and rousted everyone out of the Eight. Then they set up the TV. The women dressed up in their fanciest nightgowns for dinner and got the men to put on their decorated T-shirts.

"We were having our cocktails at camp, sitting in our sexy nightgowns and these fancy shirts, watching the TV and totally absorbed in it," Reese said. "At some point, someone said, 'We have an audience!'" About ten people stood there, mouths agape, witnessing "what really goes on" at Main Camp. "We had missed a whole bunch of people," Reese said, laughing, "and we had this audience watching us watch TV!"

As the calendar pages flipped from June to July 1981, the fair site turned into an anthill of activity along the meandering Long Tom

Main Camp guys wore T-shirts painted with ties for a special occasion (from left): Kenny Riskin, Ron Chase, Michael Killgallon, Cabal O'Dell, Mike Lions, Terry Patrick, and Wally Slocum.

River. More crafters arrived to assess winter storm damage to their booths and repair or rebuild them as necessary. Some Main Camp workers baled hay from the outer meadows to make room for public parking lots; others painted signs, erected perimeter fencing and repaired booths, and eventually rolled out the wooden barrels that would be filled with drinking water during the event. At the end of each workday, a dozen hot and dusty volunteers would sit around picnic tables to discuss the tasks left as they chowed down on the hearty dinner Jesse cooked in Main Camp Kitchen.

At home in Santa Cruz, entertainer Tom Noddy pivoted from helping prepare the Chautauqua tour to getting stage props ready for the fair. He had a plan to make the W.C. Fields Stage more friendly to bubble magic. He needed a way to block the wind for outside performances, and knew that the bubbles' rainbow colors shimmered best against a black backdrop. He started to build four eight-by-four-foot theater flats stretched with black canvas that he would also bring on the Chautauqua tour for his bubble act. By the time he left for the fair, Tom had built four frames but only one had been completed—by a friend who was showing Tom how to stretch the canvas. "We ran out of time," Tom said, "so I bundled the flats in a tarp and put it on the roof of my van, Old Van Ribber, and took off to the fair."

When he got to site, at first he couldn't find the little wooden stage he had used the year before. Finally, he came across it way down the path. The annual winter flooding of the fair site had floated the rectangular wood structure to the entrance of Chumleighland (aka the Circus Stage). Tom retrieved it with the help of friends, then secured his theater flats to it. They covered the flats with curtains from Banners Crew Coordinator Wally Slocum, who annually brought in a vast variety of cloth to use for banners.

Back at the Circus Stage, musicians gathered to practice in the "bandstand"—a large log in back and a smaller log in front with a trench dug before it to accommodate the legs of the front-row musicians. Their usual ringleader, Reverend Chumleigh, chose to take a well-paying job instead of performing at the fair that year.

"I was offered one of the best paid jobs I'd ever had," Reverend Chumleigh, aka Michael Mielnik, said. "It was in Chicago for eight weeks. I wrote to the board saying I wanted to do the fair, but could only afford it if the fair could fly me and my family out for the weekend." The fair board did not agree to those terms.

Since he wouldn't be coming to the fair, Chumleigh told the Flying Karamazov Brothers to change the name of the stage area. "Call it something else," he said. "Call it Juggler Heaven or anything, but not Chumleighland." So the Karamazovs announced to the performers that they would honor Chumleigh's wishes and rename the stage "Not Chumleighland."

Paul Magid (aka Dmitri Karamazov) took on the role of coordinating the vaudeville show logistics as they planned the order of the lineup and rehearsed their sets. Besides the Flying Karamazov Brothers, the show would feature clowns Avner the Eccentric and the Magnificent Mazuba, tap dancer Toes Tiranoff, Artis the Spoonman and juggler Roberto Morganti.

Meanwhile, entertainers had lined up two unlikely animals to be featured at the 1981 fair.

During one of their earlier perfomances at the Douglas County Fair, Howard Patterson (aka Ivan Karamazov) had stopped by the Wildlife Safari booth, where he had met Laurie Marker, head zoologist. Wildlife Safari is an animal refuge located south of

Roseburg in Winston. Howard had always considered himself a scientist who juggles, and the refuge piqued his interest.

When the Karamazov Brothers arrived in Oregon to prepare for the 1981 Oregon Country Fair, Howard and Randy (aka Alyosha Karamazov), who had rejoined the troupe for the summer, visited Laurie at Wildlife Safari. She ran the facility's veterinarian clinic, established its research arm, and headed a captive cheetah-breeding program. Laurie took Howard and Randy on a facilities tour and introduced them to some lion cubs.

"These young lions were each the size of a small German shepherd," Randy said. "They were not full-size lions, but not little cuddly cubs either." After they were let out of their cage, one of the lions suddenly shot straight for Howard, knocking Randy deftly aside as it leapt toward the slender, bearded visitor. "He put large amounts of Howard into his mouth and—rar, Rar, RAR!— made terrible noises," Randy said, adding the sound effects.

The lion cub gnawed on Howard's head a bit, "but no skin was broken," Howard recalled. "There was just a moment where we all went from 'Oh, isn't it cute, the lion likes Howard,' to realizing 'Oh, the lion's trying to EAT Howard!'" With Laurie's help, Howard shook off the cub and Laurie put the lions back in their cage.

"After the fact," Randy said, "we realized it was funny that Howard decided that day to dress as a meal. He was wearing a leather bomber jacket with a sheepskin collar, so he came attired as hors d'oeuvres."

They talked awhile with Laurie, who introduced them to Kai, a cheetah Laurie had raised from kittenhood. As a Wildlife Safari rescue cub, Kai had been raised alongside an unusual playmate: a gibbon ape. The gibbon would climb all over Kai, pull on the cat's ears and jump on her head, so Kai learned to accept playful touching that most cheetahs wouldn't tolerate. Accustomed to dealing with the monkey, Kai would patiently tolerate attention and petting from children—even rambunctious ones—making the big cat a perfect public ambassador for Wildlife Safari. (A few years later Laurie would take Kai to Africa and teach the cheetah to hunt, which had never been done before, Howard said. "In 1990 she founded and still heads the Cheetah Conservation Fund in Namibia," he added.)

As the 1981 Oregon Country Fair approached, Laurie agreed to Howard's and Randy's request to bring Kai to the event. Fairgoers could visit with Laurie, learn about Wildlife Safari, and take photos of Kai. When the fair board of directors learned of the arrangement, they were delighted. An ad for the fair published in the *Willamette Valley Observer* trumpeted "Little people's picture with Wildlife Safari cheetah."

The 1981 fair was about to take a walk on the wild side. And it got even wilder when Entertainment co-coordinator Moz Wright invited another surprise: a living unicorn named Lancelot, brought by his devoted owners Morning Glory Zell and her husband, Tim (aka Otter aka Oberon) Zell.

Lancelot was the first unicorn to emerge from the couple's Living Unicorn Project. The Zells, ordained as priestess and priest of the Church of All Worlds, worshipped the Earth as a living Goddess. They promoted neo-paganism, a term they popularized in lectures and books to describe the new-age nature-based religions that emerged during the 1960s and 1970s. In 1977 they moved to Mendocino County, where they conducted seminars and raised animals. Morning Glory and Otter studied ancient Celtic rituals and myths and discovered the "magical secret lost

Tim Zell (aka Otter aka Oberon) and Morning Glory Zell with their first "unicorn," Lancelot.

through the ages" used to create a living unicorn.

They maintained that the unicorns of ancient legends were never horses, but instead were bred from horned animals. Howard Patterson, interested as always in biology, asked for more details. Oberon said they created the unicorns by performing minor surgery on baby goats, shifting the protohorn tissue to cause it to unite into one spot. When the horn grew, it formed a single medial horn.

"Their theory was that unicorns were always a manufactured thing," Howard said. "Someone figured out the surgical procedure, but I could never get Tim to tell me exactly what it was. It somehow involved moving the horn buds of an infant goat closer together. But what it does is actually changes the shape of the skull and the animal gets more brain development. Lancelot, their first, was actually pretty smart and very attractive."

This wasn't the first time Morning Glory brought an unusual animal to the fair. In the early 1970s, she had danced as the Sensuous Serpentina with her boa constrictor Ophelia. At the time, she lived in a 1958 Chevy school bus converted to a motor home that she dubbed "The Scarlet Succubus." When she wasn't traveling, Morning Glory often parked the Scarlett Succubus at Stillstone, a commune with deep roots in the Oregon Country Fair. Several White Bird crisis workers who volunteered at the fair (including Deni Schadegg) made their home at Stillstone. The commune rented four old houses on property east of Eugene. Stillstone's proximity to Interstate 5 made it a welcome rest stop for many a fair vaudevillian traveling the West Coast circuit.

The yeasty mix of fair folks communing at Stillstone resulted in lifelong friendships and a couple of love stories. Notably, sword-swallower Moz Wright got to know Deni Schadegg during his frequent visits to the commune. After the 1980 fair, Moz and Deni planned a "uniting ceremony" and invited many fair friends to celebrate with them.

"It was especially nice to see Michael Mielnik (aka Reverend Chumleigh) and Tim Furst (aka Fyodor Karamazov) talking together at the ceremony," Tom Noddy recalled. "There had been bad blood between Chumleigh and the Karamazovs and their onstage joke rivalry had turned dark in recent years."

The festivities included a vaudeville surprise: shaving cream pies that got smooshed into the faces of the unaware bride and groom.

Tricksters Fyodor Karamazov and Chumleigh had thoughtfully held up a towel at the last minute to shield Deni's wedding dress from the mess.

Although Morning Glory had left Stillstone commune in 1977, everyone had remained good friends. In his role as Entertainment Coordinator, Moz Wright welcomed Morning Glory's offer to bring Lancelot the unicorn to the 1981 Oregon Country Fair. At the fair coordinators meeting, organizers greeted Moz's announcement with enthusiasm.

The 1981 fair opened its three-day run on a mellow Friday morning with partly cloudy skies and temperatures in the sixties. Smiling people lined up at the ticket kiosks to pay the four-dollar admission fee (three dollars for seniors, free for children twelve and younger). Rustic wood booths displaying handmade crafts lined both sides of the pathway for much of the Eight, interspersed with food booths serving cookies, drinks, falafels, pizza, burgers, fruit pies, and much more.

Fairgoers could peruse educational exhibits devoted to renewable energy at Oregon Energy Horizons or try out workshops in Community Village. They also could choose among music and vaudeville entertainment at four official stages: Main Stage, Shady Grove, Community Village Stage, and Circus Stage (aka Not Chumleighland), and at one stage not yet mentioned on the map: W.C. Fields Memorial Stage.

The consensus-run Community Village again brought together dozens of nonprofit groups in eighteen booths to offer fairgoers useful information, workshops and demonstrations. Diverse topics included herb walks (wild edibles booth), creative visualization (spirituality booth), cardiovascular fitness (health booth), raku pottery (arts booth), solar sun teas and sprout starting (self-reliance booth), computerized fund-raising (information networks booth), and tax resistance (politics booth). The Village's central meadow hosted New Games—where everybody wins—as well as music and dancing. Two Eugene cooperatives—Zoo Zoo's restaurant and Genesis Juice—worked together in the Village Restaurant.

Main Stage alternated musical acts with vaudeville entertainment. Friday began with Native American Drumming followed by comic singer Jan Luby. Other Main Stage acts delighting crowds included local favorites Balaphon marimba ensemble and

Mithrandir, clowns Avner the Eccentric and the Magnificent Mazuba, Tom Noddy's "Political, Social, and Spiritual Satire with Puppets," Sweetgrass bluegrass group, and folk singers Ramblin' Jack Elliott and Jim Page.

Three times a day, the Fighting Instruments of Karma Marching Band came blaring through the throngs to lure crowds to the Not Chumleighland stage show. In the lead with staff in hand, Tim Furst would part the crowd, followed by John Cloud, who juggled clubs in the air to help widen the pathway for the marching band.

"I used to be a juggler in front of the band," John Cloud recalled, "but juggling is hard because, you know the joke? 'Pins if you catch 'em, clubs if they hit you.' Right? You have to be very good not to be a menace to the crowd. ... We form a phalanx with Tim Furst, up front, and then the phalanx expands out, and then me [juggling] and then the front ranks: That would be flutes and piccolos, then clarinets behind, glockenspiels, then into the heavier brass instruments, percussion way at the end.

"That's the way bands have been worked out for a long time," John added. "In general, the high-register instruments are the ones that really make the band work as a whole ensemble, but if you have the high-register instruments next to the brass, they can't hear anything, so you separate them, you go from high-register, middle to low-register, with percussion at the end because nobody can hear anything close to percussion, and that's the way the band goes. So you have people with the softest instruments up front, which is not optimal for parting the crowd, hence, we got into this whole thing of just having something up there that people are going to notice."

Eben Sprinsock, who joined the band in 1978, noted how popular the marching band was. Crafters and food servers working in their booths during the fair's public hours enjoyed the daily parades as the only entertainment that passed right by. They didn't have to leave their booths to take in the performance.

"It became a feature of the fair that people liked," Eben said, "and people grew to expect this three-times-a-day parade. At that time, we were doing three shows a day. But the shows were shorter, forty minutes long. And also we were a lot younger, and had a lot more energy. ... Eventually the parade continued even after its purpose was gone. The fair got more attendance and people just naturally came to the stage areas to sit down and get away from the path, and we didn't have any trouble any more gathering crowds, but we still went out and did the parade before the show because it became expected. People wanted the parade."

Neither Kai the Ambassador Cheetah for Wildlife Safari nor Lancelot the Living Unicorn was seen much during the fair, unless someone happened to stop by at the (very separate) booths where each was tended by caretakers. Kai could be seen by anyone passing by, but Lancelot was kept hidden behind the booth; anyone who wanted to take a peek at the unicorn had to pay a fee.

"The hippies at the fair tended to fall into two categories in response to the living unicorn," Tom Noddy said. "Some declared it to be another sign of the arrival of the Aquarian Age and others thought it to be 'a goat with one horn.'"

Info Crew volunteer Indi Stern remembered her children were eager to see it. "My oldest kid about tore my arm out of my socket trying to see that unicorn," she said, "and they wouldn't let anyone see it except pay to see it. That really tweaked a lot of people." But Indi learned where Morning Glory and Otter Zell took their unicorn for walks in the evening, and managed to get her kids there to see Lancelot for free.

Howard Patterson noted that "John Cloud was always disgusted by them. He called them 'unigoats.' But the first unigoat was actually a very pretty little animal."

Robert DeSpain, who was serving on the Community Village Coordinating Council, cherished a fond memory of Lancelot. "The unicorn was very magical!" he said. "My daughter Arwen was about eight years old then. We were camping in Community Village. On Saturday night, she was very tired very early, so I hung out with her in the tent for a few hours. Curiosity got to her, so we came out of the tent, out of the brush and into the Community Village meadow, and there in the moonlight was a unicorn eating the grass! Neither of us could register that, and we were in awe as we touched it and petted it. Then, fully emerged in a Fair Magic stupor, we walked over to the tipi drum circle and got even more magic! She and I still recall that night thirty-five years later."

Otter and Morning Glory Zell were giving the unicorn a snack break in the village meadow before their starring role in the Midnight

A Wild Fair

The drum tower at the fair's Junction set the stage for enthusiastic drum jams and dancing.

Show—the annual Saturday night extravaganza put on by entertainers after the fair closes to the public. That tradition traced its roots to the first one in 1975 staged by Reverend Chumleigh and colleagues for all the crew volunteers, crafters, and food booth folks who were too busy working during the public hours to see the shows.

Every Midnight Show since the first one began with a grand torchlight parade marching around the Eight-shaped pathway to gather the crowds, then marching up on stage to start the Midnight Show with the band playing a rousing cacophony of music. This time, the parade would be led by Kai, the cheetah ambassador from Wildlife Safari.

"After a rest," Howard recalled, "Laurie brought Kai to the Midnight Parade. And the problem is that unlike other cats, cheetahs are diurnal. They aren't that comfortable running around at night. And, while Kai's very good with people, she's also an enormous, predatory cat."

"It should have led us to suspect," Randy Nelson said, "that bringing a genuine wild animal on a leash into basically, in many ways, a stone-age village at night with a tremendous number of scary things around and having that cat lead a fire-based parade in the middle of the night—that was probably an idea that needed to be considered more deeply. But that's one of the things I loved about the fair and I love about the Karamazovs. Looking back, you can see why it is that you wouldn't want to do that again. But that wouldn't stop us from doing that again, it would just let you see why you wouldn't."

Howard said that Kai was "pretty freaked out" that evening. "She started out at the front of the parade, but then she would sit down as we were trying to parade," he said. "OK, and the parade would stop. Fine. We'll all wait for the cheetah. Then she'd get up and walk again. Then she'd sit down. And the parade would stop."

Then at one juncture, Kai sat down and a couple of dancing hippies didn't notice that the parade had stopped. They danced right into Kai, who pulled her leash loose from Lauri's grasp and took off into the nighttime crowd.

Randy noted: "Certain things just march forward and a marching band is one of them. A marching band led by flaming torches just kind of rolls along toward its destination. You don't have to go back and tell the drummer, 'You know that cat that you couldn't see anyway that was leading the parade? She's off in the bushes now.' No, the parade just went along. I think everybody who didn't know about it was glad after the fact not to have known about it.

"Those of us who at the time did know that the cat had gotten loose thought: 'What are you going to do? Well, you look for it.'" Randy continued. "And then you think, 'Is it looking for me? ... Am I the prey? Am I the hunter? ... I may be brave or I may be bait.' There were a handful of us at the front of the parade who were petrified, who had no idea what to do. And we thought, 'Oh, what a bad idea this was now that it's turned into this. What a good idea it was until a minute ago, when it was the coolest thing in the world.'"

Fortunately, Laurie Marker found Kai later that evening without incident.

Meanwhile, the Midnight Show for fair staff, volunteers, and vendors had to go on, to the delight of the audience members gathered on blankets spread out in front of the stage. The show included everything from vaudeville skits to belly dancing to music. One of the last acts featured a man riding a unicycle.

For the next-to-last act, a mist of dry-ice fog swirled in the colored stage lights as mystical music blared eerily from the loudspeakers. Morning Glory and Otter Zell, in full wizardly regalia, emerged into the spotlight leading their living unicorn, Lancelot.

Suddenly, Morning Glory and Otter waved their hands yelling, "Wait! Wait! Stop the music!"

In the silence, Morning Glory said to Otter, "Wow! Did you see that guy on a unicycle?"

"That wasn't a unicycle," Otter deadpanned. "That was a bicycle with one wheel. ... What do you call a goat with one horn?" The audience laughed, the mystical music resumed, and Otter and Morning Glory continued their presentation of Lancelot.

As the music crescendoed, Morning Glory shed her clothes and posed with Lancelot at center stage, ready for the grand finalé performance of the Flying Karamazov Brothers. In what had become a Midnight Show tradition, the Brothers Karamazov stripped down and juggled naked on stage. "They culminated their elaborate juggling routine by passing a flaming torch, an egg, and a frying pan—along with several other items—through the air between them," Oberon Zell said. "In the center of all these flying objects, Morning Glory crouched, naked, holding Lancelot. The act ended with Paul [Magid] catching the frying pan in one hand, catching the egg in the pan, where it broke, and finally, catching the torch in his other hand and holding it under the pan to fry the egg. At that moment, I lit off the Roman candle fountains."

The fireworks were Paul's idea, and he quickly joined in.

"Paul did a fairly elaborate fireworks display," Howard said, "using illegal fireworks that we'd picked up in various states with looser fireworks regulations. ... We'd picked up all kinds of really scary stuff and he was setting them off. ... And Tim [aka Otter aka Oberon Zell] stood on stage in his robes with this big staff, looking like he was controlling them.

"It turned out OK," Howard added. "Nobody got hurt. But we got more and more active in future years in discouraging Paul from setting off explosives in places where there was no way of protecting anybody from them."

6   1981
Anita Sweeten and Phoenix Rising

> *"When I came to the fair, I felt really validated because here we figure out positive ways to do things and to support people in being their highest self."*
>
> —Anita Sweeten, Phoenix Rising food booth

Anita Sweeten first came to the fair in 1971 when it was still called the Oregon Renaissance Faire. "My old man—the man I was living with—said 'We're going to a gathering of the tribes.' And I said, 'Okay, that sounds like fun!'"

They teamed up with members of a couple of intentional communities in Sunny Valley and Takilma in Southern Oregon, where a large contingent of alternative-minded folks had landed during the "back to the land" movement. Anita and her husband joined these folks to set up a food booth near the Main Stage meadow at the fair.

"It was down in the area where the pizza booth and the artichoke booth and the pasta booth are now," Anita said, referring to booths there in 2007. "There was a lot more vegetation and it wasn't as wide then, but we were far enough away from Main Stage that we could barely hear. ... Main Stage wasn't amplified back then."

At the June 1971 fair, they sold yogurt sundaes. They purchased buckets of plain yogurt ahead of time from the Springfield Creamery and picked berries themselves to save money. They also bought peaches and other fruit that they mixed with honey to serve on top of the yogurt.

Then for the October 1971 fair, they cooked beans for burritos over a fire pit. "We bought really good corn tortillas from a Mexican restaurant in town," Anita said, "and we called them Bomburritos because they were pretty spicy."

In July 1972, they sold sticky buns from a friend's bakery in Ashland. They sold out early "so we had some more sent up on the Greyhound bus. … It was really really hot that year. I went around with a tray hollering, 'Sticky buns!'" she said, laughing. "And we sold them all. They were good sticky buns."

She has a fond memory from those early years of dancing naked in the moonlight with a lot of other people in the Main Stage meadow when the fair was closed for the evening. "It was so wonderful! At the time, my body looked good enough that I didn't mind doing it," she said.

From the start, Anita felt at home at the fair. She believed in changing the world in a positive way. As a freshman in 1969 at the University of Chicago, she attended a few meetings of the Students for a Democratic Society, but decided against joining because they advocated actions to tear down society without offering a vision of what would come next. "I think peaceful change is better," Anita said.

"When I came to the fair, I felt really validated," she said, "because here we figure out positive ways to do things and to support people in being in their highest self and to make things work as smoothly as possible. … and also because (the fair) culture makes it real clear that nobody cares how much money you make or what you look like. It's what you have in your heart and what you do—your energy you put out, the work that you are able to contribute to the community. I love that so much. That first year, I decided I wanted to be part of this for the rest of my life. I wanted to raise my children in this, and when I had children, I did."

After Anita had a daughter in 1973, she made it a point to bring her to the fair every year, at first as part of the paying public. Then in 1981, the Phoenix Rising food booth offered her a job at the fair. At the time, she was working at Lane Community College as the natural foods lunch program coordinator. "I've taught natural food cooking and worked in commercial kitchens," Anita said. "If I need to, I can make beans and rice for six hundred people or fifty people, whatever. I have those skills and knowledge, so they really wanted me to come and help them."

Phoenix Rising had seen a lot of turnover in cooks since its founders first established an eatery in a booth by the fair's main entrance in 1973. That first year, the food booth had no name. The 1973 incarnation began with Paxton Hoag, Helenita Kassler and two of her daughters, plus Kent Cumbo. They had run a food booth near the Springfield Creamery during the 1972 fair. Fair organizers "liked our energy," Paxton said, and offered them a large booth at the fair entrance. "The fair wanted an anchor food booth that would do breakfast, lunches and dinners," Paxton said. Not many booths offered breakfast in 1973. Most only began serving at 11:00 a.m. when the front gates opened, so crews and booth folks staying overnight had few options unless they brought their own food. Paxton and the Kassler clan agreed to open early and serve breakfast.

"That first year we pretty much used the booth construction that was there, but we brought in 200 firebricks and built a firebrick stove with a twenty-dollar cast iron stovetop that we fired with charcoal," Paxton said. "We went over to Kingsford and because the fair was nonprofit, they gave us 800 pounds of charcoal—just gave it to us. We also borrowed the grill that Northwest Natural Gas loaned out to nonprofit groups." The booth became a convenient spot for Main Campers to grab a bite to eat.

The next year when Paxton, Kent, and Helenita came to check out their booth, they were shocked to find it torn down. They would eventually find out that the Boy Scouts had rented the fair site for a jamboree campout in the autumn of 1973. The Scouts had apparently scavenged for supplies among the fair booths. Of course, booths then were supposed to be only temporary structures because the fair only rented the site each year. "They tore down our booth," Paxton said, "and we found our firebrick all over the parking lot in little round circles. They must have burned the booth as firewood." When they got to the fair and saw the destruction, Helenita, who was from Phoenix, Arizona, shouted out, "Like a phoenix, we will rise from the ashes!" And Phoenix Rising got its name.

One year Paxton and a friend, Larry Caldwell, built a cold smoker and Phoenix Rising added Pacific salmon lox to the menu. Another year they served enchiladas. But Paxton soon felt disenchanted with the hard work in a food booth. "One year I had a real bad time because I spent more time running into town shopping than at the fair," he said.

By 1977, only one original member was left, Kent Cumbo. He invited Larry Caldwell to help out.

"Joel Martin was cooking breakfast on a couple of grills he borrowed from Northwest Natural Gas and that was the only thing we sold all day," Larry said. "We were all sitting around with no customers when Joyce—last name forgotten— decided to bake a batch of cookies so we would have something to eat. Even we didn't eat at our booth. They just flew off the counter—the cookies. She ended up baking about a dozen batches of cookies and we slowly came to the realization that we should sell something people wanted to eat." For the next few years, Phoenix Rising would specialize in fresh-baked cookies.

Larry and his wife, Shawn Bussey, urged everyone to turn the booth into a collective. "Nobody agreed to that," Larry said. "But Shawn and I left our share of the profits, about seventy dollars each, in the bank account as seed money. That was the beginning of the collective. The next year I worked on recruiting people who would actually do something, and one of my first successes was Jim Larsen.

"Jim was my neighbor, a pipefitter and welder with a lot of real-world skills," Larry said. "He had a five-gallon RV water heater and a couple of food-grade fifty-five-gallon drums, so he built a water tower and plumbed it in. It was the first hot-water system at any food booth at the fair. Suddenly, we could wash dishes. The Health Department inspector was so impressed that he made all the other food booths come look at what we had done."

Like Paxton, Jim disliked the hard work of a food booth, so he moved on. Jim and his wife, Sharon, returned to the fair the next year as strolling vendors with garden carts. They used their carts to help haul gear for anyone who needed it. They knew from experience that many food booths had plenty of heavy items to ferry in every day. It was such a good idea that the next year, fair organizers purchased a fleet of garden carts to loan out to anyone who needed them.

Jim next moved to the Ritz Sauna booth, where he designed and built the boiler and water-heating system. "The flames of Phoenix Rising have caught fire all over the fair," Larry Caldwell said.

After Jim left, Kent recruited Anita Sweeten in 1981. She was in her early thirties.

"The first year I was there, I was just laughing because we

wouldn't open until 11:00," Anita said. "We were lucky to open by 11:00 because everybody had partied so hard the night before that they couldn't get up and do anything. I'm a morning person. I'm up in the summer at 5:30 a.m." She would wake up and cook breakfast. From the path, passers-by could smell the enticing aromas of fresh coffee and fried potatoes. Even though the booth window curtains were kept closed in the mornings, people still stopped and begged for breakfast.

"People really want breakfast," Anita said, "and there was no place to get breakfast because nothing was open. People really want some coffee. You need to eat." The booth purchased giant grills so they could easily serve a crowd and in 1984, added breakfast back to Phoenix Rising's morning menu. They served potatoes, eggs, pancakes, and a meat side dish from about 6:00 in the morning until the fair opened for the public at 11:00. Then the cooks switched to baking cookies until late into the evening.

The Monday after the 1984 fair, Phoenix Rising had an abundance of leftover food. Faced with hauling many pounds of heavy perishables home, Anita decided to invite the Recycling Crew over for a free breakfast. The booth welcomed the opportunity to reward a hard-working crew that helped make it possible to run a food booth—not to mention a whole fair—in a rural floodplain. Recycling Crew would end up enjoying free Monday morning breakfasts at Phoenix Rising for several years until Recycling eventually assembled its own breakfast crew right in their own camp.

That same Monday after the 1984 fair, Main Camp coordinators asked Anita to stay and cook for the post-fair crews who were putting the fair site to bed after the event. "I was getting ready to go home," Anita said. "We were using pickups and we had about four pickup loads total. We had two pickup loads hauled out. I was cleaning stuff up and getting ready to get the other ones loaded out." That's when some of the leaders at Main Camp stopped by to ask if Anita could help because the cook they had hired didn't show up. "It's an emergency," they told Anita. Since she didn't have to return to her regular job for a few days, she agreed to do it. Anita would end up serving hearty portions to post-fair crews for the next six years.

After a couple of years selling breakfasts short-order style, the Phoenix Rising crew noticed that customers had to wait a long time for their hot breakfast cooked to-order. They decided to try serving

Anita Sweeten and Phoenix Rising

Kent Cumbo's wife, Kim, brought a hand-sewn Phoenix Rising sign in 1981.

food buffet-style, cooking up big batches of scrambled eggs, potatoes, and pancakes. It would be much simpler to arrange and much more efficient for the cooks. A few in the booth worried that customers might take over-generous portions, but their fears proved groundless. Everybody in line spooned out reasonable amounts and the booth remained profitable.

Phoenix Rising evolved into a cooperative a few years after Anita joined. The first year, Kent and Anita held the booth together between them. The next year Kent proposed that he and his wife, Kim, would own two-thirds and Anita would own one-third interest in the booth. "I didn't come into this to make a profit or to own a food booth at the fair," Anita told Kent at the time. "We should do it as a cooperative, like you've talked about."

Anita eventually set up an account for the Phoenix Rising booth, with account statements for everyone who participated. "You work a shift to get your pass," Anita said. "Any profit goes into the account and we'll decide what to do with it as a group. We'll save some of it as startup money for the next year." Everyone who worked at the booth understood their only pay was a camping pass at the fair and free food. Over the years, proceeds from the booth were donated to Oregon PeaceWorks, the fair's Jill Heiman Vision Fund, and other nonprofit organizations.

In the off-season, the Phoenix Rising booth folks would enjoy getting together to meet. "We have a retreat in the fall out at the beach," Anita said. "We usually go to Cape Lookout and get in the group camps, and then we have a retreat around February just to kind of think of things. One of the things at the retreat that came up was that we wanted to get an ice cream freezer and make ice cream in the back of the booth, just for fun, family fun stuff. And so then it showed up with the little girls to crank it. They'd already done a trial run. It's sweet because the people are so wonderful. There's not one person who isn't just a treasure. They love this fair. It's a great joy to them to be here. All the volunteers are willingly donating, you know? We're basically a volunteer, nonprofit organization."

Phoenix Rising was formally incorporated into a nonprofit organization in 1998.

Anita said that more than two dozen people work throughout the year to collect what the booth needs and to take care of the equipment in storage that needs cleaning and maintenance. "We want people who really care about this and who want to take on something besides just coming down and working during the fair," she said. "Maybe you'll gather the linens, take them home, wash them and fold them up, and bring them back to the fair. Or maybe you'll make sure we have aprons that are fun—we have all kinds of different, fun aprons so somebody can go grab something that they enjoy."

Cooking large batches of food requires hard work and a lot of energy. Carrying an industrial-sized pan full of scalding potatoes and water requires a strong body. "Especially when they're hot! You have to drain potatoes when they're hot or they keep cooking," Anita said. "You have to get that water off of them so that you can cool them enough to chop them. We go through about 400 pounds of potatoes every night. We cook them, we drain them, we cool them and chop them and prep them for the grills, and store them so they're safe. We get them all ready for the grill guys. They've got these pans of prepped potatoes all covered nicely. When they get there, they can add the veggies and the onions and—breakfast is served!"

The booth serves breakfast at the fair every morning, and on Monday mornings makes a special effort to sell food. "We don't shut off our grills until Monday at noon," Anita said. "We're pushing food out, trying to get the crew to take it home in people's bellies rather than trying to refrigerate because we all live pretty far away. We donate anything that's left that we can to Main Camp Kitchen and then we donate to food banks. It's pretty hard to estimate exactly how much everybody's going to eat and we don't want to run out of anything."

Anita said they sometimes gave away food for a song, literally. "On Monday we don't care. If somebody's hungry, they can sing a song. or they can come back and wash dishes, any time. We give cookies away for people singing. Because we're not for profit and because it's not coming out of anybody's pocket, we're able to trade and to do things and just be a part of the fair, and that's real important to me," she said.

They enjoy some lighthearted booth traditions. "Instead of OM-ing, we YUM," Anita said. "We YUM, whenever we're together, at every meeting. We hold hands in a circle and we YUM. We dedicate that to being together in the highest possible way, and to making good cookies and food for people to enjoy. ... We Yum when we put our sign up.

"Our family mantra and the basic principle in the booth, is you have to be nice," she added. "You have to work hard and you have to clean up after yourself. But the 'be nice' part is hard. It's stressful, being in a food booth, and it's a lot of pressure sometimes and people get crabby. It's okay to feel crabby but go back to your tent and soak your feet. I create a foot wash station and I do foot massage because sometimes that really changes your whole perspective. People are on their feet, and our feet suffer out here a little bit."

Over the decades, the booth has become a multigenerational gathering for Phoenix Rising workers. "Our children and actually our grandchildren are old enough now to work in the kitchen," Anita said. The booth is known for training younger crew members. "I can't tell you how many kids who have learned, who have asked me for a reference for jobs for kitchen staff because they learned about washing their hands and wearing clean clothes," Anita said.

The fair is a place where people can put their ideals into practice, Anita added. "I used to cry every time the fair was over because I was so sad because I had to go back out into the world, the 'un-Fair' world." She said that prompted her to make changes in her life. "What am I getting at the fair that I don't get in the rest of my life?" she asked herself. She reached out to people she missed and started getting together with them more often, especially with people from the booth. She also bought some land with a big house on it and decided to share the house with a young family instead of living alone. She enjoyed helping the family with childcare.

"I just love to be around babies, but my grandson is in Portland," Anita said, "so I figure they're all of our children. I change and feed and hold the baby and play with both of the kids." The kids started calling her Grandma. "It makes your heart feel really good," she said.

Phoenix Rising in the mid-2000s started financing small projects to improve the fair. One of Anita's favorite was financing the rainbow-bright vinyl covering the dome to the Rabbit Hole stage. After the 2003 fair, Anita had asked General Manager Leslie Scott what fair project might need extra funding. Leslie showed Anita the diagrammed plans for the Rabbit Hole—a domed, mostly enclosed stage designed specifically to minimize wind and dust so bubble artist Tom Noddy could more easily create his fragile magic orbs for the enjoyment of all. Anita could tell it would be a lovely space, but she had a hard time describing it, sight unseen, to the Phoenix Rising folks at their annual retreat.

"It was kind of a leap of faith for everyone (in the booth) to approve it," Anita recalled, chuckling. They were asking, "What IS this? The fair needs this money for a rabbit hole?! What's a cover for a rabbit hole?"

The Rabbit Hole covering was a candy-colored confection made of ripstop nylon sewn with circles and swirls in red, orange, green, purple, white, fuschia, and yellow. From the first year it was erected in 2004, the covering—fitted snuggly over a metal dome framework—would catch people's eyes when they ambled through the bus entrance. The bright space hosted Spoken Word artists in addition to Tom Noddy's twice-daily bubble magic show.

"I love the space," Anita Sweeten said. "I've listened to wonderful lectures here. ... I wish I could be at all the Spoken Word shows. I take in as much of it as I can, plus all the music, I don't want to miss any of it, it's all so wonderful at the fair."

7   1981
A Fair Honeymoon for Bud and Jana Chase

"Great! You can play glockenspiel in the band!"
—Howard Patterson (aka Ivan Karamazov), talking to
Jana Chase in July 1981

William B. "Bud" Chase first came to the Oregon Country Fair in 1975, when he was thirty-one-years-old and living at Greenfield Ranch northwest of Ukiah in California's Mendocino County. Bud worked as caretaker of the common land and Ranch House, living in a converted shed dwelling off to the side of the barn.

Greenfield Ranch had been a cattle ranch until 1973, when Tim Baker, a progressive from Berkeley, California, purchased the 5,500 acre property in the steep verdant hills of California's Coast Range. With a vision of living in a large communal neighborhood, Tim had divided the ranch into more than fifty parcels of various sizes that he sold separately, essentially turning Greenfield Ranch into a communal association of hippie homesteads. Covenants and deeds prohibited hunting and logging on the land and restricted the use of pesticides and chemical fertilizers, among other provisions.

In his essay, "How the Greenfield Ranch Came to Be," Tim explained his plan. "Histories of Americans' earlier communal utopian societies were especially helpful. It turned out that none but the religion-based survived," he wrote. "If our community was to last, we would have to be individual owners, with our own deeds, our own stuff, and our own space. As a nucleus for community, some land and goods should be held in common. And there should be a structure whereby those who chose could unite casually or communally, but with a safety net waiting should it all go bad."

The "Ranch House" that served as a popular community center sat on 200 acres of commonly owned land, along with an abundant spring that supplied all the water for the Ranch House and for the communal gardens and orchards. The previous owners had dammed Redwood Creek, which created a large pond that the commune used for swimming. The new residents rebuilt the Pelton wheel on the dam to generate electricity for the Ranch House. A land-line pay phone —the sprawling ranch's only phone available in those pre-cellular days—could be found in an old-timey phone booth next to the Ranch House.

For his first Country Fair in 1975, Bud had offered to bring a redwood-lattice yurt he owned. Bud and some friends carried the yurt to the fair in the back of a pickup truck and set it up for Greenfield residents Bran and Moria, crafters who sculpted jewelry, pipes, and figurines.

"They sold their crafts using the yurt as their booth," Bud said, "and I just partied at the fair. ... One thing I saw at the fair that struck me was the marching band. It had just a few people and there were a lot of guitars and pennywhistles in it. I saw that band and said, 'Oh, god, they need me!' Because I played the sousaphone (a marching tuba) and I always loved marching bands."

Bud came home with an unusually lasting souvenir from the 1975 fair—a tattoo. (Soon after, health regulations would prohibit tattoo artists from inking skin in the fair's dusty outdoor setting.)

"There was a guy on the back loop doing tattoos," Bud said. "I was a brewer at the time and wanted something with hops on it. My friends and I went through all the recycling at the fair, pulling out beer cans and beer bottles, looking for depictions of hops. Moria sketched out a little hop vine. We gave that to the tattoo artist and that's what he put on my shoulder. ... The tattoo actually brought me some romance. This was before I met Jana. A young woman was watching me be tattooed and later on we ran into each other and spent a pleasant evening together."

In 1976 Jana at age twenty-one had left the home where she grew up in Fresno, California, and moved to Rich Lewis's parcel of Greenfield Ranch. Rich's site featured a small cabin on sixty acres.

Jana paid twenty-five dollars a month in rent and set up a tipi in the meadow, a bit away from the cabin.

Jana started sewing for Christopher Hale to help with his business, Christopher Crooked Stitch. Christopher lived west of Greenfield on Running Springs Ranch. "We hand-stitched fringed, beaded, batiked, and hand-dyed clothing," Jana said. When other people from Greenfield started sewing for Christopher, they all turned the enterprise into the Christopher Crooked Stitch Collective. The members divided the responsibilities evenly, leaving Christopher time to continue his design work as an equal partner.

In 1978, the clothing collective applied to the Country Fair and another fair in Los Angeles and got accepted to both. Jana's crew went to L.A. When everyone returned, the ones who went to the Oregon Country Fair raved about the experience. Jana knew she had to go there someday.

Coincidentally, Morning Glory and Tim (aka Otter) Zell also lived on a commune up the road from Greenfield Ranch for some time in the mid-1970s before moving to Allison's piece on Greenfield Ranch in July 1977. "I remember when they pulled up on the Greenfield Ranch in their bus," Jana said. "Sequoia, Bud's girlfriend at the time, said, 'They're coming in the Scarlet Succubus. Oh, Greenfield Ranch will never be the same!' She was right!"

The Pagans on the Succubus brought a more open and free lifestyle to the community, Bud noted. He had been a free-spirited Pagan for some time, and welcomed the changes that came with the Succubus. "We found (the people at) Greenfield Ranch to be more sexually conservative and less promiscuous than us Pagans," Bud said. "We Pagans had come from San Francisco and other places like that. It was wild and wonderful before AIDS and after the pill. It was the Golden Age."

Greenfield Ranch had included dozens of families with monogamous couples, as well as gays and non-monogamous singles. The new Pagans added to the cultural mix, and they were welcomed and embraced. Everyone would gather regularly at the Ranch House for meetings and parties. The Summer Solstice parties became the highlight of the year, with horse racing, swimming in the pond, choreographed water ballet, and plays put on by the kids.

"We were friends with Morning Glory and Otter and saw them

often at community events," Jana said. "They introduced the ranch community to Lancelot (the Living Unicorn) at a summer solstice party. Greenfield Ranch has huge, wonderful parties on the solstice every year." Morning Glory admired Jana's sewing skills, and she purchased one of Jana's favorite hand-made dresses.

On the Summer Solstice of June 1978, Jana and Bud started living together, moving next door from Greenfield Ranch to a new community they helped create: the Round Mountain Cooperative. "Our community was committed to equality, feminism, and ecological living," Jana said. "We wanted to live off the land with organic gardening and farming."

"We tried to fight what we called 'couple-ism,'" Bud said.

"All kinds of '-isms'," Jana added, "sexism, age-ism, couple-ism. It was working really well, I believe. Nobody in the community supposedly had more power than anyone else. We all committed an equal amount of money. We bought this large ranch with two huge barns and a beautiful lake, agricultural land, and rolling hills. Everybody had to put in an equal amount of money. We could make payments as we're paying off the rent. At the time, the ranch cost $160,000 for 800 acres. I remember thinking, 'God, my mom paid that much for a house, just a house, in Santa Cruz.'"

Round Mountain Cooperative was launched by Claude Steiner, a psychiatrist who collaborated with Eric Berne, author of *Games People Play*, to popularize Transactional Analysis. In the 1970s, Claude Steiner had developed the theory and practice of Radical Psychiatry and coined the phrases "warm fuzzies" and "emotional literacy." His books on those topics became best sellers. Claude made the huge down payment for the property with the understanding that members of the cooperative would pay him back over time.

But the money part wasn't working out so well for the thirty or so members of the community. As a group, they could barely eke out the payments of $3,000 each quarter. Then whenever members left the collective, they had to be paid back, resulting in even steeper bills for those left behind. "We were always struggling to make the payments," Jana said.

The community had envisioned creating a self-sufficient farm, with everyone working on something at the property. But working on the outside became necessary to pay for the land. Bud did pretty well as a mechanic with his Bud's Auto Repair shop located in a small garage on the property. He also laid flooring around the region to earn extra money.

A yurt shop in the barn became a real cottage industry. "David Raitt, who is a designer of yurts and (singer) Bonnie Raitt's brother, lived on Greenfield Ranch with his wife and kids," Jana said. "We made half of our barn into a workshop and we constructed small yurts for him. That was a nice community venture."

But most of the members had to leave the communal area to make money for the land payments. "Some of the members were teachers," Jana said. "I got a job at a restaurant as a waitress and then as a cocktail waitress. Then I finally decided to start Round Mountain Clothing Collective. We did mail order, mostly. We turned part of a barn into a sewing shop. … People in the community could do piecework for us and get paid by the piece. It was pretty good pay, but mostly it was myself and my partner, Maria Kaiser, who came to our community from Germany."

In 1981, Jana finally got her chance to check out the Oregon Country Fair. Their friends Bran and Moria invited her and Bud—plus Jana's business partner Maria—to join their booth at the fair. Jana and Maria could sell their handmade, hand-dyed cotton clothing in the booth. They figured Bud could help set up the booth before the fair and help tend the booth during the fair.

Jana and Bud—who, after six months of living together, had committed to each other on the Winter Solstice of 1978 under a beautiful oak tree—decided to designate this trip as their honeymoon since they never had taken one. After the fair they planned to go camping, just the two of them. They were eager to escape the long, tedious meetings that were mandatory in any community that made decisions through consensus. They also made plans to check out Alpha Farm, less than an hour's drive from the Country Fair. Alpha Farm had been founded as an intentional community in 1972 by Quakers from the East Coast and had a legendary reputation for refining the art of cooperation and consensus-building. Jana and Bud were hoping they could learn something to take back with them to facilitate the meeting dynamics at Round Mountain.

"We borrowed a friend's van that we could sleep in," Bud said, "and loaded it up with Jana's handmade clothing to sell and drove up to the Country Fair. Now I had an agenda, hidden even from myself, actually, about the band. I brought an old baritone horn. ... It wasn't really very playable. It had tape over some holes and stuff. I helped Jana set up at the fair. And the booth was all set up around noon on Thursday, and I thought to myself, 'If that band ever rehearses, they're rehearsing right now.'"

Bud added with a hearty laugh, "It was a question whether they actually did rehearse, having heard them before. So I walked into Chumleighland carrying this baritone horn and Howard [Patterson] was conducting the band. He stopped the band and said, 'a brass!' Turns out that the Flying Karamazov Brothers had an E-flat tuba, a kind of tuba that I don't normally play, and somebody was trying to play it ... and he couldn't very well. So they put me on that E-flat tuba and that's how I ended up joining the band."

After the rehearsal, Bud sheepishly went back to Jana to explain that he wouldn't have much time to help with the booth. He had agreed to perform three shows and three parades every day with the band during the fair. Jana had misgivings, but it worked out in the end. "He went off and had a great time," Jana said. Jana, Maria, Bran, and Moria would wave to Bud every time he marched by tooting his tuba.

Meanwhile, Jana and Maria enjoyed a very successful fair. "We were very busy," Jana said. "We happen to have made a bunch of brightly dyed three-tiered skirts and wrap-around pants. I had no idea those were so in vogue at the fair. Everybody was wearing them in bright colors. We had a bunch of them with us, and we sold out of those. And we made drawstring pants and hoodies."

One of Jana's favorite memories of her first fair was watching the Midnight Show. "We didn't get to see the shows during the day, and I just loved it!" Jana said. It was particularly fun seeing their friends Otter and Morning Glory present Lancelot on stage, not to mention watching the naked Flying Karamazov Brothers juggling in their fiery finale.

At the end of the fair on Sunday, Howard asked Bud if he wanted to join the fair band and entertainers on a month-long tour called Old Time New Age Chautauqua. "When I suggested this to Jana, I felt really apologetic," Bud said. "I knew what her objections were going to be."

"What? Go on the road with fifty people traveling in buses?" Jana exclaimed. "Um, we were going to have our honeymoon, honey. We were going to go off camping by ourselves, far away from people and meetings, and to visit Alpha Farm."

Trying to persuade Jana that these were fun people to hang out with, Bud took her over to meet Howard Patterson. After they were introduced, Howard abruptly asked Jana, "What do you play?" Flustered, Jana answered, "I play the piano and the guitar."

"Great!" Howard replied. "You can play glockenspiel in the band."

"What's that?" Jana asked. She had never heard of a glockenspiel—nor chautauquas—and felt a bit overwhelmed.

Howard explained that the glockenspiel, sometimes called orchestra bells, is set up similar to piano keys, making it a relatively easy instrument for pianists to learn. His wife at the time, Seiza de Tarr, who usually played the instrument, wasn't going on the tour and the band needed a glockenspiel player. However, Seiza had taken her glockenspiel home, and Jana would need to find one to play. Howard told them to think about it, and if they wanted to join the tour, to come to the Sunday night meeting at the Not Chumleighland stage.

Jana and Bud discussed it earnestly. They had their friend's van with room for them both to sleep, so they wouldn't be riding on the bus and camping with everyone. But they still wanted to check out Alpha Farm. Bud made Jana a deal: They would miss the first couple of shows on the Chautauqua tour to head to Alpha Farm, then join up with the Chautauqua tour farther north. And he promised Jana, "If at any time you want to leave, we'll leave, at that second. Whenever! If you don't want to be with these people and you don't like them, we can leave any time."

Bud's reassurances persuaded Jana to try it out. It would turn out to be a unique honeymoon trip, to say the least.

8 · 1981
The Old Time New Age Chautauqua aka The New Old Time Chautauqua

> *"Good health is a laughing matter, and that's nothing to sneeze at."*
>
> —poster for 1981 Chautauqua

Sunday evening after the 1981 Oregon Country Fair had ended, Howard Patterson (aka Ivan Karamazov) and Paul Magid (aka Dmitri Karamazov) invited entertainers to meet at the Circus Stage (aka Not Chumleighland) if they were interested in joining the inaugural Old Time New Age Chautauqua tour.

"The Chautauquas were an outcome of being at the Fair," Paul Magid recalled. "Basically, we would always do these great vaudeville shows. ... It'd finally get really good on Sunday, and then it was all over. We were with all our friends, and we're going to have to go back to the 'real world,' and we didn't want to."

The Flying Karamazov Brothers settled on a West Coast tour after their original vision for a grand cross-country trip fell through. They planned to head to Oregon's Breitenbush Hot Springs—a collective-run, rustic "resort" of natural hot springs nestled in the foothills of the Cascade Mountains—to literally get their act together before taking the show on the road. Then they would travel as far north as British Columbia for the Vancouver Folk Festival, stopping at small towns along the way.

The Karamazovs had already lined up most of the key entertainment, including themselves, clown Avner the Eccentric, sword-swallower Moz Wright, Tom Noddy the Bubble Guy, singer Jan Luby, Artis the Spoonman, Bliss Kolb (aka the Magnificent Mazuba), and tap dancer Toes Tiranoff. Dozens of entertainers came to the Sunday night meeting to express an interest in going, but space was limited. The Karamazovs ended up asking Morning Glory and Otter to bring Lancelot the Living Unicorn, and they invited a few musicians to round out the Fighting Instruments of Karma Marching Band, including Bud Chase on tuba, Twin Eagles on two trumpets, and Jana Chase on glockenspiel.

Patch Adams showed up with roommates from the Gesundheit Medical Collective on the East Coast to provide health workshops and free medical exams. But Patch also surprised everyone with some news. He had met the Love Family, a Christian communal group, at a recent Rainbow Family Gathering in the Colville National Forest in Washington and had invited them to bring their bus on the tour.

The entertainers objected, explaining that they already had lined up everyone they needed. "Patch was from Back East," Tom Noddy said, "and he didn't understand the resistance that he met among the vaudevillians and musicians of the West Coast to the Love Family's blend of New Age Christianity and hippie ethics." But Patch noted that the Love Family had a kitchen in their traveling bus and could cook meals for them. Reluctantly, the entertainers agreed to Patch's proposal.

The group spent a long time Sunday discussing logistics, including who would travel in which vehicle, and what repairs would be needed on the motley collection of old buses and cars. They finally figured it all out and caravanned to Breitenbush Hot Springs, a few hours north of the fair. They made time the next day for a relaxing dip in the hot springs, then pulled together the show and workshops. They had already planned to do a dress rehearsal in the nearby town of Detroit, Oregon.

"But time was tight," Tom Noddy said. "We would have to set up the yurt, the tipi, and the sectional stage and attached trailer and then afterward we would have to strike all of that and pack it and immediately hit the road because we had an early parade, workshops, and show ... the next day."

Paul Magid said that they had agreed to let the Love Family put on a skit before the show while the stage was being set up.

"The show went well," Tom Noddy said, "but when we tried to get a crew to work on the breakdown there was a conflicting effort to call together an Emergency Meeting. ... Morning Glory and Otter insisted that we meet and discuss the content of the Love Family's theatrical piece. The Christians had included a stock character in their piece who was a 'Wicked Witch.' The Pagans now demanded that this centuries-old slander against their kind must not be allowed to be a part of this tour."

Everyone was summoned to a circle

Rebo and Paul got married in 1980.

Visiting along the roadside during the first Chautauqua were (from left): Bud Chase (out of frame, holding the tuba), an unidentified woman, Patch Adams, Jan Luby, Howard Patterson, and Paul Magid.

to resolve this ancient religious rift. The prickly group discussion rambled amid thorny thickets of ethics as they debated "whether good intentions trumped false gods," Tom said. After it looked like the talking would never end, someone suggested that the Pagans ride in the Christian bus to continue the discussion on the road so that everyone could pack up and get to the next gig before dark. And so they did.

"When we got there, they'd solved it," Paul Magid said with a smile. "It was all done! This is the first thing that happened

Rebo Hanson's poster for the first Chautauqua.

on Chautauqua: The Christians and the Pagans resolved all their differences! We said, 'This is perfect! Next let's have the male chauvinists ride with the feminists!'"

A key co-organizer on the first Chautauqua tour—and many others to follow—was Rebecca "Rebo" Hanson (aka Rebo Flordigan), Paul Magid's wife. Paul had met Rebo the year before at a Minnesota Renaissance Faire, where the Karamazovs were performing their juggling act. The pair were smitten with each other at first sight and got married a few weeks later.

The talented and charismatic Rebo wrote witty and sensitive songs, sang like a bird, told rowdy jokes, and excelled at artistic endeavors from calligraphy to sculpting. She drew a charming poster for the inaugural tour featuring her neat, ornate calligraphy.

When she saw Twin Eagles, the trumpeter the band had picked up at the fair, crocheting on the bus, she got him to teach her how. Soon everyone was learning to crochet during the long rides between shows. Rebo could play accordion, guitar, and piano. She also played flute in the marching band. During the show, she sang "Schizophrenic Love Song" with Jan Luby.

"She was the heart of Chautauqua," Jana Chase said. "Rebo was the organizer and the manager and wore a million hats."

Jana and Bud Chase caught up with the tour on the second or third performance; they remember it being at Grande Ronde, Oregon. "I hadn't got my glockenspiel, so I wasn't part of the band yet," Jana

The Chautauqua caravan often stopped on the side of the road to regroup during the first tour.

said. "I'm more observing and trying to stay out of the way. ... Rebo and a few other women I didn't know then, probably Deni Schadegg, made lunch and invited us to have lunch back stage." But Jana politely declined. "I didn't want to make any waves."

The tour had its hiccups and confusions. They spent most nights in campgrounds and communes. Some, but not all, vehicles had CB radios to communicate on the road; signals often got crossed and much waiting ensued. Still, they usually ended up where they wanted to be. As the days passed, moving got easier as everyone fell into a routine for setting up and taking down.

Traveling with the Love Family was a source of irritation for some, entertainment for others. Deni Schadegg said they seemed like "some weird cult group. They took different names like Serenity and Courage. None of them had birthdays. They had a bunch of kids with them. And Love Israel was the leader. It was just very weird having them there because the rest of us were good friends and had been friends and wanted to develop this relationship and develop our performance with each other. And then there was this group of people that some of them were very nice. You know, they were hippies. They were very nice, but they just were doing this weird sect thing with this guy named Love that I didn't want to have anything to do with."

In contrast, Bud Chase enjoyed the spending time with the Love Family. "It was really great to have them along," Bud said. "They were not so Christian that I couldn't stand them, for a guy coming

Jana and Bud Chase dressed up for the parades.

from a Pagan background like Tim and Morning Glory. And every time they turned around, they were singing." Jana also enjoyed the singing: "We're in the kitchen cooking, they're making music for you and we all started learning the songs and singing along with them. It was kind of fun. I never had that much music in my life all the time."

Howard Patterson recalls them as "sweet, and a little terrifying." In jest, some of the entertainers adopted "Hate Family" names like Inertia, Procrastination, and Intolerance.

One communication mixup wasn't resolved until at least halfway through the tour. "Patch had told us the Love Family was coming to do food," Howard said, "but he apparently didn't make that completely clear to *them*. So each morning we'd show up at their bus, saying 'What's for breakfast?' And they'd be surprised. But being good hippie Christians, they'd come up with something for us." They would serve peanut butter sandwiches for breakfast, lunch, and dinner.

"The rest of us ended up complaining to the generous people," recalled Sam Williams (aka Smerdyakov Karamazov), "that they kept feeding us peanut butter over and over. We thought the folks who had taken on the responsibility of feeding everyone weren't handling it well. While they thought we, receiving their many gifts of food, were rather ungrateful. That Patch. What a sense of humor."

Despite the confusions, the Old Time New Age Chautauqua performers found appreciative audiences wherever they went. To drum up interest, the troupe paraded through the center of town before each show. The Living Unicorn led the way escorted by Morning Glory and Otter, followed by clowns, jugglers, and the brass marching band. The Gesundheit Collective offered workshops on basic health care, and the wild variety show had something to keep everyone entertained: a sword-swallower, a bubble blower, a tap dancer, singers, clowns, a unicorn, and crazy jugglers.

One night after a full day of shows, the group enjoyed an after-party at a commune where they would stay overnight, Folly Farm. Howard asked Jana to come with him to talk to Rebo, the "Money Buck-stopper" for Chautauqua. ("Buck-stopper," meaning the person in charge, was a phrase coined at White Bird Clinic. The phrase came to Chautauqua via Deni Schaddegg.)

"I'd never really met Rebo one-on-one," Jana said. "She was trying to be nice to me earlier. So we were in a beautiful old farmhouse, and Rebo was in the upstairs bathroom." They climbed the stairs and Howard knocked. Rebo said "Come in!" Howard walked in, motioning for Jana to follow. Rebo greeted them while bathing in a large old clawfoot bathtub. "I was all shy," Jana said.

Howard said they needed money so Jana could rent a glockenspiel. Rebo said, "Sure, let's do it."

Jana and Rebo would become good friends during the course of the Chautauqua tour. "Rebo and I were born the same year," Jana said. "I was five days older than her. And I had never met another woman who had my size of shoe, which was a size ten; and it was so fun talking to another woman who was tall as me and had the same shoe size. I just kind of fell in love with her, as everybody does who meets her."

Bud and Jana made some phone calls and found a place that would rent them a glockenspiel for a month. "Howard happened to have the strap from Seiza's glock," Jana said. "I don't know why they brought that, but they did. I liked the orchestra bells because it was set up just like a piano so I could read the music and play the bells." Jana practiced band songs over and over on the glock in the back of the borrowed van while Bud, wearing earplugs and following the Chautauqua caravan of buses and cars, drove toward their next destination: the Vancouver Folk Festival in Canada.

Worried about how the Canadian border guards would greet fifty or sixty "of us very hippie-looking-type people," Paul Magid said the group concocted a plan to play the Canadian national anthem. "What can they do?" Paul said. "All they can do is this—which is true—they have to stand at attention, they can't move! We took all the vehicles, lined up for inspection, and then we all poured out."

They lined up three-in-a row in Country Fair band formation

on the United States side of Peace Arch Park, a grassy strip of median between the northbound and southbound lanes of Interstate 5 and Highway 99. The sixty-seven-foot-high concrete Peace Arch, painted white, dominated the park at the exact border between the United States and Canada. The entire park was an international monument. The band played "The Star Spangled Banner" as they approached the arch from the U.S. side, then within the arch switched to the band's Oregon Country Fair irrational anthem, "The Chumleighland March."

Jana proudly marched in the band for the first time, playing music she had practiced on the glockenspiel. "When we were directly under the arch with the band," she said, "it just sounded amazing the way the music reflected back to us."

As they emerged on the Canadian side, the band blared out the notes to "Oh Canada" and kept marching onward, even though they had not decided in advance what they would do after exiting the arch.

"We just kept going because it's a marching band and they don't stop easily," Paul said, with a big grin. "A couple of us in the front held open the doors to the [Canadian border] office and the parade—oomph, oomph, boom, boom, 'Oh Canada'—and jugglers juggling and bubbles were blowing and we just kind of marched right through. … We played it once, sang it through, played it again." The Canadian border officials seemed to try to stand at attention, or perhaps to try to stop the band, but there was hardly any room to move as the band marched through.

That certainly impressed the Canadians, but not in the way the group had hoped. The officials insisted on searching all the vehicles.

"I'd asked everyone before we crossed the border to please not carry that funny green stuff that smells a little weird," Paul said. "But unfortunately, one guy had made this very large, clown-like spliff, and forgotten that it was in his cigarette box in his VW. The other thing we had with us was a unicorn, of course, a real living unicorn. … And first thing they do is they find the large joint. The border guard calls me to say, 'Look what I found.' And I'm thinking 'Oh my god it's the end of the trip.' But these were Canadians; they were reasonable. They said, 'You know, Just don't do it again!' … Then, they found the unicorn."

The group argued that they had to let the unicorn through since there were no rules on unicorns. But the Canadian officials insisted they saw a goat—an animal with a four-chambered stomach—not a unicorn, and the goat would need certain vaccinations before it could enter Canada.

Vancouver Folk Festival had publicized a new feature for 1981—a vaudeville Medicine show brought by the Flying Karamazov Brothers "one of the hits of last year's festival. This year they are returning with an incredible gaggle of vaudevillians, magicians, jugglers, sword swallowers, bubble blowers, and yes, folks, a unicorn."

Thinking public pressure might help their case, someone from Chautauqua called a Vancouver TV station to let them know that Lancelot, the mystical Living Unicorn slated to appear at the Vancouver Folk Festival, was stuck at the border.

"We had TV cameras come down from Vancouver and film this whole scene with the border guards and the unicorn," Paul said. "But no, the unicorn had to go back to the United States. But now the problem was, it had to go through the U.S. Customs. Fortunately the U.S. Customs doesn't have rules for unicorns and they said 'Oh, it's a unicorn. All right, it can come in.' Which I thought was kind of cool, actually."

The group stopped for a photo during the 1982 tour of the Old Time New Age Chautauqua.

Lancelot also solved one little problem: He ate the joint.

The unicorn had to stay in the United States with Oberon and Morning Glory while the rest of the troupe caravanned north to the Vancouver Folk Festival. After a delightful, music-filled weekend, the Old Time New Age Chautauqua tour headed east and wended its way back to the States, stopping to perform at a few small towns along the way. The troupe ended up adding an extra stop in Hedley, British Columbia, after their bus broke down and they had to wait a day for parts to arrive. The people at the Wooden Nickel, a hippie restaurant in Hedley, offered to let the entertainers spend the night, spreading their sleeping bags on the restaurant floor after closing time. To thank the people of Hedley for their hospitality, the performers surprised the town with a parade and show the next morning.

Everyone enjoyed the tour so much that Chautauqua became an instant post-fair tradition. They adopted Diana Leishman's "Travelin' Song," which Jan Luby sang at the shows, as their theme song:

> *Let's ride on a caravan off to the stars!*
> *Who knows where we'll land—maybe Venus or Mars.*
> *I'll show you a castle that travels on wheels*
> *And sing you a song all about how it feels.*
> *And the bells they do ring, and the pots and pans sing;*
> *If you let yourself go, you can do anything!*
> *So it's off on the road; let us lighten your load*
> *For we are the Gypsies in the traveling show!*

After a few years, the tour's name would change slightly. "We felt that a number of hucksters had given the term 'New Age' a less than wholesome patina," Tom Noddy said. "We reworked the name to New Old Time Chautauqua. That choice wasn't unanimous until it was pointed out that 'New Old Time' could be abbreviated to NOT Chautauqua, which was in keeping with other uses of the term 'Not' that we had adopted during those same years."

1982
Jill Heiman and Freedom of Assembly

> *"They tried to impose laws that applied only to the fair. ...When [County Commissioner Archie Weinstein] said, 'I don't give a damn about the fair,' Jill's eyes lit up like a Christmas tree—she knew she had him."*
> —Ron Chase, Fair Treasurer 1979-82

Jill Heiman enrolled in law school at the University of Oregon in the fall of 1972, at the forefront of a surge of women who sought to chart new destinies in male-dominated fields. The women's rights movement of the 1960s had just started to break down barriers and open the doors of education and economic independence. Young women in the 1970s wedged the doors wider. They poured into college classrooms, eager to prove their mettle.

A native of Long Island, New York, Jill had recently graduated from Case Western Reserve University in Cleveland, Ohio. She first lived with her boyfriend in a communal household outside Eugene. When their relationship broke up, Jill rented a studio apartment from Susie and Jack Delay. Jack, who volunteered as coordinator of the Information Crew at the Oregon Country Fair, introduced Jill to his friends—and stalwarts of the fair—Cindy Wooten and Sandra Bauer. The three women bonded immediately. Many an afternoon found the talkative trio at the Excelsior Restaurant, drinking house wine and solving the problems of the world.

Jill met another kindred spirit in Gretchen Miller, who started law school one year after Jill. When Gretchen graduated in 1976, the two of them set up Eugene's first all-women's law practice, Heiman & Miller. They were both in their mid-twenties. "We were right at the cusp when women were going into law," Gretchen said. "At that point, nobody in town really wanted to hire women lawyers."

Jill and Gretchen brought their passion for economic and social justice to work. They often advocated in court for low-income women. The two young attorneys would advise many small businesses in Lane County. They specialized in helping cooperative enterprises incorporate, relying on laws from the 1920s and 1930s originally intended for Oregon millworker cooperatives.

Jill Heiman, shown in Main Camp, helped the fair become a tax-exempt nonprofit.

The law partners also got involved in local Democratic politics, joining their friend Cindy Wooten, who had been active a long time. Cindy had successfully run in 1971 for the Lane Education Service board and continued to hold that post. She also had worked on local Democratic campaigns. Gretchen, Jill, and Cindy joined many other fair volunteers who campaigned in 1976 for Jerry Rust, a co-founder of the prominent Hoedads tree-planting cooperative who was running for the Lane County Board of Commissioners. Jerry won, and everyone was thrilled to have a progressive voice on the traditionally conservative county board. As commissioner, Jerry Rust always spoke up for the Oregon Country Fair, but he was often outvoted.

Jill also served as counsel for many local nonprofit organizations. One of her first clients was the McKenzie River Gathering Foundation. In 1976, Jill was invited by Leslie Brockelbank and her husband, Charles Gray, to a meeting on the banks of the McKenzie River with a group of other activists and philanthropists. Leslie had recently inherited $500,000, and the couple asked those gathered to help decide how best to use the inheritance "to deeply impact the root causes of social inequity and environmental degradation."

After considerable discussion, the group coalesced around a plan to use the inheritance to create a nonprofit foundation. The foundation would promote progressive community activism through grants to group projects. They particularly sought to empower groups considered too leftist to get mainstream funding.

(Their plan would prove to be highly successful. The foundation would last for more than four decades and was still active at this writing. By 2016 the McKenzie River Gathering would give out more than $15 million to hundreds of social justice groups around the state of Oregon.)

In 1978, Gretchen Miller ran for a seat on the Eugene City Council, with Jill as her campaign manager. At Democratic events, Jill often swapped campaign stories with Gerry Mackie, whom she had first met at the 1976 McKenzie River Gathering event. She had given Gerry a ride home after the McKenzie River meeting, but sparks didn't fly between them until two years later. "In 1978, I worked for Jerry Rust at Lane County Courthouse," Gerry Mackie said, "and at the same time, I was managing a campaign and Jill Heiman was managing the campaign of Gretchen Miller, her law partner. We started meeting in Lane County Democratic circles ... at the Democratic Party celebrations. And we started dating."

"Her network was Country Fair and [Eugene] City Council," Gerry added. "My network was Hoedads and the county. We were like a bridge between these two networks, these two giant networks. We had a lot in common that way."

Meanwhile, a series of events in the mid-1970s would draw Jill deep into the inner circle of the Oregon Country Fair. In 1976 Jill had moved out of the Delays' studio apartment to share a big house on Hendricks Hill with Sandra Bauer. When Cindy Wooten separated from Bill Wooten in the fall of 1976, she moved into the Delays' vacant studio apartment. The three women developed a strong friendship.

The friction between Bill and Cindy had become obvious at fair meetings. Nobody was surprised when they divorced in the spring of 1977. But most fair organizers were shocked to learn that Bill Wooten would remain the overall coordinator of the 1977 fair. Cindy limited her role to coordinating Admissions, which operated a booth out in the fair's parking lot. In the early years, the fair had benefited from Cindy's and Bill's divergent talents: Cindy's attention to detail helped bring Bill's broad-scope ideas to fruition. Everyone knew Bill couldn't fill both roles.

Gretchen Miller volunteered on the fair's Information Crew in the 1980s.

Behind Bill's back, a small cadre of Main Camp regulars closed ranks. Sandra Bauer, Nancy Albro, Ron Chase, and Mary Cay Liebig each took on big pieces of the fair's organizational puzzle. The turmoil made it obvious that the fair—which had functioned for years with loose, consensus-driven meetings—needed a more formal structure.

Sandra started bringing Jill to the fair's coordinator meetings. Jill took minutes at every meeting she attended. She urged the coordinators to make sure someone always took minutes at meetings. Up until then, minutes were not a main concern and often were scrawled out in longhand, if any were taken at all. On May 31, 1977, Jill officially filed with the state of Oregon to incorporate the Oregon Country Fair as a state-recognized nonprofit organization.

Later that summer at the 1977 fair, Jill and Gretchen joined Cindy on the Admissions Crew, staying mostly out in the parking lot, away from Main Camp and other fair duties. With Bill Wooten nominally in charge, the problems of a poorly run event multiplied, and so did neighbors' complaints to the county.

Immediately after the fair and well into the spring of 1978, coordinators found themselves working long and hard with county officials to try to address all of the complaints made by neighbors. Coordinators knew something had to change, and that had led them to accept Jill's suggestion to seek nonprofit status with the state of Oregon.

At fair meetings, Bill's freewheeling methods often clashed with Jill's penchant for following the rules. They shared a strong commitment to political justice, but they contrasted deeply in style and approach. Part of it could be traced to their regional differences: Bill was raised in slow-paced, rural Oklahoma; Jill grew up in fast-paced New York. But there was more to it than that. Bill was a hip, ever-serious, bearded philosopher: tall, lanky, often sloppy with paperwork and clothing, and wildly outspoken. Jill was an aspiring attorney with a dry sense of humor: petite and trim, well prepared, neatly dressed, and judiciously but energetically outspoken.

Even though Jill didn't fit the hip stereotype, she would win the respect and admiration of fair coordinators. With Jill's encouragement, the Oregon Country Fair formally elected its first board of directors in April 1979.

In September 1979, the board approved Jill's proposal to apply for federal 501(c)(3) tax-exempt status, which posed a much higher hurdle than state nonprofit status. However, the benefit to the fair becoming a recognized federal nonprofit agency would be huge. The fair owed a significant amount of money in unpaid back taxes to the U.S. government. If Jill could secure federal nonprofit designation, the Country Fair could avoid paying any taxes to Uncle Sam and the old bill would be voided.

"When the fair had to assume a legal entity," Ron Chase said, "Jill was able to gently nudge that through. ... She was the primary instrumental person in getting the 501(c)(3), which was crucial to the fair's future. Nobody else even recognized the importance of it, much less how hard it was to get." In April 1980, the Internal Revenue Service granted the Oregon Country Fair tax-exempt status, "to preserve and foster regional cultural and artistic achievement." The application emphasized the fair's demonstrations of "solar power, cooperatives, and farming" in addition to music and crafts.

Jill made a strong legal advocate for the fair at Lane County hearings. "She always dressed well," Gretchen said. "She made sure that she looked very professional and maximized her presence." Jill challenged the commissioners as they piled more conditions on the fair every year. They set the hurdles higher and higher for each fair, as if they were determined to not let it happen, Gretchen said.

In 1979, the county forced the fair to pay for extra sheriff's

Gerry Mackie, Jill Heiman, and their son Brendan visited with fair crafter Arna Shaw.

patrols. But the deputies who were supposed to be easing traffic into the fair created a massive traffic jam instead. Deputies stopped cars for any possible infraction, searching so many vehicles that traffic inched along Highway 126 for fifteen miles all the way back to Eugene. In the official report to commissioners, the sheriff's office inflated the total number of complaints filed against the fair by adding in all the complaints about the traffic jam.

In 1980 the county added yet another condition. A split board of Lane County Commissioners passed an assemblies ordinance that required the fair to post a $10,000 bond on top of the required liability insurance policy. Privately, Jill and Gretchen worried that the county could easily price the bond out of the fair's reach, and they discussed legal remedies.

During a public hearing in June 1980, Jill Heiman argued that the bond amounted to an unconstitutional restraint on freedom of assembly. She pointed out that no other group had to pay it. Lane County's assistant county counsel, Bill Van Vactor, acknowledged at the meeting that Jill might have a point.

Commissioners Archie Weinstein and Harold Rutherford, who

were leading the effort to impose the bond, said that they didn't care if the bond was unconstitutional. They said they didn't like the dirty hippies who attended the fair, or their values or lifestyles. Archie challenged Jill to take him to court if she didn't like it. Jill took up the gauntlet. On June 30, 1980, the Oregon Country Fair sued Lane County and various county officials—including Commissioners Weinstein and Rutherford—for impeding the right to assembly.

With the lawsuit pending, the county attorney advised the commissioners to suspend the bond. The 1980 Country Fair was allowed to go forward.

After the 1980 fair, organizers faced another huge turning point: The site along the Long Tom River, where the fair had been held for a decade, was offered for sale.

"The land was owned by Western Aerial Contractors," said Ron Chase, who was the fair's treasurer then. "This land investment was their retirement fund, their pension. In fact, their principal guy named Bob Nelson told me that some of them were starting to get on in years. They wanted to sell the land and that we were the logical buyers."

The property sat fifteen miles west of Eugene, past Fern Ridge Reservoir and between the bedroom communities of Veneta and Elmira. Parcels of the property closest to the main road had been sold off over the years to individual homeowners. By 1980, the land was down to 240 of the original 400 acres that the fair first leased in October 1970. The remaining low-lying woods and wetland prairies were subject to seasonal flooding from the Long Tom River that meandered through the site. The owners priced the acreage at $325,000, and asked for a down payment of $100,000.

"The land was expensive and it was way overpriced considering that there was nothing you could do with it," Ron said. The flooding made the land unsuitable for housing, and efforts at farming it had never paid off.

Fair organizers were highly interested, but the $100,000 down payment posed a sobering obstacle. After the 1981 fair, only $24,000 sat in the fair's savings account.

Community Village meetings had been filled by excited conversations about purchasing a permanent site ever since the fair's nonprofit status was approved in 1980. The Village and the fair board met together in September 1981 to further the discussion. They created a fund-raising committee and named Treasurer Ron Chase as the point person.

During a special fair-wide membership meeting held in October 1981, Ron presented a plan for a Charter Membership fund drive. Under the plan, a fair member could become a Charter Member for a contribution or loan of $300. The loans would be paid back once the land was paid off and the fair had the money. By January 1982, the fund-raising committee had collected $25,500 from Charter Memberships and T-shirt sales, an impressive sum, but combined with the $24,000 in the bank, the amount was not quite half of the $100,000 goal. Worried organizers announced a bake sale to raise more money and urged more fair participants to buy Charter memberships, or at least purchase the fund-raiser T-shirt.

Then the fair—and Jill—got excellent news. In February 1982, Lane County agreed to settle the fair's freedom of assembly lawsuit from two years earlier. The fair received a check for $19,000 in the settlement.

Fair organizers quickly recognized that the money could make a big difference on the down payment for the land. Ironically, Lane County Commissioners' attempt to put obstacles in the way of the fair would result instead in helping the fair purchase the site to use in perpetuity.

Gretchen said she helped with some background research on the lawsuit, but Jill took charge of all of it. "Jill sued the pants off of 'em! It was delightful," Gretchen said with a laugh. "It took forever, it was a huge job. It was really too big of a lawsuit for one person to do, but we were young and didn't know that."

Sandra Bauer said Jill was a "little dynamo" in court. "She was really small, but very tough," Sandra said. "She was one single lawyer against this whole battery of lawyers on the other side. She took them to court and she won."

After winning the lawsuit, Jill pivoted to facilitating the fair's land purchase. "Jill could see what was possible, whereas I couldn't imagine," Cynthia Wooten said. "She categorically outlined the process for buying the land, how to get from here to there."

Jill worked closely with Ron Chase, the fair's treasurer. "Ron was responsible for initiating the action to buy the property," Sandra Bauer said. "Lots of other people worked on the project, but he put together the basic plan to make it happen."

Longtime OCF volunteer John Stamp (Shenanigans booth, Archaeology Crew, Tree Crew) characterized the settlement payment as a "slap on the wrist to Lane County. It really wasn't much, not in the whole world scheme of things. But it was wondrous in the pressure it took off us," he said. "It allowed us to act as our community, which has always been our goal anyhow. ... to be a village that represents an alternative to the way life is lived ordinarily."

On July 8, 1982, the day before the fair opened to the public, Ron Chase signed the fair's promissory note to buy 240 acres of land along the Long Tom River for $250,000 and made the first $50,000 down payment. The note called for a second down payment of $50,000 by December 31, 1982, and for ten annual payments of $26,370 due each September 1.

Each Charter Member of the Oregon Country Fair received a signed certificate, the only tangible benefit legally allowed. But many Charter Members would later comment on the intangible benefits of their sense of personal satisfaction and ownership in the fair.

A few weeks after the 1982 fair, attorney Jill Heiman married Gerry Mackie at the Faculty Club on the University of Oregon campus. Jill's mother flew in from Long Island, New York. Sandra and Cindy helped decorate the chuppa, the traditional Jewish wedding canopy, with ribbons and flowers, and also served as bridesmaids.

10. 1982
Ibrahim Hamide and Casablanca Middle Eastern Cafe

"When I started, 'hummus' was not a household word by any stretch. I was introducing my new adopted nation to the food that I grew up on to preach its attributes."
—Ibrahim Hamide, founder of Casablanca and Café Soriah, quoted in *Eugene Weekly*, April 6, 2017

Ibrahim Hamide opened the Casablanca Middle Eastern Café in Eugene in 1981. "Ib"—(pronounced Eeb) as his friends called him—was a native Palestinian who immigrated to Oregon in 1969 to attend the University of Oregon.

At the time that he opened his restaurant at the Fifth Street Public Market, the venue's setup and atmosphere reflected Eugene's counterculture zeitgeist. Numerous local artisans displayed their wares in individual stalls in the upstairs craft mall, while small restaurants filled niches of the repurposed building with enticing food aromas that beckoned diners. Casablanca opened up in a cozy corner of the basement.

"It was Fifth Street Market/Hippie Market," Ibrahim said. "It was very much a hangout place. It was very friendly to common folk, including the ones who were making six-figure incomes." Ib got into the restaurant business because he missed the traditional foods he had eaten growing up and proudly noted that his restaurant was one of the first to serve hummus and baba ganoush in town.

"Part of the hippie movement was going back to the land and agriculture," Ib said. "Well, that's feeding the people. That's as basic as you can get as far as human rights."

Ib's large family had tended a farm east of Bethlehem when it was still part of Palestine. "We lived three to four months on this farm and the rest of the year in town, in Bethlehem," Ib said. "Farming was like mother's milk to me. It was all one hundred percent organic, one hundred percent man and animal labor. There was nothing mechanical.

"We didn't have running water, we didn't have electricity," Ib continued. "That is very much like the Country Fair. And it is where truth is present all the time because if the earth does not like a seed you put in there, a thorn comes up. If you put a seed for a garbanzo bean, a garbanzo bean comes up. You put a seed for a tomato, a tomato comes up. So there is a real honest exchange and also it's causal. If you don't plant, you don't harvest. And if you don't plant, you don't eat because that was where our food came from. ... We bought sugar, coffee, tea, rice, that's about it. The rest we grew."

Ib's family harvested fruit orchards, vegetables, and grains. They made clarified butter that would keep in the cupboard without refrigeration. "Sun-dried tomato was not a gourmet term to us," Ib said. "We preserved our tomatoes. Figs were dried and put in burlap sacks. ... It was good living and people loved each other. They were dependent on each other, helped each other with the harvest. ... Then war came and all hell breaks loose."

Israeli troops occupied his home after the Six-Day War of 1967, when Ib was seventeen years old. After that, Ib could see no good future for himself in his childhood homeland. His oldest brother had moved to the United States ten years earlier and had settled in Washington state. Ib accepted his brother's offer to help pay for the first term of his education at the University of Oregon, the same school his brother had attended.

"He sent me a suit back home," Ib said, "and I wore it so when we met at the airport, he would know who I am. I was eight when I last saw him and then I was seventeen, almost eighteen, when I saw him next. Ten years changes a lot, and we didn't have cell phones or the technology to send pictures all the time. We didn't really know how we were going to look like, either of us."

Coming to America wasn't an easy choice. Ib was leaving his loving family and everything he knew, but he found the courage to seek a better life. After reuniting with his brother in Europe and finally getting accepted to the University of Oregon, Ib arrived in Eugene in April 1969 to register for classes.

"Life was not what I envisioned it," Ib said. "Eugene in 1969 was a shock: Free love, pot smoking, demonstrations against the Vietnam War. That was all different!" He found people with common values in the peace-and-justice movement and enjoyed the freedom to express his views. He worked several jobs to help pay his way through college while studying business administration and psychology. He also found time to attend some of the early Renaissance Faires when they rolled around each year.

"The fair has that magic," Ib said. "It's got big and fat welcoming arms for just about anybody. You find the lawyer, the conservative person who's six days a week conservative but on the weekend they go and cut loose, and the ones who are children of the sixties. I came here in the midst of the hippie movement. I was just nineteen, so I'm a child of the sixties, too."

As Ib worked to pay for college, the jobs started to become more important than earning a degree. He fell in love, got married, and left school to work in restaurants.

In 1982, Ib opened the Casablanca food booth at the Oregon Country Fair at space 564 on the Upper River Loop of the Eight pathway. He served a reduced menu from his restaurant in town—falafel, tabbouleh, cucumber salad, spicy chicken, and lamb shawarma.

"Right next to us was a steel drum booth," Ib said. "I remember the first year serving those guys on the first night of being there, four-course meals on wooden planks because I didn't have trays. I didn't have anything. They were blown away. I cannot remember what foods I served, but I made a four-course, delicious, outstanding meal that they raved about. It became the beginning of a beautiful friendship with those guys—Larry Osborn, Jack Costello, Mike Metsch, and Chris Wood."

The neighbors' booth was called the Frisco Pipe Collective, and they hailed from Vancouver, Washington. Besides steel drums, they sold hats, shirts, and wood products—including pipes.

Over the years, Ib would start bringing his children to the fair.

"My daughter and son would just be tagging along with me," Ib said. "Being at the fair and just being welcomed and loved and cared for by everybody, including our neighbors. That was the beginning of that long-term relationship which still continues."

Jack Costello, a psychiatrist in the health profession, got to know Ib's children from the time they were babies.

"When my daughter Soriah got her doctoral degree in clinical psychology, when she was moving to Portland, I said, 'Look up Jack, he will give you valuable knowledge about the health industry up there,'" Ib said. "In fact, he ended up interviewing and hiring my daughter, gave her a job where she's working now [in 2018]. ... If I see Larry or Jack, it's like old friends still. That's part of the magic of the Country Fair."

The Casablanca booth developed a tradition of feeding musicians for free who would play for them. "Especially in the beginning, I had my best friend who's no longer with us, he and his girlfriend at that time," Ib said. "I also wasn't married. We'd always invite musicians. If they would come by to play music, we would feed them for free, take care of them. But we made sure they played music because we love the music."

Ib also enjoyed wandering the fair's pathways after the booth closed for the evening. He'd stop at every eatery that was open to sample their fares, and hang out at the spots where musicians gathered to jam. He would always check out the belly-dancing shows at Gypsy Caravan Stage, where he knew some of the featured dancers. Every Saturday night, he would enjoy watching the Midnight Show at the Main Stage Meadow.

The booth was hard work. "We probably take 500 pounds of lamb, 300 or 400 pounds of chicken, 200 pounds of falafel, probably similar for the hummus and the salads," Ib said. "If you add it all up, probably in the thousands of pounds. And you've got to keep it sanitary, keep it temperature controlled, hot or cold."

All the food was cooked on site. Ib said at first Casablanca had a fun-oriented, "loosey-goosey" schedule for the fair, but soon realized that did not work.

"We've streamlined it," he said. "Now we have a pre-fair meeting, where they come in there and I read them the riot act. This is a serious business when we make food. Food is something that people put into their bodies. That's an awesome responsibility. If you cannot treat it that way, you don't work at the booth."

They divided the labor so that some people took orders and money at the counter, some people brought in fresh supplies from the fair's refrigeration unit called the Reefer Truck, and some prepared food. Ib documented in a booklet the schedules, recipes, and food inventories needed for each fair.

"We've noticed that if we just do a manual, any fool with reasonable intelligence can follow it rather than have to do it over and over and over," he said. "We've been pretty good about documenting what goes out and what comes back, but it changes also."

The menu sometimes would change in response to suggestions from the fair's Food Committee. At other times, items that didn't sell well would be replaced by new offerings. "It's just like any business—you adjust, you learn from your previous experiences and you try to make it better," he said.

Ib noted that the fair improved its organization over the years, upgrading health codes and food inspection. "The food inspectors come out and make sure everyone is compliant," he said. "It is run so much better over the years; each year it seems to have gotten better and better as far as organization. ... It's almost counter-intuitive that you go out there to be free-spirited, yet have your rules and regulations. A certain amount of those are necessary."

He said they schedule workers for six-hour shifts in order to give them time each day to play at the fair.

Over the years that Ib was establishing himself as a fixture at the fair, he also started selling his hummus and baba ganoush in natural food grocery stores around Eugene. "Kiva bought my hummus in bulk for ages when I was at Fifth Street Market," Ib said. "I tried selling at Sundance [Natural Foods] but they overwhelmed me because I was a one-man show, basically. I sold them hummus, tabbouli, grape leaves, and baba ganoush—four items—and it would fly off the shelf. I would be sitting here sticking labels on it by hand, making it after work. It became very laborious and tedious. I could not keep up, so I dropped them. But Kiva took it in bulk, so it was easy to put hummus in a fifteen-pound bucket and on my way home drop it off."

In the early 1990s, Ib stopped selling to most grocery stores to concentrate on a second restaurant. In 1993, he opened Café Soriah on West Thirteenth Avenue in Eugene. Named after his daughter, the restaurant featured "Mediterranean food," which Ib said included any country that touched the Mediterranean Sea.

Out at the Oregon Country Fair, the Casablanca booth would move in 2001 to the food court of the new Chela Mela Meadow after the fair expanded to that area.

But world events in the autumn 2001 would shake up Ib's world much more seriously than the move to the fair's newest public meadow. After terrorists crashed airplanes into the World Trade Center Towers in New York City and the Pentagon in Washington, D.C. on September 11, 2001, Ib would become a de facto spokesperson in Oregon for the Palestinian people. He had already helped found the Eugene Mideast Peace Group in the mid-1980s, but he stepped up his visibility in the 2000s.

On October 11, 2001, Ib joined a few hundred other concerned people at the first Interfaith Prayer Service held in Eugene in response to the terrorist attacks. The service would bring together people of different faith traditions in prayer and support of one another. The service would become a monthly tradition in Eugene and would remain part of the city's tapestry at least until 2019. Ib would remain heavily involved throughout.

But Ib's visibility in the community also would make him a target for a few people who held prejudices that overruled any knowledge of geography. Even though Ib was not from a country that was involved in the September 11 terrorism, some bigoted Americans would blame the attack on any Arab or anyone who even looked like they might be an Arab.

In the wake of September 11, bricks and a smoke bomb were thrown into Café Soriah one night after the restaurant had closed, breaking a window. Right after that, Ib experienced an upwelling of support from friends and neighbors, who called and sent cards regretting his tribulations and wishing him well. He noted that the good responses from his neighbors far outweighed the negative act.

In 2004, Ib would be appointed by the Eugene City Council to the Human Rights Commission, where he would serve for more than a decade.

"Human rights are very dear and near to my heart," he said. "I used to focus on politics on the commission but as I get older, my view shifted. Conflicts arise when somebody dominates another person one way or the other—whether they take their land or their money or their water or try to take their freedom or whatever it is. I've come to realize that those freedoms are basic. ... Giving people basic human rights will diminish conflicts tremendously. I still care very much about the Middle East because my family lives there and I'm from there, but even that conflict I view now through a human rights prism."

Ib's son Naseem started to get more involved with the Casablanca booth at the Oregon Country Fair in the late 2000s. Naseem had been coming to the fair since he was six years old, and often helped in the booth. After Ib purchased the venerable Zenon Café in downtown Eugene when the owners retired, Naseem took on a bigger role out at the fair.

"As I get older, get softer, I miss my shower and my bed," Ib said. "I've changed, as many of us old hippies did. For the last ten years [since 2009], I've taken the bus out, I don't even drive out there." His son, who was in his twenties, and one of his employees persuaded Ib in 2009 that they could handle the booth at the fair. They noted that Ib already had his hands full running three full-time restaurants in town.

But after a few years, Ib heard complaints from his regular customers that the food at the fair was not as tasty as it used to be. He returned full-time to the booth in 2014 to restore it to his standards.

"I have my own ethics and have to live with it," Ib said. "I took my son out there and I said, 'Look, this is how it should be run, not like you or he run it.' So we did that for two years together and last year he ran it by himself. I was amazed. He did a really good job."

In 2011, Ib closed Casablanca at the Fifth Street Market and switched gears at the Café Zenon. He remodeled the restaurant at the corner of Eighth Avenue and Pearl Street and renamed it Dahlia on Broadway in honor of his daughter. He incorporated recipes from Casablanca into the menu at Dahlia's, but it didn't turn into a recipe for success at that location. Dahlia's would close in 2014.

Ib would next remodel Café Soriah to enlarge it and serve more customers.

In 2012, Naseem, then thirty-two, would join his father to relaunch a line of dips sold retail at natural grocery stores in Eugene. Under the Casablanca label, they marketed packages of baba ganoush and several flavors of hummus.

By 2016, Naseem would be handling nearly all of the production of the Casablanca dip label. Ib had hurt himself playing basketball and for several months could not help with the heavy lifting needed at the production facility. His son took over the work and did such a good job that Ib realized they didn't need him. "I was just cheap labor for them," he said. "They were doing great! So I quit. I threw in the towel. ... He makes the hummus using my recipe."

In 2018, Ib would get to enjoy being a tourist on Sunday of the Oregon Country Fair. He would drop by the booth to say hello, grab a bite, and then go wander the paths to check out all of the entertainment. The family also marked a new milestone: The Casablanca booth would embrace three generations. Naseem's son would attend the fair at age six, the same age Naseem was when Ib first brought him to the fair.

"I really respect how the folks that run the Country Fair have pulled together and upgraded," Ib said. "If you have a child lost, there's a fair person there. If you have a medical emergency they can even evacuate you out of there. The organizational nightmare that that place must be is handled with grace.

"I've never seen a child cry there, I've never seen a fist fight. It's incredible. A feather in their cap. I high-five each and every one of the volunteers for being so dedicated," he said. "It takes hard work and organization and persistence and all the ingredients to make that come off the way it does. And they have not ruffled many feathers in the process of inserting regulations that are needed. That's a fine line to walk. There's people out there half-stoned, half-free-seekers and they don't want anyone telling them, 'You can't drive your car in there,' but they do it and they manage to keep smiles on people's faces. Those are all pretty amazing accomplishments."

 1982 Celebration

> *"The Fair brings us together from all over the region to show that what we do separately can compose the image of a new and better world."*
>
> —1982 *Peach Pit*

In the weeks prior to opening day, the dozen Main Camp volunteers had fallen into the routines needed to get the site ready for the oncoming throng. With the lawsuit settled, the county permit came with no problems. Everyone anticipated the moment when Ron Chase would sign the deed and the fair could claim ownership of the land. But land ownership would usher in some unexpected changes.

As usual, crafters prepared their inventory and stopped by the site beforehand to check out what repairs would be needed to get their booths ready for fair time. But in 1982 there was a big difference. Everyone was cognizant that the fair was no longer a tenant paying rent.

Owning the land changed thinking and behavior. Instead of simply repairing their booths, crafters and food vendors built larger, sturdier structures. Many crafters took liberties to quietly expand their footprint. Defying fair policy, they cleared brush to the sides or back of

A sign welcoming people to the fair made reference to the successful land purchase.

their booths and claimed the camping space. After the fair, the board would roundly denounce the brush clearing and resulting land grabs.

Community Village expressed its exuberance for the land in a different way. "The year we bought the land, we buried a time capsule in Community Village," said Jon Silvermoon, who volunteered on the Village Coordinating Council. "We took Genesis Juice bottles and put in the bottle a camping pass, food voucher, the village schedule, some marijuana seeds, some bud, rolling paper, and some other things that a few of us contributed, wrapped it up in aluminum foil and buried it in the ground in a hole that we surrounded by charcoal so that it could be radio-carbon-dated. We said this was going to be a thousand-year time capsule. It's still sitting there in the center of the village commons, somewhere below ground."

Pre-fair, discussions bubbled up in Main Camp about how to handle illegal drug and alcohol sales along the edges of the fair's path. The problem had been only sporadically addressed during past events. When the land had been rented, fair organizers had no strong incentives to confront people. Security crews broke up only drug or alcohol sales that were flagrantly public or when people started to get out of hand. When everything ran smoothly, organizers often looked the other way. But now Main Camp folks worried that legal problems could jeopardize the fair's ownership of the land.

Strongly worded memos circulated among the crews and booths, stating that illegal drug and alcohol sales would not be tolerated at the 1982 fair.

The fourteenth Oregon Country Fair opened July 9, 1982, under partly cloudy skies with temperatures in the seventies and eighties. High spirits over the success of buying the land charged the atmosphere with a buoyant effervescence.

The Info Crew put together a Crafts Directory listing more than 300 vendors for 1982 from booth 002, Woolenwood, selling wool handicrafts and handcrafted furniture from Junction City, Oregon, through booth 979, Feet of Clay, with pottery and stoneware from Sheridan, Oregon. A crazy kaleidoscope of crafts greeted fairgoers: ironwork tools, jewelry, sandals, flutes, quilts, beadwork, pillows, pipes, mirrors, toys, puppets, futon mats, candles, candleholders, T-shirts, metal belt buckles, leather belts, and yes, even kaleidoscopes.

Celebration

Dennis Todd and Tom Agamenoni volunteered on Garbage/ Recycling Crew in the early 1980s.

Malcolm Ware and Robert DeSpain patrolled the fair paths in the early 1980s.

In its second year, Energy Park offered information on conservation and on solar, wind, hydro and solar power. This time the solar showers actually worked. People lined up for a shower first took a turn pedaling the bicycle to power the shower's water flow.

Visitors to Community Village could learn about papermaking, yoga, homeopathy, creative parenting, and polyfidelity. Activities ran from new games to square dancing. It was the first year for the Women's Grounding Circle, a daily ceremony to help women reconnect with their metaphorical roots. The grounding circle was inspired by the community grounding circles offered in Deadwood by Christine Payne-Towler. The ceremony would start with a "cleansing" of energy, such as smudging with sage or misting with lavender water. After introductions and songs, a guided meditation was offered to help women in the circle find their inner strength and wisdom.

Community Village also started a new program for the children of volunteers and crafters who camped at the fair overnight, called Youth Job Services. The program connected youths ages eight to fifteen with age-appropriate volunteer jobs around the fair, including food prep, running errands, helping people load and unload, cleaning the sauna, and stacking firewood. About forty youths worked eighty jobs. The kids and their parents liked the program so much that the fair would eventually set up an official crew for the program. The fair's Teen Crew would still be going three decades later, nurturing new generations of fair volunteers. By training fair "kids" to new jobs in different areas of the fair, Teen Crew also would help build a sense of "fair family" throughout the dispersed groups of volunteers.

Meanwhile, popular local and regional groups dominated the Main Stage lineup for 1982, including the harmonic rock of Mithrandir, Balafon marimba ensemble, folk-rockers Just Friends, and the New Age sound of Michael Hedges. A down-home vibe prevailed in the mornings, featuring Percy Hilo calling a square dance on Saturday, and Briarose and the Skinny City Cloggers dancing on Sunday.

As always, performers could be found all along the fair pathways. One fair favorite along the paths had been Dr. Atomic's Medicine Show, which campaigned against nuclear power with political comedy, satirical songs, and street theater. In 1974 after construction started on the Trojan Nuclear Plant in Rainier, Washington, Dr. Atomic's World-Famous Medicine Show & Lending Library had toured small towns around Oregon to advocate against building nuclear plants in Oregon

"Dr. Atomic's Medicine Show emerged in 1974 from a project at Eugene's Movement for a New Society called a 'macroanalysis seminar,'" original member Peter Bergel said. "After studying domestic and international problems together for half a year, a small group decided to tackle nuclear power development in Oregon. Our first project was to mount a humorous traveling comedy show pointing up the problems with nuclear power and perform it in every Oregon community (then eight) in which a nuclear power plant was proposed. We also carried educational posters and handouts that were distributed to our audiences. I'm pleased to report that not a single one of those nuclear plants was ever built."

Dr. Atomic's World Famous Medicine Show brought political theater to the fair.

Charles Gray, who would co-found the McKenzie River Gathering Foundation, was among those who acted and toured in the Medicine Show. Dr. Atomic's Medicine Show was first booked at the fair in 1974 at what was then called Kesey Park. The Medicine Show would return to the fair in 1980 and become a fair favorite for decades, often featured at Kesey Stage in Energy Park.

"The cast and the format have changed over the years," Peter said in 2018, "but the mission of Dr. Atomic's Medicine Show has remained the same: poke fun at the things in our culture that most need it. Over the years, our targets have ranged widely including: nuclear power, nuclear weapons, the arms race, any number of political figures, gambling, sexism, poor election practices, corporate greed, climate change, political cowardice, racism, advertising, and much more."

Oregon author Ken Kesey himself, then age forty-six, had participated in every fair since 1970 as part of the Springfield Creamery booth, owned by his brother and sister-in-law Chuck and Sue Kesey. He told a reporter from the *Los Angeles Times* that the fair was on "the cutting edge of civilization right now." He said the values embraced by the people who put on the fair—self-sufficiency, respect for natural resources, and making do with less—represented the best hope for the future.

Fair president Sandra Bauer agreed. "Living lightly on the Earth was the whole point" of the counter-culture revolution, she said. "I think that's still the main goal of most of the people who are involved with the fair."

The Flying Karamazov Brothers held court on the Circus Stage. In keeping with their ongoing rivalry with Reverend Chumleigh, two banners hung cross the entrance. The top one featured the juggling troup's flying heart symbol and their name in big letters; the smaller banner below proclaimed:

Chumleighland
(in memorium)
Or, Chumleigh Plays The Styx.

Once again, the Fighting Instruments of Karma Marching Band/Orchestra paraded around the Eight pathway to draw a crowd into the show. The warmup acts included mime Avner the Eccentric, silent juggler Roberto Morganti, and folksinger Faith Petric. That left most of the talking to the witty Brothers K.

Tom Noddy brought back his custom windscreen to set up the W.C. Fields Memorial Stage behind Main Camp, and signed up

The Flying Karamazov Brothers raised a banner spoofing Reverend Chumleigh's absence from the fair.

performers he saw along the paths to fill out the stage's schedule. Each morning he would place out straw bales for audience seating and each evening he'd stack the bales to the side so water trucks could rumble through to refill the empty barrels around the Eight.

Late on Saturday night long after the public left, the Flying Karamazov Brothers lined up the entertainment for the Midnight Show so the crafters and volunteers who worked all day could get a sample of the shows. The grand finale featured the Flying Karamazov Brothers juggling fire sticks while naked. The jugglers tried mightily to get everyone in the audience to remove their clothes, too. "It was about 2:00 or 3:00 a.m. and really cold," recalled Walter Renfro, who was Traffic Co-coordinator. "Nobody went along with it, and they said 'That's it!'" The Karamazov Brothers brought the show to an abrupt halt.

Sunday morning brought blue skies and temperatures in the high seventies and the entertainers had a surprise up their sleeves, so to speak. "The parade comes out with the public there—you know, grandmas, kids, everything," Walter said. "And the band didn't have a stitch of clothes on. Trumpet players, horns, just sitting there dangling wide open, right? Girls, everybody! They marched all the way through the fair. We figured that's it. We've lost the fair."

The Flying Karamazov Brothers juggled naked at the 1982 Midnight Show.

"Actually," noted Tim Furst (aka Fyodor Karamazov), "contrary to popular belief, the band was not naked. Almost everyone was wearing shoes and an instrument. Although how well-dressed a person was depended on whether they were playing piccolo or tuba."

Entertainment Coordinator Moz Wright saw the naked parade coming down the path from his spot at Main Stage. "It was cutting quite a swath," he said. "People were noticing."

Fair President Sandra Bauer certainly noticed. "I was pissed!" she said. "I go out there and I was yelling at them in the middle of the path, just screaming." But the band kept marching on, so Sandra tried to enlist Moz's help. Moz replied, "Well, I can stop them, but Sandra, they'll still be naked!" The band had to complete marching around the Eight to get back to their clothes.

For several years afterward, the Info Crew got questions from people asking where the "Naked Parade" would be held. "We explained it was a one-time experience," said Info Crew volunteer Norah Roberts. "You know, an artistic happening."

 1982 Folksinger Faith Petric

I wanna be a Geritol Gypsy, drive an RV ten yards long
I wanna roll on down the interstate just singin' a highway song
I wanna be a Geritol Gypsy underneath the open sky
I wanna be a Geritol Gypsy 'til I die!
—"Geritol Gypsy" by Peter Krug

Faith Petric first came to the Oregon Country Fair in 1982 to sing on the Not Chumleighland (aka Circus) Stage. She had met the Flying Karamazov Brothers and other fair performers the year before during the first Old Time New Age Chautauqua tour. At the time, Faith was visiting her friend and legendary activist folksinger Utah Phillips in Spokane.

"I don't know how, but we heard that the Chautauqua group was camped ... not far from Spokane," Faith said. "We went over to see them and they enthusiastically invited us to go along, which neither of us were able to do, but that led up to me getting up to the Country Fair the next year."

Faith, then age sixty-seven, had been an activist folksinger most of her life. She came equipped with an extensive repertoire of more than a thousand songs—everything from the kids' favorite "I Wanna Be a Dog" to labor songs she learned on the picket lines in the 1930s. Her friend Utah said she "harvested" folk songs.

"'Harvest' is a very good word, and once Phillips gave it to me I use it a lot," Faith said during an interview in 2003 at her multistoried Victorian Home in San Francisco. "I don't write songs. I harvest them. 'I want that one, I want that one and I'll take that one.' I just bought a CD yesterday, with a song of Holly Near's that I want. The only way I can learn it is off her CD because I still learn by ear. I don't learn by reading the music. I'm not very good at that. ...

"There's an old joke about that. They ask the leader of the band, 'Do any of your players read music?' And he says, 'Well not enough to interfere with their playing.'" Faith chuckled and added: "Traditionally, all music was passed down orally and it still is a lot."

The troupe at Not Chumleighland (aka Circus Stage) worked Faith and her songs into the skits. Over the years, she'd often sing on other stages at the fair in addition to her vaudeville gig. Some years she'd have six to eight singing performances booked each day at the fair.

Faith's impish grin and long gray hair made a striking image on stage. With her guitar, an inviting demeanor, and a bag full of serious and silly folksongs, she held court over many a sing-along. A true "Geritol Gypsy" who traveled the world to perform, she favored saucy songs with a message including "Geritol Gypsy," "If You Haven't Got a Penis then You Can't Become a Priest," and "Have You Been to Jail for Justice."

"The fair was good for me," Faith said. "It was good for me to see all these crazy people in their crazy outfits and living, with various degrees of success, in an alternative society." Faith felt right at home. "I always do at least some activist-type songs in any set that I do. I would always include something that made a statement about the condition of the world and what I want it to be."

Faith was born in a log cabin in Orofino, Idaho, in 1915, and became an unreconstructed "left winger" in the 1930s when the Great Depression descended and the Spanish Civil War flared. "A friend of mine and I ran a 'peace strike' at our school in 1936," Faith recalled. "That was in [Whitman] college [in Walla Walla, Washington]. I was very sympathetic with the war in Spain, with the Loyalists, of course. The 1930s with the Depression were a time of tremendous yeast in this country. All our people were desperate." Faith marched in picket lines to support the workers in the Newspaper Guild in Seattle, among other actions she participated in over the years to try to foster changes in society. Faith belonged to two unions for decades—the

American Federation of Musicians and the Industrial Workers of the World.

"I feel that the capitalist system doesn't work," Faith said. "I'm a radical. I believe in production for use and not for profit. Capitalism is a system of legalized greed. Socialist systems work much better and we have some successful ones in the world today. I think this country came very close to it after the Depression. Eugene Debs got over a million votes, but [Franklin] Roosevelt, much as I loved him and I think he was wonderful, but I think he saved the capitalist system. I think the country might have gone socialist."

The daughter of an itinerant Methodist preacher, Faith said she wasn't raised as a Leftist, but naturally gravitated to those values partially because of her Christian upbringing. "I would say my family was basically pretty conservative—very religious," she said. "I'm certainly the only radical in the family. ... But I've found it's not at all uncommon for a radical person to have been raised as a preacher's kid because you were taught that you were your brother's keeper—that you were responsible, that you were to help."

The church helped Faith discover how much she liked to sing. Her family attended many church services where the congregation sang hymns together. "It felt good to sing," she said. "You just opened your mouth and all that sound came rolling out."

Her parents divorced when she was thirteen and sent her to boarding school. At Whitman College, she worked several jobs to pay her tuition and graduated in 1937. She clerked in a bookstore after college, then set out to travel the world. A marriage in the early 1940s didn't work out and she became a single mother, an anomaly in those conservative times. Faith landed in San Francisco with a job at the state Department of Rehabilitation. She bought a rambling Victorian home in the Upper Haight area and took in boarders to help pay the mortgage. She wanted her daughter to meet "interesting people," she said.

Faith would sing with gusto. She became active in the San Francisco Folk Music Club in the late 1950s. The club also had roots in peace activism. "San Francisco Folk Music Club was the legitimate child of Hiroshima and the Cold War," Dave Rothkop, club founder, wrote. "Believing that music is the one language capable of transcending national egotism, a small group of idealistic and not very musically gifted high-schoolers began meeting in each others' homes in 1948."

The club became more formalized in 1959, and in 1962, Faith took responsibility for keeping it going. She started the club's newsletter, *folknik*, in 1964. For more than five decades, the club's Friday Night Jams would meet every other week at her home, starting at 8:00 p.m. and ending when the last person left after midnight. The large home, built about 1900, offered several rooms for singing, instrumental jamming, and song swaps. Instruments hung on the walls—available for impromptu playing—while comfortable, mismatched sofas and chairs invited guests to linger. Faith's house also provided office space, a mailing address, and a phone number for the San Francisco Folk Music Club.

Faith quit her job at the California State Department of Rehabilitation in 1970 at age fifty-five. She had put her daughter through college, and felt free to become a full-time folkie. Faith and five regulars from the Friday Night Jams assembled a Portable Folk Festival in 1971. They bought an old school bus and set out with fifteen people and one dog, returning three months later with eighteen people and two dogs. In that time, the Portable Folk Festival crossed the United States and into Eastern Canada, performing at music festivals, folk clubs, picnics, parking lots, and anywhere people were willing to listen.

Upon their return, Faith plunged into the Bay Area folk music scene, helping organize the nonprofit Plowshares Coffee House in San Francisco as well as the first annual Western Regional Folk Festival. She would help run the annual San Francisco Free Folk Music Festival for thirty years. She served on the board of *Sing Out!* magazine and contributed a regular column for decades. Faith also co-founded the Freedom Song Network, whose members would enliven many a protest, demonstration, and picket line with songs about workers, unions, peace, and justice.

Starting in 1982, the Oregon Country Fair became a regular gig on Faith's schedule. "At first, working at the fair was for me like any other gig. You came and did your show and left," she said. But that changed when her granddaughter, Alex Craig, started coming to the fair in the in 1988 when she was three years old.

"It was just a good experience for a child," Faith said. "All the theater and all those different kinds of cultures that are represented

Faith Petric sang at the Portable Folk Festival in 1971.

at the fair: the alternative culture, the alternative lifestyle. I thought that was very healthy and good. She just loved the theater. By the time she was four, by the second or third time she watched a show, she knew every word. I'd see her sitting there, mouthing every word as it went along. She loved that. And also, as much as possible, most years the shows were written so the kids could be involved. She was frequently on stage with me. She liked it up there and she knew the words and she would sing along with whatever I was doing."

A number of vaudeville performers brought their kids to the fair, and the kids formed friendships that transcended the distance and the years. "All these kids were friends with each other and they grew up together," Faith said of her granddaughter. "... Some of those people are still among her very best friends, although she'd see them just once a year. The rest of the year she lived in Ireland. ... We had little kids running around, and then, they were our kid gang and then it became a teenage gang, which still exists to a large extent. They've grown up and have boyfriends and girlfriends now and go off to college and different lives," but they all would return to the fair to reconnect. They spent a lot of time together during the fair and afterward on the New Old Time Chautauqua tours.

Inspired by the fair, Alex attended Circus School in Belfast on weekends for a number of years, learning circus skills. She most enjoyed performing aerial silk acrobatics. She would perform on Stage

Left at the fair and also on tour with the New Old Time Chautauqua. In the 2000s, Alex would help produce Stage Left shows along with Jasper Patterson, son of Howard Patterson of the Flying Karamazov Brothers.

Faith would perform in New Vaudeville shows at the fair for the next twenty-five years, from Chumleighland (aka Circus Stage), to W.C. Fields Stage, to Stage Left. She often got booked at the Midnight Show for a song or a sing-along. She would participate in the New Old Time Chautauqua tours for more than two decades.

She often spoke out against ageism. "When I'm introduced as eighty-six years young, I could murder," she told a reporter for the *San Francisco Chronicle* on the eve of her eighty-seventh birthday bash music jam. "I am not youthful. I'm oldful. The idea that youth is the only time you're vital and interested—that myth makes millions of dollars for people who want to make you feel there's something wrong with you. … Youth is all right, but that's only part of life."

At the fair, Faith made a point to always eat at Tofu Palace, one of her favorite food booths. She delighted in seeing people at the fair dressed up as well as people who dressed down, like the Mud People. "If you go by what's acceptable, you might as well become a vegetable," Faith commented wryly. She loved the playfulness and joy people brought to the fair.

"It has the extended family feeling about it and it's nice to be part of the Oregon Country Fair," Faith said. "… I was on a ferry once, and these three or four really tough-looking guys—I mean, they were motorbike, Hell's Angels types—came up and sat down. They were incredibly shy." They asked if she was Faith Petric. "All around me, other people were looking to see if I was going to need to be rescued!" she said, laughing. "That was good. Here are these guys who were being so shy and polite, because I was a big star, see? And they didn't want to intrude. They had seen me at the Country Fair! They just wanted to chat."

Faith last performed at the fair in 2009 at the age of 94. Even though the fair's vaudeville family made sure she had a tent with a cot, the logistics of camping and performing had grown too difficult for her to manage and still have fun. At her last Midnight Show appearance, the entertainers surprised her by serenading her with her own songs.

"We knew that she intended to close her set by singing Karl

Williams' "It's A Pleasure To Know You," Tom Noddy said. "Instead, after her other song, Cici Wilcoxon came on stage and asked for Faith's guitar and then asked her to sit. Faith was confused but Cici was an emcee so Faith agreed while remarking, 'Okay, but I won't be able to get back up.'"

Cici handed a bouquet of flowers to Faith and told her that the fair performers considered it an honor to have shared the stage with her for so many years.

"Faith was touched and distracted," Tom said. "She didn't notice the other performers and friends gather on the stage behind her. Cici along with her husband, Carl [Kraines], and Ron Bailey played and sang some altered lyrics of the song that Faith would have sung to us. It took a little while for Faith to catch on that it wasn't the audience singing the chorus with them. With a little effort she turned around to see her friends and family—her daughter Carole Craig and her granddaughter Alex were there as well—had filled the stage to join this tribute to Faith. It was one of the most memorable moments in the Midnight Show's long history."

Even though she didn't return to the fair, Faith still sang and performed whenever she got the chance for the rest of her life. She continued to host San Francisco Folk Music Club meetings at her home, wrote her column for *Sing Out!* magazine, and sang at demonstrations with the Freedom Song Network. Her friend, folk legend Pete Seeger, called her "one of the most extraordinary people in the world." By example and words, Faith debunked society's stereotypes of aging.

"When I sing a particular song, I'm in that song," Faith told the *San Francisco Chronicle* in a 2010. "I plan to keep singing until I can't sing anymore."

That she did. Faith sang for her ninety-fifth birthday gala in 2010 and at the San Francisco Free Folk Festival in 2012. She remained active until a few months before she died, when a second broken hip slowed her way down. Even then, she chafed at having to lie in bed to heal, insisting she just needed to get up and walk to get better. She died peacefully in hospice care at age ninety-eight, with her daughter Carole by her side and her granddaughter Alex on the phone.

In its tribute when she died, *Sing Out!* magazine declared, "Through her life, Faith was many things: a mother, a wife, a shipfitter, a Wobbly and a peace striker. She worked in the San

Joaquin Valley with the Farm Security Administration helping migrant workers, marched with the Civil Rights movement in Selma, visited Russia as part of a peace delegation, floated down the Amazon, and solo-backpacked around Europe. She performed throughout the U.S. at folk clubs and festivals, has been the life of British pub gatherings, and was godmother to several generations of musicians that passed through the San Francisco Folk Music Club."

1982
The Second Decadenal Field Trip

"Some shed their clothes and twisted wildly near the stage. Others reminisced under trees with an ear of corn and a marijuana cigarette."

— The *Register-Guard*, August 29, 1982

Fair treasurer Ron Chase had been working for months on a plan to help the fair meet the second down payment of $50,000 in December 1982 without using up the seed money needed to put on the 1983 fair. He spoke to Chuck and Sue Kesey, owners of the Springfield Creamery about the possibility of hosting a Grateful Dead concert in the fair's parking lot.

"We had been talking about this concert all along," Ron said. Chuck and Sue agreed to co-host the concert with the fair on August 28, 1982, ten years after the band's first legendary Field Trip to the fair site. While the 1972 Field Trip raised funds for the Springfield Creamery, the second concert would help the Oregon Country Fair make its crucial second down-payment.

Fair organizers agreed to the plan at a June 1982 board meeting, and the Springfield Creamery sold tickets from a special window at its booth at the fair in July.

Ron said that the fair had planned to partner with the Springfield Creamery on the 1982 concert and had proposed to share the risk and the profits. "But right away we started hassling," Ron said. "There were two distinctly different groups of alpha people and we just didn't get along as partners. As people we liked and respected each other, but ... it was just very hard for all of us. So finally Sue and Chuck and I sat down, and Sandra [Bauer] might've been there. We said, 'This isn't working. Why don't you just rent the land?' And we very quickly came to an agreement on what the price was and they gave, I think it was $25,000 they gave us for the rental.

"Sue Kesey is dependable and generous and honest and a hell of a lot of fun to be around, as was Chuck," Ron said. "I really enjoyed the experience of working with both of them. After we decided that we weren't cut out to be partners and we established this formal relationship, things went a lot easier then. They could deal with all of the backstage stuff or the Grateful Dead stuff and all of Ken Kesey's stuff and we never got involved with any of that. All we basically did was provide the crews and the infrastructure that was there from the fair. And in retrospect, that was a much more sensible division of labor than trying to go into this as partners."

The poster announced: "Springfield Creamery Presents The Second Decadenal Field Trip." Tickets cost $12.50. Opening acts included Peter Rowan, Robert Cray, and the Flying Karamazov Brothers. A dozen food booths would serve snacks and soft drinks to concert-goers; and fifteen buses were contracted to provide free transportation from downtown Eugene to the concert site in the fair's parking lot.

At the Springfield Creamery, volunteers refashioned a mountain of white cloth acquired from the international artist Christo's twenty-four-mile-long Running Fence project in

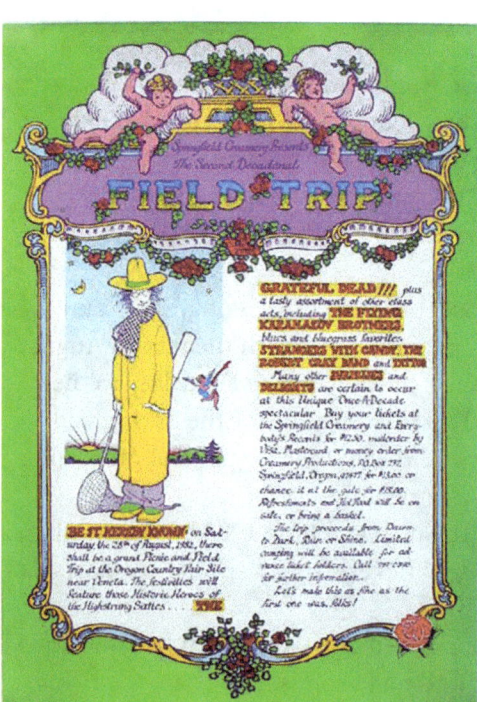

The 1982 Grateful Dead Field Trip had a colorful poster.

California (erected in September 1976 for fourteen days) into decorations for the concert venue. Fifteen volunteers tie-dyed 200 parachutes that would be hung from overhead ropes to billow brightly in the sun as concertgoers walked toward the stages from the entrance.

The Country Fair food booth for the Field Trip concert didn't work as planned. Optimistic staffers (from left) included: Gil Harrison, "Chez Ray" Sewell, Mary Wagner and Dan Maddox.

The volunteers stitched together huge swaths of white cloth to shade the main "Dead Stage." They also splashed bright rainbow tie-dye on the smaller coverings for the side "Live Stage." Long strips of white cloth were painted with blue-red-white-and-black designs by David Lundquist, who was inspired by the art of Pacific Northwest coastal tribes. One strip stretched across the front of the Dead Stage like a huge banner. The banner cloth hung between two vertical totem-pole style panels covering each sound tower. A center circle of fabric at the top of the stage featured a stylized bear.

Crew volunteers from the Oregon Country Fair enthusiastically helped erect the infrastructure for the show and handled necessary tasks from security to traffic. Members of the fair's Main Camp and Security crews built the two stages and giant sound towers. They also worked Security for the concert.

The Hoedad tree-planting collective—a group that also staffed the fair's Security Crews each year—logged tall Douglas fir tree trunks from their Cougar Mountain property to serve as a poles anchoring the metal scaffolding for the stages and sound towers. Hoedads Edd Wemple and Dave Barton hauled the poles from Cougar Mountain, south of Eugene, to the Veneta site west of Eugene. They used a self-loading log truck to set the poles upright. Off to the side of the stage in an area called "Deadland," Hoedads Ande Grahn,

Wally Jones, and Mary Barton assembled two Hoedad work yurts, one to be used as the Green Room; the other as the Hospitality Tent.

The fair's Traffic Crew coordinator, Walter Renfro, had no trouble rounding up volunteers to direct vehicles to parking places for the concert. Friends leapt at Walter's offer of free admission, a free concert crew T-shirt (featuring the red and blue Grateful Dead Lightning Skull on a white background), and a place to camp at the fair overnight. The same offer enticed other eager fair volunteers, including those with Garbage/Recycling Crew, who set up around the concert site several of the fair's barrel kiosks for recycling and trash. White Bird Clinic, which provided the medical care at every fair, brought its Rock Medicine tent for the concert, ready to help in any emergency. Water Crew members drove the tanker trucks that provided drinking water.

One glitch came in the fair's plan to feed the volunteers who were setting up the concert. Ray "Chez Ray" Sewell and Mary Wagner had teamed up to cook for the booth. Chez Ray had often served as chef for the Grateful Dead at concerts and ran a food booth at the fair. Mary had created Mama's Homefried Truckstop near the University of Oregon campus in the 1970s.

"Ray and I were supposed to do the Country Fair food booth at the '82 Field Trip," Mary said. "Our mission was two-fold. One was we were supposed to have food for the Country Fair staff that was working the Field Trip. And then we were supposed to sell food [to the public] and make money. It was a fiasco in any number of ways. … I was supposed to get the food there, Ray was supposed to get the stove there and he didn't get the stove."

"It was somewhat of a nightmare," Ray agreed. "I think the chicken came to us frozen. … We were supposed to be barbecuing, but it couldn't have been more complicated. God bless Mary Wagner. She tried her heart out. But I know that in my own wacky world and chaos that travels with me, it's sort of chaos to order. If I'm doing it on my own, I can manage my own chaos. But when you collaborate with other people, you're combining your chaos with theirs and order's a little more out of reach. So I think that that was what was going on there. But it was a terrific time. It was a great event!"

On a warm and breezy afternoon with temperatures in the seventies, fans enjoyed opening bands on the side stages. Blues and

The Second Decadenal Field Trip

Mapmaker Peter Eberhardt posed in a hat front and center in this 1982 Field Trip photo taken from the back of the concert site. The stages can barely be discerned in the background.

bluegrass favorites Strangers with Candy and Tattoo got the groove going for the dancers. Later, bluesman Robert Cray, backed up by his band, sang smooth blues.

In between sets, two dozen members of the fair's Fighting Instruments of Karma Marching Band stepped smartly to the small stage with drums beating and horns blaring. After performing songs including the crowd favorite "The Teddy Bears' Picnic," the band filed off stage, drums booming away. Accustomed to marching along the fair's crowded pathways, the band wound its sinuous way through the milling throngs in its usual thin three-in-a row parade formation—like a music carnival in motion.

The Flying Karamazov Brothers followed Robert Cray, juggling everything from clubs to musical instruments. But the Brothers K experienced "showus interuptus" when several parachutists jumped from a low-flying plane in the middle of their grand finale. "One of the organizers—no need to name names—got on a mic on the main stage, taking the liberty of interrupting the Karamazovs' finale to do whatever he already had set his mind to do when the parachutists got in range," said Sam Williams (aka Smerdyakov Karamazov). "It was rather painful. 'Twas a poor choice in theatrical priorities, but that does happen ... and one forgives family. It was a tiny blip in the day."

After all, the Karamazovs were staying as guests that week at the Pleasant Hill-area farm of author Ken Kesey. Ken's brother Chuck owned the Springfield Creamery that co-produced the show, and the "organizer" making announcements was Ken himself, dressed in white slacks, white driving cap, and black-and-white striped umpire shirt. Family, indeed.

The parachutists wowed the crowd and signaled the start to the Grateful Dead's set. "From the first chord at 2:30 p.m., the four-hour show had ... Dead fans on their feet," the local newspaper reported. "Some, like Gail Free of Milwaukee, Wisconsin, took off their clothes to dance. 'Why not,' she said. 'I think it's beautiful when everybody's this open.'"

Twenty thousand Deadheads twirled and boogied around the field to the sound-delicious beat as the parachutes flapped overhead in the gentle breeze. Lemonade from the Tibetan booth helped quench dancers' thirst. Hungry fans in bright cutoff shorts and flowing long skirts and tank tops lined up at a dozen food booths, including one selling pizza slices for a buck-fifty each. The trash and recycling kiosks got good use, keeping the grounds free of most litter.

Helped by moderate temperatures, White Bird reported a mellow concert with volunteers mainly treating cuts and bruises, "plus the people who had a little too much of whatever drugs they were using," White Bird spokesman Bob Dritz said. White Bird volunteer Norma Sax remembered having a great time. "When I wasn't giving out aspirin, I was dancing my ass off."

The Grateful Dead rocked the crowd with two legendary sets, but the music ended several hours earlier than expected. Rumors attributed the abrupt end to several causes. Some said the quickly built main Dead Stage had to be rebuilt just before the show and still remained dangerously wobbly. Others said the gritty cloud of dust kicked up by all the dancers had combined with the heat to aggravate Jerry Garcia's asthma. Whatever the reason, the early ending caught the work crews by surprise.

"My crew was ready to work, but they were told to be [back at their posts] at a certain time," Traffic Coordinator Walter Renfro said. "When the band quit early, all of my people were stuck in the crowd. ... We had one exit at that time. ... During the fair, one exit works because people trickle out at the end, they don't all leave at once. But at the concert when the music stopped, everybody wanted to leave at the same time."

Once the giant amoeba of traffic finally sorted out enough to exit, fair crew members stayed behind to camp in the Eight and party the night away.

"After the Field Trip was over, there were all these stragglers," Ray Sewell said. Barry Heath, who helped in Main Camp, drove up in one of the school buses the fair had used to shuttle people from town to the concert and back. Ray jumped on board and when they drove by the area where the food booths were, they came across five cases of unsold Monster Cookies sitting on the ground to be given away. "We loaded them up onto the bus," Ray said, "and we went around and picked up all the straggler people.

"[Ken] Kesey was with us and all of the Pranksters," Ray continued. "There was a tank of nitrous that showed up somehow and we had nitrous balloons. To get on the bus, you had to take a Monster Cookie. That was the ticket. We went around and we actually went all the way into the figure Eight ... and grabbed everybody, all the stragglers, loaded them up into the bus with Barry and everybody eating their Monster Cookies and sucking on these nitrous balloons and went back to the stage and dropped everybody off so we knew where everybody was so we could clear the place out. It was really an exciting, wonderful little moment."

A warm rain arrived overnight to drench the campers, and the Ritz Sauna at the top of the Eight stayed open all night.

Sue Kesey said that the concert was fun, but a financial disappointment. It did not make money and "the Grateful Dead basically took less money in order for it all to come out."

In a concert report to fair members in September 1982, Ron Chase wrote: "The fair was extremely lucky and fortunate to have as partners in this venture a group as responsible as the Creamery folks. While the concert was a financial success for the fair, the Creamery did little better than break even. ... Despite this ... the Creamery responded to every one of our concerns regarding health, safety and security, without regard to costs. ... It is my opinion that the fair owes the Creamery folks a lot ... for their responsible and generous approach to the concert."

The fair met the $50,000 down payment in December 1982 using $25,000 in proceeds from the Field Trip along with money raised from Charter Memberships. One hundred and forty-three Charter Members signed up. Each received a certificate and a promise from the fair to pay back the charter members' loans after the fair paid off the land in full.

1982 Grateful Dead Field Trip Set List:
Bertha
New Minglewood Blues
Tennessee Jed
Me and My Uncle
Big River
Althea
It's All Over Now
China Cat Sunflower
I Know You Rider

Day Job
Man Smart/Woman Smarter
West L.A. Fadeaway
Far From Me
Playin' in the Band
drums
The Wheel
The Other One
Truckin'
Black Peter
Playin' in the Band
One More Saturday Night

Dupree's Diamond Blues

1983
Robert DeSpain and Main Camp

"When Robert DeSpain became the president, it became more structured and more cooperative. "It evolved toward a Community Village style or character of management structure."
        —Robert Thompson, elected to OCF Board in 1983

Robert DeSpain first attended the Oregon Country Fair in 1979, when a friend in Community Village invited him to be her guest. Robert had planned to meet his friend at the fair, but she had his pass back in Community Village, an area not open to the public. "I couldn't get in," Robert recalled, "so I had to sneak in." Actually, he managed to talk his way through the Aero Road Security checkpoint. Security was more lax in those early years and crewmembers, bored by hours of standing at a quiet gate, could sometimes be persuaded with a good story.

"I talked and talked and talked and talked and talked until they finally let me go," Robert said. "It was Magic Michael at the gate out on Aero. He eventually said, 'Oh, go on in!'"

Robert, who was thirty-

Robert DeSpain earned the nickname "Robert the Red" in the early 1980s.

two-years old, was blown away by his first fair and by the spirit of cooperation he experienced in Community Village. Marshall Landman, one of the leaders in the village, invited Robert to attend their meetings that winter. "I went to these meetings and because I didn't know anything, I took minutes," Robert said. "Marshall was teaching group decision-making process and consensus process—and this was what really captured me! So I was hooked, from that fall in 1979 on. I just thought that this has got to be the most important thing that I can do in my life—learn how to work with communities like Marshall does. And to develop community, teach people how to be considerate and learn the processes so we can make decisions in large groups."

Inspired by Marshall's example, Robert rocketed into fair leadership roles. He joined the Community Village Coordinating Council and the fair's land search committee. In early 1981 he became village secretary-treasurer as well as village liaison to the fair board. In March 1981 Robert was also elected to the fair's Board of Directors while keeping his other roles in the village. In January 1982, Robert was named fair secretary and thus became scribe for both the fair board and Community Village. He attended a lot of meetings.

When Main Camp volunteers found out that Robert was a heavy equipment operator with access to machinery, they asked him for help getting the site ready for the fair.

"I had access to all this stuff that Main Camp had really never had before," Robert said. "They didn't have a backhoe or a dump truck or anything they could actually work with and change things out there." He developed working relationships with Main Camp's inner circle: Ron Chase, Sandra Bauer, Nancy Albro, Terry Patrick, and Michael Killgallon.

"I was cleaning out Indian Creek or helping to replace a bridge," Robert said. "We built roads and installed culverts to replace those old wooden bridges because they floated away constantly. Every year they'd float off into the brush and then those guys would have to drag them back and try to place them using a pickup truck. They didn't have anything else. They were thrilled to have big toys." His new Main Camp friends nicknamed him "Backhoe Bob."

But the 1982 land purchase brought upheaval to the Main Camp inner circle. That loose cadre of about a dozen had essentially run

"Backhoe Bob" DeSpain helped the fair accomplish many projects.

the fair as a collective since 1971. The group held together after the Wootens divorced, but the responsibility of making the payments on hundreds of acres of land—and taking care of that land—weighed heavily on everyone's shoulders. Tensions escalated, longtime friendships frayed. The fact that some members of Main Camp's inner circle didn't appreciate the appeal of the Grateful Dead only deepened the fractures.

"For me, the end came with the Grateful Dead concert," Nancy Albro said. "I loathed every minute of working on the concert. People who were dearly close to each other began to be at each other's throats. I just knew that it was time. I had to pull out, as much as it hurt, I couldn't stay there. … I did what I was supposed to do [at the concert], then I loaded my car and I left. I cried all the way home to Roseburg. I knew that was it."

Other Main Campers gave notice as well: Mary Cay Liebig, Terry Patrick, Amy Daycon, and Connie Epstein. "The core group began to disperse at the time that a lot of other new people arrived on the scene," Mary Cay recalled. One exception was Michael Killgallon, whom the board hired as the first fair caretaker in 1982 for the grand sum of ten dollars a day and the right to live in a dilapidated trailer "until it gets too wet."

"The old methods of governance weren't going to work and in

fact shouldn't work," Ron Chase said. "That needed to be expanded and it needed to be a much more broad-based government structure. … Robert DeSpain kind of took my place as the money person. His roots were in Community Village, which was a much more democratic and open group than Main Camp ever was. He brought that ethic into the organization as well, along with a lot of other people."

Some of the original Main Campers had planned for the future, training people to do what was needed to put on the event. Sandra Bauer noticed Sallie Edmunds' success coordinating Energy Horizons in 1981 and asked Sallie if she was interested in learning Sandra's Main Camp duties.

"Sandra told me that she was going to leave the fair," Sallie said, "and she just couldn't put in the effort that she had in the past. She had some adventures ahead of her. … So in 1982, Robert [DeSpain] was getting trained by Ron Chase and I was getting trained by Sandra, and Anya Montgomery, I find out later, was getting trained by Sandra's sister, Marcia [O'Dell]." Sandra ended up helping with the fair for a while longer as she worked to hand off her main duties.

Marcia also trained Deni Schadegg, who would step up to a role in the yurt at Main Camp, where she would coordinate distribution of passes and T-shirts in 1983. Deni had been helping Moz Wright with Entertainment Coordinator duties for several years by then.

"Moz is really good at networking, but not particularly strong at doing paperwork," Deni said. "And coordinating a group of people, you need to be able to organize paperwork. I'm good at that and so I took on that part of it, making phone calls, writing everything down, trying to keep it organized, and trying to figure out the passes, who got what and what stage they were supposed to be on and when. And then he would contact people and do all of the face-to-face work with them, making sure that their show was running smoothly. He was really good at doing that part of it."

During the spring of 1983, Deni and Marcia got into a discussion about the politics of the fair and availability of passes. Deni told Marcia that she knew of entertainers who used illegal passes to get into the fair because not enough passes were allotted.

"You know, you've got a lot of ideas and you know a lot of these people," Marcia told Deni. "I'm doing passes and T-shirts. Why don't you come and help me and I'll teach you how to do this." Deni agreed that it sounded fun.

Formal changes also came to the fair governing body. In September 1982, Ron Chase stepped down from his post as fair treasurer and the board named Robert DeSpain and Sandra Bauer as co-treasurers. At the December 1982 board meeting, Robert was appointed sole fair treasurer as Sandra stepped aside. KC Renfro, wife of Traffic Co-coordinator Walter Renfro, was named the new secretary.

At the March 1983 annual meeting, Robert DeSpain was re-elected to the fair board, along with Lucy (Kingsley) Parker. New members elected to the board were Ron Chase, Santos Narvaez, Robert Thompson, and alternate Frank Sharpy. Continuing in the second half of their terms on the board were Palmer Parker, Jon Silvermoon, Wally Slocum, Mary Wagner, Moz Wright, and alternate Dave Durant.

Most members of the new board also served as coordinators or fair officers. Robert DeSpain was treasurer; Ron Chase was longtime former treasurer; Lucy Parker was the fair representative for White Bird Medical collective; Santos Narvaez coordinated Traffic Crew; Robert Thompson had been a Security Crew co-coordinator and also worked Admissions; and Frank Sharpy served as the fair's Fire Marshall. Palmer Parker coordinated Publicity; Jon Silvermoon served on the Community Village Coordinating Council; Wally Slocum coordinated Banners; Mary Wagner coordinated Information Crew; Moz Wright coordinated Entertainment; and Dave Durant coordinated Water Crew.

When the smoke cleared, the turnover was almost total. Only three members of the board (Ron Chase, Wally Slocum and Dave Durant) had participated in Main Camp prior to 1983, and only Ron came from the original inner circle.

Palmer Parker took a break in a chair built for keeping an eye on the fair entrance.

Enjoying the 1983 fair retreat at Silver Falls were (from left): Patti Lomont, Kathleen Homa, Deni Schadegg, Jean-Marie Arnague, and an unidentified volunteer.

The announcements at the annual meeting in March 1983 reflected the extent of change: Main Camp Kitchen needed a new cook; Main Camp needed a yurt and a coordinator; Construction Crew also needed a coordinator.

In the face of so much change, the board endorsed Robert DeSpain's suggestion to hold a retreat over an April weekend in 1983 to pull together a plan. Because it was the off-season, Robert got a bargain rental rate on the Old Ranch at Silver Falls State Park near Silverton. The Old Ranch, converted from a sheep barn, had an open loft and a central fireplace on its first floor. There was no other heat; the structure mainly was used in the summertime. Fifty plain wood bunk beds, without mattresses or pillows, lined the loft. A dozen heavy timber picnic tables sat in rows on the first floor, where the restrooms and a tacked-on kitchen with running water and electric appliances could also be found.

The invitation said the fair would provide Saturday dinner and Sunday brunch, with "a pot of beans and coffee and hot water going between meals." It instructed attendees to bring bedding, warm clothing, flashlights, beverages, coolers, and extra snacks, as well as "music and instruments, games, cards, lanterns, home slides and movies, notebooks and pencils, no radios please." Organizers made it clear everyone was expected to sign up on a chore sheet to help with the event.

"The restructuring which is happening in Main Camp can be very positive," the invitation read, "if we as coordinators acquaint ourselves with the new faces and the new roles, familiarize ourselves with our functions, plan for the future, and approach this year's Fair with some unity." The invites went out to board members, officers, coordinators, and the fair attorney. About sixty people attended.

Robert used the Community Village model of consensus for the retreat. "I brought people together," he said. "I had learned a whole lot from Marshall [Landman]. We just figured it out all the way along."

Coordinators who attended formed closer bonds and came back with fond memories. "We'd have meetings all day and we'd break in the meeting into different little groups," said Walter Renfro, who was Traffic Co-coordinator. "Everybody'd come back and report what their group had talked about and then the whole group would talk about it. We'd do this for two whole days straight."

Everyone got a chance to describe their fair duties and share ideas on how the fair could run better. "The retreat was wonderful," said Patti Lomont, who volunteered in Main Camp as a sign painter. "It was really fun!"

The retreat had a full agenda. Main Camp had to be reorganized with new participants. Coordinators needed to know who to go to with questions. And the fair's land ownership created a whole new set of issues, from managing land in a floodplain to enforcing fair policies. Retreat conversations mulled over how to more strictly enforce rules that had formerly been winked at, or sometimes outright flouted. Volunteers recalled specific examples from the previous year of the difficulties they had enforcing the fair's policy banning the sales of alcohol and drugs. The groups brainstormed solutions to the agenda items for two days. Those discussions sparked immediate changes.

In April, the board approved a plan authorizing roving foot patrols on the path to watch for drug and alcohol policy violations. Each patrol would include one person from White Bird with crisis response experience and one person from the Information Crew with crisis training. The patrols would carry a radio to call Security backup if needed. "Internal security has been changed some this year to require more cooperation between various elements of the Fair

(Security, Info, White Bird, Communications) and to make the work less stressful for all involved," the plan noted.

The board established a new budget committee. Robert DeSpain was elected fair board president. Anya Montgomery replaced Robert as treasurer, and the fair's original treasurer, Ron Chase, agreed to join the Budget Committee. Ron's continued involvement on the Budget Committee would help smooth the transition.

The fair board members also wrestled with their decision-making style. Ever since the earliest days of the fair, decisions had been made by consensus. Put into practice, decisions by pure consensus—where everyone agreed to the wording of a motion—became an ideal that was hard for the board to meet. The fair's bylaws required the board to try to find consensus on a topic, and mandated that consensus be attempted for three meetings. If during the third meeting consensus could not be agreed upon, the board could pass a motion with a two-thirds majority.

When everybody got along in the early years, the process flowed smoothly. But the turnover in fair personnel in the early 1980s brought in a new batch of organizers who did not always see eye to eye. Land ownership pushed the stakes higher and made the debates more heated.

That cumbersome process dogged every discussion. Sometimes the board would reach "consensus" because those who disagreed kept their views to themselves, effectively pushing dissent underground. On the other hand, just one board member could postpone any decision for three meetings. The budget was held up by one vote in April one year, said Frank Sharpy, who served on the board then. "We passed the budget in June over the objections of a single board member," Frank added. "I thought that that was a very shortsighted way of running the fair, as did several others."

In April 1983, the board debated switching from consensus decisions to a two-thirds majority decision, but could not reach consensus on the topic. They debated the matter for two more months, and each time the decision to switch away from consensus was held up by one board member from Community Village, Jon Silvermoon, who steadfastly blocked the change.

In June 1983—the third meeting of discussion—the board approved altering the bylaws to eliminate the consensus vote requirement. Despite Jon's strenuous objections, the board voted to require a two-thirds majority to pass any motion. Jon considered the new bylaw as an abandonment of the fair's original ideals.

In a change that would reverberate with positive vibes for decades, White Bird counselors Zak Schwartz and Douglas Parker presented the first crew-wide Crisis Intervention trainings. The board strongly urged all coordinators and volunteers to attend. "White Bird found that more than half the crises we were going out to intervene in at the fair, the person we had to intervene with was wearing a staff shirt," Zak said. "The staff itself had no idea how to interact humanistically and competently at the same time."

Zak Schwartz of White Bird Clinic taught human intervention skills to hundreds of volunteers.

Since its founding in 1970, White Bird had racked up plenty of practice with handling crises. Its counselors staffed a crisis hotline, ran a walk-in help center, and provided a Bummer Squad to respond to problems on the streets of Eugene. It also provided free medical help to those in need. During the Oregon Country Fair, the White Bird booth administered medical aid as well as counseling services. White Bird had been a fixture at the fair since 1970. Established and run as a collective, the clinic operated with consensus decision-making.

Zak and Douglas led fair volunteer trainings at the fair site in late June and early July 1983. The workshops reflected the horizontal consensus process and street-response methods used at White Bird. They emphasized "staying centered" during emergencies and treating everyone with respect.

"Safety's a priority. Keep yourself safe," Zak would say to the fair volunteers gathered for training. "Let's get down to specific concepts. One is responsibility. Out here and hopefully forever in your lives, the word responsibility means 'ability to respond.' It does not mean, 'who do I hang for this?' Hear the difference? Responsibility is: ability to respond. I have options. I have choices; that's a good thing. Out here, the ideal is, 'Do not blame, do not judge, do not criticize.' There's almost no place in a good intervention for those kinds of energies. When somebody feels blame, they get defensive and pissed off. You don't want them like that. ... If I come at somebody with respect and calmness and love, they tend to be easier to deal with."

Volunteers learned techniques "to make molehills out of mountains." The training included tools for remaining centered and calm, and tips for achieving cooperation and positive solutions. The lessons would prove useful during the 1983 fair and every fair afterward.

Questions from the training prompted a couple of more changes. At a meeting in late June, the board approved a recommendation from White Bird to place a sign at the front gate to announce the policy of "no alcohol or drug sales" at the fair. The board also discussed nudity rules and reaffirmed its policy to follow county rules that prohibit genital nudity in general, and that required food servers to be fully dressed.

The coordinator potluck meetings that had been the mainstay of fair planning since 1971 remained key.

"I started giving back to the coordinators the authority for the responsibilities that they already had," Robert said. "We'd always done potlucks, but the change was that at these [new] potlucks people were coming and reporting back as to what they'd accomplished rather than waiting for direction. Because I didn't know what to tell them to do! All of those coordinators had already done it for years, or a couple years at least. ... There was always this line of experience. ...

"So I didn't have to worry about them being able to pull off their tasks. I just needed to be concerned about the coordinating of the communications and all of the contract services, like toilets and recycling and everything else that we had to provide for, the reefer [refrigeration] trucks, all those services that the General Manager does now."

At the recommendation of friends who were members of the Hoedad tree-planting cooperative, Robert hired Jessie McDonald to be Main Camp cook in 1983. Her cooking was popular with the hungry Hoedad workers. Robert also purchased for Main Camp two used yurts from the Green Thumb crew, a group of lesbian Hoedad treeplanters. Before the land purchase, fair organizers had often borrowed Hoedad yurts for use in Main Camp. Now the yurts would be fair property.

In June, fair volunteers planted native stream willow to help stabilize the banks of the wandering Long Tom River. Many a booth backed up to the banks of the Long Tom, and erosion of the banks also eroded space for the booths.

Meanwhile, volunteers set up Main Camp and started preparing the site for the 1983 fair. Sandra Bauer returned, as well as Reese Prouty and Sallie Edmunds. But with most of the Main Camp regulars out of the picture, new volunteers had to figure out a lot of tasks for themselves. Some jobs went unfilled. "By the time of the fair, there wasn't really anybody that stepped up to fully coordinate Construction, or Main Camp itself, or printing," Robert DeSpain said. "I still had all of those to do."

New volunteers struggled with effective communications as they worked on projects scattered around the fair's 240 acres. The wet spring didn't help. The fair's pathways and roads turned sticky with mud. Volunteers looked up at the gray skies and wondered when the sun would finally break through the clouds.

One of the Main Camp transitions that had been planned during the spring ended with an abrupt handoff. "In 1983, Sandra Bauer's sister Marcia O'Dell was the yurt person [responsible for staff inventory distribution] up until about a week before the fair," Robert said. "And then Marcia bailed, she left. Deni Schadegg stepped in and handled it. She completely organized the distribution of the T-shirts and food vouchers and passes in a week. It was extraordinary."

Deni said Marcia had provided her with a bit of guidance before she left. "She helped me with the initial stages of ordering things and promised that she'd be back in time to distribute and in time to do it," Deni said. "That was when we just had the little handheld passes that you put in your pocket. ... And then she went to Alaska and didn't come back." Deni figured a system out, doing the job so well that she would end up volunteering in the Main Camp yurt for decades.

One outgrowth of the Crisis Intervention training offered before each fair would be a new concert security company in Eugene. In 1983, Security Crew members Don Doolin, Steve Proffer, and Robert Thompson joined with Santos Narvaez from Main Camp to create Oregon Event Enterprises. They received guidance in their business venture from Chuck and Sue Kesey, owners of Springfield Creamery. Most of the workers came from fair Security Crews.

"We formed this crowd control company to approach concert security in a friendlier and different way from the usual approach," Robert Thompson said. "Our approach was to treat event patrons in a welcoming, friendly, non-confrontational way as we had learned from Zak's training and our experience working with crowds at the fair. It was fun de-escalating situations and creating positive outcomes."

Oregon Event Enterprises handled the security in the early years for the Eugene Celebration, an event that Cindy Wooten helped establish. The group also provided security for a 1984 Clash concert at Mac Court on the University of Oregon campus and for rock concerts at the Hult Center and Cuthbert Amphitheater.

"We handled the crowd control and back stage security for many concerts in Eugene, including the Grateful Dead, Talking Heads, Eurythmics, Tom Jones, and Huey Lewis and the News," Robert said. In 1986, Robert would step away from the company and John Doscher, another fair Security Crew volunteer, would take charge of running the enterprise. Through the 1990s, the company would provide security for the Saturday Market in Eugene as well as at numerous concerts.

1983
Who'll Stop the Rain?

"The paths were in much worse shape than they are now. I remember pulling my camping gear on a cart into the fair in ankle-deep mud and losing shoes in the mud. Oh, yeah. Using a cart in the mud's not easy. But we did it!"
—Chris "Ruby" Bauske, Information Crew volunteer talking about the 1983 fair

As a wet spring slopped into a wet summer, Robert DeSpain and other fair organizers fretted about the weather. Oregon's seasonal rains usually tapered off in May and June, with the Fourth of July traditionally marking the start of the dry season. Because the fair property sat in a floodplain, too much rain could turn the hay fields used for parking lots into mucky mud traps for vehicles. Organizers worried that if they couldn't park cars, they couldn't open the fair. If they couldn't open the fair, they couldn't make the mortgage payment on the land.

In the first six days of July, an inch of rain had fallen, four times the normal amount. It looked like winter. The rain turned the river silt on the pathways of the fair into slick mud punctuated by mucky slip-and-slide puddles at the Junction, Main Stage, and other heavily used areas round the Eight. Organizers decided to ban vehicles entering the Eight, which meant everyone had to schlep in their crafts, food, and gear by handcart. Most crafters waited until the last minute to set up their booths. Nearly everyone arrived on Thursday—

and the overcast, showery day was not reassuring.

On Thursday night, crafters and food booth workers struggled to keep their inventory covered and dry while putting finishing touches on their booths. Everyone tried to keep the mud at bay. Tarps swished over campsites as the weather put a damper on pre-fair festivities. In contrast to Thursday's usual hubbub of joyful greetings around the Eight pathway, most folks avoided the shoe-sucking mud and hunkered down at their campsites for the evening.

Paxton Hoag and his partner, Lois, snuck in on Thursday night to stay with friends. "There were literally huge puddles, lakes, in the middle of the path and people falling in them, trying to walk in at night with no lights," he said. "I wondered, how are we going to put on a fair like this?"

About that same time, coordinators and fair organizers gathered in a damp circle at Main Camp to try to answer that very question. Robert had asked Ron Chase to consult with the new Main Camp folks on what to do in case it continued to rain. Organizers came up with a plan to purchase a truckload of straw bales from a nearby farmer so they could shovel the straw over the mud in the paths. But they worried even more about the parking lots turning to mud if the rain kept up. "Really the parking lots—as opposed to the fair site—determined whether the rain would shut it down or not," Ron Chase said, "because if we couldn't get cars in there, we couldn't get paying customers in there. The buses weren't that well-used in those days."

In previous years Ron, as treasurer, would hand out food vouchers to the various fair coordinators on Thursday evening so they could distribute them to each volunteer or entertainer that started a work shift on Friday. The vouchers, meant to show appreciation, could be used like cash at any food booth in the fair. But with the rain, the fair couldn't count on the usual Friday ticket sales. If the public didn't show up to purchase tickets, it would seriously impair the fair's cash flow. Ron advised them to withhold the vouchers until they could see what happened with ticket sales on Friday.

"It rained right up through Thursday," Ron said, "and of course all of the crews wanted their food vouchers. But at the time we had just purchased the land and there was no money. There was no cash. If the fair had not withheld those food vouchers, there would have been thousands of bad checks. So we made the decision to withhold the food vouchers, which caused a great controversy at the time."

Coordinators protested, predicting correctly that the volunteer crew members and entertainers who relied on the vouchers to buy meals would be upset.

"We couldn't send out vouchers if we couldn't redeem them," Sandra Bauer said. "We couldn't do that to our food vendors." In an attempt to feed the volunteers and entertainers, organizers arranged to have Main Camp Kitchen serve snacks and sandwiches to fair folks behind the scenes on Friday.

After the meeting broke up, folks slipped backed through the mud to their tents to rest up, but most had trouble sleeping. Heavy rain pattered down on canvas tents like thousands of tiny drumbeats. "The mud got sloppier and sloppier," Robert DeSpain said. "By Friday morning we still had not cancelled the fair even though it was a constant conversation."

When the hard rain abruptly slowed to a drizzle at five o'clock Friday morning, Main Camp volunteers got up and rolling fast. About thirty people gathered around as the day began. Robert stood on top of a picnic table and declared, "Okay, here's the plan: We're going to go out and scrape the mud off the paths and we're going to replace it with straw."

Organizers dispatched a pump truck around the Eight to suck water out of the biggest holes, followed by a pickup truck packed with workers carrying shovels. At each stop, the volunteers would hop out to shovel as much muck from each hole as quickly as they could. Then they'd hop back into the back of the truck so they could catch up with the pump truck again. But everyone knew the small shoveling crew could never clear all of the mud from the paths in time.

"The order rang out at 5:00 in the morning that everybody at the fair was going to get up," recalled Chris Bauske, who was on the Info Crew. "People were going around their campsites to get everybody up out of their tents to shovel mud from the path into the bushes. In those days, there were bushes between all the craft booths. So you had a place to put the mud between the booths."

Alan Siporin—a member of CORD (Coalition Opposing Registration and the Draft) in Community Village—remembered the amazing group effort. "Everybody got out every piece of wood and implement that they could," he said, "because nobody had shovels. They cleared the paths in this kind of miraculous coming together of people. The worst fair turned out to be one of the best fairs, in terms of the memory of it. People woke up to just a nightmare of muck and mud at 4:00 or 5:00 in the morning and the public was going to be there in a few hours. Some people wanted to just cry, it seemed so insurmountable. And yet suddenly we found the power of all these people—hundreds and hundreds of people—all working together."

The astonishing effort ranged from little girls scooping out muddy water with paper cups and sticks to adults shoveling mud into wheelbarrows (originally used to ferry camping gear to campsites), then dumping the mud in the brush. Through it all, musician Percy Hilo wandered the path strumming his guitar, serenading the workers with union songs of solidarity. "I saw Percy Hilo almost be killed on the spot that day," Construction Crew volunteer Ed Moye said with a chuckle, "because he came around in his clean shirt singing songs of work, struggle, and change."

Once most of the wettest parts got scraped clear, another pickup truck lumbered through with fair volunteers in the pickup bed shoveling out straw to cover the mud like a soft blanket of gold. Sue

In an incredible group effort, nearly everyone helped scoop muddy water out of pathways (top), and volunteers spread straw on the paths to provide patrons a safe place to walk after a heavy rain on Friday morning of the 1983 fair.

Sloppy puddles remained even after volunteers laid down straw in the paths during the 1983 fair.

Kesey of Springfield Creamery said the efforts made a memorable fair.

"It actually did quit raining that morning," she said. "It was like this drippy green. It was still kind of dripping showery from the trees. But there was not a sign of mud anywhere. It was gone and there was all this clean straw on the paths."

Organizers breathed sighs of relief when the public started arriving as usual, lining up to purchase fair tickets at the gate. With its straw-covered paths ready to welcome a crowd, the fair opened to the public at 11:00 a.m. on Friday, July 8, right on time.

"The tuba player almost tripped over his umbrella," the local newspaper reported, "but the band played on as the fifteenth annual outdoor Oregon Country Fair opened with a parade and a rainstorm Friday. The Fighting Instruments of Karma Marching Chamber Band, led by the Flying Karamazov Brothers, succeeded in drumming the sun out of the clouds at least for a few hours."

When the sun came out, so did the crowds. "Finally on Friday afternoon, Ron Chase started releasing food vouchers," Sue Kesey said, "because he had enough money coming in at the gate that he knew he could cover the vouchers."

Fairgoers trodding through the soft straw could sample music and entertainment on eight stages, while perusing artful offerings at 250 craft booths and dining at any of fifty food booths. Info booths handed out the blue-inked 1983 *Peach Pit*, pointing out to fairgoers the handy map on the back and the schedules inside listing acts for all the stages and workshops at Community Village.

In Community Village, fairgoers could attend workshops on Meditation, Mime Circus, How to Sprout Sprouts, Ecotopia Emerging, Women's Grounding Circle, Men's Support Group, Dances of Universal Peace, New Games, military Draft Counseling, and much more.

Energy Park set up the popular solar-heated showers. All who wanted to shower had to first pedal a stationary bike to power the water pump for the person showering before them. The Energy Park Info Booth provided personalized advice on how to use alternative energy at home and emphasized the easiest way to help the planet: energy conservation.

A rhythmic beat pounded out by dozens of enthusiastic percussionists beckoned many a dancer to the new Drum Tower constructed at the Junction, where the Eight path crossed. Anyone could join in. Drum makers in the craft booths noted an increase in sales. Volunteers staffing the first aid stations at Info booths and White Bird ran low on the tape and bandages requested by drummers with blistered hands and fingers.

At Circus Stage, aka Not Chumleighland, the Flying Karamazov Brothers juggled pins and the puns. The troupe, now numbering five with Randy Nelson back, arrived at the fair fresh off their first-ever Broadway run and a television appearance. They had starred in *Juggling and Cheap Theatrics* at the Ritz Theatre in May and had been featured on *CBS Morning News* a week later. Earlier in the spring, the Karamazov Brothers had opened their world premiere of *Comedy of Errors* at the Goodman Theatre in Chicago. Still they made time in their traveling schedule to camp out with their vaudeville friends and put on a show at the Oregon Country Fair.

Tom Noddy also returned to the fair amid wide acclaim after his television appearance on Johnny Carson's *Tonight Show* on January 5, 1983. Carson's staff had slated Tom's act for six minutes, but Tom hadn't much experience timing his act. At the time for the one-minute-left signal, Tom was just starting his "Wonderland Bubble." Johnny called off the signal, encouraging his folks to let the act continue. That gave Tom time to do "the impossible" Bubble Cube trick and to finish up with the lively Carousel Bubble trick. Those nine minutes on Johnny Carson's show changed Tom's life. "I was performing on the streets of Santa Cruz earlier that week and then later that week again," he said. "But suddenly the phone started ringing and the offers were for gigs all over the world."

Later that spring, Tom staged a Bubble Festival at the Exploratorium in San Francisco that drew 15,000 people and international press.

Yet Tom returned with his puppets and Bubble Magic show to anchor entertainment at the W.C. Fields Stage outside of Main Camp. He looked forward to visiting with his vaudeville family of friends. As an added bonus, Paul Magid had asked Tom to join the Flying Karamazov Brothers' variety show at Not Chumleighland. Tom had helped with organizing the New Age Old Time Chautaqua tours, and everyone enjoyed performing together. Other popular returning fair entertainers included Jan Luby (music), Rhys Thomas (galactic juggling), and Roberto Morganti (juggling).

Only Main Stage had amplified sound, and that was powered by solar energy. The sound system worked as long as the sun kept shining on the array of photovoltaic cells set up in the meadow. Clouds moving in and out often reduced the power and muted the sound.

Main Stage served up folk, jazz, rock, reggae, swing and more, with Swing Shift, Jim Page, Magical Strings, Michael Hedges & Scott Cossu, and Wolf Creek. Arousing Spirit closed the Friday set with rocking reggae, Balaphon marimba topped off Saturday's shows, and Artis the Spoonman took the final bow on Main Stage on Sunday.

The straw on the path held up all three days, but by Sunday it had started to stink to high heaven as the underside began to decompose and ferment. The whole fair smelled like compost.

Chris Bauske found 1983 to be a difficult fair, especially for those who had allergies that kicked up because of the straw on the paths. "I don't know how much money we made," she said, "but it was successful enough that we were able to put on the next one. That was always the definition of a successful fair. Did we have enough in the bank that we could go and pay all our expenses the next year? It was definitely a year-to-year existence. So it did have a magical ending."

Cheryl Jones of the Community Village Coordinating Council

said it was one of her most magical fairs. "I remember all the work we did and then being at Main Stage dancing in the mist and having the sun shine through the rain and all of us dancing and smiling," she said, "because we always seem to know that we can do it ... we can make it work."

However, during and after the fair, organizers heard from quite a few volunteers who were upset with Main Camp withholding food vouchers on Friday. Some said they felt the fair had broken a promise. Entertainers said they had no time to go to Main Camp to eat meals between performances. The complaints arose at board meetings and percolated up through the Grievance Committee. Board member Wally Slocum wrote a letter that the board distributed to volunteers to explain what had happened. The letter emphasized that the board's top priority had to be paying the mortgage in order to preserve the fair. Once all the expenses and income for the 1983 fair had been accounted for, the numbers showed that withholding Friday's vouchers was key to keeping the fair solvent in 1983.

Meanwhile, the board invited all volunteers to an appreciation potluck picnic on July 24 at Traffic Camp. In essence, the picnic expanded a tradition started by Traffic Crew coordinators, who had planned a picnic after each fair that included a softball game with Security Crews. The board voted to open the event to all fair crews in 1983. In August 1984 the volunteer appreciation potluck picnic moved to the Main Stage meadow. It would later be dubbed the volunteer appreciation Teddy Bears' Picnic and would become another fair tradition that would continue for more than three decades.

16 1983
Leo de Flambeaux and Gypsy Caravan Stage

"Leo was exceptional. He was a brilliant man ... very demanding and very much a perfectionist. He was a leader in his gay community and very creative."
—Sam "Zamara" Marshall

The 1983 *Peach Pit* announced the Gypsy Stage would feature the giant puppets from the Mystic Krewe of Prince Prospero, musicians Brothers of the Baladi, and belly dancers. It actually was the fourth year that performers created a Gypsy Stage, but finding the stage was at first a puzzle because it wasn't depicted anywhere on the fair's map. This quiet genesis of Gypsy Stage can be traced to a tall, handsome, and mysterious belly dancer and puppeteer named Leo de Flambeaux (aka Leroy Howes).

"He cut a big swath," said Moz Wright, Entertainment co-coordinator. "He was a wonderful fellow, six-foot-six-inches tall with a handlebar mustache, long sideburns and very dramatic character. He had a big heart and lived celebration." Leo first came to the Fair in the late 1970s from Seattle. He was inspired to bring to the fair's pathways the mesmerizing belly dance routines he developed while performing with Seattle's Baba Karim troupe.

At the fair, he would lay a small carpet alongside the path where he would dance—wearing a turban, heavy jewelry, harem pants, and a braided bolero vest—and clang finger cymbals in rhythm. Strikingly handsome, his extraordinary presence drew people to him.

But it was one of Leo's giant Mardi Gras-style puppets at the 1979 fair that brought him to Moz's attention. The handmade puppet featured a papier-mâché head that Leo painted to depict the face of a bronze-skinned, green-eyed woman with a bright, red-lipsticked smile. She wore a yellow turban, a yellow print dress, and red shawl with gold fringe. She had articulated arms Leo could move when he donned the puppet brace like a backpack. The puppet's dress hid Leo from view.

At twelve feet tall, Leo's beautiful lady puppet stood head and shoulders above even the tallest fairgoer. She made a charming impression when she joined the parade of the Fighting Instruments of Karma Marching Band as they wound around the Eight pathway. With her arms moving in rhythm to the music, it looked like a very tall, beautiful woman was boogying behind the band.

That first year, Leo came on his own. Moz approached Leo about bringing more giant puppets to the 1980 fair as part of fair-sponsored entertainment. The fair would provide a small stipend and some overnight passes. Leo happily accepted, and also asked Moz if he could build a small stage, a performance space, for an exhibition of Oriental dance in the same area where he would keep the puppets. Moz agreed to his plan.

In July 1980 Leo invited friends he dubbed his Knights of the Mystic Krewe to help handle the giant puppets. The tiny troupe hammered together a platform of pallets to create a low stage in a clearing in the woods off the main path. Leo also invited a talented musical duo—the Brothers of the Baladi, whom he had seen perform along the path at the 1979 fair—to play music as the stage band.

The 1979 fair had been an exciting first for the Brothers of the Baladi and their belly dancing friends. The troupe would spread out rugs on the side of the path to create a small stage for the belly dancers, who shimmied barefoot as Michael Beach kept rhythm on doubek and Joseph Pusey alternated between strumming the oud and piping the nai or the mizmar. Performing to the sound of those Middle Eastern instruments were dancers Sam "Zamara" Marshall, Barbara Sellers, Karen Higgins, Ann Thompson, and Christine "Zarouhi" Otchy. Several of the dancers belonged to the troupe Gael El Rooh.

Fairgoers crowded around the carpet to get a better view of

In 1980 this smiling puppet, created and handled by Leo de Flambeaux, danced behind the marching band parade.

the show. Among them, Leo de Flambeaux watched from the sidelines and admired the musicianship of the Brothers of the Baladi.

"It was truly a magic carpet ride in all ways," Michael Beach said.

Sam Marshall said her first Oregon Country Fair enthralled her. She noted a distinct similarity between the fair and Woodstock, which she had also attended. She appreciated how the fair embraced the values of civil rights, ecology, wholesome foods, and peaceful living. "Nobody was giving alternative lifestyle a serious look except for the hippies," Sam said, "and we were living it as much as we could. The fair gave us a chance to live it for three solid days. That's the way we felt about Woodstock. ... We loved our freedom and we only had it for three days. But the Country Fair still has it every year."

Michael and Sam first performed together in 1975 in Yuma, Arizona. At the time, Sam was head of the modern division of a dance troupe in Yuma. She had been trained in modern dance as well as South American dance, ballet, and jazz. "I came into belly dancing totally by accident," she said.

Sam had signed up for a class taught by a woman from Greece, who was teaching belly dance at the same studio where Sam taught modern dance. "I'd lived in Greece for six years," Sam said. "My father was a military attaché, and I speak some Greek. I wanted to learn more, which is why I went to her class. I learned a little Greek, but I also learned belly dancing."

When the belly dance teacher moved on to San Diego, the head of the studio asked Sam to teach the class. "What? I've had three lessons!" Sam replied in shock. But thirty students had signed up for belly dance class, and the studio needed a teacher right away. Sam went to Tucson for some quick lessons. Later that summer, Sam studied belly dance in San Francisco with some of the finest teachers in the business: Jamila Salimpour (mother of international belly dance star Suhaila, who was seven years old at the time), Bert Balladine, Amira, and Aida. With a strong background in dance and choreography, Sam quickly got up to speed. She adopted the stage name Zamara and got a job on the side belly dancing at the Chilton Inn in Yuma.

Sam also started teaching belly dance and yoga at the Yuma trailer parks where "snowbirds" came to roost each winter. "Yuma would double its size in the winter," Sam said. "It'd go from 30,000 to about 64,000. ... I'd teach these senior gals, I'd charge them a dollar a lesson. I'd have over a hundred women in each class. It was great! And then I was dancing at the hotel at night and teaching classes through the studio in modern dance and belly dance. I was able to quit my job as a librarian and become a belly dancer. That became a big joke: Local librarian makes good."

Sam and Michael met through Yuma's small social circuit. "He told me that he had snakes, big boa constrictors, and that I should put those in my act," Sam said. "Michael was a P.E. teacher at the time at a local grade school. He'd bring these snakes to the school and teach kids about them."

Michael visited with Sam while wearing the snake draped around his shoulders. "He talked to me for about a half an hour while I got used to seeing this reptile on him," Sam said. When she introduced the snake into her act, it pulled huge crowds to the hotel lounge. "Oh my gosh! We had big publicity with those snakes," she said. "People would just pour in there to see me take that snake out of the basket and dance with it."

Michael started announcing the act, and Sam suggested he should join the show. He already played bongos, so Sam lent him her doumbek. "He started picking up the rhythms, drumming along with tapes that I brought," Sam said. "We started with basic four-four rhythms first and moved up to some more difficult ones. Of course, now he's a very proficient professional."

Michael had just a little formal training and a ton of natural talent. He had played snare drum in his school marching band before he took up bongos. In the early 1970s while traveling around in his van, Michael ended up at the Vancouver Folk Festival, jamming on the bongo with friends. One musician joining the jam happened to be composer and World Music pioneer David Amram, who subsequently asked Michael to "sit in" on two of his festival gigs.

But Michael didn't take up serious drumming until he started playing for Sam and founded the Brothers of the Baladi. The first incarnation of the Brothers included friends of Michael and Sam: Joshua Mertz, Colby Girard, and Peter (last name forgotten). Joshua, who also served as emcee, spontaneously named the band "Brothers of the Baladi" while introducing them for one of Zamara's shows.

In 1976, Sam moved to Grants Pass and the Brothers of the Baladi disbanded. Two years later Michael moved to Ashland and met Sam for dinner at a health-food restaurant. There they heard Joseph Pusey play Celtic and original music; it seemed he played a different instrument with every tune. Sam and Michael immediately recognized his talent.

"He could play anything," Sam said. That night they watched Joseph playing guitar, mandolin, banjo, recorders, and psaltry, a stringed instrument of the zither family. "The boy was just incredible … and his compositions were beautiful," Sam said. They struck up a conversation and became friends. Joseph soon joined Michael in a resurrected Brothers of the Baladi. They enjoyed playing all kinds of music in their own fusion style, but kept returning to Middle Eastern-style music and instruments to accompany belly dancers.

Joseph introduced Michael to the music of Kaleidoscope, a Middle Eastern fusion band featuring a musician named Sulyman "Sol" el Coyote. In 1978, Michael traveled to Santa Cruz a few times to hear Sulyman perform with the new band, Sirocco, he created with Armando Mafufo.

"Joe was married and he had to work, so he stayed home," Michael said. "But those trips were a big turning point for me. … I took one lesson from Armando. I bought an oud [Middle Eastern lute] from Sulyman, several drums, frame drums, a nai [flute], double-reed flutes, and I came back with lots of cassettes. Joseph and I used those cassettes to mold our act. Sirocco was a big influence—we all became very good friends and we played together many times over the years. I owe a lot to Sulyman and Armando. I am still very close to them."

Michael brought his doumbek to the Oregon Country Fair in

Leo de Flambeaux (left) posed with two friends (one kneeling at right behind a mask) and one of Leo's big puppets in the early 1980s.

1978, when he got the chance to sit in on a Main Stage gig with a sitar player and a belly dancer named Barbara "Varvara" Sellers. The next year, 1979, Michael convinced Joseph and Sam and dancers from the troupe Gael El Rooh to come perform at the fair.

After seeing the Brothers of the Baladi play alongside the path at the 1979 Country Fair, Leo de Flambeaux persuaded the Baba Karim dance troupe to invite the duo to Seattle to play music for their show. "We stayed with Leo," Michael said. "We hit it off, and Leo was in love with the whole package. We were the music and he saw the vision of putting it all together for the Gypsy Stage."

At the 1980 Oregon Country Fair, the musicians sat on the low platform to play while the dancers performed on bare dirt or a rug if they brought one. Leo was a featured star. "Leo was an amazing man," Sam Marshall said. "Everyone wanted to see him get on stage and twist that big mustache, raise that eyebrow, and balance a brass plate with goblets or candles on his head. ... He'd get up there with his brocaded jacket, his camel-tassels, all his jewelry draped across his chest, his turban, his belt, his shoes, and harem pants—and he was a sight!"

The Brothers of the Baladi played music as dancers took turns performing. "It was a nonstop show," Michael said. "We played all day, ate, maybe take a shower, then we'd play at night at the stage, just jamming and people would come and we'd party and play in the dark, or with a couple candles ... Then go for showers and a sauna at the Ritz, party there 'til the wee hours of the morning, if you slept at all, then you got up and had breakfast. ... And then ready to start it again around 11:00 or noon. We did that for days. Amazing times!"

For 1981, Leo sewed a colorful backdrop for Gypsy Stage that provided backstage privacy. The backdrop featured a red velvet curtain with gold brocade trim. He also sewed a checkerboard cloth to close in the space underneath the musicians' stage that he rented from Eugene's WOW Hall (which had become an entertainment venue run by the nonprofit Community Center for the Performing Arts).

In addition to their three-day gig at Gypsy Stage in 1981, the Brothers of the Baladi accompanied belly dancers on Main Stage twice in a quick turnaround—Saturday night at the Midnight Show with the full troupe, and then as opening act on Sunday morning featuring dancers "Zamara" Marshall and Barbara Sellers. In 1982 Brothers of the Baladi and dancers again performed at the Midnight Show, as well as on Sunday on the Community Village Stage.

Leo would perform once or twice a day on the Gypsy Stage, but he spent much time parading with giant puppets, as Prince Prospero with his Knights of the Mystic Krewe. The 1983 krewe included costumer Teddy Bernard, Thom "Moonsong" Dorn; Dennis Rooks, stilt-walker David Ti, and Jay Hogan.

Leo had met Jay at a Seattle coffeehouse, where Jay worked as barista. "It was before the espresso craze in Seattle," Jay said, "and it was about the only place on Broadway that had espresso machines. Leo was one of my customers. What really got his attention, I guess, was on St. Patrick's Day, I showed up in full leprechaun drag, just completely went as this Irish persona. I even hid a pint of Irish whiskey under the counter to spike certain customers' drinks, which is of course very illegal, but there were a few people I did that for, and Leo was impressed."

Leo told Jay about the Oregon Country Fair and his giant puppets. "I think you might really like it," Leo said. "You might be good at it." Later, Leo brought in a couple of puppets for Jay to try out. Jay did, indeed, like the puppets and he was charmed by Leo's artistic passion for them.

"He had a pair of twelve-foot tall puppets," Jay said. "They were sort of Indian, as in Turkish or Gypsy, Indian or Rajasthan, it was never very clear, and they were made in that French Mardi Gras style." The puppeteer would "wear" the puppet as a backpack frame, standing under the head, concealed by the costume, animating the puppet's arms by manipulating its elbows with sticks or by hand.

"They were very fun," Jay said. "I liked backpacking and it was just very fun to be in hiking boots with the twelve-foot tall puppet on. But Leo said that his puppets were a little big for me. He thought that we should make a nine-foot—three-quarter size—for my build. So I started going over to this apartment, and he taught me about papier-mâché. He had me make a large papier-mâché head, and build an armature [puppet frame]."

While they worked, Leo talked about the artistic aesthetics of the Oregon Country Fair. "He didn't describe the fair that much," Jay said. "He talked about the whole thing of vaudeville and entertainers—that people want to bring their cool act back year after year. And he said, 'It's okay to bring something back, but you should always, always, do something new.'

"He had a passion for what he was doing," Jay added. "It wasn't just a hobby or a once-a-year thing for him. He lived his life in a magical world. He had a reputation in the gay community up there— that was in the era when the gay scene was a lot of the clone look, it was short-haired men with mustaches and flannel shirts. And Leo was known for wearing kohl and finger cymbals. But he could pull it off in a way that wasn't effeminate. He was just really dramatic and mysterious."

Jay and Thom Dorn arrived ahead of the rest of the krewe in 1983, even ahead of Leo. "Thom and I came down on Wednesday night and stayed in Eugene," Jay said. "And then Thursday morning about 11:30 we arrived at the fair. It was the rainy year, 1983, and there was almost nobody here except a couple of people hammering."

Thom had made some beautiful pennants out of different kinds of fabric, but he was reluctant to hang the pennants without Leo there. "Whatever we do, Leo's going to make us take it down," he warned Jay from long experience. But late in the afternoon when Leo still hadn't shown up, the krewe started to put up the pennants and other decorations. "And, of course, Leo gets there and he's in a very bad funk, and it's all wrong and no, he makes us take it all down," Jay said. He also made Thom move his tent three times for seemingly

Zamara (aka Sam Marshall) belly-danced often to the music played by Brothers of the Baladi (from left): Steve Scaggs, Joseph Pusey, and Michael Beach. Announcer Joshua Mertz (right) looked on.

random reasons, Jay noted. "When Leo was at his best, it was like being around a magical wizard," he said. "But when we was unhappy, he could project that into the world around him as well."

The Thursday night rainfall didn't improve Leo's mood, but Jay was enchanted with the way the fair came together overnight. "Everybody had held off" from coming to the fair because of the rain, he said. "And then just all of a sudden that evening and in the morning, the fair happened!"

Jay had a blast as a puppeteer at his first Oregon Country Fair. His puppet, named Hoshigose, looked like a kind of Japanese kabuki samurai. "Mostly he was mute," Jay said. "He would bless people. But he was also a little crazed. It's hard to see in a puppet, so I can remember careening through circles at Main Stage." Jay felt like he had found the promised land.

In 1984, Leo talked the fair into building an official stage for the Gypsy Caravan show. Leo sewed a new, more elaborate backdrop to decorate the stage, and dancers brought rugs, chairs, cushions, and beautiful fabrics to make it all sumptuous.

By then Joseph Pusey had married Joanna "Kameal" Pusey, a belly dance teacher. They had met a few years earlier at a Brothers of the Baladi show, and Kameal had invited the Brothers to play at recitals for her belly dance classes. Kameal moved to Ashland with her two children, and settled for a few years into the large household where Joseph lived with Michael Beach, Michael's then-girlfriend Serena who also was a belly dancer, and their friend Leo De Flambeaux.

"We had a lot of good times then," Kameal said. Everyone in the house thrived on creativity, and Leo was an inspiration. "Leo was an extraordinary man," Kameal added. "He was just a very creative artist. He was involved with the Shakespeare Festival in Ashland. He sewed costuming and different types of things for them. He was a dancer. He was really gifted—a visionary. The man could sew like no tomorrow. He made beautiful, extraordinary things. Canopies, costuming, all kinds of stuff." He also made and sold jester hats. In Ashland, he would stand on street corners to recite Shakespeare in full regalia costumes he had sewn.

Each year the Gypsy Caravan Stage and show became bigger and better. "Because we play acoustic instruments, we started figuring out how to amplify the instruments," Michael Beach said. "The drums

The Caravan Stage (shown in 2000) became more elaborate over the years; volunteers sewed soft cushions for audience seating.

were okay, but the string instruments were quiet. So we figured out, using car batteries, some kind of battery-powered amplifiers." They found some blue curtains in a yard sale to run across the back of the stage, and started hanging cloth canopies above the stage and audience for shade. They also got bales of hay from the fair to use for seating.

The stage was set for belly dancing. Besides Leo, Zamara, Kameal, and Serena, regular dancers in the early 1980s included Christine "Zarouhi" Otchy, Barbara Sellers, Denise Gilbertson, Brenda Smith, Aziza Gerringer, and Troupe Rhajjahan's Karen Higgins and Penny "Bene Sharez" James Long. The belly dancers signed up with Leo for performance times. Soon, Leo handed off that task to Sam. Joshua Mertz, who announced for the original Brothers of the Baladi in Arizona, became emcee for the stage.

As the cast of musicians and dancers morphed over time, the Gypsy Caravan Stage continued to thrive. Sam Marshall would end up scheduling belly dancers for almost three decades. In 2009, she would become a fair Elder and respected stage advisor. She cherished many happy memories.

"Seeing my daughter grow up through the fair was very exciting," Sam said. "I've had so much fun with my friend Aziza. ... She and I have the best time. We laugh for three solid days. She is such a trouper. Not only is she an extraordinary dancer, but she just jumps in and works like a devil—all of our dancers do. They come in their overalls and their work shirts and their leather gloves and their boots, and they work like maniacs to get it all together. And then they come out [to dance] and they're these goddesses who are just so talented and so beautiful."

Sam noted that the stage would grow to include three generations of families. "Joanna [Pusey] and her daughters Emily and Celise, and now their children Kailea and Kavi, represent three generations at our stage. Joanna's son Tad has been stage crew since he was a boy. Penny James Long and her family also represent three generations of the 'tribe' and have had an enormous impact on our stage, quite literally. She collaborated with Tim Coslow and his able sons Dane and Max to produce the new, magnificent stage [in 1996]. Her daughter Jennifer is an accomplished Middle Eastern dancer and musician and has been recorded many times. ...

"There is a thread of lives and the love of the dance and the music that has been woven over time into this rich and fine fabric, strong and beautiful," Sam said. "The men, women and children who have danced their hearts out on our stage represent a legacy of artistry that could only have happened there, like that. All those people are really still near and quite dear to me. I love them all. Their efforts and contributions will not be forgotten and will forever be appreciated."

In deference to a growing awareness that "gypsy" was historically used as a pejorative phrase to describe the ancient Romani peoples, the fair in 2017 would rename that area the "Caravan Stage." It would continue to serve up a feast of sumptuous belly dancing accompanied by Middle Eastern music played live for appreciative crowds.

17 1983
Paul and Judy Fuller, Divine Balance Fruit Salad

"Hippies and cowboys unite with hay rides and magic mushrooms."
—Judy Herbert Fuller, describing the day she married Paul Fuller in 1983 at her parents' farm in Noti

Divine Balance Fruit Salad began as an enterprise of Om Farm, a commune of about a dozen people sharing a three-bedroom house on Jeans Road, west of Eugene near the Fern Ridge Reservoir. Two friends from Los Angeles who had worked at a cooperative vegetarian eatery, Our Contribution Restaurant, founded Om Farm after moving to Oregon.

"They came up here with the grandiose idea that they were going start a commune like the Love Family in Seattle," Paul Fuller said with a chuckle. "They had the idea that they were going to be kings, and they would have twelve squires and the whole scene. Well, little did they know that the people who came there, we were all kings!" Paul said Om Farm residents had no Big Purpose other than to try to live together. They observed meditation times, but also smoked pot and had fun.

Paul joined the commune by happenstance. He had come to Eugene in early June 1978 from Eureka, California, to visit a friend and to help prepare for the Gathering of the Rainbow Family in the Umpqua National Forest near Roseburg. Paul had attended the previous year's Rainbow Gathering in New Mexico, where he had met a number of kindred spirits and enjoyed the whole cooperative vibe. He was hitchhiking in Eugene to meet a friend when two guys from Om Farm picked him up. They went out for ice cream and then drove to Om Farm near Veneta. "I liked it and connected with folks and ended up going with the group to Roseburg" to help prepare the site for the Rainbow Gathering, Paul recalled.

The Rainbow Gatherings had been held in federal forests since 1972, drawing thousands of attendees. The group called itself the Rainbow Family of Living Light. In keeping with the event's free-wheeling, anti-capitalist spirit, the Rainbows never applied for permits. A nonhierarchical consortium of individuals and groups worked loosely together. A subset voluntarily would arrive early to set up the site. They would dig trenches for toilets, designate kitchen campfire areas away from the trenches, and start setting up camping areas. The Gathering embraced the virtues of communal efforts, peaceful resistance, live-and-let-live, and anti-capitalism.

They held a silent meditation circle for peace every Fourth of July, and those who attended the Gatherings often described their experience as "magical." But surrounding communities who had to deal with the aftermath and cleanup of the Gathering sites held dimmer views of the event. The Rainbows did not pay required fees and often flouted laws, so some locals derisively called them "Drainbows."

In the early years, Divine Balance Fruit Salad booth created shade with a tripod pole structure.

In 1978, the Oregon Country Fair was scheduled to start just a few days after the Rainbow Gathering ended. Fair organizers worried in a story in the local weekly paper that the Rainbow Family would descend en masse and overburden the fair's facilities. Those fears proved to be unfounded. But many Rainbow

Paul and Judy Fuller, Divine Balance Fruit Salad

Iced tea cost only 30 cents in 1979 at Divine Balance Fruit Salad.

Gathering attendees, indeed, attended the fair, including folks from Om Farm and Paul Fuller.

Paul's group left before the Gathering ended on July Fourth in order to prepare for the fair. The Om Farm folks planned to set up a fruit salad booth, figuring it would be easy to manage without anything to cook. Abe of Om Farm had claimed an available booth near Main Stage by the old Security booth (White Bird would move into that area in the 1980s). "We went out and picked local strawberries at Bergs and got the rest from Emerald Fruit," Paul said. More than a dozen Om Farm folks pitched tents behind the booth and set up a kitchen area where they could slice the fruit. They would name the booth Divine Balance Fruit Salad.

Paul found the same cooperative and groovy vibe at the Country Fair that he enjoyed at the Rainbow Gatherings. He loved the music, the entertainment, and the people. The experience left him ready to move to Oregon, but the next few months at Om Farm would test his resolve. One member of the community, Arial, who had remained until the end of the Rainbow Gathering had announced an open invitation for anyone there to stay at Om Farm.

"We ended up for like a month, two months, having twenty to fifty people there every night, just experiencing the onslaught—that's what we called it," Paul recalled decades later. "It was fun, but sanitation was sketchy. … We were filling a twenty-five-gallon barrel out of an outhouse and taking it back to a receptacle to dump, daily." The overpopulated situation led to minor outbreaks of staph, scabies, and hepatitis.

Finally the Rainbows moved on, leaving about fifteen folks living at Om Farm. Those remaining breathed a collective sigh of relief as daily life started taking on a more natural cadence. Paul went back to

California to pack his things and move north. He left a greenhouse full of pot plants behind in Eureka, considering it a good trade for his many new friends in Oregon.

Carpenters at Om Farm tore down old houses in town and recycled the wood to rebuild the main house on the farm. The group grew a huge organic vegetable garden and enjoyed the fruits of their labors. Paul settled into an old canning shed on the property. His choice of living space foretold a lifelong calling: When Paul inherited $9,000 from his great aunt Laura after moving to Om Farm, the first thing he purchased was a forty-four-quart pressure canner to preserve the bounty of the garden.

Paul met Judy Herbert at a 1979 Halloween party at the WOW Hall in Eugene. "Paul was dressed as a Bud Fairy, blessing everyone with a giant bud wand," Judy said. "I was a magic mushroom." To achieve the mushroom effect, Judy wore a sheet over her head, with eye holes cut out, and a bicycle tire around her hips. She left early with costume claustrophobia, and Paul left that party with another woman. But he came knocking on Judy's door several days later offering a magical hot springs outing, and she accepted. Judy was already familiar with Om Farm, having visited it with a friend who took her out there to swim. "They had a wonderful swimming hole, along with naked volleyball," Judy said.

When Judy showed up again at Om Farm for Thanksgiving in 1979, she and Paul fell for each other. In January 1980, Paul and Judy took a trip to Belize via Guatemala and Mexico. They found they traveled well together on that trip of a lifetime. When they returned, Judy was determined to repay money she had borrowed from Paul during the trip. She wanted to start their relationship debt-free. She joined a Hoedad tree-planting crew and began working on their reforestation contract in Washington State. But when Mount St. Helens erupted in May 1980, the volcanic ash lingering everywhere made it hard for Judy to breathe. She quit and moved to Om Farm.

Buildings at Om Farm multiplied over the years. Besides rebuilding the main house from recycled wood, the residents also built a sauna that they "packed regularly with a high vibe of singing and sweating," Judy said. The group repurposed some of the wood into cute individual cabins. Paul and Judy kept adding on to the canning shed until it became a cozy cabin. "It had a lot of character,"

Paul and Judy Fuller, Divine Balance Fruit Salad

Judy said. "Paul wanted square windows and I didn't, so that is when I learned how to build. I proceeded to make many windows, none of which were square." In some woods away from the property, Paul and Judy maintained a small marijuana patch to supply the commune with herb.

The group of young people fed themselves mostly with their huge organic vegetable garden. To make money, they mixed up peanut butter "Om Balls" to sell to health food stores in Eugene, including New Frontier, Community Market, and the West End Co-op. "We had a grinder—Godzilla—that would grind the peanuts," Judy said, laughing at the memory. "If the Om ball was just right, it would stick to the wall. We didn't sell those, of course."

In July 1980, the community at Om Farm took time off to run the Divine Balance Fruit Salad booth at the Oregon Country Fair. Judy looked forward to it. She had attended the fair in 1971 when it was known as the Oregon Renaissance Faire. She was only fourteen, and her mother and grandmother insisted on accompanying her. The 1971 fair featured a spontaneous, rustic vibe and few booths. Many crafters sold candles and pottery from blankets spread on the ground.

"One of the first things we ran into was this naked guy with a Bowie knife strapped to him and a boa constrictor wrapped around his neck," Judy said. "I was surprised that my mom and grandma still wanted to go in! ... The fair was wonderful for a country girl like me. Everyone was friendly and open. It gave me a sense of belonging."

Judy had grown up in Noti, an old logging town in west Lane County just a few miles away from Veneta and the fair site. Even though the community and her family held conservative values, she said she always had an alternative mindset. "My parents didn't know what to do with me, so they gave me the freedom to be who I was," she said.

All through high school Judy and her friends would sneak into the Oregon Country Fair. "We knew all the local people," she said. "Our friend's father owned a place right across the river, so we would just cross the river and go into the fair. I was one of the ones who didn't pay. Culturally, the fair was one of the best things that ever happened to this area. ... The fair was a very good thing for me. It changed my life in a lot of ways."

In August 1972 Judy and her friends attended the Grateful Dead

Field Trip held on the fair site. "When I first arrived, I felt a kindred spirit and kindness coming from so many folks that I set out on my own and went to the front," Judy said. Her friends remained behind. "That concert happened at a great time in my life," she said. "It gave me hope for humanity and kindness. I felt like I had found my tribe."

In 1980, Judy no longer needed to sneak in to the fair. Paul had taken on the role of booth coordinator for Divine Balance Fruit Salad and she would help. Early on, they came up with a system to run the booth. "One of the things that we pride ourselves about," Paul said with a twinkle in his eye, "is that we tried, we really tried to do a schedule. The first crew didn't show up. So we've never had a schedule for workers since then."

"And it's worked great, most of the time," Judy added, laughing.

Once during those early years, the Lane County health inspector, George Classen, spotted a display of Judy's pot-maple-nut bars and brownies in back. He asked, "What are those?" They assured him, "Oh, no, those are not for the public."

For a while in 1983, Paul and Judy moved away from Om Farm and then moved back. They got married that year at Judy's parents' farm in Noti. Judy described it as "Hippies and cowboys unite with hay rides and magic mushrooms." Around that time, the communal aspect of the Om Farm started dissipating and it became a place where people simply rented rooms and shared a kitchen. After a couple of years, Judy got pregnant. In the fall of 1985 before Zach was born, Judy and Paul moved out of Om Farm and into their own farmhouse in Noti.

That's when Paul got turned on to refrigeration work. "The recession was happening and we were going to have a kid," Paul said. "I needed to find a job. Plumbing takes five years of training, electrician takes five years, but refrigeration, you just start doing it."

Paul took a course at Lane Community College, learning enough about refrigeration to get started. He built a cooler for friends at Thistlebrook Farm and soon found himself invited to meetings to discuss creating an organic-farm cooperative. Paul met with Tom Lively, who also lived at Om Farm, and Tom's brother Dave; along with Keith Walton of Riverbrook Farm; and Jack Gray of Wintergreen Farm. They would need refrigeration to keep their produce fresh for market.

Focused on that need, Paul consulted with Chuck and Sue Kesey of the Springfield Creamery, who connected the group with a used-equipment salesman in Boise, Idaho. The man in Boise sold them an old lift, an ice machine, and cooler panels, which Paul repurposed to build the first cooler for Eugene's Organically Grown Cooperative. The refrigeration unit turned out so well that soon Paul was purchasing used coolers from major grocery stores in town and rebuilding them for farmers, local natural food stores, and food producers such as Emerald Valley Kitchen and Toby's Tofu. Organically Grown Cooperative (which would later become Organically Grown Company) kept turning to him for help as they expanded.

"I scored the old Starflower walk-in cooler," Paul said, "and we moved OGC into the old Starflower building on Broadway." Paul later built coolers for OGC on Prairie Road in Eugene, and also helped OGC with coolers when the group expanded to Portland.

Coming full circle, Paul did a lot of refrigeration repair for the Springfield Creamery. "The Keseys were just totally cool about me learning on their old equipment in Springfield," Paul said. When the old Creamery burned down in 1994, Paul would join many friends who worked eighteen-hour days in a herculean effort to get the Creamery back up and running within three weeks.

In 1995, Paul would look for ways to get out of the refrigeration business full-time because the stress was wearing on his health. He and Judy would buy land in west Lane County, near Veneta and Elmira, where they started to build a cabin. Suddenly Paul found out he had a heart condition that needed treatment. "When he found out about his heart, we had the roof off the house," Judy said. "I had to call friends to help. It was like an old-fashioned barn-raising. It was great! They all showed up and they stayed three days. They built a back porch. They built the front porch. They put the dormer on. There were people painting the siding as it was going up. It was just a real heart-warming experience."

Paul couldn't raise a hammer, but he cooked a turkey large enough to feed everyone. "There was this whole tie-in to community," Paul said. "We'd been connected with the natural food industry forever. It's what makes Eugene amazing. And the fair has been another connection that's been just an amazing, continuing thing."

At their new farm, Judy and Paul would lay the groundwork for Sweet Creek Foods, taking their commitments to organic food to another level. They would process their farm bounty in glass jars to sell at the Farmers Market in Eugene. "It was just basically Paul and I for quite a while doing everything from designing labels to making the products, before we could afford to hire anyone," Judy said. "Our son Zach was growing the cucumbers (for pickles) when he was in high school and works with us still fifteen years later (in 2018)." In 2006, Sweet Creek Foods would expand and start selling their pickles and sauces to local grocery stores.

Sweet Creek Foods also would process and pack food in glass jars for local farmers and small food businesses. The business would grow with Paul's connections to other local food producers, while giving an added-value boost to the local economy.

In the 1990s, Paul would start helping the fair maintain the refrigeration used by all the food booths, but he quickly ran into frustrating obstacles. "I donated two walk-in coolers that they never used because everyone was too scared to pour cement," Paul said. "No one wanted to pour cement because it was too permanent. I kept working at it." Finally, the cobbled-together refrigeration system broke down on a Saturday evening during the fair, and it only worked out because food was moving out fast by then as booths came to the end of their supplies on the last day of fair.

After that, the fair board designated money for a new cooler and hired Paul to build what would be dubbed Chill Ville. "I spent probably close to four months, starting in April and going right into July building Chill Ville," Paul said. He led a small crew that built the forms, poured the cement, rebuilt old containers, and set up freezer and refrigerator units. Paul placed special artwork in the cement slab. "Chuck [Kesey] gave me a piece of Egyptian sarcophagus he got when they were at a Dead show in Egypt and it is imbedded in the corner of the cement deck. Then Patti Lamont gave us a piece of glass, when she was working with Aurora glassworks." They also signed their names in the cement. Paul would help service the cooler for a while but eventually handed that duty over to someone else.

To show his support for all the hard work done by Recycling Crew, Paul started a personal tradition of loaning one of the farm's trailers to the Recycling Crew for use during the fair. "One year we loaned our Rosita, our 1957 Chevy pickup," Paul said. "That was the last time I ever loaned a truck because they drove it in granny gear the whole fair. It had fouled plugs. I drove it home with like four cylinders working." But Paul would continue loaning his trailer to the Recycling Crew every year for at least three decades.

Through it all, Paul and Judy would make time for fun every July at the Divine Balance Fruit Salad booth. As the original members of Om Farm drifted away, Paul and Judy invited their friends from other intentional communities to join them at the fair booth, including three from Butler Green Farm who would remain friends and part of the booth for decades: Mark Andrew, Robin Winfree-Andrew, and Jef "JJ" Jalof.

Booth traditions have cropped up. "The week before, we always have a decorating party," Judy said. "Everybody shows up. That's always fun. People bring food and we set up camp."

They began every morning at the fair huddled in a circle, chanting: "Fruit! Fruit! Fruit! Fruit! Fruit!"... then louder and faster ... "Fruit! Fruit! Fruit! Fruit" ... then fastest and loudest ... "Fruit! Fruit! Fruit! Fruit! Yaaayyy!!"

During the fair, booth members wore silly costumes that looked like fruits—a banana and a bunch of grapes—to draw attention of passers-by on the fair path. They created a Spinning Wheel of Balance to play with customers. Like a roulette wheel, the Spinning Wheel of Balance contained pie-shaped sections, but these featured cartoon drawings of different body parts. The player would spin the wheel that would slow down to a stop at random. Which would it be—the elbow, forehead, heel, shin, or thumb? The player was expected to balance a piece of fruit there for an entire countdown. Successful players won a free fruit bowl.

Paul and Judy Fuller stand next to their fair booth.

The Fullers' food booth made some money, but they plowed much of it back into having fun at the fair. Many years they barely broke even. "The fruit we buy and the amount we put in the bowl, and the fact that we try to keep our prices low," Paul Fuller said. "You're getting four or five dollars' worth of fruit for six dollars." In the 2000s, the Fullers would annually purchase 3,500 pounds of organic fruit each year to sell in the salads.

They would always shut down the booth for the evening so they could maintain their own fair fun time. Besides, cold fruit salad was never a big sales item after sunset, when the temperatures often plunged down to the high fifties in Oregon even in July.

The Fullers' boys, Zach and Cody, would attend every fair since they were born. To bring the generations together, the Fullers would start Saturday night buffets before the Midnight Show. The booth folks would empty the tip jar to pay for the buffet. "We have runners go get the dinner," Judy said. They would purchase large servings from different fair food booths. "People go get a whole cheesecake, whole trays of spanakopita and enchiladas to bring back to the dinner," she said. Sometimes they would drag their sofas out to the Main Stage Meadow for the Midnight Show, sending runners out for dessert as the show went on and on and on. One favorite memory of the Midnight Show was the Flaming Fart skit.

"The Flying Karamazovs are up there on stage in a four-point setup getting ready to juggle," Paul said. "They start with their backs to each other. And at that moment, this guy just kind of stonedly wanders up and gets right in the middle. They all turn around and here's this guy. If they started, he'd be pummeled on all sides. They're saying, 'Wow! That has never happened to us! I can't believe that! I've never seen that. This is the most magic amazing thing that's ever—can anyone else top that?' So this guy answers, 'Yeah, yeah, yeah.' Then he bends over and takes a lighter to his butt." A flame jetted out simultaneously with a fart sound. The audience collapsed into laughter while the Karamazovs observed: "That outdid everything!"

Judy cited 1983 as a peak fair experience. "It rained so hard on Thursday and Friday morning that the fair was going to open," she said. "I remember getting out. We had our rubber boots and we were scraping the paths with plywood pieces and anything we could find. Then we laid down straw. It ended up to be a wonderful fair except for Sunday, it smelled like compost."

A girl playing the spinning wheel game at Divine Balance Fruit Salad balanced a blueberry in whipped cream on her forehead to get a free fruit bowl.

Once in the 1980s when the fair still used hand-held passes, the pass featured a photo of Baby Gramps, a favorite fair musician. "Baby Gramps was kind of hanging with a woman in our booth," Judy said. He told them that some young guys on Security crew had stopped him at the gate, saying "You need a pass." Baby Gramps replied, "I *AM* the pass!" The boys looked at their passes, did a double-take at Baby Gramps and realized, "Wow, he is!" And let him through.

One year Judy lamented to Fyodor Karamazov, who was in line for fruit salad, that she had missed the Flying Karamazov's traditional naked juggling at the Midnight Show the night before. "So he dropped his pants and started juggling," Judy said, laughing. They gave him free fruit salad for his performance.

"That's why the fair is the most amazing place," Paul said. "There are these moments that will never happen again."

Even the start of each fair seemed magical as it took on a life of its own, Paul added. "You get all these people planning, the bureaucracies with everything that's going on," he said. "But then Wednesday or Thursday comes when all these people arrive from out of the area, setting up booths. The fair just takes over. It's like riding a wild horse. It's been tame for a long time, you've been feeding it and then suddenly it decides it's going to run. You're not going to stop it, no matter how much you try to control it. So many people. How is this all going to happen? And suddenly just, boom!" It's fair time.

18 1984 Archaeology Rocks

> "While we were buying the property, the decisions to build that highway were made and nobody objected to it. So we ... purchased the land with the highway already agreed to, and found out about it after."
> — John Stamp, OCF Archaeology Director, in 1990 report to the OCF Board

Just months after Ron Chase signed the mortgage to purchase the fair land in 1982, the event's organizers learned that the Oregon Department of Transportation had plans to reroute Highway 126 through a big chunk of the fair's parking lot.

The realignment of Highway 126 to bypass Veneta and streamline its turns and bends between Veneta and Noti had been in the works for years. For decades, the highway had followed old farm roads that avoided the meandering Long Tom River and threaded instead through the farms in the rural area.

For people driving west to the coast from Eugene, the highway doglegged at Veneta, with a sharp turn north at the Veneta stoplight. After about a mile, drivers had to take a left-hand turn at the edge of Elmira where the highway headed west again. The Elmira leg of the highway ran near the north edge of the Oregon Country Fair property. Neighboring property separated the fair site from the highway, so the fair's entrance ran between neighbors' property lines to reach Highway 126.

Initial plans called for construction of a new stretch of highway to the south of the fair site along existing railroad tracks. The southern route would go straight west from the Veneta stoplight, eliminating the need to travel north toward Elmira. Then in 1980, an Oregon archaeologist tested two sites and found evidence of Native American artifacts of cultural significance in the highway's proposed right-of-way. In response, the state decided to bypass the archaeological site by moving the highway a little further north, biting into the southern edge of the fair's property and cutting through the main parking lot. Dr. Richard Pettigrew of the Oregon State Museum of Anthropology signed off on the highway plans after finding no archaeological signs in the new right-of-way on fair property.

In September 1982, fair cartographer Peter Eberhardt visited the Department of Transportation in Salem to find out exactly what the highway department plans entailed. He reported to the board that the new route would take out more than a third of the fair's parking lots—about forty acres, a huge bite—and funnel highway noise right up to the Eight pathway. The new route would leave the fair owning a useless, long strip of inaccessible land south of the new highway. Worse still, the state planned to break ground on the highway realignment as early as 1984.

At a meeting in November 1982, the board discussed options for opposing the highway. The omens were not good. "Action to stop the highway should have been taken two or three years ago," the board was told. "The most the fair can hope for is that the highway division can be convinced to reconsider 'Option 2,' the more southerly route." In December 1982, the board sent a letter to the Department of Transportation expressing opposition to routing the highway through the fair site and outlining specific concerns about how the realignment would adversely affect the fair. But the fair didn't have a legal leg to stand on and received no response.

In September 1983 the highway division held its final hearing on the project at the Lane County Courthouse. Attorney Mary Wagner, speaking for the board, reiterated the fair's opposition to the northern route and the concerns about the project's impact on the fair itself, again to no avail.

In March 1984 at the fair's annual meeting, tempers boiled over when many members first learned about how much land the fair would lose with the new highway realignment, and how fatalistic many board members seemed to be about the outcome. The board had good reason for pessimism: The time for legally commenting on the highway had ended.

Frustrated fair volunteers sprang into action. Jon Silvermoon, who served on the board and was working as an archaeologist, and fair volunteer John Stamp figured that there had to be archaeological artifacts from the area's indigenous peoples all over the Long Tom River basin, not just in the narrow confines of the newly designated highway right-of-way.

Jon had done augur testing for Dr. Richard Pettigrew on the archaeological sites found in the Oregon Department of Transportation's original highway right-of-way proposal that ran along the railroad tracks. "I was a graduate student in anthropology/archaeology," Jon said. "I knew what had been found out there. I worked on one of the crews. ... I was fairly confident there were archaeological sites all over the place out there."

John Stamp had no training in archaeology. "But they changed the route of the highway *because* of archaeology," he said, "so the only reason I could see about getting it changed back was to find some archaeology of our own." John checked out archaeology books from the Eugene Public Library. Using what he learned from them, he gained permission from area farmers to search in their plowed fields near the fair site for artifacts. He was excited to find quite a few.

John Stamp and Jon Silvermoon joined forces and consulted with David Cole, the former director of the Oregon State Museum of Anthropology. "On a visit to [the fair] property, David was able to point out the most significant area from a half-mile away," John Stamp said. "He then showed us how to recognize and interpret successive layers of human habitation as revealed in the stratigraphy, displayed in the eight-to-ten-foot-high cut banks of the river. ... His encouragement to scientifically document our findings led to the formation of a volunteer archaeology [team] under the supervision of Jon Silvermoon."

The crew went to the site with an augur. "We started auguring along the riverbank," Jon Silvermoon said, "and sure enough, identified several locations where there were archaeological deposits, including in the location the highway was scheduled to go through."

John Stamp, Robert DeSpain, and Jim Guthrie, a longtime fair volunteer and crafter, traipsed along the bottom of the Long Tom River at low water until they found evidence of a camas oven.

"There had been an otter, or some woodland creature," Robert DeSpain said, "that had dug into the bank about nine feet below the surface, up under another old ash tree. Rocks had come out of that hole and were lying there on the bank, with charcoal mixed in. We knew these rocks were not round river rocks. They had been gathered like all the other rocks for all the other ovens. So we knew that we had found another oven, and it was right on their property line."

At the crew's request, David Cole returned to the fair property to evaluate the finding, which he verified as an authentic camas oven like those used for centuries by the indigenous peoples of the Willamette Valley. He further verified the oven was right in the line of the Highway Division's Option 2.

But the excited volunteers were met with skepticism when they presented their findings at the June 3, 1984, fair board meeting. Board member Ron Chase expressed concern that no archaeological sites had yet been found north of the proposed highway right-of-ways. "What would prevent the highway from being moved even further north onto fair property and into the Eight?" Ron asked.

The board then approved a motion by board member Moz Wright that directed the committee to keep surveying the area north of the right of way to establish more sites. Within a week, the crew spotted several more sites.

"I found one oven—it was right over here off of Chela Mela Meadow," John Stamp said, pointing toward an area of the fair. "I'd just learned that trick of looking on the banks. I looked around and I found this oven. And not only was it an oven, but it had charred camas hanging out of it in all the rock. You just couldn't argue with it. There it was, the real thing."

At the board meeting on June 10, 1984, the board voted to notify the State Highway Division of the newest findings. In August 1984, the Highway Division announced a delay in the highway realignment project until the new evidence could be evaluated.

Meanwhile, the Archaeology Crew kept up its search. The more they looked, the more they found. The fair property was littered with archaeological artifacts, confirmed as authentic by David Cole. By September 1984, the crew had found so many sites that they proposed a third alternate for a Highway 126 bypass. Robert DeSpain sent a letter to the Highway Division outlining the plan he called "Option 1½." Advantages of the plan included: It avoided the westernmost archaeological site in the southern route; decreased the state's necessary land purchases; and left standing eight acres of trees and undergrowth on the fair site that would provide a visual buffer between the fair and the new highway. It would also involve building only one bridge instead of three over the sinuous Long Tom River.

The State Highway Division decided there was only enough money to evaluate two of the sites found by the fair crew in the right-of-way. Archaeologists hired by the state determined one to be significant, but a second one was not. On November 23, 1984, the fair received a letter from the Highway Division rejecting the fair's proposed Option 1½. The letter further notified the fair that the department planned to proceed with the northern route, running Highway 126 through the fair property.

But Lady Luck had a trick up her sleeve. Thanks to an arcane provision in Oregon's 1980s land use planning rules, Oregon's attorney general had ruled that the plan to realign Highway 126 needed to go through a formal land-partitioning process with Lane County. That process would include a public hearing in front of the Lane County Planning Commission that was expected to be a mere formality. The hearing, originally set for November 27, 1984, got postponed until December 11. That two-week postponement gave fair organizers another chance to make their case against the highway realignment, after all.

The fair's Highway Committee convened an emergency meeting on November 29 to seek ways to interrupt the state process, and to focus attention on the archaeological sites the volunteers had found in the right-of-way of the northern route.

The fair board in December hired land use attorneys Bill Kloos and Al Johnson to help the fair make its case at the hearing. They also reached out to two members of the Lane County Board of Commissioners who had expressed support: Jerry Rust, one of the founders of the Hoedads tree-planting cooperative and a longtime fair participant; and Chuck Ivey, a hip new commissioner from Junction City who sported an earring and represented the west Lane County area that included the fair site. Both Chuck and Jerry pledged to talk

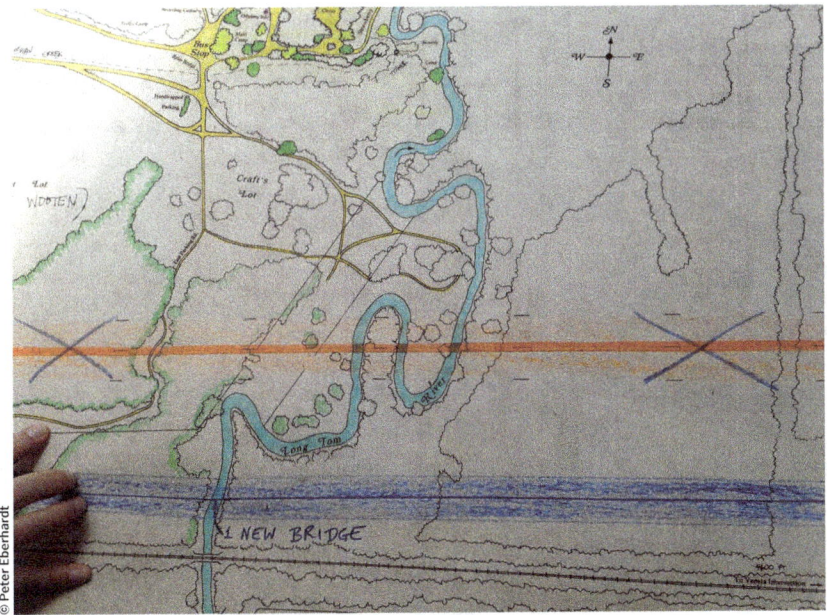

Peter Eberhardt marked a map to compare ODOT's plan to reroute Highway 126 (in blue) along the railroad tracks with ODOT's proposed realignment alternative (orange line). The alternative route would have needed three bridges to cross the Long Tom River and would have lopped off forty acres of fair property.

to the other commissioners.

"What Bill Kloos found out was that there had never been an EIS, an Environmental Impact Study," Robert DeSpain said. "So we went to the hearing, we waited our turn. And what a crew we were," Robert recalled, laughing out loud, "Jim Guthrie and John Stamp and I—all three long-haired bushy hippies—and Bill Kloos, this clean-cut attorney!

"But when we got up, we stated that we had discovered that Goal Five in this huge set of rules in the historical preservation section of the OAR (Oregon Administrative Rules) had not been satisfied," Robert said, "The state people turned around and looked at us like, 'OOOOH! You know!' They were hoping that that would never have come up."

Watching it all unfold, Jerry Rust and the other commissioners looked from one group to the other, and then Jerry told the Highway Division folks: "Looks like you guys need to go do your homework!"

As a result of that hearing on December 11, 1984, the Lane County Planning Commission recommended that the state further investigate the archaeological sites reported by the volunteers at the

Fair volunteers who checked out one of the big rigs ODOT brought in to build the highway included (from left): Ken Rodgers, Frank Sharpy with Jon and Jamie Sharpy, Ed Moye, Wally Slocum, and Robert DeSpain.

Oregon Country Fair before proceeding with the highway realignment. In the spring of 1985, Dr. Pettigrew, of the Oregon State Museum of Anthropology, started testing the sites pointed out by the fair volunteers. His tests would eventually show that four of those sites were at least as significant as the ones in the original route's right-of-way.

Many hearings followed. Wanting to make the best impression, Robert DeSpain lopped off his long red mane and trimmed his beard. He wanted to be taken seriously at the meetings when he testified as the Oregon Country Fair president. The overwhelming archaeological evidence caused the county to support the fair's position, and the state Highway Division finally relented, agreeing to route Highway 126 along the original southernmost route and leave the fair site intact.

In the fall of 1986 before the new highway was constructed, Drs. Brian O'Neill and Tom Connolly of the University of Oregon Museum of Natural & Cultural History/State Museum of Anthropology led two large-scale archaeological excavations in the highway right-of-way. (Dr. Pettigrew no longer worked at the museum.) These "data recovery" excavations were designed to mitigate for the destructive impacts of the highway construction. The findings traced prehistoric occupation of the Long Tom River area back at least 10,000 years.

In 1987, John Stamp had some interesting discussions with the city administrator in Veneta, Dave Kenny, and archaeologist Tom Connolly. Based on their talks and John's enthusiasm for the project, Tom Connolly and Dr. Patricia McDowell of the UO Department of Geography applied for a joint survey grant from the State Historic Preservation Office (SHPO). The cooperative project combined the disciplines of geography and archaeology and included the Oregon Country Fair, the University of Oregon, the city of Veneta, and SHPO.

The geographers examined the way the meandering Long Tom River created the valley and mapped its history after studying twelve-foot core samples. Historically, the successive flooding of the Long Tom River Valley had created a unique clarity of layer stratification that made it easy to study and date.

The archaeologists used a proton magnetometer to locate masses of rocks, which did not naturally occur in the floodplain. The Long Tom River ran full of silt and mud, not rocks. Nearly every rock in the floodplain had been brought in by humans. Masses of rocks underground usually indicated sites for ovens and former homes of the Kalapuya peoples.

The SHPO project documented small hearths that dated back 11,000 years, the oldest recorded archaeological evidence in Oregon's Willamette Valley. The site yielded a small number of artifacts from ancient campsites, including obsidian chips and scrapers, and charred acorn or hazelnut meats. In honor of the self-taught fair archeologist John Stamp's work on the project, one of the most significant archaeological areas was named the Stamp Site. The artifacts excavated from the sites would be housed at the UO Museum of Natural History.

By overlaying the geographic map with the magnetometer map, scientists could determine the areas on the Oregon Country Fair site that most likely harbored ancient artifacts. This would allow the fair to avoid digging in those sensitive areas in the future so they could leave the ancient record undisturbed.

Through the whole process, John Stamp and many fair volunteers gained a new appreciation for the landscape of the fair site and for the area's long history as a gathering place. "What has been learned [about the Kalapuya peoples] shows a lifestyle based on a very successful survival strategy," John Stamp reported to the fair board. "These early inhabitants lived in a well-balanced environment."

For centuries, the Kalapuya people flourished in the lush and abundant Willamette Valley. They lived in clusters of communities that shared territories defined by river drainages, archaeologist Tom Connolly said. When Lewis and Clark made their western expedition, they learned from the people living along the Columbia River that there were probably upwards of 15,000 people living in the Willamette Valley in the 1770s. The expedition learned that there had been at least two devastating epidemics, including smallpox, that had swept through the area prior to their visit.

"By looking at evidence, we know there was a giant depopulation all across North America that began hundreds of years ago," Tom said. "We don't know if the disease vector was from Columbus in 1492 or from the Norse who landed centuries before that. But European diseases came to the continent and had a devastating effect centuries before we were even thinking about it." It's possible the natural population in the Willamette Valley had been closer to 20,000 to 30,000 prior to contact with Europeans.

There were at least three different languages and thirteen different dialect groups among the Kalapuya people, derived from names on a treaty document from the 1850s. "We recognize that probably represents communities that were more numerous at one time and they consolidated into communities for the treaty document," Tom said. So there could have been perhaps twenty different communities, but certainly more than thirteen.

"The language diversity means the Kalapuya were not a single people," Tom said. "They were many different nations, basically. At least thirteen different dialects, and at least three distinct language groups. That tells us the people living in the Willamette Valley were not wandering nomads. They were not wandering all over the place. They were probably settled communities, which is the only way to get that language diversity in such a small place as the Willamette Valley."

Artifacts from the 1986 study site west of Veneta gave researchers clues to how the Kalapuyans settled the valley over time. Dating back to the oldest found site about 11,000 years ago, "there weren't that many people in the landscape," Tom said. "People moved around in family groups. They'd find a good spot to be for a while, harvest the food they could and when the pickings got a little slim, they'd move to someplace else. About 8,000 years ago things changed. The earliest camas oven we know of dates to 8,000 years old. It was found on the floor of the Fern Ridge Reservoir when it was drained. It's a site at the confluence of the Long Tom River and Hannavan Creek."

Archaeologists documented changes all over the Pacific Northwest around that time. "There's 6,000-year-old storage pits near the Northern Great Basin," Tom said. "We start seeing substantial houses. Jefferson County has one 6,800 years old. ... The landscape began filling up with people, so people accommodate to that change. They begin to extract more. When food is really abundant they'll harvest a whole lot, process it, and do something with it to store for times that are lean." They used ovens to preserve the camas bulbs and they needed houses to store the food.

"They managed a landscape and were tied to a place," Tom said. "A number of villages in any community would share a dialect. Villages would own parcels of ground and that community as a whole would own the larger landscape around them for hunting and foraging. Tualatins, for example, would hunt halfway to the mountains. ... There were recognized boundaries and a lot of trade back and forth. But there were consequences to hunting in the neighbor's land. ... The Tualatin village had sixteen known sites. That pattern was repeated through all the small watersheds in the Willamette Valley. There were clusters of villages, including obvious clustering along creeks and streams that represent distinct village communities along Fern Ridge Reservoir."

The Kalapuyans lived in a seasonal cycle, managing the landscape to improve the harvest. In the Northwest's rainy winters, they lived in permanent homes made of cedar bark and planks laid over a notched wood framework. The rectangular homes featured a central fireplace and usually housed several families. The winter sites included dome-shaped steam sweathouses for recreation and self-purification. In the drier months, the Kalapuyans camped out under the shelter of trees or large bushes and their activities cycled around hunting, fishing, and plant harvests.

They tended the camas lily fields that provided a staple to their diet. The camas bulbs grew abundantly in the wet prairies of the valley. In the springtime the lush fields of camas resembled indigo pools of water in the meadows. The women of the villages would survey the fields and dig out any white-blossomed death camas, which were poisonous. The women used curved hardwood digging sticks, fitted at the top with antler handles for better leverage. They would harvest a few fresh edible bulbs, but leave most of them for harvest several months later after the flowers had withered and the bulbs had fully ripened. Women and children all got out their digging sticks to help with the harvest.

At harvest time, they built large pit ovens from stones that people carried to the harvest site or that had been left from prior years. After a fire had heated up the stones, they would put down a layer of leaves or grass, then a layer of camas bulbs covered by a top layer of leaves and more hot stones. All of it would be topped with dirt to create a pit oven and people would keep the fire going from one to three days to slow-roast the bulbs, turning the complex carbohydrates into caramelized sugars.

"It's better to harvest your camas in August and September, when they're through making their seeds and storing up energy for the next year," John Stamp said. "Camas has little flowers, looks like an onion thing. It doesn't really have much taste at all, but if you cook it on a fire slowly for three days, it can produce starch and sugar—it's just like candy. You mix it with nuts and all kinds of stuff and berries and make a camas cake that was a big trade item here, like a cheese wheel, a fifteen-pound wheel."

The Kalapuya peoples were famous for their camas cakes, which were a valuable trade commodity. Camas cakes were taken to major trading centers like Celilo Falls and Willamette Falls. Besides the cheese-wheel-size camas cakes, the women would grind the roasted bulbs into a flour or paste, which they used in cooking all year long.

The archaeological digs near the Long Tom River in the 1980s unearthed two types of mortars. One was a mortar bowl carved of stone with a stone pestle. The other was a thick pancake-shaped rock, about six inches in diameter, with a shallow impression in the center that was used as a hopper mortar. The women used a woven basket shaped similar to a megaphone to hold the bulbs as they mashed them against the rock with a hand-held pestle.

To enhance their food supply, the Kalapuya also did "thoughtful burning," Tom Connolly said. "There were a lot of reasons for burning. One is you get a lush growth of green grass to direct the movements of game animals by timing your burning. More important than that, burning enhanced critical foods, especially the camas. ... Another one was seed-producing annual plants like tarweed. Tarweed is now considered a noxious weed. But it was cultivated in South America and was a very important staple food in the Willamette Valley."

The women harvested tarweed seeds after the fall fires, beating the seeds off the hardy plants that were left standing on the burned-over prairies. Then they would roast or parch the seeds and grind them into meal. Other important vegetable foods included many types of berries; seeds; dried hazelnuts; and wapato, a marsh plant whose tubers were harvested in the fall and stored in pits. Wapato tubers would be baked in ashes at mealtime.

The men hunted birds, small game, deer, bear, and elk. They fished for salmon, trout, and eels using nets made of plant fiber, weighted with rocks knotted into the nets. The rocks were often altered with scored lines or chipped out on the edges to hold them in place in the net.

The women were skilled at basketry. They wove storage containers, hats, and large floor mats. Men crafted tools and weapons, including bows and arrows. They also fashioned dugout canoes and paddles from fir, cottonwood, or cedar.

Archaeologists found that evidence of mound sites increased in the Willamette Valley about 3,000 to 4,000 years ago. Mound sites marked residential places where people had settled in as the population in the valley grew. People kept bringing more rocks, not only to build camas ovens, but to provide an elevated, dry base for the residence during the winter rains.

During that same period, archaeologists noted a dramatic increase in the number of projectile points, indicating a concern for defense of a home site. "The increase in points is ten-fold between 10,000 years ago and 3,000 years ago," Tom Connolly said. Ornamental items—for example, an obsidian wealth blade and whalebone clubs—started showing up in the Willamette Valley, indicating increased social stratification.

John Stamp wrote that "Local groups were interdependent on one another. Marriage ties and trading alliances linked various groups, yet no major chiefs or elite groups seem to have dominated, as was the case elsewhere in the Pacific Northwest."

In the Long Tom River area, some archaeological digs have indicated year-round villages of the Kalapuyans, principally near Hannavan Creek on the west side of what is now Fern Ridge Reservoir. At the time, the land along Hannavan Creek stood above the wintertime floods.

The Long Tom River itself is an English attempt to approximate a Kalapuyan community name, variously spelled as Lumtumbuff, Lamitambuff, Longtabuff, L'ommi tomba, Lumb Tumbles, and Long Tongue Buff. The villages of the Long Tom aka Lamitambuff villages spoke the Chelamela dialect as part of a larger community.

In 1997, the Oregon Country Fair expanded its footprint and named the new area Chela Mela Meadow to honor its original peoples. The Long Tom River borders one edge of the meadow and camas ovens have been documented nearby. It doesn't take much imagination to picture a Chelemela village or two making camp in the meadow and surrounding areas in the warm months of summertime.

The Kalapuyan peoples endured a grim fate. Diseases brought by Europeans wiped out those villages, family by family. "Look at the statistics we know," Tom Connolly said. "There were an estimated 15,000 people living in the Willamette Valley in 1770, and by the 1840s there were 600 people. This is a population decline over a couple of generations of greater than ninety-five percent! When we talk about the introduction of infectious diseases in America, we are talking about one of the greatest human disasters in the history of the world. That is not an exaggeration."

The United States government moved the few survivors of the communities to the Grand Ronde Reservation in Oregon after signing treaties in the 1850s. The first census taken at the reservation in 1856 counted eleven Kalapuyan "bands" there, with a total population of 344 men, women, and children. They were consolidated with survivors of about twenty other Oregon communities or tribes. A hundred years later, in 1956, the United States government terminated the tribes' standing, but in 1974 the tribes reorganized as the Confederated Tribes of Grand Ronde, and their federal status was restored in 1983.

1984
Richard and Debbie Bloom, Obsidian Wind Chimes

"It's my Christmas, Easter and Thanksgiving; I'd trade them all for the Country Fair. It's the best time in my life."
—Richard Bloom

"It's like a holiday."
—Debbie Bloom

Richard Bloom sold jewelry and wind chimes at a booth he shared with his friend Chris Kohler during Richard's first Oregon Renaissance Faire in September 1974. Richard had become friends with Chris, an air-brush artist, the summer of 1974 when both men sold their craftwork at the brand-new Portland Saturday Market. Chris had lined up a booth at the 1974 fair and invited Richard to join him. Chris drove down first to set things up, and Richard planned to meet him on the grounds.

"I got down to Eugene," Richard recalled, "and I'm driving around aimlessly asking people where the fair was. I pull up at a stoplight. At that time in Eugene, it was politically correct for women to go topless, which I did not know. I'm sitting there and a woman rides by on her bicycle, topless." Richard could hardly believe his eyes. "It kind of set the stage for a lot of unexpected events for the whole weekend. I eventually asked enough people that I got out to the fair."

In 1974, getting into the fair was very low key. Nobody asked for money or a pass. Richard explained to a fair greeter that he was sharing a booth with a friend and was told: "Oh, go on in, you'll find him." After wandering along the fair's meandering pathway, he came across Chris's booth in a quiet spot on Strawberry Lane at the far end of the fair from the entrance. The booth sat near a bend in the Long Tom River in an area that would later become Archaeology Park.

When the fair opened to the public, Richard laid out pieces of jewelry on a blanket and hung his obsidian wind chimes on a snowberry bush nearby. "I went to get something to eat," he said, "I think in the middle of the day on Saturday. I was gone for hours. I could not find my booth again. As a first-timer, there are plenty of places to go wrong. I was sure the booth was just around the next bend. But it was so Zen-like. The moment I gave up, when I admitted to myself that I was lost, I turn around and there was my booth."

For two years Richard shared a booth with Chris. For the next two years, he shared a booth with friends David and Alexandra. In 1978, Richard applied for a booth of his own. "It was easy," he said. "If you wanted a booth, you just went to Eugene and said, 'Can I have a booth, please?' and they said, 'Sure!' ... After people had signed up, then new people got to go in and choose from empty spots."

He found an abandoned booth to claim on Strawberry Lane that was closer to the Junction at the center of the fair's Eight-shaped path. The booth needed work, and he carted in the supplies to rebuild it before the fair began. "I don't think I really figured out the Eight until I got my own booth and had to walk the Eight to pick one," Richard said. "That's when I really got to know all the ins and outs of it."

The first year he had his own booth, his buddy Chris Kohler came by, very upset because a "Free Soul" had stolen a CO_2 canister from the back of his booth. He needed the canister for his air-brush art.

"That's too bad," Richard sympathized, "but what can you do?"

"Well, I could go and get him," Chris said. "Will you come with me?"

"But you don't know who it was," Richard said, thinking it was a person with free soul like so many others at the fair.

"Yes, I know who it was," Chris replied. "It was a Free Soul."

When the two friends arrived at a biker camp site, it suddenly dawned on Richard what Chris meant. There stood a bunch of burley men wearing denim and leather jackets with "Free Souls" scripted across the back. Richard turned to Chris aghast: "Oh, so you came to get me so I could go to a biker camp and get something back? Gee, thanks Chris."

About then a biker walked up to greet them and Chris explained his situation calmly. "I know you want to run your beer keg off of it," Chris said, "but this is how I make my living. I need my CO_2 canister." To Richard's surprise, the biker took the information in stride and said he'd see what he could do about it. The Free Souls managed to deliver a new canister to Chris by the next morning.

Richard noticed that everyone had gotten what they wanted. The Free Souls enjoyed their beer that night without interruption, and Chris's canister arrived in time for him to continue his air brush painting the next morning. Richard said he learned from that experience that by talking things over calmly—even if he felt afraid—things could be worked out.

Another event from that fair also stood out in Richard's memory. "The first time I met Artis was back when I had my own booth," he said. "I had already seen him playing spoons, but hadn't met him. I had a little space in front of this tree next to my booth."

Artis walked up and said "Hi, I'm Artis the Spoonman."

"Yeah, I know who you are," Richard replied.

"Well, do you mind if I play a really quiet set?" Artis asked.

"No, I'd love to have you," Richard said.

Artis unfolded his little bundle of utensils and placed spoons of different shapes and sizes on a small cloth on the ground. He took a deep breath and then started playing the spoons in marimba-like rhythms. "That was really a nice, cosmic moment," Richard said.

Debbie Marthaller also met Artis the Spoonman around that same time. She then owned an herb, spice, and tea shop in Old Town near the Portland Saturday Market. Artis frequently stopped by her shop as a regular customer. Her kids used to love going to the Portland Saturday Market to watch Artis create string figures as part of his act. "Today, we are still huge fans and friends of Artis and look forward to seeing him each year at the fair." Debbie said. "His wisdom and creativity and his take on life continue to inspire us."

Debbie had sold macramé creations at the Portland Saturday Market in 1974, but did not meet Richard there even though the market was still small. She went to her first Country Fair in 1975 with her then-partner, who had connections to the Mirkwood booth. Debbie spent most of one day riding a bicycle-powered blender to make smoothies at a booth near what became Community Village. "We didn't have passes," she said. "We were back behind the (smoothie) booth taking a nap at Sweep time. I was pretty worn out. When I woke up it was morning! I missed the whole Saturday night thing!

"To me the fair seemed like one giant wonderland in the woods," she added. "Wow, what are you going to see next?" Debbie noted that her sense of wonder would be rekindled at every fair she attended.

Debbie and Richard met in 1981 while participating in a personal growth/therapy group, not long after Debbie's first marriage ended. He was thirty-four and she was twenty-eight. "We dated off and on over about eight months," Debbie said. "I came as a package deal with two amazing boys—then ages one and half and four and a half—so we took some time to consider how that would all work." Richard fell in love with all three of them, and vice versa. "We tried out doing a craft fair together in June of 1982: the Fremont Solstice Fair in Seattle," Debbie said. "We all had a great time! I had a secret dream of being a fulltime craftswoman ever since my Saturday Market stint, so this was an extra fun event. The kids just *loved* it!" Not long after, they decided to become a family.

"Richard had a house-truck at the time," Debbie said. "We were going to take a trip cross-country to meet our families. The Country Fair was going to be our launching point. So by the time we got to the fair in 1982, we had all our stuff with the four of us in the house-truck, with everything else in storage."

Richard had been so distracted courting Debbie and the kids that he missed the deadline to re-apply for his booth that year. Instead, they joined friends in Booth 343 close to Main Stage. Richard brought his obsidian wind chimes. Gary Chaffin had created brass-wire mobiles. Kevin and Belinda Fulton had crafted glass sculptures with some ceramic components, including cloud chimes. They all needed space to hang their wares. "It took some negotiating to have all of our work displayed in that booth," Richard said with a smile.

It was crowded in other ways, too. "That was a very cramped little camp back there," Debbie said. "The four of us were sleeping in a regular-sized dome tent. ... And my goodness, that was a rowdy location at the fair. You could hear Main Stage. All the booths around us were into a lot of partying. And here I've got these little kids. I guess they learned to sleep anywhere in those days."

After the fair excitement, they pocketed the cash from the windchime sales and set off on the cross-country trip. While they had a lot of fun during that yearlong adventure, Richard had a more nostalgic memory of the trip than Debbie, who couldn't forget the challenges of keeping two rambunctious pre-school kids happy in a house-truck. But they toured a lot of beautiful country, met each other's families, and managed to get back in time for the 1983 Oregon Country Fair, where they again squeezed into the booth near Main Stage with friends.

In 1984, a booth space near the newly created Energy Park became available. "Our fair family then decided to make the move to Thirteenth Street," which was the main path to Main Stage, Debbie said. Their booth, number 085, included Gary and his teenage daughter Dena; Kevin and Belinda and their one-year old son, Nathan; and Richard, Debbie and their sons Shanti, age seven, and Joe, age four. The booth originally had a counter that ran across the front with a very tiny space to one side for entering. An overhanging loft blocked out most of the light, so the interior was dark.

Debbie started helping Richard create chimes around that time and they began to earn their living selling their unique wind chimes at art fairs, garden shows, and craft galleries throughout the United States. Besides traveling to shows, they drove to volcanic regions of the high desert in Oregon and Northeast California to collect obsidian. They sought out a rare form of obsidian called "needles," which occurred only in fault zones. As they traveled through the Western states, they also searched for seeds, pods, bones, thorns, and antlers to use in the wind chimes. They would look for interesting bits of nature that could be combined in the studio to make unusual and surprising chime designs.

"The chime components are all used in their natural state, save the nylon and glass beads that hold them together, Richard said. "We pride ourselves in making something with a very small footprint. ... Some materials are used exactly as found. Others are carved, drilled, filed, or polished, but all remain true to the original form, echoing nature herself."

At the Country Fair, they remodeled the booth on Thirteenth in the late 1980s. They tore down the overhanging loft and opened up the booth to more light with a new central entry. Then they erected a new loft that sat farther back from the entrance. Eventually, other modifications created places to hang wind chimes on one side and display blown glass on the other.

By then, their booth partner Gary had

Crafters Kevin Fulton (left) and Richard Bloom shared a booth at the fair for decades.

opened a Birkenstock store in Bend and stopped selling the mobiles. He and his daughter, Dena, still attended the fair for fun. Gary would later remarry and move to Florida in 1991 after Dena graduated from high school. Meanwhile, Kevin and Belinda had a second son, Alex, in 1988. In 1989, the boys' ages ranged from one to twelve. The four boys in the booth all would bring their friends to the fair, setting up "Boy Central" in the loft for many years.

"All the kids enjoyed sleeping up there," Debbie said. "You couldn't beat it for parade viewing! The sound of the band always brought cheers from each of us and we would race to the loft to see what was new this year, singing together—especially 'The Teddy Bears' Picnic'—and clapping and dancing." Booth 085 would remain their fair home for more than three decades.

Debbie and Richard said the Country Fair topped their list of favorite art shows they had attended over the years. "It's very successful for us," Debbie said. "It's one of our really good shows. What brings me back to this booth is the people who come here. They tune in to the things about your work that you're most excited about. It's the most appreciative audience, probably, of all the shows we do. That feeds us as artists."

They also praised the fair volunteers. "The fair energy is usually, first, kindness," Debbie said. "That's really prevalent here and that's really different from how the world often is, particularly when you're dealing with conflicts or problems that need solutions. The way that it all happens here, is just so sweet. ...

"I love to come here and see what's been happening the past month as Main Camp has prepared everything with such love and care," she added. "You see the flowers and the beautifully cut designs in the wood fences. All those extra things that could be just boards providing that function, but no, we make those fences into art. ... I've always been impressed with the carpenters that the Country Fair seems to draw."

The Bloom family looked forward to watching the Saturday night Midnight Show at every fair. They had caught some of the acts at the Portland Saturday Market, and had become fans of the Flying Karamazov Brothers, and Avner the Eccentric, in addition to Artis the Spoonman. "The Midnight Show was exciting because we did not get to see a lot of performances" during the fair, Richard said. Crafters were expected to tend their booths and sell their wares when the fair was open to the public. The Midnight Show's variety-show setup offered the crafters and fair volunteers a sampling of the skits, acts, and music found on the fair's many stages.

Other traditions took root over the years at the booth. They would always shop early at Gypsy Rose booth, where they could purchase fresh-cut gardenias with pins attached. "All the girls in the booth would get our gardenias," Debbie said, "We swear that's the only way you make it through the outhouse experience at the fair, smelling the gardenias."

The kids always enjoyed watching the entertainment. "Every year that my kids are here, we go see Dr. Atomic's Medicine Show together," Debbie said. "It's usually on a Friday, opening day. I absolutely love their turn of phrase. They're such a treasure. We belong to Oregon PeaceWorks, too." It took Debbie a long time to realize that Dr. Atomic's Medicine Show performances often raised funds for Oregon PeaceWorks. Medicine Show co-founder Peter Bergel served as executive director of Oregon PeaceWorks for a dozen years and was a longtime editor of its online publication, the *PeaceWorker News Magazine*. When Debbie learned about those connections, she thought, "Wow, that's pretty cool!"

Both boys took up juggling, inspired at the fair by some of their favorite acts like Rhys Thomas of Up for Grabs, Izzy Tooinsky, and the Flying Karamazov Brothers. "Our kids really did a great job of getting out to see the entertainment," Debbie said. Occasionally the adults would find time to join the boys, especially for the vaudeville variety shows at the Circus Stage.

Richard and Debbie would look forward to hearing new musical talent at the fair. Debbie discovered musical commentator Chris Chandler while watching an impromptu performance along the path. One of her favorites, Jim Page, was playing guitar while Chris Chandler performed spoken-word poetry with labor activist and singer Anne Feeney. "Oh my gosh it was so amazing," Debbie said. "I came back and said, 'You guys have got to go hear Chris Chandler. I guarantee you have never heard anyone like him!'" Everyone in the booth became huge fans and they would try to catch Chris Chandler's performance every year. "He is so relevant," Debbie said. "Each year, I can't wait to hear his commentary on what is happening in the world. He always makes me think."

They also would become fans of Trillian Green, a trio who played "psycho-tantric-juju-jazz" on flute, cello, and rhythm instruments. "It's one of those things that took our booth by storm one year, all of a sudden," Richard said. "Everyone loved Trillian Green."

During the 1990s, the booth family rekindled a Saturday night tradition that originally had been started by Gary Chaffin. "We would get everybody together from our booth after closing and go on this long walk," Richard said. "We'd stop at every food booth that looked good and didn't have too long of a line, and decide on one thing to order. We would then share it and move on to the next booth. We'd do a whole taste test, visiting ten or fifteen different food booths. We jokingly call it the Gary Chaffin Memorial Graze." They would usually end up at Main Stage to catch parts of the Midnight Show.

The tastings introduced them to new booths. One that Richard especially savored was the Mama's Momos booth by Main Stage. Mama's Momos sold Tibetan-style dumplings stuffed with spicy vegetables or beef. For many years the momo booth would donate its proceeds to causes promoting a free Tibet.

"You never really know what is going to happen at the fair," Debbie said. "We all show up with a willingness to be surprised and delighted, without ever knowing how that will take shape. This is the way we like to live every day. It is easier to do at fair." One fair in particular would stand out in their memories because of an amazing chance meeting. They were having an especially successful day of sales at that fair. Two different customers in the booth at the same time were purchasing some of the biggest pieces that Obsidian Wind Chimes had on display.

Debbie, who had been away from the booth, returned in the midst of the hubbub and stepped in to help wrap the purchased chimes for the customers. "These two sales were the equivalent of a whole fair sales total," Debbie said. "We couldn't believe it!"

As Richard was finishing up with those customers, other people came in to the booth to check out the chimes. Debbie noticed one woman studiously reading the "Artist Statement." As Debbie approached her, the woman exclaimed, "I grew up with a Richard Bloom in Aurora, Illinois." Surprised, Debbie replied, "That is where Richard is from!" Together they waited until Richard finished with the other customers. When Richard started chatting with the woman named Carol, they suddenly realized that they had been next door neighbors who had played together daily as children. It had been more than fifty years since they had seen each other.

"We lost track of each other," Richard said, "like many of us do when we grow up and move." Carol lived in Steamboat Springs, Colorado, and was in Eugene visiting a friend who brought her to the fair. Her friend had told Carol: "We are going to go to a really cool event. You never know what you will find there!" Carol stayed for a few hours in the booth chatting, meeting the Bloom family, and exchanging contact information. They all agreed it was a "true Oregon Country Fair experience."

Debbie and Richard marvel at the ways the fair changed over the decades. "It's always been about personal freedom of expression," Richard said. "But thirty years ago, we had no idea how much personal freedom we could express. It was wilder in a few ways, but I think it's a lot wilder now without as much drugs and alcohol. We've had practice, as a group. We can think of more ways to be outrageous.

"I don't think it would have occurred to any guys to wear skirts in 1975," Richard explained. "Possibly one person in full drag, maybe, but now we see all sorts of guys in skirts. You see kilts, of course, sarongs, costumes. ... I mean, nobody in 1975 would've had the idea yet to dress up twenty people in various flamingo outfits and go to the fair."

Debbie laughed, adding, "It's become an art form ... I think it's much more family-friendly now. We went through changes and had to address some things and grow up a little bit in certain areas. I think it's all for the better. I think the crowd that comes here is certainly not all people looking for a drug party scene." They both agreed that it would make a big difference in 1997 when fair organizers stopped allowing the public to bring in coolers and alcohol.

"We were pretty close to the entrance," Richard said, "And at 11:00 a.m., 11:05, you'd know that the fair was open because there'd be wagons and hand-trucks with coolers bungeed up on top and three people on each side, already falling over, headed for Main Stage. It's difficult to remove them in that state. Then what do you do? It was a conundrum."

The Blooms also noted that the fair's official rules would increase exponentially over time. "There are a lot of rules—pages and pages of rules—and there's levels and degrees of political correctness to deal with," Richard said. "But I think, for all the talk about increasing rules and regulations, it's always been about solutions."

"Like going to the advance tickets," Debbie said. "I'm so proud of us for going, okay, we can either build a bigger and bigger security force, which is kind of what we do as a country, or we can get creative and take a chance. Because going to only advance tickets took a big risk. And I think it probably has decreased attendance a little bit. But we found that we do better, probably, with a medium crowd. ... When the crowd's too thick, people get into survival mode. They're not thinking about shopping."

After sharing a booth for more than thirty years, the people in Booth 085 bonded into one big family. The two couples and their boys would enjoy a pre-fair dinner together on Wednesday nights as they finish up the booth for each fair. They often brought each other gifts. "We celebrate the fair as a major holiday," Debbie said. "We all raised our kids here." Traditions included exchanging their crafts gifts with each other. Debbie and Richard would take home a piece of blown glass, while Belinda and Kevin would take home a new obsidian wind chime.

"Our booth mates make the most beautiful blown glass," Debbie said. "We think it's the best art glass at the fair! We trade every year, so we each have huge collections of each other's work at this point. Since we live a hundred and eighty miles apart, it is fun to have the physical reminders of each other in our homes between fairs."

On Sunday nights at the end of the fair, Seattle folksinger Jim Page would often play and sing in front of a neighboring booth. Often he would be joined by other musicians in an acoustic jam. "We tend to stay open a little later on Sunday," Debbie said, "as this is a time when staff and other artists finally have a chance to shop and trades can be completed. As the music begins, we dismantle our displays and begin packing up for Monday departure. It is quite lovely to do by lantern light, with musical accompaniment. We often go to sleep in our tents with that live music as lullaby, a perfect ending to an amazing weekend."

In the 2010s, the booth would lose its loft after all the boys grew to adulthood. With the dark overhang gone the sunlight could stream in through the trees, which greatly enhanced the booth displays of brightly colored blown glass and tinkling obisidian windchimes. The boothmates would embrace a third generation when Debbie and Richard started bringing their two granddaughters to the fair. The girls enjoyed helping in the booth and loved to watch acrobatic performances, the belly dancers at Caravan Stage, and Tom Noddy's Bubble

The Blooms enjoyed introducing the fair's wonders to their granddaughters, Lauren and Sophia.

Magic Show. "Throughout his childhood, their dad was a huge fan of Tom Noddy," Debbie said, "so it is especially nostalgic and sweet to go see him with the grandkids."

Richard and Debbie said they felt fortunate in their choice of careers. "We are lucky to have such personal freedom," Debbie said. "We are free to express ourselves creatively. We have choices of selling venues and opportunities for travel, we have flexible work schedules, and we have an amazing community of artists that are our peers."

Richard chimed in: "A lot of us earn our living in the arts. It's not for everyone. There is much about it that is unpredictable. Oregon Country Fair has been and continues to be an event that gives us validation and inspiration to keep making and selling our art, and faith that it will keep working out, maybe even more beautifully than we imagined. We all show up at the fair with a willingness to be surprised and delighted, without ever knowing how that will take shape! This is the way we like to live every day; it is easier to do at the fair. This is one of the reasons we call this 'an essential event.'"

1984
Alpha Farm and Community Village

> *"The renewal of the social order, we now see, must begin with ourselves. We seek to change our basic assumptions and patterns of daily living; to accomplish this we must alter our patterns of thought. We must live ourselves into the future we seek."*
> —*Alpha Farm Prospectus*, 1972

Community Village recruited two worker-owned restaurants in Eugene—Zoo Zoo's and the Homefried Truckstop—to join the Genesis Juice cooperative in running the first village restaurant in 1977. That configuration lasted until 1982 when the wheels started to fall off the social experiments in cooperation at both Zoo Zoo's and the Truckstop.

In Zoo Zoo's case, the group's ideals of cooperatively serving great food at cheap prices yielded unsustainably low wages to its worker-owners. The worker-owners had to keep up an ungodly pace that exhausted everyone, forcing constant turnover. At the Truckstop, human nature would trump idealism: Too many worker-owners took their responsibilities less seriously than others. After crucial tasks fell through the cracks too many times, the alliance broke up.

In 1983, the Village Restaurant was co-managed by Soy World (aka Turtle Island) and Genesis Juice. Then in 1984 the Community Village Coordinating Council received an application from a group that turned out to be a great fit: Alpha Farm.

Alpha Farm had operated their vegetarian restaurant—Alpha-Bit Café—since 1972. Situated in Mapleton, Oregon, where Highway 126 took a sharp turn to follow the Siuslaw River, Alpha Bit had become a popular stop for travelers from Eugene to the Oregon Coast. The café served strong, organic coffee and delicious vegetarian soups, sandwiches, and cookies.

Alpha Farm's intentional community near Deadwood also had been founded on the ideals of making decisions by group consensus, just like Community Village. But there was one big difference between the organizations. Members of Community Village used consensus only at their monthly meetings, while Alpha Farm members wove consensus decisions into the fabric of their everyday life. The groups meshed so well that Alpha Farm would help run the Village Restaurant for the next eleven years.

Coincidentally, a chance meeting at the October 1971 Oregon Renaissance Faire (the previous incarnation of the Oregon Country Fair) played a key role in Alpha Farm's genesis.

The seeds of Alpha Farm intentional community were sown at the 1971 national conference of the American Friends Service Committee, an activist Quaker organization that historically provided international disaster relief and peace education. Many Quakers took a year or more away from their career jobs to work as paid volunteers for the AFS Committee. During the 1960s, the AFS Committee became active in the civil rights and anti-war efforts that were roiling the United States. The turmoil of the times spilled into the 1971 conference, with many groups competing against each other for the committee's time and attention.

The spectacle of liberal groups fighting among themselves disheartened Caroline Estes, a former legal secretary, and her husband, Jim Estes, a former Bay Area newspaper editor. They had dedicated themselves to peace and justice issues with the AFS Committee in Philadelphia for five years and felt frustrated by the lack of progress they saw in society. They met other Friends at the conference who felt the same way, and the small group started talking about finding a different way to effect change in the world.

"Six or eight of us agreed that for a few months we would meet weekly on Sunday night to discuss the idea of creating a small community of people," Caroline Estes said. Besides Caroline (then age forty-four) and Jim (age forty-nine), the original group in 1971 included their daughter Maria (sixteen), who attended high school; Jules Williams (fifty-four), an agronomist and former college instructor from Ohio; his wife, Kate Williams (fifty-four), who had taught pre-school in Ohio; their daughter Alice (fourteen), who attended junior high; and Glen Hovemann (twenty-three), a former newspaper journalist from Minneapolis.

For a year, the small group of Friends met in Philadelphia every Sunday night over vegetarian dinners to figure out what their ideal community might look like. Despite their urban backgrounds, they embraced the ethics of the era's back-to-the-land movement because they wanted to live simply. They made decisions using the Quaker tradition of consensus. "Consensus grows out of the Quaker process of believing that everyone has a piece of the truth," Caroline Estes explained, "and if you are able at any time to get all the pieces of truth that are available in that meeting or in that situation, then you'll make the best decision possible."

Throughout a year of meetings, the group established certain criteria. They wanted to create a self-sustaining farm community of up to twenty people. The community would emphasize group sharing but still provide separate living spaces for individual and family privacy. They felt a spiritual calling to live peacefully but not completely cut off from society. The location "had to have a growing season that was long enough to be somewhat self-efficient," Caroline said. "It had to be a university town or an area that was open to intellectual pursuits; it had to have a political system that was okay with unusual organizational people like Quakers; it had to not have earthquakes; it had to be near a large body of water."

Five of the group members took their vacation together in the fall of 1971, flying across the country to Oregon to look for farmland. "Throughout this whole journey, we had a sense of being led, that's the easiest way to say it," Caroline said. Someone along the way told them about a man living near Eugene with a large piece of property that he might be interested in selling to the group. In Eugene, the five travelers stayed with a Quaker real estate agent who ferried them around to locations he thought the group might like, but nothing he showed them fit the bill.

Finally the agent helped them contact the man "living near

Eugene" they had heard about who had property, only to learn he was not interested in selling. However, he knew a neighbor "over the hill" who wanted to sell. "You might want to go talk to him," he told the group.

So they did, and they all fell in love with the land "over the hill" at first sight. Tucked among the steep conifer-covered hills of the Oregon Coast range, the 280-acre farm stretched along a green finger of a valley bordered by Deadwood Creek. A wood bridge crossed Deadwood Creek to connect the farm to the main road. A smaller tributary creek on the land could be tapped for water. The original two-story farmhouse, plus a barn and assorted drafty outbuildings provided enough space for their needs of both privacy and togetherness. Abundant winter rainfall and dry, moderate summers made for excellent growing conditions. Located about fifty-five miles by road from Eugene and twenty-five miles from the Pacific Ocean, the land was both remote and accessible. The price was $90,000.

The group returned the next day with their real estate agent and signed the contract, putting down their last $500 and wondering how they'd come up with the rest. After they signed the contract, the five Friends happened upon the October 1971 Oregon Renaissance Faire in Veneta and stopped in to check it out. "We met a man there along the pathways who was a Friend, a Quaker," Caroline said. "We told him what we were doing, and he said he'd loan us part of the money.

"We had $500 in the bank when we signed this contract," Caroline added, laughing. "He was going to medical school, and had a certain amount of money. He said he would loan us all that money if we returned him one-fourth of it every year. So he did, and we did. That was our introduction to the Country Fair." After producing a prospectus describing their intentional community, they raised additional money from personal loans.

The first resident arrived in spring 1972. "This place was known as Alpha before we ever got here," Caroline said. "It was named for the daughter of the first post-mistress." The post-mistress had run the Alpha post office out of the front living room of her home, the original farmhouse on the property. The serendipity of the old name was perfect: Alpha Farm was born.

Alpha Farm began with thirteen community members ranging in age from newborn to their mid-fifties. The small group of singles, couples, and families struggled at the outset, dealing with frozen pipes that first harsh winter and eating bowl after bowl of beans and rice. "We were novices of the first order," Caroline said. The stark realities of a simplified rural life tested their habits of urban living as well as their spiritual commitment to consensus.

Their lofty ideals stumbled over the messiness of daily life on a farm. At first they resisted creating any rules, wanting to allow everyone to "do their own thing" and "find themselves" in the parlance of the day. They were escaping the mindless regulation and conformity of society, exploring a new way of living. They figured that everyone would simply pitch in on tasks as needed. But frustrations set in after they had worked their tails off for months on end only to find themselves still dining on beans and rice because it was all they could afford.

Reality hit hard. They needed more structure in order to create the self-sufficient, productive farm they had envisioned. They started defining jobs and scheduling work shifts. And they kept their commitment to consensus, deciding everything in family-style meetings where everyone had a voice. Meetings started with a "check in" so each member could share how he or she was doing. Then going around the circle, they discussed the agenda. The meetings often would stretch out into long hours. They would set aside a full day for certain topics—taking time out for meals—to give decisions time to reach fruition.

Even as the small group scrambled to get their act together on the farm, they opened Alpha-Bit vegetarian café and bookstore in Mapleton in the fall of 1972, six months after they arrived. The ten adults at Alpha Farm worked hard to run the café while they were still learning how to farm and live together. But they viewed the café as key to their mission of reaching out to their neighbors and the wider world.

Of course their neighbors were skeptical. After all, the back-to-the-land movement was going strong in the early 1970s, and "everyone" in rural communities had heard rumors about lazy young hippies who formed communes out in the country, using drugs, going naked, and living off handouts. But Alpha-Bit Café, with its healthy food and friendly workers, offered everyone a chance to meet these new folks. It didn't take long for the neighbors to notice that the people living at Alpha Farm didn't fit the negative stereotypes at all.

"There's always a general suspicion when something different comes to a small town," Mapleton resident Walt Huntington told a newspaper reporter in 1976. "And everybody wondered just what kind of books they were going to be selling in their bookstore. But the store has really helped people get to know them. The books are fine. Probably a few people will always be distrustful but that's not the general attitude."

Alpha members began holding monthly group meetings to cover three general areas: business, spiritual, and interpersonal development. Daily schedules listed each person's workweek, and long-range plans plotted out steps for achieving key objectives. Every member committed to work nine-hour days, five days a week. Most of it was hard, physical labor such as chopping wood for heat, tilling soil for planting, cooking meals for the whole group. The tasks assigned varied, depending on the seasons and the needs of the farm and Alpha-Bit Café.

In the early days, any visitor was welcome to the farm on the theory that the group wanted to share with as many people as possible their philosophy of living simply and peacefully in consensus with others. But the visitor policy had to be changed after Alpha Farm members found themselves outnumbered three-to-one by guests who often didn't even bother to call before showing up. Their excess of hospitality interrupted important farm work. Regretfully, members eventually agreed to limit visitors to five total, and casual drop-ins were actively discouraged.

In 1973, Alpha Farm won the contract to deliver a U.S. mail route nearby. The route provided a welcome source of income. It also created a coincidental connection to the farmhouse's pioneer past as the Alpha post office.

Alpha Farm members got active in the neighborhood in other ways, too. The kids attended local schools. Kate Williams and Caroline Estes joined the Mapleton Area Advocacy Planning Council. After several small intentional communities popped up in Deadwood Valley in 1975, Alpha folks helped set up a community co-op in the town of Deadwood, and Alpha women began a women's discussion group.

"Alpha had been there for a long time," said Karen Stingle, who moved to an intentional community in Deadwood in 1975. "And all of a sudden there was this vortex of people who arrived from all over. I remember at the first women's meeting, we went around the circle and everybody talked about how they ended up there, and it was all totally unrelated reasons. They heard about this piece of land for sale, you know, they heard about Alpha, various different reasons drew us all there. And '75 was when we started having community meetings."

Alpha's influence ended up nurturing an unintentional community of intentional communities. "Most of the new people moving in were alternative people," Caroline Estes said. "At one time we had four communities in the Deadwood area.

"Communities are not communes," Caroline clarified. "A community is usually a collection of people who made a dedication to the space that they're in, to be there, and to stay. A commune is where people come for whatever and don't particularly have commitment. Commitment's the big difference. And communities can be all kinds. Just those four [in the Deadwood area] were very different. Blue Star was mainly a spiritual community; Fir Bank was just a collection of people, not any particular belief system that I know of; Bear Creek is a collection of individual families living on the same land; and Alpha is a consensual group."

Julie Daniel, who moved to an intentional women's community in Deadwood in the late 1970s, said that "Deadwood was for the best part of two decades a very vibrant community-building space. We had childcare co-ops, a food co-op, and a library. We built a community center. We put on plays, we had women's circles, we had men's circles. It was community cultural life. Deadwood seemed a lot further from Eugene then, even though the mileage hasn't changed. When we first moved out there, the only local [telephone] calls were within the valley. You couldn't call outside the valley except long distance. There was no television. ... We shared our phone [line] with four people. It was very primitive in lots of ways. There were more dirt roads. We used to come to town about once a month. It was a great big deal."

Several of the intentional communities in Deadwood also played active roles in Community Village at the Oregon Country Fair. In 1979, Julie Daniel and her community of Deadwood women built a mud stove in the village and demonstrated making tofu from scratch. "We soaked the soy beans," Julie said. "We ground them up with a bicycle grinder, sitting on a bicycle grinding the beans. And then we made the tofu [in the mud oven] as a demonstration of appropriate technology."

Deadwood women also started a Women's Grounding Circle at Community Village that would continue for decades.

"It started out of some groups that Christine Payne-Towler used to do, and she was teaching about grounding and trance," Karen Stingle said. Other key instigators of the Women's Grounding Circle at Community Village were Darlene Colborn, Allison Klute, and Dory Sweet.

"The main goal is to provide a safe place for women to come—a place with peace and calm and strengthening and support. We do a ritual that begins with a cleansing of some sort, like smudging with sage as we're going in the door, or spraying with lavender water. We do an introduction where everybody gets to say their name and a little something about themselves."

Participants then would be invited to relax comfortably as they were led in a visualization exercise. One typical grounding exercise would invite participants to imagine becoming a flower or a tree, then visualize tracing their energetic roots connecting them to the Earth and each other as they tuned in to their inner wisdom. After the visualization, women would share their experiences and offer each other support. The Women's Circle ceremony in the village would become so popular that women would sign up to participate in monthly New Moon Grounding Circles throughout the year in Eugene.

With so many of its Deadwood neighbors already participating in Community Village, Alpha Farm fit right in as the Village Restaurant in 1984. They served vegetarian fare from the menu at Alpha-Bit Café—soups, salads, and grainburgers, plus breakfast items like muffins, granola, teas, and coffee. Genesis Juice cooperative also participated in the Village Restaurant, offering organic, raw juice. For the Village Restaurant in 1986 and 1987, Alpha-Bit worked alongside The Zoo café, reincarnated by former worker-owners of Zoo Zoo's. In subsequent years, different groups would partner with Alpha in the Village Restaurant.

Alpha Farm's experience with group consensus also helped reinforce the consensus approach in Community Village. After

Alpha Farm sold Alpha grain burgers and other vegetarian fare at the Village Restaurant for 11 years.

several Community Village co-founders—including Marshall Landman, who was a masterful facilitator—moved on to other jobs at the fair, village members often wrestled with keeping the consensus decision process moving along at meetings.

With new members arriving at village meetings every month, "blocking" became a too-common problem. For consensus to work well, blocking was supposed to be reserved for the times when a person had such a strong, compelling reason to block the decision that she or he could not bear to "step aside." At the village meetings, participants sometimes blocked decisions because they had not attended previous meetings and missed the group discussion, so they didn't understand why the decision was made. Their questions would restart the discussion, and the group would have to talk through it all over again. Meetings could drag on seemingly forever.

"If you don't have well-trained facilitators in consensus, it can be too tiring, too long, too exasperating," Caroline Estes said. "And you have to train the group to use consensus correctly, which oftentimes is not done. And that's too bad, because it leads to hierarchy, which is, I think, a mistake. In our present society, we have much too much hierarchy."

During the 1986 Oregon Country Fair, Caroline Estes taught

free, public workshops on consensus-building every day in the Village Yurt. In 1987, she began conducting annual workshops on consensus for all the participants in Community Village. She brought with her the history and structure of the Quaker model, which helped everyone become more effective at finding consensus during the meetings.

In 1987, Caroline was asked to facilitate a five-day workshop at Breitenbush Hot Springs Resort for 600 attendees. Despite the huge number, Caroline was determined to facilitate the group through consensus decisions. The process she led everyone through impressed many attendees. Next, the Green Party invited her to facilitate their national meeting in St. Paul, Minnesota. Caroline soon was inundated with requests for her workshops on consensus. In 1988 she formed the Alpha Institute with another member of Alpha Farm, Lysbeth Borie.

They often held workshops at Alpha Farm, but they also traveled to their destinations. They conducted a one-day consensus-building workshop in 1991 at Greenfield Ranch in California. In 1994 they taught workshops in Colorado, New Mexico, California, Maine, Massachusetts, Michigan, and British Columbia. Clients ranged from the Esalen Institute to Hewlett-Packard Electronics to the U.S. Forest Service. One attorney taking the course told Caroline, "You're not teaching consensus, you're teaching revolution!"

By the 1990s, the Alpha Farm community would settle into a sustainable rhythm of life. The garden would supply seventy-five percent of the vegetables served at meals. The apple orchards produced hundreds of gallons of cider. Their chickens laid abundant eggs; and the farm's cows produced enough milk to add butter, cheese, and yogurt to their diets. What they didn't produce themselves, they would obtain by buying, bartering, or trading. Sometimes they exchanged lumber for honey, or worked on a neighbor's farm in trade for used farm machinery.

Full-time members would remain close to fifteen total, with five interns living on the farm for periods of time ranging from a few months to a year. Interns who stayed a full year were called residents and at the end of the year could request to join Alpha Farm "for the foreseeable future" if all agreed.

When residents became members, they handed their personal property over to the community. Anything above $5,000 would be placed into a trust account on which Alpha received interest. Those Alpha members who later left the community would get to take with them their assets from the trust account. As members, Alpha residents gave any outside income to the farm. During the farm's first two years, the salary Jim Estes earned as a copy editor for the *Salem Statesman Journal* provided all the group's cash flow of $600 a month.

As the decades rolled by, hundreds of visitors and interns would visit and try out the lifestyle, but community life clearly wasn't for everyone. "Fifty percent of the people I know could never stand community and fifty percent of them are quite happy in a community," Caroline Estes said. "It's hard work. Creating community is very hard work. You have to be willing to do not just physical labor, but you have to be able to change yourself to be a 'we' person in place of an 'I' person. And we are trained in this society to be an 'I' person, which is the mess we're in."

In February 2016, federal working rules would force Alpha Farm to close Alpha-Bit Café forty-four years after it opened. Alpha members had run the café voluntarily as part of their work contribution to the collective. But the federal government saw them as employees, not volunteers. The café could not break even if the staff had to be paid, so they shut the doors to Alpha Bit Café after a farewell sale.

But Alpha Farm would endure as the longest continuously run intentional community in Oregon. Alpha Farm would host thirty people at its height and five people at its lowest point. As of summer 2018, eight people lived at the farm with one original group member—Caroline at age ninety-one. The former teen-agers from Philadelphia, Maria Estes and Alice Williams, had moved away after they grew up. Glen Hovemann left after a few years. Kate and Jules Williams, who were older than the others, died in the 1990s. At age ninety-one, Jim Estes died in 2013 and was buried on the farm. By 2018 the community had seen four deaths, six births, and four marriages.

"Most communes fell apart because they didn't have common commitment," Caroline said. "It's difficult to go through the hard times that we all face at some point unless you have a commitment that is larger than yourself. ... I sympathize with people who come and have a struggle living here [at Alpha Farm] because most of them come from an intellectual place, from having figured it out. Well, that's not how I got here. I got here because I was led here. It has to be a spiritual place that sustains you. All of the intellectual thinking in the world won't necessarily get you through some of the hard spots. Add in a little dash of stubbornness and it helps."

1984
The Pride of Ownership

"Maximum Personal Responsibility equals Maximum Personal Freedom."
—Moz Wright, 1984 OCF Booth Construction Guidelines

In February 1984, the fair's board of directors and coordinators held a leadership training seminar at the WOW Hall in Eugene. Because so many new people had stepped forward to assume organizing roles at the fair, board President Robert DeSpain had proposed the training to bring more cohesiveness to the group's efforts. About thirty-five people showed up, including many crew coordinators and all of the board members: DeSpain, Ron Chase, Santos Narvaez, Lucy (Kingsley) Parker, Frank Sharpy, Jon Silvermoon, Robert Thompson, Wally Slocum, Mary Wagner, and Moz Wright.

"Robert DeSpain got this woman who worked with group dynamics," Robert Thompson said. "She was a professional organizer who helps facilitate groups to define goals and that sort of thing." The trainer stood by a blackboard with chalk in her hand and asked the group what the Oregon Country Fair meant to them. She wrote down phrases, labeling them with letters.

"She was asking questions," Moz Wright said. "Why'd you come to the fair? What do you come to the Fair for? Well, what do you like about it? All this different stuff. So slowly she wrote it all down. ... It was the condensation of that big list that got us to 'psycho-spiritual rejuvenation.' And when that came out, everybody went, 'Yes! That's it!'"

The woman stood beside the blackboard with her mouth wide open as the room erupted in celebration. "That's what the fair is! Psycho-spiritual Rejuvenation!" It was option (F) on the blackboard, giving rise to another phrase coined by fair crafter and woodworker Jim Guthrie: "The Fair without 'F' is just air.'"

But organizers would need more than a feel-good phrase to get them through the challenges arising from the fair's land ownership. First, the board of directors grappled with stricter guidelines for booth construction. Now that the fair owned the land instead of renting it temporarily, the county started looking more closely at the supposedly temporary booths. Given that many of the booths had stood in place by then for more than a decade, the county began evaluating the booths as permanent structures instead of temporary ones, and found many of them lacking.

In addition, a new mindset took hold among the crafters and cooks who set up every year in their booths. Everyone "knew" the booths legally belonged to the fair, but they also felt a sense of personal ownership of the booth that they had maintained and camped behind for years. After the fair bought the land, many booth folks built sturdier, higher, and larger structures. They also cut down brush around the booths to open up more camping space. The results disheartened fair organizers. Clearing so many green zones significantly impacted the woodland ambiance of the fair. In several places where woodland shrubbery had been removed, the public could peer directly into tents behind the scenes.

A board-appointed fair committee recommended new booth construction guidelines to address the concerns and to comply with county regulations. The guidelines approved by the board in March 1984 encouraged temporary, nomadic types of structures. In a nod to what had actually been built and the county regulations, the guidelines also said booths with lofts must "be of sound construction with … poles packed in sand or gravel." The guidelines also stated clearly: "NO BRUSH CUTTING ALLOWED this year," under penalty of being expelled from the fair for a year.

Moz Wright, who served on the construction guidelines committee as a board member, wrote a letter titled "How Come?"

that was mailed out to the membership with the guidelines. The letter reminded fair members that "No One Owns the Land. The Country Fair does—and that's all of us." The letter scolded booth folks for cutting too much brush and "building little bonanzas." It encouraged people to become more aware of the group as a whole. "Let's face it," Moz wrote, "as a group we have tendencies toward self-determination and anarchy, but as a group the only way we can become personally free (no one telling you what to do), is to become aware of the effects of our actions on those around us and the Fair in general. Maximum Personal Responsibility equals Maximum Personal Freedom."

With land ownership, another new mindset blossomed among members. As long as the fair had rented property, the next fair had remained a question mark. At the end of each fair, no one was sure if the fair would happen again. But now it became clear that the fair would keep happening every year. When people realized they would be stuck with each other—or with a decision—year after year, compromise became more difficult and conflicts got more heated. In 1984 the fair board established two grievance panels—one for booths and one for staff volunteers. A call went out for volunteers to help mediate the tide of grievances that flowed in after the fair.

Conflict also arose at the fair's annual membership meeting on March 25, 1984. Speeches from two candidates for the board included harsh words about the withholding of food vouchers on the Friday of the 1983 rain fair. Board candidates George Braddock and John Parrot also accused the board of mishandling changes to the fair bylaws and cast blame by mischaracterizing the highway realignment fight.

Worse still, accusations of ballot tampering marred the 1984 board election after many ballots came in with similar handwriting, marked for the same three or four candidates. At the next board meeting, George and John apologized for their inaccurate and inflammatory remarks, and admitted to asking their supporters to vote for only the three or four people on the ballot. They attributed the similar votes to their supporters. While many at the meeting expressed skepticism at that explanation, the board reluctantly voted seven to three to approve the election results.

"I do believe a fraud was involved," Moz said. "We must improve our voting procedure so this kind of thing doesn't happen again. We have agreed we can all function as a board and to get this whole mess over with and get on with the fair, I vote yes."

Board member Ron Chase concurred, "With deep regrets I support this motion. The days when the fair could have a nonpolitical election based on trust are gone. I am voting for the motion only because we do not have time or money to go through another election. It is too close to fair time and that is what I'd like to get on with—the fair." In the months following the fair, the board would appoint an Elections Committee that would be charged with tightening the ballot-handling procedures before the next annual meeting.

In May organizers held another retreat for board members and crew coordinators to plan for the next fair and its long-term future. They discussed ways to run the fair more efficiently, land use plans, fair finances, land conservation, election standards, and the ramifications of the highway realignment through the fair's parking field. They met at Camp White Branch, a church camp nestled at the base of the McKenzie Pass. The route from Eugene wound east along a two-lane highway up the verdant McKenzie River valley into the foothills of the Cascade Range.

The facilities included electrically heated cabins and a large lodge with a kitchen and fireplace. John and Jessie McDonald agreed to cook five meals for the crowd. Robert DeSpain had hired the McDonalds as Main Camp cooks in 1983. "They are such loving, wonderful people," Robert said. "They had cooked for the Hoedads [tree-planting cooperative] and the Hoedads recommended them to me."

The invitation urged participants to "come with a cooperative, willing attitude." It also warned that the camp was affiliated with the Churches of God in Oregon, which prohibited alcoholic beverages and intoxicants on the premises. "We will not be policing our group," the invitation said, "but we expect everyone to be extremely discreet and be aware of the manager's expectations." Fortunately, all went well.

One accomplishment that emerged from the retreat in time to implement for the next fair was a proposal for an Operational Management (OM) Team. Ron Chase suggested it at the retreat after Robert DeSpain kept bringing up to the board, meeting after meeting, that he needed help during the fair event; that as the point

The fair's first Operations Management (OM) team in 1984 (from left): Robert DeSpain, Sallie Edmunds, and Moz Wright.

person, he often felt overwhelmed. People at the retreat hammered out the details of what would be expected of this new management team.

The board would end up approving the plan at its next meeting. After the retreat, the board elected to the OM Team: Robert DeSpain; Moz Wright (entertainer, Entertainment coordinator, and board member); and Sallie Edmunds (coordinator of the new Energy Park). They also approved OM Team trainees Patti Lomont (a crafter, Main Camp sign painter, and musician); Douglas Parker (White Bird counselor and fair crisis training instructor); and Wally Slocum (longtime Main Camp volunteer and Banners coordinator).

The OM Team would become an enduring piece of fair event operations. Different people have volunteered for the team over the years, with each year's membership ranging from three to a dozen people. In 1990, the team would be renamed Back Up Managers, or BUMs. For more than three decades, the fair's management team would help keep the fair running smoothly.

In the spring of 1984, Robert again took on his fair name "Backhoe Bob" to complete a big project that would improve the public's experience at Main Stage. He was finally acting on an idea he had pondered a few years before. "I was talking with Michael Killgallon one afternoon and we were both whining about the fact that we had to bring a septic pump truck into the meadow at Main

Stage to pump those toilets during the fair," Robert recalled. The trucks would distract from the entertainment on the stage. "What a drag that was, and how could we solve that problem?" they asked themselves.

Robert proposed digging holes for concrete holding tanks to temporarily hold the human waste. They would build what amounted to wooden outhouses over holes in the holding tank. After the fair was over and the public had left, the waste could be pumped out of the tanks. But Michael Killgallon poo-poohed the idea; unconvinced that it could work.

So Robert took his idea to Community Village, where he served on the Community Village Coordinating Council. The council approved a six-pack plan to be built between Community Village and the Shady Grove Stage in 1982 when the fair bought the land. "I ordered up a 1,500-gallon holding tank with six holes in the top of it and got together with Bob Dorste and Henry Kunowski in Community Village and we designed the six-pack at the Community Village that eliminated the need for a pumper to come anywhere close to that part of the fair," Robert said. Using those same plans, Ed Moye and Ted Campbell would build a six-pack of toilets near Main Camp.

The rainy weather near the 1983 fair prevented Robert from bringing heavy equipment to the fair site, but in 1984 he hauled his backhoe out to the fair to dig three large holding tanks for toilets near Main Stage. This would allow the fair to keep the sanitation trucks for the temporary toilets out of the center of the fair during the event.

"Now there's six holding tanks in there," Robert said decades later. "But the first three went in in '84 and I used the dirt from those holes—which was a lot of dirt; there was probably eighty to ninety yards of dirt—to start to fill in the rut on East Thirteenth." The fair's pathways had suffered after everyone scraped mud off them during the 1983 rain fair. The paths became even more rutted after the usual winter floodwaters washed over the fair site, scouring the soft paths.

"It was much lower than the ground around it," Robert said, "and people would slip on those sides. ... Because it was such a hazard there, we used the dirt from those tanks to fill that path up and bring it up to level."

Robert dug out holes for the next three holding tanks before the 1985 fair. In a not-very-subtle commentary, organizers dubbed the Main Stage toilet area "Politics Park." Each outhouse door got a hand-painted sign bearing the name of a contemporary politician. With each new election cycle, new names would be swapped in and out to keep Politics Park current for decades.

In June 1984, Main Camp opened as construction volunteers set to work repairing and rebuilding structures for the fair. The annual rite of preparing the land to host a big crowd had begun. Crafters and food booth folks brought working crews to the fair site to get their booths ready for the event. Most took care to meet the new booth construction guidelines the board had issued. The OM Team walked around pre-fair to keep an eye on everything, especially the brush cutting. Several booths ended up on probation for removing brush, while one booth was expelled before the fair for excessive brush removal.

For two weekends before the fair, White Bird Clinic's Zak Schwartz and Douglas Parker again offered Crisis Intervention training seminars at the WOW Hall for all fair volunteers.

The fair's news releases encouraged visitors to take the free chartered Lane Transit District buses that would run every fifteen minutes between Eugene's downtown and the fair site. Admission to the 1984 fair cost four dollars on Friday, and five dollars on Saturday and Sunday, with children under fourteen admitted free and seniors over fifty-five at half-price.

The 1984 Oregon Country Fair opened on Friday, July 13, on a warm summer day with afternoon highs expected to reach eighty-one degrees. The *Peach Pit* Crew published a sixteen-page tabloid paper welcoming fairgoers to the "Sixteenth Annual Oregon Country Fair." The *Peach Pit* listed all the stage lineups plus Community Village workshops for the three days of the fair.

The eclectic mix of musical entertainment included folk, Celtic, jazz, rock, mountain dulcimer, boogie-woogie piano, rhythm & blues, new age, a capella, marimba, and even classical. Main Stage on Saturday featured the biggest names, opening with Sandunga's Latin American folk and closing with dance band The Cashiers with special guests the Radar Angels.

Crafters on both sides of the path displayed an astonishing variety of wares and artistry: intricate wooden boxes, batik and tie-dye clothing, leather hats and vests, stone and crystal jewelry, glazed

Lunch at Main Camp was served from just one table in 1984. Sisters Chelsea and Breana Landman (front) waited not-so-patiently for their dad, Marshall Landman (center back wearing light blue fair T-shirt), to bring them a lunch plate. Other people around the table included (visible clockwise from front left): Santos Narvaez, Palmer Parker, and Zak Schwartz to the right of Marshall. Barely visible in front of Zak in a red-striped shirt was Jill Heiman.

pottery, handmade knives, pillows, quilts, wooden toys and whirly-gigs, wind chimes, stained glass windows and lamps, crochet halter tops, and even pipes and roach clips.

Food booths fired up their ovens and gas stovetops to prepare pizza, fritters, sausages, burritos, barbecue chicken, omelets, tofu wraps, eggrolls, pastries, fried rice and more. On the cold side, fairgoers could choose from ice cream and frozen yogurt, lemonade with or without strawberries, teas, coffee, or fruit smoothies.

Community Village held White Train workshops to educate the public about the transport of nuclear waste, as well as workshops on marijuana law, foot massage and reflexology, herbs for first aid, newsletter production, and master gardening, to name a few. Volunteers led herb identification walks, beehive tours, and the women's grounding circle. In the central courtyard, everyone could participate in New Games that emphasized cooperation.

In addition, the booths surrounding the village green offered fairgoers information from dozens of nonprofit organizations. Community Village also exhibited a peace quilt its members had started that would be sent after the fair to the Soviet Union in a gesture of international friendship. Fairgoers were encouraged to add a square of their own with a message of peace.

"There's hardly a hint of the bad old days," news columnist Don Bishoff noted in the *Register-Guard*. "The only nudity I saw was a bare-bottomed baby. There was a slight scent of pot near one stage, but would-be drug-dealers are evicted by the fair's 220-member security force. What prevails is the peaceful atmosphere of a happy shared experience. … The operation is organized in spades. Local government should operate with such efficiency."

Tom Noddy decorated the W.C. Fields Stage where he performed bubble magic and invited other performers to take a turn. Familiar faces included Artis the Spoonman, juggler Roberto Morganti, and folksinger Faith Petric. Also roaming the paths were Dr. Atomic's Anti-Nuclear Medicine Show, and the Royal Famille du Caniveaux.

The Flying Karamazov Brothers sandwiched in their fair gig between the end of their run in June at Chicago's Goodman Theatre of *The Three Moscowteers* (Paul Magid's musical version of *The Three Musketeeers*), and their upcoming appearance in the Olympic Arts Festival in Los Angeles in July. The U.S. Olympic Committee had tapped Chicago's Goodman Theatre to send the U.S. classical theater entry. The Goodman chose the Flying Karamazov Brothers' juggling version of *A Comedy of Errors*, which had enjoyed a successful run during the 1983 season at the Goodman.

The Brothers K enlisted folk singer Utah Phillips and Tom Noddy (for his puppet prowess) to perform with them on the Circus

Stage, which the entertainers called "Not Not Chumleighland" in order to honor Reverend Chumleigh's request to call it neither "Chumeighland" nor "Not Chumleighland" since he wasn't there. The election year inspired the troupe to present a debate of candidates for president. Stage volunteer John Cloud built a background set that turned the patterns of the American flag into abstract art.

"Utah Phillips was running on the Sloth and Indolence Party," Tom Noddy said, "and he promised that, if elected, he would sit around and scratch his ass and not do a damn thing. His point was that if we citizens wanted something done, we'd have to do it ourselves. I had a puppet candidate who first reminded people of Wavy Gravy's 1980 campaign for Nobody for President ('Who gave you better schools?' 'Nobody!' 'Who gave you a sane foreign policy?' 'Nobody!' ...) but my puppet complained that the problem was that Reagan was elected and therefore 'Nobody Won!' My puppet called on us to vote for 'Anybody! ... Anybody but Reagan.'"

After the fair, the Flying Karamazovs flew to Los Angeles to represent the United States in the Art Olympics. From there, they would travel in their bus to Port Townsend, Washington, to join their Country Fair friends for the 1984 tour of the New Age Old Time Chautauqua.

 ## 1980s
Toby's Tofu Palace

"He couldn't eat dairy products or peanut butter or wheat or nuts. It was a nightmare for a vegetarian."
—Toby Alves, about cooking for her son Olem

The challenges Toby Alves faced in dealing with her son's food allergies would fortuitously lead to a booming family business specializing in tofu products in the 1980s. But the road to get there started inside a humble house-bus, where Toby roasted nuts and seeds on the family wood stove. In 1973 when Toby was twenty-five, she was living in the forested hills of the McKenzie River valley east of Eugene in a converted school bus with her then-husband, Onesmo "Oney" Alves, and their three-year-old son, Jonah.

In the 1970s crafters often converted vehicles into homes to live in as they traveled around the country. "We had lived in various vehicles, but the school bus was the final one," Toby said. Oney and Toby had modified the bus by removing the seats to make room for living quarters and a small kitchen inside, complete with wood stove, upright cabinets, and sink. The raised roof created ample standing room, and a bed accessible by ladder was tucked up under the roofline that extended over the driver's seat of the bus. Oney and Toby painted the outside of the bus a warm shade of brown and trimmed it in cedar shakes. They covered the inside walls with wood paneling, making the space feel like a cozy den.

The couple had joined a group of like-minded nomads traveling the country to sell their wares. "We had a business in our bus called The Cook Stove," Toby said. They coated nuts and seeds in soy sauce and roasted the concoction in small batches on the wood stove. By 1973 they had stopped traveling and settled in the McKenzie River area.

In December 1973 Oney and Toby participated in the Olde English Christmas Fair at the Lane County Fairgrounds. The couple set up a table at the fair to sell their healthy, protein-packed snacks. The Christmas fair was coordinated by Bill and Cindy Wooten and their friend Sandra Bauer, who also coordinated the Oregon Renaissance Faire, the early incarnation of the Oregon Country Fair. At Cindy Wooten's suggestion, Toby signed up for the September 1974 Renaissance Faire, where she sold the roasted nuts in a shared booth.

In late 1974, Toby whipped up a new product—carob clusters—and she and Oney created the Oregon Candy Company. The clusters were placed for sale near the cash registers at natural food stores around Eugene and sold well. For the 1974 Christmas Fair, Toby and Oney packaged gift boxes of roasted nuts and carob clusters.

The next year, the Alves family moved to Eugene so Jonah could attend public school in town. They accepted an invitation from Bill and Cindy Wooten to park their bus in the big yard at the house the Wootens rented on Willakenzie Road in north Eugene.

Toby Alves sold packages of roasted nuts from a shared booth at the 1974 Renaissance Faire.

For the 1975 Oregon Country Renaissance Faire, Toby and Oney built a mobile food cart so they could sell the carob clusters as a frozen treat. "It was unbelievably difficult," Toby said. "They were very popular, but they were really a nighttime item so we had to stay up late. It's just hard to do a cart because you have no place to store your stuff. It was labor-intensive. We did that for a year and we did fine, but it was just too exhausting!" Making it more difficult, Toby was eight-months pregnant with their second son, Olem.

After Olem was born, the Alveses bought property from a

friend near Whiteaker Elementary School. They parked their bus on the land and continued to live in it while Oney converted one room of the shack on the property into a commercially licensed kitchen. "That's where we made our carob clusters," Toby said, "and that's how we got that little business going."

The clusters became so popular that Fred Meyer stores came calling. The company wanted the Alveses to produce enough candy to stock all of the stores in the huge Northwest chain. "But to do that, we'd have to make a lot of big changes," Toby said. "We decided to put an ad in the paper for one week to try to sell the business. If it didn't sell, then we'd make the big plunge. We'd try to borrow some money and do the Fred Meyer thing. Believe it or not, within one week we got a call from two attorneys and two nurses, two different couples. … They bought our business for twenty grand. It was just uncanny because in those days, that was a lot of money."

Meanwhile, Oney and Toby, who were strict vegetarians, had discovered that their son Olem had a number of food allergies. "He couldn't eat dairy products or peanut butter or wheat or nuts," Toby said. "It was a nightmare for a vegetarian. That's how I got involved with tofu. I just started experimenting. I've always been the kind of cook who never followed recipes, just kind of looked at a recipe and got a guideline and went from there. That's how I developed the Tofu Tia. I started putting different spices in with tofu while cooking at home. Then in 1978 we heard that the Country Fair was going to open up to more food booths."

During those years the fair launched what came to be called the "land rush." Fair coordinators would mark the areas where they wanted food booths to go, and prospective booth folks would check them out on a Saturday in springtime. Then on Sunday morning, everyone lined up at the starting point. Coordinators yelled "On your mark, get set, go!" and people ran to their favored booth spot. Oney and Toby landed the location where Toby's Tofu Palace would be found for nearly three decades: next to the Odyssey booth and close to the main entrance of that period. "That was really good for us because a lot of people would hit our booth right at the beginning," Toby said. "Or they'd hit it at the end [on their way home]. That's been a really good spot."

Oney Alves built a second story to the new Toby's Tofu Palace booth in 1979.

The first Tofu Palace menu was relatively limited. The Tofu Tia, consisting of spiced tofu and lettuce wrapped in a corn tortilla, cost sixty-five cents. They offered a drink called the Palace Cooler that "was more like a root beer drink, with sassafras and spearmint," Toby said. After a few years, the Palace Cooler recipe would evolve to an herbal iced tea mixture of hibiscus, lemongrass, and peppermint.

In 1979, Toby joined Mary Wagner as co-coordinators of the food booths for the fair. They worked with county officials and food vendors to develop guidelines for safe food handling under the unusual circumstances found at the fair site.

"The county had absolutely no rules that covered temporary restaurants," Toby said. At the time, there weren't very many events held outside except for the Lane County Fair, which was in an urban area. "We didn't fall under those guidelines because we didn't have running water, we didn't have electricity," Toby said. "We had nothing. Basically, we had to educate George Classen [of the Lane County Health Department] that we were capable of pulling this event off. Thank goodness, he was really quite open-minded. He worked with us and he could see that even though we didn't have running water and we didn't have garbage disposals and all that, we were innovative enough to find alternative ways to make it work."

For example, to create running water, food vendors would hide large water receptacles in the upper rafters of their booths with clean lines running to sink faucets below. Gravity would let water flow into the sinks when the prep folks turned on the faucet. Food booth members would dig French drains at the base of the sinks to contain the water runoff.

In 1980, Oney and Toby split up. They weren't getting along, partly because Oney was a loner and Toby enjoyed being around crowds and doing events like the Oregon Country Fair. "He didn't like it," Toby said. "It was too stressful for him. He just doesn't like being around a lot of people." When they split Oney got the house-bus, where he would live for decades, dedicated to a simplified lifestyle.

For the 1980 Country Fair, a friend of the Alveses, John Cameron, agreed to help Toby with the Tofu Palace booth strictly as a business venture. "That was sort of the beginning of us getting together," Toby said. They found they worked together well at that fair, fell in love, and became romantic partners for the next fifteen years.

Also that year, Toby opened the Blair Island Restaurant in the Whiteaker neighborhood in Eugene, investing her money from the candy company sale. The restaurant derived its name from its location—it was the only building occupying a small, triangular city block on Blair Boulevard. Toby had six partners in the business. "We operated on consensus and it was pretty nuts," she said with a chuckle. The Blair Island group also helped Toby run the Tofu Palace at the fair every July.

Even though it was doing a booming business, Blair Island closed its doors in the fall of 1983. Toby was pregnant, and the ownership group couldn't find anyone to fill her shoes while she took maternity leave. "We tried to sell the restaurant," Toby said. "We tried to hire people to take my place when I had maternity leave. But nobody really wanted to do it without me."

After daughter Chelsea was born, Toby stayed home for a while to take care of the baby. But she needed to figure out a way to make an income to supplement John's house-painting job. "That's when I invented the Tofu Paté," Toby said. She was forty-two when she got her home kitchen commercially licensed and started selling the paté, then called Tofu Salad, to local health food stores. "Because I'd already sold the carob clusters in the stores, I knew a lot of the store owners, so it was really pretty easy to get in," she said.

In the spring of 1984, Toby heard that the Saturday Market was expanding, so she applied and was accepted to operate a new food booth. Between the income from the Saturday Market and the Country Fair, the Tofu Palace booth became a profitable business for Toby and her family. Toby incorporated her business as Tofu Palace Products in 1984. The business made a huge leap when Safeway grocers started selling Toby's Tofu Paté in 1985.

"As the boys got bigger, they became more involved," Toby said. They started out in the food booth. "One of the jobs that has become really important, is called a 'cooler kid'. ... They stand in the front and put ice in the cup, and then they put the drink in the cup and garnish it with mint and orange. That's the way we got our boys to work. When they were young, we were always working. When we had the restaurant, if they wanted to see me, they pretty much had to come down to the restaurant. It was only a few blocks away from our house. ... I just always have worked a lot. It's part of who I am."

All three of Toby's children have come up through the ranks in the booth. "They worked every job," Toby said. "They were cooler kids at first and then became rollers, the people who assembled the orders, and then they became counter people." Toby's daughter Chelsea would eventually help manage the Saturday Market booth.

Toby's son Jonah would earn a business degree in college and take on responsibilities as president of Toby's Family Foods in 1994. In that capacity, he would oversee a considerable expansion of the business, including the building of a new warehouse in Springfield and the purchase of the Genesis Organic Juice product line.

Toby's other son, Olem, helped part-time with the family business, and would play music professionally as an adult. Olem first learned to play guitar from James Thornbury, a dishwasher at Blair Island who performed with several bands. Olem continued to study music, eventually graduating from the University of Oregon School of Music. Olem and his bands would perform frequently at the Oregon Country Fair, the Saturday Market, and the Holiday Market.

The Tofu Palace booth at the Oregon Country Fair would become a big family event and reunion for Blair Island workers. "The fair just got bigger and bigger for us," Toby said. "As my children got older, we would hire their friends. A lot of them would start at the Saturday Market and then they would work at the fair and they would all love it. As they got older, it was like a big family affair where we had a lot of our kids' friends and a lot of our friends. Then people who

Toby served long lines of customers at the Tofu Palace in 1985.

had worked at the [Blair Island] restaurant moved away to California, and they would come up once a year for the fair."

Over the decades, a number of traditions evolved at Tofu Palace. During the fair, "the counter people always dress up," Toby said, "and we try to get everybody on some theme or some color. ... One year we decided to make things out of duct tape. Everybody made all these wild head gear and costumes out of duct tape. So that's really a fun thing. The hard thing about our booth is we're so busy. ... It's a lot of pressure and we expect them to work really hard. ...

"Another of the big things that we do is to have a beautiful dining room where people can come and sit and get away from it all," Toby said. "We always do a big thing with flowers and we have a decorator. Somebody's always in charge of putting tapestries up. We have a couple boxes of things that we always use, but we give people a chance to express themselves and to make the booth look really beautiful."

Tofu Palace workers were always dedicated recyclers. The booth would win the Oregon Country Fair Recycling award several times. Toby often handed out free tofu and coffee in the morning to the Recycling Crew as they made their rounds, as thanks for their hard work. "Talk about a horrible, hard job. ... I mean, people just don't realize. They have to sort everything and it's kind of gross," Toby said. "We really appreciate what they do because it's really hard. Everybody works hard there."

Toby would serve for nearly three decades on the OCF Food Committee with Springfield Creamery's Sue Kesey and other food booth representatives. Toby's family life also would revolve around the fair for more than three decades. "Everyone kind of lived for the fair," Toby said. "You would go out there for as long as you could and just basically live in this other society where you got away from everything that you plugged into. ... As everybody got older and things got more conservative, hippies kind of had to evolve. They cut their hair because they had to get jobs. You know, things just changed. Yet in the summer, people could always go back to the fair. For us, it is our roots."

Toby's Tofu Palace took a one-year hiatus for the 2018 Oregon Country Fair while Toby dealt with health issues, including a recurrence of cancer. The family was planning to reopen Toby's Tofu Palace for the fair's fiftieth anniversary in 2019.

1984
Silk-Screen Artist Diane McWhorter

"All of us, we have this huge, deep emotional investment. We're all so invested in the Country Fair that I'm amazed at how well we interact and cooperate and coordinate."
—Diane McWhorter, silk-screen artist and longtime OCF crafter

In the spring of 1984, Diane McWhorter's new romantic and business partner, Mike Martin, built a sturdy booth near the junction of the Oregon Country Fair's Eight pathway that would become Diane's fair craft "home" for decades. Diane, then age thirty-one, and Mike, thirty-six, had met at Diane's Saturday Market booth, where she sold her hand-designed cards, calendars, and stationery.

Diane stood out at Saturday Market with her small, portable booth that she transported by bicycle. Every Saturday morning she would pack up a box of her artwork, fold and bundle the booth pieces together, and attach it all to her bike. Depending on the weather, she'd bundle herself up as well. She'd haul the entire load by bicycle along the two-mile route from her house to the Saturday Market. Then she'd unpack it and set it up. At the end of the day, the whole procedure would repeat in reverse. For Diane, the weekly bike commute put into practice her belief of living simply to limit her impact on the environment.

She first landed in Eugene in 1975 after a whirlwind series of personal upheavals. Diane had dropped out of college on the East

Coast after majoring in "protesting and civil rights." She felt drawn to head west. Inspired by Woody Guthrie's biography describing his life as a traveling sign painter, she set up a portable sign-painting business. The winds of whimsy and a romance with a cowboy whirled her from Colorado to California. When the cowboy life got a bit too real (brandings and cooking bull "nuts" turned her off), Diane split the scene and headed north to the refuge of an aunt's home.

In Eugene she quickly found her community. Saturday Market perfectly meshed with her talents. Diane kept painting signs—including one for local business Humble Bagel—while adding cards and stationery to sell at the market. She built a portable booth and experimented early on with ways to transport everything by bicycle. Her own makeshift bike transports worked only clumsily, so she asked a friend for help. George Braddock—a construction contractor who also ran the Ritz Sauna booth at the Oregon Country Fair—handcrafted a bicycle cart that Diane would use to ride to market for years. During that time she got more involved with Saturday Market governance, where she learned about the many nuances of making decisions by group consensus. In the early 1980s Diane served as chair of the board of the Saturday Market.

In the meantime, she had sold her artwork at the Oregon Country Fair each summer in a booth she shared with friends. That booth sat near the top of the fair's eight-shaped pathway at Maple Commons, a wide area by a mature maple tree draped in moss and ferns. Far from the bustling Main Stage, this area had a sweet vibe during the fair, with meandering shoppers and strolling musicians. But after a few years, changes in the booth dynamics prompted Diane to move on.

This new booth, new boyfriend, and new business would mark a fresh start in 1984. The booth sidled up to a small vine maple tree and a mature Oregon ash that kept the premises shaded and cool during the fair.

Together, Mike and Diane created a business printing graphics on T-shirts. Unbelievable as it may seem, Americans mainly wore plain T-shirts for underwear until the mid-1980s, when decorated T-shirts started trending as fashion. The young couple found themselves on the cutting edge. Mike built the equipment and worked out technical aspects; Diane designed and printed the shirts.

Diane had already experimented with silk-screened T-shirts to sell in her Saturday Market booth. In 1984, they hired a designer who came up with twenty-five shirt designs. "One of them was a fish," Diane said. Several years later, Mike suggested turning the fish vertical like a tie, and drawing a shirt collar up to the fishtail. "Those tuxedo T-shirts had come out by then," Diane said, "so it was sort of based on that concept."

The Fish-Tie T-shirt drew considerable attention at the wholesale gift shows and sold phenomenally well. One time Diane wore it to a T-shirt trade show at the Denver Convention Center. A sales representative walked up to her and said, "I can sell a million of those shirts. Here's my card." He ended up marketing the Fish Tie T-shirt in his territory spanning the West Coast from California to Alaska. The Fish Tie shirt proved especially popular with the Japanese tourists in Alaska, Diane said.

"I followed up the Fish Tie concept with my Pocket-O-Slugs, which expanded into a line of pocket designs," she said. "It included birds like chickadees and puffins and that was super successful." Mike experimented with fractal designs. "We were doing the first fractal T-shirts available, and we were selling those to MIT and the Boston Art Museum," she said. "I mean, it was something. And it was amazing!"

Eventually they diversified into art ties made of silk. "We got into this little silk manufacturing business, which was pretty fun. They were expensive and we never really made a lot off of those, but they put us into another niche market," Diane said. "We made handmade slug ties and flamingo ties and quite a lot of different fish ties." The silk ties qualified them for craft fairs for several years once the decorated T-shirts lost their artsy novelty. Diane and Mike also brought the designs every summer to their booth at the Oregon Country Fair. Every winter, they ran a booth at the Saturday Market's indoor Holiday Market.

The insane pace of production combined with all the travel to craft shows left them scrambling to keep up with orders. "From '85 to '90 we were just jamming," Diane said. "But we had no clue how to handle it. We got tired of it because you have to have a brand new line every six months—with all new designs—and there was no way I could keep up with that." The workload only got harder after Diane and Mike had a son, John McMartin, in January 1990. Not long after, major pieces of the business started to fall through the cracks. The whole business fell apart by 1992 when Diane and Mike split and went their separate ways.

Diane got the house, the business, and the debt. She shouldered the challenge, relying on her graphic artist skills and sales at the Saturday Market to make ends meet. She also kept the booth at the Oregon Country Fair.

"I had this huge network at Saturday Market and Country Fair," she said. "As a subculture of crafts people in Eugene, we have a really wonderful setup. I stopped doing all the other fairs; I just do Country Fair and Holiday Market and the Saturday Market every week, and because of that and my screen-printing business, it's quite sufficient and I've been doing it for all this time. It's really quite a great foundation."

When John was young, Diane volunteered at his schools, and contacts there opened more doors. "I got to use my skills," she said. "I taught art projects. I hooked up with Paul Otte, the silk artist, and learned how to do silk painting, so that was quite fortuitous. And all this time, I've also been a job artist." She would gladly take a job painting a special sign or silk-screening a batch of shirts or hats when asked.

For a half-dozen years she quit setting up at Saturday Market every week, instead concentrating on rebuilding her old house. But Saturday Market always beckoned, and for decades she commuted by bicycle.

In the 1990s Diane started producing shirts that gently poked fun at Oregon Country Fair culture. "The first one I did was the 'Oregon Country Fair Geezer,'" she said, "and that was a collaboration with my friend Willy Gibboney," a drum maker who sold his drums at Saturday Market and the Oregon Country Fair. Willy drew a cartoon of an old hippie guy saying "This is my billionth fair!"

"The second one was the Curmudgeon," Diane said, "which has a little guy wearing a beer T-shirt and he says, 'There's too damn much magic around here.'" One year Diane created a shirt featuring the Fairy Olympics. Jen-Lin Hodgden, a member of Community Village at the fair, had come across the Pressed Faeries Calendar and brought it to Diane's attention. "On the date of the Country Fair was the 'Millennial Faerie Olympics,'" Diane said. "Seriously, right there. We both said 'Hey!'" Diane dreamed up a bunch of events for the Oregon Country Faerie Olympics and scripted them across the back of a T-shirt. Events included "Fire Juggling, Parade Preparedness, Figure 8 Trotting, Creative Sixpack Line Jumping, Midnight Path Recreation, Om Circle Hand Holding, Rumor Relay, Realtime Re-entry…" The front featured a whimsical drawing of a fairy riding a dragonfly encircled by fairies frolicking in a woodland setting.

Large trees for many years shaded Diane McWhorter's booth 175, shown in springtime.

"One year, we were rebuilding our booth and I did the This Old Booth, which was a comic strip version of 'This Old House,'" she said. "I still love it, and I made a gazillion of those because I thought every crafts person is going to buy one of these. But of course crafts people buy very few crafts, mostly because they have no time to shop. So, yeah, I still have many, many This Old Booth T-shirts." Another year she made Mall of the Woods, "an apocalyptic vision of the future of the fair when it became a mall and there was one lone tree left," Diane said. "All the hippie-dippie things had been all commercialized and co-opted." Another time she riffed on the fair's logo by drawing her own version of a peach upside down, making it more than slightly resemble a person's upturned rear-end. "I did it on the thirtieth anniversary," she said. "I turned it upside down. I made it really beautiful with a tie-dye sort of background. It said, 'Turning the Sacred Upside Down.'"

Diane also got fair approval to sell items screen-printed with the fair's official peach logo. At first, she screen-printed and hand-painted the logo on silk scarves and flags. Later she got the OK to screen-print the peach logo on tote bags to sell at the fair.

In the 2000s, Diane would start screen-printing T-shirts for the *Fair Family News*, the crew that published the fair's newsletter. Other fair crews, including Construction and Child Care, asked her to screen-print special designs on the back of their Oregon Country Fair staff T-shirts. In 2017 the fair Elders especially requested one of her designs for their shirts: two old folks living in a peach.

"I'm working with lots of other volunteers," Diane said. "They'll bring me a design and I'll print it on the back and it's a quick and easy thing. It always happens right at the end, of course, because nobody ever had their T-shirts early and it created a lot of drama right before the fair. I always have a lot of work that's connected to the fair that all has to be done by the deadline and then trying to do my own stuff, too. It's always a very intense period."

Besides the money she made, she experienced a different kind of payoff whenever she would see someone along the fair's path wearing a crew T-shirt she had worked on. "I feel a connection with the people who wear them," she said. "When I see them on the path, I get a little thrill."

In 2011, fair organizers decided to get staff shirts printed as locally as possible. Diane made a bid and won part of the contract, giving her a big job during a relatively slow time in her production schedule before the last-minute orders arrived. While she enjoyed working with fair groups, she also felt an internal dissatisfaction crop up during each fair when she had to deal with rules and hassles as she set up her booth.

"As a long-time craftsperson, I have a completely different feeling about my fair than a volunteer can have because I have a home there," Diane said. "I have a piece of land there, which the fair can tell me a million times that the fair owns the booth and I am using it, but that is not how my emotions are about it. … It's my home. I go out there and I sink right in. I want to do what I want to do. I feel that I should be able to operate as an independent person out there. I shouldn't have to ask anybody any permission.

"But the fair has changed," she said. "The fair has a structure and a hierarchy and a government and a bureaucracy. These feelings that I have are not true. I can't operate independently out there. I do have to ask permission. I do have to follow all the rules. Even when I don't agree with something, I can't necessarily change it. I may have to just do it. ...And I didn't feel right about my conflict. How can I love the fair and still have this complaining side?"

Diane would start volunteering at the fair to try to understand things better. In 2011 she would join the Scribe Tribe, a group of volunteers who would take minutes for fair committees. She first took minutes for Peach Power, a program set up by the fair in the 2000s where ticket-buyers could opt to donate funds to finance alternative power sources at the fair. The Peach Power committee decided where the funds should be spent, such as for solar-powered sound systems for the fair's stages.

Diane also would volunteer to take minutes for the Craft Committee. "Meeting the people, seeing who they were, connecting the names with the faces, seeing how they spoke to me, seeing how they operated, seeing what they were doing," changed Diane's perspectives. She settled in as the Scribe for the Craft Committee, where she would volunteer for many years.

"I didn't know anything about Peach Power," she said. "I had no idea there was all this great energy stuff going on. ... As I started to broaden my knowledge about the fair and realize what volunteers actually did, I saw it wasn't just a bunch of teenage boys driving around in gators in the pathway getting in my way. ... You see how little any individual can do, yet how hard they try and how dedicated everybody is. How truly people come from the heart. Then all the dysfunction melts away for me and becomes hilarious, amusing, and just a natural part of the human interaction."

Her new perspective would come in handy in 2012 when the large Oregon ash next to her booth toppled in the floods the winter before. It knocked out her neighbor's booth, but her booth was mostly spared. The absence of the branches overhead, however, would allow sunlight to flood down and heat the space like an oven. That year, Diane was also struggling with a broken foot that limited her mobility. She scrambled by cell phone to ask friends to bring enough cloth so she could improvise some shade. "It was the worst adjustment we've really had to make," Diane said. "I slept under that tree for so many years." The shade cloth worked and would be reinstalled each year afterward for shade.

As the years clicked by, Diane's appreciation deepened for the fair's organization. "There are so many random things going off and so many people with wild ideas," she said. "So many creative people going off in their own directions without checking with each other, it's amazing that they manage to make that event happen as smoothly as it does, the safe way that it does. I like the psychospiritual rejuvenation idea. It does take all of us and everybody gets so much credit. It's just terrific.

"Even the people who screw up and cause the problems, you learn something from that," she added. "You can make it easier. There are things that can go better. As soon as we pitch in, we realize that it can be what we make it. It totally is ours. It's still a hands-on life, and that pretty much sums me up as a craftsperson. I have built my life, I built my house, I built my family, I built my world. I didn't do it by myself at all, but I feel very powerful in it."

24 1985
Happy Zones

"Many of us who commit our volunteer energy organizing the Fair work year-round at the task. Through our contributions, we actually create a small community complete with water delivery, disposal facilities, recycling, handwashing stands, child care, communications networks, traffic management, information services, security, a Board of Directors, and an Operations Management (OM) Team."
—Marshall Landman, "Welcome to 1985 Oregon Country Fair" in the *Peach Pit*

In its first order of business in 1985, the Oregon Country Fair Board of Directors turned its attention to running a cleaner board election than the year before. An Elections Committee formed in September 1984 recommended changes to the fair's bylaws, setting up an election panel to oversee all aspects of the voting—from preparation of the ballots and a voters' pamphlet to the final count. The new bylaws for the first time made provisions for absentee voting, allowing fair members who could not get to Eugene for the annual meeting to still exercise their right to vote.

The annual meeting on March 31 involved a failed attempt to recall board members George Braddock and John Parrot for their alleged role in the previous years' ballot-marking irregularities. Given that friction, the meeting went relatively smoothly and a new board took shape. Notably, Ron Chase, the stalwart former treasurer who had stayed on since the days of Bill and Cindy Wooten, stepped down from all his fair duties. New board members included Zak Schwartz, White Bird liaison and key presenter for the fair's Crisis Intervention trainings; Patti Lomont, a performer, Main Camp sign-painter, and 1984 OM (Operations Management) Team trainee; and Marshall Landman, one of the original founders of Community Village and an OM Team member.

Continuing board members were Mary Wagner, Moz Wright, Brian Rohter, George Braddock, John Parrott, Robert DeSpain, Frank Sharpy, and alternate Lucy Kingsley Parker.

Robert DeSpain was again elected president, and Anya Montgomery became Treasurer. Secretary KC Renfro resigned in April after Brian Rohter, John Parrot, and George Braddock complained that the minutes KC took for the board were "slanted and editorialized" over the last year. Lucy Kingsley Parker, a White Bird volunteer and Douglas Parker's wife, was named the new secretary. The OM Team for 1985 included Marshall Landman, Moz Wright, Barbara Stern, and Douglas Parker.

Toward the end of April, Robert DeSpain announced his intention to resign as board president as of October 1, 1985. At the same time, he lobbied for the board to change the annual membership meeting from the spring to the fall in order to give each new board more than a couple of months to get organized and plan for the fair. The board approved the new annual meeting timeline at its May 19 meeting.

Also in May, Robert reported to the board that the outlook for routing the highway to the southern alignment was looking better after a big meeting with the Oregon Department of Transportation in Salem. Everyone welcomed the news, while teasing Robert about his new short haircut. The minutes drolly note that Robert now resembled John Foster Dulles (the U.S. secretary of state for Ike Eisenhower). With the highway fight still taking center stage, the board skipped the annual retreat they had held for the three prior years and focused on the basics of putting on the fair.

White Bird's Zak Schwartz and Douglas Parker again led Crisis Intervention trainings for all fair volunteers who dealt with the public. Main Camp opened in June and the annual mowing and hay-baling got underway in the fields that would become parking lots for the event. Crafters and restauranteurs came out to check their booths and make repairs. All the pieces were clicking into place in the run-up to the fair, except for one piece of the entertainment schedule.

For the first time since 1975, the Flying Karamazov Brothers would not perform at the Oregon Country Fair. Instead, they were in Europe filming a movie, *The Jewel of the Nile*, with Michael Douglas, Kathleen Turner, and Danny DeVito, as well as their friend-in-comedy Avner the Eccentric (who played The Jewel, a scene-stealing holy man). The hit comedy film was a sequel to *Romancing the Stone*. The Brothers K lent their juggling prowess to a parade of ludicrous situations in the film and enjoyed the experience immensely, even at the cost of missing the fair.

In the absence of the famed jugglers, fair Entertainment coordinators invited Bliss Kolb and Bob Venezia, who called themselves Laughing Moon Theater, to produce the show at the Circus Stage (aka Not-Not-Chumleighland). The Flying Karamazov Brothers generously offered the pair a free ride to the fair from California's Bay Area, where they lived, on the official FKB bus driven by Bud Chase.

Bud had by then become part of the juggling troupe's traveling entourage, playing in the Kamikazi band for the Flying Karamazov Brothers' stage performances. Bud's first gig with them was in 1982, for Paul "Dmitri" Magid's vaudeville version of *The Comedy of Errors* at the Goodman Theatre in Chicago. Bud played sousaphone and juggled on the timpani drums. Soon Jana Chase flew out from their Round Mountain Farm commune in California to join Bud. Jana's sewing skills came in handy, and they both were welcomed into the Karamazov stage family.

In 1984 the Flying Karamazov Brothers flew Bud and Jana out to Duluth, Iowa, so that Bud—who still ran his auto repair shop at Round Mountain Farm—could inspect a 1954 Scenicruiser bus that the Karamazovs wanted to purchase. The old bus checked out, so the Brothers K hired Bud and Jana to drive the bus back to the West Coast. The busy jugglers had to get there earlier, so they would fly back to participate in the Oregon Country Fair. Everyone was supposed to meet at the fair, but the bus wasn't in quite as good repair as first appearances suggested. The Scenicruiser broke down in Council Bluffs, Iowa, and the delay caused Bud and Jana to miss the fair. Instead, they drove the repaired bus directly to Los Angeles, where the Brothers K would be representing the United States at the Olympics Arts Festival, performing *The Comedy of Errors* right after their gig at the Country Fair. Bud played in the Kamikazi band for the

Karamazov's show at the Art Olympics.

In 1985, Bud and Jana were dispatched in the Scenicruiser to drive Bliss Kolb and Bob Venezia to the fair. "I really liked Bob and Bliss," Bud said, "and I was looking forward to hanging out with them and visiting on the bus. But those bastards spent the whole time [at the back of the bus] writing. They wrote their show! They wrote this great show." The clever pair based their script for the Gen-Con show on the premise of a multinational corporation called General Conglomerate that planned to modernize the fair with cement bleachers and Astroturf. When a player in the show pointed out that the fair had already purchased the land, the corporate shills pulled out a contract trumping that claim, showing that Gen-Con owned the mineral rights.

"Rebo [Hanson] wrote a great song that went with the show," Jana Chase said, singing a few lines: "Gen-Con, we're the people's people, your friendly multinational cor-por-a-tion. Where would you be-e-e without us? Gen-Con, we're the people's people."

Tom Noddy noted that the show was rewritten after the first few performances. "Bliss had actually written the show in such a way that it ended with us on the losing end," Tom said. "These hilarious corporate clowns had the power and we had none, the idea being that we, fair family, had to not be complacent and still had work to do if we wanted to own our labor and our creativity.

"But Bliss conceded after one or two shows that that theatrical idea just fell flat in this context. We changed over to an ending whereby Jan Luby and Faith Petric led a revolt and called on the audience to join us in taking back our fair! And they could help right now by putting money into the hats that were then passed among them," Tom said. "This allowed our happy audiences to leave our area of the fair and go on to other happy zones."

And happy zones abounded for fairgoers. Temperatures in the high 80s and blue skies welcomed everyone to enjoy a glorious summer weekend at the 1985 Oregon Country Fair. Folk music predominated on the stages, including Seattle performer Jim Page with his folk song commentaries, the Eugene Peace Choir, Ron Lloyd & Friends, pianist Scott Cossu of Windham Hill, Baby Gramps singing in cartoon voices, and the fun harmonies of Girls Who Wear Glasses (Jan Luby and Rebecca "Rebo" Hanson). Main Stage got the

People hiked from the parking lot fields to the front entrance of the fair.

Ron Lloyd played the Shady Grove Stage in 1986.

dance beat going with marimba from Shumba and Balafon, Ritmo Tropicale's Latin salsa, the Jackals' rockabilly, and the J-Walkers' ska rock.

Energy Park expanded its exhibitors. A booth on easy ways to conserve energy at home was sponsored by the Bonneville Power Administration, which operates the Columbia River hydroelectric dams that provide energy to the region. Across the way in a different

Energy Park booth, the Northwest Power Planning Council offered information on protecting fish from the dams' turbines. Agricultural issues were highlighted by Tilth, the certifier of organic produce in Oregon and Organically Grown Cooperative, a consortium of local organic farmers that by then had been going for eight years. Lane Transit District and the City of Eugene Carpool Program showed people how they could use less gas for transportation.

Community Village workshops for fairgoers included consensus decision-making, tarot reading, child development, community organizing, and introduction to nonviolent action. Activities ranged from Tai Chi and New Games in the Commons to face painting in the Arts Booth.

Fairgoers took in a sensual symphony, wandering along the eight-shaped path and stopping to check out the rustic booths stuffed with colorful crafts: batik clothing, natural wind chimes, intricate hand-carved boxes, hand-tooled leather belts, beaded bags, bright hairclips.

Twice a day, the Fighting Instruments of Karma Marching Chamber Band/Orchestra paraded through the Eight—drums booming and horns blaring—to entice an audience to the show at Circus Stage. Fairgoers pointed and smiled at the giant puppets dancing along behind the band. The parade remained highly popular among the crafters.

"To me, the parade every year is an absolute high fair moment," said Peter Eberhardt, who ran a map booth at Upper River Loop and also did cartography for the fair. "That just absolutely does it for me, to see the band that ends up getting down to the Circus playing the 'The Teddy Bear's Picnic.' We have a booth etiquette where everyone stops what we're doing, comes to the front, and claps and sings with them. We take pictures. It's grand to see the giant puppets stroll through and all the costumed folks. It's just exhilarating!"

Tom Noddy stayed busy with the Gen-Con show, but the fair continued using the W.C. Fields Stage that Tom had started in 1981. Taking a tip from previous years, new Entertainment Coordinator Marge Wise booked comedy vaudeville acts every thirty minutes at the W.C. Fields Stage and another small platform set up at Daredevil Meadow. Bob Venezia and Bliss Kolb managed enough time away from Gen-Con to perform as Laughing Moon Theater. The stages also featured Girls Who Wear Glasses, the Mud Bay Jugglers, Dr.

Peter Eberhardt's map booth in 1983 along Upper River Loop.

Atomic's Medicine Show, Rachel the Storyteller, and juggling jokester Izzy Tooinksy. The two small vaudeville stages at opposite ends of the Eight provided welcome venues, getting some entertainers out of the clogged-up paths.

Even without the Flying Karamazov Brothers, the fair operated on the premise that the shows must go on and the Midnight Show was no exception. After the crowds had gone home, a bevy of acts got a chance to strut their stuff on stage to the delight of the crafters and volunteers lounging on blankets in front of Main Stage, laughing and enjoying the good times with good friends.

This time there would be a difference, though. Paul Magid, aka Dmitri Karamazov, had been running the Midnight Show ever since Reverend Chumleigh left in 1981. Paul would let anyone up on Main Stage. He signed up all comers at 7:30 Saturday evening before the show. The entire production grew longer and longer each year, eventually lasting until dawn and thoroughly frying the performers who still had shows to stage on Sunday.

In 1985, Tom Noddy saw his chance to run the Midnight show while Paul Magid and all the other Flying Karamazovs were away filming *The Jewel of the Nile*. Tom had devised a plan to shorten the show. He sent a letter to all the performers titled "Midnight Show Information."

In the beginning there was Reverend Chumleigh and he was good. Chumleigh begat Chumleighland and it was good. Chumleighland begat the Midnight Show and it was good. The Midnight Show did grow and prosper and it was good. It did come to pass that the Midnight Show outgrew Chumleighland and it was banished from the Garden and did move onto the barren stage called Main. There on Main Stage, the Midnight Show acts did multiply and it was good. Jugglers begat jugglers, musicians begat musicians, Spoonman begat Spoonboy, poets begat storytellers, dancers begat dancers, magicians begat magicians and it was still pretty good. The commandment came from Someone or Something on high to someone high on something:
    THOU SHALT NOT COMMIT A SHOW LATER THAN TWO O'CLOCK A.M.
    The theologians who study these matters did interpret this commandment to mean that the show should begin earlier. This was done and still the show ended at 3:30 a.m.

The letter went on to explain that the show would be limited to four hours and there was not enough time to include every great act at the fair. It noted that excellent acts would have to be excluded because "there is simply too much talent at this fair." Those who were chosen to be in the Midnight Show received a blue "draft notice" that indicated they would be on the list to perform. Tom signed the letter *Coordinator of Anarchy*.

Tom also held a meeting on Friday night of the fair to give anyone a chance to speak up and stop what he was doing. Only four people came, and they all just wanted to be in the show. Tom happened to have brought exactly four draft notices with him. The vaudeville-heavy Midnight Show ran from 10:00 p.m. until 2:00 a.m. and everyone left happy.

At the July board meeting after the fair, Robert DeSpain reported that attendance topped 15,000 people in 1985, and that the fair would just about break even on income, counting all expenses. In August, the board approved new bylaws that formalized the decision to move the annual membership meeting to the fall. At that first fall meeting in September 1985, board members explained why they had switched the dates. The previous schedule—with elections in April and Main Camp opening in June—had left precious little time for new board members and officers to get up to speed in their new roles, resulting in a lot of stress during the fair. The new schedule would allow nine months for people to grow into their roles and establish working relationships before the next fair rolled around.

No new board members were elected at the annual meeting in order to not cut short any elected terms. Instead, terms were extended and elections were set for fall 1986. Robert triumphantly noted that the fight over the highway route to the Oregon Coast had concluded favorably to the fair. The new Highway 126 would stretch south of the fair property, significantly reducing the impact on the fair's parking lot and sound ambiance.

Also at the annual meeting, Peter Eberhardt announced he would coordinate the fair's entry into the Eugene Celebration Parade in September. He had already lined up the Horse Crew (who patrolled traffic during the fair) and the giant puppets, and he invited any member interested to show up wearing their Oregon Country Fair staff shirt to march with the group. The Fighting Instruments of Karma Marching Chamber Band/Orchestra agreed to participate.

The fair's entry would make quite a splash on the streets of downtown Eugene, with a marching band, giant puppets, equestrians, and dozens of people sporting Oregon Country Fair staff T-shirts.

The Oregon Country Fair often won prizes in the 1980s for its entries in the Eugene Celebration Parade.

They had so much fun, Peter agreed to coordinate the fair's entry to the Eugene Celebration Parade for the next two years, and the entry got bigger and better each time. In 1986, the fair won first place for Marching Bands. In 1987, the fair's entry in the Eugene Celebration Parade won three blue ribbons—Best Costumes, Best Non-Commercial, Best Non-Float—and the Grand Prize trophy. In 1988, Don Hathaway of Energy Park stepped up to coordinate the fair's entry into the Eugene Celebration Parade, where the fair again placed first among the Non-Commercial and Non-Float entries.

1985
Jay Hogan and Risk of Change

"I cry out
I'm going to take the risk to change.
What I know
is that it's never ever gonna be the same."
 —chorus of Parachute Club's song "Act of an Innocent,"
 from the album, *At the Feet of the Moon*

Jay Hogan had so much fun at the 1983 Oregon Country Fair wearing the giant puppet Hoshigose and interacting with the crowds that he wrote a thank-you note to mentor Leo de Flambeaux. "I told him what a good time I had at the fair and how much I really wanted to be there again," Jay said. Meanwhile, Jay moved to Portland from Seattle and introduced his friend Glen Corson to the giant puppet. They had a blast taking turns wearing Hoshigose at the Art Quake in Portland. Jay said Glen "was just a natural. He had the total enthusiasm for doing the puppetry in the crowds."

In previous years, Glen had managed to sneak in to the fair overnight by hiding out during the Sweep, when Security Crews ushered the public out of the fair. Jay invited Glen to come out to the 1984 fair to see if they could persuade Leo to let Glen help with the puppets to earn one of the few coveted overnight passes in Leo's hands. "You should bring a really nice food offering to just show up contributing," Jay advised Glen. Jay later noted: "It turned out to be this perfect moment when we arrived. Glen brought this tray that was the most gorgeous fruit tray you've ever seen. It looked like a Hindu temple offering."

Jay told Leo that Glen had talent working the giant puppets and without hesitating, Leo agreed to give him a pass. "Leo was terribly nonchalant about it," Glen recalled. "He said, 'yeah sure, here it is.' I get it now, but I didn't know what this was all about."

"You can imagine how this was," Jay observed, "because I'm pretty sure Leo only got eight passes. At the time he had a few puppeteers, a few belly dancers and a couple of musicians. We had a great year. ... They called us the Mystic Krewe of Prince Prospero of the Knights of the Lost Realm."

But in 1985, Prince Prospero (aka Leo) stayed home from the fair. "He said he was tired of being broke," Jay said. "He'd often quit his job to do the fair, and I think there might have been more to it—the burnout factor." Leo's perfectionism could generate creative tension with other performers, and he frequently clashed with the two musicians of the Brothers of the Baladi. "When Leo was unhappy, he had a dark cloud," Jay said. "And that's not an unusual thing in a really creative person with a big personality."

David Ti (pronounced "tea"), a stilt-walker who had joined Leo's Mystic Krewe at the 1982 fair, took up the role of liaison between the puppeteers and the fair. "Ti was really creative," Jay said. "He was the only one in our group who had any money. He had his own business. The rest of us were pretty poor hippies at the time." Jay, Glen, and Glen's boyfriend Tom Hambleton started driving up nearly every weekend from Portland to Ti's house in Seattle to work on their puppets. Their creativity clicked, and they often stayed up all night talking about their visions and the creative process. "We brought different things to the group process," Jay said. "We worked really well together, and we all were passionate about the fair. ...

"We had this grandiose idea of doing a twenty-eight-foot-long giant koi puppet, kind of like a Korean dragon," Jay said. The giant koi would make its debut on the paths of the 1985 Oregon Country Fair. "It was enormous. Ti had a windsock business—making giant fish windsocks—so for him it was like doing this giant parade version." Everyone worked on the large papier-mâché head. At the same time, Jay and Glen also built two giant Rastafarian puppets named Jahman and Rastafaerie, and Tom crafted Odo, a round-faced puppet

Odo first appeared at the fair in 1985 in a shaman's outfit sewn by Tom Hambleton.

with bright paint splotches on his cheeks and a mouth perpetually puckered in a surprised "O." That first year, Odo was dressed in a simple, brown robe. The next year, Odo would get a new "patchy-patchy" robe covered with bright-colored strips of cloth that danced in the air with every step.

Another friend, Teddy Bernard, joined them with his belly-dancing puppet. "Teddy comes to his first fair with the troupe and brings this amazing belly dancer with the hips all loose," Jay said. "Her name was Fatima." With so many giant puppets, the troupe got in the way of the belly dancing scene around Gypsy Caravan Stage, so they moved their tents and puppet-staging area next to the public path. There, Ti and Jay built a screen to help keep the campsite out of view from the passing throngs. Not everyone's tent fit in such a tiny space, so a few puppeteers set up their tents farther back in the woods.

"The thing about the puppets is, they're a lot of work," Jay said. "It's like having babies, only they're twelve feet tall and they have no muscle control. You have to do everything. And their clothes need to be ironed, washed, and neatly folded. All those kinds of things."

With Ti on stilts, parading through the fair became even more of a challenge. "It was strange doing stilts and giant puppets because the crowd often cannot tell the difference," Jay said. "Yet to anyone who does it, there's a big difference to whether you're nine feet tall or you're underneath something. But we loved it! It was such a fun way to see the fair, to put on a puppet and go run through the Eight. You got to see everybody there. ... And 1985 was such an amazing year. The group energy! That year I met Peter Eberhardt, and he told me how much he loved the puppets. Especially Hoshigose is one of his favorite things about the fair, and we had a really nice connection."

After the fair, Peter, the fair's cartographer, volunteered to organize the OCF's entry into the 1985 Eugene Celebration Parade in September. He offered the puppeteers gas money to bring the puppets to Eugene. They packed up Hoshigose and the two giant Rasta puppets to parade down the streets with the Fighting Instruments of Karma Marching Band/Orchestra leading the way, followed by dozens of fair volunteers. The Traffic Equestrian Crew brought up the rear.

Around that same time, the puppeteers went on a retreat to the Oregon Coast to revel in their good fair times and plan their future. The Country Fair had paid the group fifty dollars for their performances. They spent their earnings on clam chowder at a restaurant in Florence. Then they drove along Oregon's coastline—where evergreen-covered mountains gave way to miles of sand dunes—with the car's tape deck blasting Caribbean-beat pop tunes from *At the Feet of the Moon*, by the Canadian band Parachute Club.

They set up their tents among the sand dunes at the edge of the Pacific Ocean. With the waves whooshing in the background, they talked, toked, drank, and bonded. "We talked a lot about what we were doing," Glen recalled. "You know how you feel after the fair—that it went so fast and you didn't get to hug everybody. We communed with ourselves. ... We were casting about for who we were becoming, because we knew we were moving beyond Leo's patriarchal structure. We had created something of our own and we decided that what we were doing was mutiny."

Jay felt the same way. "We realized that we were no longer what Leo had as the Mystic Krewe, and we wondered what to call ourselves. Ti had an album we were listening to that year as we made the puppets, from the Parachute Club." One track in particular struck a chord: "The Act of an Innocent." The lyrics to the breakup song seemed apt.

"I cry out
I'm gonna take the risk to change.
What I know
is that I'm never ever gonna be the same."

The phrase "Risk to Change" resonated deeply with the nascent troupe. Jay suggested changing "to" to "of," and everyone agreed on their new name: Risk of Change.

But they would eventually learn that fair organizers didn't get the memo. Only a few people at the fair knew they had been the Mystic Krewe of Prince Prospero of the Knights of the Lost Realm. Without Prince Prospero (aka Leo de Flambeaux) at the helm, the troupe would discover they were both mysterious and invisible to fair coordinators.

"In the 1985 fair, we were really cramped," Jay said. "We had these sweaty costumes and they all got dirty" from resting on bare ground next to people's tents. "We had this idea of building a little platform, a floor," he said. Tom Hambleton was a carpenter. A friend donated some tongue-and-groove cedar for the project and Tom contacted the fair's Construction Crew early and often to get signoff on building a small platform for their wardrobe area back in the woods near Gypsy Caravan Stage. They were eager to follow all the rules and thought they had covered their bases, but about two weeks before the fair, an alarmed coordinator phoned David Ti in Seattle. "Excuse me, what is this?" the volunteer asked him. "You know performers do not have booths."

"Somebody came around and said, 'What the hell is this? There's no stage here. Who's doing this?'" Jay recalled. "I don't know about now, but back then the shit would hit the fan every year about a week or two before the fair about something. That year it was us: Who is this group? We didn't fit in any category. We were part of Entertainment but we didn't camp at Entertainment Camp. We weren't stage performers, and because we'd had this Mystic Crew non persona, nobody knew who we were except [former Entertainment Coordinator] Moz [Wright] and a couple of other people.

"And suddenly, it was up in the air. People said, 'No, this can't be here.' Suddenly we were this hot potato," Jay said. "We had no real billing, we just appeared out of nowhere. … I don't know if you can imagine what it was like for those of us committed to working on puppets all year. We felt evicted. We didn't fit into any categories." New name or not, to the fair they remained truly in a Lost Realm.

Jay contacted 1986 Entertainment Coordinator Marge Wise to plead the case for the troupe. "We felt like we were the in-house puppet troupe, and it was a big to-do," Jay said. Jay, Tom, and Glen drove down to Eugene the weekend before the fair to try to work things out. They strategized over a breakfast at the Keystone Café in Eugene and then headed out to the fair site west of town. Luckily, on site they ran into Don Hathaway, a volunteer with Energy Park who was happy to see them.

"Hey, I've got an idea," Don said. "Energy Park has been threatened with being moved out to the parking lot because we're such a boring spot in the fair, and we would like to adopt you. We're a separate part within the fair, so we can give you this spot to camp." Energy Park had experienced troubles in previous years with people sneaking in to a part of their camping area on the periphery near an access road. They offered the area to the puppeteers for camping. Risk of Change would gain a home at the fair. Their new campsite would block off the flow of people sneaking into Energy Park, while also bringing in the bright, active energy of giant puppets parading in and out of Energy Park. It was a true win-win situation.

"We pulled the floor up, which we had sunk with rebar into the ground," Jay said. "We carried the whole platform to Energy Park, twenty people walking our floor over. … We called it Puppetland because it was home, it was *land*. At the fair, that's a big deal." The arrangement turned into such a success that Energy Park would continue to host Puppetland for decades to come. "Energy Park took us in," Jay said. "We had eighty people taking us in as family, telling us how much they loved us, how much they loved our energy."

To bring even more good energy to Energy Park, volunteers established Kesey Stage, named in honor of the Kesey family who ran the Springfield Creamery booth at the entrance to Energy Park. The stage often booked marimba bands, and as the puppets emerged from their camp sites to go parade on the paths of the Eight, they would delight the crowds by dancing to the music all the way to the path. "We always did the Circus parades," Jay said. "That was the main focus. We would take the puppets and characters out just to wander on their own, but the main focus was to follow each Circus parade and the Torchlight parade for the Midnight Show."

In 1987, Peter Eberthardt made sure the troupe would be noticed and recognized by fair organizers. He drew a likeness of Jahman, the giant Rasta puppet, on the fair map at the far edge of Energy Park, and noted at that spot: "Risk of Change, Giant Puppets."

Ironically, Risk of Change wore completely different costumes in 1987. Teddy, who was a professional costumer, had just finished working on a production in Idaho of *A Midsummer Night's Dream*. He brought a bunch of the Fairy World costumes for the troupe to wear and they put fairies on parade. Instead of wearing a giant puppet, Jay loped along the path on his new stilts as a tiny fairy. David Ti had taught him how to walk on stilts, and Jay had practiced all year.

When not worn, Risk of Change's giant puppets lived in Energy Park (from left): Odo, wearing his bright new "patchy-patchy" robe; Rastafaerie; and Fatima, the belly-dancing puppet made by Teddy Bernard. The Risk of Change Mummers banner (in background) marked the entrance to Puppetland.

"Instead of trying to make myself look like I was really big, I tried to make myself look like I was really small," Jay said. "I wore black and my stilts were all black with black flat pants." His outfit featured fairy wings and tiny fake fairy legs emerging from his back. The costume created the illusion of a tiny fairy flying above the path. "I even took it out at night. In the dark, the illusion really worked," Jay said

Mummers and friends in the early 1990s (from left); Canis Millican, Naomi Singer, Jay Hogan, Todd Hildebrandt, and David Horste aka Leo Sunshine. Naomi wore a beard wig harvested from Todd's face some year earlier. Jay dressed up like Saturday Night Live character Father Guido Sarducci because he was singing backup at the fair for Mother Zosima, who dressed as a nun.

with a chuckle. "After that fair, somebody came by and said, 'You're that guy! You blew one of my friends so far away he still hasn't come down.' I had a lot of fun with that."

The puppet troupe would grow closer each year. The tight circle of friends—Glen, Tom, Ti, and Jay—threw large "amazing" dance parties for their friends. They would clear out all the furniture and decorate lavishly. In the mid-1980s, Jay moved in with Glen and his roommates to a place they called Savier House in Portland. "That kind of became our Fair Central," Jay said. "We had a basement and Glen and I were there and Tom was around a lot. We had parties and I started to see this really magical thing we were doing. It seemed like the characters that we were creating were having an effect on our personalities, that we were manifesting, channeling these different energies."

The basement became their creative studio. They started to add other characters to their giant puppets and stilt-walkers as their concept of "character" expanded to "creations utilizing mask, costuming, improvisation, and spectacle including, but not limited to, puppets," Glen said. Their name morphed to Risk of Change Mask and Giant Puppet Troupe. Also in the troupe were Canis Millican, Cyn Holder, Helen DeNormanville, Jeff Bale aka Judy Jensen, and Eric Slade.

"Every January, I would start it up," Jay said. "I would start asking all my housemates: 'So, who are you going to be at the fair this year? What are you working on?' Especially with papier-mâché, there is a huge amount of work to be done. You really need to be working on it months ahead. At first people were like, 'God, why are you so intense about this? It's six months away!' But for me, I definitely thought about it year-round, and wanted to stir up passion for what we were doing."

Every year, they would bring something new to the fair. By the early 1990s, the troupe would branch out beyond just following the Circus parade and started creating their own parade "jams." One year they all brought black-and-white costumes. "Black-and-white optical is one of my favorite things," Jay said. "It's so high contrast with all the rainbow colors at the fair. So for many years, Risk of Change has done a black and white jam." Dave McKay created a giant skeleton bride puppet, inspired by imagery from Dias de los Muertos. Another year, the troupe created a child Rastafarian, named Irie, for Rastafaerie and Jahman.

Even though Jahman was featured for several years on the fair map, Jay considered Odo, created by Tom Hambleton, as the group's signature puppet. "He's just so colorful, lightweight, and really fun," Jay said. Fairgoers would be able to spot Odo's cheerful face rising above the crowds for decades to come.

"One of the weird things about doing giant puppets is people want to hug you," Jay said. "They reach around you and there's this big backpack frame you're all encased in. That's what they get and it's always really weird. We tried padding the puppets to make them a little friendlier to hug, but it didn't help much." Soon they were designing tree puppets, made to be soft and accessible for hugging.

One fair they dressed up to resemble the Maxfield Parrish painting of the lantern-bearers. "It's a very popular image," Jay said. "They're wearing these white-and-black Pierrot costumes. It's twilight and they carry these round Japanese paper lanterns. Terry had the idea to do it collectively. By that time, the level of costume-making and mask-making was really high in the group, plus we were all getting along still.…. We did a twilight procession. People at the fair loved it. That was a really sweet one."

About the same time, the troupe would start parading in a "morning jam" for the overnight campers before the public came in. "The Javacrucian parade was a really memorable one," Jay said with a smile. The troupe fashioned out of papier-mâché a giant marijuana spliff, giant cups of coffee, and a giant pipe. Troupe members wore silly pajamas, fuzzy slippers, and wild hairdos looking like they had just woken up, which was true for many of them.

"We had this whole thing about coffee and marijuana for breakfast: 'The breakfast of champions,'" Jay recalled, laughing. "We had chants: 'Wake up, get up, wake up, get up, grind it up, perk it up, stir it up, drink it up, java, java, java, java, java, java, java, java!' We'd all start chanting and we would go out at 9:00 a.m. to get coffee. … We all worshipped the black bean, god caffeine. The crowd, oh, people loved it! For one thing, people weren't working the crowd at 9:00 a.m., and it was really wild."

For several years in the 1990s, the troupe would parade as trolls. Dave made the first one, Troll de Bogen. "We loved it," Jay said. "Troll de Bogen was the most delightful character. He was so much fun." They would create a troll family the next year. "That's what Risk of Change was really good at," Jay said. "We sometimes did things where we were remarkably similar, but mostly we had a theme and everybody was uniquely similar. So everybody made troll characters."

Jay would create a troll lady, Troll de Mor. "She went out flirting with guys," Jay said. "She had an articulated mouth with cow teeth. It's a very fun mask. She had real silicon breasts and padded hips. The funniest thing is, you can see how homely I was. But the guys went ga-ga! I had guys fondling me—like can't they tell? Come on, that I'm really a guy? And that this is all fake and that I have the scariest teeth you've ever seen in your life!"

The next year, they would stage a troll wedding even though the loving feeling in the troupe was starting to fade. Some of the trolls developed an attitude. "While some of the trolls were sort of dear, kind of Norwegian, loving trolls, a lot of them were not very nice trolls," Jay said. "In a way, that was the start of Risk of Change not getting along. It was doing the trolls, we started manifesting cantankerousness."

Leo de Flambeaux returned to the fair in 1988 to hang out with his friends in the troupe and to perform his belly dancing routine along the path. He would come back once more in 1993 for a poignant visit when he knew he was dying of AIDS. "We hadn't seen him in years," Jay said. "He'd been living in Ashland, and I did visit him during that time. But in 1993 he knew he was dying. He looked really good still. He came to the fair and he did a ceremony—a give-away." Leo handed Jay a favorite jacket and distributed other treasures among the gathered circle of friends. Leo died later that year.

By the mid-1990s the troupe had tragically lost five of its members—plus dozens of friends—to the AIDS epidemic that was sweeping the nation. Risk of Change created a Mardi Gras funeral procession to honor those who had passed to the other side. "Traditionally in New Orleans, when they had the funeral procession to the cemetery," Jay said, "they'd play a dirge, and then on the way to the wake—the party afterward—they'd play the same music, real happy. And so we did that. We asked the band to send us a musician, or musicians, and only one person shows up—it's Morgen (Spiess), with his clown nose and the instrument he has is a metal clarinet." (Morgen played clarinet for the fair's Sweep each evening for many decades.)

For the funeral procession, the Risk of Change troupe wore all-white blousy Pierrot-clown-style costumes with their faces painted white. They carried white paper lanterns suspended from long bamboo poles. Jay brought a metal clarinet with a kazoo inside, since he couldn't actually play clarinet. He and Morgen improvised a duet funeral dirge to lead the procession. Slowly parading behind them, the rest of the troop quietly chanted the names of those who had departed. "We did this whole ceremony," Jay said. "We recognized that we weren't just doing a masquerade. This wasn't just like frolicking on the path—'Hey, everybody look at me.' It was shamanic ritual. We were doing this very meaningful—playful and silly, yes, but also significant working to transform the world."

Info Crew volunteer Chris Bauske vividly remembered that particular parade; it imprinted on her one of her most poignant fair memories. "They were dressed in these most ethereal costumes of white," she said, "which at the fair was unheard of because everything was so dirty all the time you really couldn't keep things white. ... They were chanting and humming, very ethereal, very soothing, very like elvish music. I stood there and each of them wove around me humming and very quietly singing lullabyes, religious chants, and sacred chants, and interwoven among these words were the names of humans. I don't remember the names, but every person in that troupe had names to tell. It was very sad and very touching. But I didn't know what was going on. They went past me and they went off into the fair toward Main Stage. I was struck by this deeply spiritual and earth-shaking sadness."

Later at that fair or the next one, Chris wasn't exactly sure which, she would learn more about that parade at a coincidental meeting in the sauna. "This guy comes up to me in the sauna," Chris recalled, "and says something like, 'Hi, I saw you in the grove last year, didn't I?' I kind of looked at him and of course he's in the sauna, so he's naked. Not in white face, definitely. And I said, 'Were you one of the Pierrots?' And he said, 'Yes!' I said, 'Oh.' He said, 'I remember you. You were really good with us.' I said, 'I was?' He said, 'Yeah. I think you got what we were doing.' I said, 'Um, what were you doing?' He said, 'Honey, we were reciting the names of the first victims of AIDS. We had lost partners, we lost kids.'

"And for many years after that, I'd see this guy in the sauna." Chris said in 2004. "Every year we'd check in. I haven't seen him for several years. I haven't been going to the sauna as much as I used to. It was a wonderful touchstone for me, to always see him. Never knew his name."

In 1994 the fair asked Risk of Change to create a giant peach for the fair's twenty-fifth anniversary celebration that year. The troupe took pride in the quality of its costuming, and the fair's commission showed faith in those high standards.

The Giant Peach before it was brought to the fair to hang at the top of the Spirit Tower in 1994.

"We didn't want it to be to the level of Disney," Jay said. "We didn't want automatons. We wanted it to be folk art done to a really high level of artistry and sophistication, where it looks really good at close range. ...

"The fair offered us $500 and we took to calling it the $5,000 peach, counting the time we put into it," Jay said. "It's made with special batting that's mildew-proof. Wendy was dyeing fabric for the Seattle Ballet, so she dyed the silk velvet that makes the peach. People did different parts of it. It was stippled by hand; I did the leaves."

In 1988 Jay moved to Takilma, Oregon, with another member of the troupe, Kevin Moore. About that time, Jay started seeing Todd Hildebrandt, who would become his life partner, and Kevin dated a girlfriend named Shannon.

Friends in Takilma who had a craft booth at the Country Fair became huge fans of the troupe—mask-makers Jill Birmingham and Newman (he used only one name). They started making their own giant puppets, dubbed themselves the "Illuminated Fools," and joined in on the puppet parades.

Newman noted that Leo had created a unique design for his giant puppets, which other groups used when they created their own giant puppets. "The basic design for the giant puppets made by the Mystic Krewe of Prince Prospero, Risk of Change, the Illuminated Fools, and Coyote Rising—with arms operated from inside the puppet—was different from the usual giant puppet technique, where the arms either hung loose, or were moved by folks outside the main body," Newman said. "Brought to the Country Fair by Leo, these puppets have become iconic fair images."

But more turned out to not necessarily be merrier for the puppeteers. "It was the same old story," Jay said. "I was struck about how universal it is. Like wow, no wonder the world is such a mess! If twelve puppeteers have this much trouble doing a three-day event once a year, it's no wonder that parts of the world have troubles. This is really the human condition. Once the group got to a certain size, it kind of fragmented into cliques that worked together, but it wasn't the same happiness of the early era."

Ironically, changes would spark friction amid the ranks of Risk of Change.

"By the mid-nineties, a lot of us are not getting along," Jay said. "There was a big rift between Ti and me, who had been really powerfully close friends. Ti wanted to be the patriarch in the group, and I was really clear that I didn't want to be in a group that had a patriarch. ... This is a creative collective. We're a collective. So we started growing apart." Eventually, Glen, Tom, and Ti left the troupe. In 1999 Jay would be the last of the original members to "graduate" from Risk of Change.

In 2000, Jay and his life partner, Todd Hildebrandt, would arrange a separate gig at the fair, performing as tree puppets. They enjoyed the simplicity and freedom of setting their own schedules as a duo. Best of all: They made the tree puppets easy to hug. "I made it so that you can see my face," Jay said. "That's part of what makes it so alive—my eyes and mouth are there. And it's a curious thing: If you stand still in a tree puppet, you disappear. I've had people lean on me and be totally spooked, because they think I'm a tree! For people at the fair who may be over-stimulated, it's just very magical everywhere. And suddenly, they see a live tree!" Jay laughed, adding. "The costumes are lightweight and really designed for hugging."

In the 2010s, Jay and his partner, Todd, would move on from puppeteering to coordinating the fair's Ambiance Crew, which oversees the creation and installation of art pieces on the paths. By then, they lived together in a farm in Veneta, not far from the fair site.

After Jay left Risk of Change, the troupe would continue to bring wildly festive and silly parades to the Oregon Country Fair for at least two more decades, changing and growing and always fueled by a collective creativity. But that's another story.

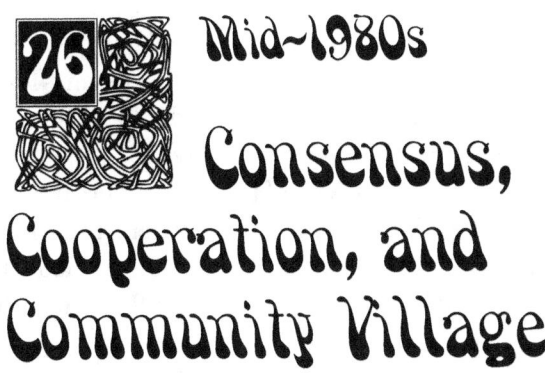

Mid-1980s
Consensus, Cooperation, and Community Village

> *"Community Village is an endeavor within the Fair by members of the local cooperative community to facilitate positive social change by creating an environment which will enable participants and fairgoers alike to experience firsthand the benefits of working cooperatively."*
> —The *Village Vision*, Friday, July 13, 1984

Community Village flowed along in the 1980s with its proven formula: grouping representatives of like-minded organizations together in shared booths. This method enhanced the organizations' connections with each other at the fair and afterward in the community. The nonprofits and worker-owned businesses enjoyed the opportunity to get their messages out to fairgoers who would come to Community Village for the music or workshops and who would then often linger to check out the informational booths.

Christine Frazer, who had left Starflower in the late 1970s, started attending Community Village meetings in the 1980s as a representative of Country VW, which participated in the village Economic Cooperation booth.

"After about two years with Starflower and one year in the Lane Community College Auto program, I landed at Country VW through their co-op work experience program," Christine said. Country VW was an all-women's worker-owned cooperative that ran an automotive shop. The co-op members dedicated themselves to conserving resources by keeping vehicles running well as long as possible.

Jill Heiman, the Oregon Country Fair's attorney, had become a local expert on setting up cooperative businesses. She helped Country VW incorporate as a worker-owned cooperative. In the mid-1980s, when laws passed by the Reagan administration doubled the taxes on cooperative businesses, Jill Heiman would advise Country VW to reorganize as an S corporation. Instead of being members in a co-op, the workers became shareholders in the S corporation. The company, in turn, would pass through all corporate income, losses, deductions, and credits to their shareholders for tax purposes. Jill handled the legal details.

"We were members of OUR Credit Union," Christine said, as she explained a vehicle inspection plan for credit union members. "For a twenty-five dollar fee, we'd go over the car bumper to bumper estimating the cost to fix it and the timeframes. Then a person could decide whether to put the money into the vehicle or to part it out and buy new. Eighty percent of the time, it was more sound to keep the car. Our clientele were people with low incomes and university people." Country VW could do any repairs except transmissions. They had an agreement to refer transmission business to Friendly Street Automotive, another worker-owned shop.

"Eugene was a community of all kinds of worker-owned businesses back then," Christine said. Christine's friend and co-worker from Starflower, Jain Elliott, had suggested that Country VW join the village's Economic Cooperation booth. "We did demonstrations and wore our T-shirts," Christine said. "We had flyers about keeping your car running well for as long as you can, instead of trading it in every year."

Hilary Anthony got involved with Community Village in 1982. She had moved to Eugene that spring, a couple of years after she had graduated from college in Florida. In Eugene, she joined the Growers Market cooperative and signed up as their member produce buyer. Other members of the Growers Market asked her to represent them at an upcoming Community Village meeting.

"I sat down next to Jain Elliott, who became a close friend of mine after that," Hilary said. "I'd never met her before." Jain asked

Hilary if she'd be willing to coordinate the Local Self-Reliance booth at Community Village, the booth that included Growers Market, Starflower, Queenright Beekeepers, and a few other groups. Hilary agreed to do it.

"I went home from that meeting and I'd been in town about a month," Hilary said. "I was living in this big old group house. I didn't even know the right name, but I was saying, 'Well, there's this village, community thing, and I'm doing this and I'm going to camp out.' And all these people who'd been living in Eugene for a long time here in this house were like, 'What, you've got a camping pass to the Country Fair?' So I went out there a couple times before the fair and was just thrilled and excited."

Hilary also got to know a few fair entertainers that spring through her hobby of juggling. She often practiced with other jugglers in a city park in the afternoons. That's where she met fair performers Rhys Thomas and David Lichtenstein. Through her friendships with jugglers, she got to go backstage at the Circus Stage during performances.

In the late 1980s Hilary took a few years off from the fair to complete a degree in accounting. By then she was ready to move on from Community Village. "A lot of the times, the meetings felt hard and consensus felt like a very challenging way to make decisions in a big group," she said. In 1992 she landed on the Vaudeville Crew as a co-coordinator with Tim Miller.

In 1994 the fair board would put Hilary's accounting degree to use, appointing her fair co-treasurer with Steve "Grumpy" Gorham. "We had different and complementary skills," Hilary said. "I think we both really enjoy sharing the position because it's a lot of work." She would remain the fair's co-treasurer for more than two decades. In 1997 Hilary would be asked by the Path Planning group, in which she had participated for two years, to coordinate the new Chela Mela Meadow area, another key fair position that Hilary would still be handling in 2019.

After her stint with Starflower, Jain stepped up to help with the village's Little People's booth in 1986. The Little People's booth offered free child care for parents who wanted a break while they spent time perusing the booths and workshops in the village. At the time, Jain, age thirty-seven, was a single parent with a two-year-old son, Forest, so her booth duties made a perfect fit.

"Forest loved it," Jain said. Each year, Forest's boundaries at the fair got more permissive as he matured. "He marked the first year he could remember where the Springfield Creamery booth was," Jain said. Another year, Jain made a mandala button to signal that her son was old enough to come and go from the Little People's booth whenever he wanted. The year Forest could find his way alone all the way to Toby's Tofu Palace for a Tofu Tia marked another big milestone.

When he got older, Forest loved participating in the Teen Crew program. Volunteers often paid him cash tips when he delivered ice to crews and food booths. One year he saved enough to surprise Jain with a beautiful crystal rock. Another year, he treated Jain to dinner out at the fair. "When he was in high school, he decided the fair wasn't cool," Jain said. "Then his senior year, the fair was suddenly cool again and he came back." Forest (who later renamed himself Elliott Farren) would end up volunteering at the fair for many years; Jain would volunteer in the village for decades.

"I was drawn again and again to Community Village," she said. "It seemed to me to be the most interesting part of the fair. I loved playing the New Games. ... Many of us in the village are so pushy. We want to convert everybody. The Moon Lodge people want all women to be blissed out about their biological connection to the Earth. Peace and Justice wants everybody to know that there are ways that we can make change, right now. ... We're a little more laid back at Little People. We just want to have fun with your kids. But you know, we kind of like it if you're bopping about checking out our booths while we're watching the kids."

Community Village would become an influential force in the fair in the 1980s. The Community Village Coordinating Council had already incubated several ideas that would be adopted by the fair. In 1981-82 the council invited the fair board to brainstorm ideas to raise funds for the down payment on the land. In 1982, Community Village began Youth Job Services, which would eventually be implemented fair-wide as the Teen Crew program.

Quite a few members of the village council would go on to fair leadership roles. Village co-founder Marshall Landman started that trend when he was elected to the fair's board of directors in 1979. He also volunteered at Main Camp and in 1985 served on the fair's OM (Operations Management) Team.

A prime indicator of Community Village influence on the larger fair organization was the election of village scribe Robert DeSpain to the fair board of directors in 1983. Shortly after, he was elected board president. Robert would shoulder a leadership role at the fair for many years.

Patti Lomont also volunteered in Main Camp after serving on the village council. She started out painting signs at Community Village and because of her talent, she was recruited to paint signs in Main Camp in late 1978. That's when veteran Sandra Bauer recruited Patti to join the team that worked to smooth out relationships and issues with the fair's neighbors.

"Right away, Sandra Bauer whisked me off to visit neighbors," Patti said. "They had a policy that nobody would go out to visit neighbors by themselves. ... I was just in Main Camp, painting, and she said, 'Hey, I need somebody to go visit neighbors with,' and we went off."

Patti was elected to the fair's board in 1985. She also was hired a few months later as an art teacher in the Fern Ridge Middle School, which served the Elmira and Veneta areas. Patti had just graduated from the University of Oregon in June with a degree in art education. "I went out for the interview with the principal and was dressed in a suit and high heels," Patti said. "Then I went out to Main Camp all dressed up like that, and freaked everybody out. It was very funny! But I did get that job. I was up-front on my resume. I didn't want anything to come up later with parents saying 'Oh, she's involved with Country Fair.'"

One time the school connection helped Patti nab a fair vandal. "We had been having some problems with vandalism at the fair site and we'd just figured it was local kids," Patti said, "but we never ever could catch anybody." Then one day at school a student came up to Patti in the hall and said, "Miss Lomont! I found your name on the fair site."

Patti realized the students had to have been climbing the Spirit Tower in Community Village where the names of the original coordinating council had been carved into the wood. She turned to the student and demanded: "What were you doing at the fair?" As he stammered out a response and confessed to climbing the tower, she thought to herself, "You're busted!"

"This kid was a troublemaker and I was sure that he could have been one of our culprits," Patti said. She read him the riot act, threatening to call his parents. It worked—the vandalism abated for a while after that.

Patti would continue to serve as Sign Coordinator for Main Camp for several years, and would visit fair neighbors as the "Neighbor Liaison" for twenty-eight years. She helped form the fair's Poster Committee in 1983 and was still active as of 2019. She also sold her beautiful glass jewelry and artwork in several different booths for more than forty years after she started in 1977.

During the 1980s, Community Village held monthly meetings November through July. Every year, the November and January meetings of Community Village would be sparsely attended. As fair time neared, more people showed up every month. The Call to Council went out in February to find out who would serve on the Community Village Coordinating Council for the next year. "The number of people on council ranges from eight to twelve," Jain Elliott said. "Nine to eleven is ideal."

New leaders rising to the helm of the Community Village Coordinating Council in the mid-1980s included Kathryn Madden, Norma Sax, Diane Albino, Michael "Coyote" Connelly, Jain Elliott,

Community Village leaders reunited in 1991, from left: (first row) Percy Hilo and Michael Mooney; (second row) Michael Connelly, Norma Sax, Marshall Landman, Diane Albino, Darlene Colborn, and Jean-Marie Arnague; (third row) Dick Stewart (guest), Skeeter Duke, Cheryl Jones, Craig Patterson, and Robert DeSpain.

Consensus, Cooperation, and Community Village

Darlene Colborn, Jon Silvermoon, Bob Fennessy, "Planet" Janet Tarver, David Hoffman, Rich Toymil, and Martha Evans. Quite a few of them would also rise to influential positions in the fair.

Every meeting was run by consensus. "Our meetings were all about decision-making for sure," said Michael Connelly. "However, the uniqueness of it and what I feel is the strength of what we did, is that everyone had the opportunity to participate. Everyone's voice was respected in the process. If somebody wanted to block consensus—if you had a hundred people at a meeting and ninety-eight people were in favor of something and one person wasn't—we would not move on until we either resolved the issue or the person chose to stand aside. ... If they had a strong enough feeling that this was not the proper decision, then we would move on [to something else]. It reinforced the reality that it was the process rather than the outcome that was important. It was the way that we did things rather than what we did."

The meetings could go on a long time, but they always ended with "The Hokey Pokey" dance and a huge group hug.

Michael first volunteered in Community Village in 1978 as part of a group called the Coalition Opposing Registration and the Draft—or CORD. "In 1977 and 1978, they were considering bringing back the draft," Michael said. "I got very politically active on the University of Oregon campus and with Clergy and Laity Concerned. ... It was a wonderful coalition with representatives from Congressman Jim Weaver's office. Peter DeFazio, who was Weaver's aide, may have been one of those people. Dave Fidanque from American Civil Liberties Union, Jerry Rust was a county commissioner, and Marion Malcolm from Clergy and Laity Concerned—we had a lot of very powerful people."

A few representatives from CORD joined other groups to build the Peace and Justice booth in Community Village in 1978. Michael and his then-partner, Peg Peoples, set up a tipi in the village camping area behind the yurt. "That's where Skeeter [Duke], Norma, Diane [Albino] and Marshall all camped," Michael said. "It was really sweet in the morning to be able to wake up and see your fellow workers. Marshall was always there, making his coffee and we'd always have a little pre-fair time in the mornings."

Every morning before the fair, the village gathered in the commons for announcements and a village Om Circle. Every Sunday morning of the fair, Community Village instigators would head out to the path to blow their conches to call the fair family to the fair-wide Om Circle. The goal was to have people holding hands along the complete Eight pathway at 10:00 a.m Sunday, with everyone chanting "Om." Sometimes it actually connected as planned. Whether it connected or not, those participating still could savor the good vibes of a feel-good moment.

As symbolized in the Om Circle ritual, Michael noted that one of the real strengths of the village was its inclusiveness.

"The word 'community,' if you break it down, it's "common unity"—we really looked toward commonalities and building on our vision," he said. "We were a gathering of nonprofit agencies, educational agencies, child care agencies, environmental groups, health groups, anti-war pro-peace groups. The village encouraged dialogue among peoples and agencies and groups that wasn't much happening in Eugene.

"We spent time together under the stars and we had days and nights when we got to know one another," Michael added. "Our influence in the local community is undeniable. We're like morning glory—we're everywhere."

Michael would volunteer in Community Village for more than fifteen years. In 1996, he started volunteering for the Neighborhood Response Team to help out fair neighbors who reported problems such as trespassing during the fair.

Martha Evans joined the Peace and Justice booth of Community Village in 1979 as a representative of the local chapter of the National Lawyers Guild. She had just completed her second year of law school at the University of Oregon and it was her second fair. In 1978, she had gone to her first Country Fair with friends from the university, and had run into a law school friend, Mary Wagner, who was staffing the Information Booth at Main Stage.

Mary came out from the booth to hug Martha, exclaiming, "Oh Martha! I'm so glad you're here." Mary borrowed a T-shirt from another Info staffer and handed it to Martha, saying, "Go home and get a sleeping bag. This'll get you back in to spend the night." In those years, fair staff T-shirts served as a volunteer's pass to get in after hours.

"So my first fair, I was snuck in to the fair by a friend to spend the night," Martha said. "All you needed was the right T-shirt to do that. And I loved it! The romance, the beauty, the people, the community! It was not like a law school keg party. From the very beginning, it seemed like people who were trying to create something. ... I never was really a hippie. But in my heart I always was. Here were people taking those values and saying there are alternative ways to have fun, alternative ways to dress, alternative ways to organize ourselves, alternative views on drugs, alternative ways to make music. Let's come together and do those things we love to do and show other people how it's done. Let's give people a chance to see hippies aren't really unwashed radicals. They're creative, wonderful, thoughtful, artistic, musical, funny, laughing, peaceful people."

In 1980 Martha graduated from law school and came to the fair for a few years after that to help a friend with his orange juice cart. In 1984, she returned to the Peace and Justice booth in Community Village as part of WAND (Women's Action for Nuclear Disarmament). That's when she got more involved in the monthly village meetings.

"We'd sit in a big circle," Martha said. "We'd have somebody from Alpha Farm come explain consensus decision-making probably every other year. Then we'd go around and speak our piece and talk and talk and talk and talk. Two meetings later somebody who hadn't been at that meeting who had an interest in the topic would bring it up again! We'd talk it back and forth again. It was really committed to the process more than to the outcome. So anybody could make anything revisited. ...

"It irritated me at first," Martha allowed. "People who weren't very articulate could go on and on and on and on. Nobody would say, 'Okay, we got your point.' But in fact, I learned to really appreciate that as respectful of people's input, whatever form it took. It was contrary to my lawyer's training that you're succinct, you're efficient, you make your point, you advocate, somebody decides. ... I learned to be more nonjudgmental. ... I got to know them, not just as points of view on an issue, but as real people with all their stuff."

Soon Martha was facilitating the village meetings, making sure everyone was heard so consensus could be reached. Community Village required every participating group to attend at least three village meetings.

"Part of that idea was that to really call ourselves a village, we wanted to get to know each other and to work together during the year," Martha said. "It was a way to spend time with each other, get to know each other, and really build community. That was fun, facilitating those meetings. That was a good experience for me. Honoring the process and honoring everybody who was there so that you didn't let one person dominate over and over, meeting after meeting, with one point of view. Trying to learn how to be gentle with people but respectful of the other people in the room."

While serving on the village coordinating council, Martha learned there was more to the Oregon Country Fair staff shirts in the 1980s than she first realized. She noticed some of the T-shirts had little googly eyes pasted on the peach, another year a jeweled sequin appeared on the peach of certain shirts. One year there was a squashed mosquito. Each of those embellishments signaled that the person wearing the T-shirt had permission to enter Main Camp, where fair Security staff stopped most volunteers at the gate.

Martha became one of Community Village's liaisons to the fair board meetings. She would later run for the board and serve from 1993 to 1995. In the 2000s, she often acted as the fair board's moderator.

Village council member Jon Silvermoon helped create the fair's Archaeology Crew to fight the highway realignment throughout the 1980s and was elected to the fair's board of directors in 1982. At a board meeting in the spring of 1983, Jon raised the issue of how the board made decisions. Some members of the board had expressed frustration with the consensus process under fair bylaws, where one person could block a board decision. Jon advocated keeping the consensus process, but he was met with resistance.

Board member Robert Thompson moved to change the fair's bylaws to allow the board to pass a measure by a two-thirds vote instead of by consensus, but the board was bound by the consensus process and Jon blocked that decision.

"The bylaws said after the third meeting they could pass it with a two-thirds vote," Jon said. "So I blocked consensus every meeting until the meeting that they could change it. That angered some of the people, but I felt strongly that the vote to move away from consensus was a key changing point in the way the fair conducts business. If you do everything by consensus, then you need to involve everybody in the decision. You need to inform people about what's going on, and people have to have their say."

On June 12, 1983, the board approved making all decisions by a two-thirds vote, a provision that would remain in effect more than three decades later. Jon didn't like the results. "Cohesiveness was sacrificed on the altar of expediency," he said. The board would, indeed, have a difficult time finding cohesiveness over the years. However, it's debatable whether consensus decisions would have helped or exacerbated the issues the board would face.

Kathryn Madden first volunteered in Community Village in 1981 as part of the Health Booth when her son, Ethan, was still a toddler. Because of her organizational skills, she found herself coordinating the booth the next year and joining the Community Village Coordinating Council.

"One year, we actually turned down a group that came to us to be a part of the Community Village," Kathryn said. "It's a pretty big deal, I think, to have the village say, 'No, you're too weird for us.' It was the Revolutionary Communist Youth Brigade—they wanted to come and be part of the village."

The village coordinating council already had some concerns about the youth brigade, but planned to hear them out when the group came to plead their case at a council meeting. The council started the meeting in their traditional way—sitting in a circle and holding hands for moment of silence. But this time the silence was interrupted.

"The kids from the Revolutionary Communist Youth Brigade sat there and snickered and laughed at us!" Kathryn said. As a result, "they were ix-nayed, man. We weren't going to let them in if they laughed at us. That was an easy decision."

The process to rebuild the Integral House in 1988 impressed Kathryn for how the group handled it. The annual winter floods had taken their toll on the original 1980 structure, which was falling apart.

"It was really entirely a consensus decision," she said. "Some of those village meetings have fifty or sixty people. We held hands and got quiet before we began the meeting. I was way into it; I loved it! We talked about the purpose of the Integral House, what its historical purpose was, what did we want it to be for us now and future generations, what was the function, who was going to live there, how should it be made. We did that all in meetings of fifty or sixty

Community Village Coordinating Council in 1986 included, from left: (first row) Jon Silvermoon, Norma Sax, and Kathryn Madden; (second row) Janet Tarver, Diane Albino, David Hoffman, and Paula Jamison.

people. We came up with a design through consensus. It was a pretty amazing project to have done that.

"Then we built it," she added. "We went out to the Alpha Farm in Deadwood and helped them take down a bunch of their trees for poles, and brought them in." In 1988, Kathryn would successfully run for the fair board of directors and start to transition out of Community Village to Main Camp.

David Hoffman joined the Community Village in 1983 as a representative of the Master Gardener program for the Oregon State University Extension Program. Lane County had cut funding for the Extension Program but voters had passed a serial levy to keep the program going on a shoestring. That's when OSU staff initiated the Master Gardening program to relieve the agricultural agents from repeatedly answering the public's most common questions. Even with reduced OSU staff, the public could still get answers to questions about plants, soil, and gardening techniques.

"I was not a Master Gardener," David said, "but I coordinated their being in the village by registering, doing the village meetings and work parties; scheduling the actual Master Gardeners; and providing a sign, chair, reference books, and one plant for the booth in the Integral House. In 1984 I became a Master Gardener."

In 1985 David joined the Community Village Coordinating Council, where he would serve for more than three decades. In 1988 he coordinated the project to rebuild the Integral House in Community Village. "The original Integral House was modeled after the Berkeley example and had the Aprovecho Clay Stove (pre-Rocket Stove), greenhouse, solar showers, and composting toilet," David said.

Out of all the displays, the composting toilet was ill-suited for massive use during the three days of the fair. "The toilet was a bit much," David said, "so Robert DeSpain designed and built the first six-pack/vault toilet at Shady Grove" right next to Community Village.

The original Integral House included a substantial deck on the second story for public meetings, but after the county started evaluating booths for integrity in the early 1980s, officials cracked down on public use of fair booth lofts.

"With trees overgrowing solar access and more community folks joining the village, Energy Park moved to its present location led by Sallie Edmunds," David said. Energy Park had piped water showers, so the Integral House with batch showers was decommissioned and replaced with the Come Unity House.

David noted that the consensus process to build the new structure worked smoothly in the long run. "Consensus is often seen as a long, boring waste of time," he said. "However, it crosses bridges before we get there as people speak their piece and more issues are settled ahead of time, so consensus can actually save time and emotions in the long run." After the village participants rebuilt the structure, they renamed it the Come Unity House.

In the late 1980s David would help found the VegManEC (Vegetation Management and Erosion Control) team that would work proactively to keep the fair's green spaces intact. In the 2000s David would successfully advocate for construction of urinals at the fair— for women as well as men— to provide a quick alternative to the long lines at the toilets.

While not part of the coordinating council, Robert Leo Heilman joined David Hoffman and a few others to initiate a program offering people with disabilities better access at the fair. Robert first volunteered in the Community Village Information booth in 1985. At the time, he was doing interviews and writing for the Siskiyou Project, a bioregional organization based in Takilma, Oregon.

"Community Village Info Booth was staffed by radical press organizations," Robert said. "We had a set of passes for our organization." Most of the Siskiyou Project group lived in the Rogue Valley, but Robert lived near Roseburg, the closest member to the fair. He became the contact from the group and attended the Community Village meetings in Eugene.

In 1985 the meetings were still held on the second floor of Growers Market in downtown Eugene, where the village had been meeting for years. Kathryn Madden, who was the village's liaison to the fair board, announced at the meeting that the fair wanted to do an accessibility study. "A good friend of mine by the name of Midge Campbell, who has cerebral palsy, was working in Roseburg for the county at the time doing accessibility studies, checking out the county buildings and such," Robert said. He suggested the fair contact her and they did.

Midge and a small committee did an accessibility study in 1985 for the fair. "Community Village invited them back the next year, 1986," Robert said, "and in 1987, it was established as a Main Camp crew to start providing services that they'd recommended as needed."

The crew was named Four-A for Alter-Abled Access Advocacy and would serve the fair for more than three decades.

Around that time the coordinating council became concerned that the second floor of the Growers Market was not handicap-accessible, so they moved Community Village meetings to school buildings and other places with universal access.

Robert Leo Heilman would become Four-A Crew co-coordinator in 1998. "We do a ton of things that are centered around accessibility," Robert said, "including site studies, reports, recommendations to the Construction

Starting in the 1980s, Community Village offered an accessible rest stop.

Consensus, Cooperation, and Community Village

Crew, assistance coming in from the parking lot and back out to the parking lot, and wheelchair loans. We also provide the sign language interpreters for the stages." He would volunteer with Four-A Crew for decades.

Norma Sax was volunteering with White Bird Clinic at the fair when she also started volunteering as a representative of the Rape Crisis Network in Community Village's Health and Human Services booth. "In 1981, Marshall, who was the big cheese in the Community Village, asked if I wanted to be on the Community Village Coordinating Council. He thought I'd be good at it." Norma agreed, and she would become close friends with several people on the council, including Marshall.

Some of her favorite memories in the 1980s involved writing the Community Village newsletter, the *Village Vision*. The small staff—Norma, Michael Connelly, Skeeter Duke, and Cheryl Jones—would sit at the top level of Integral House on dusty afternoons to pull it together for the next morning's edition. They used manual typewriters and mimeograph machines to complete the project on the spot.

"The thing is full of typos because there's no way to correct it," Norma said, "or you'd have to erase the thing and then it would tear. We would feature a group that was in the village and write about it, like Womenspace or Lane Arts Council. Or we'd feature a person. There was the entertainment schedule and a schedule of the workshops, demos, and the New Games at the village."

Michael also remembered the newsletter work fondly. "Norma and I had some great laughs together," he said. "The memories that I have of her and me and Skeeter up there in the top of the Integral House! We'd be up there on a Saturday afternoon in the dust with everything going on and typing out these stories on an old typewriter and ditto-ing them off and then stapling them together so that we'd be able to get it out there for Sunday morning. Then walking around the Eight at 8:30 on a Sunday morning. We had to get going early. We had to be back for the 9:30 village circle because we were on the council, too."

The newsletter was well-received. "Michael would take one side of the path and I would take the other," Norma said. "He had this big beautiful leather bag that he would carry the papers in. We would put one at each booth and say good morning to everybody, give them to people on the path. It was just a wonderful thing to do first thing in the morning, while everybody's waking up. Everybody would love to see us and everybody would be so happy."

In the mid-1980s, Norma and Kathryn Madden from the village started going out to the fair site in the early summer to help in Main Camp, forming the Brush Babes. "Brush Babes were pre-fair," Norma said. "Reese Prouty, Kathryn Madden, Sandra Bauer, Sallie Edmunds, and I used to go around the Eight in the ratty old pickup truck and pick up brush along the way. We'd put it into the truck and take it out to the burn pile. We had so much fun! We were the Brush Babes from Hell. It was a lot of hard work but it was one of my fondest memories of the fair."

Reese Prouty said the Brush Babes recruited cute young men to ride with them. "We had Dave-Babe and then there was Pea-Bob," Reese recalled. "We'd make them our hood ornaments. We'd always have some token boy that had to ride around with us on the hood of the car without his shirt on. It was always some buff young kid."

In 1988, Norma would become the fair board's secretary, where she would serve for seven years. In 1995, she was hired as the fair's

"Brush Babes" at work and play (from left): Kathryn Madden, Sallie Edmunds, Reese Prouty, Norma Sax, and Sandra Bauer.

paid administrative assistant, a job she would hold for more than two decades.

Toward the end of the 1980s, the Community Village Coordinating Council would get its moment of fame in the spotlight at the Midnight Show. "We told them what we were going to do," said "Planet Janet" Tarver, laughing. "Some of us were already backstage and all of us jumped on the stage. We did 'The Hokey Pokey.' For the last part, we flipped around and gave everybody the moon! 'You put your moon in, you put your moon out!' There was a big circle of us and we got big laughs."

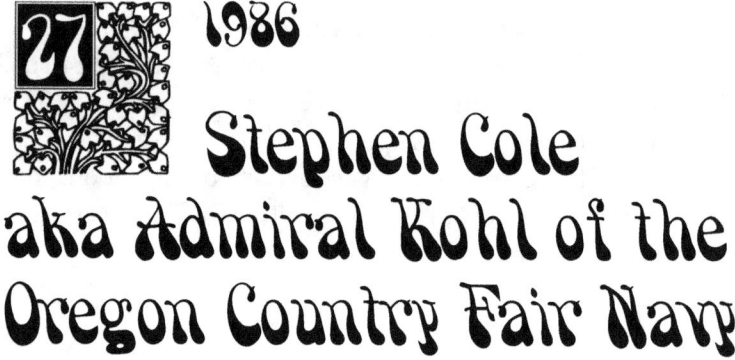

1986
Stephen Cole aka Admiral Kohl of the Oregon Country Fair Navy

*"If you don't know these facts
then you may not know your larboard
from your starboard.
Keep learning or all hope is dashed.
Stay curious—that's an order!*

—Oregon Country Fair Navy,
Hellbenders Training Manual

Stephen Cole was attending college at the University of Kentucky the spring in 1970 when the Kent State shootings shocked the nation. National Guardsmen from Ohio opened fire on unarmed students during demonstrations against the U.S. military bombing of Cambodia. Bullets fired by the National Guardsmen killed four students and injured nine. The incident also shocked Stephen—who had grown up in a middle-class Republican household in Ohio—into a more radical view of the world.

After graduating, Stephen took off traveling across Europe and Asia at age twenty-three.

He gravitated to a Full Moon Festival in Goa, India, in 1973 that he found transformational. Timothy Leary was on the bill, but he was detained in Kabul. The festival went on without him and featured a "big bonfire, huge speakers powered by underground generators blasting recordings of live concerts by Pink Floyd, Led Zeppelin, the Who, and the Rolling Stones," Stephen said. "Free LSD was provided by a branch of Wavy Gravy's Hog Farm, therefore it was Owsley's liquid sunshine." Fireworks punctuated the end of the rock 'n' roll extravaganza.

In the mid-1970s, Stephen would visit his sister in Portland, Oregon, every summer, then he would loop down south to winter in Yucatan and Key West. He moved to Oregon for good in 1977, when he first attended the Oregon Country Fair. He had just found a job with the Hoedads, a cooperative organization of tree-planting crews, and many of his new co-workers volunteered on the Security Crew at the fair.

The tree-planters had served as the Security Crew for the fair since 1972, when a half-dozen brawny Hoedads successfully stopped a fight brewing at the Free Souls' biker camp one night. The next year, the Hoedads began organizing shifts to annually provide security for various venues within the fair. They also helped run the fair's Sweep at closing time. When it was time for the public to leave, tree-planters would link arms and walk down the path so no one could pass them, urging people to leave.

In 1978 Stephen, then age twenty-eight, volunteered for the Admissions Crew, and in 1979 he joined his fellow Hoedads on the Security Crew. He coordinated the midnight to 6:00 a.m. shift at the fair entrance on Highway 126 (renamed Suttle Road when the state realigned the highway in the late 1980s). "That was my first coordinator position," Stephen said. "That was your foot-in-the-door type position." Bob Leash worked Admissions Crew during the same shift, and the two would often check in with each other over the radio to combat boredom. "Click, click. Radio check, time check, temperature check, admissions numbers today check, weather tomorrow check." Their radio conversations woke up fair organizers at Main Camp who were trying to sleep but had kept their radios on to listen for emergencies.

"We got dressed down several times about sucking up the batteries so badly," Stephen said. "Then we'd get new batteries and that would be another half-hour's worth of conversation. … It was really lonely. You had to make your own fun."

In 1982, Stephen began coordinating the 6:00 a.m. to 10:00 a.m. Security shift at Admissions. "It was a mellow shift, but things would start heating up because everybody starts mobilizing pretty heavily at 8:00 or 9:00 a.m. to get open by 11:00 a.m."

Stephen asked to be transferred to the Sweep Security Crew in 1986 because he didn't like what he saw when the Sweep barreled down the paths at closing time. "The problem was these big guys who just wouldn't negotiate," Stephen said. "The paying public had no idea what was going on. Here comes this line of people yelling, 'Turn around and get out!' Then: 'I'm not turning around!' 'Oh yes you are!'" Sometimes the yelling match turned into physical confrontation. People who tried to bust through the line often found themselves held in a headlock by a Hoedad.

Stephen decided there had to be a better way. He had a banner made by the fair's Banner Crew that said: "The Fair is Closing. Please Exit Behind You." Then he changed the lineup for how the Sweep would proceed down the path. "I got two big guys down each side who were gentle and persistent to check everybody," Stephen said. "Then everybody else can just hang out pretty much behind the sign. But two guys right down the side. Nobody could bust through Red Rover, Red Rover like we had before the banner. Let them know what's going on."

To attract more attention and soften the message, Stephen enlisted fair kids to help hold the banner and he added musicians to play as the Sweep Band. "Before [the new configuration], somebody

The Sweep banner helped soften the message at fair closing time.

would turn around and try to exit through the banner," Stephen said. "But kids and musicians really demilitarized the Sweep. …We created our own fog that made things mellow and happy." The new Sweep configuration would become the standard for more than three decades.

"I did that for a few years," Stephen said. "It was a thankless job. I got out of it just about the time Strider was getting kicked out of the fair with the River Rats because he was using it to get all his friends in free." The River Rats—aka the Oregon Country Fair Navy—patrolled the Long Tom River by boat to prevent people from sneaking into the fair. But instead of due diligence, Strider (real name unknown) had helped many friends avoid the Sweep. When that was discovered, Strider was relieved of his duties.

Stephen had helped the Navy out before and he also knew many of the craftspeople in the booths that backed up to the Long Tom. Stephen requested to join the Navy and got the assignment in 1990. The Navy was integral to the fair's perimeter security because the steep, overgrown banks of the Long Tom River provided ample areas for sneakers to hide.

"A lot of people tried to hide from the Sweep, especially on Saturday night, by creeping down to the river bank and hiding in the tall grass," Stephen said. "It was a great place to hide, I'm sure, in the '70s, '80s." But Stephen enlisted the Navy to work in concert with the Sweep to watch for sneakers. Even when they didn't have radio contact during the early years, they could tell where the Sweep was by listening for the music played by the Sweep Band. The Navy also had special maps marking booth locations and booth numbers from the river side—the back side—of the booths, so the Navy could keep track of boat locations relative to the Eight path.

After the Navy coordinated with the Sweep, the number of riverbank sneakers started decreasing. "We used to get eighty, ninety, a hundred people a night" in the 1980s, Stephen said. "And we've seen this go down to sixty, fifty, forty, thirty and twenty a night" by the 2000s. "We used to go up there on the banks—just this sea of grass, you know—and say, 'All right, we see you! Come on out!' And two or three people would pop up," he said, chuckling. "So that works." In later years, the crew would enlist volunteer "Brush Bunnies" to beat the brush along the banks to ensure they found everyone.

As coordinator of the Navy, Stephen was dubbed Admiral Kohl.

Spectators lined up across the opposite high bank of the Long Tom River to watch the OCF Navy's Changing of the Guard.

Under his command the OCF Navy settled into a routine, with half working the shorter morning shift and half working the longer evening shift. The morning shift got a shorter schedule because those volunteers would pitch in an additional hour each evening to help with the Sweep. They developed a tradition to mark the shift changes.

"We have a changing-of-the-guard ceremony every day about 2:30 or so," Admiral Kohl said. "The a.m. crew hands the paddles over to the p.m. crew amidst much fanfare and bagpipes, precision marching and singing. … We have bagpipes, and we sing a song from [the comic opera] *H.M.S. Pinafore.*" Stephen spontaneously broke out singing the OCF Navy's "Changing of the Guard Song," based on Gilbert and Sullivan's "We Sail The Ocean Blue."

> *We sail the ocean blue*
> *in our saucy ships of beauty.*
> *We're sober and we're true*
> *and attentive to our duty.*
> *When the balls whistle free*
> *O'er the bright blue sea,*
> *We stand to our paddles all day.*

*When at anchor we ride
On the Pike Street tide,
We have plenty of time for play.
Ahoy, ahoy, ahoy, ahoy!
We sail the ocean blue
in our saucy ships of beauty.
We're sober and we're true
and attentive to our duty.
We're sober and we're true.
We sail the ocean blue!
Huzzah!*

Over the years, the Navy campsite, Smirkwood, evolved from a place of "toasting and boasting around the grog circle to a live music venue," Stephen said. The group enjoyed creating themes for their fair campsite every year. Not only would they decorate their camp, they also would dress the part.

"We started off with Robin Hood because we like hiking around in the dingly dell and the bosky glade," Stephen said. "We went to Fairies after that because this place is a lot like a fairyland. We went to Camelot after that because we were actually trying to accomplish deeds of valor and be a good crew. ... The fourth one was Navy. We figured, well, we should get an aquatic theme and so the fifth one was Privateers and Buccaneers. And then we went to Druids. I think then Highlanders. That's where the kilts came from. We went to Vikings. That's where the helms came from. Shakespeare might have got mixed in there—a person of the woods and streams or springs. But after about ten of them, we kind of ran out of ideas, so we started recycling them. We had Robin Hood II, Fairies Again, Camelot Also, Navy Navy. Next year (2005) it'll be Privateers and Buccaneers Again, or Pirates."

The 2004 theme was Navy Navy. "It's really a themeless theme because we're always Navy. ...We have grog rations, of course, being in the Navy," he said. "We have toasts and boasts and I've always tried to incorporate the themes into the toasts: 'Is the sun over the yardarms yet? Somewhere in the world it is! Time for a drink yet?' Or: 'Splice the main brace!' We get an extra ration of grog if you're the one who has to do the difficult job of using a marlin spike to splice the main brace."

Stephen said the Navy had to substitute a couple of people into the ceremony one Friday after some crew members had been delayed because of their work outside the fair. "I gave one guy a twelve-minute warning," Stephen said, switching to a booming voice: "'You are impressed into the Navy! Get out there and put that kilt on and sing this song! March around! Hand that paddle over! Get off the beach now! Twelve minutes!'" Stephen added with a laugh: "He was impressed into the service. He's a volunteer, so he went willingly."

Stephen cited two members of the Navy who particularly stood out for their years of service. Brian Keith Kelley, aka Ensign Kelley, handled a lot of the details for the crew. "He got stuff done," Stephen said. Ensign Kelly procured radios and handled paperwork for the crew. He left the Navy after twenty years when he moved back East with his spouse to care for her aging father.

Another commendable member, "Sir Kenneth" Thompson, served in the Navy for twenty-five years. "He was the heart and soul of the Oregon Country Fair Navy," Stephen said. "I met him in 1978 when I picked up him and his friend and dog hitchhiking. He was a huge person, in size and magnanimity, red hair and beard; a poet, sketch artist, music lover, and all-around beautiful person." Sadly, Sir Kenneth died of a heart attack while driving home from the 2015 fair. "We have a permanent chair for him in our grog circle, under the portrait of him in full Viking regalia," Stephen said.

Over the years, the Navy developed a close relationship with one fair booth in particular: Peter Eberhardt's Map Gallery on the Upper River Loop. Peter's unique "No Trace" booth was perched at the top of a steep bank that had no room to camp behind it. So Peter's friend Stephen "Bear" Pitts helped create a booth with decks on the riverbanks below. They would completely remove the booth after the fair every year to let the river run its course, and rebuild it again before each fair. And every year, Bear's design had to be modified to match the changing, eroding contours of the steep, sandy banks.

The top floor cantilevered over the river, and the bottom deck had direct river access. Bear always brought a keg of beer to the fair and generously shared with the Navy volunteers, who enjoyed pulling up to the riverside deck for a drop of grog and a visit when things got slow on the Long Tom.

In 1993, the friendship with the folks in Peter's booth helped the OCF Navy solve a problem with some local juvenile delinquents. "For a while, we'd heard rumors of a small band of rogues yelling and throwing things at fairgoers from across the Long Tom, near the Upper River Loop, around midnight on Saturdays," Admiral Kohl said. "One reported incident resulted in cuts and bruises, and even a bit of bloodshed. In 1993, I and a few of the OCF Navy Crew members happened to be visiting a friend at booth 491, the Map Gallery, and witnessed some of this taunting. Mustering a canoe, we stormed the scalawags, chased them off and confiscated their arsenal of rocks, eggs, rotten produce, and Ball Park Franks.

"In 1994, we devised a plan to stake out the beach from which these perpetrators perpetrated," the admiral continued. "So while everyone else was enjoying the climax of the fair's festivities, Ensign Paul, Ensign Dave, and I silently paddled across the river to wait for the rogues, who might or might not show up." Stephen and Paul took their positions near the beach while Dave hid in some bushes a bit farther back to cut off their escape route.

As they waited, Dave and Stephen amused themselves by attempting to call in a screech owl that they had heard. When the screech owl heeded the calls and perched on a nearby tree branch, calling out persistently, Dave and Stephen fell silent. They knew from experience that the screech owl would be apt to dive bomb them with its talons if the bird figured out he had answered the call of humans instead of a willing mate.

"Waiting to see if the rogues returned, we were missing a hell of a party in the fair," Stephen recalled. "We were taking a chance in the cold, swarmed with mosquitoes. It's pretty breezy." Suddenly Stephen heard the snap of a twig. The screech owl ceased calling and flew away. "There was much crunching, cracking, crashing, and cussing, as the wretched miscreants trooped toward the beach with boxes of rocks, eggs, and produce in tow. No Ball Park Franks this year," he said with a chuckle. "As we crouched in a small depression nearby, Paul and I could see three males making their way along the cow path in front of us toward the beach."

The members of the Navy silently bided their time until they saw the troublemakers walk out on the sand, letting them get as close to the river and the fair as they could. "Before their feet could settle into the sand, a blinding light flashed from the heaven, as if the Sun itself had decided to pop out of hiding," Admiral Kohl said. "Actually, it was Ensign Tim, another OCF Navy Crew member, who had missed the midnight rendezvous due to a headache, and his million-candle-powered handheld spotlight, from the fair side.

"The hoodlums reacted as if they had been hit by lightning, taking off for the supposed safety and shelter of the nearby woods," the admiral said. "However, Paul and I too were spurred into action and we came bubbling out of our hiding place yelling, 'Security! Freeze!'" That only spurred the trio to run faster.

"You hate to put your hands on somebody, but we really wanted it to stop," Stephen said. Paul caught one. Stephen was chasing the other two when he saw two more scalawags crouching behind a bush. "So I stopped chasing the ones who were running and just trained my mace and flashlight on the ones who were crouched," Stephen said. After nabbing three of the five intruders, they were instructed by fair Security Crew coordinators to transport the teens across the river to deliver them to the Path Rove Crew, who would take the trespassers to the Admissions area and notify their parents.

"Now, if you think crossing the Long Tom, after several days of revelry, in midnight darkness, under unusual circumstances is risky, try it with three novice passengers who really don't want to be there, not to mention the watchful eyes of what seemed like a hundred people who had now gathered on the fair side of the river," Stephen said. "I pointed out to my reluctant passengers that the river was very deep in this spot and they had better relax and stay calm if they wished to stay dry. The malcontents were delivered to the Path Crew amidst a surprising round of cheers and applause."

From there the trio met the fair attorney, who called their parents, who came to pick up their kids. "It was some local kids who were pretty embarrassed," Stephen said. "We got photos of them and displayed them prominently on the sides of our canoes for years. ... The annual practice of 'Bowling for Hippies' was put to rest."

Stephen's favorite fair story happened in 1991. The Navy had only four members that year, and they all helped with the Saturday night Sweep. Stephen's cousin, Vice Admiral Navy Davy, was sitting in a canoe near Pike Street as Admiral Kohl stood above at the top of the steep shoreline. Dave reported by radio that a man wouldn't leave his spot on the banks of the river near Pike Street, even after Dave warned him that the Sweep was coming. Stephen went to check it out.

"As I walked by the fence, I hear, 'Cur-splash!' Like a cannonball.

Stephen Cole aka Admiral Kohl of the OCF Navy

As I got around the corner to look, I see this guy swimming across the river, his hat bobbing nearby," Stephen said. He also noticed Navy Davy and Ensign Richard hanging on to the boat as it rocked in the wake of the guy's splash. Dave reported that the guy had performed a back flip and almost landed in the canoe. "The Flipper exited the river and waded through the grass and out of sight," Stephen said. "It was then I looked down at the place from which he'd leapt and couldn't help but notice several twenty-dollar bills." Stephen pocketed the money to share later with the other crew members. Dave fished the guy's knit hat out of the river.

"That was not the end of that fellow's story, however," Stephen said. "We had heard stories about a guy matching the leaper's description giving away twenty-dollar bills at the Admissions area, burning some and eating some."

A month later at the annual Teddy Bears' Picnic for fair volunteers, Dave and Stephen were hanging out at the Navy campsite, Smirkwood on Smile Lane, when they noticed someone walking slowly along the path, approaching them with his head down. He walked up, looked at them, and said, "I followed the glitter trail."

"For the record," Stephen explained, "we had already incurred the wrath of the Recycling Crew for our daughters' use of glitter to mark the way to our camp." The glitter would shine in the beam of their flashlights at night. "We couldn't help notice that the glitter follower was wearing a hospital gown and booties, and he was carrying a bag from the Sacred Wallet Pharmacy," Stephen said. "We chatted for a few minutes before we realized that this was the guy who nearly sank one of our canoes a month earlier. At that time, Dave had draped the hat that he'd fished out of the water over a sacred stick in camp, and when the glitter follower saw it he said, 'There's my hat. I've been looking for that.' That clinched it. We told him we were the ones who confronted him during the fair."

"Could you show me where I jumped from?" the guy asked. "I left a jacket with $250 of food stamps in it on the other side of the river." Stephen and Dave agreed to take him there and as they approached the river bank, the guy pointed to the ground and said, "There! Right there God was born."

"We took this to mean that was where he dropped the acid that made him flip out," Stephen said. "I showed him the exact place from which he'd launched himself, explaining what I'd done with the cash he'd left, and he said that was cool by him."

The guy scrambled down the steep bank, swam across the river, and searched through the tall grass until he yelled, "Here it is! And the food stamps are still here! Now I think I know where my guitar is! Thanks guys!" As the man took off walking upriver, Dave and Stephen wandered back to the Teddy Bears' Picnic, shaking their heads in disbelief.

The OCF Navy Hellbenders 2002, from left: (front row) Joanne "Lady JoJo" Lubin, "Ensign Brian" Keith Kelley, Dave "Vice Admiral Navy Davy" Cole, and Holly "Dolphin" Hill; (back row) Stephen "Admiral Kohl" Cole, "Ensign Paul" Walker, "Ensign Tim" Justis, and "Sir Kenneth" Thompson.

28. 1986
Mark Miller and the University of Oregon Drug Information Center

"Everything but where."
—Slogan on Drug Information Center T-shirts

The University of Oregon Drug Information Center originated in April 1972 as a student-run educational group sponsored by the Associated Students of the University of Oregon. Mark Miller, a pre-med student, secured funds from the student incidental fee committee to start a drug-education library in the basement of the Erb Memorial Union building. The center's charter stated it was to be a source of accurate and current drug information, but was not to counsel or moralize about drug use. By 1973, the Drug Information Center would staff an informational booth at the Oregon Renaissance Faire, the predecessor to the Oregon Country Fair.

In 1969 and 1970, Mark had volunteered at Night Flight, which helped runaways, and at White Bird, where local overdose cases often landed. He had seen how problems often got worse when overdose cases ended up in a hospital emergency room, where the medical personnel were unfamiliar with how to treat patients freaked out on hallucinogens and other drugs.

In 1971, he shared his concerns with Dr. Fay Meyns, a physician and medical librarian for Sacred Heart Hospital in Eugene. Together, they researched and wrote a book detailing the best emergency procedures for treating drug overdoses. In the late 1960s and early 1970s, there was no guide or manual for handling the epidemic of overdose cases that landed in hospital emergency rooms. When their book was rejected by conventional publishers, Mark asked the ASUO incidental fee committee to finance it for distribution to area hospitals for use by medical personnel, on the premise that many students then were experimenting with drugs and some were ending up in hospitals with overdoses.

After their request won approval and the book was published, UO student body president William Wyatt approached Mark with an idea. The university and White Bird had hatched a plan two years before for a Drug Information Center, but it had never been implemented. He asked Mark if he would help launch it.

After securing initial funding for a drug library, the Drug Information Center settled into an office in the EMU basement. The group ordered an extensive collection of pharmacology and medical texts to provide students with accurate, current information. The center recruited student volunteers for drug education training. Trained student volunteers would help the center reach more people with services.

The University of Oregon Committee for Protection of Human Subjects, which oversaw all student and university outreach services, issued guidelines that prevented the center from offering any form of counseling. Instead, center volunteers would give out factual information about drugs and drug safety.

The committee also required the center to form an advisory panel of professionals. "We had a doctor, a pharmacist, drug treatment educators, and other members of the community including ministers and juvenile counselors," Mark said. "The doctor and the pharmacist gave us a lot of advice on how drugs could be hazardous, and how people made frequent mistakes in understanding how drugs work. It started becoming evident that a simplified system could be taught to people that would minimize more than ninety percent of the drug mistakes—either intentional or incidental—that were occurring."

The center started its seminars with a discussion of the drugs most likely to cause harm or death. Statistics showed that legal drugs killed more people than illegal drugs, so the center's presentations first focused on the dangers of using or misusing prescription drugs, alcohol, or nicotine. Then they addressed illegal drug use. The UO Drug Information Center quickly established a reputation for offering a common-sense program on making responsible decisions about the use of any drug, legal or illegal.

"Most drug use was not illegal drug use, but that's where most of the education is centered because of concerns about the kids using illegal drugs," Mark said. "Our society doesn't teach them how to make responsible decisions to minimize harm from prescription, over-the-counter, or other legal or illegal drugs. A prominent example in our presentations was the use of alcohol. In this society, we've developed the ethos that we drink to get drunk. No one has ever been taught the one-drink-per-hour rule, where you can get relief from anxiety without the other negative effects." The Drug Information Center's programs filled in the gaps.

Mark noted that three-quarters of a million of people die in the United States every year from nicotine, alcohol, and prescription drugs. "Fifty-eight million people a year are harmed by mainly legal drugs," he said. "We started pointing this out in the 1970s and at that time it was considered radical to dare to point out that most of the danger came from the drugs that were most widely available." The center's curriculum focused on reducing harm and deaths instead of moralizing about drugs.

In the fall of 1972, the Drug Information Center started offering anonymous drug testing through a private company, PharmChem. The company had just won a court case that let it continue offering anonymous drug analyses at concerts in California. "PharmChem had shown something amazing at the concerts," Mark said. "Sixty to ninety percent of the time the drugs they were analyzing weren't what they claimed. That was a surprise to people. It was either outright misrepresented or it might be hazardous substances."

The Drug Info Center won approval from Lane County District Attorney Pat Horton to run an anonymous drug analysis program. The UO student association and the Lane County Health Department came through with funding so the testing could be offered free. Anyone could arrange—through an anonymous phone call—to have a drug sample sent to a private laboratory for testing to see what the drug actually contained. Local newspapers published the results every week, using codes to anonymously identify each sample tested.

In 1973 the Drug Information Center signed up for the Oregon Renaissance Faire to expand its outreach even further. The center's volunteers built a booth next to a little yew tree along Shady Lane in the loop of the upper Eight path near Shady Grove. "We brought our library out to the fair," Mark said. "Everybody was very supportive of us, and we had a wonderful time."

Fairgoers who walked up to the Drug Info booth often asked, "Where?" They'd get the reply: "We can tell you everything but where. We can tell you about the drug. We can tell you about its effects. We can show you what you need to know to make a responsible decision, but we don't know where," Mark noted. Eventually the center staffers got special T-shirts just for the fair. The front said: "University of Oregon Drug Info Center." The back said: "Everything but where."

Center volunteers also brought out a blackboard to create a Drug Information board. "People would come by and they would say what they had seen at the fair and whether it was OK or not," Mark said. "We couldn't do testing at the fair, so we started listing all the drugs people reported, their price, and whether people perceived they

The Drug Information Center sign made the booth easy to locate.

were harmful or not. This became a point of contention with fair staff because they perceived it might be promoting drug use." But Mark compared the drug board to the drug analysis system supported by the district attorney. He pointed out to fair organizers that if the DA could understand and endorse the concept of drug safety information, certainly the fair should.

Also in 1973, Mark and the center's Assistant Director Dale Gordon started teaching drug education seminars to the beginning health classes required of all UO students. "Dr. Warren Smith and Dr. Richard Schlaadt saw the wisdom to bring us into the Health Ed Department," Mark said. "The instructors didn't like how they had to deal with the section on drugs. So instead they would say, 'We've got the Drug Information Center, they've got this amazing drug

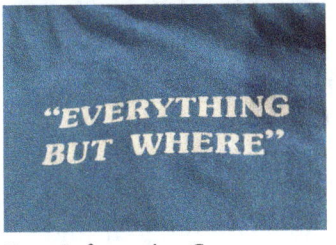

Drug Information Center volunteers wore special T-shirts at the Country Fair.

consumer safety approach that's been recognized nationwide. They've got it in plain language. We can bring in the Drug Information Center staff to give the three-hour component on drugs.'" Mark and Dale offered drug safety education to thousands of UO students every year.

In 1975 the Department of Health, Education, and Welfare deemed the Drug Information Center's educational program to be a model that would be replicated across the country. President Jimmy Carter's administration also designated the center as the statewide Drug Abuse Communications Network (DRACON) affiliate. "We set a standard not just in the state, but

Mark Miller (pictured in the 1980s) noted that the Drug Information blackboard in the booth remained popular with fairgoers.

in the nation," Mark said. "The center was recognized as a replicable model: Something that could be taken to other places in the country, be implemented, and casualties would be reduced."

In recognition of the large volume of student and public requests for services, the University of Oregon decided to change the Drug Information Center from a student-run organization into a faculty-run part of the university's Department of Health Education. By then, Mark and Dale had been teaching the drug safety courses for three years and the UO welcomed them both officially as university faculty members.

Next, the UO Department of Education asked center volunteers to help teach the drug consumer safety course required for student teachers. The ripples from that decision would extend the Drug Information Center's outreach even further into the community.

Teachers who had graduated from the UO and were hired at area schools would ask the center to send someone to talk to their classes about drug safety. The Junior League heard about the program and asked to have their volunteers trained so the women could teach the course in the classrooms. "For the next ten years in Eugene, we trained the Junior League women to go into the elementary schools at the fifth- and sixth-grade level where it could start being effective in teaching basic drug consumer safety concepts," Mark said. "I can't even start to guesstimate the thousands of students that were served this way."

By 1977 the Drug Information Center budget had blossomed to more than $100,000 annually, supporting a full-time staff of ten and numerous trained student volunteers. Its mission had expanded beyond campus to provide drug information and education statewide. The center's library would grow to a thousand volumes and be the largest available to the public on the West Coast. The state of Oregon had also commissioned the center to produce all its alcohol and drug fact sheets. The center started to coordinate local publicity for National Poison Week each year, again working with the Junior League. Meanwhile, the drug analysis program continued to expand.

"The nice thing about the drug analysis project was when we found something dangerous we could put out alerts all through AP [Associated Press], UPI [United Press International], the television stations," Mark said. "The drug analysis project showed something that we had never expected. We fully expected that kids were going to use it to test illegal drugs. What we didn't expect was for senior citizens to start using it on such a large scale for prescriptions. Nobody did, and it was a revelation.

"At this time, seniors were going down to Mexico in the belief that they could get drugs that weren't available in the United States," he added. "This was also the time when Laetrile was hitting, you know—the alleged anti-cancer properties of Laetrile."

Older people began calling the center to see if they could have pharmaceutical drugs tested. Lots of seniors started submitting samples. "We found out that, in fact, these drugs were available in the U.S. readily, but were not being prescribed in large dosages or for lengthy periods of time because of the dangerous side effects, especially in the elderly, who are more prone to them," Mark said. Sometimes the "Laetrile" turned out to be steroids or minor tranquilizers. The center subsequently developed a program on drug safety for the elderly, and began visiting nursing homes, gerontology centers, and hospitals.

For the 1977 Oregon Country Fair, the Drug Information Center added a new attraction to the booth. "We brought our psilocybin mushroom photographs," Mark said. "Gary Menser had just published the *Field Guide to Psychedelic Mushrooms*. Everybody in the world was out there hunting, but they didn't know what they looked like. We had Gary Menser's original eight-by-ten color monographs from his book displayed out there." Fairgoers crowded in to check out the magic mushroom photos. A few folks might have dropped by with a sample to compare to be sure they had the right stuff.

As director of the center, Mark worked with up to twenty staffers to deliver education, information, and instructional services on prescription, over-the-counter, recreational, commercial, and illegal drugs. By the early 1980s the center was directly serving 150,000 Oregonians. The materials emphasized accurate drug information and responsible decision-making skills.

"The police came down from Monmouth from the Board on Police Standards and Training," Mark said. "They had heard of what we were doing. They certified all the police officers in this state. They asked me to come up and give a sample course of what we might teach to the officers." When police saw the presentation, "they were blown away," Mark said.

"My god," they told Mark, "we won't be called 'pigs' in the classroom if we teach it this way." State police appreciated the program's approach, which treated people as responsible adults who simply needed information on making decisions about drugs.

The Coast Guard requested seminars especially focused on handling alcohol risks. Coast Guard members often had to deal with boat operators who had been drinking. "They would come and pick me up in a helicopter at Hayward Field, fly me out to the various stations up and down the Oregon Coast," Mark said. "I'd stop at each one. You can't imagine the thrill of getting into a helicopter and seeing the coast from the air."

Mark once had a "just incredible" experience when his Coast Guard chopper had to suddenly respond to a beach emergency while they were en route to Mark's next stop. "The pilot kicked in the jets and we're moving like crazy," Mark recalled. "Another bird comes alongside us to help with the rescue. Apparently, some guy has fallen off Elephant Rock near Lincoln City."

Coincidentally, Mark knew the pilot, Commander Driscoll, who had served with Mark's father in Vietnam. When they had recognized each other, Commander Driscoll invited Mark to move to the co-pilot seat before they took off. Now that seating arrangement came in handy. A couple of times during the hour-long rescue, the pilot asked Mark to "take the stick" and hold it at a certain angle to keep the chopper steady while the pilot attended a rescue task. Later with the rescue underway, Commander Driscoll "hands me a huge Nikon with a zoom," Mark said, "and tells me to stick my head out of the cockpit and start taking the rescue photos."

That rescue had a happy outcome, but Mark learned from Commander Driscoll that's not always the case. "The North Bend air station does more rescues than anywhere in the country other than Alaska," Mark said. "We lose guys here. The Coast Guard here pays a very, very heavy price and I was never aware of it until then."

The quieter thrills of the Oregon Country Fair would remain on the radar screen for Mark and his cohorts at the Drug Information Center. "The moment you're there—the beauty of it, the feelings that people have, the evidence of the work and how it's being done—everything shows that this is a loving, caring place that is different than everywhere else," Mark said. For many years, a husband-and-wife duo from Seattle would pluck their dual dulcimers as they stood in a nook beside the booth. "They played the most beautiful music and would attract so many people," Mark said. "It was just amazing."

An artist on the center staff painted a sign for the fair booth with the group's name written in nice calligraphy. "At night, that part of the fair was completely unlit, so we would put candles out," Mark said. "Our signs would show up in the night out of the blue and we could hear people say as they walked by: 'Oh, Drug Info Center, cool, now we know where we are.'" The booth would stay open late into the evenings to answer people's questions.

But 1986 would be the last year for the Drug Info Center booth at the Oregon Country Fair. The center had to shut down even though University of Oregon officials fought for three years to keep it open. The center lost key state funding after Nancy Reagan's "Just Say No" to drugs campaign gained traction across the country. The group's dispassionate analysis of facts got tossed in favor of a moralistic slogan.

Already frustrated at the outcome, Mark got a sinking feeling that he had been blacklisted by powers-that-be when he had a hard time landing another job. He would eventually create his own computer services company in Portland, attracting numerous high-tech clients. Mark would later find work as an engineer at Tektronix and as research associate at the Oregon Health Sciences University, where he would help create the Biomedical Information and Communications Center.

Mark also would volunteer with Mothers Against Misuse and Abuse, working with Sandee Burbank of Mosier, Oregon, to direct drug education services. That organization would promote the Drug Consumer Safety formats that had been developed during the heyday of the UO Drug Information Center. At MAMA, Mark would continue to write and produce drug consumer safety presentations and publications. He noted that others also would continue to carry the torch of the Drug Information Center's mission. Notably, staff member Jerry Beck would become a doctor and principal investigator for National Institute on Drug Abuse.

29 1987
Option F: Psychospiritual Rejuvenation

"The Fair without F is just air."
—Jim Guthrie, woodworker and longtime OCF crafter

After Robert DeSpain stepped down as president of the Oregon Country Fair in 1985, the organization struggled to fill his position. Robert had complained to the fair board many times that the job of managing the fair had grown too big for one volunteer to handle. In short, he burned out trying to do it all.

Nevertheless, the board elected as its next president Douglas Parker—a fair board member, former Operations Management Team member, and White Bird volunteer who for years had led the Crisis Intervention training with Zak Schwartz. The board gave Douglas all the responsibilities that Robert had shouldered. Robert handed Douglas a spiral notebook listing twenty-three key items that the fair president needed to do to set up for the event. The handwritten list ran twelve pages. That's all the training Douglas received.

The kids hanging around Main Camp had a hard time pronouncing Douglas's name, and called him "Dog Lips." The nickname got around and the adults picked it up, too—at first in jest and later in frustration.

Douglas would serve as board president for only one year.

Distracted by a romantic affair during Main Camp of the 1986 fair, he shirked many of his duties. Once again, Robert was asked to step up to help the OM Team calm the chaos behind the scenes. That year the OM Team included Anya Montgomery, Palmer Parker, and Sallie Edmunds. They held things together when Douglas went missing.

Douglas "was totally distracted," Robert said. "He wasn't holding any meetings and he wasn't doing anything with his management team. He didn't even have a clue. We held a meeting the Friday morning of the fair and we removed him. I was effectively the general manager again in '86 because of his incompetence."

For the 1987 fair, the board stumbled into a different approach by not coordinating efforts very well. A few board members talked to Bedo Crafts—who had been an Admissions Crew coordinator and had helped in Main Camp—about running for president.

Toward the end of the 1986 fair when they were dealing with Douglas, Bedo was visiting with board members Frank Sharpy and Robert DeSpain, and Main Camp stalwart Palmer Parker (no relation to Douglas). "Doug Parker never really should have been in that job," Bedo said. "He got talked into it and he was not at all prepared for it. We were talking about what a poor job poor Doug had done, and I in my flippant way said, 'I could do a better job than that.' There was this dead silence and I went 'uh oh.' I said: 'No no no! I didn't say anything.'

"They promised me they wouldn't say a word," Bedo added, "but of course within a couple of hours, people on the path came up to me and said, 'Hey, I heard you were going to run for president.'"

Ed Moye and other Main Camp regulars recruited Sallie Edmunds—who had coordinated Energy Park, had been active in Main Camp, and had volunteered on the OM Team for three years—to be fair president. Sallie was living in Hawaii and for several years had been flying to Oregon to spend a month before every fair volunteering in Main Camp. When Sallie and Bedo realized they both had been asked to do the same job, "Bedo and I got together and tried to figure out how to share the work," Sallie said.

That would mark the first time the job of fair board president had been separated from the duties of a general manager. "The fundamental change came about when Sallie and I split the job," Bedo said. Sallie moved back to Eugene and opened a small energy consulting business. She and fair Treasurer Anya Montgomery met with Bedo every Friday afternoon after work for months while they figured out how to carve one job into two.

Bedo knew her strengths would be working with the board and the public. Sallie had much more experience running the event from her years working pre-fair in Main Camp and volunteering with the OM Team. Bedo took the president piece, Sallie took the general manager piece, and the board ratified their fair titles at a meeting on January 25, 1987.

Right off, Bedo challenged a fair tradition. "It used to be that the phone number for the fair was the president's home number," Bedo noted. "I said, 'No, no, no not me!' I changed that right away. We had an answering machine."

The first item on Sallie's list that spring was hiring a new Main Camp cook, who would prepare hot meals for the people working and camping out on the fair property during the month of Main Camp prior to the fair. The cook had to keep a diverse group of people with big appetites happy, which often meant offering a separate vegetarian entree for those who did not eat meat. The previous Main Camp cook who was hired by Douglas Parker, Tove Vils, had moved on to cook for the New Old Time Chautauqua tours.

The fair board placed a classified ad in the *Willamette Valley Observer*, a free weekly newspaper based in Eugene: "Cook needed at Oregon Country Fair, one month, $900."

"Several people applied," Sallie said. "Each one had to audition by cooking dinner. We gave them a certain amount of money, told them how many people to cook for, and what their budget was per person for these meals. One cook made spaghetti for us, and we were just totally unimpressed. The next cook candidate to come in was Ande Grahn. She made the most amazing meal. She kept within the same budget and she was a total delight."

Ande Grahn had been a tree-planter with the Hoedads cooperative, and had also cooked numerous camp dinners for tree-planters after their long, hard days on the slopes. She had learned to cook hearty meals from former fair Main Camp cook Jessie McDonald when they both cooked for a Hoedad crew in 1984 and 1985. In 1986, Ande lived in Eugene with her baby daughter Aster and her husband, Roger, who planted trees for a spin-off company, Trickle Down Reforestation. When Ande saw the fair advertisement in the

Option F: Psychospiritual Rejuvenation

Willamette Valley Observer, she applied because the job sounded fun. She made the tryouts.

"I had to go to Anya's house to cook a meal," Ande said. "Anya Montgomery was the fair treasurer at the time. She let me in at noon. She came home for lunch and unlocked her house and had given me a budget to make dinner for nine people. I went grocery shopping and got all this stuff."

Ande baked two kinds of stuffed cannelloni—vegetarian and meat—plus vegetables and salad. Taste-testers were Anya, Sallie, Quartermaster Fred Silvestri, Main Camp coordinator Ed Moye, Construction Crew Co-coordinators Kenny Rodgers and Santos Narvaez, board Chair Frank Sharpy, OM Team Trainee Jeanne Sharpy, and one other person whose name has been lost in the mists of time.

On top of serving a delicious meal, Ande visited all around the table, telling jokes and sharing stories. The Main Camp stalwarts were impressed to see how easily Ande got along with everyone, despite all the quirky personalities among them. They offered her the job on the spot.

"These guys had hired me," Ande would later note, "and they told me, 'Well, you'll be feeding nine or ten people before the fair and then at the end you'll feed like forty people.' And it turned out that at those last meals I was feeding 120 people. I was by myself and people were so apologetic. More people came out to camp and we didn't know how to not feed people."

Ande welcomed the kitchen help volunteered by Laura (Stuart) Warden, who lived in Walton with her daughter, Crow, and would drive to the fair site to lend a hand with food prep and dishwashing. For a place to sleep before the fair, Ande had erected a sixteen-foot metal frame dome that had a canvas cover. Because the weather was rainy and cool, she brought in a woodstove for heat. Ande hired the girlfriend of one of the fair Construction workers to baby-sit Aster, who was eight months old, and Crow, who was ten months old. During rainy days, the little ones would hang out in the cozy dome.

Everyone appreciated Ande's cooking prowess and organizing skills, and she would serve as Main Camp Kitchen coordinator for the next dozen years.

In the spring of 1987, the board set up a long-range planning committee to consider major infrastructure projects. Erosion control of the banks of the Long Tom River had become a concern as the flooding had started to eat away at the eastern edge of the Eight, especially toward the top where whole booths were about to collapse into the river.

The board considered ways to replace the huge water trucks that lumbered through the tight turns in the fair's pathways each morning to fill up the water containers at food booths and replenish the oak water barrels that served the public. Getting rid of the water trucks by piping water underground seemed like a better idea, but it would take time and resources.

Organizers also sought ways to control the dust that got kicked up into the air during every fair. After a little trial and error, they found what helped best was encouraging grass to grow on the paths and limiting vehicle access to the Eight. Back in September, Frank Sharpy and some friends had sowed grass seed on the paths and at the Main Stage meadow before the fall rains came. After fertilizing and mowing several times in the fall and spring, Frank's efforts had been rewarded with lush green blades.

New peach carts were freshly painted by Jeanne Sharpy in 1987.

Option F: Psychospiritual Rejuvenation

To protect the tender grass, fair organizers instituted a policy to limit craftspeople bringing vehicles into the Eight. The fair purchased several dozen large garden carts so that crafters and volunteers could ferry their camping gear and goods to their booth or camping spot. Because food vendors needed to carry heavy materials to their booths, they were allowed to drive fully loaded vehicles into the Eight. Those measures served to preserve the grass on the paths at least until the first day of the fair, somewhat keeping the dust down.

In the meantime, the fair's internal leadership struggles had not gone unnoticed. A small group of fair coordinators and vaudeville folks formed a group called Club Molimo in 1984 to help combat negative energy and to raise money to supplement the pay for entertainers, whose compensation from the fair sometimes barely covered expenses.

Club Molimo could trace its beginnings to the "F Team," a group of fair friends who flew on vacation to Hawaii to visit Sallie Edmunds when she lived there. They cooked up a plan to promote more fun at the fair. The "F Team" adopted their name after the 1984 board retreat, where everyone chose Option F—"psycho-social-spiritual rejuvenation"—as the fair's main purpose.

"We were upset," said Robert Thompson, who was on Security Crew. "Ed Moye, Moz [Wright], Anya [Montgomery] and Sallie Edmunds—we were upset with the stuff that was starting to happen with the fair."

The F Team made tongue-in-cheek proposals to the board. One called for the board to relocate its annual retreat to Hawaii. "Sallie was living in Hawaii," Patti Lomont said. "And Sallie and Ed and Robert [Thompson] and I and Anya put together these bizarre proposals." For example, The Results of the F Team Motto Contest Winner:

Fair without F is air,
Frank without F is rank,
Cut the crap,
Fun without F is un,
F it out, the F be with you,
You gotta be kidding,
Shit without F is still shit.

"At that time, the fair was starting to swirl the toilet bowl," said

Ed Moye, who was Main Camp coordinator. "There was not enough money—less every year. Crews were having to be cut back. We looked around camp and there wasn't anybody in camp who was under thirty and had a good back. We couldn't figure out who was going to pick up all that and we were really quite concerned."

The F Team switched gears from poking fun at the fair to organizing more fun at the fair. They wanted to generate more magic and excitement after hours.

Their inspiration came from reading about the Molimo ceremony of the Mbuti pygmies in an area of Africa now called the Democratic Republic of the Congo. "If things were not going quite right, the pygmies believed it was because the forest was asleep and therefore was not watching over them," a Club Molimo flier said. "They would take to the woods and create music and noise to wake the forest, making the world right again."

That idea of waking the forest resonated with everyone. "The F Team decided to adopt the name Club Molimo," Ed said, "and set about organizing entertainment along the nighttime path. 'Wake the Forest' became our goal."

The group reached out to other fair coordinators—people with Security, White Bird, and Entertainment all joined. The group sold T-shirts to raise money and also to increase awareness of their idea of "waking the forest."

Club Molimo made plans for a parade at night in 1985 after the crowds had gone home. The parade would start up on the far end of the fair and would wind its way through the Eight to gather people to various shows along the way. After that, the parade would lead everyone out into the parking lot where a stage would be set up for a big finale.

"We'd have a bunch of cars to beam their headlights," Ed said. "We'd light it up and put on a party. The idea was to fire up the path and to get some money to help with entertainment."

But the first one in 1985 was "an abysmal failure," Ed admits. Entertainment Coordinator Moz Wright said that the person who was helping him handle the nighttime entertainment for Club Molimo dropped the ball. The entertainers didn't end up where they were supposed to be at the right time.

In addition, many fair folks felt skeptical of following a parade out of the Eight and into the parking lot. People worried that the

Option F: Psychospiritual Rejuvenation

whole thing was a scheme to double-check fair passes once they were out of the Eight. At the time, people often would share their paper pass with several folks who could use it to sneak in. Nobody wanted to leave the Eight.

For 1986 and 1987, Club Molimo scaled back the spectacle and focused on quality entertainment. To raise funds, they sold Club Molimo T-shirts and sweatshirts that had been silkscreened by Mike Martin, Diane McWhorter's then-husband.

Poster for the first OCF Spring Fling, co-sponsored by Club Molimo.

Club Molimo funneled the profits from the shirts into paying entertainers at the fair. Musicians that Club Molimo helped bring to the fair in 1986 included Scott Cossu, Shumba, Ritmo Tropical, the Soulsations, and Mithrandir. They also paid for musicians to perform at the staff Teddy Bears' Picnic in August.

In 1987, Club Molimo sent a letter to the board revisiting the Hawaiian retreat proposal:

"Dear Board Member,

"... Several years ago, the Fair membership chose Option F as that which most closely described what the event meant to them. Option F is/was psycho-social-spiritual rejuvenation. The enclosed document was drafted by the elusive F Team in November 1984 and addressed the reinstitution of psycho-social-spiritual rejuvenation. Please review this proposal and bring your questions to the March 2, 1987, board of directors meeting. ... Thank you for your time and consideration."

The enclosed document detailing the Hawaii retreat was titled: "Retreat relocation initiative preliminary draft sent to the president of the Oregon Country Fair, prepared by the Executive Committee of the Reintroduction of Psycho-Social-Spiritual Rejuvenation Option F."

While the board didn't vote for the retreat, the board did approve Moz Wright's motion to make "Psycho-spiritual rejuvenation one of the major reasons we hold this fair each year." Moz removed "social" from the phrase, shortening it. The motion became part of the fair bylaws and the word would join the fair's lexicon. Fairgoers for decades would look forward to getting their "psychospiritual rejuvenation" with each fair.

In May 1987, Club Molimo co-sponsored the first Spring Fling for Oregon Country Fair members at the WOW Hall in Eugene. Featuring live music, vaudeville entertainment, a raffle, and camaraderie, the Spring Fling was so successful that it would become a fair-sponsored annual tradition for more than thirty years.

Notably, Club Molimo's offer of extra pay to entertainers would play a key role in the return of Reverend Chumleigh, aka Michael Mielnick, to the 1987 Oregon Country Fair, his first time back in six years. Reverend Chumleigh had missed the 1981 fair because he was working a lucrative gig in Chicago. He had offered to come to Oregon if the fair would purchase plane tickets, but the board turned him down. Later, Michael would blame Entertainment Coordinator Moz Wright for standing in his way. Michael said Moz's lack of support upset him so much that he stayed away for five years.

However, rumors swirled around Entertainment Camp that Chumleigh's absence from the fair may have had something to do with his strong feelings of professional rivalry with the Flying Karamazov Brothers, and in particular Michael's personal friction with Howard Patterson and Paul Magid. The fact that Reverend Chumleigh first returned to the fair in a year when the Flying Karamazov Brothers would be absent only served to reinforce that impression.

The Brothers K would miss the fair in 1987 because they were busy with a six-week run on Broadway, staging their madcap jugglers' version of Shakespeare's *The Comedy of Errors* to much acclaim at the Vivian Beaumont Theater.

Without the Karamazovs to anchor the Circus Stage, entertainers

Option F: Psychospiritual Rejuvenation

again turned to Laughing Moon Theater—Bliss Kolb and Bob Venezia—to write the script for their variety show. The performers invited Reverend Chumleigh to join them in the show at the fair, but no one knew if he really would come. Bliss and Bob penned the Heaven Show in two versions: Plan A in case Chumleigh actually showed up and Plan B if he decided to stay away. The performers also dropped the "Not Chumleighland" jokes that Chumleigh had always disliked. Instead, they nicknamed the stage, "Not the Circus."

Fortunately, the stars aligned for Reverend Chumleigh's return. Michael felt touched that Club Molimo's donations came from crafters and volunteers at the fair. Plan A it would be. The show opened with angels in Heaven planning a telethon because times were hard. Each act became a part of the telethon show. Faith Petric sang like an angel and got everyone to sing along. Artis pulled multiple spoons out of his bag to play heavenly rhythms. Izzi Tooinsky joked and juggled. For one fleeting moment, Tom Noddy encased a young girl angel in a giant rainbow-vibrant bubble. And then came the magic of flight.

"Bob [Venezia] had died and gone to the Pearly Gates where he was met by Bliss Kolb, the angel at the gate," Tom Noddy recalled. Bob received "what we all get if we choose heaven for your afterlife experience"—a white gown, halo and harp. Then

In the "Heaven Show," Faith Petric (left) played guitar and sang; Tom Noddy (right) surrounded angel Paloma Vils-Small (daughter of Tove Vils, a cook for New Old Time Chautauqua) with a giant bubble.

angel Bliss gave angel Bob a sip of the magical elixir from a barely disguised bottle of Jack Daniels with a little cloud glued to the label. Just one sip delivered the miracle of flight! "That cued the heavenly music and the wonderfully mixed voices of Rebo, Teresa Koon, and Jan Luby," Tom said. "It also cued the emergence of the rope." A half-dozen men stood ready offstage to hoist Bob aloft.

"It was the fair's first-ever aerial rigging," Tom said. "As befits that distinction, it was primitive. Bob only went up. The rope was tied off and he hung there in his elegant sheet, halo, and hightop Keds. Like a yo-yo that is not spinning, there was no reason for his body to stay oriented in one position, so he slowly spun around. He would run his long legs in an effort to hurry the spin to bring himself back around to a position that showed off the full outfit. Only then would he strike a pose of playing the harp. Then he would slowly spin some more."

In Plan B, the story would've ended there after a few words from angel Bob. Instead, angel Bob, still hanging from the rigging, introduced the fabulous, stupendous, Reverend Chumleigh and pointed to stage right. But Chumleigh wasn't there. Angel Bob kicked his legs to reorient himself and re-introduced the fabulous, stupendous Reverend Chumleigh while pointing to stage left. Not there, either.

"Then," Tom Noddy said, "from the back of the crowd, we all heard Chumleigh's voice as he climbed over people and made his way to the stage, along with his trained dog Brodie that was wearing sheep's clothing to hide her from the fair's anti-dog authorities." (In fact, OCF President Bedo Crafts had forbidden Michael from bringing Brodie into the fair since dogs were prohibited in the guidelines, but Chumleigh managed to get around that somehow.)

Reverend Chumleigh leapt up onstage to explain why he had arrived late to the show. "It was a marvelous story," Tom recalled, "that involved a conspiracy by the Good Reverend's rival religious leaders including Sun Myong Moon and Guru Maharaji, a deep burial in the catacombs of Springfield, a straitjacket escape, dematerialization, and other mystical matters."

Chumleigh enlisted a kid volunteer from the audience for a mind-reading trick involving a Magic Word. When the volunteer got the Magic Word right, angel Bob finally got lowered back to the stage. Chumleigh brought out "Brodie, Dog of the Future, the World's Only

Option F: Psychospiritual Rejuvenation

Dog with a Ph.D.," for a few tricks. Then for the finale, Chumleigh stripped down to a leopard-spotted singlet and ascended a slack rope. A group of volunteers held one end of the rope; the other was tied to a tree behind the audience. When Reverend Chumleigh made it to his "prayer tower" in the tree, he did his best Oral Roberts impression, exhorting the audience to dig deep for donations to the angelic entertainers among them passing the hat. Everyone had a heavenly time at the Heaven Show.

Club Molimo also sponsored music on Main Stage in 1987, including folk musicians Mary McCaslin and Jim Ringer, soloist Peter Alsop, famed harmonica player Norton Buffalo and his band the Knockouts, pianist Scott Cossu, and the South African dance group Zulu Spear. Other groups playing on Main Stage ranged from Caliente and the Soulsations, to the steel drums of Bakra Bata from Seattle.

Fair favorites Jim Page and Baby Gramps sang at Shady Grove and along the fair's pathways. At the Gypsy Stage, Scirroco joined the Brothers of the Baladi to accompany the belly dance performances. The W.C. Fields Stage showcased the antics of the Mud Bay Jugglers, the political skits of Dr. Atomic's Medicine Show, and the sublimely silly Reduced Shakespeare Theatre. Some of those same acts also played the Daredevil Meadow Stage toward the top of the Eight. The Royal Famille du Caniveaux closed out the Daredevil Meadow show each evening with their bawdy skits, jokes, songs, and dancing.

Community Village again welcomed New Games to the Village Green. The Alter Abled Access Area got prominent space in the village to help meet people's needs. Village workshops included consensus process for environmental activists, tai chi, women's grounding circle, soft exercises for older folks, juggling lessons, and more. Energy Park featured solar energy demonstrations on cooking, water heating, and electricity. Energy Park folks booked Kesey Stage with vaudeville shows and prominently promoted in the *Peach Pit* the giant puppets on parade.

When the fair neared closing time each evening, the volunteers in the fair's Sweep would begin their rounds at Main Stage and funnel fair guests toward the exit at the other end of the Eight. Friday night, after the crowds departed, the forest would awake with extra entertainment sponsored by Club Molimo all around the Eight.

Saturday night, the craftspeople and volunteers would enjoy another amazing Midnight Show. Tom Noddy made sure the last bows were taken by 2:00 a.m.

◫ ◩ ◉

During the Oregon Country Fair's fortieth anniversary in 2009, the fair would erect a temporary stage in Pyrates Cove of the parking lot for special music productions at the end of the fair day. The stage would be dubbed Club Molimo in honor of the first group that had set out to "wake the forest" with a show for everyone in the parking lot.

30 1988

Royal Famille Du Caniveaux and Daredevil Vaudeville Palace Stage aka Du Caniveaux Vaudeville Palace Stage

There's a party at the Fair, everybody knows.
There's a party at the Fair, everybody goes.
Everybody will be laughin'
It always seems to happen.
We're so glad you're at the party at the Fair!
  —Chorus from "Party at the Fair," by R.W. Bailey and Mark Ettinger

Fair coordinators in 1988 decided to move the small stage at Daredevil Vaudeville Meadow to a new location at Upper River Loop. The Long Tom River over time had eroded the meadow, leaving less room for an audience to gather. During popular performances, people watching a show would partially block the main pathway of the Eight.

The new location sat in a natural bowl—known as Toad Hollow—that was scoured out every winter by floodwaters from the Long Tom River. Before the 1988 fair, Ed Moye, who coordinated the project for Construction Crew, hauled in heavy equipment to clear out trees and underbrush.

To line up entertainment for the new stage, former fair president Robert DeSpain and Entertainment Coordinator Lucy Lynch approached Ron Bailey of the Royal Famille Du Caniveaux to find out what it would take for the troupe to anchor the new venue. By 1988, the troupe had been performing for years along the fair's paths and at the Daredevil Meadow. They welcomed the chance to establish a home stage.

"We made two conditions," Ron said. "One was that we get to design and build the stage, which we've done every year since then. And then the second condition was that we get to do two shows a day at the time of our choosing. That's been the agreement ever since, and it's just worked really well except for one thing. We're always trying to have them name the stage 'Du Caniveaux Vaudeville Palace.' … But whoever is in the hierarchy keeps fighting us on that, even though we've put up that stage all these years." Fair organizers settled on calling it Daredevil Vaudeville Palace. The Royal Famille Du Caniveaux would stage wildly popular song-and-dance revues at the Daredevil Palace for more than three decades.

Two members of the Du Caniveaux troupe had first set down roots at the Oregon Country Fair in 1979, when Cathy Sutherland and Rebecca Chace caravanned to the fair from La Conner, Washington, with Michael Mielnik (aka Reverend Chumleigh). Michael had invited them to join about two dozen other entertainers and band members to put on shows at Chumleighland (aka Circus Stage). The lithe young gymnasts had been performing as the Daring Deviante Sisters at Reverend Chumleigh's Alligator Palace in La Conner. They brought their tumbling routine to the fair, delighting audiences.

In 1980 while the Daring Deviante Sisters were performing at the Alligator Palace, Cathy and Beka started dating two singer-songwriters. "At the time, Rebecca Chace was dating P.K. Dwyer," recalled guitarist and vocalist Ron Bailey, "and I think I was just beginning to date Cathy. They were saying how great the fair was and that we should come down." P.K. sang and wrote funny folk songs with the group The Throbbing Gems. Ron sang with the Dynamic Logs, a musical group in Seattle.

P.K. and Ron attended the 1980 fair with Beka and Cathy. Cathy and Beka sketched out vaudeville comedy routines with the

Laughing Moon Theater duo, Sam Williams and Bliss Kolb. The quartet's sketches garnered rousing laughter along the fair's pathways and at Chumleighland Stage. Cathy and Beka also performed their signature Daring Deviante Sisters gymnastics and tumbling stunts at Chumleighland.

In the meantime, Ron and P.K. performed with friends. "We formed a little group to play the paths called the Gutter People," Ron said. "We worked our asses off. We spent the whole day going all over that fair, just like they still do, setting up in some corner to play." P.K. Dwyer had written a bawdy song titled "Extramarital Relations" that caught the attention of other entertainers. Paul Magid (aka Dmitri Karamzov) invited them to sing it at the Midnight Show.

Afterward, when the summer season ended at Alligator Palace, the Daring Deviantes enrolled in a circus school in Paris to learn flying trapeze and horseback tricks. They had signed a two-year contract, but when they arrived at the school they were disappointed.

"We go up to the circus to watch it, and the circus is pretty bad," Cathy said. "The girls had to do really dumb, sexist things. ... At one point this little pony comes out and the pony's running around and he's really fat. He looks so embarrassed to be with the circus that I started laughing. ... The clowns think we're laughing at them, so they come over and they're doing all their antics in front of us, and that makes me laugh harder. When we leave there, I'm still laughing so hard I'm crying."

Beka asked Cathy, "What's so funny?"

"That was funny," Cathy replied, "but you know what? We're not joining that circus."

Beka couldn't believe it. "Are you serious?" she asked.

"Oh, yeah, I'm serious, I'm not joining that circus," Cathy said. "They're not going to let us do flying trapeze. It's a family-run business and you know they were not going to teach us two little Americans their family skills." Cathy saw the writing on the wall, so they switched over to the mime theatrical side of the school.

Meanwhile, P.K. Dwyer and Ron Bailey had followed Beka and Cathy to Paris. They had brought along friends Jennifer Collins and Lou Hevly, who would perform with them as the Gutter People on the streets of Paris. Once, when Lou was walking his dog, he noticed the French signs instructing that dogs should "go" in the gutter. He realized that "gutter" in French translated to "caniveaux" (pronounced CAN-iv-oh). He promptly dubbed himself "Gens Du Caniveaux." When he told the others, they agreed to rename the troupe the Royal Famille Du Caniveaux (Royal Family of the Gutter), and they crowned Jenny as queen and Louie as king.

Cathy and Beka would eventually drop out of mime school and join the Royal Famille Du Caniveaux. The troupe traveled to Amsterdam and sang in the streets there, passing the hat for cash. In 1981 the troupe won the First Annual Amsterdam Street Performers Competition while singing songs written by P.K. and Ron. For three months, the three couples squatted in an apartment slated to be demolished. Just as the building was about to be torn down, they were invited to perform a New Year's Eve show at the Globus Bar in Manresa, Spain, near Barcelona. Afterward, P.K., Beka, and Jenny would return to the United States, but Ron, Cathy, and Louie stayed in Spain. When Ron and Cathy flew back to the United States in 1982, Louie would remain behind, making Manresa his home.

The Royal Famille Du Caniveaux first performed on the pathways of the Oregon Country Fair in either 1982 or 1983. No one remembered exactly which year. They placed all their props in a decorated box the troupe would carry with poles down the fair's path. A few years later they attached bicycle wheels, transforming the box to a gypsy wagon pushcart. As they pushed the heavy wagon through the throngs on the path, they'd shout: "Make way for the Royal Cart!" When the troupe stopped to set up, crowds would gather in anticipation, then laugh at their joke-filled skits and songs with suggestive lyrics.

"We'd carry all our costumes and props in our cart and we'd set up and we'd perform," recalled Rhonda Sable, a dancer who joined the troupe in 1984. By then, the Royal Famille had grown from three couples to more than a dozen performers. "It was crazy, with this many people and that many props and costumes, performing on the paths," she said.

But Rhonda loved her first fair. "I graduated from high school in the Summer of Love in 1967 and went to New York University in Greenwich Village in 1967, right in the middle of the Vietnam War," she said. "I was involved in a lot of protests, so I was right in the smack-middle of the hippie thing. Then in the eighties, when I came here, it was just like it was in the sixties. ... The fair felt very familiar to me. It was like home, and I loved it. ... I felt like I was in Narnia. I just couldn't believe there was anything like this. This was a whole new event for me and it was really fantastic. I've been coming nearly every year since."

In 1986 Ron, then thirty-nine, and Cathy, age twenty-nine, brought their four-month-old daughter Caela to the fair, where they discovered their daughter had an adventurous streak. "She'd be on a big blanket and we'd be rehearsing something as we're throwing a show together, and I'd look down and she would've squirmed a good ten feet away," Cathy recalled. "At four months, she would've wiggled off into the bushes, and we'd all go, 'Where's Caela?'"

When the troupe performed at the Midnight Show, Cathy turned a guitar case into a cradle, where she carefully placed the sleeping baby for warmth and protection. Their performance lasted less than five minutes, but when Cathy returned backstage, she didn't see Caela and panicked. "People had stacked their coats high on top of the guitar case!" Cathy said. "I look at it like, oh my god! And I'm throwing these coats off!" At the bottom of the pile of coats, there was Caela, softly snoring and still safe in the guitar case.

The precocious child would soon join the act. "I have a picture of Caela, two years old, and she's on the stage," Cathy said. "She has these little blue Converse All-stars on, this little dress and her hair's up, and she's going, 'pooh!' Singing."

Members of the troupe pulled together lumber and plans for their new stage in 1988 and traveled early from their home base in Seattle south to the fair in Veneta so they'd have time to build it. "A group of us—Ron Bailey, Mark Ettinger, Bill Shaw, John Olufs and myself went and built the first stage so that we could perform there," recalled Randy Minkler, who had joined the troupe that year. They also prepared skits for the show.

"Some of the ideas came while we were in the shower and the sauna before the fair, while we were working on the stage," Randy said. "We made up a routine called the 'Eight Balls' with the four of us. It was four guys in the sauna and one was 'om-ing.' And it turned into [the song] 'The Lion Sleeps Tonight,' except we changed the words to 'The Sauna's Hot Tonight.'" In the skit, four guys sat on a long bench with white towels wrapped around their waists. Making exaggerated eye movements (the Eight Balls), they joked about the passing parade of naked people—invisible to the audience—in the sauna.

"It was a funny routine," Randy said. "We ended up doing it in the Midnight Show that year. That was my first year. It was really fun and I kept going." Randy would perform with the troupe for at least three decades.

The Royal Famille quickly fell into a rhythm as they prepared each year to put on a song-and-dance show with funny skits at the fair. Every year, troupe members would gather in Seattle before the fair to brainstorm ideas and delegate tasks. Cathy and Rhonda, who both had dance training, often would collaborate on the choreography. Others would work together on songs and skits. The ideas that made the show would include "whatever makes us laugh the hardest," Rhonda said. Randy agreed: "It's just good friends hanging out and joking around with each other. Somebody will say something that will turn into a skit." One time Ron, Randy, and long-term troupe member Danny O'Brien started riffing on the idea of the funny bone and that turned into the "Funny Bone" song.

The songs, the music, and the band always spiced up the Du Caniveaux shows. John Olufs and Mark Ettinger would lead the funky, rockin', ragtag band every year, show after show. Mark and John would contribute songs and incidental show music. Randy

Members of the Royal Famille Du Caniveaux danced and sang at their show at the 1989 fair.

also would sing with the group and help write songs. Guitarist Dave Conant, the now-departed Sir Loin, was regarded as the band's master funkster. Ron regularly played in the band.

In 1989, the Royal Famille Du Caniveaux staged a show called Realville, based on the troupe's experiences when they had traveled back to Barcelona to perform with King Louie. It had elaborate sets and a full story. "The next year, 1990, we did something called Cirque Du Caniveaux," Randy said, "which was a takeoff on Cirque Du Soleil. We needed a clown, so I created the Godfrey character."

Godfrey Daniel specialized in making easy things—like tossing a balloon—look hard.

Randy borrowed Godfrey Daniel's name from W.C. Fields, who used the words in his comedy routine in place of a curse. Materials for Godfrey's head came from a costume shop. Randy's friend Paula Togawa sewed Godfrey's green-and-white striped pants and brightly checkered shirt. On stage, Godfrey would lope out and play with a big balloon, tossing it with slow, effortful motion. The simple schtick evoked humor and poignance. Fairgoers quickly warmed to the character.

"I created something I thought was funny, but he kind of comes to life and has his own personality," Randy observed. "Cathy Sutherland helped me choreograph the first versions of it. I've added things and it's developed a lot through the years. ... It looks a lot harder than it is, and that's the idea of it. He makes easy things look very difficult. ... Just the last couple of years, doing it so often in front of audiences, I've learned how to relax and take my time and listen to the audience."

In the early 1990s, Randy wanted to explore the dramatic and humorous possibilities of having more than one Godfrey on stage. He created Girl Free (aka Claudine, aka Mamie Sunday), a female version of Godfrey with red balloon lips, a blue hair bow, and yellow pearls. She wore a pink dress with white polka-dots. Randy also added more adult male Godfreys. Then in 2004, a little Godfrey would debut, played by four-year-old Isak Moon, son of longtime Du Caniveaux member Shannon Moon. "Isak grew up knowing Godfrey, so he was pretty excited to get to be a Godfrey," Randy said. "He loved it! He didn't want to get off the stage."

Randy also would portray other memorable Du Caniveaux characters. "In '97, I did the Hypnomatic, where I hypnotized the crowd and took them back to the Summer of Love," he said with a wicked laugh. "We're going back, back, back to 1967, thirty years ago! Now look around you. What do you seeee? Tie-dye and hippies!" Of course, at the fair in the nineties, most every audience still would include long-hair guys and people wearing tie-dye. For the Millennial scare in 1999, Randy played the Millennium Lounge Monster, a crooner sporting a pompadour hairdo, gold lamé suit, and an eight-foot-long green tail.

Other popular Du Caniveaux skits included the Du Caniveaux Dancing Bears doing the "Bear A** Waltz" featuring cute lady dancing bears with unusual cleavage, and the Fearless Kundalinis,

Audiences always laughed while watching "The Bear A** Waltz."

an "acrobatic" show starring Chez Ray Sewell. In 2005, fiddler Billy Oskay would wrangle the band into his Big Red studio to record the only CD of Du Caniveaux songs, including favorites "Funny Bone," "Hypnomatic," and "Party at the Fair."

From the beginning, the fair's vaudeville community welcomed the troupe with open arms. In the evenings, they would sit around fair campfires, sharing stories, songs, and jokes. The performers would become closer each year as they gathered at the fair for more than three decades. Over the years, the Royal Famille Du Caniveaux would welcome more than a hundred guest performers to be part of their shows and part of the fun.

Those bonds also brought them together beyond the fair. Often, Tom Noddy, the Bubble Guy, would make his way to Seattle and look up the Dynamic Logs, Ron Bailey's band. "Whenever I was in Seattle as a street performer—me or Artis the Spoonman or Avner the Eccentric—we were always looking for someplace to perform at night, where we could pass the hat between sets," Tom said. "It's often up to the band. If we saw that the Dynamic Logs were playing, then boom! We knew we were in. … R.B. was just really happy to see us, and there'd be a little scene happening there."

Tom Noddy later became friends with a clown in Berlin named Hacki Ginda. "One year Hacki put together a comedy/Varieté festival," Tom said. "He got a [big] sponsor who offered airline tickets. So he offered me two tickets to bring my girlfriend. And my girlfriend couldn't get away, so I offered my girlfriend's ticket to Ron Bailey of Du Caniveaux."

Ron said that Tom surprised him with the airline ticket in 1996. "I was thrilled and inspired by the event!" Ron said. "Every day and night there was unique and wonderful entertainment in two tents, one large theater, and smaller venues in midtown Berlin. We dreamed about someday bringing a festival like that to the people in Seattle."

After that trip to Germany, Hacki sometimes would fly to the states to perform with the Du Caniveaux troupe and the other entertainers at the Oregon Country Fair. The Du Caniveaux family welcomed him into their fold. The physical comedy of Hacki's mime routines needed no translations. One favorite Hacki trick at the fair involved carrying a raining umbrella through the audience on a hot day as he made his way up to the stage. Hacki's umbrella contraption sported an overturned gallon jug of water on top, from which wet drops would cascade down the umbrella and over the edges. People would laugh and try to dodge the "rain" as Hacki bumbled forward through the crowd.

In 2004, Ron Bailey and Maque DaVis would see their dream (inspired by the acts at OCF) of a vaudeville festival in Seattle come true in a very big way. They teamed up with several other Seattle and Oregon Country Fair performers to present the first Moisture Festival. Key organizers included Maque DaVis of Cirque de Flambe and The Fremont Players; Ron Bailey of Du Caniveaux; Sandy Palmer and Simon Neale of The Fremont Players; and Tim Furst, aka Fyodor Karamazov, a former Flying Karamazov Brother. They were assisted by Randy Minkler, Rhonda Sable, Danny O'Brien, John Olufs, Cathy Sutherland, and other members of the Du Caniveaux troupe; the Fremonster Theatrical troupe; and many fair performers. What started as two weekends of Varietè performances would eventually stretch into a four-week extravaganza of vaudeville, Varietè, and burlesque. In 2018, the Moisture Festival would mark its fifteenth anniversary. In 2019, Moisture Festival still would reign as the premier vaudeville showcase in Seattle.

Work on the Moisture Festival would take a lot of Ron Bailey's time away from his regular job, so much so that in 2007 he had to miss the Country Fair. That's the year Caela and the other Du Caniveaux kids truly stepped up to keep the fair spirit going. Cathy recalled that Caela was adamant. "You have to go to the fair," Caela told Cathy. "this is important to me, I want to go do this." The Du Caniveaux "kids" promised to do most of the work. They wrote the script and Caela, then age twenty-one, coordinated rehearsals. Notably, Caela and the other "kids" were almost the same ages as their parents had been when the Gutter People first performed at the fair in 1980.

The 2007 show would turn out great, just as enjoyable as all the others. Cathy found the energy to join them on stage that year, after all.

Over the decades, the troupe would grow and change. "Actually, Cathy and I are the only couple that stayed together," Ron said. "Still, most of the couples remain friends. ... And then we started having kids. Almost all of the kids came to the fair the first year of their lives, and they grew up around the troupe performing at the fair. As soon as they were able to be in a 'bit,' they were on stage."

The second generation of Du Caniveaux "kids" who grew up at the fair would include Mark Ettinger's and Queen Jenny Collin's daughters, Caroline and Kate; Paul Magid's and Beka Chace's daughters, Pesha and Rebecca; Dave Conant's and Dee Dee Crane-Conant's daughter, Vivian; Shannon Moon's son, Isak; Moeppi and Rebekah Ginda's son, Diemo; Billy and Jackie Oskay's daughter, Lauren; and Craig Sutherland's and Jennifer Sutherland Potter's kids, Henry and Chloe. Years later, the second generation of the Du Caniveaux family would laugh around the Entertainment campfire as they recalled the roles they created as children.

"We had one year where the kids got to rebel against us, our ways," Cathy said. "It was the parents versus the kids and we had a whole crazy, nutty skit. ... And the kids got to say, 'We don't want to do your stuff,' and the parents said 'Do your homework!' The adults would say 'We know funny!' and the kids would say 'That's right! You no funny!' ... Now, Caela has a band called Caela and the Dangerous Flares and I'm her backup singer. She sings all her dad's songs." Kate Copeland has her solo singer/songwriter career. The other kids do well in their adult careers and always stay connected because of their shared times at the Country Fair.

Caela would be thirty-three at the fair in 2019. "Caela was four months old when I first came to the Fair," Rhonda noted. "The kids have all grown up. Now all of a sudden, they're starting to take a larger role in the show and it's really different. We started here as single people with no kids or maybe little babies, and now we have young people who have a voice and want to be in the show and want their parts and want to say what we do in the Midnight Show. ...

"It's funny," Rhonda added, "in spite of how much it's changed, it just feels a lot the same to me. ... I come here and we get to camp in the woods and see our friends that we don't see for a whole year and perform these crazy shows ... with a great audience who just adores us. And it's a lot the same."

Ron Bailey said their children are crucial to the show. "I think the troupe probably wouldn't have lasted as long if it weren't for the kids," he said. Just about the time some of the troupe felt like taking a break, "the kids were always so excited to go that we said, 'Oh, we have to go because the kids all want to go.' They helped us renew that feeling that everyone has when they first go the fair," Ron said.

Ron would return to the fair for many more years as everyone pitched in to create a romping, stomping show. "It's amazing," Cathy said. "I feel so lucky that my kid wants to be with me at the Oregon Country Fair!" In 2019, Cathy would turn sixty-two and mark forty years of performing vigorous dance and acrobatics at the fair, with no sign of letting up.

In 2018, Ron, then age seventy-one, sang a song he wrote honoring the dear, departed Faith Petric called "Do You Believe?"

Have you heard Faith? She's over ninety.
She sings her songs and you sing along too.
I saw her last night, strolling the Eight in her nightie.
She made me believe that singing is the fountain of youth!

Ron Bailey would keep writing songs and performing in Seattle and at the fair for four decades. As of 2019: John Olufs still played regularly with several Seattle bands; Randy Minkler would still bring Godfrey Daniel to life; Mark Ettinger played and recorded in New York City; Kate (Ettinger) Copeland lived and performed in Los Angeles; Caela Bailey sang and hosted shows in Seattle; and Cathy Sutherland still did aerial performances and taught gymnastics. All of the Du Caniveaux troupe would remain active in the arts. While they lived all over the map, when the summer rolled around, their creative thoughts would always turn to the fair.

"I feel lucky that we all still want to be together, and we owe it all to the Oregon Country Fair," Ron said.

In 2019, the troupe would get to see a longtime dream come true. For the fair's fiftieth anniversary, the Daredevil Vaudeville Palace would be renamed the Du Caniveaux Vaudeville Stage.

1988
Troubled Waters

"It became clear that this job really needed somebody who was able to give it full-time, year-round focus."
—Sallie Edmunds, Volunteer General Manager of the Oregon Country Fair

As the Oregon Country Fair chugged along in the late 1980s toward its twentieth anniversary, everything seemed to be going smoothly. The highway fight finally came to a satisfactory conclusion, the fair had only a few payments left to make on the property, and attendance kept increasing every year. To most of the people who came, every fair seemed more magical than the one before.

But behind the scenes, the friction among various fair crews, coordinators, and board members was heating up. Despite Club Molimo's efforts to emphasize "psychospiritual rejuvenation" among the organizers, clashes inevitably arose over differing visions of How Things Should Be Run at the fair and their conflicting ideas of the fair's path to the future.

The fair organization had come to a crossroads. Volunteer General Manager Sallie Edmunds in 1988 echoed Robert DeSpain's desperate pleas to the board that the GM job had become too big to be handled by one volunteer. She also emphasized that even after the job had been separated from the fair president's duties, there was more than enough work to justify paying an employee a salary. But Sallie also met resistance. Many fair members and some organizers felt strongly that the fair should remain an all-volunteer organization.

At the same time, land ownership created new challenges that made it clear the fair needed a caretaker for the property. Local kids would often bypass the locked gates to vandalize the booths when no one was around. More troublesome, vandals once started a fire in a booth that was put out by neighbors who noticed it. In 1983, the board had named Chuck Jensen as caretaker. He visited the site from time to time, but that was an ineffective deterrent.

In December 1987, the board named one of its own members, John Winslow, to the caretaker position. "We invested the caretaker with certain sets of things to do," said Frank Sharpy, who was on the board then. "There was a photo journal that he kept and a journal of what was going on on the property." The caretaker's many challenges included dealing with herds of neighbors' cows that would cross the Long Tom River and wander through the figure Eight. He had to contact neighbors to help get the cows back where they belonged.

John Winslow became the first paid caretaker at the Country Fair.

The caretaker's contract stipulated that the fair would provide $300 a month for living expenses and a mobile home on site for living quarters. John Winslow had found a small mobile home for sale for a few thousand dollars, and the board had already approved its purchase and the cost to relocate it to the site. At first the rickety trailer home had no electricity and no running water.

In February 1988, efforts to install a standard three-phase electric line to the fair site did not pan out when a neighbor decided to charge an exorbitant fee for easement access. Instead, Construction Coordinator Ken Rodgers worked with the Emerald People's Utility District to run a less powerful line of single-phase electricity down Chickadee Lane to the caretaker's trailer in March. Ken was assisted by Communications Co-coordinators Chris "Ichabod" Murray and R. "Sparks" Scott, plus the new volunteer electrician, Jim Sahr, who was a longtime crafter at the Shenanigans booth. By May the trailer was finally connected to running water, in addition to the new electric line.

In a controversial move, the board also authorized an electric line to Main Stage to replace the solar electric panels that had been used to power its sound system. The power from the solar panels often would fluctuate—depending on the configuration of the sun, clouds, and shadows—which created problems for musicians' electronic equipment.

The fair board had already debated adding electric power to the Eight in 1987. "Much discussion centered around the role that the OCF has always played in showcasing alternative lifestyles and energy sources," the board minutes noted in April 1987. "It was stressed that the OCF does not want to change this focus. The relative costs of various types of alternative energy were discussed from all angles and vantages."

Board President Bedo Crafts said the meetings got intense. "We had these heated arguments," she said. "Before electricity, the fair was a little village at night."

Sallie Edmunds, with her background in solar energy, opposed the plan. "It was one of those hard things for me," Sallie said. "I wanted the fair to use alternative energy sources and not plug into the grid. I wanted the fair to invest in that. Well, the board had a different opinion."

Even the fair's volunteer electrician argued against wiring more of the fair. "I thought we should have enough to take care of the caretaker's needs," Jim Sahr said. "But then everything else they had to talk me into. Of course, I wasn't the final say. I just would have my arguments. Sometimes I would prevail in some parts of it and sometimes I wouldn't. Then when it was over, I would do whatever it was I was supposed to do. Of course, immediately Main Stage wanted power."

The board considered it an advantage that electricity in the Veneta area came from Emerald People's Utility District, a community-organized utility that broke away from the corporate Pacific Power & Light company in the mid-1970s. The board also liked that EPUD donated a percentage of its profits to causes opposed to nuclear energy. Board members discussed electric power again at their June 1, 1987, meeting. At that point they clarified that electric power would be limited to the refrigerator trucks, the barn, Main Stage backup, White Bird, the ice truck, "and caretaker when we have one." But that did not settle the issue.

"There were many people who were very adamant they did not want electricity coming into the figure Eight," Main Camp Coordinator Ed Moye said. "They did not want it going anywhere in there. The fair was supposed to be pre-electricity. It was supposed to be a medieval village ... even the Main Stage, where we were frying musicians' expensive equipment with the fluctuations of our solar-powered electricity. Solar power was a great PR thing, but about that time all this digital equipment started hitting music. These guys are coming in with thousand-dollar rigs and they were scared to plug it in."

After the 1988 fair ended, Main Stage Entertainment Coordinator David Paul Black would thank the board for getting electricity to Main Stage because "it really made a big difference," he said. "It was the best year yet."

And indeed, the 1988 Oregon Country Fair featured plenty of fun and festivities for the 25,000 fairgoers who would attend, most of them unaware of the simmering philosophical disputes among fair leaders and volunteers. Perfect summer weather prevailed on three sunny days with temperatures in the low eighties. David Paul booked a sonic variety on Main Stage from reggae to rock to salsa to new age to jazz.

Inspired by Robin Williams' recent hit film, *Good Morning, Vietnam*, Main Stage emcee Denny Guehler welcomed the public with his Oregon Country Fair rendition of the actor's line, bellowing: "Good morning, Oregon Country Fair!" Thus began a fair tradition that would continue for three decades.

Reverend Chumleigh livened up the Saturday morning opening slot on Main Stage with "Church of the Incandescent Resurrection" featuring his irreverent humor and wild antics. Chumleigh also got a starring guest role with the Royal Famille Du Caniveaux at their brand-new Daredevil Palace.

Over at the Circus Stage, the Flying Karamazov Brothers joined with a cast of friends to produce the "Little Nemo" show. A young Jasper Patterson—the son of Howard Patterson aka Ivan Karamazov—played Little Nemo. When Little Nemo went to sleep in the play, his vivid dreams would be acted out on stage by the adults. Of course his dreams included crazy juggling by the Flying Karamazov Brothers, plus a series of acts by Artis the Spoonman,

Faith Petric, Girls Who Wear Glasses, Laughing Moon Theater, Tom Noddy's Bubble Magic, and Magical Mystical Michael.

Community Village invited fairgoers to "Participate in the essence of the fair. ...Come to Community Village and surprise yourself." Energy Park added Ag Alley, a new booth that promoted ideas on organic farming and gardening, including organic weed and pest control. It was staffed by Tilth, Organically Grown Co-op, and Integrated Pest Management.

Crafters again laid out their amazing array of batik and tie-dye clothing, beaded barrettes, leatherwork purses, crystal pendants, fancy hats, and hand-painted ceramics. The food booths fired up their stoves to cook up tasty blintzes, samosas, enchiladas, stir fries, and more. Fairgoers could encounter around any corner the Risk of Change Puppet Theater; Leo de Flambeaux; the Radar Angels; or singers Baby Gramps, Jim Page, and Amber Tide. Jugglers and clowns took to W.C. Fields Stage, including box juggler Charlie Brown, the Mud Bay Jugglers, mime Russ Fish, and Clowning Around.

Out in the parking lot, fairgoers could enjoy camel rides sponsored by Oasis natural grocery store in Eugene as a fund-raiser for Unity School. Bedo remembered well her visit that year with the insurance salesman that handled the fair's account.

"Every year as president, I had to go to Portland to deal with insurance," she said. "One year we had camels. We also always had the pony rides. I came in and said, 'Oh by the way, we also have camels.' And he said, 'Oh no, no please.' I'll never forget it. He just put down his pen and said 'Are you serious?' And I said, 'Yes, I am.'

"We didn't realize what the liability would be," Bedo added, "having all these kids ride the camel saying 'look ma, look pa!' We were really truly hippies not knowing what we were doing. We were doing it all by the seat of our pants."

In August 1988, the board approved a huge infrastructure project to add underground water pipes to deliver fresh water around the fair. The idea had been percolating along for a while to provide safe water easily to all parts of the Eight.

The project took on greater urgency after the Lane County Health Department raised serious concerns about the safety of the fair's water supply. In particular, the department noted that the oak water barrels posed a high risk of possible contamination and that

Ry Newsom (left) and Forest Elliott (aka Elliott Farren) at the fair's water barrels.

food vendors were at risk of not having enough water to provide adequate sanitation.

The first part of the project would cost $10,000 and would involve digging trenches for pipes along one side of the Eight—starting by Daredevil Palace Stage at the top of the Eight, running along the East Thirteenth corridor and ending near the Patti's Pies booth and a Dunk Tank. The board also approved burying internal telephone communications wires underground with the piping.

Usually, action on business and budget items on the fair board's agenda took two meetings: New Business would be noted on the agenda to alert members it was coming up; but the board would discuss and vote on an agenda item at the second meeting, when it came up again as Old Business. Coordinator Ken Rodgers and the Construction Crew sought the variance to the usual board process so that digging the trenches for the pipes could begin right away and be completed before the rainy season set in. Ken and Ed Moye had recruited Tim Wolden—a civil engineering student at Oregon State University who had participated in Energy Park—to help design the plans.

"After a brief meeting with the Water Crew coordinators to determine how much water was needed and where the demand was greatest," Tim Wolden said, "I designed a multiple loop pumped system that would theoretically provide ample water to three hose carts at a total flow of fifty gallons per minute. With outlets spaced every 150 feet, water would be available for Fire Crew and whatever the future would bring."

But the project got off to a rocky start.

Ed said that at the first meeting, Water Crew Co-coordinator Chris Howe wanted the whole plan to be approved by Community Village. While the need to put the pipes in place was urgent, Community Village was known for talking for hours on end to reach consensus. That approach did not sit well with Ed, who was worried about completing the massive project on time.

"We put together the water project the same way we'd done other things," Ed said. "We got people on the crews who were involved together and we'd sit down and talk. ... Dave Corcker from the Water Crew was part of that design group. He was a fair water truck driver and he had some experience in construction, so he spoke the language. We decided to make him the Water Crew representative."

Three months later in November, the committee overseeing the water project complained to the board of directors that the Construction Crew had not followed the right process in doing the job. At the same meeting, members of the Water Crew accused Ed of not listening to their concerns. Water Crew Co-coordinators Henry and Chris Howe resigned over the incident.

The board appointed a mediation team of Kathryn Madden and Dahinda Meda to meet with the water system project committee to resolve the disagreements. That's when Ed met Kathryn, a board member whose involvement had started in Community Village. "She was assigned to interview the asshole who was pushing everybody around," Ed said.

"At that point, I was on the board and there was this huge stink about the water project," Kathryn said. "How there were horrible feelings and this guy Ed Moye—Evil Ed Moye—his name was key there. So the board of directors decided to assign Dahinda and me to interview all the players and kind of see what happened, then to type up their statements and present some sort of report. And that was a very interesting little process.

"But I did meet with Ed, that was the first time," Kathryn added. "I knew who he was. I thought he was a loud-mouth asshole from

Main Camp, actually, and he thought I was the queen of the hokey-pokey people, some hippie chick from Community Village, some airy fairy hippie. I remember sitting down with Ed at the French Horn [restaurant in Eugene] and interviewing him, and listening to him tell his whole side of the story. I believe there was a lot of defusion because we took the time to listen and write it up. But then nothing ever really happened."

Disgruntled feelings spread like wildfire among the fair family that fall. More than eighty fair crafters banded together in a Crafts Guild to challenge the fair over the difficulty of getting new craft items juried in as well as other issues. In response, the fair board authorized a Craft Committee—composed of five board-appointed members and five representatives from the Crafts Guild—to sort it all out.

Also that autumn, the caretaker's trailer needed repairs on a leaky roof and unsafe railings. John Winslow rebuilt the railings and used plastic sheeting held with duct tape to fix the roof. John also regaled the board with stories of how hard he had been working on site, yet he failed to credit the volunteers who had helped him.

At the November meeting, the board approved the Personnel Committee's recommendation to create two paid positions: a general manager and a caretaker. In a move they would later regret, the board also approved back pay for a full year for the caretaker.

Construction Coordinator Ken Rodgers resigned his post to protest the board's decision on the caretaker, among other concerns.

In December 1988, Sallie Edmunds resigned as the volunteer general manager, announcing she was moving back to Hawaii. She had accepted a job with the National Park Service. The board's decision to offer back pay to only one employee confirmed for her that she had made the right choice.

Adding to their troubles, Jill Heiman resigned as the fair's attorney. Her close friends no longer helped organize the fair, and she knew that the fair would need additional legal guidance when the organization hired paid staff. She recommended Eugene attorney Russell Poppe to handle the fair's legal matters and promised to consult with Russell as needed.

The board sent a letter thanking Jill for her years of work and appointed a committee to make an independent search for an attorney. In the end, the board would accept Jill's recommendation to hire Russell. Fair organizers had their hands full trying to find and hire a new paid general manager.

At the board's first meeting of 1989, Ken Rodgers filed a grievance over the board's approval of retroactive pay to John Winslow. Longtime Banners Coordinator Wally Slocum submitted a letter arguing against paying a general manager.

The board also wrestled with its own process and adopted rules limiting the length of the meeting. As a result, the first meeting of the year had to be continued the following week. That's when the board approved a motion by Marshall Landman to extend an apology to Sallie Edmunds and Ken Rodgers for not handling the compensation question very well. The motion noted that the board should have developed a compensation policy before granting John Winslow back pay.

In February 1989 the board approved the Personnel Committee's recommended job description and pay scale for the general manager. Sallie said she considered applying. "I really thought long and hard about whether or not I wanted to be the first paid manager of this organization with everything that would come with that, and all of what would be expected," Sallie said. "All of a sudden somebody's getting paid to do this, and it just to me seemed like a huge nightmare." Instead, Sallie settled into her job in Hawaii.

1989 Twentieth Anniversary Fair

"May the Peach be with you."
—Ad for Organically Grown Co-op in the 1989 *Peach Pit*

In April 1989 the board hired longtime fair artisan Arna Shaw as the fair's first paid general manager. A weaver, Arna happened to be married to Ron Chase, the fair's former treasurer and board member. She and some friends shared a booth at the fair in 1970 and later joined the Big Elk booth on Shady Lane of the fair's Upper River Loop. Arna had sold handwoven clothing at the fair for almost two decades.

Arna had met many of the fair's key organizers through Ron, but she had avoided fair politics until the Crafts Guild formed to protest the fair's jurying process. Arna joined the guild and started attending board meetings. That's when she heard about the general manager job.

"It came at the right time in my life," Arna said. "My back was hurting from weaving, which is very hard on you physically. My daughter was leaving for college. It just seemed like the right time to try something different and that seemed like a job I could do. I knew the fair really well. I understood the issues from having been around it for all those years. And I'd also done crafts shows my whole life. I made my living doing crafts shows."

Arna knew there had been contentious discussions over whether the general manager should be paid or not. "I don't know why I was naïve about their politics," Arna said. "I'd watched it enough. I walked into this total can of worms, just by being hired."

A month after she took the job, Arna received a letter from Lane County reminding the fair that all new permanent structures constructed at the fair site would need county permits and proper plans before work began. The letter also noted complaints from a "concerned Veneta resident" about previous fairs and proposed a meeting to discuss the issues: blocked roads in the neighborhoods, inadequate access for emergency vehicles because of the traffic jams, uninvited cars parked on private property, and uninvited campers on private property.

For years fair organizers had tried to address neighbors' concerns. Sandra Bauer, Patti Lomont, and other Main Camp volunteers would visit neighbors ahead of the fair every year to try to smooth the relationships. They would listen to neighbors' complaints and try to find ways to address them. Fair organizers had been distributing hand-painted signs for the neighbors to display in their driveways to discourage unwanted parking and camping.

The fair also worked with the county and state to post special no-parking signs during the event. "I met with law enforcement, local and federal, every year," said Bedo Crafts, who was still fair board president. "I had a meeting with cookies and coffee for the officers so we could talk about what they could do for us and what was our own responsibility." The county sheriff's department stepped up law enforcement during the event. But neighbors still persistently reported that traffic jams gridlocked their streets and that fairgoers trespassed on private property.

Arna managed from the beginning to implement key changes at the fair. Right after the board hired her, at that same meeting, Arna proposed to create a Teen Crew for the 1989 fair with consultation with the OM Team. Arna had gotten the idea from talking with Ron, but the Community Village's Youth Job Services program had paved the way by placing dozens of teens with fair crews. The OCF Teen Crew would bring more structure and fair resources to the process of connecting teens with crews.

"I created the Teen Crew the very first year," Arna said. "I can't stand moving at the rate of molasses. I'm not good at it. I'm a doer. ... I'd seen all these teens who hung out in groups. I really saw a need to harness this energy. I didn't see the fair going anywhere without it. ...

"But had I asked for money, it would've taken another two years to get it going," she added. "If I'd asked them to fund a program, they would've put a committee together to study it. So I just did it. We may have run for a year or two without food vouchers and then they went to the board, to get food vouchers for the teens. By then they were so well established and so popular, it was kind of impossible for the board to say no. It's actually, I think, the best thing I ever did."

In the long term, the Teen Crew would help ensure the success of the fair's volunteer crew system. Many Teen Crew members would find regular volunteer jobs among the fair crews after they "graduated" to adult status. And in the decades to follow, many new crew coordinators could trace their first fair jobs to Teen Crew.

With the fair coming up only three months after she was hired, Arna threw herself into the fair's organization, figuring things out as she went. She assembled a seasoned Operations Management Team to help her out: Sallie Edmunds, Marshall Landman, Frank Sharpy, and Lucy Lynch. All but Lucy had served on the OM Team before.

"As usual, the crews pretty much knew what they were doing," Arna said.

A month after she was hired, Arna faced a challenge related to the county permit system. "There was a little scene with George Braddock that year really early on," Arna said. "He'd been told he couldn't enlarge his holding tank without a permit. I got a call before Main Camp opened that George was doing what he was told not to do and he wouldn't stop work. He had a crew in there that wouldn't stop work. Would I come out and deal with it?"

Construction Co-coordinator Dennis Todd was the caller who brought Arna to the site. "George tried to do an end run around on Memorial weekend and we busted him and had to bring out Arna to get him off site," Dennis said. "Arna stood by me in the confrontation with George at the sauna. He tried to do an end run around my direct instructions that he had to get a building permit if he was going to change his water reservoir at all."

Instead of simply replacing a wall of the reservoir, George and his construction workers had placed the new wall two feet further out, enlarging the reservoir, Dennis said.

"I have great respect for George," Arna said. "He's a real asset to the fair. He does a really good job at the sauna. But George—at least in those days—he always wanted to push his boundaries and see how far he could go. One of the things I always liked about George is that he's really kind of in your face about it. I knew where he stood."

Arna drove out to the site and spoke with George. She pointed out that he was not following his own construction proposal. George agreed to stop the work.

At the June 5 meeting, the board voted down a recommendation from the OM Team to put the sauna on probation for one year for not getting the required county permits before starting construction. But the board approved a follow-up motion by Marshall Landman, who served on the board and the OM Team, stating that all booths must get county building permits whenever required for construction before doing the work.

Ande Grahn returned to head up Main Camp Kitchen in 1989 and Laura (Stuart) Warden came back to help Ande out. The years when organizers built the water system remained among some of Ande's fondest memories of pre-fair. Her daughter Aster was a toddler by then. "We were doing this big water infrastructure project," Ande said. "Tim Wolden would be out here to work on it and he had just a passle of kids. Anna Wolden was the same age as my daughter Aster and Laura's daughter Crow. ... They just were little girls growing up in Main Camp for a couple years. So sweet."

In those days, organizers stored hay bales in Main Camp until they could be distributed for use around the fair. "The kids would go into the pile of hay bales," Ande said, "and they would hollow it out and make these incredible forts, two and three stories. They would camp in it at night. It was really fun."

For many months before the fair, crews had met to formulate ways to make the 1989 fair the best ever for the twentieth anniversary celebration. The Water Crew had to figure out how to distribute water from the new underground system along the East Thirteenth stretch of the Eight. Each morning before the fair opened to the public and each evening after it closed, Water Crew members would use hose carts, connecting the hose to various outlets in the pressurized water system so they could fill the water reservoirs in each food booth. They also would use the hose carts to top off the oak barrels that still served for drinking water.

However, they found a few glitches in the new system right before the fair.

"The first year that we had it, we had this complicated system of three pumps in the well-house," said Dennis Todd, who had jumped in to help on the project. "We had a recurrent problem with an airlock in the system. The water pressure would drop and the pumps would shut off. Right up until Thursday night we were wrestling with it. I got maybe three hours of sleep Thursday night, and Friday morning Tim Wolden and I got up and we finally resolved the issue, but it was touch-and-go that first day."

At the same time, the Water Crew had to keep its old procedures for the river side of the Eight. Every morning and every evening, a large tanker truck full of water rumbled into the Eight and maneuvered along the thinnest, curviest parts of the path that followed the Long Tom River so the Water Crew could deliver to food booths and water barrels on that side of the fair. These would mark the last few times any water truck driver would make that treacherous drive through the pedestrian throngs of fair volunteers, crafters, and entertainers milling in the pathway.

Traffic Crew also faced a big and exciting challenge: staffing the new entrance to the fair site from the newly rerouted Highway 126. The rebuilt highway traveled due west from a stoplight intersection in Veneta along the fair's southernmost border, cutting off a small corner of fair property.

In fact, just before the highway opened to the public, the fair pulled a little prank on the portion of the highway that was built on the fair's corner. "We lost a little part of the fair to Highway 126," said Bedo Crafts. "The night before the highway was opened to the public [Frank] Sharpy and the other boys wanted to set off fireworks on the road."

Bedo told them to go for it. "It's ours now still," she noted. They parked the Peach Truck with its tank full of water nearby for safety. "So we had fireworks on that part of Highway 126," Bedo said. "Every time I drive over that stretch of 126, I laugh."

The highway previously had followed county roads, taking a sharp turn north at the Veneta stoplight before turning west on Suttle Road, which ran near the fair's north side.

Traffic Crew would designate the old Suttle Road entrance for fair volunteers and for the city buses that brought fairgoers out to the site during the event. For the new public entrance on the south side, Traffic Crew crafted a plan to open a wide area so they could bring in vehicles off the highway as quickly as possible and then park them.

Twentieth Anniversary Fair

They hoped the new traffic plans would minimize the backups that had plagued fair neighbors for two decades.

Archaeology Crew erected a new exhibit at the old Daredevil Meadow along the Upper River Loop of the Eight that featured information on the archaeological sites found on and around the fair property during the highway relocation fight. Archaeology Crew would curate the exhibit for many years after that. Over the next three decades, the archaeology exhibit would be enlarged and expanded to encompass split-cedar structures and life skills demonstrations such as fire-starting and basket-weaving. In 1994 the meadow would be dubbed Archaeology Park, aka Ark Park.

Fun surprises awaiting fairgoers to the twentieth anniversary celebration included a new Children's Stage near Child Care, extra parades, and a Country Fair birthday card.

Another sweet surprise: Fair co-founders and ex-spouses Bill and Cindy Wooten would get together again during the 1989 fair and rekindle their romance. Bill had been living in Florida since 1982 with his wife, Eileen, but they had recently gotten divorced. Gerry Mackie, Jill Heiman's husband, had been in touch with Bill and persuaded him to come back to Oregon to celebrate the fair's twentieth anniversary. Early Main Camp stalwarts Sandra Bauer and Cindy had helped plan an opening ceremony to mark the fair's anniversary, and Bill would join them Friday morning on Main Stage.

The twentieth annual Oregon Country Fair opened on a perfect summer day with blue skies, sunshine, and temperatures headed for the mid-eighties. The new highway entrance got fairgoers' vehicles off the highway in record time with virtually no traffic backups for the first time ever.

The Fighting Instruments of Karma Marching Chamber Band/Orchestra led a parade to Main Stage playing "Happy Birthday," followed by the giant puppets of Risk of Change, to launch the twentieth anniversary ceremony at Main Stage at 11:30 Friday morning. The celebration featured a six-tier carrot cake with cream cheese frosting that would serve a good portion of the gathered crowd. Kim Murphy, owner of Fall Creek Bakery, said the birthday cake required fifty pounds of flour, thirty-five pounds of carrots, twenty-five pounds of honey, and took three days to make.

Cindy Wooten spoke first and praised the event as "this great

Tim Furst (aka Fyodor Karamazov) led the marching band parade to Main Stage for the twentieth anniversary celebration.

The tiered anniversary cake looked great before the top tiers started to slip off.

tribal reunion that bears both cultural and political significance." Bill Wooten told the boisterous crowd that the first fairs were intended as a political statement on how a community can live in peace using fewer resources.

Steve Elliott, who volunteered on Main Stage Crew, remembered the celebration didn't go quite as smoothly as organizers had hoped.

"We had a company bringing us in a cake, it was like four feet high or something," Steve said. "Robert Painter was still on the crew. He built a riser for the cake to sit on, but then they had a couple of people standing on that riser to put the top parts of the cake together, and it couldn't take that. The riser tipped and the cake slid. We kind

Twentieth Anniversary Fair

Cindy Wooten (left) and Bill Wooten (center) spoke about the values that brought people together to create the fair. Ken Kesey (right) railed against the Sweep from Main Stage during the fair's twentieth anniversary celebration.

of restacked it, got it together. From out in the house you couldn't see the cake all that well. Then they had all of us ferrying cake to get it out into the crowd real fast, you know, take big chunks and run it out. I tripped with a piece. Then I was carrying a piece and somebody had their legs out. I went over that, lost another piece out in the field."

Denny Guehler, who was Main Stage emcee, also remembered the glitches in the ceremony. "Cindy got out and talked and Sandra got up and talked and Bill got up and talked," Denny said. "And Ken Kesey was there." A friend pulled Denny aside and said, "Make sure Ken gets a chance to talk." Denny agreed to hand him the mike as the cake was being served.

"Ken got up there and just absolutely tore the fair a new asshole." Denny said. "He was fucked up and he was on a tangent about he wanted the fair open to the public. It's kind of like Chumleigh's thing, you know, that the fair was run by a bunch of hippie elitist fascists. Kesey thought that entertainment like the Midnight Show should be available for everyone. And if they couldn't do it within the Eight, then it should be out in the parking lot. And on and on and on and on."

Ken specifically ranted about the fair's Sweep that cleared out the public every evening. He said it caused an us-versus-them mentality that was un-Fair-like. Ken exhorted the crowd to resist the Sweep en masse.

Steve Elliott said he found the whole thing humorous. "Kesey's such an iconic figure here at the fair. Everybody in the crowd was loving what he was saying," Steve said. "But the staff, of course, they were all behind the stage pouting. They weren't as happy about the idea of making it a free fair."

Board President Bedo Crafts said she was livid. "I'd known Ken Kesey a long time and when he said we did not need the Sweep, I almost broke down right there," she said. "This was dangerous—simply dangerous! There were hundreds of people in all stages of inebriation who wanted to be at the fair. It was really irresponsible for him to rant against the Sweep."

In the middle of his diatribe, Ken suddenly turned to look at Denny Guehler standing to one side off stage and shouted "You! You big emcee! You think you can pull me off this stage? I used to be a wrestler at the U of O!"

"No Ken! Just go ahead!" Denny responded.

"He warned me not to try and physically pull him off the stage, which was the furthest thing from my mind," Denny said. "When he got done, I just walked over to the microphone and I said, 'Ken Kesey, Oregon's poet laureate.' And he left and a lot of people laughed."

Afterward David Paul Black, Main Stage coordinator, congratulated Denny on handling the prickly situation perfectly. By ignoring Kesey's inflammatory comments, Denny kept the handoff positive and neutral.

"Chez Ray" Sewell, the restauranteur, also remembered that day well.

"It really should be recognized the influence that Kesey had on the Country Fair," Ray said. "The whole idea behind the Pranksters and the bus and its quest was to expose people to new ideas and thoughts and notions of freedom in somewhat of an in-your-face rebellious way. It was, I think, a difficult dance for the fair to manage. Kesey was somebody you just can't manage. He was very much a pain in the ass. But I think the fair needs that pain in the ass. We all do. It's a pain in the ass to get out of the comfort zone, but if you stay in the comfort zone, nothing happens."

Ken Kesey would often stop by Ray's booth during the fair. After the anniversary event where he called for an end to the Sweep, he went to visit Ray. "Ken had some huge moments with the fair on the Main Stage," Ray said. "Then he'd come back to my booth and say, 'Oh, I think I did it this time!' He'd said something that had really pushed it over the edge. You know, it was hard for him in a lot of ways."

Bedo Crafts said she got back at Ken. "I started a rumor in well-placed places that Kesey had offered his place for a party after the Sweep that night," Bedo said. "I don't know what happened because I'm at the fair, but I got a call from Ken saying, 'Bedo, what the hell are you doing?' Apparently people showed up."

Reese Prouty, a volunteer with Fair Central, also had become livid when Ken Kesey denounced the Sweep. She said she helped make sure the rumor got spread around. "I was standing there thinking, 'My job is hard enough doing the Sweep without you antagonizing all these people out here,'" Reese said. "I don't even remember whose idea it was, but we went into town and made posters that said the Grateful Dead were playing at an impromptu party that same night. We put Kesey's address on it and we distributed them around the fair!"

Back at the Main Stage meadow on Friday, Entertainment Co-coordinator Moz Wright marveled as the hot air balloon project continued the fair's twentieth anniversary celebration. Artist Robert Dunniford crafted the balloons from tissue paper and Elmer's glue, and used a small heat source to fill them with warm air. Moz would later list it among his peak fair memories. "What an experience!" Moz enthused. "It's in the great meadow and you see those things rise and fly. Everybody in the meadow looked on in amazement."

Moz said he got to ride on the back of a motorcycle to retrieve one of the balloons that had remained intact. "That was one of those other high points," he said. "I had to hunt down one of those and fly it again. It's the only one that I know of that ever came down. There were so many trees, you know. We got to take it back over and fly it again."

Energy Park upped its game with daily demonstrations of solar refrigeration, solar cooking, solar water heating, solar-generating electricity, and a bicycle-powered radio. "The focus of this year's Energy Park is Planet Earth, a system that is being overtaxed today," Energy Park volunteer Gaelen Laue wrote in the *Peach Pit*. "We will be presenting information on global warming and other energy issues from national and international sources." This expanded their focus from just regional energy to a much larger picture. It was also the first time Energy Park literature warned about global warming, decades before climate change would make its way into the national consciousness.

To attract crowds, Energy Park booked a festive lineup at Kesey Stage that ranged from music to juggling to mime. Friday and Saturday the music of marimba bands Balafon and Shumba would beckon fairgoers to dance along to the poly-rhythmic beat.

Community Village offered the usual New Games and tai chi on the village green, while workshops invited fairgoers to explore Lucid Dreaming, Safer Sex, Origami, Bioregionalism in Pacific Cascadia, Peace and Justice by Computer, Women's Grounding Circle, Altared Life, and other eclectic topics.

"In the midst of sparkling crystals, aromatic foods, and the river of people that is the figure Eight, rests an island of idealism, the Community Village," The *Village Vision* stated in its issue for Friday, July 7, 1989. "At the heart of the Oregon Country Fair, the Community Village stands for social-environmental awareness by providing a forum for the free communication of ideas."

At the still-new Daredevil Vaudeville Palace, the Royal Famille Du Caniveaux staged their musical comedy revue twice daily, and Reverend Chumleigh (aka Michael Mielnik) joined Laughing Moon Theater (aka Bliss Kolb and Bob Venezia) for a theatrical magician set.

Over at Circus Stage, the Flying Karamazov Brothers and guests presented "It's A Wonderful Fair," written by Paul Magid. Guests included bubble guy Tom Noddy, Artis the Spoonman, magician Magical Mystical Michael, music duo Girls Who Wear Glasses, and tap dancer Toes Tiranoff.

John Cloud, on top of the ladder, helped hang a banner for the Circus Stage show, "It's a Wonderful Fair."

Tom Noddy and Mousie performed in "It's a Wonderful Fair."

In the show, Smerdyakov Karamzov (aka Sam Williams) had come on hard times. "In a brilliant comic soliloquy he bemoaned his life at the Oregon Country Fair," Tom Noddy said. "He wished that he had 'never come to the fair.' There was a musical interlude where sets changed and other mystical events took place and when it was over, we saw the horrible fair that would have resulted had Smerdyakov never attended." Of course, the play's ending mirrored the movie's and everybody left happy.

Saturday night the performers again joined forces to present a stupendous Midnight Show for all the fair volunteers and booth folks. Tom Noddy said Ken Kesey's speech on opening day sparked ideas among the vaudeville family. "That year there was an effort—inspired by Kesey—that the Midnight Show parade would march to the back of the crowd and it would keep going. We were going to have a flatbed truck set up outside so that we would do the Midnight Show outside the gates. …

"I liked the anarchic idea," Tom said, "but that would also come to the point where the show was over and there would be Security people at the gate, separating those with passes from those without and then those without would all be gathered in a crowd on one side of a line of Security people. I don't like that picture."

Instead Tom teased Ken from the stage of the Midnight Show.

"The parade, as I understand it, is going to march through to the back of the crowd," Tom announced. "Then they're going to keep marching outside. Then they're going to keep going all the way to Springfield, where we're going to go to Ken's farm, and bring all the hippies in the Northwest to Ken's property."

The plan drew wild cheers and guffaws from the crowd, but everyone kept their seats in the Main Stage meadow. Nobody wanted to miss the Midnight Show.

The twentieth anniversary event would bring in a record attendance of more than 35,000 people over three days. That was almost 10,000 more attendees than previous years. Arna Shaw's first year as general manager had gone well. "Attendance was very high," Arna said. "We had some problems just from that. But things went really smoothly."

But even a successful fair could not smooth the turmoil roiling behind the scenes among fair organizers. A week after the fair ended, Marshall Landman resigned from the board and all his other fair positions—OM Team, Budget Committee, Personnel Committee, Special Events (Picnic) Coordinator, Bus Crew coordinator, and Archaeology Crew.

In his resignation letter Marshall wrote, "While I could go on and on about the concerns I have, let me just state that the major reason that I am resigning is that I do not feel that I had on-site authority to go along with the responsibility that the board of directors vested in me." Arna would note in a letter to the board after the fair that Marshall's resignation "left a huge hole" in the organization.

Arna and board member Kathryn Madden met with the neighbors and the county staff for a debriefing after the fair, where nobody mentioned traffic jams. The new highway entrance had mostly solved that problem. But the neighbors still voiced complaints about trespassers on their property, illegal parking along the roads, and the use of drugs by fairgoers.

Arna reported to the board that the county had asked the fair to pay for the "no parking" signs posted on the county roads. More alarmingly, the county raised the possibility that officials would require the fair to sign a contract for the sheriffs to patrol on fair property.

"I did not agree to this," Arna wrote the fair board, "and told them I would talk to the board. The county counsel replied that if we did not do this voluntarily, the commissioners could enact laws forcing us to contract for these services. I pointed out that any law would also apply to all Lane County events. This could prove extremely unpopular and possibly bankrupt smaller events such as the Creswell Air Show, the Dexter Boat Races, and the Applegate Trail Days."

Arna brought to Lane County officials' attention that the county spent $1,200 dollars posting "no parking" signs on county roads, but that the Oregon State Highway Department spent less than $100 posting similar signs on state roads. She questioned the huge disparity.

In her letter to the board, Arna concluded "You may remember that once before the county tried to single us out and Jill took them to court and won a cash settlement from them. My attitude with the county is to be cooperative but not let them push us around."

In September the board approved a proposal by new Construction Co-coordinator Dennis Todd to complete the water system project on the river side of the Eight as soon as possible. Dennis worked with the new Water Crew coordinators, John Anthony and Ulee Yanok plus Energy Park consultant Tim Wolden and a few volunteers to dig more trenches and lay more piping on the river side of the Eight. The final section was laid on the Upper River Loop side of the Eight on Shady Lane in front of what was then Dana's Cheesecake booth.

"Tim Wolden and I had been laying what seemed like miles and miles of this big PVC pipe in the figure Eight," Dennis said. "We came to the last coupling and it was almost dark. We were muddy and dirty. We painted the last coupling purple because we didn't have a 'golden spike.' We glued it in place and did high fives!"

In November 1989, John Winslow announced that the system had been extended with three spurs "so now the Water Crew can reach anywhere in the figure Eight with carts and hoses. Assuming the system works OK, no more water trucks!"

The new water system would enhance the safety and ambiance of the fair immensely. For starters, Frank Sharpy used it to irrigate the grass. "I built a hundred-foot PVC pipe with sprinkler heads every fifteen feet that had a length of flex hose to quick-connect to those water taps. One person could drag the whole thing down the path," he said.

They began sowing grass seed in August, with the goal of mowing three or four times before heavy rains came. This method would let the grass roots grow deep enough to withstand the winter floods.

Tim Wolden admired the "purple link"—the last piece needed to finish the fair's water system—before he and Dennis Todd installed it.

The water system would also deliver more water faster to all the food booths around the fair every year. Beginning in 1990, dozens of Water Crew volunteers would use hoses to deliver water to the food booths. The new water system also featured drinking fountains along the paths and handwashing stations near the toilets.

"The first few drinking fountains were fabricated by a local copper artisan and used air pressure nozzles for delivery," Tim Wolden said. "The learning curve was steep on how to supply the public with fountains and these fountains were soon replaced by a series of rock fountains and eventually the more compostable straw-bale fountains."

In the weeks leading up to the 1990 fair, Tim designed an 18,000-gallon concrete reservoir and got county approval to build it. Tim, his friend James Prull and a guy named Peter—who Tim had met at breakfast in the Keystone Café one morning—poured, formed and stripped the tank walls. "Another fair family friend, Rainbow Walker, finished the lid on top of the reservoir within a short time," Tim said. They named it Wolden Pond.

1989
The Radar Angels

> "It was an easy step from the dress-up teas to the signature wings, masks, wigs, and wacky costumes that are an integral part of the Radar Angels' public and private personae."
>
> —Lois Wadworth, "Radar Angels Do Jello," *What's Happening*, March 30, 1989

The Radar Angels performance art troupe traced its beginning to a series of "Frivolous Teas" held in 1978 by friends seeking a whimsical outlet from their serious side.

"It consolidated out of about five different groups," original member Indi Stern recalled. "Some were arts people, some were political, some were philosophical, quite a few were students at the University of Oregon. Most of these other meetings and groups were very serious. A few of us came together for somebody's birthday or something. We were talking about all our groups being so serious and it'd be fun just to chew the fat and let our hair down."

At the time, Indi worked part time for the Northwest Wine and Cheese Shop and had access to leftover wine bottles that had been opened for tastings. "I knew my boss wasn't going to do anything with them," she said. "They'd sit there for months and if they were turning, we'd just dump it." Indi took home about three cases of opened wine and asked everyone to bring chocolate. "We had our first Frivolous Tea with chocolate and wine," Indi said. "It was quite an event!" Everyone dressed up in fancy or silly thrift-store dresses and vintage hats.

"The teas became a major source of fun," said Angela Pershnokov, another original member of the group. "The teas spread to various restaurants like The Excelsior, where we would take over a whole room. The waiters would help out by doing such things as donning ladies underwear for a cap." The waiters who joined in the fun "got well tipped for their enthusiasm," she said.

An early poster for one of the teas referred to the "Old Social Aid and Pleasure Club" but the group would quickly settle on a new name in January 1979, when the friends gathered to watch the Super Bowl.

The broadcast of the football game was interrupted with a special CBS news spot featuring Walter Cronkite reporting on Unidentified Flying Objects. The idea of visitors from outer space had grabbed people's imaginations in the late 1970s after the CIA had declassified reports of "flying saucers." News outlets had reported UFO sightings in South Africa, New Zealand, Australia, and Canada.

"We were all enthralled," Indi said. "You could tell Walter Cronkite was trying to keep from laughing." Walter introduced an aerospace engineer, who launched into an explanation about swamp gas and public hysteria and then added, "Of course, it could easily be those well-known radar angels."

"Huh? What the hell?" Angela said. "He didn't even say what a radar angel was."

"Well, I know what it would be good for," Indi responded, "a great name for our teas, our group." Everyone at the party enthusiastically agreed, and the Radar Angels took wing.

The term actually came out of World War II, when military leaders in Britain and the United States used it to describe false signals that appeared as blips on the radar when nothing could be seen in the skies. Different postwar studies attributed the puzzling phenomena to flocks of birds or to radar echoes caused by atmospheric disturbances.

For the friends in Eugene, Radar Angels came to mean "a state of mind," Indi said. "Anarchy and irreverence are some words that come to mind. Anything goes. Most people have seen us on the paths of the Country Fair and we're a bit irreverent."

They ran a series of free personal classified ads in the *Willamette Valley Observer*, Eugene's alternative community weekly in the late 1970s. Inscrutable messages such as "How many Radar Angels can dance on the head of a pin?" attracted the interest of artistic types.

A pregnant Indi Stern took a break to enjoy her lunch at fair in 1979.

Some ads were more suggestive: "How do you know if you've had a Radar Angel in your bed? ... Glitter on the sheets!"

Many Angels had formal training in theater, dance, or music, and it seemed natural to put on a show. They wanted to share their talents, raise money for a good cause, and have fun transforming a space "to feel like a different reality," Angela said. They also wanted to give women without a performance background a chance to "get up on stage to spread their wings," she added. "The idea was always to empower women to do what made them feel good about themselves."

In October 1979 the Radar Angels staged their first public event, Some Tainted Evening, at the WOW Hall as a benefit for the Rape Crisis Center. The evening promised a movie, dancing, costumes, prizes, and the rock 'n' roll Radar Angel revue.

Other fund-raisers would follow for the WOW Hall and for the nuclear arms freeze movement. In April 1980 the Radar Angels began their April Foolies series, which incorporated serious art performance, poetry reading, and dance.

"Breaking down traditional female roles was always a big part of the message," Angela said. "It was one that many people weren't ready to hear. The Radar Angels were essentially doing burlesque, long before the current trend. Some feminists—which the Angels considered ourselves to be—were not ready for the idea that a woman could be a feminist and sport lingerie in public. We were doing this right from our very first event, quite a while before Madonna made it popular. One time our posters were torn down by someone who thought the feminist cause was being subverted."

The Radar Angels added another spice to the stew of irreverent art and theater projects that flowed into Eugene's stages and streets in the late 1970s and early 1980s. Around that same time, the zany Live Matinee ensemble was showing weird home movies and performing comedy routines at the art film house Cinema 7 in the Atrium Building in downtown Eugene. Across the hall, Oregon Repertory Theatre's Midnight Mafia staged avant-garde plays.

"Art was getting stapled up on any convenient telephone pole or other surface, inspiring yet more art," Angela said. "The Art Maggots was a group of mostly male cartoonists, animators, and illustrators who put their signature stickers all over town on everything from dead birds to political posters. They made and distributed 'zines'—homemade magazines, Xerox art, and mail art. The Radar Angels jumped right in with raids on Xerox art shows."

During their art show "raids," the Angels—in full costume—would storm in, grab artists they knew, stand them next to their art, and staple their clothes to the wall. In the mayhem, some of the Angels also got stapled against the wall. "Everyone's feet were still on the floor," Angela explained. "The stapling was really symbolic. … The idea was to interact with the art viewers as art pieces for a while, until we got tired of being stapled up!"

From the start, the Radar Angels did their best to remain mostly anonymous. Indi Stern often spoke for them in public. "I can't tell you their names," Indi said. "There are Angels all over the place. They're in medicine, they're in county and city government, they're politically active, they're artists, they're craftspeople, they're writers, they're mothers, and some of us are performers as well."

In 1983 the Angels took their act to the paths of the Oregon Country Fair and sang as "The Lemmon Sisters," a goofy takeoff on the Lennon Sisters who had been frequently featured on *The Lawrence Welk Show* back in the day.

In 1984 they introduced the "Fairy Klutzes" on the fair paths. "We would goof around and bump into each other and entwine our antennas," Indi said. "We had these giant clunky boots on. I can't believe that we tromped around the fair in those things, but we did." Like many fair performers, after each performance on the path they would pass the hat to help pay for their expenses. That Saturday evening, they danced their Klondike Can-Can Review on Main Stage as the popular local group The Cashiers rocked the crowd.

The Radar Angels noticed on the paths that the children didn't

The Radar Angels

see them as funny or klutzy; they saw pretty fairies. "That blew us away," Indi said. "So we decided back up at camp after our first full Saturday of being fairies that we might as well really be fairies. We might as well be comfortable. So our invite was, anybody could join us as long as they had magic wands, wings, and antennae."

But over the years, they came to realize that some children felt terrified instead of friendly toward the fairies. The Angels started making new recruits aware of the situation and tutored each other with lessons on respecting personal space to avoid upsetting children. "There are also parents who go, 'Oh look, the fairies!'" Indi said. "Then they drag their poor little kid and shove them up into you, and the kid is just falling apart. The parent is not even aware. So we've learned some very interesting things about personal space.

"Little boys are threatened by you and hit you," she added. "We had a punk fairy one year. She was wonderful! As soon as we had any little boys who were confrontational, she would turn on them. They were terrified of her—it was great! She had this spiked wristband on. All fairies are invited to develop their own personae, their own name, their little story or song. That was kind of another requisite. We've had big fairies and little fairies."

In 1985 the Radar Angels presented a skit called "Ms. Fit America Pageant" at the Daredevil Meadow and along the pathways of the fair. "They did an outstanding show one year," said Charlene Tremayne, who volunteered in Community Village. "They had Ms.

Radar Angels, dressed as fairies, sang and danced at the 1998 fair.

Performing "Oh Brother" at the Hoarse Chorale Stage in 2004 were (from left): Indi Stern-Hayworth; Rita Monasterio; Kate Barry; Joan Gold Cypress; Karen Howard; Shawn Fontain; Larry Lynch in back with long feathers; Tim Howard; and Roger Wood.

Hap, Ms. Deed, Ms. Information—and it was a spoof on a beauty pageant." The emcee was of ambiguous gender.

The Angels had found a performance rhythm at the fair. "Normally Friday and Sunday we do what we call our yearly act," Indi said. "And then Saturdays we're fairies and that's our gift to the fair. We do not pass the hat, we do not take tips. We are there completely for the children and entertainment."'

That routine would change in the 2010s when Entertainment coordinators would book the Radar Angels in the mornings to welcome fairgoers with silly songs outside the gates and in the evenings to serenade people as they went home. As paid greeters, they no longer would pass the hat.

The Radar Angels also played a pivotal role in creating the first dragon parades at the Country Fair. They staged the first in 1981 as an offshoot of one of their events in town. "The Radar Angels were deep into large-scale productions," Angela Pershnokov said, "and one of our favorite things to do was to mish-mash celebrations together."

In February 1980, they put on a program called "Mardi Gras Plus" to celebrate Mardi Gras, Feast of Ishtar, Valentine's Day, and the Year of the Monkey. Angela created a Chinese-style dragon with a papier-mâché head and a long, cloth-covered body that the Radar Angels used for a dragon dance at the event.

That summer, Angela brought the dragon to the fair, where she shared a craft booth with Charlene Cuc. Once each day, Angela and some friends would bring out the dragon for a small parade around one loop of the Eight. "We were already longtime friends of Moz's [Wright] at that time," Angela said, "and I'm sure he knew about our little parade."

In the mid-1980s, the fair's Ambiance Entertainment Co-coordinator Moz Wright enlisted the Radar Angels to create Peachi the Dragon. "He and Jennifern Taylor were the driving forces behind the later, more official version, and we all pitched in," Angela said. "I think Jennifern was the main design person."

Moz envisioned a dragon parade as adding a touch of magic to the paths of the Country Fair. The Radar Angels—particularly Jennifern, Angela, and Stephanie Griffis-Means—brought that magic to fruition with help from dozens of friends. They fashioned a papier-mâché head that was so heavy, two people had to carry it. They sewed the long body out of fabric covered with colorful diamond shapes representing scales. Fringe decorated the bottom of the long body, and diamond-shaped foam "spikes" were sewn on top.

For the first Peachi the Dragon parades (most likely at the 1986 fair), a dozen young men brought the dragon's body to life. Moz helped another guy carry the head, but they could not see very far. Wendy J. Frades, dressed as a fairy, led the dragon along the path. By following the fairy, the dragon could stay on course. The Radar Angels dressed up as fairies and walked alongside the dragon to clear a pathway for Peachi to maneuver, chanting: "Beware! Beware! Beware the Dragon!"

Peachi the Dragon would materialize for parades at the fair for more than thirty years in different incarnations. Wendy would play a fairy with the Radar Angels for a few more years before she went on to perform with the tall puppets and stilt-walkers. The Radar Angels also would move on to concentrate on their own performances, and other people would bring Peachi to life along the fair's pathways.

Over the years, Peachi would be outfitted with newer, lighter-weight heads and more colorful bodies. She would emerge from different lairs around the fair site. (In the 1990s, Peachi often would leave from Community Village, where dragon fans could decorate themselves with body paint before following Peachi on her parade route. In the 2000s, Peachi's home would move to the new Chela Mela Meadow, where she would attract other followers: The Lime Green

Peachi the Dragon made her way behind the scenes to the fair's Ware Barn after parading the paths the first time in 1987.

Parade. But that's a story for another time.) Peachi's handlers would change the chant to a friendlier warning emphasized by drumbeats: "Make way! [Boom-BOOM] Make way! [Boom-BOOM] Make Way for the magic of the dragon!"

In 1988 the Radar Angels transformed their April Foolies series into the first of their Jello Art Shows. Held on or near April Fools' Day, the art show raised funds for both the Maude Kerns Art Center in Eugene and for the Radar Angels' performances. The Angels would make temporary art out of gelatin and welcomed entries from the community at large. Examples included a dead fish with jewels for eyes "floating" with plastic flowers in an aquarium full of light blue gelatin; or a dozen gelatin "eggs" decorated with odd embellishments. The Jello Art Show would become an annual tradition at Maude Kerns Art Center for more than three decades.

Also in 1988, a couple of the Radar Angels posed for photographer David Joyce and were included in his 1989 art installation—called "Flight Patterns" and popularly known as "Flying People"—at Eugene's airport. Joanie Cypress, who joined the Radar Angels in 1983 when she moved to Eugene, initiated the Angels' participation.

The Radar Angels

"When we heard there was going to be a photo shoot for the airport art project, I called a bunch of Radar Angels, but most of them had to work," Joanie said. "So Shawn [Fontain] and I were running around downtown on a cold, wet day, in little fairy outfits."

When they walked in, David Joyce was so impressed with their costuming that he got out his personal camera to take their photos in addition to the ones he took for the art project. "Flight Patterns" featured more than a hundred large black-and-white photographic cutouts of people posing with their arms out as if flying. The artist posed the volunteers on a padded mat and took their photos from the top of a ladder.

"He really liked the fairies," Joanie said. "Months go by. I've gone back to Nashville, where I was born and bred. When I came home, [my husband] Marvin and the kids greet me at the airport." Joanie asked them if they had seen any of the photos.

"Mom, you are not going to believe it!" the kids said. As they walked back down the concourse, Joanie could see that David placed the Radar Angels wearing fairy outfits at each end of the art installation. "My gosh, there we are at the beginning and the end of it," Joanie marveled. "Bless David's heart."

David later attended one of the annual Jello Art Shows at Maude Kerns Art Center. When Joanie greeted him, she asked "Do you remember me?"

"Oh yes, you're my angel!" David said.

For the fair's twentieth anniversary in 1989, the Radar Angels planned something special and completely different. They staged an Endangered Species Ritual called "That We May Live" at Main Stage on Friday evening after the fair closed to the public.

The idea for the ritual emerged from a jungle dream where Shawn Fontain had a visit from a jaguar who told a story. "Out of that came: 'Hear our song that we may live,'" Shawn told the group.

"We spent a mammoth amount of time," Indi said. Some members held personal rituals to choose an animal or creature from the Endangered Species List. Each individual Radar Angel researched her creature, created a costume and a dance, and wrote up a brief description of what they represented. From the written descriptions, poet Stephanie Griffis (later Means), crafted poetry that she would recite during the Radar Angels' performance.

Angela served as artistic director for the project. The Angels recruited Nicki Scully, a shamanic practitioner and teacher, to help give their ritual cohesion. "Very interestingly and unbeknownst to us, Thursday when we got there and we were finishing dress rehearsal and setting up camp, there were all these Native Americans there watching us," Indi said. "They stayed up in Entertainment Camp. A man came over and told us they watched our rehearsal and they watched Nicki to make sure that we weren't doing something that would in any way be sacrosanct. And we received their okay, which gave me chills."

The troupe ventured out in their species costumes all three days of the fair. They had proposed the ritual for Friday night because it was less busy than Thursday, when everyone was still preparing for Friday morning's opening. Also, it would give members time to get into their animal character Friday during the fair before the ritual that evening.

"Because the Oregon Country Fair is a wildlife sanctuary when the fair is not operating, we feel it is appropriate to commemorate the endangered species of this planet for the Twentieth Anniversary," the proposal said. "Our intent is to create a sacred ritual that invokes the archetypes of endangered animals that are disappearing from the Earth."

A few weeks after that fair, Indi heard people talking about the Endangered Species Ritual at a party. "I just sat there eating my food, listening," Indi said. "My hostess said, 'Well that was the Radar Angels.'"

"Oh no it wasn't," a man replied. "I know it wasn't them. This was not a funny group."

"Oh, but I think it *was* the Radar Angels," the hostess said. The man started arguing with her, his voice getting louder and louder until he's yelling at the hostess.

Finally the hostess turned to Indi and smacked her knee, "Tell him it was the Radar Angels!" she insisted.

"No, I don't think so," Indi replied. "They weren't funny. Probably wasn't. Couldn't have been. They weren't funny."

The Radar Angels would get the opportunity to perform the ritual a couple of more times at the University of Oregon: once at Earth Day, and once at the Environmental Law Conference, where singer and fair regular Joanne Rand lent her musical voice to the piece.

The Radar Angels

A late-blooming Radar Angel would be Christine Frazer, who would return to the fair in 1997 as a Bumblebee Fairy at age fifty-two, long after Country VW had folded and her stint in Community Village had ended. After years of performing along the paths with the other Angels, Christine's family talked her into using an accessibility cart at the fair in 2004. "I have thirty years on damaged feet," Christine said. "I would be lame for a month after the fair. The accessibility cart has been a blessing."

One year, Christine got acquainted with the fair's Four-A program—Alter-Abled Access Advocacy. "They are wonderful and a great addition to the fair," Christine said. "My cart broke down Thursday night when I had a chaotic tent thing." She drove to town to buy a smaller air mattress for her tiny tent. When she returned on Friday morning, she put on her Bumblebee Fairy outfit so she would be ready to join the Radar Angels' performance that morning.

But the electrical connections on her cart were short-circuited by wet grass in the parking lot. "Now my cart wouldn't go!" Christine said. "A Security guy finds me and calls a tow truck. Well, that's not what I needed! He didn't get it. I finally got somebody on Traffic Crew to call Fair Central, who said, 'Call Four-A.' A Four-A team guy with a bike and a lowboy sidecar trailer comes out and puts my cart in the trailer. He pedals me up the back road to the Ware Barn and didn't break a sweat! It was fantastic."

Still, Christine would miss the Radar Angels performances that day. "Finally, I figured out that no one else would know how to fix my cart better than me, the ex-mechanic," she said. "Radar Angles camp right next to the Ware Barn. I got out of the Bumble Bee costume and went back to my cart at the Ware Barn. I pulled the batteries and put them on chargers, blew out all the electrical connections, dried it all out, and everything worked out.

"I didn't get to do the Youth Stage show or any bumblebee play that day at all," she said. "It's hard on the paths for everyone. Even in a cart, it's hard on my neck and arms, but I couldn't do much of the fair if I had to do it on my injured feet, so I'm thankful for the cart and the fair's support."

Graphic artist Diane McWhorter joined the Radar Angels early on, mostly in roles behind the scenes. At first she'd help by designing the signs and silk-screening T-shirts for the Jello Art Shows

The Radar Angels often performed in bee outfits.

at Maude Kerns Art Center. But she satisfied her artistic muse by entering gelatin art pieces in every show. "I've used it to express what was going on in my life," she said. "A Barbie doll was my alter ego, remodeling a bread box with building materials made of Jell-O."

Diane discovered that thin sheets of gelatin would dry and hold up relatively well over time. That allowed her to construct elaborate sculptures that lasted, and to create fanciful hair ornaments and flowers from dried gelatin.

For the Jello Art Show in 2012, the Radar Angels had a surprise in store that had been planned for a year. Diane, then age sixty-two, complicated the plot when she broke her foot a few months before the event. She had strict orders from her doctor to stay seated.

"Indi set me up right in the main hall with my table of shirts and all of my [dried gelatin art] that I had been selling at the Saturday Market last season," Diane said. "I had shirts from previous years, and hung my wings on the wall. I had my foot on a pillow and jello flowers in my hair."

The Radar Angels performed a skit based on "Jello Queen for a Day" with four outlandish candidates who reflected current events. One was Newt Gingrich's wife, another resembled Sarah Palin. A third candidate, who resembled Paula Deen, swore that she lost weight on a deep-fried Jell-O diet. A fourth candidate sort of played the ukulele and sang sweetly. None received enough "uptwinkles" (borrowed from the hand signals used by the Occupy Wall Street movement) to win.

"Finally the lovely assistant and the guy on piano [aka Rico Suave] announced that there was 'No clear winner!'" Diane said. Instead, they crowned Diane.

"For a year they had kept the fabulous secret," Diane said. "They brought me the royal crutches and a box of tissues and put me on stage in a throne with a cape, scepter, and bouquet of Jell-O boxes. I babbled some sort of a speech in my giggly confusion. I didn't stop grinning for an hour at least.

"They proceeded to sing a special song, 'Time Warp,' and I got to sing along, fulfilling a lifelong dream to actually be one of the performing Angels, something I'm always too chicken to do," Diane said. She would thenceforth perform on stage annually with the Radar Angels at the Jello Art Show.

The Radar Angels surprised Diane McWhorter (seated, wearing a crown of Jell-O Boxes) during their "Jello Queen for a Day" skit at Maude Kerns Arts Center in 2012.

Over the decades the Radar Angels would poke fun at cultural conventions—particularly traditional women's roles—with performances including "Beach Blanket Bimbos," "Bridal Passion Fashion Show," "The Debuhaunts," and "Ode to Carmen Miranda."

"We're a family act for the Country Fair," Indi said. "We have a lot of double entendres and innuendos so that we entertain the adults and children. We always throw in a poop or a fart joke because it makes everyone laugh. We try to pick some themes that are poignant for the times. We did 'Angels Incorporated' in 2002 and that was a direct stab at Enron. We did 'The Spaced Ozdyssey,' which was a spoof on *The Wizard of Oz* in 2001, which was Frank Oz's hundredth birthday. And then sometimes we've just done things because they've been fun. …

"We did a little stab with science fiction with 'The Mixed Galactica Pageant,'" Indi added. "That was probably one of our more outstanding series of creative costumes. Even I was impressed. We had one woman, Asha, who made herself an eight-legged spider. Angela was the one-eyed, one-horned flying purple people-eater. That was just great stuff, great costumes, and so fun!"

In the 1980s and 1990s, the troupe performed at the Eugene Celebration and regularly created entries for the Eugene Celebration Parade. But the Oregon Country Fair "is one of our biggest venues," Indi said in 2018. "We used to do a big event at the WOW Hall a couple times a year and we've had some pretty big private parties. For a long time even the Eugene Celebration was right up there, but now besides the fair, we primarily do the Jello Show at Maude Kerns and shows for Lane Independent Living Alliance."

34 1990
Dahinda Meda and the VegManECs

"The VegManECs make the backdrop for everything. The whole world's a stage and we're the actors, but somebody's got to be the stagehand and make the stage. Creating that ambience is a long-term project."
—Dahinda Meda, describing the role of the VegManECs

Board member Dahinda Meda was named coordinator of the "Vegetation Management Committee" at the fair board's February 1990 meeting. With the vote, the board simply acknowledged reality: Dahinda had been leading volunteers who tended the fair's landscaping since he moved to Eugene in 1987.

However, the board secretary got the group's name wrong, which happened often. The volunteers had given themselves a tricky moniker—the VegManECs—which stood for Vegetation Management and Erosion Control. "It's Veg-Man-*EC*s," Dahinda said. "It's not Veg-Maniacs. It's not Veg-Mania. It's not Vegematics, although we're called all of those by people."

The committee came together out of their shared concerns over the heavy impact the fair event made each year on the natural landscape.

"As the fair family grew, campers arriving to prepare for the fair would cut down small trees and bushes with abandon," Dahinda said. "The fair people were putting more importance on the one-week-a-year event than on the other fifty-one weeks for the wildlife and the habitat. Fair folks started cutting a whole lot more brush after the fair bought the property."

Dahinda said the group thought the fair needed a landscape crew based on the principles of conservation. Dahinda said the group of concerned folks included John Winslow, John Doscher, John "Chewie" Burgess, Kirk Shultz, Susan Bryan, and David Hoffman. Before the landscape crew members named themselves the VegManECs, they were just volunteers who helped the caretaker.

"When we first started, we debated about our pruning standards," Dahinda said. "One person suggested the 'four Ds,'—disease, dying, dangerous, and dead. … I introduced the three S's—safety, shade, and stilts. … First we can make it safe and second, we try to provide shade, but we can still make it safe. … And then from the path, we have to maintain at least a four-foot-wide space that's twelve feet high so that the stilt people can get around."

They also studied the winter flooding patterns and sedimentation. "We started the practice of putting in straw-bale check dams on the paths in winter," Dahinda said. "When it floods, there's a lot of silt in the water, which smothers the grass the fair wants on the pathways. The straw bales captured the silt and helped get the grass established."

They would anchor the bales with steel rods. Susan Bryan, a Security Crew volunteer who joined the VegManECs in 1991, said the straw bales could serve other purposes, as well. "We'd watch the

The 1986 paper camping pass featured a photo of the fair flooded in the off-season.

Susan Bryan joined the VegManEcs in 1991.

patterns of the river so that the hay bales will hopefully move the water into an area to prevent the collapsing of booths, or to try to channel the flood into the natural creeks on the property rather than having it come down our lanes that we create by walking through our structural play land. If we can do that, then we save the grass or the soil that's in our walkways and put that liquid back into the creeks, where it's a natural action."

Dahinda had first attended the fair in 1977 when his friend John Cloud (stage manager for Chumleighland aka the Circus) invited him. They had met when they worked together maintaining hiking trails in the Sierra Nevada Mountains of California, where Dahinda lived. The first fair was so much fun that in 1978 Dahinda returned and joined the Security Crew with some Hoedad tree-planting friends he had met working in the woods. In 1978 when the fair ran more informally, the Hoedads had been tapped by organizers to serve as the fair's Security Crew.

After that, Dahinda would return year after year to volunteer at the fair. He brought his children, Erica Lerch, who was twelve years old when she first attended in 1979, and John Lerch, who was eleven. Dahinda and their mom had divorced in 1972 when Dahinda was thirty-two.

After the divorce, Dahinda had moved to property he bought in Mendocino County, changed his name (previously Albert Lerch), became a vegetarian, and swore off sugar.

"I guess I pretty much went full hippie after the divorce," he acknowledged. "For a while there I had my nude period where I went naked for weeks at a time, even greeting visitors wearing nothing but sandals." He built a five-story post-and-beam structure off the grid on his property, which he dubbed Terrarium.

Before the divorce, Dahinda had worked as an architect and

urban planner, but he chucked the fast lane when he moved north. He joined New Growth Forestry, a worker-owned cooperative, which in the late 1970s had won the contract to design and build parts of the Pacific Crest Trail in the John Muir Wilderness.

At Terrarium, Dahinda also grew marijuana for personal consumption and for gifts to friends. One Christmas, he mailed a wreath made of pot leaves to his Hoedad friends in Eugene. "I used the male plants," he said with a laugh. Those are the plants he pulled up so the female buds could ripen without setting seed.

In 1982, Dahinda celebrated with everyone else when the fair signed the papers to buy the land. He returned to Eugene from his home in Northern California to help provide security for the Grateful Dead concert in the fair's parking lot in August 1982. "My friends John Doscher and John Winslow and I were on the concert security crew together," Dahinda said. "Afterward, there was a huge party on the site that lasted well into the night."

Eventually Dahinda left the Security Crew for Admissions Crew. "I was always anti-authoritarian," he said, "and I had trouble with the hierarchy in Security."

At Admissions, Dahinda worked crowd control at the fair's entrance to the Eight pathways. Every morning of the fair, pedestrians swarmed the area. People lined up to purchase tickets then looked for the line to get into the fair, which could be confused with the line to the Solutions window at Main Camp. "The pathway was only half as wide as it is now, creating a constant traffic jam, always a congregation of people," Dahinda said. "I spent my time herding people. I became the greeter."

Wearing a rolled-up bandana as a headband to keep sweat and his wild hair out of his eyes, Dahinda would stand in front of the entrance to the Eight to direct foot traffic. "Here's the entrance to the Oregon Country Fair!" he would shout, smiling broadly as he pointed in the correct direction. "No one can get in without a smile! Get your smile out! If you don't have one, go back and get it!" Local TV crews often focused on Dahinda in action, featuring his smiling spiel in their evening news broadcasts covering the fair.

Dahinda moved to Eugene in the fall of 1987 and purchased a blueberry farm on Royal Avenue just west of Eugene. He joined Tilth, a nonprofit that certifies organic farms in Oregon, and named his farm Royal Blueberries.

Dahinda Meda and the VegManECs

Shortly after Dahinda moved, his friend John Winslow became the fair's caretaker. Dahinda enjoyed visiting John and spending time on the fair site in the off season. "It felt like a sacred site to me as well as some other like-minded people," he said. "We felt drawn to spend time out there."

In March 1988, the fair purchased a riding lawnmower with four-foot-wide blades to help manage the grass growing in the paths of the Eight. John started to train volunteers to help with the work that Frank Sharpy had done mostly alone. Frank compared John's technique to enlist volunteers with Tom Sawyer's successful effort to get his friends to paint a fence for him.

"We'd come out and there'd be a big barbecue," Frank said. John would park the lawn mower nearby. People would notice it and ask if they could try it out. "Okay, yeah, but you've got to cut the grass over here," they'd be told. "Soon there was a crew of people who were showing up regularly to run the lawn mower," Frank said. That became the VegManECs a few years later.

"I am their grandpa!" Frank claimed.

Like many generations who disagreed with their grandparents' old-fashioned ways, the VegManECs found fault with Frank's grass-growing methods, particularly his use of conventional fertilizer.

"A contingent of organic people began bitching about my fertilizer," Frank said. "They wanted to use fish meal, which is okay but not quick enough or strong enough for high-production grass growing. ... When faced with these obstacles, I was done. After all, my only expertise was professionally growing and maintaining turf grass for over thirty years. ... I had over-wintered and growing grass on East Thirteenth for three or four years, much of which survived both the fair and floods."

In the fall of 1988, the group helped dig trenches for the water piping project.

Also that fall of 1988, John Winslow told Dahinda about a five-acre parcel of land on the northwest edge of the fair site that had been put up for sale. Originally set at $30,000, the price had just been lowered to less than half—$14,500. "An interested buyer had already tagged all of the trees he was going to log off to make the down payment," Dahinda said. "He planned to sell it off as a subdivision lot."

John Doscher (left) and Dahinda Meda reminisced about the old days during the 2013 Teddy Bears Picnic at Main Stage meadow.

Dahinda talked to board President Bedo Crafts and other members of the fair's board of directors. Nobody wanted that land to become a subdivision right next to the fair. "Timing was the issue, as the property was about to sell and the fair needed to act soon," Dahinda said.

But the fair board's process was not set up for swift action, even though the fair had enough money in reserve for the down payment. If the board followed its normal procedure, the land purchase would need to be brought forward as new business at one meeting, and then be voted on a month later as old business. Another glitch complicated the timing. The property price was reduced the first week of October, and the board's annual meeting later that month meant a likely turnover in the board before the process could even start.

"The organization was like a dinosaur where you kick its tail and three weeks later it gets the message in its brain," Dahinda said. "So I bought the land and then sold it to the fair in January or February when they could get their trip together. I was the owner for three and a half months." The property would be dubbed "Dahinda's Acres."

The purchase of that piece of land made it possible for the fair to run a new access road along that edge of the fair site and to increase the land available for camping. The road extended Green Bus Road, which formerly had run into a dead end in the woods. Coincidentally, the new access road passed along the back side of Frank Sharpy's family campsite, replacing a placid woodland view with constant traffic.

"It was my campsite that was going to be forever altered," Frank said. "You could not get there then unless you belonged there. And to be perfectly greedy and honest, it was really nice. Really quiet and really safe."

Walter Renfro, former Traffic Crew co-coordinator, remembered when the road went in. "A lot of the elders lived [camped] on Green Bus Road, except that was never open to anybody," Walter said. "Frank Sharpy, a good friend of mine, lives [camps] there. But he sniveled, he whined, and he fought and fought and fought. He did not want half of the fair walking by his camp site every day."

Fair volunteers named the section of the new access road that passed Frank's camping spot "Snivel Lane" in honor of Frank. They also placed a sign on a curve declaring "Sharpy Curve," and poured a concrete plaque at the entrance to Frank's campsite, which they inscribed before the concrete dried: "Here Snivelled Sharpy."

October 1988 proved to be a key month in Dahinda's relationship with the fair. He put his name in the hat to join the fair's board of directors and was elected at the annual meeting. "I really jumped in at the fair that year," he said. "There was a just a lot of stuff that I guess was a burr under my saddle, in terms of the way things were going and what needed to be done. Besides my training and background in planning and urban design, I had plenty of experience out in the field and trenches."

Around that same time Dahinda also ran for the board of directors of NCAP (Northwest Center for Alternatives to Pesticides), a nonprofit he had long supported financially. He fell in love with the NCAP director, a savvy activist named Norma Grier. In 1989, Norma moved to the blueberry farm, and they would marry in a ceremony at the farm in 1996.

In 1989 Dahinda also launched a coffee distribution business, Café Mam, to sell organic coffee beans grown by a social solidarity cooperative in Chiapas, Mexico, called ISMAM. The cooperatives' name stood for Indigenas de la Sierra Madre de Motozintla. Dahinda set up Café Mam so that two percent of all coffee sales would go to pesticide reform.

Within a few years, Dahinda's son John Lerch joined the blueberry business. John and his cousin Brad Lerch also became partners with Dahinda in Café Mam.

Café Mam coffee made its first appearance at the Oregon Country Fair when several food booths started serving it in 1991. It even became the coffee served at Main Camp. In 2015, Café Mam would open its own booth along East Thirteenth at the fair.

Erica Lerch, John Lerch, and Dahinda Meda paused for a photo in the new Café Mam booth at the Country Fair in 2015.

Meanwhile, the VegManECs continued to help the caretaker with the land. In October of 1991 they created a clubhouse for themselves at the fair site, a place to get out of the weather and enjoy lunch and take breaks together. "In 1991 we repurposed a little trailer [house-truck] that had been left at the fair," Susan Bryan said. "We pushed it from one side of the site to what was an old compost heap at the top of fair property. ... Then I redesigned it. I made it from being a house into being a clubhouse, so that we had benches and we had places to store things. During the wintertime, especially, we have our meetings in there, we have little luncheons."

The porch of the clubhouse got put to a different use during the fair, when stilt-walkers would perch on the high back porch to rest.

They could easily remove their stilts to give their legs a break and then simply strap their stilts back on again when they were ready to return to the Eight to entertain the crowds.

Each year, after the fair closed, the VegManECs returned on weekends to prepare the site for winter.

"Our new year starts the weekend after fair is over," Susan said. "We start with taking down and fixing up and preparing and planting. ... One of the things in our autumn, right after the fair, is to walk through and find things that could float. ... The flood flows both ways, it flows one direction and then it can come back and flow the other direction as it drains back into Fern Ridge Dam area. And if you have any kind of floating structure, it will bump up against trees and damage them." The VegManECs also would make sure that all the vegetation they tied up for the fair had been untied for the winter.

When the fair undertook projects to expand the footprint beyond the original Eight pathway, the VegManECs participated to help protect the landscaping. The group would show up nearly every weekend between fairs to care for the land. Still, volunteers with the VegManECs also kept their gig on other fair crews to earn a T-shirt and overnight pass.

After working hard on projects to expand the Eight pathways, it started to rankle the group that they weren't earning their pass through VegManECs. To make the point that they worked just like a crew, Dahinda brought in batches of long-sleeved shirts and sweatshirts imprinted with a VegManEC logo for the volunteers to wear during their weekend shifts.

Bill Verner was a Security Crew volunteer when he started working with the VegManECs in 1991. "There's a number of shirts with logos that were produced to let those in power know that there was some definite weird feelings about being stewards of the land and taking care of the land year-round and not getting any crew status," Bill said. "Dahinda basically bought a whole load of shirts for a number of years ... all supporting the VegManEC cause. We did that on our own just to show who we were."

The group finally got crew status in 1993 and would remain integral for decades to keeping the landscape of the fair in as natural a state as possible.

After all their work, springtime would bring sweet payoffs. "We can help to maintain vegetation and keep it within its own wildlife status," Susan Bryan said. "Like keeping our trilliums, keeping the delphiniums, keeping the serviceberry that feeds the birds and the filberts that feed our ground squirrels. We can help to keep a lot of that at the same time as accommodating what we like to do as humans playing at the fair."

In 2012, Dahinda Meda and Norma Grier would be honored with the David Brower Lifetime Achievement Award at the Public Interest Environmental Law Conference at the University of Oregon. The award recognized the couple for their lifetime of work dedicated to protecting the environment.

Four days before his seventy-sixth birthday in 2016, Dahinda passed away at home on his blueberry farm. He had suffered two strokes and had battled cancer for six years. Surrounded by love, he remained a warrior to the end.

The businesses established by Dahinda, Royal Blue Organics and Café Mam, would continue to thrive for years, guided by his son John and nephew Brad.

1991
The Left Bank

"It was a time of change when we opened the Left Bank. It was challenging but the family rose to it."
—Kirk Shultz, minutes from OCF Path Planning Committee, March 16, 2014

When Kathryn Madden ran for the fair's board of directors in the fall of 1987, she still served on the Community Village Coordinating Council. "I was friends with some people from Main Camp and with the Construction Crew coordinator, Ken Rodgers, who was really interested in me being a bridge between policy and operations. The board would make all these weird decisions that showed they clearly didn't have a clue about what really went on during the event. So my big claim to fame was that I understood how things should happen on the ground."

Kathryn remained a board liaison to Community Village for two years, but as she got deeper into her role on the board, she started to spend more time in Main Camp.

"I would follow [then-General Manager] Sallie Edmunds around during the event," Kathryn said. She started camping with early fair stalwart Sandra Bauer, and hanging out with Sallie, Sandra, and Fair Central volunteer Reese Prouty. "I got very quickly absorbed into all of the administrative ends of the fair," Kathryn said.

In the spring of 1988, Kathryn noticed that Main Camp and Construction Crew had decided without consulting the board to punch through a new course for the path near Upper River Loop to move that section away from the eroding riverbank.

Main Camp volunteers had been talking about it for quite a while. "People kept falling in the river there," Construction Crew volunteer Ed Moye said, "and the erosion was making it worse. We had to do something about it. I came up with the idea of putting a path around the back side of the existing booths so they wouldn't have to rebuild. Then we'd have area on the other side we could move booths into." That became Abbey Rode on the fair map.

"I was very full of myself," Kathryn said, "I think it's a disease you get once you're on the board of directors of the Oregon Country Fair. I remember lecturing Ken Rodgers, who was then construction coordinator, about how it was horrible that they had punched in that road without consulting the board of directors. And I remember Ken walking out of my house just totally disgusted with me." At least in this case, the person that Ken had encouraged to run for the board didn't seem to get "how things should happen on the ground," after all.

In early 1989 Marshall Landman—the Community Village co-founder who had also moved on to volunteer in Main Camp—pulled Kathryn into the Personnel Committee that had been tasked with hiring a general manager for the fair. "I was on the Personnel Committee that hired our first paid general manager, who was Arna [Shaw]," Kathryn said.

In the fall of 1989, Kathryn was elected board president for the 1990 fair. When Main Camp rolled around the next summer, her day job had kept her away from Main Camp during the week. However, she had heard rumors that people in Main Camp were partying after hours and riding the fair's water tank truck (dubbed the Peach Truck because of the peach painted on the tank) in the parking lot.

"I was very concerned about the liabilities of having lots of people riding around on the top of the Peach Truck," Kathryn said. "I was feeling that I needed to insert myself quite a bit because I was looking out for the fair's fiduciary responsibility."

One evening in June 1990, Arna phoned Kathryn to invite her to an important meeting at Main Camp a few days later. When Kathryn showed up, organizers poured her a gin and tonic to enjoy with the delicious dinner cooked by Ande Grahn in the Main Camp Kitchen. After dinner, everyone sat around Main Camp to discuss the optimal placement of the recycling barrel stands. The conversation went on and on and on.

"I remember thinking, 'Is this the discussion they wanted to have with me, about where we're going to put the recycle barrels?'" Kathryn recalled. "This didn't seem quite as pivotal as I had thought."

Then she noticed Deni Schadegg and Robert DeSpain walking into Main Camp carrying armloads of colorful items. Suddenly they grabbed Kathryn and put her legs into a pair of hip-boot waders that they had embellished with glitter and paint to spell out "Madame President."

Next, they hung around Kathryn's neck a wooden toilet seat that had been painted with glitter that declared "Madame President." They stuffed her hands into sequined rubber gloves and gave her a "royal scepter"—a toilet brush. Someone started tossing rose petals at Kathryn and someone else popped open champagne bottles as they presented her with her throne, an eight-foot-tall chair that they hoisted her up on before she could figure out what was happening.

With Kathryn perched on her throne, Robert DeSpain explained everything. When he became fair president, he had come up with a tradition that he felt was incumbent on all future presidents to continue. In order to maintain their humility and their connection with the heart of the fair, future presidents of the Oregon Country Fair would always from thenceforth and for all time be required to clean the toilets at Main Camp.

Robert had, in fact, cleaned the toilets in Main Camp during his presidency. Bedo Crafts had been pressed into duty as well. Kathryn would eventually take her turn.

After they explained her duties, they lifted Kathryn up to the top of the Peach Truck. She rode up there with a group of other volunteers—sharing champagne and maybe a toke or two—as the Peach Truck driver took them on "perimeter patrol" around the fair property.

"I remember driving back to town that night," Kathryn said, "and I was sort of horrified, because I didn't really know those people. I kind of knew who they were from seeing them over the years, but I didn't *really know* them. Part of me was tickled pink and another part of me was horrified."

Kathryn said her son Ethan, who was ten at the time and had accompanied her, got upset about the toilet seat prank. He could see that Kathryn was laughing, but he got mad that they were making fun of his mom—especially putting a toilet seat over her head.

"Yet it was so funny!" Kathryn said. "It was one of the best pranks that I've ever seen out there. Later that year, I got into walking around the fair wearing my toilet seat, waving my scepter, and making proclamations. I did clean the shitters and then the president after me was J.R. [Robinson] and he refused" to continue the tradition.

In May 1990 Arna replaced the OM Team system with a similar one she called Back Up Managers. The board approved her choices of Sallie Edmunds and Kathryn Madden to be the fair's first BUMs. The BUM system, staffed with helpful volunteers picked by the general manager, would remain in place for decades.

Besides the fun and hijinks, Main Camp helped create significant new fair landmarks during Kathryn's presidency and Arna Shaw's term as general manager. In fourteen months, fair volunteers would complete a path expansion that came to be known as The Left Bank.

In January 1990, the fair's Planning Committee had recommended enlarging the public fairgrounds beyond the two loops of the Eight. Some trees and a few craft booths along Strawberry Lane had already fallen into the Long Tom River and almost two dozen more booths sat too close to the eroded bank. The new area would offer space where those crafters could relocate their booths. The area could also accommodate more booths as the river continued to nibble away at the Eight over the years.

Organizers began work shortly before the 1990 fair, when the Construction Crew, with help from "Backhoe Bob" DeSpain, built a new bridge over Indian Creek to connect to the new area and added a second entrance to the fair on the south side of Main Camp. The original fair entrance sat on the north side of Main Camp. The new bridge would be named DeSpain Bridge on DeSpain Lane. At Robert's request, "his" bridge was dedicated to all fair volunteers.

The remainder of the work began in the fall of 1990. But first, fair organizers would celebrate a landmark occasion: The final payment on the original site. At the board meeting on August 6, 1990, fair Treasurer Lucy Lynch reported "last land payment $8,900."

Arna, Kathryn, Ed Moye, and board member Palmer Parker arrived at the mortgage company carrying a bunch of balloons and the final check. Arna savored how she and her husband, former fair Treasurer Ron Chase, bookended the fair's land purchase. "I always liked that Ron wrote the check for the down payment on the property," Arna said, "and I wrote the check for the final payment. There was a certain symmetry to it for me."

Afterward, they celebrated at a local bar to toast the fair's accomplishment. At the volunteer-appreciation Teddy Bears' Picnic a few weeks later in August, Arna and Caretaker John Winslow burned the mortgage in a roundly applauded ceremony at Main Stage meadow.

(From left): Kathryn Madden, John Winslow, Arna Shaw, and Ed Moye burned the fair's mortgage at a ceremony during the Teddy Bears' Picnic in 1990.

Then Arna turned her attention to the new loop and to the resulting relocation of some booths. "We did the grounds work that fall," Arna said. "We wanted whatever brush clearing we had done to start to come back and look nice again. I started talking with the people who were moving and doing all the negotiations with them. At that point, that was the largest move that had ever happened." For 1991, around twenty booths would move.

"We did it pretty quickly," Arna said. "I put together a really good group of people who I thought had a good sense of design planning. Kirk [Shultz], Ed Moye, Dennis Todd, and Dahinda Meda were all on it." Greg Prull, a volunteer from Energy Park, came for only one meeting but made a big contribution.

"What you're talking about is finding all the really big trees in your area and connecting the dots between the big trees for your path," Greg told the committee.

"We were just like, 'Ohhhhhhh. Yeah!'" Arna said. "We kept saying we want to be in the shade because booths need shade mostly. Nobody wants to sit for eight hours in full sun. ... So we ended up laying out this route and then we cleared it."

Bill Verner, who volunteered on Security Crew and with the VegManECs, said the group decided together how to handle clearing the paths. "To take hawthorn and some nasty types of shrubs and create clearings without totally destroying the environment with the plants and making it work sometimes takes a little bit of creativity," Bill said. "The creativity came from everybody. It was never any one person's grandiose idea. Dahinda would talk to us and give us what his idea was. Then we either went along with it or wanted to make changes for one reason or another. A lot of times the changes were all good and accepted. It was everybody's call. It wasn't one person making all the decisions."

Early in the spring, Arna invited the relocating crafters out to the fair site to assess the new area. They asked the crafters what they were looking for and tried to accommodate their booth needs.

As the fair's first paid general manager, Arna Shaw oversaw the fair's first expansion beyond the Eight pathway to the Left Bank.

"At that point, the VegManECs were really kind of sticky on not clearing stuff," Arna said. "I was trying to get sympathetic VegManECs to say, 'Oh! This pile of brush that's in the entranceway of your booth or the middle of your booth, well, yeah, we can clear it out!' But there were some VegManECs who were really dogmatic."

Main Camp opened a month early in 1991 to give the fair's Construction Crews time to build all the new infrastructure needed

John Winslow inspected a booth that fell after floodwaters eroded the bank of the Long Tom River.

in the new loop and to give the crafters time to erect their booths. At first only a few food booths joined the craft booths on the Left Bank: Ritta's Burritos, New Day Bakery, and Golden Avatar.

"It was very hard work," Arna said. "It was such a long Main Camp. We did a ton of work. The Water Crew got water over there. They were laying pipe. There were so many logistics in terms of figuring out where everything was going to lay, putting in the service road, moving campers.

"We displaced all these Security Crew campers," Arna said. "We had to move them up to Dahinda's Acres. That was a whole other thing to deal with. And we took over Recycling's camping area and we had to move them to what's now Recycling camp."

Kirk Shultz, who had volunteered on Construction Crew since 1987, redesigned the Drum Tower and also helped design the new Dragon Plaza entryway. Dennis Todd asked Kirk to create a design for the long fence planned for the plaza at the new entry to Left Bank. Construction Crew originally imagined a "Village Square Entry with booths breaking up the long fence."

But late one night as he enjoyed a few glasses of red wine, inspiration struck Kirk via a book on Feng Shui, the Chinese design philosophy. Instead of a village square, he envisioned a dragon along the fence line—a "Laughing Dragon Gate." When Kirk presented his idea to the group, everyone loved it except the general manager.

"We can't get this done in time," Arna objected. "Why don't you just build the basic shape, you know, build it so that we can do the dragon the next year." But the group's excitement won out.

"The next thing I knew, they're building this dragon!" Arna said. "And I'm like, okay so much for my authority! It got done! Oh they were thatching that thing up to the morning we opened, but it was very cool. I'm glad they did it."

Dennis Todd put Kirk in touch with Jack Makarchek, who helped guide and build the Dragon. "Art is Controversial," Jack said, adding that he thought it shouldn't be a Chinese Dragon, but a Hippie Dragon. He proposed using thatch for the dragon's spine. Andy Strickland, who would later become fair caretaker, also added artistic touches like painting the teeth and toenails.

"It was a time of change when we opened the Left Bank," Kirk said. "It was challenging, but the family rose to it and marked the shift from the first era of fair to the next. The Dragon became a symbol of that transition."

A second bridge that connected the Left Bank to the entrance of the Circus Stage (later renamed W.C. Fields) would become another symbol of transition. It was dubbed "Jill's Crossing" in a bittersweet ceremony held Friday afternoon of the 1991 fair. The ceremony and the bridge's name honored Jill Heiman, the fair's former attorney—whose death on January 1, 1991, from complications of childbirth had been a huge shock.

Cynthia Wooten recalled how upset everyone was at the news. "Her parents came immediately," Cynthia said. "Because Jill is Jewish, we sat shiva at her house and began making arrangements for the funeral. … We were all just numb, you know. We couldn't believe it." Hundreds of people attended the funeral. Jill's survivors included her husband, Gerry Mackie, and her seven-year-old son, Brendan Mackie.

Over the years, the fair would progress from its earlier hand-to-mouth financial straits. In 1996, Arna Shaw and Ron Chase would spearhead a plan to get the fair board to donate more money to the community. Ron and Arna invited a few fair friends over to their house to discuss the proposal. "It started as a way to help the fair spend its money," said Kathryn Madden, who attended the meetings. "We believed that the fair wasn't putting enough of its money to charity." The group decided to name the program in honor of Jill Heiman.

"It seemed natural to name it after Jill," Arna said. "Jill was essential in the creation of the fair. It was Jill who got the fair its tax-exempt status, ... and who—by suing the county—helped get the money for the down payment for the land. ... Jill believed the fair could help the larger community. We felt that by donating money to nonprofits, we were following Jill's vision."

Besides Ron, Arna, and Kathryn, "Jill's Group" would include former board President Robert DeSpain; Main Stage Coordinator David Paul Black and his wife, volunteer Brenda Black; Main Camp volunteers Santos Narvaez, Palmer Parker, and Deni Schadegg; and Fair Central volunteer Michele Sharpy.

The group proposed to place boxes at Information booths around the fair to gather donations to benefit nonprofit programs. They set up a plan where fair members could vote on which category the donations from the next year's fair would go. Categories included homelessness, basic needs, environment, education, the arts, and more. The group asked the board to count food vouchers as donations to the fair, and to match the donations with profits from the event.

Ron proposed the Jill Heiman Vision Fund to the board in May 1996. Ron reminded the board that in the early days before the fair purchased the land, organizers had always donated proceeds after each fair to nonprofit organizations chosen by consensus. He said organizers had assumed back in the 1980s that once the land was paid off and fair finances had stabilized, that the fair would return to its tradition of being a contributing member of the community.

Some board members expressed surprise that the very first fairs gave away money to nonprofit groups, a practice that faded during the years in which resources were directed to paying off the mortgage on the fair land. Several liked the idea of members choosing the categories by vote. That made it easier to commit to spending the fair's funds, one person said. But many expressed concern that if the program became too successful, the board's matching funds could rise beyond what the fair could afford. In the end, Ron won approval from a skeptical board for a one-year trial.

"They did not want to do it at first," Arna said. "But we kind of shamed them into doing it."

That first year, fair volunteers donated more than a thousand food vouchers. With the fair's one-to-one match, the Jill Heiman Vision Fund in August 1996 made its first grant—more than $5,000—to FOOD for Lane County to combat hunger.

After the fair in 1996, the group behind the Jill Heiman Vision Fund met with the fair's treasurers to come up with a more detailed plan to satisfy the concerns expressed by the board back in May. But when the board reviewed the proposal in September 1996, the debate lasted long into the night as members quibbled over the particulars. Even though the proposal had strong support from the Financial Planning Committee, the fair treasurers, and the general manager, the board voted it down: six in favor; four opposed.

At the October 1996 meeting, board members who had opposed the group's detailed proposal offered a new motion to continue the Jill Heiman Vision Fund as it had run the first year with two changes: cash would be accepted and the fair would cap its match at $10,000. The board approved the motion. Like the first year, it would be limited to one year only.

"The board was more than a little suspicious," Kathryn Madden said, "but we got them to agree, finally, that they would cap their share."

Frustrated that the board refused to approve the vision fund in perpetuity—chief among other reasons—Arna Shaw would put her name in the hat for the board of directors' election at the annual meeting in October 1996. She won an alternate position. In January 1997, the board approved a Recipients Committee to evaluate and choose grant applicants to the Jill Heiman Vision Fund. Arna, who was on the list, had recruited the committee that included Ted Campbell, a crafter and early Jill's Group member; Leslie Scott, general manager; Anne Henry from the board; Hilary Anthony, fair treasurer; Julie Cherry, a craftsperson; and Richie Weinman, a booth representative.

Donations to the Vision Fund doubled the second year. With the board's match, the fund collected more than $12,000. More than half went to First Place Center to purchase a new van to transport homeless families in their shelter network. The rest financed an English as a Second Language program at Centro Latino Americano.

In August 1997 after two successful years, the board approved Arna's motion to keep the Jill Heiman Vision Fund as a continuing philanthropic program of the Oregon Country Fair. Jill's Group, who were all fair volunteers, had finally prevailed.

"It's pretty powerful when the organization steps in and says they'll match what an individual gives," Kathryn said.

Over the years, a number of food and craft booths would donate part or most of their profits to the Jill Heiman Vision Fund. "It is really fun to go around and talk to the crews and talk to the booths about it," Arna said. "We get a very positive reception."

"The food booths are really incredibly generous," Kathryn noted.

The fair board would eventually raise its match to two-to-one and in 2018 would increase the cap to $25,000. Over more than two decades, fair members most often would choose "basic needs" as the category for giving. In 2018, twenty-one years after it started, the Jill Heiman Vision Fund had donated more than half a million dollars to nonprofit groups. Many years, donations were granted to nonprofit agencies serving the Veneta and Elmira areas near the fair. The grants would help usher in a time of more harmony between the fair and its neighbors.

1990–91
State of the Peach: Bruised

"Will it be the end of the Fair as we know it??? The end of the world????"
—Minutes of OCF Board meeting, October 7, 1991, by Secretary Heidi Doscher

While the fair continued to run smoothly each year, behind the scenes the scope and pace of changes sparked deep discord on the fair board.

During the first few years after the fair board hired the organization's first paid employees, board members struggled with their new responsibilities and other effects of the transition. It didn't help that significant pockets of resistance persisted among the membership and among board members to having any paid job in the Country Fair organization.

Other contentious issues divided the fair board as well, including where to use electricity on site and how to fix the fair's pass system that had left so many people sneaking in every year. Many issues split the board so evenly that members couldn't reach the required two-thirds vote to make a decision.

In March 1990, former board President Bedo Crafts along with current President Kathryn Madden co-wrote a letter to the board expressing concern with the group's process "or lack thereof." They recommended setting up a board training session and appointing Michael Connelly, a counselor with Lane Mental Health Services and a member of Community Village, to facilitate the meetings instead of having it facilitated by a board member.

In May, the board attended a training session. Separately, Michael Connelly offered comments and suggestions on the board process, including sticking to a set agenda and limiting discussion times. But he also noted "content issues" and emphasized that the board needed to start treating each other with courtesy and respect at meetings and needed to reduce cross-talk. Still, the strident tenor of the meetings only worsened as time went on.

In early 1990, the board took up a recommendation by the Planning Committee on how to handle the problem of too many people sneaking into the fair at night. For many years, sneaking into the fair had become a rite of passage for multitudes of people. The fair's strict limits on overnight passes almost guaranteed cheating because the passes fell far short of what various groups needed—especially crafters, food booths, and entertainers.

Vaudeville entertainers in particular had pleaded their case for years to get more passes. Quite a few members of the Fighting Instruments of Karma Marching Chamber Band/Orchestra had been reduced to sneaking in to march in the band because there were not enough passes for them all.

Food booths had to sneak in enough workers to cover all their shifts, and craft booths sometimes hid family members in lofts or tents when the Sweep passed by each evening. On top of that, the fair family started to become a collection of families instead of single people and couples with toddlers. Those toddlers had grown into teen-agers and more kids came to the fair with their parents every year. The fair's overnight pass rules were still geared to young adults and made no provisions for older kids.

The Planning Committee recommended that anyone who earned a fair pass by volunteering could purchase a Significant Other pass. Anyone could be designated as a significant other, not just a spouse. They also recommended increasing the number of passes available to booths. The S.O. pass price would help cover the cost of the services that the fair provided to people who stayed overnight. In March 1990 the board approved the plan, noting that it provided a way to account for fair fans who already had been staying overnight and would "make honest people out of them."

In April 1990, board member and Entertainment Co-coordinator Moz Wright brought several proposals to the board to try to bring more equity to the vaudeville performers, who were paid a fee that barely covered their expenses.

The old system had worked when all entertainers came separately to the fair to perform, but now the vaudeville family helped produce shows on two stages at the fair, working together in large groups long before the fair began. Vaudeville folks also helped erect two stages each year. Moz proposed that their sweat equity should be considered equal to the fair volunteers' sweat equity, and that those vaudeville performers deserved the perks offered to fair volunteers, particularly the ability to purchase Significant Other passes.

But the motion to give vaudeville entertainers parity with volunteers failed. The board then approved unanimously a motion by Kathryn Madden that a committee be set up to address the issue of equity for entertainers. In May, the board named a group to the committee, but the committee apparently never met and never reported back to the board. The issue of entertainer equity would remain a sticking point for several more years.

The tussle over Significant Other passes spilled over into 1991. In February J.R. Robinson, a co-coordinator of Traffic Crew who had recently been elected to the board, made a motion to discontinue the S.O. passes. The board voted six in favor and four against to discontinue the passes, but the motion failed because the vote count didn't reach the required two-thirds majority.

In April 1990, fair co-founder Cynthia Wooten asked the board to use the fair mailing list to send out campaign flyers in her race for Lane County commissioner. The board turned down the proposal with five voting in favor, four against, and one abstention. Even so, several fair members wrote the board afterward expressing alarm that the board would even consider giving out the fair's mailing list.

That spring the board also grappled with an issue that had been a problem for nearly ten years. An informal barter fair had cropped up among the fair crafters at the end of every fair. It started as informal "blanket sales" by a few fair crafters at Main Stage in the late 1970s.

Ascha Gellman (later Champie), who had sold beaded barrettes and other beaded crafts from her booth near the Main Stage meadow since 1977, had always sold strands of top-quality beads to other crafters after hours and after the fair. Once the fair purchased the property and crafters could stay through Monday mornings, Ascha spread out a blanket in Main Stage meadow to accommodate the buyers who crowded her booth.

Other crafters joined Ascha in the meadow to barter and sell items. The informal barter fair offerings included imports and other merchandise that was not handmade by the sellers—items that were not allowed to be sold at the fair during public hours. But the bargains and imports attracted a legion of fans among those who camped overnight at the fair. As packing got underway at all the campsites on Monday morning, eager buyers and traders congregated around the blankets. Commerce was brisk.

After a few years, fair organizers moved the barter fair to the parking lot to try to get everyone out of the inside loops of the Eight and off the property on Monday mornings after the fair was over. The board had set up a task force to review the barter fair, and the task force concluded that the barter fair drained fair resources to increase the profits of a few. It didn't help that the barter fair's inclusion of inexpensive imports violated the creative spirit of the fair. In May 1990, the board voted to disallow the barter fair.

Barter fair fans fought back, presenting a petition at the June 1990 board meeting signed by thirty-eight crafters requesting the board to reinstate the barter fair. The heated discussion included "some yells of SHUT UP!" Even though the board stood by its earlier decision, crafters would continue for decades to lobby the board to support a barter fair.

(The board would

Ascha Gellman Champie, shown in the early 1980s, sold beadwork at the Country Fair for decades.

eventually allow the barter fair to resume during the 1990s and early 2000s, only to call a halt to it again. The crews that had to work longer and harder after the fair was over because of the barter event—particularly Recycling, Security, Traffic, and the Deconstruction crews—objected loudly to the increased workload. The board sided with the crews and stopped the barter fair in 2013.)

The board in 1990 also renewed the fight over electricity in the Eight. Once power ran to the Main Stage sound system, White Bird Clinic's fair medical center sat only a hop, skip, and jump away.

White Bird volunteers provided medical and counseling services to fair visitors during the three-day event, as well as to volunteers and booth people who stayed overnight. The clinic never closed during the fair, staying open all night in case of emergencies. White Bird's tent included an urgent care area (aka the White Bird hospital) that used electricity from a gas-powered generator behind the tent. But White Bird's request for access to the electric line to replace their generator sparked more controversy.

At the June 1990 meeting, the board first turned down White Bird's request with a vote of four in favor, two against, and two abstaining. Several board members were not present for the vote, including Frank Sharpy, who had long questioned why White Bird's hospital needed to be next to Main Stage. He wondered why the urgent care center couldn't be moved to a quieter spot away from all the action where electricity could be provided without invading the Eight?

Mindful of Frank's arguments and that many fair members agreed with him, the board approved Darrel Sink's motion that "a temporary power line for this year's fair only go to the White Bird hospital with no visible light outside the medical tent on condition that the whole issue of electricity for and/or moving White Bird be re-examined in the fall."

The board then approved George Braddock's request to run electricity to the sauna reservoir so water could be pumped to the showers without using a "noisy and polluting" generator.

The next week, Frank Sharpy resigned from the board over the electricity votes. "I remember the commitment we made to *never* allow power to booths or into the inside of the figure Eight," his resignation letter said. "I can't live with these decisions, so I tender my resignation to the board of directors." Still, Frank would continue to volunteer in Main Camp during the fair for decades.

As promised, the board revisited the White Bird debate in December 1990. Zak Schwartz and other White Bird volunteers attended to present their case. They told the board that the

Frank Sharpy and Kathryn Madden were friends and key participants in Main Camp in the late 1980s.

doctors in charge did not want to split up the hospital from White Bird's service area at Main Stage. They wanted the hospital to stay with the rest of their operations in the middle of the fair where it could be easily found. The motion to allow power to White Bird "for the foreseeable future" divided the board exactly in half: five to five, leaving the issue unresolved.

The board again discussed allowing electricity to White Bird in May 1991, and once more kicked the can forward. The board voted to allow the electricity for only one year, "on the condition the whole issue be re-examined in the fall." That discussion would not take place until years later. The issue of White Bird and electricity in the Eight would be eclipsed by the growing personal discord and dysfunction that brought the board to a stalemate in October 1991.

The issues that deeply divided the board in the fall of 1991 had roots in the deteriorating relationship between the general manager and the caretaker. It was clear as early as the fall of 1990 that Arna Shaw and John Winslow did not get along, and the situation worsened when Arna found fault with John's work performance. At the same time, board members remained at odds over how to handle the situation. They collectively had very little experience as employers and certainly made missteps in the process of trying to reach a resolution.

"At most nonprofit agencies, the manager hires and fires," Arna said. "The Country Fair is one of the few places that the manager doesn't have that kind of ability. Even for crews. Even for anything. That's where it all fell apart."

Rumors of the discord had swirled for months among volunteer organizers. The Personnel Committee set up an Executive Session with the board to discuss it in October 1990. The Personnel Committee recommended that Arna get a raise and a twelve-month contract and that John get a three-month contract at the same wage with "a plan of correction to work out job performance problems."

Nevertheless, at the October 1990 regular board meeting, it took much conversation and four votes to sort out what to do. Volunteers and crafters, who had heard rumors about the disagreements between the general manager and the caretaker, had already started taking sides. The board first considered extending both contracts for three months while both parties worked to mediate the differences between them, but that motion failed with a split vote.

After much debate, the board voted to extend John Winslow's contract as caretaker for three months with a plan to correct work performance problems. During the discussion, it came to light that John had experienced an injury that made it difficult for him to complete many of his job requirements. The board also required John to participate in mediation with the general manager.

Next the board bickered over how to handle Arna's contract. Board members ultimately approved renewing Arna's contract for a year with a salary review in three months, and required her to "participate in mediation sessions with the caretaker."

But the personal quarrels quickly spread beyond the board to include fair volunteers. On Dec. 31, 1990, John Winslow filed a grievance against Construction Crew volunteer Ed Moye for harassment. John also filed grievances that day against Arna Shaw and members of the fair's Personnel Committee—Kathryn Madden, Sue Kesey, and George Braddock—for not responding to John's previous complaints about Moye.

John accused Moye of of targeting him with critical, hostile, and false statements. His grievance filing argued that Arna had done nothing about Ed's harassment even though John had brought it up several times. John also accused the Personnel Committee of failing to take his complaints seriously.

Dennis Todd, Construction Crew co-coordinator, got involved because Ed was a friend and worked on his crew. "Ed Moye pointed out that John Winslow couldn't do his job," Dennis said, "and Ed doesn't know when to quit. ... I told Ed, 'Hey, just back off a bit.' But he wouldn't."

The board at the January 1991 meeting referred John's complaint to a grievance committee. The board also voted against renewing John's contract because of medical reasons. The board asked John to stay until the end of March and restricted his work duties, as per his doctor's orders, in order to smooth the transition to the next caretaker. John agreed.

But fair board members themselves made the transition to a new caretaker difficult. Their behavior at the March 1991 meeting before a large audience of fair coordinators and members offered a glimpse into the board's recurrent dysfunction. The board process allowed fair members to comment often, prolonging all the discussions.

The Personnel Committee had recommended that the board hire Scott Ballin as caretaker. He was a fair volunteer with a "good background in grounds maintenance and knowledge of erosion control," the PC told the board. "He has also been working as a carpenter and has experience in safety procedures."

Dahinda Meda, who represented the VegManECs (Vegetation Management and Erosion Control) on the Personnel Committee, presented the board with a minority report. Dahinda said that the VegManECs, who worked very closely with the caretaker, preferred a different candidate who had been turned down by the rest of the committee at meetings held when Dahinda had been out of town on business.

A member of the Personnel Committee (unnamed in the fair minutes) responded that "Dahinda had abdicated his responsibility by leaving when he did, knowing they had three more people to interview."

Part of the hiring decision rested on whether the caretaker could live on site all year round, a requirement of the job description. The VegManECs' preferred candidate had proposed to live off site for part of the year, and that was why a majority of the Personnel Committee had dropped him—albeit reluctantly—from the list.

But the board voted against the recommendation to hire Scott Ballin with four in favor, one opposed, and five abstentions. The board had no procedure or precedent for what to do next after they turned down the Personnel Committee's preferred candidate. Board members and the large group of fair members and coordinators attending the meeting launched into an extensive debate over the hiring process—so heated that at one point a board member admonished Santos Narvaez, a Main Camp volunteer, for bringing his "home boys" in to harass the board.

After extending the meeting, the board voted against requiring the caretaker to live on site. Board member Michael Goldhammer went home, letting alternate Dean Felders vote.

The board passed a motion to have the Personnel Committee negotiate the resident-on-site schedule for the caretaker. The discussion wore on and the board again extended the meeting.

Once more, the board voted on hiring Scott as caretaker, and once again the motion failed: four in favor, one opposed, and five abstentions. The board again extended the meeting. Discussions raged on and on, pushing toward 11:00 p.m.

A motion to hire Scott on a seven-month contract also failed, with six in favor and four opposed. Then another board member went home.

With only nine board members left, the board again considered a motion to require the caretaker to live on site. Now a quirk in the board's two-thirds majority rule emerged. This time the motion passed with six in favor. Normally six votes would not be enough to pass a motion, but with only nine people voting, six votes equaled two-thirds.

Then Kathryn Madden moved to hire Scott Ballin as caretaker for seven months. Before they could vote, they had to agree to extend the meeting past 11:00 p.m. At that point, another board member left for home.

Finally, the shrinking board voted to hire Ballin, with six votes in favor and two opposed. The minutes noted: "It was about 11:30 when the secretary turned off the recorder and fled."

From that point forward, division and acrimony among the board members and fair coordinators would grow like thistles—fertilized with personal grievances, rumors, and gossip.

"There was one grievance after another," Dennis Todd, Construction co-coordinator said. Over the next month, a flurry of correspondence inundated board members' mailboxes.

Main Camp volunteer Darrell Nealon filed a grievance against John Winslow for allegedly spreading lies about Darrell's connection to Arna. Darrell said the lies implied his friendship with Arna was something much more. Dennis Todd filed a grievance alleging that John Winslow had spread lies about Dennis and had slandered the Construction Crew.

Bedo Crafts wrote a letter to the board protesting the process followed in hiring Scott Ballin and advocating for the candidate that the VegManECs liked. To top it off, board alternate Dean Felders wrote a proposal to remove the general manager for failing to follow the fair's Code of Conduct. Dean accused Arna Shaw of bringing in a cohort of her supporters to the March 1991 meeting to insult board members and disrupt the proceedings.

Two letters came in pleading for a better board process. Board member Mary Wagner's letter asked members to treat each other kindly and with respect. Main Camp volunteer Palmer Parker beseeched board members to hold themselves to a higher standard of conduct.

At the April 1991 meeting, the board weighed in on John Winslow's original December 1990 grievance against Ed Moye, Arna Shaw, and Personnel Committee members Kathryn Madden, Sue Kesey, and George Braddock.

Decades before videos became ubiquitous, Construction Crew Coordinator Ken Rodgers set up a video-film camera on a tripod and pointed it at the board to record the proceedings. Santos Narvaez waved a hand-lettered sign proudly declaring "HOME BOY" in defiance of the board member who had admonished him the month before for bringing so many Main Camp friends to the meeting to allegedly harass the board. Ed Moye showed up wearing red-sequined devil's horns and an impish grin, humorously embracing the nickname "Evil Ed."

The board first voted decisively against the Grievance Committee's full recommendation, which contained four parts. Next the board voted separately on each section. They agreed to hold Arna and the Personnel Committee accountable for not handling John Winslow's complaint well.

After much debate, the board also approved the Grievance Committee's recommendation to improve the grievance process and to stop spreading gossip and rumors.

But the portion recommending that Ed Moye be suspended for a year from working on any fair crew drew loud pushback from the many crew volunteers assembled at the meeting. Construction Crew Co-coordinator Jim Richmond even drove all the way from Arizona to defend Ed. Numerous other crew coordinators spoke up for Ed, insisting that Ed expressing his opinion about John Winslow didn't rise to the level of harassment.

The board voted against suspending Ed but continued to talk about it. Five board members walked out of the meeting in the middle of the discussion and "the audience expressed disappointment" the minutes note.

After consulting the bylaws, the six remaining board members determined they still had a quorum. They debated putting Ed on probation instead of suspending him. Again the board voted against sanctioning Ed and the meeting adjourned as the clock ticked toward midnight.

Meanwhile, fair members were getting fed up with the board's dysfunction. In May the board received three membership petitions. One called for the board to not make any more decisions dealing with the general manager, the caretaker, or any structural change until after the 1991 fair. It was signed by 151 fair members. A letter of support for Arna Shaw circulated by fair coordinators came to the board with 169 signatures. A third letter, written by Robert DeSpain and signed by 123 people, begged the board to refrain from name calling. In this pre-email era, gathering that many signatures demonstrated considerable determination and hard work on the part of the board critics.

Nevertheless, at the May meeting the board turned down a motion to express board "confidence" in Arna Shaw with five voting in favor, two opposed, and three abstaining. A follow-up motion expressing "support" for Arna passed after long discussion, seven in favor, two opposed, and one abstention. Arna expressed her disappointment, noting that "support" fell far short of "confidence."

Before the June meeting, Mary Wagner resigned from the board with a letter stating her reasons. "It seems to me that many members of the board, the general manager, and the president have become so caught up in their respective politics—politics of pettiness, self-interest, inflexibility, and paranoia—that they are no longer providing the leadership the fair needs so badly," Mary's letter said. "... For myself, I feel that I have nothing to offer to resolve this ugly dilemma. The efforts I have made have been fruitless."

Despite all the behind-the-scenes backstabbing, the 1991 fair was a huge success. More than 45,000 people attended, breaking the old record by 10,000 people. The new Left Bank expansion opened without a hitch and the fair ran smoothly. Even so, some board members groused that the fair had gotten too big and too crowded.

The first meeting after the fair—held early in August—started out on an upbeat note. Wren Davidson, representing crafters who had met to discuss fair issues, reported to the board that the crafters' "general feeling is that the fair is getting better and better, and the last few years have shown a lot of improvement."

But after the committee reports, the veneer of civility vanished. Dean Felders moved and Dahinda Meda seconded a motion to fire Arna Shaw. Angry debate broke out with many people pointing out the motion should have at least waited until after Arna's evaluation, which was coming up in a few weeks. Ultimately the motion failed, six in favor and four opposed.

A few weeks later at the annual Teddy Bears' Picnic held in the Main Stage Meadow, Dennis Todd and several other volunteers circulated a petition to recall every person on the fair's board of directors. On the board were Rene Knowles, Dahinda Meda, J.R. Robinson, Darrel Sink, Wally Slocum, Janine Alea, Michael Goldhammer, Bedo Crafts, Kathryn Madden, Dean Felders, and Jeanne Sharpy (alternate). With Mary Wagner's resignation, the board had ten members and one alternate instead of twelve members.

"I wrote the petition," Dennis said. "I was the lead circulator. I wanted to start over. I wanted the fair to purge all top-level staff, including my own job. I knew that being a construction coordinator was a position of power and I did not want to emerge from it as a victor because I knew there were no victors, there were only losers.

"When I started that petition," Dennis added, "I told everyone I'm taking this on not to consolidate my power. I am going to resign as coordinator after this is done, no matter how it comes out, as soon as we can train our replacements."

However, the petitioners themselves added to the rifts in the fair. At the picnic, they approached Frank Sharpy about signing even though his wife, Jeanne, served on the board as an alternate and would be subject to the recall. As an alternate, Jeanne had only gotten the chance to vote a few times during the whole fiasco.

"Get the fuck out of my sight!" Frank yelled at them. Decades later he would remain bitter about the recall petitioners. "I lost a lot of respect for the peace-and-love Woodstock shit about the fair then," he said. "I knew that a line had been crossed."

Dennis presented the recall petition containing 128 signatures to the board at the September meeting. Also at that meeting, Dahinda Meda resigned from the board, citing his lack of trust in Arna. Rene Knowles announced his intention to resign after the October meeting.

"Several board members resigned even though they were in the middle of their term," Dennis noted, "so that they could be re-nominated at the election that was coming up."

Board President Kathryn Madden read an open letter to the membership at the September meeting acknowledging "a crisis in confidence and trust that permeates the organization. ... It is an ugly situation that has been building for over a year." In the letter, Kathryn apologized to the members for "the pain, the drama, and the conflict" that have taken their toll. She urged members to become involved and work to shape a positive solution.

At the October 1991 board meeting, Jim Guthrie announced that he finally had found someone to certify the November board election, including the results of the recall. Jim recommended John Sundquist, one of the original founders of the Hoedads tree-planting cooperative, "who is willing to do the all-nighter and who is emotionally unattached to the fair right now."

John had volunteered on Traffic and Security crews at the early fairs and worked at his own organic farm, but had not been active in the fair since 1979. "Wren Davidson and another friend from the fair walked up to me at Saturday Market one day," John said. "They asked me if I could help them, if I could help the fair, by counting ballots at the next annual meeting. I said sure." The board approved his appointment.

The board also accepted Moz Wright's resignation from the board and from his duties as Entertainment and Ambiance/Shady Grove coordinator. In his resignation letter, Moz complained that over the years since he and Deni Schadegg broke up in late 1985, he had been harassed over the Entertainment budgets he submitted and that other Entertainment co-coordinators quit cooperating with him. Moz had also aired his complaints to the fair family at large during his performance at the 1991 Midnight Show.

The contentious mood of the meeting only intensified when board members reached an impasse as they turned to employee evaluations. The Personnel Committee recommended not rehiring Scott Ballin. The board accepted that recommendation and voted to not renew Scott's contract.

However, the board voted down the committee's recommendation to keep Arna for three months in her general manager post while making plans to hire a new general manager by January. During long hard debate, the board tried to figure out what to do next.

First the board extended the meeting until 11:00 p.m. Next it approved a motion seeking volunteers to help take care of the property. Then members voted to initiate a caretaker job search.

But the people who served on the Personnel Committee told the board that they could not initiate a hiring process unless they got reappointed that night. Then the motion to reappoint the Personnel Committee failed.

At this point secretary Heidi Doscher wrote in the minutes: "Are you still with us? Right now we have no P.C., no Caretaker, no General Manager. Will it be the end of the Fair as we know it??? The end of the world????"

Finally Darrel Sink moved that the president form an ad hoc transitional team to serve until the November board meeting when the new board would take office. Kathryn objected that she had mixed feelings about it, but the motion passed. Kathryn agreed to do it because she felt a "responsibility to the organization."

Arna noted that "Everything was in turmoil. Almost every board meeting from the fair on to October, they tried to fire me. God, it was horrible! ... They didn't have the votes. They tried to fire me and the word would go out among the coordinators that they were trying to fire me and people would come in my support. I actually had a lot of support among coordinators. The board just never had enough votes to fire me. But they didn't have enough votes to re-hire me either."

The Elections Committee scrambled to assemble a fair

and balanced 1991 *Voters Pamphlet*. In addition to the standard candidates' statements, the fifty-eight-page pamphlet included viewpoint pieces from the petitioners and from those who were targeted in the recall, attempting to present all sides of the contentious issues. Notably, the statement from the petitioners for recall asked voters to not recall three board members who were credited with seeking middle ground: J.R. Robinson, Kathryn Madden, and Michael Goldhammer.

Besides wrestling with a huge *Voters Pamphlet*, the Elections Committee struggled with how to conduct the vote that would involve both a recall and an election at the same meeting. There were no guidelines for the situation in the fair's bylaws.

The Elections Committee printed two separate ballots, one for the recall and one with all the candidates for the election. With two separate ballots, voters faced a complex situation. On one ballot, they would be asked to recall sitting board members. On a second, they would be asked to select a new board from a list of candidates. Oddly, that second ballot included some people who were on the recall ballot, raising at least a theoretical possibility that a current board member could be both recalled and re-elected at the same meeting.

In all, six board members facing recall also ran for re-election. Bedo Crafts and Janine Alea, whose terms were expiring, ran again for the board. Dahinda Meda, Dean Felders, and Wally Slocum resigned from the board to avoid the recall and also sought re-election. Jeanne Sharpy, who served as an alternate, ran for a full board position. A dozen other fair members put their names up to challenge the incumbents for slots on the board.

Kathryn Madden didn't run for re-election, opting to step down at the end of her term. Two other board members also did not seek a second term: Michael Goldhammer and Darrel Sink. Rene Knowles resigned in the middle of his term. Only J.R. Robinson faced the recall in the middle of his board term without resigning.

No one affiliated with the fair would count the ballots because too many people had taken sides in the ugly debates to find credible, neutral tabulators among the fair membership. John Sundquist, who had been appointed by the board, recruited his wife, Marsha; her cousin Ben; and friend Frank Florian to help count the ballots. Ben and Frank "were good with numbers," John said. "They had a system." None of them were affiliated with the fair.

State of the Peach: Bruised

The fair's annual meeting in October 1991 attracted more members than it had in many years. Volunteers donned their oldest fair staff T-shirts to stake their claims to credibility. In her "State of the Peach" address, President Kathryn Madden lamented "a hell of a year" and shouldered responsibility for not being able to turn things around.

When it came time to cast votes, members were instructed to treat each ballot differently. On the recall ballot, they could check off as many board members as they wanted to recall, or leave it blank to recall none of them. On the election ballot they were instructed to vote for twelve out of the nineteen candidates, numbering one to twelve in their order of preference.

After the votes were cast, John Sundquist's crew first would count the recall votes. Once they determined how many directors got recalled, they could tally votes from the election ballots up to the number needed to fill the remaining slots on the board. The number of votes counted off each election ballot would depend on how many slots were left open by the recall.

At the crowded annual meeting, heated discussions about the recall and the board candidates ran every which way. The outcome, though, came through loud and clear. Only two board members survived the recall: J.R. Robinson, who remained a full board member, and Jeanne Sharpy, who remained an alternate.

The other ten board of director positions were filled by new people: Kelly Campbell (Crane) (Teen Crew coordinator), Steve Gorham (Traffic Crew), Anne Henry (Charter Member crafter and *Peach Pit* coordinator), Margo Schaefer (Advertising coordinator), Steve Wisnovsky (Traffic Crew), Thom Chambliss (Registration Crew—Craft Inventory), Daniel Dillon (Blintz Booth, Charter Member), Bob Durnell (Recycling Crew), and Paxton Hoag (Water Crew), with alternate Jim Sahr (Charter Member crafter and fair electrician).

The recall year fractured longtime fair friendships. Many former friends would remain estranged for decades. But with new leadership, the fair organization would begin a new era.

 ## 1992 Fair Family News

"Most of us who work so hard to put on this 'essential event,' as Artis the Spoonman calls it, have a strange and fierce commitment to keeping the magic going. We think a year-round newsletter is one way to make that happen."
—Norma Sax, "Welcome to the Oregon Country Fair Newsletter," Volume 1, Issue 1, May 1992

Amidst the uproar over the 1991 recall election, many fair members agreed that they needed a better way to publicly and openly communicate with each other all year long.

On November 21, just a month after the annual meeting, fair Secretary Norma Sax hosted a gathering of fair friends at her house to talk about presenting a fair newsletter plan to the board.

"There was no real way to provide input to the board," said Mary (Doyon) Shuler, who volunteered on Traffic then. "We talked about it at the planning meetings."

Mary's husband, Michael Ottenhausen, agreed. "There wasn't any way to voice opinions to the entire group without going to endless amounts of meetings," he said.

The group included Carol Bull, Kelly Campbell (now Crane), Dahinda Meda's daughter Erica Lerch, Dahinda's nephew Brad Lerch, Wally Slocum, Michael Ottenhausen, Mary Doyon Shuler, and Norma. Anne Henry acted as board liaison. Heidi Doscher volunteered to be the mailing list coordinator. They met for months and finally firmed up a plan.

"Everybody was great," Norma said. "It was Erica's idea to use newsprint, running eight to twelve pages. My vision was to have about five pages on eight-and-a half-by-eleven-inch paper. But Erica did the research, and said that we could sell it to the board by including the minutes and that using newsprint would be a lot cheaper."

The first issue of *Fair Family Flashes* debuted in tabloid newsprint format in May 1992. Mary said the temporary name came from "an old hippie saying, 'Oh man, I just had a flash,' meaning an insight or thought."

The May 1992 issue opened with a welcome letter written by Norma, and a "name the newsletter" contest on page one. Readers found articles inside about the fair phone system (by Sparks Scott), reverence for the land (by VegManEC Co-coordinator John Doscher), plus the board minutes. Several crews and individuals wrote to praise the new newsletter, including an article by Tom Noddy that spoofed fair politics and revealed "The Secret Circus Plan to take over the Fair!"

Zak Schwartz, the White Bird medical coordinator who had been offering Crisis Intervention training to the volunteers for years, contributed "Healthy Thoughts." In it, Zak addressed the uneasy feelings among fair members that the organization had not lived up to its lofty ideals:

> Well, I say to you that the pain of these little imperfections is a function not of their existence but rather of our expectation that ideals will, and should be perfectly manifest in the reality of the event. Perfection that embodies these ideals remain in our souls, hearts, and minds where it belongs. Ever striving to create realities closer to them is an essential aspect of experiencing value and meaning in a manifest world. It is in that space between ideal concept and imperfect manifestation that love and caring flows. Where would we be without room to improve?
>
> Each of us exists in a subjective world built of the 'maps' of our memories and perceptions that we imperfectly store within us. 'Objective reality' (what is actually real) is a term with little or no meaning to me. Truth and sincerity are one and the same. Expressing our subjectivity with no deliberate fabrication is as honest as it gets. 'Fact' is liquid in solid clothing. When thousands of us relatively independent forces work together all

year to manifest one tight, interdependent event, we must try to do so with respect for each of our worlds, understanding that the product is a collage of these.

Each of us must work on our abilities to be both assertive and considerate simultaneously.

The June 1992 issue covered pre-fair information that would help everything run more smoothly. Erica Lerch wrote an article about registration booths' hours and processes. She offered advice on fire safety and suggested items for volunteers' packing lists: "sun protection, warm hat & blanket, insect repellent/relief, patience, small penlights, chocolate, a cart, a smile, water & squirt gun."

The second issue included the newsletter's first advertisers: ACE Contracting by Michael Ottenhausen; Café Mam; Royal Blueberries; Chez Ray; CPA Chris Bauske; Summit University by Cerredwen Harper; and Oregon Event Enterprises by Don Doolin, Dean Felders, and John Doscher.

Among the "unclassified ads" that month, careful readers found a few spoofs and jokes:

"Lost: 9 ft. python at '91 Fair, Contact bellydancers.
Wanted: mosquito-free camping spot for '92 Fair, will pay cash ..."
"How many Main Campers does it take to change a lightbulb? Only one, they hold the lightbulb and the world revolves around them. How many Security people does it take to change a lightbulb? None, Security people aren't afraid of the dark! How many Energy Park people does it take to change a lightbulb? Change a lightbulb? Change to solar! How many White Birds does it take to change a lightbulb? Only one, but the lightbulb has to really want to change."

By popular vote, the newsletter's name changed to the *Fair Family News* in September 1992. And in October 1992, the phrase "One Creative Family" was added to the masthead after Brad Lerch suggested it as a play on the letters "OCF."

The *Fair Family News* would report on fair-related events all year long. The newsletter's cover photo in January 1993 featured the brand new yurt that volunteers had assembled for the caretaker. The fair had purchased the pre-fabricated yurt from Oregon Yurtworks, whose owner Morgan Reiter brought a small yurt every year to erect at the fair for his booth. Morgan's yurts were juried in as a craft.

But the *Fair Family News* did not carry a report about how crucial the new yurt would be for Caretaker Bill Verner and his health. The caretaker's mobile home had become uninhabitable.

The old mobile home "was long and narrow and had mice living in between the flooring," Bill recalled decades later. He had taken to sleeping on a mattress on the floor because the legs of the bed threatened to break through the rotting floor. In fact, the floor would fail in a place they had never considered.

One morning Bill woke up to the smell of horrendous exhaust fumes. He quickly evacuated from the trailer to sit in the cab of his truck. When morning dawned, he called board members and the general manager and asked them to come out to the site to help him find the cause of the fumes.

They would discover that the floor had rotted underneath the propane-fired hot water heater and it had fallen through the floor. That caused the exhaust pipe on the water heater to break and release exhaust between the walls and roof of the old mobile home. To everyone's horror, they found black soot covering the insulation between the walls. The problem had been going on for some time.

"Everybody was surprised as to how bad it was," Bill said. He would take a month-long vacation until the yurt could be completed.

A year and a half after he was hired, Bill would finally move into the yurt in May 1993 when fair volunteers finished installing electricity, plumbing, a porch, and other essentials. Bill said he felt beyond relieved.

In March 1996 the *Fair Family News* reported that a major flood on the fair site had downed trees and damaged many of the structures along the path. The article invited fair members to a work party later that month. In April 1996 the newsletter ran a photo spread and story detailing how 100 volunteers came together to help clean up the damage on the site.

In August 1996, the newsletter ran a sampling of the clever "red tag" notices written by Construction Crew volunteers to inform booth folks about repairs that needed to be made prior to the fair. Construction Crew volunteer Ed Moye specialized in rhyming versions of the notices, written on red construction paper (hence the name red tags).

Because of the flood damage, booth folks found more red tags than usual in 1996:

Though this note may make you sore
And this project makes you fried
There are problems with your floor
That cannot be denied.

When you see past loft's illusions, there lies the danger.
When your perfect structure looks built by a perfect fool,
And you go ranting off at the rhymes of a perfect stranger,
As the dry rot seems to spring from your booth
Like a fountain of drool.
Fountain of dry rot, fountain of spite,
You've know the empty feeling of your hand rail in flight.
You've had to suffer some, but now you're all right,
And it's good to see your swollen face here tonight.
   Apologies to J. Browne

There once was a booth at the fair
Whose structure was mostly of air
A wonder to see
But oh, golly gee
Don't anyone climb in up there.

In May 1997, the newsletter ran several articles introducing another expansion to the fair's pathways: Chela Mela Meadow. The new area would provide room for more participatory activities. Fairgoers could hang out, create art, learn to juggle, join a parade, or catch a show. The article noted that Back Up Manager Sallie Edmunds spearheaded an inclusive planning process, replete with workshops and meetings. Soon they formed a Path Planning Committee to lead the way. The committee would tap Hilary Anthony, the fair's co-treasurer who had participated in the planning process for two years, to coordinate Chela Mela Meadow.

Fair family members were invited to check out all the new offerings in the meadow, including a yurt where Tom Noddy could complete his more complicated bubble tricks without being disturbed by the wind.

The *Fair Family News* crew's playfulness would spawn several traditions over the years. The crew started playing with the staff box listing in May 1994, when everyone added "bear" to their titles (Editor Bear, Layout Bear, Assistant Bear, etc.) The different names each month poked fun at the "fair names" many volunteers adopted at fair time.

An April Fools' tradition of tomfoolery with photos and stories started in 1995. As an April Fools' joke in 1997, the crew tried to make the pages look as dirty and messy as possible.

"We spent twenty-five or thirty minutes at least messing the pages up," Michael said. "We were doing all the stuff we had forbidden everyone to do. ... We put coffee stains on it, ink smudges, fingerprints. We even took it and stomped on it!"

But the workers at the print shop, who weren't clued in on the joke, cleaned up most of the pages, and the crew ended up feeling like the joke was on them. In the final print, all that remained of the mess were a few fingerprint smudges, some stray paperclips and a single strand of Sheila Landry's long hair copied onto the April Fools' page.

Other fun crew traditions would include staff parties for Winter Solstice in December and the newsletter anniversary every spring.

Over the years, the crew would remain remarkably steady. Brad, Mary, Michael, and Norma all would remain involved more than two decades after the first organizational meeting. Sheila Landry volunteered for twelve years. Other people who volunteered for five years or more included: Heidi Doscher, Mira Rainy, Cynde Leathers, Kevin Dougherty, Dominic DeFazio, Joseph Newton, Suzi Prozanski, Niki Harris, Dan Cohn, and Kim Griggs.

Dick Stewart, while not "officially" listed among the crew, helped his sweetheart Norma Sax edit and mail the board minutes before the *Fair Family News* was created, and he continued helping with the monthly newsletter mailings for years. "I licked a lot of stamps or put 'em on a sponge," Dick said of the early days. "We also used to use sticks to fold the paper," an arduous task that finally ended in the 2000s when money was budgeted to pay for the press to fold the paper automatically. By 2015, fair organizers would allocate enough funds to have the newsletter mailed by the press instead of bringing in volunteers to slap labels on every month.

When the newsletter started in 1992, the fair office didn't have the equipment needed to produce it, so crew members would sneak

Fair Family News volunteers in 1996 (left, from left): Michael Ottenhausen, Mary (Doyon) Shuler, Brad Lerch, Sheila Landry, Norma Sax, and Heidi Doscher. Crew photo in 1997 (right) included Kevin Dougherty (at left).

back into their day-job workplaces after hours to use computers to print out type. Everyone spent a lot of late nights pasting up pages at the twenty-four-hour Kinko's.

With advances in technology, newsletter crew members began to produce the type for the newsletter using computers at the fair office and at volunteers' homes. When the fair office moved to Lawrence Street in 1999, the crew created a place in the basement to paste up the pages. On paste-up nights, they would play Grateful Dead music and other groovy tunes as they placed art and headlines on each page. Sheila and Norma often spontaneously broke out go-go dancing.

The *Fair Family News* staff box nicknames in September 1999 referenced the move to the basement of the new office:

FFN Cellar Dwellers   Sump Pump Shuler
                               Song of the Deep Songchild
   Headbanger Lerch   Foundation Dougherty
   Vintage Wine Ottenhausen   Underground Landry
   Coal Bin Sax   Storage Dunbar

The hands-on layout would end in 2006 when the *Fair Family News* went to using desktop computers to create the layouts. The first newsletter went out to three or four hundred people, Norma said. In

2018 the mailing list would top 3,000, with thousands more accessing the electronic version online since 2006 (www.oregoncountryfair.net).

While the newsletter would experience significant changes in technology, the guiding philosophy would remain the same: "the creation of an open forum for ideas and information related to, contributed by and distributed to the OCF family." Members would write letters discussing and debating the issues that came before the board, offering an outlet to air views beyond the board meetings. The calendar listings and committee reports would help fair members keep up with what was happening behind the scenes between fairs.

Even after other forms of electronic communication emerged, the *Fair Family News* would remain a touchstone of reliable information ranging from fair board elections to path planning, from pictures to poems.

As the wheel of life continued to turn for the "Fair Family," the news crew would enjoy the pleasure of printing birth announcements with baby photos and would feel the grief of writing "Fair Thee Well" tributes for fair folks who passed on to the other side.

For the fair's fiftieth anniversary celebration in 2019, the newsletter would run dozens of nostalgic stories from volunteers, crafters, and entertainers recalling many magical moments from years past.

Volunteers for *Fair Family News* gathered for a reunion party in 2007 (left). Annual May birthday covers sometimes featured crew members heads collaged onto others' bodies. A new masthead was introduced in 2012 for the twentieth birthday.

1992
Leslie Scott and the Fair's Neighbors

> *"My graduate program required all kinds of curriculum development work on peace and conflict resolution, community development, and community relations. That's why I was drawn to the job. What struck me in this interview is that they didn't ask me anything about it."*
> —Leslie Scott, describing her 1992 interview with the fair's Personnel Committee

The Oregon Country Fair's new board of directors wasted no time filling the caretaker and general manager jobs. At the December 1991 meeting they set up a process for hiring and put out requests and ads for applicants. At the start of the new year, they filled the caretaker slot by hiring Bill Verner, a Security Crew member who also had been volunteering at the fair site every weekend as a member of the VegManECs team.

Board members next turned to hiring the general manager. At their January meeting, they set up a process that they would follow in February. They agreed that no straw vote would be taken during an executive session when the Hiring Committee would present the board with a list of its top three candidates listed in order of preference. That meant the board would be required to conduct the entire hiring process at the open meeting in public view.

At the public board meeting following that executive session, the process called for a board member to nominate the Hiring

Committee's top candidate. If that person was not approved, the board would be free to nominate from the other two candidates. If neither of those candidates won approval, the Hiring Committee would be instructed to start over.

The Hiring Committee interviewed five candidates and asked three finalists to come to the February board meeting where the decision would be made. One finalist dropped out, leaving temporary General Manager Arna Shaw and fair participant Leslie Scott as the two top candidates. When the time came, fair members filled the chairs in the audience and two applicants sat in nervous anticipation of the decision.

"There was so much tension in the room, people could hardly breathe," Leslie Scott said. "The room was packed to the walls." Leslie was sitting next to Andrew Harvey, a friend she had served with on the Council for Human Rights in Latin America, a nonprofit based in Eugene. When she first sat down Andrew asked her, "What are you doing here?"

"I'm one of the candidates," she said.

"YOU?!" Andrew exclaimed as he burst out laughing. Leslie was wearing a black sweater with a pink spiral on it, like a labyrinth, but Andrew told her it looked like a target. "That sweater's perfect," he said. "Just turn it around so the design's on your back."

"I was completely unknown," Leslie said. When someone mentioned Main Camp during the discussion, she turned to Andrew and asked, "What's Main Camp?" Andrew burst out laughing again.

The board first heard routine announcements and reports, then turned to the hiring process. Tension built when the board moved to hire the first-ranked candidate, Arna.

Members immediately jumped into a debate of what they had meant when they had voted to "Heal the Peach" at October's annual meeting amid the turmoil of the recall vote. They argued over whether that meant staying the course with Arna or starting completely over. Board members weighed in with a spectrum of viewpoints. The new board resembled the old board when it split its votes down the middle: five in favor, five opposed.

The crowd audibly gasped. Some people clapped; others cried. A group of Arna's supporters left the room. The board then voted unanimously to hire Leslie Scott for general manager for one year, even though several board members expressed reservations that Leslie

431

was an unknown who had never volunteered at Main Camp.

Immediately after the vote to hire Leslie, J.R. Robinson resigned from the board but kept his post as fair president. A Traffic Crew volunteer for more than fifteen years with a balanced approach to the last two years of mayhem, J.R. had earned the respect of the fair's membership. His resignation letter pointed out that he had spoken in favor of the recall at the annual meeting and with everything that had been accomplished since then, he felt it was time for a new board of directors and general manager to take the lead. Board members tried without success to persuade J.R. to change his mind.

Leslie may have been unknown to the board, but she wasn't exactly a newcomer to the fair. She first participated in Community Village in 1979 when her then-husband, Tom Scott, helped design the Integral House in the village. Tom shared his expertise in solar energy, earning them day passes in 1979. The next year, Tom helped build the Integral House and Leslie participated in the Politics Booth in the village as a representative of the Council for Human Rights in Latin America.

"I'll never forget my first night sleeping in a loft in Community Village," Leslie said. "Going to sleep to all the sounds. Especially listening to the sound of a piano in Shady Grove. It might have been Johnny Hahn playing. ... We spent the one night that year, and had this magical, magical sleep in that loft under the stars. It almost feels like my whole life changed as a result of that one-night's sleep. Feeling like we had found home: This is it; these are our people; this is our place."

Partly inspired by the fair and the Integral House, Leslie and Tom looked for land and purchased a homestead east of Eugene near Finn Rock in the McKenzie River valley. They built their home out of three other houses they tore down. Tom hooked the house up to solar energy and they went completely off the grid. Water came from a gravity-fed system on a stream on the land. Solar energy provided electricity and heated water, and a woodstove kept them cozy when the cool rains arrived each autumn.

"People from the university, people from the Country Fair, and people who were involved in solar energy and all these other experimental projects—we were real involved with self-reliance," Leslie said. "It was the days of the Foxfire books and *Chop Wood,*

Carry Water, all these things."

Leslie worked part time at their solar energy store, handling research and bookkeeping. That gave her enough free time to cultivate a garden big enough to supply much of their food. Tom worked at the store and installed solar energy arrays in people's homes. He also taught at Lane Community College, where he helped write the grant that initiated the community college's alternative energy technician training program.

After a few years on the farm, Leslie felt increasingly isolated. She grew restless. "I wasn't psychologically or emotionally prepared for that lifestyle," she said. "I'm so social and into people."

Leslie had gotten more involved with the Council for Human Rights in Eugene and wanted to go back to college; Tom wanted to stay on the homestead. They eventually split up amicably. At the fair, Tom would continue to volunteer at Energy Park, while Leslie returned as a fair participant in the Birthsong Midwifery booth on East Thirteenth. She had trained as a midwife and remained involved with the Birthsong Booth through 1991.

In the fall of 1991, Leslie completed her master's degree in community cultural development with an emphasis on peace studies at the University of Oregon. That's when she came across the fair's advertisement in the local weekly *What's Happening*, seeking general manager applicants. Friends had encouraged her to apply.

After she was hired, Leslie worked on establishing good relationships with the board and on putting the past tumult from the painful board recall behind them. She held open houses to meet fair members and to listen to their concerns. Her peace studies came in handy as she forged ways to bridge the differences between people. Her educational background also helped Leslie as she took on the task of reaching out to the fair's neighboring communities, which she considered one of the board's main blind spots.

"Their absolute focus was not on the nonprofit part of the organization at all, but on the three-day event," she noted. Leslie had pushed back on that notion even before she was hired. She had told the board in her thank-you letter after her interview that if she were hired, she wanted to work on the fair's community relations with neighbors. "I felt like how the fair navigated those waters would determine its future in many ways," she said.

She attended Veneta City Council meetings to hear neighbors' concerns and to provide a fair presence. She and the new caretaker, Bill Verner, walked door to door to introduce themselves to the fair's immediate neighbors. Leslie relied on a collaborative approach to consensus-building to help people feel empowered.

"I tried to look at the context of the fair and the way the fair was embedded in all of these different communities and the relationships that needed to be built," Leslie said. "It was really fun and creative and really hard and complex at times, and frustrating. But the thing that really worked with the community was active participation and walking our talk."

In June, the board approved Leslie's recommendation to create a Neighborhood Response Team to address neighbors' concerns about trespassers and other nuisances that routinely arose during each fair. Previously the fair's organizers reached out to neighbors prior to the fair, but during the fair the neighbors had to either handle problems themselves or call the county sheriff.

The response team would include trained peacekeeping teams who would respond to neighbors' requests during the fair and go to neighbors' properties to ask trespassers to leave. If the trespassers refused, the team would call the sheriff's office and a tow truck when necessary.

John Doscher—a volunteer with the fair Security Crew and the VegManECs team who lived in the Veneta area—helped inspire the Neighborhood Response Team. "He is the one who told me about the extent of the neighbors' issues and problems," Leslie said. John enlisted the first NRT volunteers from other crews who had mediation training and were already on the fair site, including Norma Sax and Michael Connelly. They used John's truck to cruise the neighborhood.

In 1993 the NRTs (they called themselves "Nerts") would coordinate efforts with the Veneta-area Neighborhood Watch program, providing another avenue for fair volunteers and the community to work together. The neighbors heartily welcomed the help when they had problems during the fair, and the Neighborhood Response Team would remain a crucial fair service for decades.

In July of 1992, Leslie survived her first Main Camp and her first fair as general manager by assembling a good team around her. "I still knew barely anything about Main Camp and how it actually worked. I just knew that in my job description I had to live out there. Ande Grahn came down to coordinate Main Camp Kitchen. I spent lots of time at coordinator potlucks."

Leslie had heard that she needed to line up Back-Up Managers, or BUMs, to help her. Luckily, she counted among her acquaintances several key fair folks. She knew Sallie Edmunds through their solar energy connections. Sallie and Leslie's then-husband, Tom, both had belonged to the Willamette Valley Solar Energy Association. "We used to call her 'Solar Sallie,'" Leslie said.

Next, Leslie asked her friends Robert DeSpain and Marshall Landman to join her BUM team. Robert said yes. Although Marshall turned down her offer to rejoin the BUM team, he would remain one of Leslie's close advisers.

She also asked Andrew Harvey, who "had been one of Arna's right-hand people. He knew Main Camp inside and out," Leslie said.

General Manager Leslie Scott and Security Co-coordinator Don Doolin worked together at the fair in the early 1990s.

"Those were the people I drew around me, the people I knew. As it turns out, they had the most amazing, perfect experience at the fair."

Sallie and Robert both had experience serving as the fair general manager, and both had been on the BUM or OM Team. Andrew had served in the key Main Camp position of Quartermaster. "I don't know how I ever could have gotten through the first Main Camp without them," Leslie said. "We were connected at the hip. They all worked so hard."

After the fair, Leslie helped get the endowment program rolling so that the fair could invest in its neighbors. Former fair treasurer Ron Chase had first presented the Planning Committee's endowment proposal to the board in May 1990. At that time, the board took the very preliminary step of approving a nominating committee to set up the endowment committee. But that effort languished amid all the disputes that led to the 1991 recall of the board.

Leslie's efforts to champion the endowment got a boost from History Booth Coordinator Camille Cole, a professional educator. Camille was concerned about budget cutbacks in the schools that had been necessary after Oregon voters approved a tax-limit initiative, Measure 5, in November 1990. The citizens' initiative rolled back funding for the states' school districts. Camille anticipated that the endowment could help local schools bridge some of the gap in their budgets.

In September 1992, the board formally approved an endowment to fund arts and environmental educational activities in the fair's neighborhood—the Fern Ridge community of West Lane County. The board stipulated that the endowment would contribute to local cultural resources, to promote the arts, and to support grass-roots community organizations "consistent with the fair's ideals of a peaceful, just, and environmentally sound society."

But board members declined to fund the endowment until they had a better accounting of how much excess revenue the fair had on hand after the 1992 event. In November 1992 the fair deposited the first $30,000 into the endowment fund.

The first grant cycle of the OCF Endowment program began in 1993. Over the next three decades, the endowment would hand out hundreds of thousands of dollars to finance art, music, and nature programs in every school of the Fern Ridge School District; plus art for the new Fern Ridge Library; student-created art at the Veneta Skatepark; and programs and equipment for Camp Wilani.

In 1992, the fund was renamed the Bill Wooten Memorial Endowment to honor a key co-founder of the fair. Bill Wooten later died in January 1995 at age sixty from complications of a lung infection, with Cynthia Wooten and the rest of his family by his side.

While the fair board dealt with several internal issues in 1993, Leslie kept looking out toward the neighborhood. In search of a holistic solution to the problems the neighbors had experienced with trespassers, Leslie teamed up with a great ally she had met at the Veneta City Council meetings—Galen Carpenter, a Veneta city councilor.

Galen and her family had gotten a big taste of the downside of living near the fair during the second weekend in July.

"Back then there were few, if any, legal campgrounds nearby for fairgoers," Galen said, "so all these people who couldn't spend the night at the Country Fair really had no place to go. They wound up camping in the city park, school grounds, people's yards—all against the rules. They brought in a lot of trash. They were using local yards as bathrooms. They were sleeping in ditches alongside the road. Suttle Road was just packed with people and campers along the side of the road. ... It was very disruptive to the community."

Galen knew the fair from the inside, as well. She first attended the fair in 1976. "I had an absolute ball," she said. "I was amazed at all the food and fun and booths." In 1984 Galen and her partner, Greg Prull, participated in Energy Park, where they offered information about Integrated Pest Management.

Leslie Scott reached out to Galen and they worked together to build bridges to the community and instigate collaboration with the fair, the city of Veneta, and the fair's neighbors.

"Leslie and I served on some committees together," Galen said, "talking about what we could do to help the problems with the need for camping in the area, the illegal camping, the parking." Their alliance helped foster creative solutions to some persistent community problems.

In May 1993, Leslie hosted the fair's first open house for neighbors, inviting people from Veneta and Elmira to the site for ice cream and a tour. Patti Lomont and other members of the pre-fair Neighborhood Liaison Crew helped with logistics.

That same year, Galen spearheaded the organization of a campground for fairgoers at Zumwalt Park just a few miles from the fair site. The picturesque park, located on the shores of Fern Ridge Reservoir, was run by the U.S. Army Corps of Engineers. The city of Veneta jumped through several bureaucratic hoops to rent the park from the federal agency.

"We started out with a core group of about twenty volunteers from Veneta," Galen said. "We didn't really know what we were doing." They welcomed Leslie's advice on the logistics of providing water and toilets to the camp. They relied on fair Security Crew volunteer John Doscher to handle traffic and security.

"We were pretty excited about it," Galen said. "The fair

advertised Zumwalt Campground. The Sign Crew at the fair made some beautiful signs for us to put on the highway, a series of Burma Shave-style signs that rhymed. ... Some of our campers who came down from Washington state for the first time were real 'alternative' types living in their trucks, just really country folks living out there off the grid. They came down and they worked so hard on the campground with us."

That first year, the camp was overwhelmingly popular. Zumwalt volunteers had planned for a few hundred campers, but more than a thousand inundated the park.

"We stretched all our services to the max," Galen said. "The campers were absolutely wonderful, but there was a lot of traffic and a lot of noise. We were doing a real service to the community by providing the campers with a good, safe place, and getting them off the street. But we had no idea that so many people were going to show up. Security and everybody involved felt like, just pack 'em in as safely as we can. Do it without a fire hazard. Better that than have them camp down at the shopping center. But it was a double-edged sword: Yes, we took care of the problem, but also it was very crowded and some neighbors didn't like that."

Another shock the first year was the amount of garbage the campers left behind. "We hadn't really thought that through, about providing enough bins and cans," Galen said. "We did not plan for recycling very well." The next year they collected and painted fifty-five-gallon drums for trash and recycling. One of the school clubs offered to recycle bottles and cans from the campground as a fund-raiser.

Galen credits Leslie with coming up with the idea for a shuttle bus to ferry the campers to the fair, helping reduce traffic.

The fair would continue to contribute ideas and people-power to improve the Zumwalt campsite. "We did a lot of signage for Zumwalt in addition to the Burma Shave-style signs," Leslie said. "The fair helped with all of their booth and directional signs. We did weekend work parties with Zumwalt to help them build their admissions booths and stuff like that, too. It built a lot of relationships with people working together on something creative."

Zumwalt Campground proved popular with fairgoers from the get-go. Many of the campers—who called themselves "Zumis," (rhymes with "roomies")—would return year after year. The campground offered special T-shirts each year, food booths, a fire pit to gather around, plus other amenities.

"We have hired entertainment Thursday, Friday, and Saturday nights since it started," Galen said. "Everything from Gaelic bands to belly dancing, drumming, blues, reggae. It is nice because they can spend all day at the fair and go back, jump in the lake or have their kids relax and just rest there. It's a nice quiet park with an incredible view. A lot of people coming from out-of-state, they're looking out across the lake facing east and can see the Three Sisters [mountains], the moonrises and sunrises. ... We take that for granted, but for people from all over the country—it's so beautiful! Some people actually don't go to the fair on Saturday because they choose to attend Friday, hang out at Zumwalt on Saturday, then go back to the fair on Sunday."

Almost from the start, the campground paid for itself and generated income for the city of Veneta. Over the years Veneta has funneled Zumwalt Campground proceeds to parks projects, library services, and arts and recreation programs.

While attending the Veneta City Council meetings, Leslie learned that the city had problems dealing with its wastewater and was contemplating moving its sewer system with a sewage lagoon right next door to the fair.

"There was a huge worry about eminent domain," Leslie said, "and where they were going to get the land and all of this. ... They'd already dug that burrow pit completely without any archeological permits or anything. It was outside the urban growth boundary, but they had done it anyway. It was on land that Bernie Larson owned." The city had been spraying effluent to irrigate the Larson land, which he used for cattle grazing. The cattle also trampled and degraded the riverbank on that side.

Leslie met with Les Clark, the city manager of Veneta, and they consulted a landscape architect. "We got together with Ann Bettman," Leslie said, "and her then-business partner and life partner, Richard Britz, and started on this long, long process of doing grant writing to figure out how to do a more environmentally friendly sewage plant for the city of Veneta and to do something ecologically, hopefully not only neutral, but valuable, on what we now call the Far Side."

Leslie talked the board into purchasing the last thirty-six acres of the Larson property that was inside the Veneta urban growth boundaries, where most of the effluent spraying took place.

"That was a huge leap of faith for the board because it was not connected to any fair land," Leslie said. "… I figured if we could own that, then it would give us huge leverage. It would become a natural collaboration, a natural partnership for us to work together because we had definitely common interests at that point." The city owned the land situated directly across the Long Tom River from the fair's Eight pathway.

The city of Veneta and the Oregon Country Fair wrote grant applications with Region Ten of the U.S. Environmental Protection Agency, Cascade Pacific Resource Conservation & Development, the University of Oregon's Landscape Architecture Department, and Oregon's Watershed Enhancement Board. "We got every grant we wrote, the first five grants," Leslie said. "It was amazing. We had a broad public/private collaborative partnership."

By 1996, the fair and the city would swap landholdings so that Veneta would own the former Larson property inside the urban growth boundary, and the fair would own the land across the Long Tom River from the original fair site. Over the years, the fair population had grown to the point where the land across the Long Tom would be useful for additional fair campsites. Leslie had looked into it, and found it would be possible to put up a temporary footbridge to give those campers access to the fair's pathways.

Meanwhile, everyone had noticed that the Zumwalt Campground had not yet solved the problem of fairgoers trespassing on neighbors' properties. In addition, many neighbors for years had quietly allowed illegal camping on their farms. Leslie proposed that the fair apply for an umbrella camping permit to cover not only Zumwalt, but also the fair's Far Side plus any of the neighbors who wanted to host camps on their property during the fair.

"We had a very friendly head of Land Use Management then," Leslie said, "so we took advantage of that. He waived all the individual property owners' fees so that we paid one umbrella permit and went through one hearing process as a group. … They licensed all these neighborhood campgrounds, including Zumwalt, simultaneously in the spring of 1996."

That was also the first year fair volunteers and crafters camped on the Far Side.

Among the fair neighbors, Cindy Darling had hosted camps for fairgoers—under the county radar—after she bought her home in Veneta in 1987. It was one of the first neighborhood campsites. When the 1987 fair rolled around, Cindy had saddled her horse and gotten ready.

"I charged five dollars a carload, and it would be like a clown car pulling in with fourteen people piling out of it," Cindy said with a laugh. She'd ride her horse to show them where to camp, then gallop back to the entrance to collect money from the next car. She brought in an outhouse to serve the people who stayed with their cars overnight.

The pasture where people camped offered plenty of shade from scattered stands of pine, oak, fir, cottonwood, and cedar.

When Lane County permitted multiple neighborhood campsites in the mass approval of 1996, Cindy increased the amenities she offered her campers. She opened a kitchen to serve coffee, drinks, and light meals, and hired bands to play in the evenings.

Darling Reunion Camp would become so popular with repeat campers that Cindy would turn it into an invitation-only, private campsite. "If someone causes problems, they don't get to come back," she said. By 2018, she had a crew of 100 folks who would host 1,200 campers each year.

"People come from all over the world," Cindy said. "People's kids grow up coming here. There's been a lot of weddings and engagements. It's really become like a family." People who camped near each other year after year would become good friends who looked forward to seeing each other at their annual fair reunions.

Eventually, about a dozen neighbors would also offer campsites that would become popular with fairgoers—from EZ Camp to Quiet Camp. At long last, many neighbors would make peace with the fair.

39 1993
Stage Left and the Fighting Instruments of Karma Marching Chamber Band/Orchestra

> "Chumleigh started calling [the band] Fightin' Instruments of Karma. ... By free association, I called it a lot of different things each time I'd introduce it. Usually Chamber Band, Marching, and Orchestra were in there somewhere. This is what it settled into."
>
> —Howard Patterson, on how the fair band got its name

Fair leaders negotiated with organizers of Chumleighland (aka the Circus, aka Not Chumleighland) to move their stage from its original location to a new spot in the Left Bank Loop for the 1993 Oregon Country Fair. The crafters who had to move their booths to the new loop worried that without popular attractions on the Left Bank, the public would continue to frequent the original Eight without exploring further, so fair volunteers proposed the change.

"They wanted to get some proven fair favorites and persuade them to move," said John Cloud, the stage manager for the Circus. "The idea was, the fans would follow their favorite enterprises over to the new area."

The troupe's first performance on the new stage didn't

disappoint. "It turns out that in constructing that site, we'd disturbed the burial grounds of the ancient Egyptian god Thoth," said bubble-blower and puppeteer Tom Noddy. "I myself, acting as emcee of that show, was skeptical of the whole idea despite the fact that the Ibis-beaked god himself had appeared in a puff of smoke to tell us this. ... But I pointed out that there were no Egyptians in the New World."

Thoth, speaking with a lisp, responded, "Then how do you explain the pyramids of the Mayans?" Tom had no answer.

In the course of the show, German clown Hacki Ginda, a good friend of Tom's, made his first appearance at the Oregon Country Fair. Hacki carried an Egyptian idol "who wore an Egyptian pharaoh-style headdress and a jewel in his navel, but otherwise was readily recognizable to the audience as a large Troll Doll," Tom Noddy said. "The idol was said to be related to the great sun gods Ra and Aten and Amen. He was, we were told, the highest of them all, though. He was the Top Ra-amen." Hacki set the Top Ra-amen atop a sarcophagus.

Later on Tom would open the sarcophagus only to find a tiny "mummy" inside. "This was not in the script," Tom said. "It was a surprise for me the first time." It turned out to be Tom's favorite puppet Mousie wrapped in an Ace Bandage. "I had to take it off to show the audience it was Mousie," Tom said. "While I did, the band naturally went into "The Stripper" music. That cracked me and the audience up! The whole band was dressed in pharaoh hats and the set was a gorgeous sand and pyramid scene."

The move in 1993 had a domino effect on other stages. The old Circus Stage, which would host more vaudeville acts, was renamed W.C. Fields. The original W.C. Fields stage that was first established by Tom Noddy in 1981 got moved over a bit and was renamed Next Stage, and would feature entertainment by and for young people. After a few years, Next Stage was renamed the Youth Stage.

Mose Mosely, who had volunteered at the Circus Stage as assistant stage manager to John Cloud since the early 1980s, negotiated the design of the new Stage Left with the fair's Construction Crew. The performers had a solid idea of what they wanted: a bandstand built level with the stage.

John Cloud, who had helped build the bandstands at the original Circus, noted that at Chumleighland, "the band was on the same level as the stage, off to the side, not down in the pit. That's so the band could participate, essentially equally, with what was going on on the stage, with all kinds of witty repartee, call and response, that kind of stuff. We definitely wanted to continue that at Stage Left. The stage integrates with the band. The Fighting Instruments of Karma are really the heart of everything we've done."

Indeed, the marching band had been integral to the show since the very beginning of Chumleighland, when the band would march around the Eight to round up an audience for the nearly hidden stage. In the years since, the parade had become highly popular with the crafters and cooks who tended their booths all day long and had little time to catch the stage acts. The twice-daily musical and visual spectacle gave everyone along the path a colorful dose of fair entertainment. Often the parade was the only "show" many crafters would see all day.

"There's something great about being in the parade," said Heather Weihl, who joined the band in 1988. "You're out in the fair and I think it's great for the people who have booths. We are entertainment for them since we're mobile. I think they really appreciate us. There's something great about the communication you develop with your audience, although you're going by them. It's really true that everyone loves a parade!"

Over the years the Chumleighland band had gradually grown from its lowly beginning of a half-dozen marchers playing instruments—including a violin—to a four-dozen-strong full-fledged marching band with brass instruments, bass drums, and glockenspiels. Howard Patterson (aka Ivan Karamazov) became the band leader early on when the original band leader brought in by Reverend Chumleigh, Carl Spaethe (aka Thaddeus Spae), bowed out of the role. Carl had composed the Chumleighland March for the band, a favored tune for decades.

Howard always enjoyed parading in the fair's band.

"The thing that I love most about the Oregon Country Fair is playing in the band when it's marching," he said. "I never marched in high school at all. I was in the wind ensemble and we had more interesting music to play." The militaristic aspects of marching in a band at football games never had appealed to Howard, but he thoroughly enjoyed mixing cultures at the fair.

"We were taking elements of mass culture and co-opting it to our own use," he said. "I love doing that. Any way we can do that is great. The whole idea of a marching band is so mass culture, and turning it into a micro-culture thing was an incredible delight for me. That's where it starts from, but then over the years we've had these glimmers of actually playing well."

Howard credits music composer Doug Wieselman with helping the band sound its best. Howard and Doug had become friends in college when they sang in a madrigal quartet at Renaissance Faires in California. Doug had moved to New York but would travel to the fair every few years to play in the marching band. Howard tapped Doug to compose instrumental arrangements for the band. Doug composed arrangements of a samba called "Radio Brazil," a marching band version of "Revolution" from the Beatles' White Album, a quasi-Arabic tune called "La Pregunta," and another Brazilian-flavored piece called "Black Orpheus," among other numbers.

Howard Patterson played sousaphone in the marching band.

Doug Wieselman also arranged one of the band's most iconic musical pieces: "The Teddy Bears' Picnic." Doug dashed off an arrangement after his first fair playing in the band in 1976 or 1977. "I knew the tune, I think from *Captain Kangaroo*," Howard said. "I was delighted by the wonderful irony of druggy hippies playing this innocent tune in the woods. For the kids who grew up hearing us play it, the irony layer is largely missing—which is in itself ironic."

The band wrestled with the physical arrangements of the marching band. "How do you make a guerilla marching band going through the woods sound (A) like something, and (B) sound like something cool?" Howard asked. "It doesn't have to be straight square rhythm. If we find where the groove is, we can make band music incredibly groovy, like when we play cumbias and sambas."

They gradually evolved a system to balance out the sounds of the band as it wound its way along the path, three-by-three. Musicians usually preferred to play with the same instruments grouped together, Howard said, but that didn't produce an ensemble sound in the long, thin parade. Howard had the musicians mix in with each other, but still grouped by the tone of their instruments.

The high-pitched instruments like flute and piccolo would lead the way, with the glockenspiels up the middle next to the mid-range instruments like clarinets and saxophones. Howard played euphonium toward the middle, followed by some of the percussion instruments. Next came trumpets and trombones and another percussion section, with a tuba bringing up the rear, like a caboose on a train.

"I have the bass drummer behind me and I train him to watch my left foot," Howard said. "Here is the beat and that's your most important job because I can change it. You know, if he's paying enough attention and the flutes start to rush, I can hang behind the beat just a little bit. …

"When Doug is there, I like to have Doug on bari sax on one side of me and a tuba on the other side," Howard said. "Doug is the source of groove. He's the grooviest player on the planet. To take that groove, translate it through my body to the drummers and have the tuba player broadcast it to everybody else is what actually makes the groove of the band actually happen. That's when we're at our grooviest."

During one show at the fair, though, Howard had a too-groovy moment as bandleader. The Circus Stage troupe put on a "Pirate Show" in 1991, revisiting a popular theme from 1986. Fairgoers raved over both shows. All fair long, fairgoers could be heard talking like a pirate—"Arr!"

"I've always loved captaining the band," Howard said. "The pirate show was about me being the band leader and being tied up and dragged into the show, no longer part of the band. … And the key to performance is from the time you start, we are completely aware of time at all times. That's the thing the Karamazovs do best—being aware of the flow of things, of the laugh, of the joke, of the timing of when you've said your thing and then they respond when the next thing has to start relative to their response, so that you don't lose the energy of the show.

"But I was standing on the deck—the band platform—feeling

Howard Patterson, Sam Williams, and Paul Magid performed in the "Pirate Show" in 1986, and again in 1991.

like I was on the prow of a ship. I had taken mushrooms and time was not really passing for me. I knew it was for everybody else. And it was actually an incredibly liberating experience," Howard said. "Time is not passing. I'm just here and I loved it. But I realized that I wasn't going to do what the show needed, necessarily. So I spoke to the band very quietly and I said, 'Uncle Howie has had too much medicine. I will continue to conduct, but our concert master henceforth will tell us where the cues are.'"

First clarinetist Eben Sprinsock was the concert master. "I was gung-ho about the band at the fair, and so I quickly became Howard's assistant or concert master," Eben said. "I volunteered to help Howard and I got to know how the band worked." After the mushroom incident, Howard passed the baton along to Eben, who stepped up to his new duties as bandleader.

"It was a scary thing," Eben said, "because here are all these great musicians that I really admire and I know I'm not nearly as good as, and I'm going to lead them? But everybody was so gracious. Everybody cooperated. ... They all acknowledged that someone had to be the leader and no one else wanted to do it. ... I got to develop my skills as a band leader and an on-stage presence, totally through doing it. And professional performers let me do it, let me screw up, just because I was a friend of theirs. I got to learn by doing."

Eben started sending music charts out a month or two before the fair so that people could practice their parts. For the fair parades and shows, Eben always dressed to the nines in a red fez and white suit. Depending on the day and the occasion, he added tie-dye or logo T-shirts underneath, or a white button-down collared shirt with a musical-score-theme tie.

During fair marches, the fair's bandleader didn't lead the parade from the front. Eben would signal songs by blowing a whistle, wherever he was in the lineup. At show time when the band came back from marching around the loops—blaring its musical way through the audience—it always set a rousing tone. "Having the band march in is a great way to start the show," Eben said. "It just starts the show with a lot of energy."

As Howard noted, the fair's bandleader also played a key role in the stage performances. "There's a stage manager and an emcee who make sure things work correctly backstage and that cues happen," Eben said. "But the bandleader, for our shows, sort of paces the show, making sure the show runs smoothly. Mostly that's in managing the transitions between acts. The band covers the transitions and makes the transitions seamless. Or if they don't do it right, they don't. And it can affect the pace and the length of the show."

Eben fondly remembered when his daughter Betsy played a part in the "Little Nemo" show in 1988. Eben and his wife were sharing a house in San Francisco with Howard and his then-wife, Seiza, and their son Jasper. "Betsy and Jasper grew up going to the fair together," Eben said. Both kids found themselves cast in the "Little Nemo" show.

"The way the show was constructed, during Awake Time it was Jasper who was on stage," Eben said. "But during sleep—during Dream Time—an adult actor took his place. Jasper was this kid star of the show. And of course in 'Little Nemo' he meets a princess in his dreams. At the end of the show, the princess comes into his real, waking life. Betsy, at the end of the show, played the princess. So the last scene of the show had Jasper waking up in bed and Betsy popping up underneath the covers—there's the princess! And she's a little girl! That was a lot of fun."

When Betsy went back to school that year, her third-grade teacher gave the class the prototypical assignment: What did you do on your summer vacation?

"Betsy wrote this little essay about how she went to a fair in the woods where her father led the marching band and she was the princess in the show," Eben recalled, chuckling. "Well, she got the paper back with a big star on it, and the teacher had written on it, 'It's fun to pretend, isn't it?' Betsy told the literal truth and her teacher thought she was making it up, which just shows you what a magical experience the fair is. We never bothered to set the teacher straight."

Eben would use the band-leading skills he picked up at the fair to make music in his own community in Seattle. "I played in my high school marching band and symphonic band, so the fair was not my first experience with being in a band," Eben said. "But it was through the fair that I learned how to lead a band, and grew to love doing it. I eventually led the [New Old Time] Chautauqua band. Here in Seattle I created and still lead the house band for the SANCA circus school. That band is called Doc Sprinsock and the SANCApators." (SANCA is the School of Acrobatics and New Circus Arts located in Seattle.)

Eben would remain the bandleader of the Fighting Instruments of Karma Marching Chamber Band/Orchestra for two decades. When he stepped down in 2011, he would pass the baton of leadership back to Howard in a ceremony held on Main Stage at that year's Midnight Show.

Heather Weihl first came to the fair in1988 when she was invited by Tim Furst (aka Fyodor Karmazov) whom she had known since high school. It took years for Tim and other friends to convince Heather to go to the Oregon Country Fair.

"I was a tiny bit skeptical, actually," Heather said. "I used to work at the Renaissance Faire in California when I was a teenager. So I thought, 'Oh, god! Hot, dusty little booths in the woods. How special can it be?'"

The year she graduated from veterinary school, she had some time off and agreed to go. "It wasn't what I was expecting at all. I brought a book!" Heather said, chuckling. "I thought I was going to be bored—really, honestly—it's so funny now! And from the moment I set foot on the property, I was enchanted with it."

When Heather first heard the Fighting Instruments of Karma Marching Band practicing at Chumleighland, she knew she wanted to join the band and the parade. That first year the musicians loaned her a pair of maracas and had her march with the percussion section.

She enjoyed it so much, she was determined to return to march in the band, even though she didn't know how to play an instrument.

"What do you need in the band?" Heather asked Howard. "I have to do this! What can I learn to play that you need?"

"How about tuba?" Howard offered.

"Oh, no tuba! That's too big for me," Heather said. "but I'll try the trombone." She went home and made time after her veterinarian practice to take lessons and practice on the trombone.

"When I came back, I'd been playing for nine months," Heather said. "I was a baby trombone player, and they were incredibly supportive. Bud Chase, who plays tuba, said as long as you kept getting better, that was the whole thing. They were terrific about it. The band has been great! The band has great musicians and some deadly great ringers, and they have always been lovely and supportive."

Howard said the band welcomed different skill sets and playing levels. "In the Fighting Instruments of Karma, virtuosity is a virtue but not the only one," he said. "To be with a bunch of people who were making this incredibly magical music, regardless of their musical ability—that's what I love about the Fighting Instruments of Karma. The band ranges from players like Thaddeus Spae, Doug Wieselman, and Stephen Bernstein—these incredible players—all the way to people who played clarinet a little bit in high school. And they're all welcome."

Heather said the dynamics of playing music while marching along a narrow path would get interesting at times. "You're in this long snake of a band, so you hear mostly what's right around you," she said. "You don't necessarily get to hear all the pieces of it. There are folks in the center who are trying to send signals to keep everybody all together. ... But there have been times when the front half of the band is playing one song and the back half is playing another and we can't hear each other well enough to know, so the middle has to come back to get us together. Trombones play in the back of the band, so it's a unique perspective."

Heather allowed that marching is hot, tired, dusty work. "There's like a lot of physical challenge about it," she said, "and you want it to be your best effort because that's what you're there for. It's still great because people are so receptive to it."

To help connect more with the audience as they passed by,

Heather took up wearing oddly glamorous costumes.

"I'd try to make some fabulous costume to wear that also gives a surprise, gives a great experience to the people who see it as we go by," she said. "One of my costumes is what we call the Snake Lady. It's a snake-print body suit. I have a false arm on the costume and then my real arm goes in a snake and the snake holds in place the trombone slide. Then there are coils of stuffed snake that wrap around me, so that it fills the eye, especially in this glance, people think it's a real snake. It creates a great experience when they see it."

Another costume featured the open frame of a hoop skirt, with the framework wrapped in red fabric with yellow polka dots. Underneath, Heather's bright yellow stockings could be seen in contrast, and she wore a red top.

"People wanted to come over and talk to me about it, it was very successful," she said. "They wanted to touch it. They would try to catch my eye and talk to me while I was playing, and interact about it. It was very cool. It really caught people's attention. And my band members, I must say for the record, were incredibly kind about it because it whacked into their ankles and stuff because it's really huge. The thing's springing around and whacking the trumpet players. They were lovely. They're very good, our trumpet players."

Heather participated in the New Old Time Chautauqua tours right away in 1989. "We go in a group of fifty or sixty people, usually, camping the whole way, pulling a kitchen, and visiting small communities that don't have good access to the arts," Heather said.

Most tours traveled to rural areas in Washington state and parts of Oregon. In 1992 the group toured small towns in Alaska.

At each community, the troupe would conduct a three-day residency that included a parade, free workshops, and a big show. They also booked performances in prisons, nursing homes, or hospitals in the communities they visited. One year they worked in a community garden.

Heather was impressed with how their small efforts seemed to open doors for change in their wake. "It's a great organization, it's really powerful," she said. "Some people say we're changing the world one town at a time.

"First of all, they see us working in community," Heather said. "It's like a little portable Country Fair. It's a very volunteer-driven organization. This year [2004] we ranged in age from three-and-one-half to eighty-nine-and-three-quarters! People see us doing this thing together, making it happen, putting it together as a group. The process is very evident, and I think that's incredibly powerful. They go, 'Wow, we could do that.'"

All the acts also made it fun for the audiences. With juggling, joking, singing, and bubble-blowing, Chautauqua shows served up a feast of laughter. Howard always enjoyed heckling from the sidelines to prove it was a live show.

"When we do Chautauqua shows, I consider it my primary duty to get Tom Noddy to laugh while he's blowing bubbles," Howard said. "If you can just sneak it in at just the right moment, you can make him go *cchhhnnnnkk!!*—and all the bubbles! That's one of my favorite things to do."

Many times the communities' volunteer-based organizations that helped schedule the Chautauqua visit would find new ways to incorporate the arts in their lives. "We get fabulous letters back from the kids in the detention center," Heather said. "We teach them to juggle and to drum and then we put them in the show." The kids' letters expressed appreciation for being shown that they could actually do something good and worthwhile. They wrote that the Chautauqua experience changed their self-perception and opened their eyes to new possibilities.

Howard said that Rebo aka Rebecca Hanson helped keep the Chautauqua tours running smoothly. "Rebo's official title was always Queen. She was the Queen of Chautauqua," he said. "She didn't really have a huge amount of decision-making power, but she had a lot of influence with the board and people basically did what she thought we should do and trusted her love and her judgment."

Trumpet player Dave Bender said that Rebo seemed to be the hub of Chautauqua. "She was the one who made contact and friends with everybody in any group," Dave said. "She was always drawing people in."

Everyone mourned deeply when Rebo died in 1997 of non-Hodgkin's lymphoma in Seattle at age forty-two. In the months before she passed, her fair friends help her record a CD of her own music, *Feb-ru-ary*. That same year, fair volunteers would build and name "Rebo Gazebo" in the new Chela Mela Meadow in her honor.

"We were all so broken when she passed," Tom Noddy said. "The next fair would be the first one without her. It was hard to imagine."

The dedication ceremony for Rebo Gazebo took place Friday morning on the fair's opening day of 1997, which also marked the debut of Chela Mela Meadow. Ande Grahn, who had cooked for many Chautauqua tours in addition to her role as cook in Main Camp Kitchen, hung a collection of clarinets from the gazebo in honor of Rebo's missing clarinet in the marching band. The Fighting Instruments of Karma Marching Chamber Band/Orchestra played a few songs and tears were shed before the gathered vaudevillians dispersed to their appointed shows.

Mose Moseley said that the dedication of the Rebo Gazebo was poignant. "I go sit in that gazebo and think of her every year," Mose said. "She was an extremely talented, beautiful woman who embraced me and allowed me to become involved in the Country Fair Circus and also a part of the New Old Time Chautauqua."

Even without Rebo to help with organization, the New Old Time Chautauqua tours would remain an annual tradition for decades.

Through the years, Heather cherished her friendships that developed with the other entertainers at the fair. "I wouldn't get to sit up all night around the Du Caniveaux campfire, having special, special, magical times if it weren't for the fair," she said. "That's one

Everyone with the 1990 New Old Time Chautauqua tour posed for a photo; at far left, Rebecca "Rebo" Hanson waved at the camera.

of my magic moments, our campfire. Even my first year there when I didn't know any of those guys, there was something really special. … They had all those guys playing guitars and this incredible music that just poured out of them all night long."

The jokes and pranks between the Du Caniveaux troupe and the Stage Left troupe would escalate as their friendships grew deeper and richer with time. In 2001, Stage Left would put on a show written by Paul Magid called "The Road to Uranus" that set off a minor brouhaha.

"For some reason, Paul Magid wanted us to keep it a big fat secret," Heather said. "It's all on the QT. We're not allowed to talk about it. They're not going to know anything about it."

But something went amiss. Unbeknownst to the Stage Left troupe, a member of the Royal Famille Du Caniveaux got hold of the script and began plotting.

The Du Caniveaux troupe popped their surprise during the traditional occasional Thursday night cocktail soire that the Stage Left troupe hosted in their camping area for all the vaudeville entertainers. As it was getting dark, the troupe members gathered together at one end of the party and recited the lines from the ending of the "Road to Uranus."

"It was smashingly great!" Heather said.

But Paul stood up on the food table to object to the reading, shouting: "This is abominous! Who told?" Nobody would spill the beans, so Paul called for a trial. Declaring himself "Judge Smudge," Sam Williams (aka Smerdyakov Karamazov) climbed on the food table next to Paul and pointed his finger at likely suspects.

Heather was accused because she marched in the band, and also performed with the Du Caniveaux troupe. She firmly denied being the rat. After more accusations and denials, Judge Smudge confidently pointed to Howard's son, Jasper "because he did, after all, live in the Howard household, but he was performing with Du Caniveaux that year," Sam said. Like the others, Jasper denied the charge.

Finally the Du Caniveaux troupe revealed the culprit, turning their flashlights toward Howard to illuminate his puzzled face. He protested that he was innocent.

"Au contraire!" the Du Caniveaux troupe countered. Howard had doomed the secret when he stayed at the home of Rhonda Sable, the company manager for the Flying Karamazov Brothers who also performed with the Royal Famille Du Caniveaux.

Howard had slept in the office in Rhonda's home while they were rehearsing the show for the fair. "Quite unbeknownst to him, he left his script out in plain sight," Sam said. "After Howard left to go off to rehearsal, she came in to work at her desk and here right in front of her was sitting this script that such a big deal was being made about not letting any Du Caniveaux see it. So she took it and Xeroxed it and put it back."

Laughing, Sam noted: "Howard gave it away without knowing about it!"

By the 2010s, the Fighting Instruments of Karma Marching Chamber Band/Orchestra had been parading along the fair's paths for forty years.

1997
The Line in the Sand

"We first approached this from the alcohol point of view. We realized that people were bringing beer into the event in enormous quantities in coolers and going up to the Main Stage and parking for the whole day and just getting toasted."

—Daniel Dillon, OCF President, 1993-1998

As he had promised, J.R. Robinson relinquished his role as president of the board in November 1992, and the board elected Daniel Dillon to fill the post. Daniel—a former Hoedad tree-planter who helped start the Blintz Booth at the fair—was elected during the 1991 recall.

Daniel noted that several of the people who were elected during the recall had come together before the annual meeting to discuss ways to change the board's culture. "We were willing to commit to not bringing our personal agenda," he said. "We were willing to commit to working for the good of the organization. We were committed to cleaning up the backlog of work that needed to get done for the organization and we were committed to setting up a plan to move the organization forward."

They all abided by their commitments after the election, Daniel said. "It has been one of the finest groups of people that I've had the experience of working with, to have that commitment established beforehand. Then to have the actual experience of focusing on what was best for this organization and to leave our personal agendas behind was really fantastic," he said.

For a year, the board met twice a month to catch up on the backlog of work that had languished when the previous board devolved into dysfunction. Each board member also committed to join at least two fair committees, putting more hands on deck.

When he became president of the fair, Daniel invited members to visit with him about any concerns. At the Blintz Booth he put up a sign that said, "Home of the President of the Oregon Country Fair. Come Talk at Any Time." He also arranged to visit with crew members before the fair with an event he dubbed "Breakfast with the President" held on July Fourth.

"I worked it out with the kitchen," he said. "They built me a special booth with this grill and we made omelets. We made everybody line up and they put all the raw stuff on their plate. They would give me their plate. Right there they would stand and they had an opportunity to talk with the president of the organization while I made them an omelet.

"I put their stuff on the grill, poured the eggs on, we mixed it all up, you know. 'What do you want to talk about?' This is it. Face to face. … It was a huge success. I did that for five or six years. Martha Evans and I did that together for a while."

Daniel Dillon cooked blintzes in the Blintz Booth at the 1979 fair.

Daniel had served on the Personnel Committee that interviewed Leslie Scott. He was impressed with Leslie's insistence that the fair needed to improve its relationship with its neighbors and surrounding community to survive in the long-term. After he became president, he met with Leslie to discuss the fair's future. For nearly a decade the board and members had been focused on purchasing the land. Now that the land was paid off, "there was no focus," Daniel said.

Leslie pointed out that the fair's 501(c)(3) application listed the fair's mission as educational. "So that started to become the focal point of what we wanted to do with this organization," Daniel said. That emphasis propelled the board's approval of the Endowment Fund, which would finance arts and ecology educational programs in all the schools in the fair's Fern Ridge neighborhood.

The outreach to the community was critical, Leslie said.

"The fair had become a new marginalized stereotyped group," she said. "It was a new target for bias, for what was wrong with the world. It was the heyday of the backlash against the sixties. We had come through Iran-Contra and Republican administrations and rejection of everything the sixties stood for. There was active rejection of feminism, condemnation of everything alternative. It was the beginning of a very strange, authoritarian culture."

Leslie said a quote from Terrance McKenna—"*Real life exists in the boundary between either and or*"—helped clarify the fair's situation for her. "I thought that's exactly where the fair lives," she said. "It's not just an alternative to the dominant culture. It's an absolute reflection of the dominant culture, but it shows how you can live happily and successfully and beautifully very differently inside the dominant culture and have an influence. It shows you how you change culture and how you create culture."

After it dawned on Leslie that the fair actively generated culture, she began to share that message with the community. "We're here. We're not going away," she said. "We have a lot to offer. We want to be friends. We want to be collaborators and partners where we can."

When Measure 5 budget cuts caused the local schools to trim back extracurricular activities, the fair's endowment program indeed helped bridge the gap. For a few years, the Oregon Country Fair's Endowment would provide more than ninety percent of the funding for arts programs in the Fern Ridge School District.

The new fair board took stock of the event's internal problems. Leslie helped call the board's attention to the number of people who camped overnight in the fair parking lots, some of whom never purchased tickets to the event and repeatedly tried to sneak in. People in the parking lot also sold alcohol and drugs illegally and posed safety issues.

Fair President J.R. Robinson noted in his "State of the Peach" address at the annual meeting in October 1992 that violence had increased markedly in the parking lots during the last fair. Organizers had resorted to calling the sheriff's office to the site to help maintain safety. Usually the fair's Security Crew handled all kinds of situations, but that year it had gotten too rough and dangerous.

Daniel Dillon had checked out the problems in the parking lot during the 1992 fair after his wife opened his eyes to the situation. She usually left the fair on Friday night so she could bring in more food supplies Saturday morning for the Blintz Booth. But one year she told him, "I don't want to walk to the car anymore by myself. I am scared out there!"

"Well, that sends a message home," Daniel recalled. "If you haven't gotten it by that point, when your wife tells you that it's not safe, that message comes home loud and clear."

Daniel went out to see for himself. "I was just horrified," he said. "About every fifty feet there was somebody with a cooler that had a whole new designer drug that they were trying to market. And then people walked up to the families in line, offering them pot and acid and all this stuff! I was like, 'Oh, my god!'"

After that, Daniel explored some ideas that he thought could help. He made plans to attend Reggae on the River—a music event with camping held annually in August on the Eel River in Humboldt County, California. "There was talk around that Reggae had wristbands," Daniel said. "I wanted to see how that worked. They also had paid parking for people with passes and tickets and that was of great interest to us also."

Ascha Karen Champie, a bead crafter with a booth near Main Stage, worked in the office for Reggae on the River. Daniel contacted Ascha, and they agreed to trade a couple of passes so the two groups could learn from one another.

Daniel said that the venue's setup differed from the fair's. The main event was enclosed by a fence, and campers found spots around the outside. "Wristbands were necessary to get into the venue," Daniel said. Around the perimeter of the venue, local organizations, nonprofits, churches, and restaurants sold food, drinks, crafts, and other items. That was one way Reggae on the River involved the community and helped mitigate the impact of the event. Reggae also helped fund community activities during the rest of the year.

"I learned several things at Reggae and brought them back to the fair," Daniel said. "Paid parking was doable. It only took a little space off the highway and took organization and planning. It was also another revenue stream. Wristbands at registration was a no-brainer. This event did it and everyone accepted and appreciated that only paying customers and staff were allowed on site. Camping was safe."

Daniel took note of how Reggae on the River had involved the surrounding community. "I learned that the Oregon Country Fair had a superiority attitude and didn't care how the community felt about our event and the stress we put on the community," Daniel said. "I knew that would come back to bite us in the future."

In February 1993, the fair board took decisive action to make it harder to sneak in by trading passes. They approved issuing wristbands to replace the T-shirt passes used by volunteers, and the paper passes for booth people and entertainers. Then the board approved restructuring Security and Traffic crews to create a Lot Crew specifically to deal with issues in the parking lot. Nobody would be allowed to stay overnight in the parking lot without a wristband.

A firestorm of protest arose among the fair membership when organizers announced that wristbands would be used for 1993. Two petitions called for a vote on the matter before the 1993 fair. Debates raged in letters to the *Fair Family News*, the fair's new newsletter.

Several hundred people gathered for the June 4 meeting to vote on the petitions. Many members acknowledged that the number of shared passes had gotten out of hand. Some said resorting to wristbands showed "a lack of trust." Others objected to wearing plastic. Marshall Landman, who volunteered on Craft Inventory, said he thought wristbands could be the key to restoring the old fair magic, when the paths at night were less crowded.

Leslie told the members that the decision had arisen from the notable problems with overcrowding from too many guests at the fair overnight. "This is bigger than wristbands," Leslie said. "This is about facing change with integrity and honor." In the end, members voted to affirm the board's decision to use wristbands for the 1993 fair.

Despite members' initial misgivings, the 1993 wristband solution worked out very well. "That was really one of the very big things that took place after I became president," Daniel said.

"Even though there were a great number of people who thought that wristbands were a very bad idea," he said, "after they happened, many more people came and said what a great idea that was to be able to actually identify who needs to leave and sweep them out. Wristbands gave us space to breathe again overnight to refresh for the morning. We had better control on how many people are on-site."

After the 1993 fair, members wrote letters to the *Fair Family News* praising the wristbands solution for restoring a mellower nighttime flavor to the fair.

All of the fair's efforts to solve problems in the surrounding neighborhoods still failed to fix everything. The citizens of Veneta, Elimira, and the surrounding community continued to be plagued by hangers-on and trespassers during the fair every year. A tipping point came during the 1996 fair. Presale tickets went like hotcakes and the fair sold out by opening time, 11:00 Friday morning. People without tickets got turned away at the gate.

Subsequently, a big group of hangers-on gathered in the parking lot of the shopping center in Veneta to camp out. They used the restrooms at the local businesses, often without purchasing anything. Some were accused of shoplifting at the supermarket. The owner of the Dairy Queen, Christine Rush, objected to the crowds and locked the restaurant's bathrooms. Someone threw a rock and broke the Dairy Queen's glass menu at the restaurant's drive-through lane. Afterward, Christine Rush went on a media tirade, blaming the Oregon Country Fair for the damage to her business and for the problems at the shopping center parking lot.

A few weeks after the fair was over, Christine Rush organized a community forum to discuss the persistent problems the neighbors dealt with from anti-social fairgoers in their neighborhoods. She invited state Representative Jim Welsh to moderate.

Before the gathering, Daniel Dillon called Jim Welsh to ask how he planned to run the meeting. Jim said he didn't know and asked Daniel what he had in mind.

"We should establish a registration when people arrive," Daniel said. "If they want to speak, they need to sign up as pro, neutral, or con. And then we should go between these three positions and have a person talk from each one and then around and around. It is not going to be fair if you set it up so everybody talks against the Country Fair and we don't have a chance, or if somebody sets up a meeting and talks about how great the Country Fair is and nobody has a chance to air their complaints." Jim agreed to Daniel's suggestion.

About 200 people attended the forum held at the end of July at the Fern Ridge Middle School in Veneta. Leslie Scott stood in front of the crowd and began the conversation with an apology. "We did have kind of an attitude," she admitted to the crowd. "We would come in, do our thing, and leave. We didn't do very much to mitigate the impact of our event and I apologize to you for that. …

"The fair has a history here," she said. "We want to work this out. We want to make changes. I won't pretend to tell you we've solved the problems. But we want to."

Daniel made a point to sit in the first row. "The media was there—cameras everywhere," Daniel said. "It was just amazing. I had decided that I was going to put a face on the fair. I sat directly in front of the podium where everybody had to get up and speak. If they were going to look at the fair and tell us that we were shitheads, I wanted them to see a real face."

County Commissioner Ellie Dumdi played a crucial role at the meeting. Fair organizers had forged a relationship with her over four years and she had attended the fair as a welcome guest. When the meeting started to devolve into anger and ugly name calling about "filthy hippies," Commissioner Dumdi stood up and said the meeting was not about shutting down the fair. She noted that the fair had a right to exist, and the meeting needed to focus on solving problems. She was booed by some in the crowd, but stood her ground.

Daniel's strategy of trying to set up a balanced meeting also helped. He had contacted everyone he knew with connections to the community and asked them to speak up for the fair at the meeting. They did.

The *West Lane News* reported that "The tone was neighborly, with certain exceptions, and the underlying assumption was that the problems could be solved." Neighbors listed concerns about drug abuse, illegal parking, noise, vandalism, shoplifting, litter, lack of water, cleanup problems, and lack of security.

Toward the end of the comments, Jim Welsh took the microphone. With the media cameras still rolling, the state representative began criticizing the Oregon Country Fair. Daniel quickly sized up what was going on. He stood up to object.

"Wait a second Jim," Daniel said. "What's going on here? You are supposed to be facilitating the meeting, not having a show. What needs to happen now is we need to form a committee to figure out how to solve these problems. Where is a piece of paper? I want to be the first one to sign up."

Dozens of people clamored to sign up for the task force, essentially ending the forum.

"An incredible group of people signed up—a county commissioner at the time was at the table, the state police came, the local police came to the table, local ministers were there, the people from the shopping center—the owners of the businesses—they came," Daniel said.

The meeting created the Respect Our Community Committee, which first met on September 10, 1996. Members of the committee also included organizer Christine Rush, Lane County Commissioner Dumdi, Elmira resident and fair participant Paul Fuller, fair neighbors Floyd Henderson and Ron Johnson, Veneta Mayor Galen Carpenter, and Leslie Scott.

"We all sat down and it really felt like that was a group, a community, that had a purpose," Daniel said. "We learned a lot of things. The community here learned that they did not have any posted signs in the parking lot that says, 'This is private property. You have to leave at this hour.' They never had any sign that said, 'We have the right under this or that statute to tow you.'" Neighbors also requested that fair organizers provide more liaison contacts during the event. Daniel and the fair obliged.

Before the 1997 fair, Daniel contacted the most vocal neighbors who had trouble with the fair. "Here is my pager number, here is a phone number," Daniel said. "If you have any problem whatsoever, I want you to call me personally. I will see that something happens."

Also in late 1996, the fair's board began looking for ways to address the persistent problems that cropped up along the fair's pathways. "We first approached this from the alcohol point of view," Daniel said. "We realized that people were bringing beer into the event in enormous quantities in coolers and going up to the Main Stage and parking for the whole day and just getting toasted."

Security had come to the board after the 1996 fair asking them to do something about the alcohol problem. "We have a nightmare trying to get these people out of the event," coordinators told the board. "You've got the wristbands—that's great! But now that we know that they don't belong here, they're all drunk and we have to herd these drunk people out. You've got to help us do something. It's beyond our control."

More ominously, the board had received a tip from a reliable source that Lane County District Attorney Doug Harcleroad was researching a draconian solution to the neighborhood problems that cropped up around the fair, Leslie said. The board was told at their annual retreat that the district attorney and the county sheriff were considering a federally approved process known as asset forfeiture. Under the law's provisions, they could seize the fair's land based on allegations of drug trafficking at the fair; they didn't have to prove their case before they took the property.

Through the fall of 1996, the board worked on solutions. Daniel had allies on the board to advocate for change, chief among them Tom Alexander. Tom worked at Nearly Normal's, a renowned vegetarian restaurant in Corvallis that also had a booth selling falafels and salads at the Oregon Country Fair.

During the 1980s, Tom had published the magazine *Sinsemilla Tips*, which he first had distributed from a booth in Community Village in 1980. He had signed up enough subscribers at the 1980 Oregon Country Fair to start monthly publication. The magazine would soon become known as an authoritative source for cannabis growers. Sales took off and the media came calling. Tom appeared on numerous television programs, from *Donahue* to *Nightline*.

"In September 1989 the Drug Enforcement Administration targeted garden and grow shops in nationwide raids called Operation Green Merchant," Tom said. "I owned one of the garden stores in Corvallis—Full Moon Farm Products— that was stolen by the government through civil forfeiture. These raided garden stores were the main advertisers in *Sinsemilla Tips*. Without advertisers, the magazine folded a year later."

His experiences would profoundly shape Tom's views about what the government could do to average citizens.

Board member Martha Evans also felt concerned. "My friend Mary Drew had told me about her school's practice of being a Racism Free Zone," Martha said. "That didn't mean that there wasn't racism, but that all aspired to eliminate racism. ... We knew something needed to change, so I suggested being a drug-free zone."

At the December 1996 meeting, Martha's motion to make the fair a drug- and alcohol-free event sparked heated debate. With such strong pushback, the board tabled the motion until the next month. In January 1997 Martha made the same motion and the discussion raged on.

Several fair members declared that prohibition just wouldn't work among the "community of anarchists" who attended the fair. Some worried about creating "a police state" to enforce the policy that would ruin the fair's magic.

Volunteers with Security Crew testified to how difficult their jobs had become and urged the board to pass the measure. Martha said the motion was directed not at the "fair family, but at the other population that comes to the fair to get away with as much as possible." The motion would make the rules clear to everyone, even if they don't read fair guidelines, she said.

Tom Alexander told members that he was worried the fair might face property forfeiture under federal drug laws if the board didn't take a public stance against illegal drugs. Tom shared what had happened to him.

"I personally had a concern about that," Tom later said. "I had a garden store up in Corvallis taken from me in 1989 when it was deemed the lights and garden supplies were drug paraphernalia. I was a big supporter of the 'no drugs, no alcohol' policy. People in the fair family didn't know what was going on. They called us fascists and dictators and all kinds of other things. Our main purpose was to save the fair land. That's the main reason we instituted that policy."

After the new policy prohibiting drugs and alcohol was approved, Leslie and fair volunteers jumped into action to get everything in place in time. Leslie worked with Security and Lot crews to set up a checkpoint for backpacks and coolers. They would call it the Line in the Sand. Zak Schwartz—the White Bird volunteer who had taught Crisis Intervention and Human Intervention trainings at the fair for decades—updated the training sessions to emphasize the importance of enforcing the new policy and to provide volunteers with ways to handle difficult situations that could crop up.

Separately, Leslie instituted an operational change that put an end to ticket sales on site. Fairgoers would be required to purchase a ticket off site before they would be allowed on the property. That also required Leslie and fair leaders to find a ticket vendor, work with the neighborhood campgrounds to be sure everyone camping there had fair tickets, and spread the word to the public. Moving all ticket sales off site would prove key to the fair finally gaining control over its own parking lot.

In late May 1997, the Oregon Country Fair received a certified letter from Lane County District Attorney Doug Harcleroad. The letter said the fair site "constitutes a nuisance" as defined under state law, that the county narcotics team had "conclusively documented substantial trafficking in controlled substances" in prior years, and that "your prompt correction of this problem is expected." It threatened the fair with possible property forfeiture if more drug sales were observed at the fair site.

Underscoring the threat, the district attorney and the county sheriff called the fair attorney and Leslie to a meeting to demand that Lane County sheriff deputies be allowed to patrol the fair's property to handle security and prevent drug use. The county expected the fair to pay for the sheriff deputies' time.

Fair attorney Russell Poppe responded with an absolute no. Russell noted that the fair was fully prepared to provide its own security just like the fair had always done. Russell and Leslie asked the sheriff to alert fair organizers of any controlled substance transaction they became aware of so that the fair could put a stop to it. Russell and Leslie also provided key phone numbers and arranged with the sheriff's office to have sheriff's transportation available in the fair's parking lot in case anyone had to be removed.

Even after being warned it could happen, and even after making all the pre-fair preparations and changes in policy, the district attorney's letter hit the board like a lightning bolt. It struck home that the fair could very well lose its land if the district attorney followed through.

Every fair member received a letter in the mail that underscored the importance of following the new policy prohibiting drugs and alcohol at the fair. Fair organizers also reached out to the public, hiring for the first time a public relations firm to help ensure that word of the new policy got out.

"We put a huge publicity campaign together that went to the media," Daniel said. It emphasized the policies banning drugs and alcohol, and told fairgoers to be sure to purchase their tickets early because none would be sold on site. Fairgoers were told to expect to have their backpacks checked at the gate.

The board stressed the seriousness of the situation to all the fair crews. Security Crews took on extra volunteers to get a handle on anything that came their way. Security Crews and other volunteers who interacted with the public received Zak's training updates on how to police the situation kindly but firmly. Anyone who was seen using drugs would be confronted with a similar script:

"You are jeopardizing the fair. The district attorney has threatened to take the land for drug forfeiture. You have got to stop now. You can throw it in the toilet yourself while I watch, or you can crush it out and stomp it into the ground right here, right now. Or you can walk with me and I'm going to escort you out. If we need more security, they're at a moment's notice."

Word got around and the policies contributed to one of the mellowest fairs in years. The public mostly left the alcohol and drugs at home. Anything brought to the gate that was not allowed was tossed into a nearby dumpster. The fair's volunteers, booth folks, and entertainers all cooperated and followed the rules.

"I had this little experience that year," Daniel said. "I was walking back in the woods. I wanted to keep checking in the woods, because I walked everywhere when I was president."

All of a sudden he saw a couple of teens sitting on a log in the woods, holding a lit joint. Daniel strode over to confront them: "What are you doing? What are you thinking about? Have you not heard what is going on?"

The teens acknowledged they had heard about the no-drug policy.

"I got a letter personally, threatening me because of what you are doing right now," Daniel told them. "You have got to put this out. You can have three choices. You can stomp it out on the ground right now. You can throw it in the toilet or I'm walking you all out of here."

The teens opted to stomp it out, and suddenly applause erupted from the tents all around the clearing. "Way to go! Right on! You tell 'em!" people yelled out.

"Everybody bought into this plan to save the fair," Daniel said. "Drugs and alcohol were not the important part here. The life of the fair was."

The main disruptions that year came from the sheriff's helicopters buzzing low for a closer view of the fair site. Otherwise, everything was much mellower than usual.

White Bird reported that their workload at the fair's medical tent decreased by more than fifty percent in 1997 compared to recent fairs. They attributed the difference to the new policies, especially no alcohol and the pre-fair ticket sales that kept non-ticket-holders off the property.

"It was a tremendous success," Daniel said. "Everybody bought into the idea that they wanted the fair to exist."

The district attorney wasn't through yet, though. Doug Harcleroad followed up afterward with a letter to the fair noting some improvements during the event that he attributed mostly to the efforts of neighbors and the sheriff. But the letter alleged that undercover officers had procured drugs "from two of your security staff" and again threatened the fair with action if steps weren't taken to halt drug sales at the event. In addition, the district attorney's letter requested reimbursement for extra sheriff's patrols.

The fair's attorney, Russell Poppe, responded with a letter disputing Harcleroad's allegations. Russell noted the agreements they had made with the county prior to the fair and pointed out that the sheriff had not notified fair organizers of any drug problems during the event. Everything had gone so well that the sheriff's transportation on site wasn't used even once.

Russell questioned whether the sheriff's office was truly interested in stopping illegal activity or if the county was using the issue to force payment for more law enforcement under the threat of forfeiture. Russell pointed out that the extra sheriff's patrols had not been agreed to by the fair, and that it looked as though the county—once again—was singling out the fair and treating it differently than any other event.

The dispute showed up in the local newspaper headlines. The *Register-Guard*'s editorial board weighed in on the fair's side.

"Lane County Sheriff Jan Clements says the Oregon Country Fair has a 'moral obligation' to pay $7,622 for patrols and other services his office provided during last month's event," the editorial said. "He has to call it a moral obligation, because it's clearly not a legal one. And calling it an obligation of any sort is quite a stretch. …

"No event planner can sign blank checks for police services, agreeing to pay whatever amount law enforcement agencies later determine is warranted," the editorial continued. "And in fact, the Country Fair did agree in advance to pay public agencies for specific types of assistance from government agencies, including $3,950 to the sheriff's office for help in the parking lot."

The county dropped the threat, but the fair remained vigilant in enforcing the policies. Even after marijuana was legalized in Oregon in 2014, federal forfeiture would remain a threat. The policies and enforcement stayed in place.

Leslie Scott was proud of how the fair handled the difficult situation. "This group can do anything it wants to do," she said. "We truly acted on faith and pulled off one of the best fairs even while many eyes, entities, and microphones were watching and recording us. We remained true to ourselves and acted with heart, integrity, and good humor. Everyone worked so well together. It was an extraordinary example of commitment and teamwork from beginning to end."

Residents of Veneta agreed with the fair that the event went well and that the county's use of helicopters circling overhead was disruptively over-the-top. "Thrifty taxpayers among Fern Ridge residents saw the helicopters as an unnecessary expense and an unwarranted intrusion," the *West Lane News* reported.

After the 1997 fair, even Christine Rush sounded conciliatory. "My sales were down from last year, but in the long run I think that we can be proud of what we accomplished," she told the *West Lane News*. "It shows people what we can do when we all come together. … Sitting down at the table together was key."

Respect Our Community Committee would remain active for several years until the problems tapered off enough that the group opted to disband.

Epilogue

The Oregon Country Fair would defy everyone's original expectations and reach its fiftieth anniversary in 2019. Organizers would once again plan a huge celebration for "The Best Fair Ever." Dedicated volunteers spanning several generations would continue to staff key positions and keep the fair running like a well-oiled cuckoo clock.

Through the 1990s and 2000s, the fair's paid staff would remain remarkably stable, with Leslie Scott serving as general manager and former board Secretary Norma Sax as administrative assistant. Former board member Steve Wisnovsky would become the fair's longest-serving site manager during those same years. In 2001, Leslie would persuade the fair board to approve a fair-sponsored youth summer camp called Culture Jam. The week-long camp, which would still be ongoing in 2019, would empower youth campers with arts-based, creative community experiences.

Also in 2001, former fair President Robert DeSpain would spearhead the drive to add a Spoken Word program to bring in speakers, poets, and performers to smaller

Robert DeSpain enjoyed visiting with Peter Yarrow, who performed in the Spoken Word program in the 2000s.

stages. As co-coordinators of Spoken Word, Robert and his wife, Laura Stuart, would pack the schedule with a diverse range of topics such as juggling, social change, global warming, anti-GMO information, get-out-the-vote discussions, alchemical healing, and hip-hop poetry. Counterculture luminaries who accepted invitations to speak at the fair included Patch Adams; folksinger Peter Yarrow of Peter, Paul, and Mary; Stephen Gaskin, co-founder of The Farm commune; comic Swami Beyondananda; and Robert's favorite, Ram Dass, author of *Be Here Now*.

By 2019 the Oregon Country Fair would evolve into a highly successful nonprofit that continually gave back to its community. Over the years, the Bill Wooten Memorial Endowment and the Jill Heiman Vision Fund would donate more than a million dollars to various area schools and nonprofits. Culture Jam would serve dozens of youths each summer, with many of them on scholarships.

The fair would remain an "Essential Event"—as Artis the Spoonman so eloquently put it—by providing psychospiritual rejuvenation for thousands of people year after year. To accommodate the crush of fairgoers, volunteers would expand the fair's pathways two more times to encompass Chela Mela Meadow in 1997 and Xavanadu in 2015. Also in 2015 KOCF, the fair-sponsored low-powered FM radio station, began broadcasting to the West Lane County area.

For years, rumors had swirled that the Grateful Dead would perform on Main Stage. While that never happened, in the new century Grateful Dead drummer Bill Kreutzmann would play percussion several times on Main Stage in various eclectic rock ensembles. For 2019, Phil Lesh & The Terrapin Family Band were booked on Main Stage.

The fair also would help manifest a longtime dream of co-founders Bill and Cindy Wooten, who envisioned offering a place where artisans could make a living creating beautiful crafts with their hands instead of laboring for corporations.

Indeed, the regular annual income from the Country Fair would enable hundreds of artisans, crafters, artists, musicians, and food vendors to establish viable small businesses. The lifestyle wasn't without its problems, especially with the scarcity of affordable health insurance for the self-employed in the United States. Still, people managed to live the artful life of their dreams because the Oregon Country Fair, along with other craft fairs that cropped up around the

Northwest, provided reliable venues for their products.

Through the years, the fair incubated artistic collaborations among performers that would result in creative liaisons that flourished well beyond the three days of the event. Two key artistic nonprofits founded by fair performers still going at this writing include Seattle's Moisture Festival and the New Old Time Chautauqua, with its annual tours around the Northwest.

Another entire book could be written about the aforementioned events that unfolded from the 1990s to 2019. Those stories will have to wait until another day.

Meanwhile, here's one more story that has roots in the past while pointing to the fair's future. A third artistic nonprofit—Girl Circus—would spring to life at the fair in the 2000s with hard work from longtime fair entertainers Darcy DuRuz and her husband, Dave Bender. Their children, Walter and Coco Bender, would also play a part.

Girl Circus shows just one of the ways the fair made efforts to include the next generation. Among other innovations, the fair launched in the 2000s a Youth Craft Booth, where fair kids could sell their handcrafts, and the Youth Stage, located across the path from Tom Noddy's original W.C. Fields Stage, where young people could perform for other kids.

2001
The Fair Must Go On: Girl Circus

Dave Bender was blown away by the Flying Karamazov Brothers' juggling and jokes the first time he attended the Oregon Country Fair in 1977. He had recently moved to Eugene, where his brother lived. His family had attended the 1976 Country Fair, and with wide grins they told Dave stories about encountering uninhibited, naked people walking along the fair's pathways.

Dave also witnessed nudity along the fair's paths in 1977, but he became more fascinated with the entertainment at the fair. He especially enjoyed the variety show at the Chumleighland stage, where Reverend Chumleigh acted as ringmaster with his sidekick "Brodie, Dog of the Future."

"The Karamazov Brothers were hilarious," Dave said. "Their

execution of things was just perfect. Everything was thrilling. It was so fresh! At that time, just about every time they played a show they got a standing ovation. People would leap to their feet. ... It had a lot to do with their rap. It was really fast, it was really funny, but they all have big voices and enunciate well so you always heard it all. Without amplification, that was an amazing thing."

The next few years, Dave found fair "jobs" with different food and craft booths. Then from 1981 to 1984, he joined Community Village in the Local Self-Reliance booth, representing Surata Soy Foods, a company based in Eugene. But what Dave really wanted to do was to play in the marching band at the fair.

"The Flying Karamazov Brothers inspired me to become a musician, to go back to music," Dave said. In January 1984, he took a trumpet class at Lane Community College. That same year, he packed his cornet (a smaller trumpet-like instrument) along with his camping gear when he went to the fair.

"I heard that their regular trumpet player couldn't make it, that they needed a trumpet player," Dave said. "I went over to—I think at that time it was called Not-Chumleighland, because Chumleigh didn't come—so I went over there and did a little audition and got hired to play in the Fighting Instruments of Karma."

Dave and three other musicians from the marching band would quickly become friends and form a band they named Unstuck in Time.

Darcy DuRuz first came to the fair in 1988 to meet Dave Bender, but he wasn't expecting her. "I had moved to Eugene in 1987 and met Dave," Darcy said. "We kind of had a little fling and he had told me about the fair, how wonderful it was and how great it was. Then he off-handedly said, 'You should come!' I had moved back to Seattle but I decided to come without actually talking to him on the phone about it."

But Darcy started worrying as she drove toward Veneta and the Country Fair on opening day. After she parked in the fair's parking field and walked to the gate, she learned the fair would not open to the public for a few more hours. She returned to her car and opened the bottle of whiskey she had brought to share with Dave.

"By 11 o'clock in the morning I was kind of drunk," Darcy said. "I was staggering around, trying to find the stage—it was just huge out there. I thought, 'Oh my god, what if he doesn't want me to be here?'" Suddenly she heard the band play, and she headed in that direction.

"It must've been Friday morning," Darcy said. "I go up and I stand by the stage." Eben Sprinsock's wife, Sylvia—who kept her eye out for uninvited guests encroaching on the fair's entertainment camp—walked up to Darcy and asked who she was. Seeing what was going on, Dave materialized by Darcy's side and said, "She's with me."

"Yeah, I'm with him," Darcy agreed, swaying slightly.

Quickly assessing the situation, Dave told Darcy: "You go in the tent and lie down. It's the green tent. You look like you need some sleep while the band practices." Sylvia Sprinsock produced a paper pass for Darcy, who took it to Dave's tent and passed out.

"I wasn't prepared at all to camp out," Darcy said. "I had my backpack, an extra pair of underwear, I wore a dress, and a little sweater. I had some Chapstick and this big bottle of whiskey. I just showed up and David's oh, so gracious: 'My tent *est votre* tent.' We had a lot of fun that year!"

The next year, Darcy jumped in to help backstage, but that didn't really utilize her talents. When the other entertainers learned she was a trained soprano with a master's degree in vocal performance, they added her into the script and gave her a part to sing during most shows staged in the 1990s.

In 1993, Darcy stunned the Midnight Show crowd with an amazing rendition of Mozart's "Queen of the Night Aria," a difficult piece from the opera *The Magic Flute* that requires a voice capable of spanning two octaves. Darcy's virtuoso performance was accompanied by Unstuck in Time. Dave had arranged the Mozart piece for the quartet: trumpet, saxophone, valve trombone, and sousaphone. When Darcy finished singing the last challenging notes, the audience leapt to a roaring, standing ovation.

At first oblivious to her reception, Darcy walked off stage. A member of the band stopped her, saying, "Darcy, you better go out there and take another bow! They're screaming!" She got back on stage to acknowledge the accolades. "I felt like a rock star," Darcy said.

In the early 1990s Dave and Darcy started their family: Walter was born in 1992 and Coco arrived in 1994. The kids would grow up at Stage Left and would watch their parents perform year after year. It wouldn't be long before they both joined their parents on stage.

Epilogue

Walter landed his first fair job sweeping the stage in 1997 when he was five. In 1998, when Walter was six and Coco was four, they played rats harassing an elephant in the "Guys and Dolls" revue.

In 1999, the entertainers on Stage Left presented the "Cuba Show." The silly production featured characters based on Lucy and Ricky Ricardo, Fidel Castro, and giant dancing bananas. Darcy portrayed a nightclub singer while Walter and Coco played monkeys who were her sidekicks.

Walter gave a synopsis of the Cuba Show plot in 2004 when he was twelve years old. "She [Darcy] was in a big house with important politicians," Walter said. "Then out in the woods was Fidel Castro. All the Flying Karamazov Brothers were his generals. They played baseball and then invaded the big house. 'Fifty years ago next Thursday we found liberty,' they said."

The giant banana props for the 1999 "Cuba" show filled a tent.

The dancing bananas looked realistic, said Heather Weihl, the trombonist in the marching band. "We have these great artists who work with us who paint these incredible sets," Heather said. "That year, Laurie Childers made us these giant bananas. When we got to the Country Fair—this is another one of my favorite moments—she unzipped the tent and here are these bananas!"

When the kids were young, Darcy, Coco, and Walter would climb the loft of the Information booth near Stage Left twice a day in time to watch the Fighting Instruments of Karma Marching Chamber Band/Orchestra parade by. They would look for Dave, and as he paraded by, he would turn around to march backward, playing his trumpet up toward his family, who would wave to him from the loft. The family would continue the tradition even as the kids grew older and could roam the fair on their own. The three would meet at the loft twice a day to check in and to wave to Dave in the marching band.

475

All four enjoyed marching in the torchlight parade on Saturday night for the Midnight Show. In later years because of safety concerns, the fire torches would be traded in for portable electric art that was attached to instruments or held in the air by hands raised high.

Over the years, the vaudeville family at Stage Left and the Royal Famille Du Caniveaux established another tradition. They adjusted the Sunday stage schedules so that each troupe could watch the other's final performance at the fair. Darcy, Dave, Coco, and Walter always joined the fun. One year when Hacki Ginda performed on the Du Caniveaux stage, he brought out his raining umbrella for the last show. After making his entrance from the back of the audience, Hacki took his sweet time inching his way through the section where Stage Left folks sat together. Darcy recalled that they were drenched and laughed uproariously at the prank.

In 2001, Darcy would launch the family on a different trajectory. She gained approval from the fair's Entertainment Co-coordinator Marge Wise to start a new show at the fair called Girl Circus. Darcy said the fair took a leap of faith with her proposal. She wanted to provide a venue for girls to shine on stage through acrobatics and other performance skills.

"I was really grateful to the fair, on the strength of my past performance at Stage Left, that they said, yeah, go ahead, bring it on," Darcy said. "They gave me some money. They gave me the stage and the time. It was really very pivotal in my development as an artist."

Darcy switched from being an individual with a four-minute part in a show to being the artistic creator and director of a fifty-minute production involving dozens of people. Dave would contribute his talents by assembling a band and composing original music for the shows.

"It takes a lot of courage on our part," Darcy said, "but it takes a big leap of faith that the fair is saying, 'We will give you the venue.' I started feeling that this idea of Fair Family, it's really manifesting for me now. My idea that I can gather together all these performers, who are people at the fair already, and all these children, and give them work and artistic vision—a job, a purpose, a reason for being there, a real involvement—and that the fair is also saying, 'Yeah, your artistic vision is great, we want it.' That's pretty big."

Girl Circus features girls of all ages doing tumbling, dancing, singing, acrobatics, and silly skits, accompanied by music from a live, ten-member band led by Dave. The shows mostly revolve around a loose theme. From the start, Coco then age seven, participated on stage and Walter, age nine, played percussion in the band.

But the family didn't cut ties with their original vaudeville friends. Dave continued to parade twice a day playing trumpet with the Fighting Instruments of Karma. Walter soon joined the parade too, playing percussion. Walter also took small parts on Stage Left, dividing his time at the fair between marching in the parade, appearing in Stage Left shows, and playing in the band for Girl Circus.

By 2006, Coco had become an accomplished performer at age twelve. She and her good friend Rya Giudici would plan and rehearse their act together for Girl Circus. Rya lived in Eugene and her parents ran the Rising Moon Ravioli food booth at the fair. That year Rya and Coco practiced for more than three months on two performance pieces: fan juggling as geishas and stage combat as Evil Mutant Ninjas of Doom. The show's theme was "Flying with Girl Circus."

"They were fan juggling, which is a little bit crazy because it's really hard to juggle fans outdoors," Darcy said. "When they're in the wind, that was a little problematic. ... but they also had to do stage combat with fake kung fu fighting."

"Evil Mutant Ninja fighting, Mom," Coco corrected.

"Yes, Evil Mutant Ninja fighting," Darcy agreed with a smile. "And that is really difficult and takes a lot of skill so that nobody gets hurt. They worked so hard on that."

Coco and Rya created their own costumes as well as costumes and hats for other girls. They dubbed their small operation Maiden Designs. Sometimes the two friends came up with ideas for Girl Circus. One year they wrote a skit called "Mommy Mummy." The evil Mommy was a robot that gave terrible answers to questions from pre-teen girls. In the skit, the girls figure out how to turn Mommy Mummy off and claim their personal power to find their own answers in life.

"From an artistic point of view, people are freer to take bigger risks at the Country Fair," Darcy said. "That really feeds an artist so that that is a place where you can really try something new, something wild, something crazy without fear of being censored, or censoring yourself. ... The audiences are forgiving and welcoming

The "Mommy Mummy" skit at Girl Circus in 2005 featured (from left) Coco Bender, Darcy DuRuz, and Rya Giudici.

simultaneously."

Girl Circus would become so popular at the fair that those in the know would arrive early for the show. People who came right at showtime would find no space to squeeze in and would have to stand at the back of the crowd. Darcy would invite girls who had trained in aerial acrobatics to perform trapeze and silk-climbing in the show. The lithe, talented aerialists could be seen even from the back.

By 2018, Darcy's yearly calendar would revolve around Girl Circus performances at the fair. In the fall after each fair, she would incubate the kernel of an idea for a show that she would workshop with other performers to get feedback. In January she would run the idea by all the teachers who would be committing to the show. Then Darcy would sketch out the show and outline the individual routines while Dave composed original music to complement the theme.

As of 2019, about thirty Girl Circus performers gather in two separate geographical groups to train. The group that meets in Portland includes two girls who drive south from Seattle. The group meeting in Eugene includes girls who travel from California and Southern Oregon.

"In February, March, April, and May, I do trainings one time a month with each of those groups," Darcy said. "I go to Portland four

Epilogue

The whole Girl Circus cast for 2018 gathered on stage for a group portrait.

times and then those other girls come up here. … You can see the show looks pretty snappy and put-together. We're trying to create choreography earlier, so that means Dave and I have to write the show and the music earlier."

After the four training sessions, Darcy and Dave schedule a performance camp in Eugene for everyone in the show. That's when they put all the show components together and finish the set pieces. They also schedule a couple of rehearsals right before the fair in July. "We try to get [the routines] on YouTube so people can watch films," Darcy said. "We do our best to keep elevating the level before we can really present. It's super fun."

Besides the thirty girls, the troupe counts six to eight adult performers. Adrienne Wise, daughter of fair entertainment volunteer Marge Wise, grew up in Girl Circus and would also become an adult adviser. "Adrienne Wise teaches in Eugene," Darcy said. "She's been in Girl Circus since she was seven years old. She's been my assistant director for probably nine years now."

One of the adult performers helps train the aerialists year-round. Adding aerialists also meant the troupe had to purchase extra insurance for the show. In 2018, the fair provided additional funding. "Every single girl who goes up in the air has to have a million-dollar insurance policy at the fair," Darcy said. "They gave me a grant to help with that."

Darcy would branch out beyond the key Girl Circus troupe to offer Girl Circus summer camps for any girl interested. In 2012, Girl Circus camps became a recognized federal 501(c)(3) nonprofit. In 2018, Darcy would offer camps in Portland and Eugene, as well as on Lopez Island, Washington.

"For the regular camps we do partner acrobatics, introductory gymnastics, hooping, juggling, poi-spinning, circus fans, ribbon baton, and improvisation," Darcy said. "It's a lot. It's busy, busy. We work a ton on strength building, too. Strength building and teamwork are the two big things. ... My really big effort in those camps has been two sided: one is to reach rural populations who don't have as much enrichment, and two is to reach nontraditional camp-goers, which is First Nation girls, Latina girls, LGBT girls. I put a lot of energy into that."

Darcy writes grants to help fund the outreach programs of Girl Circus. "I'm totally supporting girls," Darcy said. "I'm empowering girls. I am giving girls a good dose of being strong and believing in their own creativity." She added that reaching the girls in elementary school helps instill confidence before they reach the critical teenage years in middle school. In circus camp, the girls learn that they can do something very hard if they let themselves fail again and again, but keep at it until they get it right.

"Circus is really what teaches you that there are a lot of different ways to be a part of a group," Darcy said, "and a lot of different ways to understand your own strength. As the girls get older, that is potent and relevant, especially with what's going on with the world these days."

In the meantime, the Girl Circus performance troupe would remain remarkably steady over the years. "People don't leave the core," Darcy said, "so I haven't accepted many new people. The core performers' ages range from six to eighteen. Counting the adults, the ages range from six to sixty-six."

Coco stopped performing on stage in 2010. Her friend Rya had gotten involved with her family's food booth, Rising Moon Ravioli, and stopped actively participating in Girl Circus. In 2018 at age twenty-four, Coco plays piano with the Girl Circus Band and twice daily grabs her piccolo to join her father and her brother as they parade with the Fighting Instruments of Karma Marching Chamber Band/Orchestra. In 2019, Coco was still creating fanciful hats, flower

EPILOGUE

Adrienne Wise, who grew up performing in Girl Circus, learned silk-climbing and aerial acrobatics. In the 2010s, she became an adult advisor.

crowns, and headdresses.

Walter stopped performing for a while when he hit his teens. Toward his senior year in high school, he returned to play percussion in the Girl Circus Band. In 2018 at age twenty-six, Walter plays percussion with the Girl Circus Band and marches as a drummer with the Fighting Instruments of Karma. He has joined his dad in composing music for Girl Circus, as well. "I've written a couple of songs," Walter said. "Some of the stuff from early shows were based on silly things I was humming when I was a kid. More recently I've actually composed music, which is still based on things that I was just humming."

In 2019, Walter attends the University of Oregon, studying Eastern European history and Russian language. Coco teaches piano and plays piano professionally in Portland, Oregon. Dave continues to compose original music for the Girl Circus Band. During the fair, he plays trumpet with the marching band and Girl Circus.

After all these years, the family still feels recharged with every fair.

"I like the element that it really is a family," Darcy said. "We have our kids with us, some people have babies, some people have teenagers, some teenagers have boyfriends and girlfriends. We're all camping together and we're all working hard together, and there's no ageism. It's not a party just for adults, it's not a day camp just for kids. It really is all blended in with all the ages. It's natural. Kids have to learn to be quiet at shows, adults have to learn to listen to kids."

Dave agreed. "There is a lot of love at the fair," he said. "There's a lot of lovemaking going on. It is a party—and there's a lot of work going on, of course. But people are doing the work in order to celebrate. …

"It's happening in the same spot every year," Dave added. "There is no other word for it. That is hallowed ground! It's got its own vibe, and that vibe is very loving. What's being put into that land is not hate and tension and anger and angst. Those things happen because we're humans, but people are going there with really good intentions and you can feel it."

Fair Thee Well

Susan (Downing) Bryan, one of the original members of the Vegetation Management and Erosion Control team (VegManECs) at the Oregon Country Fair, was born in 1949 in McMinnville, Oregon, and died in March 2014 in Eugene at age sixty-four. She first attended the Oregon Renaissance Faire in 1972, and joined the Garbage Crew (before it became Recycling Crew) in 1983—the year of the big rain. Over the years she would volunteer for Bus Admissions Security, Watergate Security, Pre-Post Security, and VegManECs. She also participated in the OCF highway cleanups, Neighborhood Response Team, and Construction. She had three children: Susanna Hathorn (who predeceased her), Jennifer Hathorn Baumeister, and Gil Hathorn. Outside the fair she joined other Security Crew members working at Oregon Event Enterprises providing security to area concerts and shows. She also worked as a waitress, seamstress, and clerk. (Chapter 34)

Dominic DeFazio, a longtime fair toymaker and *Fair Family News* photographer, grew up near Niagara Falls, New York, and earned a degree in photography from Rochester Institute of Technology. After three years of taking photographs for the aerospace industry, he followed his sister Carol to the West Coast where he met his wife, Susanna. In 1974 Dominic and Susanna settled into a homestead in the Coast Range forests west of Eugene. They made a living selling handmade wooden toys at the Saturday Market and the Oregon Country Fair, among other places. They had a daughter, Diana, and a son, Daniel. A lifelong hiker, Dominic died of a heart attack at age sixty-seven while hiking with his wife up a mountain on the Olympic Peninsula in August 2009. (Introduction, Chapter 37, and numerous photos)

Robert DeSpain was a sixth-generation Oregonian born in Pendleton, Oregon, in 1947. He earned a bachelor's of science in music composition and theory at Oregon State University. He had a daughter, Arwen, in 1972 with his then-wife, Linda. In his day job he excavated land, specializing in cleaning up soil around leaking oil tanks. Inspired during his first fair in 1979 by Community Village luminary Marshall Landman, Robert went on to serve as a scribe for the village and secretary for the fair board of directors in the 1980s, was elected fair president from 1983 to 1985, and volunteered with the fair's Operation Management team numerous years. In 2001 he co-founded the fair's Spoken Word program with his wife, Laura Stuart. Robert said his favorite Spoken Word artist was Ram Dass, who came to the fair in 2002. Robert died in September 2018 at age seventy-one. (Multiple chapters)

John Doscher was born in 1949 in Boise, Idaho, and grew up in Eugene. He graduated from South Eugene High School; married his first wife, Vivian; and served in the Army during the Vietnam War. John and Vivian had son Christopher in 1969. John attended Lane Community College and worked as a welder, a skill he later taught at LCC. He married Laurie (known at the fair as Heidi) in 1983, and helped raised Michael and Noah Power. John volunteered on the Fair's Security Crew and co-founded the Vegetation Management and Erosion Control team (aka the VegManECs). He helped create the Neighborhood Response Team and initiated the fair's participation in the highway pickup program on Highway 126. In 1996 and 1997 John served as the OCF caretaker. Beyond the fair, John co-owned and managed Oregon Event Enterprises, which provided security services at Zumwalt Campground during the fair as well as at music and sports events throughout Western Oregon. He died in 2013 at age sixty-three. (Chapters 14, 34, 37, 38)

Leo de Flambeaux (aka Leroy James Howes): See Chapters 16 and 25.

Ande Grahn was born Andrea Lee Kauffman in 1951, in Merced, California, and grew up in a suburb of Seattle. In 1983 Ande sneaked into the fair as part of a Hoedad crew that had loaned its yurt to Main Camp; she hid under a crafter's table to avoid the Sweep. She and her husband, tree-planter Roger Grahn, had daughter Aster in 1984. Ande served as coordinator for the Country Fair's Main Camp Kitchen from 1986 until 1998, then switched to communications and other Main Camp duties for another dozen years. After she and Roger divorced, Ande helped manage the Pine Street Theater nightclub in Portland. During the 1980s and 1990s, she cooked on tour for the New Old Time Chautauqua as well as for performers, including Eric Clapton, Carlos Santana, and—with "Chez Ray" Sewell—for the Grateful Dead. In the early 1990s, Ande ran the Arcadia Country Inn and the Palindrome for the Flying Karamazov Brothers in Port Townsend, Washington. She next worked for Abundant Life Seed Foundation. After serving on the Port Townsend County Planning Commission, she switched to a career in urban planning. She died at age fifty-nine in November 2010. (Chapters 13, 29, 32, 35, 38)

Rebecca Hanson, aka Rebo Flordigan, was born in Minneapolis in 1955 and graduated from the University of Minnesota with a bachelor's degree in design. In 1980 she met Paul Magid of the Flying Karamazov Brothers at the Minnesota Renaissance Faire, where they both were performing: He was juggling; she was singing with a madrigal group. They got married shortly afterward and divorced in the early 1990s. Rebo, as she was known, helped co-found and manage the New Old Time Chautauqua traveling vaudeville show and also performed for years at the Oregon Country Fair as part of Girls Who Wear Glasses (with Jan Luby) and the Rodz Sisters (with CiCi Wilcoxon). Rebo wrote and performed poignant and funny songs. She died in 1997 of non-Hodgkins lymphoma after recording a CD of her original songs, *Feb-ru-ary*. In the summer of 1997, Rebo Gazebo was built in the Country Fair's Chela Mela Meadow in her honor. (Chapters 1, 8, 24, 29, 39)

Gil Harrison, pottery artist, was born and raised in New York City, but always felt like a country boy out of place. He fell in love with Oregon while working on a fire suppression crew in the mid-1960s in the Umpqua National Forest. After he graduated from Cornell University in 1968 with a bachelor's degree in wildlife conservation, he moved to Eugene and enrolled in ceramics classes at Maude Kerns Art Center. In 1969 he became an original member of the Eugene Crafts Guild and sold pottery at the first Saturday Market. He also sold his pottery at the first Renaissance Faires. He volunteered on the fair's first Info Crew in 1971, served as Quartermaster from 1976 through the early 1980s, and served on the fair board from 1977 to 1981. Gil became known for his futuristic pottery glazed in deep hues of black and brown with jewel-tone highlights. A stage set on *Star Trek: Voyager* in 1997 featured one of his ethereal vases. He was active in the Oregon Potters Association and showed his work in juried fine art festivals and exhibits from coast to coast. He enjoyed playing marimba with the group Shumba. He died in January 2013 at age sixty-eight. (Preface)

Jill Heiman, the fair attorney from 1977 to 1988, consulted as an attorney for many nonprofit organizations and for small, alternative businesses in Eugene. A native of Long Island, New York, she graduated from Case Western University in Cleveland, Ohio, and in 1975, graduated from law school at the University of Oregon. In 1976, she and Gretchen Miller established Heiman & Miller, the first all-women's law practice in Eugene. Jill played a key role as the attorney for the Oregon Country Fair, ushering the organization through the legal hoops to incorporate as a state nonprofit, then as a federal 501(c)(3) organization. She also won a key lawsuit against Lane County that allowed the fair to continue, and she handled the legal work for purchasing the fair site in the early 1980s. Jill married Gerry Mackie in 1982 and they had son Brendan in 1984. In January 1991 Jill died during childbirth at age forty. In her honor, a bridge at the fair was named "Jill's Crossing," and in 1996 fair participants established the Jill Heiman Vision Fund. The fund donated more than $500,000 to nonprofit organizations in the region from 1996 to 2018, and remains an ongoing program of the fair. (Multiple chapters)

Anne Henry moved to Oregon in 1976 after growing up on the East Coast. She sold her handmade clothing at Saturday Market. In 1977, she shared booth 606 on Upper Shady Lane at the Country Fair with two other Saturday Market crafters. The booth, which she dubbed Grandmother's Potlatch, would become her fair home for more than three decades. Anne was born in 1953 in Waterbury, Connecticut, and graduated from Bennington College in Vermont. She earned a master's degree in education from the University of Oregon in Eugene and taught middle school and high school in the Eugene School District. She had a son and a daughter, who grew up at the fair. Anne helped start the *Fair Family News* and served as editor of the *Peach Pit* for many years. She also served on the fair board, the Crafts Committee, and the Planning Committee, and coordinated Feedback. Anne died in 2008 of cancer at age fifty-five. (Chapters 35, 36, 37)

Wally Jones was an early member of the Hoedads tree-planting cooperative, joining in 1975. He served as president of the Hoedads in 1985 and 1986, and worked with them until the cooperative disbanded in 1994. He was born in 1946 in Grants Pass, Oregon, to Ellis and Barbara Jones, and spent most of his life in Eugene. He graduated from Sheldon High School in 1963 and attended the University of Oregon. At the Country Fair, Wally worked Security Crew in the 1970s, later moving on to Construction Crew before joining Recycling Crew in 1986, where he remained until he earned Fair Elder status. Wally was a fair Charter Member. He could often be found around the Blintz booth after hours at the fair, jamming on his guitar with other musicians. He and his ex, Janis Davis, had twin daughters, Darcy and Miel. In the 2000s, Wally logged many hours volunteering for Path Planning Committee. He died of a heart attack in May 2011. In 2013, a new kids' play loop at the fair that Wally had helped plan was named Wally's Way in his honor. (Introduction, Chapter 13)

Ken Kesey, the popular Oregon author of *One Flew Over the Cuckoo's Nest* and *Sometimes a Great Notion*, grew up on a family farm in Pleasant Hill, Oregon, and attended the University of Oregon, where he was a wrestling champion. His legendary place in hippie history sprang from his 1964 cross-country trip with the Merry Pranksters in a wildly painted bus that was documented in Tom Wolfe's *The Electric Kool-Aid Acid Test*. Chief Merry Prankster Kesey participated in the second Oregon Renaissance Faire held in May 1970 as part of the Springfield Creamery booth, owned by his brother and sister-in-law, Chuck and Sue Kesey. Ken remained an active participant in the fair for more than three decades until his death in November 2001 at age sixty-six. (Chapters 1, 2, 11, 13, 32)

Marshall Landman moved from Los Angeles to Eugene in 1972 to work on a farm. That year he attended his first Oregon Renaissance

Faire. In 1974 he was hired to develop a community gardens program for the city of Eugene. In 1975 he organized the first Harvest Fair for the city and helped co-found the Eugene Beekeepers Cooperative, later renamed Queenright Beekeepers Cooperative. In 1976 he joined many others to stage the Leap Year Conference near Portland. Soon Marshall and Brian Livingston created the Cascadian Regional Library (CAREL), a nonprofit that networked alternative groups through publications and conferences. Through CAREL, Marshall participated in 1976 in the Appropriate Technology (APT) area of the Oregon Country Fair. Marshall helped found Community Village in 1977. That same year, he married Mary Cole. They had two daughters, Chelsea and Breana. When CAREL folded, Marshall sold health insurance. He served on the fair's board of directors in 1979-1980 and 1985-1989, and on the Operations Management (OM) team in 1985 and 1987. He volunteered in Main Camp through the 1980s. In the late 1990s, he spearheaded the creation of the Hospitality Crew (aka Crew Services). He died in 2003 at age fifty-four. (Numerous chapters)

Dahinda Meda: See Chapter 34. (Chapters 31, 34, 35, 36, 37)

Robert Painter spent his childhood on a small family farm in Arkansas and graduated from Louisiana State University before moving to Eugene in the late 1960s to attend the University of Oregon. After earning an MBA, Robert became a self-employed carpenter, remodeler, and landlord. Starting in 1972, he restored numerous vintage homes, moving several of them from their original location to the Whiteaker neighborhood. Robert would creatively remodel the houses, using recycled materials and fixtures whenever possible. He relished creating cooperative housing communities and making friends with his tenants. Service and community-building were central to his life. Robert visited the Renaissance Faire in 1973, and in 1974 joined Admissions Crew. A few years later, he transferred to the Garbage Crew (later named Recycling Crew), where he volunteered for almost four decades. Robert served as Recycling coordinator for ten years. He and his life partner, Linda Frohbach, ran his rental business and raised their four children together in Eugene. He died at home with his family by his side in 2016, at age sixty-eight. (Chapter 32)

Faith Petric: See Chapter 12. (Numerous chapters)

Fair Thee Well

Tom Scott grew up in Florida and earned a degree in civil engineering from the University of Florida. He opened a business after college, selling and installing glass doors and windows, which led to building and installing solar water heating systems for customers. He fell in love with Oregon during a vacation trip, and moved to Eugene in the summer of 1977. He plunged into the solar energy field that was in its infancy at the time. Tom opened his first solar business, Energia, in the late 1970s. He taught classes in solar energy at Lane Community College starting in the 1970s and helped establish the school's energy management program. His expertise was also in demand at the Oregon Country Fair, where he shared information about solar energy at Community Village and Energy Park for almost forty years. Beyond the fair, he became a partner in Sage Advance, which manufactured, marketed and installed a passive solar water heater called the Copper Cricket. Later he became a partner in the Energy Service Company, and then helped establish the Green Store, again focusing on solar energy installations. He also was known for his penchant to recycle, repurpose, or reuse everything possible. He died in his sleep in 2018 at age eighty-one. (Chapters 2, 38)

Ray Sewell was born on Oct. 26, 1950, and grew up in an apartment his mother rented above the legendary City of Lights bookstore in San Francisco during the heyday of the Beat Generation. Trained in classic French cooking, "Chez Ray" opened a food booth at the Saturday Market when he moved to Eugene in 1972. Soon afterward, he built the Gritz La Ritz booth at the 1972 Renaissance Faire and a month later, Chez Ray found himself cooking backstage at the Grateful Dead's 1972 Field Trip concert after being advised to "find something to do" by Merry Prankster Page Browning. Ray would cook on tour with the Grateful Dead through the 1970s and early 1980s. Chez Ray also "ran away with the circus" as chef for the New Old Time Chautauqua. Ray met his wife, Dawn, when she applied to work at his first Eugene restaurant, La Primavera. They had a daughter, Jennifer Shine Sewell. Always generous, Ray would help cook free meals for the Whiteaker Thanksgiving Dinner in Eugene from 1982 until November 2018. He died in his sleep a week later at age sixty-eight. (Chapters 13, 30, 32)

Wally Slocum was born in Springfield, Illinois, in 1937. After numerous moves because his dad served in the Air Force, his family settled in Lebanon, Oregon, where he attended high school. Wally graduated from the University of Oregon in 1960 with a bachelor's degree in journalism. He later earned a Master of Library Science and worked at the UO Law Library for more than thirty years. Active in the Oregon Country Fair's Main Camp in the 1970s, Wally coordinated banners for the fair for four decades. He served on the fair board from 1980 to 1991. For three decades, he would coordinate the Teddy Bears' Picnic held in August for volunteer appreciation. After every fair, Wally would walk the site before leaving, meticulously picking up cigarette butts and other debris. At the age of seventy-two, he died the day before the 2009 Teddy Bears' Picnic. (Multiple chapters)

John Stamp was born in 1946 in Washington state, where he grew up. He served in the Vietnam War in 1966-1967 and moved to Oregon in 1968. John enjoyed his first Renaissance Faire in 1972 and in 1974, he helped build the Shenanigans booth (No. 192) out of yew wood for friends and crafters Jim Sahr and Joanne Jones. John worked as a machinist, ran a shake mill, and worked as a timber faller. At the fair, he helped found the Tree Crew, which he coordinated for many years. He studied archaeology and was instrumental in locating key archaeological sites at the fair. University of Oregon archaeologists named a research find in his honor: the Stamp Site. He died in February 2008 at age sixty-one. (Chapters 9, 18)

"Planet Janet" Tarver, was born in Seattle in 1947 and raised in San Francisco. In the late 1960s, she took part in the San Francisco Diggers' free food giveaways and attended many Grateful Dead concerts. Janet sold handmade dresses from a blanket at the Renaissance Faire in 1971 with a communal group from Takilma, Oregon. In the mid-1970s, she missed the fair a few years while attending Oregon State College in Ashland, where she earned a degree in social sciences. In college she met her future husband, Steve Tarver, and they shared their lives for the next thirty-five years. Janet joined Community Village in 1982, representing Active Bethel Citizens in the Neighborhoods and Communities booth. She next joined the Spirit booth, then served for more than two decades on the

Community Village Coordinating Council. She designed the artwork on many of the village T-shirts. Janet also helped establish the fair's Elder group, where longtime fair folks could retire from their posts so younger people could step up. Outside the fair, Janet taught special education. She died in November 2011 at the age of sixty-four. She was survived by her husband, one son, two daughters, and nine grandchildren. (Preface, Chapter 26)

Edd Wemple, one of the original Hoedad tree planters and fair Security Crew volunteers in the 1970s, later advocated against nuclear power and was among dozens who helped found the Emerald People's Utility District. He died of an aneurism at age thirty-six in 1985. By then, he and his wife, Betsy, owned more than 300 acres on Cougar Mountain, southeast of Eugene. Cougar Farm is now home to Betsy's and Edd's son Noah and his family, and it remains a popular gathering place for former members of the Hoedads tree-planting cooperative. (Chapter 13)

Sam Williams began his career as a street-juggling jokester in 1973 in Seattle, where he grew up. In early 1979, Samwise and The Magnificent Mazuba (aka Bliss Kolb) co-founded Laughing Moon Theater. They amicably parted ways in 1980 when Sam joined the Flying Karamazov Brothers. Performing as Smerdyakov Karamazov, Sam juggled with the Karamazovs for nearly two decades. He left the group to care for his cancer-stricken wife, Barbara J. Warren, and then to raise their twin sons, Joshua and Zachary. Experienced with driving the Karamazov tour bus, Sam worked as a bus driver for King County Metro Transit in Seattle. At Christmas he often wore a Santa hat to complement his snow-white hair and beard. Sam died at age sixty-three in 2016 while driving his bus route. In his last few lucid moments, he kept passengers safe by slowing the bus and signaling to riders that he was having a heart attack. His passengers leapt to action and brought the bus to a halt inches from the railing of the Alaskan Way Viaduct. (Chapters 3, 8, 13, 30, 32, 39)

John Winslow, the original Caretaker of the Oregon Country Fair site in the 1980s, also helped established the VegManEC Crew. He served as Traffic Co-Coordinator in the 1980s and on the fair's Board of Directors. Over the years, John volunteered with Security,

Water and Main Camp crews. Beyond the fair, John worked backstage at music performances and festivals. He founded several successful businesses, including Wind Arts Kites and the pioneering herbal product company Om-Chi Herbs, which specialized in Ayurvedic and Chinese herbal formulas. He and his wife, Barbara Neuhaus, had a son, Seth. John died in 2013. (Chapters 31, 32, 34, 35, 36)

Bill Wooten helped coordinate the Renaissance Faires and Oregon Country Fair through most of the 1970s with his then-wife, Cindy Wooten. After their divorce, he moved with his second wife, Eileen, to Florida. They later divorced and at the fair's twentieth anniversary in 1989, he reconnected with Cindy and moved back to Eugene. They lived together a year and organized community events, including Springfield's Filbert Festival. But they soon once again forged separate paths. Bill moved to Seattle for a job in high-tech sales, sharing a house there with their longtime friend, Sandra Bauer. In 1992, the fair board established the Bill Wooten Endowment Fund in his honor. Bill died in Bellville, Washington, in January 1995 at age sixty of complications from a lung infection, with Cynthia Wooten and the rest of his family by his side. (Introduction plus Chapters 2, 5, 9, 32, 38)

Morning Glory Zell-Ravenheart was born Diana Moore in Long Beach, California in 1948. She performed at the 1973 Renaissance Faire as a snake-dancer and in the late 1970s parked her Succubus from time to time at Stillstone commune east of Eugene. She became an American Pagan and Goddess historian, and a priestess in the pagan Church of all Worlds founded by her husband and life partner, Oberon Zell. They popularized the term "polyamory," describing their open marriage. She and her husband in February 2014 published a book about their lives, *The Wizard and the Witch: Seven Decades of Counterculture, Magick & Paganism,* that was co-authored by John C. Sulak. Morning Glory died in May 2014 at age sixty-six. (Chapters 5, 7, 8, 26)

Notes & Sources

The author extends her heartfelt thanks to everyone who generously shared copies of original fair documents and clips of news stories about the Oregon Country Fair. Those resources helped preserve the historical record. While many fair folks offered documents, special thanks go to: Brian and Chris Bauske, Robert DeSpain, Peter Eberhardt for his maps, Chelsea Landman for Marshall Landman's documents, Kathryn Madden, Palmer Parker, and Wally Slocum.

This book could not be written without the help and cooperation of hundreds of interviewees. Their contributions are invaluable to the oral history of the Oregon Country Fair. The vast majority of these interviews were made in person by the author in people's homes, at the fair, and at coffee shops. A few were conducted by telephone. Many interviewees answered follow-up emails. In addition, the History booth taped about three dozen interviews at the 2004 Oregon Country Fair; interviewers included Hal Hartzell, Bonny Ross (Bettman) McCornack, Joshua Binus, Kehn Gibson, and the author.

Interviewees: Barry "Plunkr" Adams, Diane Albino, Nancy Albro, Tom Alexander, Toby Alves, Mark Andrew, Hilary Anthony, Wren Arrington, Artis the Spoonman, Ken Babbs, Ron Bailey, Barbara Bartel, Sandra Bauer, Colleen Bauman, Brian Bauske, Chris "Ruby" Bauske, Michael Beach, Nancy Bebout, Maida Belove, Coco Bender, Dave Bender, Walter Bender, Jim Bitle, Debbie Bloom, Richard Bloom, Robb Bokich, George Braddock, Tomas Brandt, Bill Brewer, Susan Bryan, Cathy Calisch, Heron Calisch-Dolen, Ted Campbell, Galen Carpenter, Rebecca Chace, Ascha Karen (Gellman) Champie, Bud Chase, Jana Chase, Ron Chase, John Cloud, Cynthia Wooten Cohen, Stephen Cole, Michael Connelly, Cathy Coulson-Keegan, Virgil Courtright, Bedo Crafts, Brian Cutean, Joan Gold Cypress, Julie Daniel, Carol DeFazio, Dominic DeFazio, Susanna DeFazio, Jack Delay, Reggie deSoto, Robert DeSpain, Seiza De Tarr, Daniel Dillon, Connie Epstein Dinneen, Diana Dorsett, Mary Doyon, Skeeter Duke, Bob Durnell, Darcy DuRuz, Peter Eberhardt, Sallie Edmunds, Dennis Ekanger, Jain Elliott, Steve Elliott, Caroline Estes, Martha Evans,

Ben Farrell, Christine Frazer, Judy Herbert Fuller, Paul Fuller, Tim Furst, Kathy Ging, Ann Goddard, Steve "Grumpy" Gorham, Ande Grahn, Doug Green, Denny Guehler, Jim Guthrie, Allison Halderman, Ibrahim Hamide, Gil Harrison, Hal Hartzell, Betsy Vaughn (Wemple) Hartzell, Robert Leo Heilman, , Julia Herson, Rick Herson, Percy Hilo,

Paxton Hoag, Conrad Hodson, Jay Hogan, Robyn Hayes (Partridge) (Milich) Ingram, Sue Jakabosky, Jef "JJ" Jaloff, Penny James Long, Cheryl Jones, Wally Jones, Chuck Kesey, Sue Kesey, Lucy (Parker) Kingsley, Robin Richardson (Ulrich) Kinkley, Bliss Kolb, Chelsea Landman, Gary Lenz, Jimbo Lesiak, Mary Cay Liebig, Andy Lifschutz, Barbara Lifschutz, Thomas Lifschutz, Patty Linn, Brian Livingston, Patti Lomont, Sheri Hamilton (Teasdale) Lundell,

Gerry Mackie, Kathryn Madden, Paul Magid, Sam Marshall, "Bob-1" Maynard, Robert "Mouseman" McCarthy, Bonnie Ross (Bettman) McCornack, Diane McWhorter, Dahinda Meda, Michael "Chumleigh" Mielnik, Gretchen Miller, Mark Miller, Randy Minkler, Mose Mosely, Ed Moye, Chris "Ichabod" Murray, Santos Narvaez, Randy Nelson, Jenny Newtson, Tom Noddy, Ron Norton, Paul Otte, Michael Ottenhausen, Palmer Parker, Craig Patterson, George Patterson, Howard Patterson, Faith Petric, Jon Pincus, PJ "Peachez" Pitts, Stephen "Bear" Pitts, Randy Poole, LiBette Porter, Reese Prouty, Joanna Pusey, Steve Raymen, Walter Renfro, Jim Rich, Sara Rich, Ryan Ritchey, Norah Roberts, Bennett Rogers, D.J. Rogers, Lowell Rose, Jerry Rust,

Rhonda Sable, Jim Sahr, Ron Saylor, Norma Sax, Deni Schadegg, Tod Schneider, "Bob-O" Schultz, Zak Schwartz, Anna Scott, Leslie Scott, Tom Scott, Nicki Scully, "Chez Ray" Sewell, Marsha Shadbolt, Mike Shadbolt, Frank Sharpy, Arna Shaw, Sally Sheklow, Jon Silvermoon, Alan Siporin, Wally Slocum, Etienne M. Smith, Janie Smith, Merrill Smith, Sandahbeth Spae, Thaddeus Spae, Eben Sprinsock, John Stamp, Fiora Starchild-Wolf, George Victor Stathakis, Barb Stern, Indi Stern, Dick Stewart, Kim Still, Karen Stingle, Anthony Stoppiello, Victoria Stoppiello, Lyndia Storey, Lotte Streisinger, Tina Stupasky, John Sundquist, Anita Sweeten, Cathy Sutherland, "Planet Janet" Tarver, Joyce Theios, Robert Thompson, Charlie Tilden, Michael "Toes" Tiranoff, Dennis Todd, Charlene Tremayne, Jan Tritten, Jeff Turk, Bill Verner, Mary Wagner, Dana Wajnarowicz, Heather Weihl, Margaret Weller, Peggy Wendel, Ongkar Whalen, Sam Williams, Robin Winfree-Andrew, John Winslow, Steve Wisnovsky, Bill Wright, Moz Wright, James Wyant, Brad Yazzolino, Bob Zagorin.

Introduction

Information about Children's House, which staged the first Oregon Renaissance Faire, came from an interview on July 6, 2005, with Sheri Hamilton (later known by the last names Teasdale and Lundell), who taught there. Sheri said the Children's House curriculum was based on the teaching principles of A.S. Neill, founder of the Summerhill School in southern England and author of *Summerhill: A Radical Approach to Childhood*. Neill advocated the child's right to play. Information about the Summerhill teaching philosophy came from the organization's online site: www.summerhillschool.co.uk

Background information on the movement of free-spirited young people in the late 1960s from the Bay Area and around the country to Oregon was gleaned from books by: Charles Perry, *Haight-Ashbury, a History,* Wenner Books, © 2005; Peter Braunstein and Michael William Doyle, editors, *The American Counterculture of the 1960s and '70s,* Routledge, © 2002; Steven Hager, *Adventures in the Counterculture: From Hip-Hop to High Times,* High Times Books, © 2002; and Tom Wolfe, *The Electric Kool-Aid Acid Test,* Ferrar Straus and Giroux, Inc., © 1968.

Facts and background on peace protests at the University of Oregon and about Oregon's U.S. Sen. Wayne Morse's anti-war stance came from numerous articles in the *Eugene Register-Guard* on April 18, 1965; February 6, 1966; October 19, 1969; November 12, 1969; November 14, 1969; April 24, 1970; April 27, 1970; April 28, 1970; April 29, 1970; April 30, 1970; May 7, 1970; May 9, 1970; May 7, 1971; May 8, 1971; April 23, 1972; May 3, 1972; May 5, 1972; November 18, 1973; and October 12, 1975.

Information on Senator Morse came from: "Wayne Morse Sets Filibuster Record," April 24-25, 1953, Senate Stories, Art and History, www.senate.gov; an interview of George Victor Stathakis by Hal Hartzell at the fair History booth on July 11, 2004; and the National Radio Project *Making Contact,* © October 13, 1999, Transcript: #41-99 "War Stories: The Gulf of Tonkin and Wayne Morse," www.radioproject.org/transcript/1999/9941.html.

Details on the first fair emerged from the *Augur,* April 14, 1970, and June 4, 1970; and Bill Wooten's article "Oregon Country Fair: The Early Years." Interviews with teacher Robyn Hayes Partridge Milich Ingram on August 24, 2004; parent Robin Richardson Ulrich Kinkley on November 22, 2003; and student Alison Halderman on July 7, 2007, added information. Background also came from the author's previous book about the fair: *Fruit of the Sixties: A History of the Oregon Country Fair,* Coincidental Communications, © 2009 Suzi Prozanski.

Interviewees who participated in the Oregon Renaissance Faire held on Crow Road in May 1970 were key sources: Robin Richardson Ulrich Kinkley on November 22, 2003; Jim Bitle on July 20, 2007; Dick Stewart and Gil Harrison on November 3, 2002; Lucy Kingsley on July 17, 2004; Chuck Kesey and Sue Kesey on April 26, 2005; Reggie DeSoto on March 12, 2003; Mary Cay Liebig on July 10, 2003; Jimbo Lesiak on August 12, 2004; Ron Saylor on April 10, 2004; Reese Prouty on March 27, 2007; Hal Hartzell on November 22, 2002, and February 28, 2006; and Brian Livingston on April 1, 2004.

Other facts were gleaned from an email from Lyndia Story on March 31, 2006; emails from Ken Babbs on November 3 and 15, 2005; Bill Wooten's written account, "Oregon Country Fair: The Early Years;"

articles in the *Augur* on April 14, 1970, and June 4, 1970; and the *Eugene Register-Guard* on May 27, 1970; May 29, 1970; May 30, 1970; and May 31, 1970. The chapter directly quotes from the euphoric report of the event printed in the *Augur* on June 4, 1970.

Information about Vortex I came from the Oregon Historical Society's online website on Vortex I https://oregonencyclopedia.org/articles/vortex_i/; the author's interview with Barry "Plunkr" Adams on July 14, 2018; the Woodstock Museum's online interview of Barry "Plunkr" Adams by Nathan "White Buffalo" Koenig, www.youtube.com/watch?v=aineLwDlixc, that was recorded at the Woodstock Museum www.woodstockmuseum.com; Matt Love, *The Far Out Story of Vortex I*, Nestucca Spit Press, © 2004; Garrick Beck, *True Stories: Tales from the Generation of a New World Culture,"* iUniverse, © 2017; and Steven Hager, *Adventures in the Counterculture: From Hip-Hop to High Times*, High Times Books, © 2002.

Details on the third fair held at the site along the Long Tom River were found in the *Augur* on September 24, 1970, October 8, 1970, and October 22, 1971; Wooten, "Oregon Country Fair;" plus interviewees Connie Epstein Dinneen on August 31, 2003; Ron Saylor on April 10, 2004; Cynthia Wooten on October 24, 2003; Reese Prouty on February 26, 2007; Jim Sahr on August 14, 2004; Paxton Hoag on July 11, 2004, and April 12, 2009; Gil Harrison and Dick Stewart on November 3, 2002; Reggie DeSoto on March 12, 2003; and Nancy Albro on February 9, 2003. Background information also came from Sandra Bauer on July 10, 2003, and Lyndia Storey's email on March, 31, 2006.

Confirmation of the Rainbow Family's help with the first Main Camp Kitchen came from an article written by Bill Wooten about fair history for the 1981 *Peach Pit*. Interviews with Reggie DeSoto and Barry "Plunkr" Adams added further information. Details about pulling vehicles out of mud came from interviews with Nancy Albro and Cynthia Wooten, plus Wooten's "Oregon Country Fair." Articles in the *Augur* on May 18, 1970, and November 19, 1970, reported on fair donations.

Chapter 1—1980, Tom Noddy and the W.C. Fields Memorial Stage

Tom Noddy provided most of the information in this chapter at various times, including the author's interview with Tom Noddy on July 9, 2004, and at the Oregon Country Fair Spoken Word program, July 12, 2015; Tom's Facebook posts "facts about me" on November 20, 2014, and December 3, 2014; Facebook post of a photo showing a young Tom and his old car from the 1960s on July 20, 2017; Facebook post about the July 20, 1969, moon landing; and leaving college post on Facebook July 3, 2014; plus February 24, 2016, email reply from Tom Noddy on who helped with the W.C. Fields Memorial Stage.

Further information was gleaned from Tom Noddy's online biography from his website: www.tomnoddy.com; interview with Moz Wright on April 8, 2008; interview with Deni Schadegg on April 22, 2008; the OCF Board of Directors Meeting Minutes of 1980; the New Age Old Time Chautauqua 1984 participants list, hand-calligraphed by Rebecca "Rebo" Hanson; and two articles in the *Register-Guard:* "Fair to Showcase Energy Ideas," published July 3, 1980; and "Curry, Quilts, Flutist All Part of Country Fair," by Ron Bellamy, published July 12, 1980.

Chapter 2—1981, Oregon Energy Horizons aka Energy Park

The Oregon Country Fair Board of Directors Meeting Minutes note that the Oregon Energy Horizons Committee members in 1981 included Palmer Parker, Sandra Bauer, Jon Pincus, and Robert DeSpain. Kathy Ging, who worked for Sunergi in Ashland, said in her interview on August 10, 2006, that the fair committee asked her to head the project, but she was too busy coordinating the Oregon State Fair's alternative energy area that summer. Kathy recommended Sallie Edmunds, whom she knew through the Alternative Technology booth in Community Village, to fill the slot. Kathy prepared a three-page handout for Oregon Energy Horizons listing organizations and publications that offered information on solar energy, wind energy, energy conservation, recycling, ride-sharing, and more.

Most of the information on Energy Park came from a group interview with key members of Energy Park on July 12, 2017: Sue Jakabosky, Nancy Bebout, Tom Scott, "Bob-O" Schultz, "Bob-1" Maynard, Anna Scott, and George Patterson; plus interviews with Anthony and Victoria Stoppiello on December 12, 2007; Sallie Edmunds on August 15, 2005; Joyce Theios on November 14, 2006; Craig Patterson on July 10, 2004; and Kathy Ging on August 10, 2006.

More information was gleaned from the 1976 *APT Guide* at the Oregon Country Fair; "Country Fair Ready to Open," the *Register-Guard,* June 24, 1976; "Country Fair Adds Booths on Energy Use," the *Register-Guard,* July 7, 1981; "Country Fair Begins Run near Elmira," the *Register-Guard,* July 10, 1981; Palmer Parker's "OCF Geosite Name" document; the 1981 and 1982 issues of the OCF *Peach Pit*; the 1981 Oregon Energy Horizons handout; "Energizing the Fair," *Willamette Valley Observer,* July 2, 1981; "Peach Power Solar Project," *Fair Family News,* August 2007; and OCF Board of Directors Meeting Minutes of April 1981. Some facts about Bob-O Schultz came from his former Electron Connection home page www.electronconnection.com. Net metering information came from the June 2005 *Net Metering Fact Sheet* produced by the Oregon Department of Energy.

Chapter 3—1981, The Flying Karamazov Brothers

Interviews for this chapter came from Howard Patterson on August 15, 2005; Tim Furst in November 2015; Randy Nelson on November 28, 2005; Sam Williams on September 7, 2005; Michael Mielnik on January 24, 2009; Peggy Wendel, Bliss Kolb, and Cathy Sutherland on September 6, 2008; Jana and Bud Chase on September 6, 2015, and May 6, 2016; and Tom Noddy at OCF Spoken Word, July 12, 2015.

Information also emerged from interviews of Seiza de Tarr and Peggy Wendel, by Hal Hartzell on July 10, 2004; Paul Magid's Spoken Word talk at the Oregon Country Fair, July 10, 2010; Tom Noddy's report on Chautauqua in *Fair Family News*, December 2011; an email from Howard Patterson on June 21, 2018; Howard Patterson's post in Facebook on February 16, 2009, remarking on Ann Goddard's photo of Thaddeus Spae's Volkswagen in front of Alligator Palace; the Oregon Country Fair Board of Directors Meeting Minutes from July 1980; and the 1982 Old Time New Age Chautauqua flyer, hand-calligraphed by Rebecca "Rebo" Hanson.

Facts about Chumleigh's "around-the-world tour" came largely from Howard Patterson's account of Flying Karamazov history posted in 2005 and 2010 on the Flying Karamazov Brothers website, www.fkb.com. Details of the Flying Karamazov Brothers' performance schedules and awards also came from the troupe's website.

Background information arose from Don Bishoff's column, "Woodland Burlesque," the *Register-Guard*, July 11, 1986; and David Arnold, "Catch as Catch Can," the *Register-Guard*, July 13, 1980.

Grateful Dead information came from numerous online sources, including the Grateful Dead archives: https://archive.org/details/gd1979-12-31.sonyecm-walker.walker-scotton-miller.88768.flac16; www.dead.net/show/december-31-1979; www.gdao.org/items/show/275969; and www.dead.net/show/march-28-1981.

Facts about the schedule of the Flying Karamazov Brothers were gleaned from several websites, including www.abouttheartists.com/artists/44289-flying-karamazov-brothers; the Goodman Theatre site, www.goodmantheatre.org; the Arena Theatre site, www.arenastage.org; *People Magazine* online , November 3, 1980, www.imdb.com/title/tt0344479/?ref_=nmbio_mbio.

Information about Oregon Event Enterprises came from email interviews of Robert Thompson on March 1, 2017, and November 23, 2018.

NOTES & SOURCES

Chapter 4—1981, Starflower and Community Village

Poems reprinted with permission from Sally Sheklow's *Hayfield's Collection of Starflower Ditties*, © 1977-1984 Sally Sheklow.

Interviews with Sally Sheklow in April 2014; Jain Elliott on July 7, 2004; and Christine Frazer on July 29, 2007, provided information for this chapter. Clarifying emails came from Sally on May 28, 2018, and June 25, 2018; from Jain on May 28, 2018, and June 25, 2018; and from Christine on June 2, 2018.

Other information was derived from the Community Village Coordinating Council Meeting Minutes on April 15, 1981. The 1981 Information Crew "Database Directory" provided names of groups new to Community Village in 1981.

Further information on Starflower came from the exhibition catalogue for *Tie Dye & Tofu: How Mainstream Eugene Became a Counterculture Haven*," curator Mary Dole, Lane County History Museum, pp.65-66, and from Brian Livingston, "Starflower: Working Together," *Willamette Valley Observer*, circa 1975, from the Lane County History Museum collection.

Participation of Wymprov! was confirmed in the 2001 *Peach Pit*. Other facts came from Sally Sheklow's web page, www.tributewebdesign.com/sally/whos-sally.html; and the Wymprov! page on Facebook: www.facebook.com/pg/WYMPROV.

Chapter 5— 1981, A Wild Fair
1981 Oregon Country Fair Coordinators
(compiled from the 1981 Oregon Country Fair Board of Directors Meeting Minutes)
Energy Horizons: Sallie Edmunds
Entertainment: Moz Wright
Fire Marshall: Frank Sharpy
Food Booths: Toby Alves
Information: Larry Moran, Jack Delay
Publicity: Palmer Parker
Quartermaster: Gil Harrison
Registration: Amy Daycon
Main Camp: Nancy Albro
Medical: Lucy (Kingsley) Parker
Traffic: Santos Narvaez

Tom Noddy offered many delightful details of the pie prank the vaudevillians played at the uniting ceremony of Deni Schadegg and Moz Wright in July 1980. Here is Tom's long version sent by email on August 30, 2018:

Surprise at Moz & Deni's Uniting Ceremony
By Tom Noddy

It was nice to be in the company of so many vaudevillians during the "off-season." No Country Fair and no show planned, just a gathering in a park in Eugene for Moz and Deni's wedding. I'm sure that I looked my usual shabby chic but overall, people were dressed beautifully. Award-winning juggler Roberto Morganti was there in a tall and wide top hat and his wasn't the only one. The women, of course, were gorgeous—as hippie girls and women often are.

Deni made her own wedding dress. Her hair was braided into a frame around her face. She was truly a beautiful bride. Deni also sewed the outfit that Moz wore. I don't remember his shirt or jacket, but I remember the pants he wore. We called them "Stupid Pants"—the sort worn on stage by the Flying Karamazov Brothers—wide and baggy wraparound pants. Made from a single piece of sewn cloth that wraps around the waist, the broad cloth at the legs are bundled together and tied in a big knot at each leg. The ones Moz wore weren't the normal black cotton ones but made of a fancy material with liner.

It was especially nice to see Michael Mielnik (aka Reverend Chumleigh) and Tim Furst (aka Fyodor Karamazov) talking together. There had been bad blood between Chumleigh and the Karamazovs and their onstage joke rivalry had turned dark in recent years.

The ceremony took place; it was sweet. Then there was a reception in that same park. Deni's parents came out from Minnesota. They looked a bit like fish-out-of-water at first, but they took it all in with such sweet spirit that they quickly fit right in.

There was food and music and then at some point Reverend Chumleigh announced that, in honor of this wedding, he was going to present his version of a notorious old vaudeville piece, The Dance of the Seven Veils.

Deni and Moz sat on one of the park picnic benches with wide smiles while Chumleigh held a towel in front of the lower half of his face and held everyone's attention while he leapt and turned and hummed the tune. Deni and everyone else was surprised when Chumleigh jumped behind her and pulled the towel around her shoulders, covering her dress while Fyodor Karamazov stepped forward with one of those shaving cream pies.

Fyodor mooshed the pie, ever so gently, into the side of Deni's face. His care and Chumleigh's towel ensured that not a single blob of shaving cream fell onto Deni's dress or got into her beautifully braided hair.

The towel was soon held out to allow her to clean her face. The laughs hadn't died down and Moz was laughing as much as anyone. But it suddenly dawned on Moz what the next logical step would be after the pieing of the bride. He took off, hoping to outrun the inevitable pieing of the groom.

I and others leapt up to hold him. When we grabbed him, the ties holding up the Stupid Pants on one side broke! Suddenly the groom's pants were coming undone in front of the wedding party and in front of her parents! He pleaded with those of us holding him to let him get a pin and fix it. He promised to take his pie like a vaudevillian.

Someone came up with the pin and we brought Moz back to his place, in front of Deni and everyone. Just in case, I still held his arm from one side and Chumleigh held him on the other side. Tim smiled, faced Moz, took his second pie and … went for Chumleigh!

It was a great move! Chumleigh isn't often (ever?) pied, but he was quick! He saw it coming and he ducked. The pie went to the grass leaving only a slight streak of cream in Chumleigh's hair. He came up smiling and congratulating Tim on the good idea. They shook hands. But then Moz noticed the pie on the grass. He picked it up and everyone backed away in one quick rush. "The pie! …The pie! …The groom has the pie!"

Moz, relishing the moment, smiled and rose to the occasion. Like many of us (ahem) he could be long winded and now he had everyone's attention. He held the pie at waist height and raised his voice to be heard by all. "I notice that many people are very reluctant …" and at that moment a guy came out of the crowd to push Moz's hand up, delivering the pie into Moz's own face!

Like a script from one of those early pie fight movies where they keep looking for novel new ways to deliver the mess, this was the punchline that the event needed. Everyone fell apart in hilarity. Later, as I was walking past the table where Deni's parents sat, I heard her father asking one of the vaudevillians "So, just how old is this tradition of pieing the bride?"

Confirmation of the participation of the Wildlife Safari cheetah at the 1981 Oregon Country Fair came from the OCF Board of Directors Meeting Minutes of June 28, 1981, and the fair's advertising in the *Willamette Valley Observer* on July 9, 1981.

OCF Board of Directors Meeting Minutes from May 13, 1981, detail Jill Heiman's report on the Lane County Outdoor Assembly ordinance hearing and the fair's settlement offer.

Interviewees contributing to this chapter include Barbara Stern on June 27, 2005; Chris Bauske on July 11, 2004; Brian Bauske on June 26, 2013; Reese Prouty on February 26, 2007; Howard Patterson, on August 15, 2005; Randy Nelson on November 28, 2005; Eben Sprinsock on September 25, 2005; Toes Tiranoff on April 30, 2007; Michael Beach on August 16, 2005; John Cloud on July 12, 2011; and John Cloud talking to Hal Hartzell in the OCF History booth on July 9, 2004.

Other information came from Reese Prouty's 1981 photos of Main Camp and the Country Fair; Paul Magid's Spoken Word talk at the July 10, 2010, Oregon Country Fair; email from Tom Noddy on August 29, 2018; email from Robert DeSpain on April 30, 2015; email from Michael Mielnik on November 19, 2003; Facebook post on February 18, 2009, by Tom Noddy on Ann Goddard's photo of a unicorn goat; Tom Noddy's private message to the author on Facebook on February 24, 2016; Mike Martin's comments on the 1981 Midnight Show photo posted on Facebook on March 10, 2017; and Howard Patterson's comments about the 1981 Wildlife Safari visit posted on Facebook on March 10, 2017.

The 1981 OCF *Peach Pit* provided details for this chapter, as did the fair's Board of Directors Meeting Minutes from 1981 and the 1981 Information Crew "Database Directory." Weather details came from the *Register-Guard,* July 10-13, 1981. The name of the fair's marching band that year—Fighting Instruments of Karma Marching Band (without the Chamber/Orchestra part)—was verified by the 1981 New Age Old Time Chautauqua tour poster calligraphed by Rebecca "Rebo" Hanson.

More information about Laurie Marker was gleaned from a news article by Mark Baker, "Out of Africa," the *Register-Guard,* February 3, 2008.

Oberon Zell-Ravenhart described how he created the unicorns in a video interview by Rev. Don Lewis in "Living the Wiccan Life" published by Magick TV on January 15, 2009, on YouTube (www.youtube.com/watch?v=qVQ7BOD86j). Background, quotes and other information about Oberon/Otter and Morning Glory Zell also came from George Knowles' biography online, www.controverscial.com; Morning Glory's obituary by Antonia Blumbert, "Morning Glory Zell-Ravenheart Dead: Pioneering Pagan, Polyamory Leader Dies at 66," *Huffington Post,* July 14, 2014; her obituary in the *Telegraph* in July 21, 2014, which also included a link to the 2008 film of Oberon and Morning Glory: www.telegraph.co.uk/news/obituaries/10980913/Morning-Glory-Zell-Ravenheart-obituary.html; Oberon's comments on the 1981 Midnight Show posted on Facebook on September 5, 2011; and the Church of All Worlds website, http://caw.org.

Chapter 6—1981, Anita Sweeten and Phoenix Rising

Phoenix Rising members who have passed on: Bruce Brooks, Deon and Lynn Kassler, Dan Allen, Nancy Feldman, Henry Howe, Janina Kassler. (List from Larry Caldwell's account of Phoenix Rising history, "The Magic Begins.")

◻ ◘ ◉

Information in this chapter came mostly from an interview with Anita Sweeten at the Oregon Country Fair on July 11, 2007, and an interview with Paxton Hoag at the fair on July 11, 2004. Other details came from Larry Caldwell's "The Magic Begins," unknown publishing date; Larry's post in 2016 on the Unofficial OCF Facebook page about Jim Larsen and Peach Carts; and an email from Shelly Devine, OCF Caretaker, on February 22, 2018, describing the fabric of the Rabbit Hole covering.

Chapter 7—1981, A Fair Honeymoon for Bud and Jana Chase

Bud and Jana Chase provided most of the information for this chapter in interviews on November 6, 2015, and May 6, 2016; and in an email from Jana on June 11, 2018.

Thanks to Jana and Bud for sharing the book: *Greenfield Ranch 25th Anniversary 1972-1997: A Celebration of a Quarter Century of Living in Community,* compiled and edited by Kirsten Ellen Johnsen, Karen Lease Hensley, Zephyr Bergera, Susan Pepperwood, Dale Glaser, Marylyn Motherbear Scott, Yoli Rose, Yvonne Kramer, © 1997 by The Greenfield Ranch Association. The book verified it had been a cattle ranch, not a sheep ranch as Jana had said. It also contained details about Morning Glory and Oberon's time at the ranch and their work with Lancelot the Living Unicorn.

Other information about Morning Glory and Oberon in the 1970s and 1980s came from the Church of All Words website: caw.org. Information about Claude Steiner emerged from his website ww.claudesteiner.com.

Chapter 8—1981, The Old Time New Age Chautauqua aka The New Old Time Chautauqua

Interviewees contributing to this chapter include Jana and Bud Chase on May 6, 2016; Howard Patterson on August 15, 2005; Sam Williams on September 7, 2005; Toes Tiranoff on April 30, 2007; Dave Bender and Darcy DuRuz on November 1, 2006; Artis the Spoonman on July 7, 2004; Chez Ray Sewell on July 3, 2006; and Tom Noddy at OCF Spoken Word on July 12, 2015. Paul Magid also discussed the first New Age Old Time Chautauqua at his OCF Spoken Word program on July 10, 2010.

Jana Chase's email from June 11, 2018, detailed the lyrics to Diana Leishman's "Travelin' Song." Jana's copy of the 1981 Chautauqua poster caligraphed by Rebecca "Rebo" Hanson confirmed some details of the trip.

Information gleaned from websites also added to this story, including the Vancouver Folk Musical Festival archives http://thefestival.bc.ca/festival-archives/1981-arists/, and Patch Adams' information on the Gesundheit Collective www.patchadams.org/gesundheit/timeline/.

Further information emerged from postings on Facebook, including posts about that first Chautauqua on September 5, 2011, made by Tom Noddy, Oberon Zell, Howard Patterson, Tod Schneider, Bud Chase, Jan Luby, and Sam Williams. Tom Noddy also answered a private message question on Facebook on February 24, 2016.

Chapter 9—1982, Jill Heiman and Freedom of Assembly

Information for this chapter came from the author's interviews with Gerry Mackie, Hal Hartzell, and Betsy Vaughn Wemple Hartzell at Cougar Mountain on August 7, 2004; with Cynthia Wooten on March 12, 2008; with Sandra Bauer and Mary Cay Liebig on July 10, 2003; with Gretchen Miller in 2008; with Jack Delay on January 24, 2009; and with Ron Chase on March 18, 2004. Other interviews of Gerry Mackie by Hal Hartzell at the Oregon Country Fair History booth on July 9, 2004; and of Bonnie (Ross) Bettman (now McCornack) by Gerry Mackie at the fair's History booth on July 10, 2004, also provided quotes and information.

Facts about the fair's legal incorporation and its lawsuit filed against Lane County were found in the *Oregon Country Fair Articles of Incorporation* filed with the state of Oregon on May 31, 1977; the January 1982 and May 1982 newsletters to OCF members (from Brian Bauske's collection); and the Lane County Board of Commissioners Meeting Minutes of June 13, 1979, June 9 and 10, 1980, June 25, 1980, and July 7, 1980; the Oregon Country Fair Board of Directors Meeting Minutes and the Community Village Coordinating Council Meeting Minutes spanning 1980 to 1981; and notes documenting the terms of sale handwritten by Indi Stern on her copy of the October 18, 1981, OCF Board of Directors Meeting Minutes.

More information emerged from the two Lane County waivers allowing the Oregon Country Fair to take place signed on July 15, 1980, and July 2, 1981; and documents from the signed settlement agreement in U.S. District Court for the District of Oregon Case No. 80-6162-E filed on February 12, 1982: The Oregon Country Fair, an Oregon nonprofit corporation vs. Lane County, Oregon; Otto t'Hooft, Vance Freeman, Gerald Rust Jr., Harold Rutherford, and Archie Weinstein as the Board of County Commissioners of Lane County; Harold Rutherford and Archie Weinstein, individually; and David Burks in his capacity as

NOTES & SOURCES

Director of Public Safety of Lane County, Oregon.

Further information emerged from the *APT* newsletter of June 1977; the *McKenzie River Gathering 1976-1978 Two Year Report; McKenzie River Gathering Foundation 10 Years of Funding Social Change,* 1976-1986; Peter Bergel's editorial, "So Long, Charles Gray," the *Peaceworker,* the newsletter for Oregon PeaceWorks, September 2006; Richard Moeschl, "The McKenzie River Gathering Foundation Turns 30," *Sentient Times,* October/November 2006; and the website of the McKenzie River Gathering Foundation, www.mrgfoundation.org.

Chapter 10—1982, Ibrahim Hamide

The author's interview with Ibrahim Hamide at Café Soriah on April 23, 2018, provided the bulk of the information for this chapter. Other facts were gleaned from Ib's talk on International Human Rights Day on December 5, 2012, in Eugene; Cheryl Rade, "A Little Taste of Home: Restaurateur Sells his Famous Middle Eastern Dips," the *Register-Guard,* January 11, 2012; William Kennedy, "Food Ambassador: Chef Ibrahim Hamide Recalls Nearly 50 Years in Eugene," "Chow" section of *Eugene Weekly,* April 6, 2017; TV station KVAL's report on May 5, 2017, kval.com/features/tasty-tuesday/tasty-tuesday-cafe-soriah-05-05-2017; *Human Rights Retrospective Project,* published by the City of Eugene in November 2011; and from the website for the monthly post-9-11 Interfaith Services in Eugene, www.internationalpeacegroup.com/about/us/.

Chapter 11—1982, Celebration

An article titled "Oregon Country Fair Opens Friday," the *Register-Guard,* July 8, 1982; weather forecasts published in the *Register Guard* on July 10, 11, 12, and 13, 1982; and an article by Robert W. Stewart, "Annual Gathering Draws an Outpouring of Hippies," *Los Angeles Times,* July 15, 1982, yielded information for this chapter, along with the 1982 Oregon Country Fair *Peach Pit* and the OCF Board of Directors Meeting Minutes of 1982.

Further information emerged from interviews with Karen Stingle on March 2, 2006, and March 9, 2006; Julie Daniel on August 17, 2005; Walter Renfro on January 24, 2006; Tim Furst on October 13, 2003; Sandra Bauer and Mary Cay Liebig on July 10, 2003; Moz Wright on April 8, 2008; Norah Roberts on June 2, 2003; and Jon Silvermoon on October 19, 2005. The exact wording of the Circus Stage signage came from a photo of the signs taken by Robert Thompson in 1982.

The Spoken Word biography of Dr. Atomic's Medicine Show in the 2014 OCF *Peach Pit* verified that the show began in 1974 "as they toured every town in Oregon where a nuclear power plant was proposed." Emails from Peter Bergel on December 29 and 31, 2018, added quotes and clarifications. Issues of the *Peach Pit* from 1982 to 2018 detailed how frequently the act came to the fair. Other facts on the Medicine Show were gleaned from the website of the McKenzie River Foundation, www.mrgfoundation.org. Information about the Trojan Nuclear Power Plant came from the Oregon Encyclopedia, https://oregonencyclopedia.org/articles/trojan_nuclear_power_plant/.

Chapter 12—1982, Folksinger Faith Petric

An earlier version of the chapter appeared in the August 2009 issue of *Fair Family News* in the Fair Luminaries series, "Faith Embraces a Life of Music and Activism," by the author. That was Faith's last year to perform at the Oregon Country Fair.

This chapter is largely based on the author's interview with Faith Petric on October 26, 2003, in her beautiful home in San Francisco. Other details were gleaned from the website for the San Francisco Folk Music Club, www.sffmc.org; from Faith Petric's now-defunct website; from Tom Noddy's post about Faith's death on Facebook on October 26, 2013; and from news articles: Rona Marech, "Profile: Faith Petric," *San Francisco Chronicle*, September 30, 2002; Meredith May, "Faith Petric: Bay Area Folk's Enduring Voice," *San Francisco Chronicle*, September 28, 2010; "Faith Petric Passes at 98," *Singout! Magazine*, October 25, 2013.

Chapter 13—1982, The Second Decadenal Field Trip

With special thanks to Peter Eberhardt for sharing the detailed planning maps he drew for the 1982 Dead Show for show producers Sue and Chuck Kesey of the Springfield Creamery, and for stage manager David Paul Black.

Interviews contributing to this chapter include those from: Ron Chase on April 15, 2004; Sandra Bauer on July 10, 2003; Sue and Chuck Kesey on April 26, 2005; Mary Wagner on May 27, 2003; Ray Sewell on July 3, 2006; Walter Renfro on January 24, 2006; John Sundquist on February 12, 2003; Ron Saylor on April 10, 2004; Peter Eberhardt on June 5, 2017; Reggie DeSoto on March 12, 2004; and Hilary Anthony on May 5, 2005.

Oregon Country Fair Board of Directors Meeting Minutes from 1981 and 1982 provided more details, as did the 1982 Field Trip Poster; an article on the concert published in the *Register-Guard* on August 29, 1982; and a film of the 1982 Field Trip posted on YouTube by Charles Mullen on January 8, 2015: www.youtube.com/watch?v=_cBjhxmkjcQ&feature=youtu.be&t=1619.

Other details emerged from discussions on Facebook posts about the Field Trip on April 12, 2010, by Ande Grahn; on March 3, 2012, by Norma Sax; on April 28, 2016, from Anita Sweeten, Nancy Ledivow, Ann Goddard, Sam Williams, Mary Barton, Dick Stewart, and Yvonne Rose;

and on May 2010 and May 4, 2016, from Ben Ferrell, Jana Chase, and Yvonne Rose.

Information on the Running Fence came from Christo Jeanne Claude's website, http://christojeanneclaude.net/projects/running-fence, and from the Wikipedia listing of the Running Fence. The set list was found on the Grateful Dead's website, www.dead.net/show/august-28-1982.

Chapter 14—1983, Robert DeSpain

A host of interviewees contributed to this chapter, including: Nancy Albro, Mary Cay Liebig, and Connie Epstein Dineen on August 31, 2003; Sallie Edmunds on August 15, 2005; Patti Lomont on February 13, 2004; Patti Lomont and Robert Thompson on April 7, 2004; Frank Sharpy on July 26, 2010; Moz Wright on April 8, 2008; Robert DeSpain on April 13, 2004; Sue and Chuck Kesey on April 26, 2005; Ron Chase on April 15, 2004; Frank Sharpy on July 2, 2010; Sandra Bauer on July 10, 2003; and Deni Schadegg on April 22, 2008.

Further information in this chapter emerged out of an OCF document titled "More on the Retreat, April 2-3, 1983;" the OCF Board of Directors Meeting Minutes from 1980 to 1983; Oregon State Parks' website on the Old Ranch at Silver Falls, www.oregonstateparks.com; Zak Schwartz's Human Intervention training recorded at the fair site on June 27, 2004; and the 1987 *OCF Crisis Intervention Training Manual*.

Chapter 15—1983, The Rain Fair

Interviews providing information in this chapter included: Robert DeSpain on April 13, 2004; Chris Bauske on July 11, 2004; Sue and Chuck Kesey on April 26, 2005; Tom Noddy on July 9, 2004; Paxton Hoag on July 11, 2004; Ron Chase on April 15, 2004; Ed Moye and Kathryn Madden on May 13, 2006; Sandra Bauer on July 10, 2003; Cheryl Jones on August 14, 2004; and Alan Siporin on July 10, 2004.

News sources included "Oregon Country Fair 1983," *What's Happening* weekly newspaper in Eugene, July 7-20, 1983; "Gates Swing Open Friday for 15th Country Fair," the *Register-Guard*, July 7, 1983; and "Fair Radiates Its Own Sunshine," the *Register-Guard*, July 9, 1983.

Tom Noddy's email in April 2009 detailed his 1983 appearance on *The Tonight Show Starring Johnny Carson*. Further information came from Tom Noddy's post on Facebook on September 30, 2016, where he shared a YouTube video of his appearance on *The Tonight Show*, www.youtube.com/watch?v=pDhryITm7hc; and Tom's Facebook post on May 25, 2012.

The OCF 1983 *Peach Pit* provided background information and facts about the 1983 fair. More information was gleaned from John Beaufort's article, "Karamazov Brothers: Flying Objects and Flying

Gags," *Christian Science Monitor*, May 18, 1983, www.csmonitor.com/1983/0518/051800.html.

Chapter 16—1983, Gypsy Caravan Stage

Information in this chapter emerged from interviews with Jay Hogan on August 21, 2010; Moz Wright on April 8, 2008; Michael Beach on August 16, 2005; Sam Marshall on September 27, 2008; Penny James Long on January 2, 2010; and Joanna Pusey on January 5, 2010. More details came from Jay Hogan's emails on August 8 and 9, 2010; and Michael Beach's email in December 2009.

Background facts on the Brothers of the Baladi came from the group's website, www.baladi.com; and from www.ishimmy.com, which republished an article by Oberon, "Dancer to Musician with Michael Beach," *The Belly Dancer Magazine*, February 21, 2004.

A letter handwritten on February 20, 1987, by Leo de Flambeaux to Marge Wise, then Entertainment coordinator at the Oregon Country Fair, gave key insights into Leo's fair history. Issues of the OCF *Peach Pit* for 1981, 1982, and 1983 also added details.

Chapter 17—1983, Divine Balance Fruit Salad

The majority of the information in this chapter came from an interview with Paul and Judy Fuller on March 14, 2018, from emails from Judy Fuller on May 3, 2018, and Paul Fuller on May 7, 2018; and from the Organically Grown Company's website, www.organicgrown.com.

The author's interview with Brian Livingston on April 1, 2004, added more details, as did news reports in the *Willamette Valley Observer* on June 30, 1978, and July 14, 1978; an editorial titled "Drainbows at the Fair? Country Fair Shouldn't Take the Rap," the *Register-Guard*, July 19, 1997; and the book by Steven Hager, *Adventures in the Counterculture: From Hip-Hop to High Times*, High Times Books, © 2002.

Chapter 18—1984, Archaeology Rocks

Deep gratitude to Dr. Tom Connolly, archaeologist with the University of Oregon Museum of Natural History, for reviewing this chapter for accuracy and for providing the following citations on the archaeological study sites:

The two sites containing earthen ovens and significant cultural resources found in 1980 in the original proposal right-of-way for Highway 126 were 35LA439 (the Long Tom site) and 35LA440 (the RP2 site).

In the fall of 1984, the two sites tested on Oregon Country Fair property were 35LA658 (the Stamp site) and 35LA758 (Country Fair #1 site). The Stamp site was found to be significant; the Country Fair #1 site was not.

In the spring of 1985, more locations pointed out by fair volunteers were evaluated. Of those, 35LA760 (Country Fair #4 site) and 35LA420 (the Chalker site) were tested and found to be significant. Further testing at site 35LA439 (the Long Tom site) expanded this site's boundaries. In early 1986 site 35LA759 (the East Park site) was tested and found to be significant.

In the fall of 1986 before the new highway was constructed, Drs. Brian O'Neill and Tom Connolly led two large-scale archaeological excavations at sites 35LA420 (the Chalker site) and 35LA439 (the Long Tom site). These were "data recovery" excavations at these two significant sites designed as mitigation for the destructive impacts of highway construction.

Two master's theses resulted from the State Historic Preservation Office grant: one by Dorothy "Dolly" Freidel who described the landform history and identified a series of deposition and erosion events throughout the last ca. 12,000 years in which the archaeological materials were found; the other was by Lynn Peterson, who described the archaeological findings. There was also a report completed in 1989 for SHPO to satisfy the grant obligations by Freidel, Peterson, McDowell, and Connolly.

◘ ◘ ◙

Special thanks to Kathryn Madden for sharing John Stamp's 1990 archaeology report to the Oregon Country Fair Board of Directors, to Peter Eberhardt for sharing the 1983 Planning Map he drew for the OCF board showing the two proposed highway routes, and also to Robert DeSpain for sharing the following key documents:

The letter from the Oregon Country Fair to the state Highway Division dated December 28, 1982; the *Work Session & Public Hearing Agenda* for the Lane County Planning Commission on December 11, 1984; David Cole's report to the fair's board of directors at the December 11, 1984, meeting; "Delay Expected in Bid for Bypass," the *Register-Guard*, August 31,1984; "Country Fair Begins Run near Elmira," the *Register-Guard*, July 10, 1981; the Meeting Minutes of the Lane County Planning Commission on January 15, 1985; the reply filed by the Oregon Country Fair on January 15, 1985, over archaeological resources found on highway routes and goal; the memo dated January 22, 1985, from Jim Mann, Senior Planner to Lane County Planning Commission Members on Summary of Goal 5 compliance; and copies of the *Goal 5 Compliance Process* (per OAR Ch. 660, Division 16), specifically—Goal 5: Open spaces, Scenic and Historical Areas and Natural Resources; Goal 5: 16.213(1) Natural Resource Zone & Rural Comprehension Plan; and Goal 5: 16.233(5) Historic Structures of Sites Combing Zone & Rural Comprehension Plan.

Interviews contributing to this chapter include those with Jon

Silvermoon on October 19, 2005; John Stamp on June 24, 2006; Robert DeSpain on April 13, 2004; Peter Eberhardt on June 6, 2017; and the fair's Archaeology Crew—Virgil Courtright, Bennett Rogers, Ryan Ritchey, D.J. Rogers, Randy Poole, and Ron Norton—on August 14, 2004.

Two talks at public meetings also contributed information and insight: One given on March 28, 2017, by David Turner and Dr. Tom Connolly on the history of the Long Tom River at the Long Tom Watershed meeting in Veneta, Oregon; and another by Dr. Connolly on the Kalapuyan peoples given on January 30, 2018, at Ninkasi in Eugene and hosted by the University of Oregon Museum of Natural History and the Lane County History Museum. Dr. Connolly's email of June 11, 2018, offered fact-checks, background resources, and further information on the archaeological digs.

Further information emerged from the OCF Board of Directors Meeting Minutes from 1982 to 1986, Robert DeSpain's notes for his Highway Report at the OCF board meeting on December 8, 1984; the author's notes taken on May 23, 2012, on the exhibits at the University of Oregon Museum of Natural History that detailed the tools and the lifestyles of Oregon's indigenous tribes; David Turner, *Along the Long Tom River: Observations from the Past and Present,* Paw Print Press, © 2017, chapters one through three; Melvin C. Aikens, Thomas J. Connolly, and Dennis L. Jenkins, *Oregon Archaeology,* Oregon State University Press, © 2011; Richard D. Cheatham, *Late Archaic Settlement Pattern in the Long Tom Sub-Basin, Upper Willamette Valley, Oregon,* University of Oregon Anthropological Papers 39, © 1988.

Online sources included David G. Lewis, "Kalapuyan Tribal History," ndnhistoryresearch.com, blog, accessed in 2018; the Salem Public Library's history website on Native American Oregonians, www.salemhistory.net/people/native_americans.htm; and the *Oregon Encyclopedia* entry on Kalapuyan peoples written by Henry Zenk, author of *Kalapuyans,* Wayne Suttles, ed., Handbook of North American Indians, Vol. 7: Northwest Coast, 547-553, Washington, D.C.: Smithsonian Institution, 1990, www.oregonencyclopedia.org/entry/view/kalapuyan_peoples/.

Further thanks go to Dr. Tom Connolly for sharing the following list of published papers detailing the findings at the archaeological digs made in the Veneta area at the time of the rerouting of Highway 126:

Thomas J. Connolly, "Noti-Veneta Borrow Area Monitoring," letter report on file at the Oregon State Historic Preservation Office, Salem, 1986.

Thomas J. Connolly and Patricia F. McDowell, "The Oregon Country Fair/City of Veneta Archaeological Project," research proposal submitted to the Oregon State Historic Preservation Office, Salem, 1987.

Dorothy E. Freidel, "Alluvial Stratigraphy in Relation to Archaeological Features on the Long Tom River Floodplain, Veneta, Oregon," master's thesis, Department of Geography, University of Oregon, Eugene, 1989.

Dorothy E. Freidel, Lynn Peterson, Patricia J. McDowell, and Thomas J. Connolly, "Alluvial Stratigraphy and Human Prehistory of the Veneta Area, Long Tom River Valley, Oregon: The Final Report of the Country Fair/Veneta Archaeological Project," report to the USDI National Park Service and the Oregon State Historic Preservation Office, on file at the State Historic Preservation Office, Salem, 1989.

Brian L. O'Neill, "Noti-Veneta Borrow Area Monitoring," letter report on file at the Oregon State Historic Preservation Office, Salem; and 1987, "Archaeological Reconnaissance and Testing in the Noti-Veneta Section of the Florence-Eugene Highway, Lane County, Oregon." Oregon State Museum of Anthropology Report 87-6, University of Oregon, Eugene, 1987.

Brian L. O'Neill, Thomas J. Connolly, and Dorothy E. Freidel, "A Holocene Geoarchaeological Record for the Upper Willamette Valley, Oregon: The Long Tom and Chalker Sites," University of Oregon Anthropological Papers 61, Eugene, 2004.

Lynn Peterson, "Nine Thousand Years of Human Occupation in Relation to Geomorphic Features and Processes in the Long Tom River Sub-Basin, Willamette Valley, Oregon," M.A. Thesis, Department of Anthropology, University of Oregon, Eugene, 1989.

Richard M. Pettigrew, "The Archaeological Survey (Phase I) of the Noti-Veneta Section of the Florence-Eugene Highway," letter report on file at the Oregon State Historic Preservation Office, Salem, 1980; "Additional Site Explorations (Phase II) for the Noti-Veneta Section of the Florence-Eugene Highway," letter report on file at the Oregon State Historic Preservation Office, Salem, 1981; and "Test Excavation of Locality CF1 on Currently Proposed Alignment of the Noti-Veneta Section of the Florence-Eugene Highway," letter report on file at the Oregon State Historic Preservation Office, Salem, 1984.

Chapter 19—1984, Obsidian Windchimes

The author's interview with Richard and Debbie Bloom in their beautiful booth at the Oregon Country Fair on July 6, 2006, provided the basis for this chapter. Further clarifications came from email correspondence with Richard and Debbie Bloom on April 3, 2018; June 28, 2018; and June 29, 2018.Other information came out an interview with Sheri Hamilton Teasdale Lundell at the fair on July 6, 2005; from emails from Peter Bergel on December 29 and 31, 2018; from the Portland Saturday Market website, www.portlandsaturdaymarket.com; from the 1996 OCF *Peach Pit* describing Trillian Green's music; from the

2000 *Peach Pit* listing Chris Chandler's Magical Minstrel Show & Flying Poetry Circus; and from the author's personal memory of the late-night fair performances of Chris Chandler and Anne Feeney at the fair's Library.

Chapter 20—1984, Alpha Farm

This chapter is based on interviews with: Caroline Estes on August 26, 2010; Karen Stingle on March 2, 2006, and March 9, 2006; Julie Daniel on August 17, 2005; and Norma Sax on December 20, 2005.

Details were gleaned from: the Information Crew "Database Directories" of 1981, 1982 and 1983; the Community Village Coordinating Council Meeting Minutes in 1984; an article by Mike Thoele, "Alpha," the *Register-Guard*, January 11, 1976; George Howe Colt, photo essay by Eugene Richards, "For the Foreseeable Future," *Life Magazine*. December 1991, part six of "The American Family" series; a Business Beat report on Alpha-Bit closing published in *Eugene Weekly* on March 17, 2016; Jim Estes's obituary, the *Register-Guard*, October 20, 2013; and a brief notation found in *Greenfield Ranch 25th Anniversary 1972-1997: A Celebration of a Quarter Century of Living in Community*, compiled and edited by Kirsten Ellen Johnsen, Karen Lease Hensley, Zephyr Bergera, Susan Pepperwood, Dale Glaser, Marylyn Motherbear Scott, Yoli Rose, Yvonne Kramer, © 1997 by The Greenfield Ranch Association.

Online sources included the Alpha Farm website, http://members.pioneer.net/~alpha; the Alpha Institute website, http://members.pioneer.net/~alpha/ai-info.html; Oregon Public Broadcasting website for the *Oregon Field Guide* program on Alpha Farm that originally aired February 6, 2018, Season 29, Episode 11: https://watch.opb.org/show/oregon-field-guide/; and from Robyn Braverman and Thelma Garza, "Moving With ZooZoo's," *In Context* magazine, Spring 1983, www.context.org.

Chapter 21—1984, The Pride of Ownership

1984 Booth Construction Guidelines Committee: George Braddock, Santos Narvaez, Kaz Sussman, Jim Guthrie, Ed Moye, Douglas Parker, Moz Wright

🖽 🖸 ◉

Much gratitude to Tom Noddy for sharing his "Fair Show Timeline Notes," which provided entertaining and informative show details for this and future chapters.

Interviews with Ron Saylor on April 10, 2004; Robert DeSpain on April 13, 2004; Robert Thompson on April 7, 2004; and Moz Wright on April 8, 2008, contributed to this chapter.

NOTES & SOURCES

Details emerged from the 1984 OCF Board of Directors Meeting Minutes; the 1984 *Peach Pit;* issues of the *Village Vision* dated July 12, 13, 14, and July 15, 1984; the 1984 Information Crew "Database Directory;" the *Register-Guard* weather pages on July 14, 15, and 16, 1984; "Oregon Country Fair Starts Friday," the *Register-Guard,* July 12, 1984; and Don Bishoff's column, "Fair's Still Got Magic," the *Register-Guard,* July 14, 1984.

Online sources included Misha Berson, "Juggling Two Worlds—The Flying Karamazov Brothers Hang in Port Townsend, Balancing Freedom With Success," the *Seattle Times,* January 24, 1993, http://community.seattletimes.nwsource.com/archive/?date=19930124&slug=1681587; and the Goodman Theatre archives—www.goodmantheatre.org/Artists-Archive/production-timeline/1980-1989/.

Chapter 22—1984, Toby's Tofu Palace

Information for this chapter emerged out of: the author's interview with Toby Alves on February 28, 2009; the website for Toby's Family Foods, www.tobysfamilyfoods.com; Roger D. Beck, *Some Turtles Have Nice Shells,* Trucking Turtle Publishing, © 2002; Don Kahle, "Toby's Troubles Are Our Own," the *Register-Guard,* June 20, 2008; and Toby Alves' biography information on Facebook.

Chapter 23—1984, Diane McWhorter

The author's interview with Diane McWhorter on May 13, 2013, provided the key basis for this chapter, along with her emails on March 7, 2018; March 10, 2018; March 13, 2018; and June 25, 2018.

Chapter 24—1985, Happy zones

Interviewees who contributed to this chapter include Robert DeSpain on April 13, 2004; Peter Eberhardt on July 3, 2004; and Jana and Bud Chase on May 6, 2016.

Details were gleaned from Tom Noddy's "Fair Show Timeline Notes;" Tom Noddy's emails on August 2, 2018, that included photos of the show, and August 18, 2018; the Oregon Country Fair Board of Directors Meeting Minutes of 1985, 1986, 1987, and 1988; the 1985 *Peach Pit;* "The Country Fair," the *Register-Guard,* July 11, 1985; Joe Mosely, "As usual, Festive Country Fair Packs 'em in," the *Register-Guard,* July 13, 1985; Bill Bishop's article on the 1986 Eugene Celebration Parade, the *Register-Guard,* September 29, 1986; and Avner the Eccentric's website, www.avnertheeccentric.com.

Chapter 25—1985, Risk of Change

This chapter is based on the author's interviews with: Jay Hogan during the Teddy Bears' Picnic on the fair site on August 21, 2010; Chris

513

Bauske at the fair on July 11, 2004; and Michael Beach in his music studio on August 16, 2005; plus emails from Jay Hogan, Glen Corson, and David Ti on August 10, 2010; and a transcript from the 1993 Blue Moon stage meeting of Risk of Change attended by Jay Hogan, David Ti, Newman, Glen Corson, and Rebeccca Rae, where they discussed their collective history.

Further details emerged from the 1988 OCF *Peach Pit*; Paxton Hoag's video of the Java Parade titled "1993 OCF Coffee Chant," published February 17, 2018, on YouTube: www.youtube.com/watch?v=v9uubIK-9v8; the author's personal memories of the Java Parade; a film of the 1985 Oregon Country Fair made by Community Cable Television Center Cable Access Corporation that included a clip of the giant koi puppet traveling down the path; Newman's email on December 13, 2018; and the 1908 Maxfield Parrish painting, *The Lantern-Bearers*, that appeared as frontispiece of *Collier's Weekly*, December 10, 1910.

Chapter 26—1980s, Community Village Consensus

1986 members of the Community Village Coordinating Council
(from the Community Village Scrapbook)

Michael Connelly, Bob Fennessy, Janet Tarver, Diane Albino, Jerry Westphal, Darlene Colborn, David Hoffman, Charlene Tremayne, Jain Elliott, Kathryn Madden, Jon Silvermoon, Jim Linn, Norma Sax, and Barbara Vitasek

1988 Community Village Coordinating Council
(from OCF Board of Directors Meeting Minutes of February 1, 1988)

Norma Sax, Michael Connelly, David Hoffman, Jon Silvermoon, Kathryn Madden, Bob Fennessy, Diane Albino, and Janet Tarver

1989 Community Village Coordinating Council
(from Community Village Coordinating Council Meeting Minutes, April 5, 1989)

Diane Albino, Darlene Colborn, Bob Fennessy, "Water Paul" Henderson, Mark Goldby, David Hoffman, Kathryn Madden, and Janet Tarver

Information for this chapter was compiled from interviews with Patti Lomont on February 13, 2004, and April 7, 2004; Martha Evans on September 24, 2005; Jain Elliott on July 7, 2004; Hilary Anthony on May 5, 2005; Christine Frazer on July 29, 2007; Michael Connelly on September 1, 2010; Jon Silvermoon on October 19, 2005; Reese Prouty on March 27, 2007; and Kathryn Madden on May 13, 2006. David

Hoffman's emails on April 25, 2014, December 13, 2018, and December 16, 2018, also added quotes and details.

Other sources included the 1983 OCF Board of Directors Meeting Minutes; the Information Crew "Database Directories" from the 1980s; the *Village Vision* of July 13, 1984; the Community Village Coordinating Council Meeting Minutes; and the Community Village Scrapbook compiled by "Planet Janet" Tarver. The website of the IRS helped explain elements of an S corporation: www.irs.gov/businesses/small-businesses-self-employed/s-corporations.

Chapter 27—1986, OCF Navy

This chapter is mainly based on an interview with Stephen Cole by Hal Hartzell at the OCF History booth July 10, 2004. Further information emerged from: the website of the OCF Navy, www.Ocfnavy.com; emails from Stephen Cole on April 4, 2018, and June 11, 2018; the author's interviews with Peter Eberhardt on July 3, 2004, and Stephen "Bear" Pitts on July 13, 2012.

Chapter 28—1986, Drug Info Center

Members of the University of Oregon Drug Information Center Advisory Board

Glenn Brigham—Lane County Juvenile Department
James Buie, M.D.—Lane County Medical Society
Carl Carmichael—University of Oregon Speech and Communications Department
Michael Connelly—Indian Alcohol Program
Dennis Ekanger—Lane County Mental Health Department and past White Bird Director
Wayne Harger—Oregon Resources, Inc., and past DIC staff member
Janet Kallstrom—Pharmacist, Eugene Clinic
Don McLoud—Attorney
Wesley Nicholson—Minister, First Congregational Church of Eugene
Dr. Richard Schlaadt—University of Oregon Health Education Department
Dr. Warren Smith—University of Oregon Health Education Department

Some of the full-time staff at University of Oregon Drug Information Center

Mark Miller—Director
Dale Gordon—Assistant Director
Joe Coss—Administration and Finance Coordinator
Jerome Beck—Information Specialist
Lori Allen—Information Specialist

Sandy Norris—Librarian and former librarian of STASH (Student Association for the Study of Hallucinogens)
Nancy Rodrigues—CETA* employee
Debra Shepard—CETA* employee

*The Comprehensive Employment and Training Act (CETA) passed by Congress in 1973 financed job creation in areas like Lane County with high seasonal unemployment.

◘ ◘ ◙

The author's interviews with Mark Miller in April 2014 and at the OCF Spoken Word program on July 11, 2014, provided the bulk of information for this chapter. More details were gleaned from Mark Miller's emails on July 6, 2018, July 27, 2018, and August 7, 2018; the website for Mothers Against Misuse and Abuse, www.mamas.org; Gary P. Menser, *Hallucinogenic and Poisonous Mushroom Field Guide*, Ronin Publishing, Inc., 1977; and from a story in the *Register-Guard*, May 27, 1983, that provided background facts on the Comprehensive Employment and Training Act.

Chapter 29—1987, Psychospiritual Rejuvenation
1987 OM Team
Bedo Crafts (president), Sallie Edmunds (general manager), Anya Montgomery, Mary Wagner, John Winslow

1987 Coordinators

Roy Lisi	Admissions
Mel Urban	Advertising
Peter Eberhardt	Cartography
Mary Jo Garner	Child Care
Jill Liberty	Child Care
Ichabod	Comunications
Kathryn Madden	Community Village
Diane Albino	Community Village
Palmer Parker	Computer Consultant
Ken Rodgers	Construction
Nancy Bebout	Energy Park
Moz Wright	Entertainment—Ambiance
David Paul Black	Entertainment—Main Stage
Lucy Lynch	Entertainment—Vaudeville
Deni Schadegg	Entertainment—Vaudeville
Les Lauridsen	Fire Crew
Frank Sharpy	Fire Marshall
Sue Kesey	Food Committee
Toby Alves	Food Committee

Bernie Bradvica	Highway flaggers
Camille Cole	History booth
Norah Roberts	Information
Ed Moye	Main Camp
Fred Silvestri	Main Camp
Anne Henry	*Peach Pit*
Robert DeSpain	Printing
Dick Stewart	Recycling
Rod Roehnelt	Refer truck
Mary Wagner	Registration
Barbara Neuhaus	Registration
Chuck Corlett	Registration
Tom Wenk	Security
Nancy "Elf" Snyder	Security
Don Doolin	Security
Mary Beth Havel	Security
Amos Breach	Security
Walter Renfro	Traffic
Don Tadda	Traffic
J.R. Robinson	Traffic
Henry Howe	Water
Chris Howe	Water
Jon Pincus	Water
Zakariah Schwartz	White Bird
Kim Davidson	Youth Jobs
Jeff Budd	Youth Jobs
Jon Silvermoon	Youth Jobs

◧ ◉ ◉

Interviews contributing to this chapter include: Sallie Edmunds on August 15, 2005; Ande Grahn on June 27, 2004; Frank Sharpy on July 26, 2010; Michael Mielnik (aka Reverend Chumleigh) on January 12, 2004; Tom Noddy on July 9, 2004; Ed Moye on May 13, 2006; and Moz Wright on April 8, 2008. Clarifications came in emails from Frank Sharpy on August 18, 2018; Michael Mielnik on November 19, 2003; and Tom Noddy on July 9, 2008, and August 1, 2018.

Other facts and information emerged from Tom Noddy's "Fair Show Timeline Notes," the 1987 OCF *Peach Pit*; the OCF Board of Directors Meeting Minutes; and a 1987 photo of the "Heaven Show" cast posted by Eben Sprinsock on Facebook on August, 27, 2016.

Chapter 30—1988, Royal Famille Du Caniveaux

Lyrics to "Party at the Fair," by R.W. Bailey and Mark Ettinger, from *Du Caniveaux 25 Years Collectors' Edition CD*, © 2005, reprinted with permission.

Interviewees for this chapter include: Ron Bailey in December 2008; Cathy Sutherland with Peggy Wendel and Bliss Kolb on September 6, 2008; Rhonda Sable at the fair in July 2008; Randy Minkler on April 23, 2005; Tom Noddy on July 9, 2008; and Rebecca Chace on July 9, 2010.

Further information emerged from Randy Minkler's email in March 2010; the Moisture Festival website, http://moisturefestival.org; and the article, "Cirque du Silly: Juggler Tim Furst Loves Vaudeville Acts—and He's Made a Haven for Them at Seattle's Moisture Festival," *Stanford Alumni Magazine*, March-April 2011.

Background information was gathered during the author's personal experiences watching and taking notes at fair shows of the Royal Famille Du Caniveaux from 1988 to 2018 and from attending shows at the 2010 Moisture Festival in Seattle.

Chapter 31—1988, Troubled Waters

This chapter relied on interviews with Sallie Edmunds on August 15, 2005; Frank Sharpy on July 26, 2010; Kathryn Madden and Ed Moye on May 13, 2006; Jim Sahr on August 14, 2004; Bedo Crafts on August 15, 2018; and Denny Guehler on August 14, 2003.

More information was gleaned from Tim Wolden, "How Water Grew the Fair," *Fair Family News*, June 2018; the 1988 *Peach Pit*; and the OCF Board of Directors Meeting Minutes of 1987 and 1988.

Chapter 32—1989, 20th Anniversary Fair

Numerous interviewees contributed to this chapter, including Arna Shaw on September 21, 2004; Denny Guehler on August 14, 2003; Ray Sewell on July 3, 2006; Tom Noddy on July 9, 2004; Moz Wright on April 8, 2008; Ande Grahn on June 27, 2004; Bedo Crafts on August 15, 2018; Reese Prouty on March 27, 2007; Dennis Todd on April 25, 2014; Sallie Edmunds on August 15, 2005; Cynthia Wooten on October 24 and 25, 2003; and Steve Elliott, who was interviewed at the fair History booth by Hal Hartzell and Bonnie Bettman on July 11, 2004.

More details were revealed in Marshall Landman's resignation letter to Bedo Crafts, President of the OCF Board of Directors, dated July 18, 1989; Tom Noddy's Facebook post on May 19, 2016; Tom Noddy's "Fair Show Timeline Notes;" Tim Wolden, "How Water Grew the Fair," *Fair Family News*, June 2018; the 1989 OCF *Peach Pit*; the 1994 *Peach Pit*; the OCF Board of Directors Meeting Minutes of 1989; and Jeff Wright, "20th Birthday Celebration Has Country Fair Rockin'," the *Register-Guard*, July 8, 1989.

Chapter 33—1989, Radar Angels

This account is based on interviews with Indi Stern on March

1, 2005; Diane McWhorter on May 13, 2013; and Charlene Tremayne on July 25, 2007. Angela Pershnokov added key details with emails on October 26, 2018; November 17, 2018; February 28, 2019; and March 10, 2019. Indi Stern's email of February 28, 2019, helped with name spelling and other facts. Diane McWhorter's online blog in April 2012 also contributed: gelatinacea.blogspot.com.

Several articles in the Eugene alternative weekly magazine *What's Happening* (aka *Eugene Weekly*) also added information: Lois Wadsworth, "Radar Angels do Jello," *What's Happening*, March 30, 1989; Paul Neevel, "Happening People: Diane McWhorter," *Eugene Weekly*, March 29, 2018; and Paul Neevel, "Happening People: Joanie Cypress," *Eugene Weekly*, August 5, 2005.

Online sources on UFO sightings and radar angels included Wikipedia's list of UFO sightings, https://en.wikipedia.org/wiki/List_of_reported_UFO_sightings; the American Meteorology Society website, https://journals.ametsoc.org/, which had a link to the study by T.H. Roelofs, "Characteristics of Trackable Radar Angels," Center for Radiophysics and Space Research, Cornell University, Ithaca, New York, CRSR REPORT NO. **137**, Project 8622, TASK 86222, Scientific Report No. 2, Contract No. AF19(604)-6160, January 16, 1963. Prepared for Geophysics Research Directorate, Air Force Cambridge Research Laboratories, Office of Aerospace Research, United States Air Force, Bedford, Massachusetts. The American Meteorology Society website also had a link to the study by David Atlas, "Meteorological 'Angel' Echoes," Geophysics Research Directorate, Air Force Cambridge Research Center. (Manuscript received 13 January 1958), Journal of Meteorology; and the website of Dr. David Clarke, a lecturer in journalism at Sheffield Hallam University in South Yorkshire, United Kingdom, https://drdavidclarke.co.uk/secret-files/radar-angels/, which listed a story on radar angels that was originally published in *Fortean Times* issue 195 in 2005.

Chapter 34—1990, Dahinda Meda and the VegManECs

Interviewees in this chapter include Dahinda Meda at the fair's History booth by Hal Hartzell on July 1, 2004; Susan Bryan at the fair's History booth by Joshua Binus on July 13, 2004; Frank Sharpy on July 26, 2010, by the author; and Walter Renfro on January 24, 2006, by the author. More details emerged from David Hoffman's email on April 25, 2014; Frank Sharpy's email on August 18, 2018; and Mary Doyon's email on December 14, 2018.

The story of Dahinda's life came primarily from his autobiography as told to Mary Doyon: *Dahinda Meda, a Memoir*, Coincidental Communications, © 2016. The crew status of the VegManECs was confirmed in the May 1993 OCF Board of Directors Meeting Minutes in comments made by board member Margo Schaefer.

Chapter 35—1991, The Left Bank
1990 OCF Planning Committee
Dahinda Meda, Ron Chase, Toby Alves, Tom Wenk, Jim Larsen, Darrel Sink, and Charlene Tremayne.

◼ ◘ ◉

Interviewees contributing to this chapter include Kathryn Madden and Ed Moye on May 13, 2006; Charlene Tremayne on July 25, 2007; Arna Shaw on September 21, 2004; Dennis Todd on April 25, 2014; and Cynthia Wooten on March 12, 2008. Emails adding clarifications and facts came from Arna Shaw on August 28, 2018; and Kathryn Madden on August 28, 2018.

Contemporary accounts also served up dates, quotes, and facts: the OCF Board Meeting Minutes of 1990 and 1991; the "OCF Planning Committee Report" submitted on January 4, 1990; the 1991 *Peach Pit*; J.M. Jones, "Before the Fair," *What's Happening*, July 3, 1991; and Ron Chase, "Jill Heiman Vision Fund Approved," *Fair Family News*, June 1996. Kirk Shultz's descriptions of the 1991 construction projects, especially of the Dragon Plaza, came from the OCF Path Planning Committee Meeting Minutes of March 16, 2014.

Chapter 36—1990-91, State of the Peach: Bruised
Special thanks to Kathryn Madden for sharing key documents from her time as fair president.

The description of the recall vote system was based on the recollection of Mary Doyon and Michael Ottenhuasen and on how the fair's Election Committee has conducted other Board of Directors recall votes at the Oregon Country Fair annual meetings over the years. The *OCF 1991 Voters Pamphlet* said the method was yet to be determined, and numerous sources said they could not remember the details.

Much information for this chapter came from the OCF Board Meeting Minutes of 1990-1991 (for the meeting strife leading up to the recall) and from 2011-2012 (for the Barter Fair). The *OCF 1991 Voters Pamphlet* also provided key details, viewpoints, and facts, as did Kathryn Madden's letter to the board in September 1991 and Kathryn's handwritten notes for her "State of the Peach" address at the annual meeting on October 21, 1991.

Interviewees providing quotes and insights included Arna Shaw on September 21, 2004; Frank Sharpy on July 26, 2010; Paxton Hoag on July 11, 2004; Dennis Todd on April 25, 2014; Ascha Champie at the 2013 Oregon Country Fair; and John Sundquist on November 21, 2018. Clarifications came in emails from Kathryn Madden on October 6, 2018; Jeanne Sharpy on November 20 and 21, 2018; and Mary Doyon on November 23, 2018.

Notes & Sources

Chapter 37—1992, Fair Family News

A special thank you goes to Palmer "Poodle" Parker, who graciously donated a nearly complete set of every *Fair Family News* published, filed neatly by date. Deep appreciation also to Wally Slocum for saving and sharing the prototype of the first *Fair Family Flashes* that was presented to the Oregon Country Fair Board of Directors, and to Janet Tarver for sharing a copy of the 1984 OCF newsletter from her archives.

◘ ◘ ◙

This chapter was based largely on issues of the *Fair Flashes* and *Fair Family News* from 1992 to 2018, including the original prototype found in Wally Slocum's collection. Further information and quotes came from interviews with: Mary Doyon and Michael Ottenhausen in April 2007; Norma Sax on December 20, 2005; and Bill Verner on July 4, 2006. The OCF Board of Directors Meeting Minutes of 1992 and the 2002 *Peach Pit* provided additional facts. The author's personal experiences volunteering for *Fair Family News* for the last fifteen years added to the author's general knowledge of this piece of the fair's history.

Chapter 38—1992, Leslie Scott and the Fair's Neighbors

Interviewees contributing to this chapter included Leslie Scott on December 6, 2007; Cynthia Wooten on March 12, 2008; Galen Carpenter on July 27, 2007; and Cindy Darling on July 23, 2018. Emails adding insights came from Leslie Scott on October 7, 2018; October 21, 2018; October 31, 2018; and November 1, 2018.

Print sources included the OCF Board of Directors Meeting Minutes from 1992 to 1997; and a flier from the Oregon Country Fair titled "Greetings Neighbors!!!" inviting people to the second annual West Lane County Open House in June 1994 at the fair site.

News accounts offered up more background details and confirmation of facts in this chapter: Karen Smith's letter to the editor, "Fair Caused Problems," the *Register-Guard,* July 21, 1988; Mary Shuler (Doyon), "Wristband Meeting Report," *Fair Family News,* June 1993; Judy Hunt, "Country Fair Folk Set Open House for Neighbors," *West Lane News,* April 15, 1993; "Nice Folks, Gorgeous Weather Highlights OCF Open House," *West Lane News,* May 1993; Lynn Fogus, "Veneta Councilors Take the Plunge with OCF Camping," *West Lane News,* May 1993; Joe Kidd, "Neighbors Getting a Fair Shake," the *Register-Guard,* July 11, 1993; Bill Wooten's obituary published in the *Register-Guard* on January 31, 1995; Ed Hawley, "Country Fair Apologizes: 200 Attend Forum to Hunt for Solutions," *West Lane News,* August 1, 1996; an opinion piece by state Rep. Jim Welsh, "A Good Example of Addressing Local Concern," *West Lane News,* August 9, 1996; "19 Named to Citizen's Country Fair Steering Committee," *West Lane News,* August 15, 1996;

and Noah Campbell, "Fair Manager Looks Forward to Dialogue with Neighbors," *West Lane News,* September 19, 1996.

More news accounts included: Ari Seligmann, "Fair Days Ahead: Oregon Country Fair Takes Steps to Correct Last Year's Fair-Related Problems," *Eugene Weekly,* June 19, 1997; Ed Hawley, "Veneta and the Fair: Can They Ever Be Friends?" July 10, 1997; Eileen Stewart, "Oregon Country Fair Staff Undergoes Expanded Training for Extra Security," *West Lane News,* July 10, 1997; Janelle Hartman, "This Year's Fair Pleases Veneta Neighbors," the *Register-Guard;* July 13, 1997; Ed Hawley, "This Year It Was Better, Much Better, as New Calm Comes to Country Fair," *West Lane News,* July 17, 1997; Christine Rush's letter to the editor, "A Giant Leap ...," *West Lane News,* July 17, 1997; letter to the editor from Pat Coy, manager of Ray's Food Place, "Great Strides in the Right Direction," *West Lane News,* July 17, 1997; Christine Rush's letter to the editor, "This Year's Fair," *West Lane News,* June 18, 1998; letter to the editor from Joan, Sherry, Kathy and Mac, "Zumwalt Park Open for Camping," July 23, 1998; Steve Gray, "ROC Committee Discusses Upcoming Country Fair," *West Lane News,* June 3, 1999; and Mayor Galen Carpenter's "State of Veneta" article, "Mayor Carpenter: 'Many Things Begun, Many Things Completed,'" *West Lane News,* January 2, 1999.

Thanks to Palmer Parker for sharing news articles that added facts and background on the Veneta effluent project and the land exchange between the Oregon Country Fair and the city of Veneta: "Land Use Plan Forum May 12," *West Lane News,* April 23, 1998; Steve Gray, "Veneta, Fair Plan Swap of 35 Acres," *West Lane News,* October 8, 1998; "Veneta Given $128,385 in Grant Funding," *West Lane News,* January 21, 1999; Steve Gray, "CLUE to Present Periodic Review Recommendations," *West Lane News,* September 30, 1999; and "City, Fair Agree to Land Swap," *West Lane News,* December 2, 1999.

Chapter 39—1993, Stage Left and the Fighting Instruments of Karma Marching Chamber Band/Orchestra

Past and present members of the Fighting Instruments of Karma Marching Chamber Band/Orchestra as of 2008, posted on the 2008 New Old Time Chautauqua web page (no longer available online)

> The Fighting Instruments of Karma Marching Chamber Band/Orchestra has been an integral part of the New Old Time Chautauqua since even before our Chautauqua existed. You figure it out.
>
> We would like to take a little space here to thank the various incarnations of our live band from over the years. Fortunately, musicians are accustomed to little thanks. We would even like to thank each and every person who has ever played music in the band, but, unfortunately, nobody can remember them all. Perhaps it should be noted, so as not to frighten away the musically squeamish, that, of the

Notes & Sources

sixty-plus musicians mentioned below, never have more than around half of them played together at any one time.

Finally, here are some of them, past and present, in something like alphabetical order:

Jeffrey Alberts, *Percussion*
Robyn Albro, *Flute, Flautiste, Long Tubular Thingy*
Dave Bender, *Trumpet, featured character on "Futurama"*
Stephen Bent, *That Bone which Troms*
Steven Bernstein, *Trumpet, Cornet, leader of the Jazzicians, "Sex Mob"*
Paul Black, *Percussion, Guitar and Laughing Shill*
Diane Chaplin, *Cello, Flute, member Colorado String Quartet*
Jana Rose Chase, *Glockenspiel and Various Other Spiels*
Bud Chase, *Sousaphone, Upright/Downtown Bass*
Doug Clark, *Trombone, Lone Arranger*
Will Clark, *Percussion? Yes He Will*
Jennifer Collins, *Saxophone, Flute*
Pom Collins, *Fiddle and Faddle*
Adam Danoff, *Piccolo which is rather Piccohigh*
Cici Dawn, *Cycymbals*
David de la Rocha, *Sousaphones and Smiles*
Seiza de Tarr, *Glockenspiel and Various Other Glocks*
Gavi de Tarr, *Trumpet, Teen Babe Magnet*
Mac Dolecki, *Trumpet*
Liz Dreisbach, *Clarinet*
Dan Duggin, *Accordion, and how!*
Mark Ettinger, *Baritone Horn, Deus Ex Machina*
Phillip Farrell, *Clarinet, even after hearing his father play the thing*
Ben Farrell, *Clarinetist, Universitarian*
Jennifer Freelan, *French Horn*
Stefan Freelan, *Percussion*
Mark Gowan, *Percussion, Ah Gowan!*
Steve Horstman, *Saxophone*
Richard Karst, *Trumpet, Keyboards, CD Producer*
Miles Kennedy, *Percussion*
Roderick Kimball, *Trumpet of the Schwans*
Sasha Landis, *Percussion*
Coire Ready Langham, *Trumpet, Unlikely Name*
Mary Langham, *Flute*
John Langham, *Percussion*
Gina Leishman, *Piccolo, Accordion, Bass Clarinet, British Accent*
Nancy Levidow, *Flute, Finances and Fun*
Barney Lindsley, *Saxophone*
Kathleen Luther, *Assorted Percussion and Polka Dots*
Lisa Lystad, *Percussion, Eyeballs*
Paul "It's the Reed" Magid, *Clarinet, Saxophone*
Djuna Mascall, *Flute, The Silver Blow Gun*
Nicholas Mayer, *Bass Drum*
Michael Mielnik, *Trombone, Reverend Chumleigh-for-hire*
Marie Mileto, *Saxophone, Big Eyes, Big Mouth*

Mose Mosely, *Third Cymbalist*
Daniel Neville, *Saxophone, Flute, Piccolo, Back-up Band Leader*
Ben Neville, *Saxophone, Handsome Young Devil*
Todd Nordling, *Trumpet and Pinch-Hit Trombone*
Howard Patterson, *Euphonium, Trombone*
Jasper Patterson, *Percussion, Concussion, Seatcussion*
Jenny Pipia, *Clarinet*
Cynthia Pitts, *Flute, Piccolo*
Mary Ramsay, *Flute and Foreign Relations*
John Sanders, *Percussion*
Sid Small, *Washboard, avec tout le Bells and Whistles*
Thaddeus Spae, *Trombone, Composer, Arranger*
Eben Sprinsock, *Clarinet, Band Leader, It's All His Fault*
Oliver Steck, *Trumpet, Accordion to Hoyle*
Lito Tabora, *Portable Keyboards*
Mark Warren, *Percussion, Shrinkage*
Heather Weihl, *Trombone, Interior Design*
Doug Wieselman, *Clarinet, Saxophone, Arranger, Cool Guy*
Andrea Williams, *Bass Drum, Energy*
Sam Williams, *Alto Horn, Faux French Horn*
Shelley Winship, *Actual French Horn, Latin Percussion, Beloved Toiler*
And Many, Many More...

◘ ◙ ◎

Information for this chapter came mainly from interviews with: John Cloud on July 12, 2011; and of John Cloud on July 9, 2004, by Hal Hartzell in the OCF History booth; Howard Patterson on August 15, 2005; Eben Sprinsock on September 25, 2005; Heather Weihl on September 24, 2005; Mose Moseley on November 15, 2005; Sam Williams on September 7, 2005; and Darcy DuRuz and Dave Bender on September 1, 2006. Emails from Howard Patterson on October 26, 2018; Heather Weihl on October 29, 2018; Tom Noddy on December 21, 2018; and Hilary Anthony on February 2, 2019, helped clarify facts.

Further details were gleaned from Tom Noddy's "Fair Show Timeline Notes;" the obituary by Janet I-Chin Tu, "Rebecca Hanson, 42, Singer, Songwriter, Vaudeville Trouper," *Seattle Times,* May 13, 1997; film clips from 1992 New Old Time Chautauqua tour of Alaska shown at the Celebration of Life for Chez Ray Sewell at the McDonald Theatre on December 16, 2018; the author's article about Eben Sprinsock retiring as band leader, "The Baton is Passed: The Band Marches On," *Fair Family News,* August 2011; and the author's memories of fairgoers on the pathways talking like a pirate—"AAARRG!"—the years the pirate shows were staged at Knot-Not Chumleighland.

Chapter 40—1997, Line in the Sand

Special thanks to Palmer Parker for sharing his 1990s files full of Oregon Country Fair notes, letters, memos, planning documents from the fair's Security Crew, and other key background documents concerning the fair's interaction with the Lane County district attorney and sheriff's offices over the drug forfeiture threat.

Information for this chapter emerged from interviews with: Daniel Dillon on July 9, 2004; Leslie Scott on December 6, 2007; Wally Jones on December 27, 2005; and Tom Alexander at the fair's Spoken Word program in July 2014. Emails that helped clarify details came from Martha Evans on December 9, 2018; Daniel Dillon on October 12, 2018; and Leslie Scott on October 7, 2018, October 22, 2018, and October 31, 2018.

Other print sources included "Interview: Tom Alexander," by Bob LaBrasca and Dean Latimer, *High Times*, December 1983; Tom Alexander's autobiography for the 2014 OCF Spoken Word program; *Fair Family News* from 1992 to 1997; and fair board minutes from 1992 to 1997.

Extensive news sources provided confirmation of facts and timelines: "Country Fair Responds to Warnings about Drugs," by Joe Mosley, the *Register-Guard*, June 22, 1997; "Reminder: Fair Tickets Must Be Pre-purchased," by Ed Hawley, *West Lane News*, June 26, 1997; "Fair Warning: Tickets Must Be Bought Ahead," by AnneElena Foster, the *Register-Guard*, June 29, 1997; "For the Country Fair, a Year of Challenge," *West Lane News*, July 3, 1997; "Annual Counterculture Festival Told It Better Clean Up Its Act," by Dana Tims, the *Oregonian*; July 3, 1997; an opinion article titled "Country Fair Represents Community," by Leslie Scott, OCF general manager, the *Register-Guard*, July 9, 1997; "Fair Organizers, Police Cooperate on Security Issues," by Joe Mosley, the *Register-Guard*, July 11, 1997; "Country Fair Taking a Turn," by Joe Mosley, the *Register-Guard*, July 12, 1997; "'Magic Is Back' at the Fair," by Suzanne Hurt, the *Register Guard*, July 14, 1997; "This Year It Was Better, Much Better, as New Calm Comes to Country Fair," *West Lane News*, July 17, 1997; "Patrols Sweep Veneta Country Fair," *Trooper News*, August 1997; "Fair Urged to Pay Deputies," the *Register-Guard*, August 23, 1997; and an editorial "Next Time, a Contract: Sheriff Is Reaching with Country Fair Bill," the *Register-Guard*, August 23, 1997.

Epilogue, 2001, Girl Circus

The first part of the Epilogue relied on numerous sources throughout the previous chapters, but especially *Fair Family News* publications from 1997 to February 2019, the 1997 *Peach Pit* and *OCF Guidelines*, the 2001 *Peach Pit*, and the 2015 *Peach Pit*.

Girl Circus details emerged from three interviews over a fourteen-year span with members of the DuRuz-Bender family at their home: with Darcy DuRuz, Dave Bender, and Coco and Walter Bender on February 18, 2004; with Darcy DuRuz, Dave Bender, and Coco and Walter Bender, on September 1, 2006; and with Darcy DuRuz and Walter Bender on September 7, 2018. Heather Weihl's interview at her home in Seattle on September 24, 2005, also contributed. Further information was gleaned from Tom Noddy's "Fair Show Timeline Notes" and the Girl Circus website: www.girlcircus.com.

Fair Thee Well

Information for these Fair Thee Wells came mainly from interviews and "Fair Thee Well" notices in the *Fair Family News*. Sources included an interview of Susan Bryan by Joshua Binus in the Oregon Country Fair History booth on July 13, 2004; issues of *Fair Family News* in March 2013 and April 2014; Dominic DeFazio's "Fair Thee Well" in *Fair Family News* in September 2009; author's interview with Dominic and Susanna DeFazio at their rural property outside Walton, Oregon, on August 1, 2005; an interview with Robert DeSpain on April 13, 2004; Robert DeSpain's "Fair Thee Well" in *Fair Family News* on September 2018; John Doscher's "Fair Thee Well" in *Fair Family News*, on March 2013; an email from Robert Thompson on November 23, 2018; the Oregon Country Fair Board of Directors Meeting Minutes in the 1990s; Ande Grahn's interview on June 27, 2004; and Ande's "Fair Thee Well" in *Fair Family News* in December 2010.

Information on Rebecca "Rebo Flordigan" Hanson came from interviews with Howard Patterson on August 15, 2005; with Darcy DuRuz, Dave Bender, Coco Bender, and Walter Bender, on September 1, 2006; with Ben Farrell on March 15, 2005; with Rhonda Sable in July 2008; and from "Rebecca Hanson, 42, Singer, Songwriter, Vaudeville Trouper," by Janet I-Chin Tu, *Seattle Times*, May 13, 1997.

Gil Harrison's information emerged from an interview on November 3, 2002; his "Fair Thee Well" in *Fair Family News* in February 2013; and the Oregon Country Fair Board of Directors Meeting Minutes from 1978 to 1981.

Jill Heiman's biography was gleaned from interviews with Gerry Mackie, Hal Hartzell, and Betsy Vaughn Wemple Hartzell on August 7, 2004; with Cynthia Wooten on March 12, 2008; with Sandra Bauer and Mary Cay Liebig on July 10, 2003; with Gretchen Miller in 2008; and with Jack Delay on January 24, 2009.

Anne Henry's information came from an emailed interview in September 2003, and her obituary in the Register-Guard.

Details on Ken Kesey came from an interview with Chuck and Sue Kesey on April 26, 2005; from his obituary in the *Register*-Guard by Bob Keefer and Susan Palmer published on November 11, 2001; and from the book, *The Electric Kool-Aid Acid Test*, © 1968 by Tom Wolfe, Ferrar Straus and Giroux, Inc.

Marshall Landman's information emerged from an interview with Brian Livingston on April 1, 2004; the Community Village Coordinating Council Meeting Minutes from late 1977 through the 1980s; *APT* newsletter 1976 and 1977; 1980s issues of the *Village Vision*; the Oregon Country Fair Board of Directors Meeting Minutes from 1978 to 2003; and from Marshal's obituary in the *Register-Guard* on March 27, 2003.

Tom Scott's details derived from a group interview with key members of Energy Park on July 12, 2017: Sue Jakabosky, Nancy Bebout, Tom Scott, "Bob-O" Schultz, "Bob-1" Maynard, Anna Scott, and George Patterson; and Tom's "Fair Thee Well" in the February 2019 issue of *Fair Family News*.

Other sources in this section include an interview with "Chez Ray" Sewell on July 3, 2006; Ray's "Fair Thee Well" in the January 2019 *Fair Family News*; his obituary in the *Register-Guard* on December 2, 2018: "Eugene Says Goodbye to Hippie Icon, Chef Chez Ray Sewell;" interviews with Wally Slocum on Dec. 3, 2002, March 18, 2004, and August 23, 2006; Wally's "Fair Thee Well" in *Fair Family News*, September 2009; John Stamp's interview at fair site on June 24, 2006; John's "Fair Thee Well" in the March 2008 *Fair Family News*; Janet Tarver's interview on April 7, 2006; and her "Fair Thee Well" in the December 2011 *Fair Family News*.

Edd Wemple's information came from interviews with Hal Hartzell on November 22, 2002, and February 28, 2006; Hal Hartzell's book, *Birth of a Cooperative Hoedads, Inc.: A Worker Owned Forest Labor Co-op.*, a Yew Book published by Hulogos'i Communications, © 1987; and a story on Cougar Mountain Farm published in the *Eugene Daily News* in March 2012: http://eugenedailynews.com/2012/03/cougar-mountain-farm-and-its-40-years-of-sustainabilty/.

Sam Williams' interview on September 7, 2005, contributed to this chapter, as well as a series of emails from Sam on April 4-10, 2009; his "Fair Thee Well" in *Fair Family News*, December 2016; and Mike Lindblom, "Bus Riders Step In as Driver Has Fatal Heart Attack on Viaduct," the *Seattle Times*, November 18, 2016.

The "Fair Thee Well" for John Winslow in *Fair Family News*, November 2013, and the Oregon Country Fair Board of Directors Meeting Minutes for the 1980s yielded more information.

Facts on Bill Wooten emerged from interviews with Cynthia Wooten on October 24 and 25, 2003, and March 12, 2008; with Sandra Bauer on July 10, 2003; and notes from the program for Bill Wooten's memorial service.

Information about Morning Glory Zell-Ravenheart came from interviews with Christine Frazer on July 28, 2007; with Zak Schwartz on August 17, 2006; with Alison Halderman on July 9, 2007; and follow-up emails from Alison Halderman in 2007. Online sources included Antonia Blumbert, "Morning Glory Zell-Ravenheart Dead: Pioneering Pagan, Polyamory Leader Dies At 66," the *Huffington Post*, May 14, 2014; Morning Glory's obituary published in the *Telegraph* in the United Kingdom on July 21, 2014, www.telegraph.co.uk/news/obituaries/10980913/Morning-Glory-Zell-Ravenheart-obituary.html; and the website for the Church of All Words, www.caw.org.

Index

Bold-face page numbers refer to photos.

Abbey Rode, 396
Abundant Life Seed Foundation, 485
ACE Contracting, 424
Active Bethel Citizens, 490
Adams, Patch, 58, 105, **106**, 471
Adams, Barry "Plunkr," 15-27
Admiral Kohl. *See* Cole, Stephen
Admissions Crew, 117, 159, 303, 310, 311, 323, 388, 488, 516
Advertising coordinator, 421, 516
Agamenoni, Tom, 133
Alberts, Jeffrey, 523
Albino, Diane, 290, 291, **296**, 514, 516
Albro, Nancy, 75, **76**, 117, 156, 157, 499
Albro, Robyn, 523
Alea, Janine, 417, 420
Alexander, Tom, 464-465
Allen, Dan, 501
Allen, Lori, 515
Alligator Palace, 56, 57, 336-337
Alpha-Bit Café, 224, 227-228, 230, 233
Alpha Farm, 101, 103, 223-234, **231**, 293, 296
Alpha Institute, 232
Alsop, Peter, 333
Alter-Abled Access Advocacy, 297-299, 333, 381
Alternative Technology booth at Community Village, 39
Alves, Chelsea, 249-250
Alves, Jonah, 245-246, 250
Alves, Olem, 245, 246-247, 250
Alves, Onesmo "Oney," 245-247, **248,**
Alves, Toby, 245-252, **246**, 499, 516, 520
Amber Tide, 351. *See also* Spae, Thaddeus

Ambiance Crew, 284, 377, 517
American Civil Liberties Union, 291
Amsterdam Street Performers Competition, First Annual, 338
Anthony, Hilary, 286-287, 404, 426
Anthony, John, 369
anti-nuclear activism, 40, 134-135, 243, 293, 349, 373, 491
Appropriate Technology area, 40, 229-230, 488. *See also* Community Village, Energy Park
Aprovecho, 297
Arcadia Country Inn, 485
Archaeology Crew, 122, 200-201, 294, 361, 368
archaeology study sites, 508-509
Arnague, Jean-Marie, **160, 290**
Art booth, Community Village, 61, 266
Art Maggots, the, 374
Artis (aka Artis the Spoonman), 422, 471
  as street performer, 33, 213, 343, 422, 471
  at fair, 49, 78, 173, 213, 217, 242, 350, 366
  with New Old Time Chautauqua, 105
Avner "the Eccentric." *See* Eisenberg, Avner

Baba Karim dance troupe, 175, 180
Baby Gramps, 197, 264, 333, 351
back to the land movement, 15, 88, 124, 225
Bailey, Caela, 339, 344-346
Bailey, Ron, 145, 335-346. *See also* Dynamic Logs, Royal Famille Du Caniveaux, Moisture Festival

529

Baker, Tim, 97-98
Bakra Bata, 333
Balaphon, 82, 173
Bale, Jeff (aka Judy Jensen), 279
Ballin, Scott, 413-414, 415, 419
Banners Crew and coordinator, 48, 75, 78, 159, 239, 304, 355, 490
Barry, Kate, **376**
Barton, Mary, 150
Bauer, Sandra, 114, 116, 121, 158, 159, 169, 246, 289, 300, **300**, 361, 363, 395, 492, 497
  as Main Camp volunteer 75, **76,** 117, 156, 158, 165, **300,** 357, 361
  photo credits, 119, 170, 386
  as president of the fair, 37, 39, 40, 136, 138
Baumeister, Jennifer Hathorn, 483
Bauske, Brian, 73, 74
Bauske, Chris "Ruby," 13,73, 281-282, 424
Beach, Michael, 184, 176, 177, **183**. *See also* Brothers of the Baladi
Bebout, Nancy, 495, 516
Beck, Jerome "Jerry," 321, 515
Bender, Coco, 472, 474-475, 476-477, **478,** 480-481
Bender, Dave, 452, 472-482, 523
Bender, Walter, 472, 474-477, 478
Bent, Stephen, 523
Bergel, Peter, 134-135, 217
Bernard, Teddy, 181, 273, 277, **277**
Bernstein, Steven, 450, 523
Bettman, Ann, 439
Beyondananda, Swami, 471
Big Elk Booth, 356
Bill Wooten Memorial Endowment, 435-436, 458, 471, 492
Birdalone, 51-52
Birmingham, Jill, 283
Birthsong Midwifery booth, 433
Bishoff, Don, 243
Black, Brenda, 403
Black, David Paul, 350, 364, 403, 516
Black, Paul, 523
Blair Island Restaurant, 249, 250-251
Blintz Booth, 421, 456, 457, 459, 487
Bloom, Debbie (Marthaller), 211-222
Bloom, Richard, 211-222, **216**
Bonneville Power Administration, 265

Booth Construction Guidelines, 235, 236, 241
Booth Construction Guidelines Committee, 512
Bolton, Jesse, 75-77
Borie, Lysbeth, 232
Braddock, George, 237, 254, 261-262, 358-359, 410, 412, 415, 512
Bradvica, Bernie, 517
Bradvica, Rebecca, 13
Breach, Amos, 517
Bread and Roses, 57
Breitenbush Hot Springs, 104, 105, 232
Brigham, Glenn, 515
BRING, 20
Britz, Richard, 439
Brockelbank, Leslie, 115
Brodie, Dog of the Future, World's Only Dog with a Ph.D., 332-333, 472
Brooks, Bruce, 503
Brothers of the Baladi, 175,176, 177, 179, 180, 181, 183, **183**, 185
Browning, Page, 489
Brush Babes, 300, **300**
Bryan, Susan, 386, **387,** 392-393, 394, 483
Budd, Jeff, 517
Budget Committee, 368
Buie, James, M.D., 515
Bull, Carol, 422
Bummer Squad, 163. *See also* White Bird
BUMs (aka Back Up Managers) 13, 398, 435. *See also* OM Team (aka Operations Management Team)
Burgess, John "Chewie," 386
Bus Crew, 368
Bussey, Shawn, 91

C

Café Mam, 391-392, **392,** 394, 424
Café Soriah, 123, 127, 128, 129
Café Zenon, 129
Caldwell, Larry, 90-91, 503
Caliente, 333
camel rides, 351
Cameron, Chelsea, 249
Cameron, John, 249
Campbell, Midge, 298
Campbell, Ted, 240, 404
Carmichael, Carl, 515

Index

Carpenter, Galen, 436-439, 463
Cartography Crew, 73, 199, 517
Casablanca food booth, 123-130
Cascade Pacific Resource Conservation & Development, 440
Cascadian Regional Library (CAREL), 488
Cashiers, the, 374
Centro Latino Americano, 404
Chambliss, Thom, 421
Chace, Rebecca "Beka," 336, 337, 338, 345. *See also* Daring Deviante Sisters
Chalker Site (archaeology site 35LA420), 509
Chaffin, Dena, 216
Chaffin, Gary, 214, 216, 218
Champie, Ascha Karen (Gellman), 408-409, **409**, 459
Chandler, Chris, 218
"Changing of the Guard Song," 306-307
Chaplin, Diane, 523
Charlie Brown, 351. *See also* Miller, Tim
Charter members, 121, 122, 154, 421, 487
Chase, Jana, 13, 97-102, 263-264, 523
  with New Old Time Chautauqua, 102-103, 105, 107-112, **109, 112**
  photo credits, 106, 107, 108, 109, 453
Chase, Ron, 114, 118, 153, 261, 356, 402-403, 435, 520
  as board member, 159, 201, 235, 238, 262
  and land purchase, 120-121, 122, 131, 147, 198, 399
  and Main Camp, 75, **77**, 117, 156, 157-158, 168
  as treasurer, 158, 159, 162, 168, 171, 399
Chase, William B. "Bud," 13, 97-103, 263-264, 450, 523
  and New Old Time Chautauqua, 105, **106**, 107-110, **109**, 112
Cheetah Conservation Fund, 79
Chela Mela Meadow, 128, 201, 210, 287, 377, 426, 452-453, 471, 485
Cherry, Julie, 404
Chicano Affairs, 60
Child Care Crew, 258, 261, 361, 517
Childers, Laurie, 475
Children's House, 16, 17
Children's Stage, 361
Chill Ville, 194
Christopher Crooked Stitch Collective, 99
Chumleigh (aka Michael Mielnik aka the Flaming Zucchini aka Major Chumleigh aka Reverend Chumleigh), 12, 25, 32, 33, 37, 49, 81, 336, 363, 442, 444, 500-501, 523
  at Alligator Palace, 57, 336
  absence from fair, 49, 78, 136, **136,** 244, 267, 330, 473
  at Circus Stage (aka Chumleighland), 34, 49, 50-51, 85, 330-333, 336, 472
  at Daredevil Palace, 350, 366
  and the Flying Karamazov Brothers, 50-53, 78, 81, 136, **136,** 330, 442
  at Main Stage, 350
  and Midnight Show, 51, 85, 267-268
Chumleighland. *See* Circus Stage
"Chumleighland March, The," 111
Church of All Worlds, 80, 492
Circus Stage (aka Chumleighland aka Not Chumleighland, aka Not Not Chumleighland), 12, 50-51, **58**, 82, 102, 103, 104, 111, **136**, 218, 243-244, 263-264, 268, 287, 330-333, 336, 337, 350-351, 366-367, **366, 367,** 387, 402, 442-444, 448, 453, 472-473, 476. *See also* Stage Left
  and Faith Petric, 139, 140, 144, 331
  and the Flying Karamazov Brothers, 12, 49, 78, 83, 136, 172, 173, 350, 366, 446-447, **447**
  and the Fighting Instruments of Karma Marching Chamber Band/Orchestra, 83, 136, 266, 444-448, 449-450, 473
  and Reverend Chumleigh, 34, 49, 78, 244, 331-333, 336, 472
  and Tom Noddy, 34, **38,** 78, 173, 244, 264, 268, 331, 423, 443
Cirque de Flambe, 344
Citizens for Safe Energy, 60
civil rights movement, 30, 146, 177, 224, 253-254
Clark, Doug, 523
Clark, Les, 439
Clark, Will, 523
Clarke, David, 521
Classen, George, 192, 248

Clergy and Laity Concerned (later Community Alliance of Lane County), 291
Cloud, John, 83, 84, 244, **366**, 387, 442, 443-444
Clowning Around, 351
Club Molimo, 327-331, **329**, 333, 334, 347
Coalition Opposing Registration and the Draft, 169, 291
Cohn, Dan, 427
Colborn, Darlene, 230, **290**, 291, 514
Cole, Camille, 436, 517
Cole, David (with Oregon State Museum of Anthropology), 200, 201
Cole, Dave (aka Vice Admiral Navy Davy), 310-312, **312**
Cole, Mary, 488
Cole, Stephen (aka Admiral Kohl), 302-312, **312,** *photo credit, 312*
Collins, Jennifer, 337, 523
Collins, Pom, 523
Come Unity House, 297. *See also* Community Village
communes, 15-16, 18, 19, 20, 81-82, 97-101, 105, 108, 110, 114, 187, 188, 191, 192, 227, 229, 233, 263, 471, 491. *See also* intentional communities
Communications coordinator, 517
Community Center for the Performing Arts (aka CCPA aka WOW Hall), 181. *See also* WOW Hall
Community Market, 191
Community Village, 39-40, 60-62, 65-66, **70, 71,** 74, 84, 120, 132-134, 159, 169, 214, 223-224, 229-232, **231,** 240, 256, 262, 286, 291, **298**, 300, 351, 353, 354, 375, 377, 381, 396, 407, 432, 464, 473, 516. *See also* Appropriate Technology area, APT newsletter; Alpha Farm, Integral House, Starflower, Village Restaurant, *Village Vision* newsletter, Village yurt, separate listings by village booth name
    coordinating council and members, 60, 61, 84, 132, 156, 159, 173, 223, 240, 288-291, **290,** 294, 295, **296,** 297, 298, 299, 301, 395, 514
    Fair Thee Well, 484, 489, 490, 491
    and Four-A, 298, 298-299, 333
    governing structure and consensus, 62, 82, 155-156, 158, 161, 224, 231-232, 285-301, 353
    Information booth, 298, **298**
    members of fair board, 156, 159, 162, 289, 294, 296, 354, 395
    Om Circle, 257, 291-292
    workshops, 12, 82, 133, 172, 173, 241, 243, 266, 287, 333, 366
    youth job program, 134, 288, 357
Community Village Stage, 74, 82, 172, 181
Conant, Dave, 341, 345
Conant, Vivian "Oblivion," 345
Connelly, Michael "Coyote," **290**, 291-292, **296**, 299, 406-407, 434, 514, 515
    photo credits, 117, 163, 165, 290
Connolly, Tom, 204, 205, 206, 208, 209, 210, 508-509, 510
Consensus 11, 24, 62, 63, 65, 10, 117, 156, 161, 162, 163, 224, 225, 227, 228, 230, 231, 232, 249, 254, 403, 434
Construction Crew, 170, 241, 258, 275, 298-299, 325, 335, 352-353, 395-396, 398, 400, 401, 412, 415, 443
    coordinators, 160, 165, 325, 335, 348, 352, 354, 358, 369, 395, 396, 412, 414, 415, 416, 417, 516
    Fair Thee Well, 483, 487
    and red tags, 425-426
Cooperative Fruit booth, **70**
cooperatives, 20, 82, 115, 118, 388, 391
coordinator potlucks, 16, 22, 23, 164, 435
Copeland, Kate, 345, 346
Copper Cricket, 488
Corcker, Dave, 353
Corlett, Chuck, 518
Corson, Glen, 271
Coslow, Dane, 185
Coslow, Max, 185
Coslow, Tim, 185
Coss, Joe, 515
Cossu, Scott, 173, 264, 329, 333
Costello, Jack, 125-126
Council for Human Rights in Latin America, 431, 432, 433
Country Fair #1 Site (archaeology site 35LA758), 508
Country Fair #4 Site (archaeology site 35LA760), 509
Country VW co-op, 285, 286, 381

INDEX

Coyote Rising, 283
Craft Committee, 259, 354, 487
Crafters, 11-12, 14, 16-17, 26, 34, 48, 72, 74, 76-77, 82, 83, 85, 118, 131-132, 134, 137, 167-168, 172, 191, 236-237, 239, 241, 245, 262, 266, 267, 305, 327, 331, 351, 354, 374, 405, 407, 417, 440, 471, 472, 473
  and the barter fair 408-410
  specific crafters, 98, **119,** 201, 211-222, 236, 253-260, 283, 322, 348, 356, 376-377, 404, 408-409, **409,** 421, 425, 459, 490
  move to Left Bank, 398, 400-401, 442, 444
Craft Inventory Crew, 421, 460
Crafts, Bedo, 406, 415, 417, 420
  as president of fair, 323-324, 332, 349, 351, 357, 360, 364-365, 390, 397, 516
Crafts Directory, 132
Crafts Guild, 354, 356
Craig, Alex, 142, 143-144, 145
Craig, Carole, 145
Crane-Conant, Dee Dee, 345
Crane, Kelly (Campbell), 421, 422
Crane, Vivian, 345
Cray, Robert, 148, 151
Crew Services. *See* Hospitality Crew
Cuc, Charlene, 377
Cumbo, Kent, 90-91, 93
Cumbo, Kim, 93, **93**
Cypress, Joan Gold, **376**

D

Dahlia on Broadway, 129
Dana's Cheesecake booth, 369
Daniel, Godfrey, **341,** 341-342, 346
Daniel, Julie, 229-230
Danoff, Adam, 523
Daredevil Meadow, 266, 333, 335, 336, 361, 375
Daredevil Vaudeville Palace Stage (aka Du Caniveaux Palace Stage), 335-336, 339-343, **340, 341, 342,** 350, 352, 366
Daring Deviante Sisters, 34, 336-337. *See also* Chace, Rebecca; Sutherland, Cathy
Darling Reunion Camp, 441

Darling, Cindy, 441, 523
David Brower Lifetime Achievement Award, 394
David the Minstrel, 35
Davidson, Kim, 517
Davidson, Wren, 417, 418
Davis, Janis, 487
DaVis, Maque, 344
Dawn, Cici. *See* Wilcoxon, Cici
Daycon, Amy, 157, 499
Debs, Eugene, 141
Deconstruction crew, 410
DeFazio, Carol, 483
DeFazio, Daniel, 483
DeFazio, Diana, 483
DeFazio, Dominic, 427, 483
  photo credits, 331, 341, 342
DeFazio, Susanna, 483
de Flambeaux, Leo, (aka Prince Prospero, aka Leroy James Howes), 175-177, **177, 180,** 180-186, 271-272, 274-275, 281, 283, 351, 484
Dahinda's Acres, 390, 401
de la Rocha, David, 523
Delay, Jack, 72, 73, 114, 499
DeNormanville, Helen, 279
DeSpain, Arwen, 84, 484
DeSpain Bridge, 398
DeSpain Lane, 398
DeSpain, Linda, 484
DeSpain, Robert (aka Robert the Red aka Backhoe Bob), 13, **133, 155, 157,** 238-241, 336, 347, 397, 398, 403, 416, **470,** 470-471, 484, 497, 517
  as board member, 156, 159, 160, 235, 262, 323
  and Community Village, 61, 84, 155-156, 158, 240, 289, **290,** 297
  as fair co-treasurer, 158-159
  as fair president, 162, 235, 262, 268, 322, 397
  and highway bypass, 201-204, **204,** 262, 269
  and Main Camp, 155-166, 167-169
  as OM/BUM Team member, 238-39, **239, 323,** 435
de Tarr, Gavi, 523
de Tarr, Seiza, 51-53, 103, 110, 448, 523
Diggers, 490
Dillon, Daniel, 421, **457,** 459-460

as fair president, 456-458, 461-463, 464, 467-468
Divine Balance Fruit Salad, 187-197, **188, 189, 195, 197,** 508
Dr. Atomic's Medicine Show (aka Doctor Atomic's World Famous Medicine Show), 134, **135,** 135, 217, 243, 333
"Do You Believe," 346
Doc Sprinsock and the SANCApators, 449
Dolecki, Mac, 523
Doolin, Don, 165, 424, **435,** 517
Dorn, Thom "Moonsong," 181
Dorste, Bob, 240
Doscher, Christopher, 484
Doscher, Laurie (aka Heidi), 406, 419, 422, 427, **428,** 484
Doscher, John, 166, 386, 388, **390,** 423, 424, 434, 437, 484
Doscher, Vivian, 484
Dougherty, Kevin, 427-428, **428**
Doyon, Mary (Shuler), 422-423, 427-428, **428**
Drew, Mary, 465
Dreisbach, Liz, 523
Dritz, Bob, 152
Drug Abuse Community Network, 317
Drug Information Center, 313-321, **316, 317,** 515-516
Drum Tower. (*See also* Junction), **85,** 172, 401
Duggin, Dan, 523
Duke, Skeeter, 61, **290,** 291, 299
Dumdi, Ellie, Lane County commissioner, 462, 463
dunk tank booth, 352
Dunniford, Robert, 365
Durant, Dave, 159
Durnell, Bob, 421
DuRuz, Darcy, 472, 473-482, **478,** *photo credits, 478, 479*
Dwyer, P. K., 336-338
Dynamic Logs, 336, 343

E

Eagles, Twin, 105, 107
East Park (archaeology site 35LA759), 509
Eberhardt, Peter, **151,** 266, **267,** 269, 274, 308, 493
fair cartographer, 73-74, 199, *photo credit, 203*, **203,** 516
Economic Cooperation booth, 285, 286
Edmunds, Sallie, 158, 165, 300, **300,** 324, 327, 355, 435
and Energy Park (aka Oregon Energy Horizons), 39, 42, 158, 165, 297, 495, 498
as fair general manager, 323-324, 347, 349, 354-355, 395, 516
as OM/BUM member, 239, **239,** 323, 358, 398, 426
Eisenberg, Avner "the Eccentric," 29, 33, 35, 49, 78, 82, 105, 136, 217, 263, 343
Ekanger, Dennis, 515
el Coyote, Sulyman "Sol," 179
Elders at the fair, 185, 258, 391, 487. 491
Elections Committee, 238, 261, 419-420
Electron Connection, 45
Elliott, Iain, 61-62, **61,** 63, 64, 286, 287-288, 290, 514
photo credits, 61, 67, 70, 71, 352
Elliott, Ramblin' Jack, 83
Elliott, Steve, 362-364
Emerald People's Utility District (EPUD), 348, 349-350, 491
Emerald Valley Kitchen, 193
Energia, 489
Energy Outfitters, 45
Energy Park (aka Oregon Energy Horizons), 12, 36, 39-46, **41, 44, 46,** 133, 215, 239, 265, 270, 297, 323, 352, 369, 399, 424, 433, 437, 489, 516
displays and activities, 133, 172, 265-266, 333, 351, 365
home for giant puppets, 276-277, **277,** 351
Kesey Stage, 135, 333, 366
Energy Park Electric Company, 43, 44
Energy Service Company, 489
Entertainment Camp, 275, 330, 345, 380
Entertainment coordinators, 35, 49, 80, 82, 138, 158, 159, 175, 239, 263, 266, 275-276, 328, 330, 336, 365, 376, 408, 418-419, 476, 499
Ambiance coordinator, 377, 418-419, 516
Main Stage coordinator, 350, 364, 516
Vaudeville coordinator, 287, 516

Index

Epstein, Connie (now Dinneen), 157
Essential Event, 222, 422, 471. *See* Oregon Country Fair. *See also*, Artis the Spoonman
Estes, Caroline, 224-229
   and Alpha Farm, 224-229, 233-234
   and consensus, 225, 227, 228, 230-232
   and Community Village, 231-232
Estes, Jim, 224-225, 233
Estes, Maria, 225, 233
Ettinger, Caroline, 345
Ettinger, Kate, 345
Ettinger, Mark, 335, 339, 340, 345, 346, 523
Eugene Beekeepers Cooperative, 488. *See also* Queenright Beekeepers
Eugene Carpool Program, City of, 266
Eugene Celebration, 166, 269, 274, 384
Eugene Celebration Parade, **269,** 269-270, 274, 384
Eugene City Council, 116, 128
Eugene Crafts Guild, 485
Eugene Human Rights Commission, 128
Eugene Mideast Peace Group, 128
Eugene Peace Choir, 264
Eugene Public Library, 200
Eugene Saturday Market, 25, 166, 418
   Fair Thee Well, 483, 485, 486, 489
   vendors (craft and food booths), 249-250, 253, 254, 255- 256, 382
Evans, Martha, 291, 292-294, 457, 465
EZ Camp, 441

F

Fabulous Dyketones, 66
Fair Central, 74, 278, 365, 381, 395, 403
Fair Family Flashes, 423
Fair Family News, 13, 258, 422-429, **428, 429,** 460, 461,
   Fair Thee Well, 483, 487
Fall Creek Bakery, 361
Family Shelter House, 60
Farrell, Ben, 523
Farrell, Phillip, 523
Farren, Elliott, **352**
Far Side, the, 439-440
Fatima, 273, **277**
Feb-ru-ary, 452, 485
Feedback Coordinator, 487

Feeney, Anne, 218
Feet of Clay, 132
Felders, Dean, 414, 415, 417, 420, 424
Feldman, Nancy, 503
Fennessy, Bob, 291, 514
Fern Ridge community, 436, 469
Fern Ridge Library, 436
Fern Ridge Middle School, 289, 462
Fern Ridge Reservoir, 120, 187, 207, 210, 393, 437
Fern Ridge School District, 436, 458
Fidanque, Dave, 291
Fifth Street Public Market, 123, 127, 129
Fighting Instruments of Karma Marching Chamber Band/Orchestra (aka *too many permutations to list*), 83-84, 105, 136, 137-138, 151, 171, 176, 266, 269, 274, 361, **362,** 407, 442-455, **445,** 475, 477, 480, 481, 522-524
   mentioned as "band," but not named, 25, 51, 58, 98, 113, 177, 216, 281, 473-474
   and New Old Time Chautauqua, 97, 102, 103, 105, 107-111
   in the Midnight Parade, 85-86, 277, 368, 475-476
Financial Planning Committee, 404
Fire Crew, 353, 516
Fire Marshall at the fair, 159, 499, 516
First Place Family Center, 404
Fish, Russ, 351
Flaming Zucchini. *See* Chumleigh
Flordigan, Rebo. *See* Hanson, Rebecca
Florian, Frank, 420
Flying Karamazov Brothers, 29, 32, 47-59, **58,** 81, 144, 148, 151, 171, 217, 218, 263, 454-455, 472-473, 485, 491, 500. *See also*, Furst, Tim; Kamikazi band; Magid, Paul; Nelson, Randy; Patterson, Howard; Williams, Sam
   and Bread and Roses, 57
   and *CBS Morning News,* 172
   at Circus Stage (aka Chumleighland) 12, 34, 78, 102, 136, **136,** 172, 173, 244, 350, 366-367, **447**
   and Chumleigh, 25, 49-53, 78, 81, 136, 330, 442

and the Fighting Instruments of
   Karma Marching Chamber Band/
   Orchestra, 102, 137-138, 171, 362,
   362, 444-446, **445,** 473
and the Grateful Dead, 47-48, 55-56,
   148, 151-152
and *Jewel of the Nile,* 263
and Midnight Show, 87, 102, 137, **137,**
   197, 267
and New Old Time Chautauqua, 58-
   59, 97, 104-107, 109-113, 139, 244
and Olympics Art Festival, the, 243,
   244, 263-264
at Stage Left, 475
and theater performances, 47-48, 56,
   172, 243, 330
food booths, 62, 73, 85, 168, 172, 194,
   218, 241, 288, 392, 401, 405, 407,
   477, 480, 489. *See also* Casablanca,
   Divine Balance Fruit Salad,
   Phoenix Rising, Toby's Tofu Palace
and electricity, 44
at the Grateful Dead Second
   Decadenal Field Trip, **149,** 150, 152,
   153
types of food, 82, 242, 351
and water, 91, 248-249, 326, 359-360,
   370
at Zumwalt Campground, 439
Food Booth coordinators, 248, 499
Food Committee, 127, 248, 252, 498, 516
FOOD for Lane County, 404
Fontain, Shawn, **376,** 379
Four-A. *See* Altered Able Access
   Advocacy, Community Village
Frades, Wendy J., 377
Frazer, Christine, 63, 285-286, 381
Free Souls motorcycle club, 212-213, 303
Free, Gail, 152
Freedom Song Network, 142, 145
Freelan, Jennifer, 523
Freelan, Stefan, 523
Freidel, Dorothy "Dolly," 509
Fremonster Theatrical Troupe, 344
Fremont Players, The, 344
Fremont Solstice Fair, 214
Frisco Pipe Collective, 125-126
Frohback, Linda, 488
"F Team," 327-329. *See also* Club Molimo
Fuller, Cody, 196

Fuller, Judy Herbert, 187-197, *photo credit, 197*
Fuller, Paul, 187-197, 463
Fuller, Zach, 196
Fulton, Alex, 216
Fulton, Belinda, 214, 215, 216, 220-221
Fulton, Kevin, 214, 215, **216,** 216, 220-221
Fulton, Nathan, 215
Furst, Tim (aka Fyodor Karamazov),
   47-48, 53-55, 81, 83, 138, 344, **362,**
   449, 499, 500-501. *See also* Flying
   Karamazov Brothers, Moisture
   Festival

G

Gael El Rooh, 176, 180
Garbage Crew, **133,** 150, 483, 488. *See also* Recycling Crew
Garcia, Jerry, 152. *See also* Grateful Dead
Garner, Mary Jo, 516
Gaskin, Stephen, 471
Gay Hotline, 60
Gellman, Crow, *photo credit, 409*
Genesis Juice (aka Genesis Organic
   Juice), 82, 132, 223, 230, 250
Gerringer, Azza, 185
Gesundheit Health Collective (aka
   Gesundheit Medical Collective), 59,
   105, 109
Gibboney, Willy, 256
Gilbertson, Denise, 185
Ginda, Diemo, 345
Ginda, Hacki, 343-344, 443, 476
Ginda, Myron "Moeppi," 345
Ginda, Rebekah, 345
Ging, Kathy, 497
Girl Circus, 472, 476-482, **478, 479, 481**
Girls Who Wear Glasses, 264, 266,
   351, 366, 485. *See also* Luby, Jan;
   Hanson, Rebecca
Giudici, Rya, 477, **478,** 480
global warming, 365
Goddard, Ann, *photo credit, 317*
Goldby, Mark, 514
Golden Avatar, 401
Goldhammer, Michael, 414, 417, 420
Goodman Theatre, 48, 56, 172, 243
Gordon, Dale, 316, 515
Gorham, Steve, 287, 421

INDEX

Gowan, Mark, 523
Grahn, Ande, 149-150, 324-325, 359, 396 435, 453, 484-485
Grahn, Aster, 324, 325, 359, 485
Grahn, Roger, 485
Grandmother's Potlatch, 486
Grand Ronde Reservation, 210
Grateful Dead, the, 16, 166, 191-192, 194, 365, 428, 471, 485, 489, 490
  and the Flying Karamazov Brothers, 47-48, 55-56
  and the Second Decadenal Field Trip, 147-154, **148**, 157, 388, 489
Gray, Charles, 115, 135
Gray, Jack, 192
Greenfield Ranch, 97-101, 232
Green Store, the, 489
Grier, Norma, 391, 394
Griffis-Means, Stephanie, 377, 379
Griggs, Kim, 427
Gritz la Ritz, 489
Growers Market, 60, 61, 62, 286, 287, 298
Guehler, Denny, 350, 363, 364
Guthrie, Jim, 201, 203, 236, 322, 418, 512
Gutter People, The, 337-338. *See also* Royal Famille Du Caniveaux
Gypsy Caravan Stage (aka Caravan Stage), 126, 175-186, **183, 184,** 221, 273, 275, 333
Gypsy Rose booth, 217

H

Hacki. *See* Ginda, Hacki
Hagan, Michael, 40
Hahn, Johnny, 432
Hale, Christopher, 99
Hamide, Ibrahim, 123-130
Hamide, Dahlia, 129
Hamide, Naseem, 129-130
Hamide, Soriah, 126
Hanson, Rebecca (aka Rebo Flordigan), 35, **106,** 264, 332, 452-453, 485. *See also* Girls Who Wear Glasses, Rebo Gazebo
  and the New Old Time Chautauqua, 107-108, 110, 452-453, **453**
Harcleroad, District Attorney Doug, 464, 466-468
Harger, Wayne, 515

Harris, Niki, 14, 427, *photo credit, 429*
Harrison, Gil, 12, **149,** *photo credit, 149,* 485-486, 499
Hart, Mickey, 47
Hartzell, Hal, 13
Hartzell, Betsy Vaughn Wemple, 491
Harvest Fair, 487
Harvey, Andrew, 431, 435
Hathaway, Don, 270, 276
Hathorn, Susanna, 483
Hathorn, Gil, 483
Havel, Mary Beth, 517
Hayfield. *See* Sheklow, Sally
Head Start, 60
Health booth in Community Village (aka Health and Human Services booth), 61, 82, 295, 299
Heath, Barry, 153
Hedges, Michael, 134, 173
Heilman, Robert Leo, 297-298
Heiman, Jill, 40, **76,** 114-118, **115, 119,** 121, 122, **242,** 286, 354-355, 361, 402-403, 486. *See also* Jill Heiman Vision Fund
  and fair's freedom of assembly lawsuit against Lane County, 75, 118-120, 121
  and fair's nonprofit incorporation, 25, 117, 118
Heiman & Miller, 115, 116, 486
Henderson, Floyd, 463
Henderson, "Water Paul," 514
Henry, Anne, 404, 421, 422, 486, 517
Hevly, Lou, (aka Gens Du Caniveaux, aka King Louie) 337-338, 341
Higgins, Karen, 176, 185
Highway Committee, 202
Highway Flaggers Coordinator, 517
Hildebrandt, Todd, **278,** 283, 284
Hill, Holly "Dolphin," **312**
Hilo, Percy, 134, 170, **290**
Hippies, 27, 30, 32, 61-62, 84, 86, 110, 113, 120, 123, 129, 177, 187, 192, 203, 227, 256, 272, 310, 342, 351, 354, 363, 368, 402, 423, 445, 462
  lifestyle and movement, 20, 97, 124, 125, 177, 252, 257, 293, 338, 387, 487
Hiring Committee, 430-431
History booth, 436, 517
Hoag, Paxton, 90, 91, 168, 421

photo credits, 58, 135, 137, 170, 177, 340, 362, 363, 366
Hodgden, Jen-Lin, 256
Hoedads, 115, 116, 164, 190, 202, 303, 324, 387, 388, 418, 456
  Fair Thee Well, 484, 487, 491
  and fair's Main Camp cooks, 164, 238, 324-325
  and fair Security, 303-304, 387
  and the Grateful Dead's Second Decadenal Field Trip 149-150
Hoffman, David, 291, **296**, 296-297, 386, 514
Hogan, Jay, 181, 271-284, **278**, *photo credit,* 282
"Hokey Pokey, The," 66, 291, 301
Holder, Cyn, 279
Holiday Market, 250, 255, 256
Homa, Kathleen, 160
Homefried Truckstop, 223. *See also* Mama's Homefried Truckstop
Horse Crew. *See* Traffic Equestrian Crew
Horste, David (aka Leo Sunshine), **278**
Horstman, Steve, 523
Horton, Pat, Lane County District Attorney, 315
Hoshigose, 183, 271, 274
Hospitality Crew (aka Crew Services), 488
Hovemann, Glen, 225, 233
Howard, Karen, **376**
Howard, Tim **376**
Howe, Chris, 353, 517
Howe, Henry, 353, 503, 517
Howes, Leroy James. *See* de Flambeaux, Leo
Human rights, 124, 128, 129, 431, 432, 433
Human Services booth in Community Village, 60
Huntington, Walt, 228

Ichabod. *See* Murray, Chris (aka Ichabod)
Illuminated Fools, 283
Indian Creek, 156, 398
Industrial Workers of the World (aka IWW aka Wobblies), 141, 145
Information booth at Community Village, 298

Information booth at Energy Park, 172
Information Crew (aka Info Crew), 13, 72-74, 84, **117,** 132, 138, 161, 167, 169, 172, 281, 292, 403, 475, 486
  coordinators, 72, 73, 114, 159, 499, 517
Integral House**,** 40, 295-296, **297,** 299, 432. *See also* Come Unity House, Community Village
Integrated Pest Management, 351, 437
intentional communities, 88, 101, 195, 224-229, 232-233
Interfaith Prayer Service, 128
Ivey, Chuck, 202

Jackals, 265
Jakabosky, Sue, 41-42, 43, 45
Jalof, Jef "JJ," 195
James Long, Jennifer, 185
James Long, Penny (aka Bene Sharez), 185
Jamison, Paula, **296**
Jello Art Show, 371, 378, 379, 381-383, **383,** 384
Jensen, Chuck, 348
Jensen, Judy. *See* Bale, Jeff
Jewel of the Nile, The, 263, 267
Jill Heiman Vision Fund, 93, 403-405, 471, 486
Jill's Crossing, 402, 486
Johnson, Al, 202
Johnson, Ron, 463
Jones, Cheryl, 173, **290,** 299
Jones, Darcy, 487
Jones, Joann, 490
Jones, Miel, 487
Jones, Wally, 17, 18, 150, 487
Joyce, David, 378-379
Junior League, 318
Justis, Tim (aka Ensign Tim), 310, **312**
J-Walkers, 265

Kalapuya peoples, 205-208, 210
Kallstrom, Janet, 515
Kamikazi band, 263
Karamazov, Alyosha. *See* Nelson, Randy
Karamazov, Dmitri. *See* Magid, Paul
Karamazov, Fyodor. *See* Furst, Tim

Index

Karamazov, Ivan. *See* Patterson, Howard
Karamazov, Smerdyakov. *See* Williams, Sam
Karamazovs. *See* Flying Karamazov Brothers
Karst, Richard, 523
Kassler, Deon, 503
Kassler, Helenita, 90
Kassler, Janina, 503
Kassler, Lynn, 503
Kauffman, Andrea Lee. *See* Grahn, Ande
Kelly, Brian Keith Kelley (aka Ensign Kelley), 308, **312**
Kennedy, Miles, 523
Kenny, Dave, 206
Kent State University shootings, 19, 302
Kesey Park, 40, 135
Kesey Stage, 43, 135, 276, 333, 366
Kesey, Chuck, 36, 40, 135, 147-148, 152, 165, 193, 194, 487. *See also* Springfield Creamery
Kesey, Ken, 16, 36, 40-41, **41,** 135, 148, 152, 153, **363,** 363-365, 367, 487
Kesey, Sue, 147-148, 153, 165, 193, 412, 415, 487. *See also* Springfield Creamery
at the fair, 36, 40, 135, 170-171, 252, 516
Killgallon, Michael, 75, **77,** 156, 157, 239-240
Kimball, Roderick, 523
Kingsley, Lucy (Parker), 159, 235, 262, 336, 499
Kinkley, Robin Richardson Ulrich, 16, 18
Kloos, Bill, 202-203
Klute, Allison, 230
Knowles, Rene, 417, 418, 420
KOCF, 471
Kohler, Chris, 211, 212-213
Kolb, Bliss (aka the Magnificent Mazuba), 49, 78, 82, 264, 331-332, 366, 490
and Laughing Moon Theater, 57, 263, 266, 331, 337, 366
and the New Old Time Chautauqua, 105
Koon, Teresa, 332
Kraines, Carl (aka Red Rhodes), 145
Kreutzmann, Bill, 47, 471
Krug, Peter, 139
Kunowski, Henry, 240

L

Landman, Breana, **242,** 488
Landman, Chelsea, 13, **242,** 488
Landman, Marshall, 13, **242,** 261, 288-289, 291, 396, 460, 488
and Community Village, 156, 161, 231, 288, **290,** 291, 299, 484
on fair board, 262, 355, 359, 368
as OM/BUM Team member, 262, 289, 358, 435, 368
Landry, Sheila, 427-428, **428**
Land Search Committee, 156
Landis, Sasha, 523
Lane Arts Council, 299
Lane Community College, 42, 89, 192, 285, 433, 473, 484, 489
Automobile repair program, 285
Energy Research Group, 42
Lane County, 12, 115, 116, 117, 118, 164, 236, 246, 248, 296, 297, 315, 351, 357, 358-359, 368-369, 370, 441, 466
assemblies ordinance and permit, 75, 131
Board of Commissioners, 25, 75, 114, 115, 116, 119, 121, 202, 291, 408, 462-463, 464
district attorney, 315, 316, 464, 466-467, 468-469
Health Department, 192, 248, 315, 351
and highway realignment, 202-204, 360
Oregon Country Fair lawsuit against, 25, 75, 119-120, 121-122, 403
Planning Commission, 202-203, 509
sheriff and sheriff's deputies, 25, 118-119, 357, 368, 434, 459, 464, 466, 468-469
Lane County Fair, 248
Lane Education Service board, 115
Lane Transit District, 241, 266
Langham, Coire Ready, 523
Langham, John, 523
Langham, Mary, 523
La Primavera, 489
Larsen, Jim, 91, 520
Larson, Bernie, 439-440
Laue, Gaelen, 365
Laughing Moon Theater, 57, 263, 266,

539

331, 337, 351, 366, 490. *See also* Kolb, Bliss; Venezia, Bob; Williams, Sam
Lauridsen, Les, 516
Leash, Bob, 303
Leathers, Cynde, 427
Left Bank, the, 395, 398-402, 417, 442, 520
Leishman, Diana, 113
Leishman, Gina, 523
Lerch, Albert. *See* Meda, Dahinda
Lerch, Brad, 392, 394, 422, 424, 427, 428, **428**
Lerch, Erica, 387, **392,** 422-423, 424
Lerch, John, 387, **392,** 392, 394
Lesh, Phil, 471
Levidow, Nancy, 523
Liberty, Jill, 516
Lichtenstein, David, 287
Liebig, Mary Cay, 117
Life-Long Learning Booth, 61
Lindsley, Barney, 523
Linn, Jim, 514
Lions, Mike, **77**
Lisi, Roy, 516
Little People's booth at Community Village, 287-288
Lively, Dave, 197
Lively, Tom, 192
Live Matinee, 374
Livingston, Brian, 13
Lloyd, Ron, 264, **265**
Local Self-Reliance Booth, 61, 287, 473
Lomont, Patti, **160,** 161, 239, 262, 289-290, 327, 357, 437
  photo credits, 133, 136, 160
Long Tom River, 11, 24, 25, 48, 76, 122, 348, 360, 440
  and fair site archaeology, 200-201, 204, 205, 207-208, 210, 212
  and fair Navy, 305, **306,** 308-310
  and highway re-alignment, 198, 202, **203**
  flooding and erosion, 21, 120, 165, 205, 326, 335, 398, **401**
Long Tom site (archaeology site 35LA439), 509
Lot Crew, 460, 465
Love Family, 105-106, 108-109, 187
Lubin, Joanne (aka Lady Jojo), **312**
Luby, Jan, 34, 35, 38, 49, 59, 82, 173, 264,

332, 485. *See also* Girls Who Wear Glasses
  and New Old Time Chautauqua 105, **106,** 107, 113
Lundquist, David, 149
Luther, Kathleen, 523
Lynch, Larry, **376**
Lynch, Lucy, 336, 358, 398, 516
Lystad, Lisa, 523

M

Mackie, Brendan, **119,** 402, 486
Mackie, Gerry, 116, **119,** 122, 361, 402, 486
Madden, Ethan, 295, 397-398
Madden, Kathryn, 13, 353-354, 403-405, **411,** 412, 415
  as board member, 368, 395-396, 408, 414, 417, 420
  as board president, 396-398, **399,** 406, 418, 419, 421
  and Community Village, 290, 295-296, **296,** 298, 300, **300,** 354, 514, 516
Maddox, Dan, **149**
Mafufo, Armando, 179
Magical Mystical Michael, 29, 35, 351, 366
Magical Strings, 173
Magid, Paul (aka Dmitri Karamazov), 49-51, 53, 54, 78, 173, 267, 330, 337, 345, 454-455, 485
  in the Fighting Instruments of Karma Marching Chamber Band/Orchestra, 523
  as a Flying Karamazov Brother, 32, 49, 53, 55-57, 87, 243-244, 263, 267, 366, **447**
  and New Old Time Chautauqua, 58-59, 104-107, **106,** 110-112
Magid, Pesha, 345
Magid, Rebecca, 345
Magnificent Mazuba. *See* Kolb, Bliss
Main Camp, 13, 73, 74, 92, 136, 160-161, 164, 173, 174, 240, 322-323, 358, 388, 395-398, 431-432, 484
  coordinators, 75, 92, 165, 325, 328, 350, 499, 517
  and entertainers, 37-38, 173, 174
  fair operations hub, 75, 77, 117, 131,

132, 156-160, 165, 168-169, 217, 241, 262, 268, 294, 298, 300, 303, 357, 398, 434-435
and the Left Bank expansion, 400-402
volunteers at, 13, 38, 75-77, **76, 77,** **115,** 117, 149, 153, 156-158, 159, 161, 165, 239, **242,** 262, 289-290, 296, 300, **300,** 323-325, 353-354, 360, 395-396, 304, 403, 411, **411,** 414, 415, 484-485, 488, 490, 492

Main Camp Kitchen, 24, 48, 77, 95, 169, 325, 359, 392, 396, 435
cooks at, 75, 92, 160, 164, 238, 324-325, 359, 396, 435, 453, 485

Main Stage, 22, 27, 82, 88, 89, 128, 167, 174, 183, 189, 214-215, 220, 239, 240, 254, 282, 292, 326, 350, **390, 399,** 456, 459, 464, 517. See also Politics Park
and barter fair, 408-409
electric power at, 173, 349-350, 410-411
and the fair's twentieth anniversary, 361-365
and Midnight Show, 126, 196, 218, 267-268, 367-368, 449
performances at, 22, 82-83, 134, 173, 180, 181, 241, 264-265, 333, 350, 374, 379, 471
and Teddy Bears' Picnic, 174, 399, 417

Makarchek, Jack, 402
Malcolm, Marion, 291
Mama's Homefried Truckstop, 64, 150. See also Homefried Truckstop
Mama's Momos, 218
Map Gallery booth, 266, 267, 308-309. See also Eberhardt, Peter
Mapleton Area Advocacy Planning Council, 228
Marijuana (aka pot aka cannabis), 12, 19, 125, 132, 147, 187, 190, 191, 192, 243, 280, 388, 459, 469
Marker, Laurie, 78-80, 85-86
Marshall, Jennifer, 185
Marshall, Sam "Zamora," 175, 176-180, **183,** 185-186
photo credits, 180, 183, 184
Marthaller, Debbie. See Bloom, Debbie (Marthaller)
Marthaller, Joe, 215
Marthaller, Shanti, 215

Martin, Joel, 91
Martin, Mike, 75, 253-256, 329
Mascall, Djuna, 523
Maude Kerns Art Center, 378, 379, 382, 383, 384, 485
Mayer, Nicholas, 523
Maynard, Bob-1, 43-44, 45-46
McAllister, Tom. See Noddy, Tom
McCall, Tom Governor, 19, 20
McCaslin, Mary, 333
McKay, Dave, 279, 280
McDonald, Jessie, 164, 238, 324
McDonald, John, 238, 324
McDowell, Patricia, 205, 509
McKenzie River Gathering, 115-116, 135
McLoud, Don, 515
McMartin, John, 255-256
McWhorter, Diane, 253-260, 381-383, **383**
Meda, Dahinda, 353, 385-394, **390, 392,** 413, 487, 520
as board member, 391, 417, 418, 420
and Café Mam, 391-392
and Dahinda's Acres, 389-390
and VegManECs, 385-386, 393, 399-400, 413
Menser, Gary, 319
Merry Pranksters, 16, 40-41, 153, 364, 487, 489. See also Kesey, Ken
Mertz, Joshua, 179, **183,** 185
Metsch, Mike, 125
Meyns, Fay, 313
Midnight Show, 51, 56, 66, 71, 102, 126, 137, **137,** 144-145, 181, 196, 197, 217, 218, 267-268, 301, 334, 337, 339, 340, 345, 363, 367-368, 419, 449, 474
and the torchlight parade, 85-87, 277, 475-476
Mielnik, Michael. See Chumleigh
Mileto, Marie, 523
Miller, Gretchen, 114-115, 116, **117,** 486
Miller, Mark, 313-321, **317,** 515
Miller, Tim (aka Charlie Brown), 287, 351
Millican, Canis, **278,** 279
Minkler, Randy, 339-342, 344, 346. See also Daniel, Godfrey
Mirkwood booth, 214
Mirkwood Forest, 32
Mithrandir, 82, 134, 329

Moisture Festival, 344, 472
Monasterio, Rita, **376**
Monster Cookies, 153
Montgomery, Anya, 158, 162, 262, 323-324, 325, 327, 516
Moon, Isak. 342, 345
Moon, Shannon, 342, 345
Mooney, Michael, **290**
Moon Lodge at Community Village, 288
Moore, Diana. *See* Zell-Ravenheart, Morning Glory
Moore, Kevin, 283
Moran, Larry, 499
Morganti, Roberto, 35, 49, 78, 136, 173, 243, 500
Mosely, Mose, 443, 524
Mothers Against Misuse and Abuse, 321
Mother Zosima, 278
Mousie, **367,** 443. *See also* Tom Noddy
Movement for a New Society, 134
Moye, Ed, 170, **204,** 323, 353-354, 398, 399, **399,** 412-413, 415-416
   and Club Molimo, 327-328
   and Construction Crew, 240, 335, 352-353, 396, 412, 425-426, 512
   as Main Camp coordinator, 325, 350, 517
Mud Bay Jugglers, 266, 333, 351
Mud People, 144
Murphy, Kim, 361
Murray, Chris (aka Ichabod), 348, 516
Mystic Krewe of Prince Prospero of the Knights of the Lost Realm, 175-176, 181, 272, 274-275, 283. *See also* de Flambeaux, Leo

N

Narvaez, Santos (aka Toes), 159, 165, **242,** 325, 414, 415, 499, 512
   as board member 159, 235, 403
National Lawyers Guild, 292
natural foods, 16, 19, 61, 62-65, 66, 70, 89, 124, 127, 177, 179, 191-193, 194, 206-209, 223-224, 227, 245-250, 288, 391-392
Navy at the fair. *See* Security Crew
Neale, Simon, 344
Nealon, Darrell, 415
Nearly Normal's, 464

Neighbor Liaison Crew, 290, 437
Neighborhood Response Team (aka NRTs), 292, 434, 483, 484
Neighborhoods and Community booth at Community Village, 490
neighbors of the fair site, 198, 348, 458, 461-463, 468. *See also* Respect Our Community Committee, Zumwalt Campground
campgrounds, 405, 437-439, 440-441
complaints about the fair, 117, 357, 368, 461
outreach from fair 289-290, 292, 357, 361, 368, 405, 433-435, 436-441, 458, 462
Nelson, Randy (aka Alyosha Karamazov), 49, 53-57, 85-86, 172. *See also* Flying Karamazov Brothers
Neuhaus, Barbara, 492, 517
Neville, Ben, 524
Neville, Daniel, 524
New Day Bakery, 401
New Frontier Market, 191
New Games, 243, 266, 288, 299, 333, 366
New Growth Forestry, 388
Newman (mask-maker and giant puppeteer), 283
Newman, Gary, **41**
New Moon Grounding Circle, 230
New Old Time Chautauqua (aka Old Time New Age Chautauqua), 58-59, 77, 102-103, 104-113, **106, 107, 108, 109, 112,** 139-140, 143-144, 244, 324, 449, 451-453, **453,** 472, 522-524
   Fair Thee Well, 485, 489
Newsom, Ry, **352**
Newton, Joseph, 427
New Vaudeville, 25, 28-29, 32-33, 34-38, 48-49, 57-59, 78, 81, 82, 86, 104, 112, 140, 143-144, 172-173, 182, 218, 263, 266-268, 287, 327, 330, 333, 335-346, 366-368, 407-408, 443-444, 452-455, 476-482, 485
Nicholson, Wesley, 515
Night Flight, 313
Noddy, Tom (aka the Bubble Guy aka Tom McAllister), 13, 28-38, **38,** 49, 57, 77-78, 81, 83, 84, 96, 221-222, 343, 423, 426, 499-501

INDEX

and Circus Stage (aka Not
  Chumleighland), 243-244, 264,
  266, **331,** 331-332, 351, 366-368, **367,**
  443, 452-453
and the Midnight Show, 71, 144-145,
  267-268, 334
and New Old Time Chautauqua, 59,
  105-106, 113, 452
on the *Tonight Show Starring Johnny
  Carson*, 172-173
and the W.C. Fields (Memorial) Stage,
  35-38, **36,** 136, 243, 443, 472
and Westwind Travelin' Vaudeville,
  34-35
Nordling, Todd, 524
Norris, Sandy, 516
Northwest Center or Alternatives to
  Pesticides (NCAP) 391
Northwest Power Planning Council, 266
Norton Buffalo and the Knockouts, 323
Norton, Ron, 510
Not Chumleighland. *See* Circus Stage
Noti, Oregon, 187, 191, 192, 198
nuclear energy. *See* anti-nuclear activism

O

Oasis, 351
O'Brien, Danny, 340, 344
Obsidian Wind Chimes, 211-222, **216,
  221**
"Ode to Paula Jo," by Sally Sheklow aka
  Hayfield, 66-70
O'Dell, Cabal, **77**
O'Dell, Marcia (later Masters), 75, **76,**
  158, 165
Odo, 272-273, **273, 277,** 279
Odyssey Coffee House, 11, 20
Odyssey Info Booth, 73-74, 247
Officer, Shandra Goodpasture, *photo
  credits, 36, 41, 85, 93, 231, 304, 447*
Olde English Christmas Fair aka Dickens
  Faire, 246
Old Time New Age Chautauqua. *See*
  New Old Time Chautauqua
Olufs, John, 339, 340, 344, 346
Olympic Arts Festival, 243-244
Om-Chi Herbs, 492
Om Circle, 257, 291-292
Om Farm, 187, 189-192, 195

OM Team (aka Operations Management
  Team), 238-239, **239,** 241, 261-262,
  289, 323, 324, 325, 357, 358, 359,
  368, 435. *See also* BUMs (aka Back
  Up Managers)
Fair Thee Well, 484, 488
O'Neill, Brian, 204, 509
Oregon Candy Company, 246-247, 249
Oregon Country Fair. *See also:* Oregon
  Country Renaissance Fair,
  Renaissance Faire in Oregon, crews
  and committees listed separately
  by name
alter-abled accessibility, 297-298, 333,
  381
annual membership meeting, 159,
  237-238, 261-262, 268-269, 391, 456
barter fair, 408-410
board of directors, 40, 44, 78, 80, 132,
  147, 156, 174, 194, 199, 202, 235,
  237-239, 261, 268-269, 288, 289, 294,
  296, 322, 324, 326, 329-330, 347,
  353-354, 355, 358, 359, 368-369, 385,
  390, 391, 395-396, 402, 404-405,
  406-421, 422, 430, 433, 439-440,
  456-457, 459, 460-461, 470; Fair
  Thee Well, 486, 487, 489, 491
booth construction guidelines, 235,
  236-237, 241, 359
bus service, 96, 129, 241, 266, 368, 438,
  483
bylaws, 162, 237, 261, 268, 294, 330,
  416, 420
camping passes, 34, 93, 132, 158, 165,
  176, 197, 214, 271-272, 287, 292, 298,
  329, 367, **386,** 393, 407, 408, 459,
  460-461
caretaker, 157, 348, **348,** 349, 354, 386,
  389, 392, 402, 411, 412-414, 416, 419,
  424, 425, 430, 434, 484, 491
Code of Conduct, 415
donations, 402-405, 435-436
drug and alcohol policy, 132, 161, 164,
  220, 456, 459, 463-469
electric power to fair site, 348-350,
  406, 410-411, 425
general manager, 323-324, 347, 354-
  355, 356-357, 368, 396, 398, **400,**
  402, 412, 415, 419, 430-432, 433,
  434-435, **435,** 470

543

governing structure, 118, 155, 160-162, 294-295, 352, 355
grievances, 174, 237-238, 353-354, 355, 412-413, 415-416
Guidelines, 332, 465
highway construction fight, 198-204, 237, 238, 262, 269, 294, 303, 347, 360-361, 368
land purchases, 120-122, 131-132, 153-154, 156-157, 198, 288, 389-391, 398-399, 403, 439-440, 486
lawsuit against Lane County, 75, 118-120, 121, 486
name change, 24
as a nonprofit, 12, 25, 27, 90, 117, 118, 120, 433, 471, 486
officers, 121, 147, 159, 162, 204, 262, 287, 289, 300, 322-324, 357, 390, 396-398, 398-399, 404, 406, 418-419, 432, 456, 484
rain fairs, 22-23, 167-174, 183, 237, 240, 483
Recycling Award, 251
retreats, **160,** 160-161, 238-239, 262, 327, 329-330, 464
traffic problems, 18, 21, 119, 153, 357, 361, 368, 437-438
water supply, 37, 77, 137, 150, 159, 248-249, 261, 326, 348, 351-353, **352,** 358-360, 369-370, **370,** 389, 401
Oregon Country Fair Adopt-A-Highway Pickup, 483, 484
Oregon Country Renaissance Faire, 24, 246
Oregon Department of Transportation, 198, 199-200, 262
Oregon Drug Information Center, 313-321, 516-517
Oregon Energy Horizons Committee, 497, 499. *See also* Energy Park
Oregon Event Enterprises, 165-166, 424, 483, 484
Oregon PeaceWorks, 93, 217. *See also Peaceworker News Magazine*
Oregon Potters Association, 486
Oregon State Highway Division, 201-202, 204, 369

Oregon State Museum of Anthropology, 199, 200, 204

Oregon State University, 352, 484
Oregon State University Extension Master Gardeners Program, 296-297
Oregon Yurtworks, 424-425
Organically Grown Cooperative (aka Organically Grown Company), 193, 266, 351, 356
Osborn, Larry, 125
Oskay, Billy, 343
Oskay, Jackie, 345
Oskay, Lauren, 345
Otchy, Christine (aka Zarouhi), 176, 185
Otte, Paul, 256
Ottenhausen, Michael, 422, 424, 427, 428, **428**
OUR Credit Union, 286

P

Page, Jim, 83, 173, 218, 221, 264, 333, 351
Painter, Robert, 362, 488
Palindrome, the, 485
Parades, 151, 257, 272, 328, 323, 377, 426. *See also* Eugene Celebration Parade and the Fighting Instruments of Karma Marching Chamber Band/Orchestra, 51, 83-84, 137-138, 171, 176, 177, 216, 266, 279, 361, **362,** 368, 444, 446-449, 475, 477, 480
giant puppets at the fair, 276-277, 333
Lime Green parade, 377-378
midnight torchlight parade (aka Midnight Show parade), 85-86, 367
at New Old Time Chautauqua, 59, 106, 111, 113, 451
Peachi Dragon parade, 377-378
Risk of Change, 276-277, 279. 280-282, 333
Parker, Douglas, 262, 322-323, 324, 512
Parker, Lucy. *See* Kingsley, Lucy Parker
Parker, Palmer, 13, 64, 159, **159, 242,** 323, 398, 403, 415, 497, 499, 516
Parrot, John, 237, 261, 262
"Party at the Fair," 335
Pate, Tim, *photo credit,* 428
Path Rove Crew, 310
Path Planning Committee. *See* Planning Committee
Patrick, Terry 75, **77,** 156, 157
Patterson, Craig, 40, **290,** 495

INDEX

Patterson, George, 44, 46
Patterson, Howard (aka Ivan Karamazov), 51, 78-79, 81, 84, 97, 144, 330, 350, 454-455
  in the Fighting Instruments of Karma Marching Chamber Band/Orchestra 102, 103, 442, 444-447, **445, 447,** 448, 449, 450, 452, 524
  as a Flying Karamazov Brother, 32, 49-50, 51-56, 78-80, 81
  with New Old Time Chautauqua, 102-103, 104, **106,** 109-110, 452
Patterson, Jasper, 144, 350, 448, 454, 524
Patti's Pies, 352
Payne-Towler, Christine, 133, 230
Peace Arch Park, 111
Peace and Justice booth in Community Village, 288, 291, 292, 293
Peace and justice movement, 28. 71, 115-116, 118, 125, 217-218, 224, 362, 418
  at Community Village 243, 288, 291-293, 366
  and Faith Petric, 140-141, 142, 145-146
  and the Rainbow Family, 16, 19-20, 22, 24, 26
  and Leslie Scott, 430, 433
PeaceWorker News Magazine, 218. *See also* Oregon Peaceworks
Peachi the Dragon, 377-378, **378**
Peach Pit, the, 39, 43, 72, 74, 131, 172, 175, 241, 261, 333, 356, 365
  coordinators, 421, 487, 517
  Fair Thee Well, 487
Peach Power Fund, 44, 46, 259
Peach Truck, 360, 396, 397
People for Prison Alternatives, 60
Peoples, Peg, 291
Pershnokov, Angela, 372-374, 376-377, 380, 384. *See also* Radar Angels
Personnel Committee, 354, 355, 368, 396, 412-414, 415, 419, 430, 458
Peter, Paul, and Mary, 471
Peterson, Lynn, 509
Petric, Faith, 136, 139-146, **143,** 243, 264, 331, **331,** 346, 351, 488
Pettigrew, Richard, 199, 200, 204
PharmChem, 315
Phillips, Utah, 139, 243-244
Phoenix Rising booth, 88-96, 503

Pincus, Jon, 497, 517
Pipia, Jenny, 524
Pitts, Cynthia, 524
Pitts, Stephen "Bear," 308
Planning Committee (aka Path Planning Committee), 287, 326, 395, 398, 404, 407, 426, 429, 435, 487, 520
Plunkr, Barry. *See* Adams, Barry Plunkr
Politics booth in Community Village, 432
Politics Park, 240-241
pony rides, 351
Poole, Randy, 510
Poppe, Russell, 354-355, 466, 468
Portland Saturday Market, 211, 213-214, 217
Portland Sun, 41-42
Poster Committee, 290
Pot. *See* Marijuana
Potter, Jennifer Sutherland, 345
Power, Michael, 484
Power, Noah, 484
Pranksters. *See* Merry Pranksters
Printing coordinator, 517
Proffer, Steve, 165,
Prouty, Reese, 75-76, **76,** 165, 300, **300,** 365, 395
  photo credits, 76, 77, 216, 248, 251, 373, 399, 457
Prozanski, Floyd, *photo credit,* 428
Prozanski, Suzi, *photo credit,* 26, 427
Prull, Greg, 399, 437
Prull, James, 370
psychospiritual rejuvenation (aka psycho-social-spiritual rejuvenation), 236, 260, 322, 327, 329-330, 347, 471
Publicity Coordinator, 159, 499
puppets, 17-18, 183, 271, 284
  and Leo de Flambeaux, 176-177, **177,** 181-182, 271
  and Illuminated Fools, 283
  and Tom Noddy, 28, 29, 32, 243, 244, 443
  and Risk of Change, 272-274, 276, 277, **277,** 278-279, 351
Pusey, Celise, 185
Pusey, Emily, 185
Pusey, Joanna (aka Kameal), 183-184, 185
Pusey, Joseph, 176, 179, **183,** 183-184

Quartermaster at the fair, 325, 435, 486, 499
Queenright Beekeepers, 287, 488. *See also* Eugene Beekeepers Cooperative
Quiet Camp, 441

R

Rabbit Hole, 96
Rachel the Storyteller, 267
Radar Angels, 241, 351, 371-384, **375, 376, 382, 383**
Rainbow Family, 19-20, 21, 22, 23-25, 26, 105, 187-189
Rainbow Farm, 23
Rainbow Gathering, 24-25, 26, 105, 187-189
Rainbow House, 23
Rainy, Mira, 427
Ram Dass, 471, 484
Ramsay, Mary, 524
Rand, Joanne, 380
Rape Crisis Network (aka Rape Crisis Center), 299, 373
Rastafaerie, 272, **277,** 279
Rebo Gazebo, 452-453, 485
Recycling Crew, 37, 74, 92, **133,** 150, 194-195, 251, 311, 401, 410, 421, 483, 517. *See also* Garbage Crew
Fair Thee Well, 486, 488
Refer Truck crew, 517
Reggae on the River, 459-460
Registration Crew, 74, 421, 424, 460, 461, 499, 517
Reiter, Morgan, 424-425
Renaissance Faire, 50, 107, 485
  in California, 16, 49-50, 445, 449
  in Minnesota, 107, 485
  in Oregon, 11, 16-18, 21-23, 24, 88-90, 125, 191, 211, 224, 226, 246, **246,** 314, 316, 483, 485, 486, 487, 488, 490, 492
Renfro, KC, 159, 262
Renfro, Walter, 137, 150, 152, 159, 161, 391, 517
Respect Our Community Committee, 463, 469
Reverend Chumleigh. *See* Chumleigh

Revolutionary Communist Youth Brigade, 295
Richmond, Jim, 416
Ringer, Jim, 333
Rising Moon Ravioli booth, 477, 480
Risk of Change, 271-284, 351, 361
Riskin, Kenny, **77**
Ritchey, Ryan, 510
Ritmo Tropicale, 265, 329
Ritta's Burritos, 401
Ritz Sauna at the fair, 91, 153, 180-181, 254, 282, 339-340, 358-359, 410. *See also* Braddock, George
Riven, Laurie, 50
Riverbrook Farm, 192
Roberts, Norah, 138, 517
Robinson, J.R., 398, 408, 417, 420, 421, 432, 456, 459, 517
Rodgers, Ken "Kenny," **204,** 325, 348, 352, 354, 355, 395, 396, 415, 516
Rodrigues, Nancy, 516
Rodz Sisters, the, 485. *See also* Hanson, Rebecca; Wilcoxon, CiCi
Roehnelt, Rod, 517
Rogers, Bennett, 510
Rogers, D.J., 510
Rohter, Brian, 262
Ron Lloyd & Friends, 264, **265**
Rooks, Dennis, 181
Rothkop, Dave, 141
Round Mountain Cooperative, 100
Rowan, Peter, 148
Royal Blueberries, 388, 424
Royal Blue Organics, 394
Royal Famille du Caniveaux, 243, 333, 335-346, 350, 366, 453-455, 476
Rush, Christine, 461, 463, 469
Rust, Jerry (Gerald), Lane County Commissioner, 115, 116, 202, 203, 291
Rutherford, Harold, Lane County Commissioner, 119-120

Sable, Rhonda, 338, 340, 344, 345, 454-455
Sage Advance, 489
Sahr, Jim, 348, 349, 421, 490
Sanders, John, 524

Index

Sandunga, 241
San Francisco Cabaret, 32
San Francisco Folk Music Club, 141-142, 145, 146
San Francisco Free Folk Music Festival, 142, 145
Saturday Market. *See* Eugene Saturday Market, Portland Saturday Market
Sauna at the fair. S*ee Ritz Sauna*
Sax, Norma, 14, 152, **300**, 300-301, 434, 470
   and Community Village, **290**, 290, 291, **296**, 296, 299-300, 514
   and *Fair Family News,* 422-423, 427-428, **428, 429**
Saylor, Ron, 13
Scaggs, Steve, **183**
Schadegg, Deni, 34, 81-82, **160**, 403, 418, 499-501
   Entertainment co-coordinator, 35, 49, 158, 516
   at Main Camp, 37-38, 158-159, 165, 397
   and New Old Time Chautauqua, 108, 110, 158
Schaefer, Margo, 421
Schlaadt, Richard, 316, 515
School of Acrobats and New Circus Arts (SANCA), 449
Schultz, Bob-O, 43, 45-46
Schwartz, Zak, **163, 242,** 262, 411, 423, 517
   and Crisis Intervention (aka Human Intervention aka HI) training, 163-164, 166, 241, 262, 322, 465, 467
Scott, Anna, 44, 96
Scott, Leslie, 13, 404, 430-440, 470
Scott, R. "Sparks," 348, 423
Scott, Tom, 42, 432-433, 435, 489
Scribe Tribe, 259
Scully, Nicki, 380
Second Decadenal Field Trip, 147-154. *See also* Grateful Dead, the
Security Crew, 74, 132, 149, 155, 159, 161, 174, 189, 197, 294, 303, 310, 327, 328, 367, 381, 401, 410, 418, 424, 437, 434, **435**, 437, 438, 459, 517
   alcohol- and drug-free event, 460, 464-465, 467
   and Bus Admissions, 483

Fair Thee Well, 483, 484, 487, 490, 491
   and the Navy at the fair, 305-312, **306, 312**
   and Oregon Event Enterprises, 165-166, 483
   and the Sweep, 23, 214, 271, 281, **304,** 303-306, 310, 333, 363-365, 407, 461, 484
   and VegManECs, 386-387, 388, 393, 400, 430
Sellers, Barbara (aka Varvara), 176, 180, 181, 185
Sewell, Dawn, 489
Sewell, Jennifer Shine, 489
Sewell, Ray "Chez Ray," **149**, 150, 153, 343, 364, 485, 489
Shady Grove Stage, 82, 240, **265**, 297, 316, 333, 418, 432
Sharpy, Frank, **204**, 323, 358, 360, 391, **411**, 418
   as board member, 159, 162, 235, 262, 323, 325, 348, 410-411
   as Fire Marshall, 159, 499, 516
   and grass at the fair, 326-327, 369-370, 389
Sharpy, Jamie, **204**
Sharpy, Jeanne, 325, 417-418, 420, 421, 522
   photo credits, 36, 44, 155, 204, 242, 265, 269, 273, 277, 326, 362, 367, 400, 401, 411, 435, 445
Sharpy, Jon, **204**
Sharpy, Michelle, 403
Sharpy Curve, 391
Shaw, Arna, **119,** 396, 402-405
   as fair general manager, 356-359, 368-369, 398-405, **399, 400,** 411-412, 415, 416, 417, 418, 419, 431, 435
Shaw, Bill, 339
Sheklow, Sally (aka Hayfield), 60-62, **61,** 64-71
Shenanigans booth, 122, 348, 490
Shepard, Debra, 516
Showers at the fair, 42-43, 133, 172, 180-181, 297, 410
Shuler, Mary. *See* Doyon, Mary
Shultz, Kirk, 386, 395, 399, 401-402, 522
Shumba, 265, 329, 366, 486
Sign Crew, 290, 304, 438
Significant Other passes, 13, 407, 408
Silver Falls State Park, 160

547

Silvermoon Jon, 132, 159, 162, 200, 235, 291, 294-295, **296,** 514, 517
Silvestri, Fred, 325, 517
Singer, Naomi, **278**
Single Men's Support Group, 60
Sink, Darrel, 410, 417, 419, 420, 520
Sinsemilla Tips, 464
Siporin, Alan, 169
Siskiyou Project, 298
Slade, Eric, 279
Slocum, Wally, 13, 75, **77,** 78, 159, 174, **204,** 239, 355, 422, 490, 523
  as board member, 159, 235, 417, 420
  photo credits, 41, 115, 157, 159, 239
Small, Sid, 524
Smirkwood campsite, 307, 311
Smith, Brenda, 185
Smith, Karen, 523
Smith, Warren, 316, 515
Snyder, Nancy "Elf," 517
solar energy, 39-45, 173, 333, 349, 432-433, 435, 489, 495. *See also* Energy Park.
Solar Energy Resources Group, 41, 42
Solutions booth, 388
Soulsations, 329, 333
Soy World (aka Turtle Island), 223
Spae, Thaddeus (aka Carl Spaeth aka Professor Tibbs), 49, 51-52, 444, 450, 524. *See also* Amber Tide
Spaeth, Carl. *See* Spae, Thaddeus
Speiss, Morgen, 281
Spirit booth in Community Village, 490
Spirit Tower in Community Village, 289
Spirit Tower on the Left Bank, 282
Spoken Word, 96, 470-471, 484
Springfield Creamery, 88, 165, 193, 252
  and the Grateful Dead's Second Decadenal Field Trip, 147-148, 152
  at the Oregon Country Fair, 36, 40, 42, 90, 135, 171, 276, 288, 487
Spring Fling, **329,** 330
Sprinsock, Betsy, 448-449
Sprinsock, Eben, 83, 447-449, 474, 524
Sprinsock, Sylvia, 474
Stage Left, 144, 442-455, 474, 475, 476, 477. *See also* Circus Stage
Stamp, John, 122, 198, 200-201, 203, 205, 208, 209, 489-490
Stamp site (archaeology site 35LA658), 205, 490, 508

Starflower, 60-71, 193, 285, 286, 287
"Starflower Natural Anthem," by Sally Sheklow aka Hayfield, 65
Star Trek: Voyager, 486
State Historic Preservation Office (SHPO), 205, 509
Steck, Oliver, 527
Stern, Barbara, 74, 262, 500
Stern, Indi (also Indi Stern-Hayworth), 13, 84, 371, 373, 374, 376, **376.** *See also* Radar Angels
  photo credit, 375, 378
Stewart, Dick, **290,** 427, *photo credit, 428,* 517
Stingle, Karen, 228-229, 230
Stoppiello, Anthony, 42, 43, 45, 495
Stoppiello, Victoria, 495
Strangers with Candy, 151
Strawberry Lane, 212, 398
Strickland, Andy, 402
Stuart, Laura Warden, 325, 359, *photo credit, 470,* 471, 484
Students for a Democratic Society, 89
Suave, Rico, 383
Succubus (aka the Scarlett Succubus), 81, 99, 492
Summer of Love, 15, 338, 342
Sundquist, John, 418, 420, 421
Sundquist, Marsha, 420
Sunergi, 41-42, 497
Sunny Valley, Oregon, 88
Surata Soyfoods, 473
Sussman, Kaz, 512
Sutherland, Cathy, 336-338, 339, 340, 341, 344-345, 346. *See also* Daring Deviante Sisters, Royal Famille Du Caniveaux, Moisture Festival
Sutherland, Chloe, 345
Sutherland, Craig, 345
Sutherland, Henry, 345
Sutherland, Jennifer. *See* Potter, Jennifer Sutherland
Sweep, the. *See* Security Crew
Sweet Creek Foods, 194
Sweet, Dory, 230
Sweeten, Anita, 88-96
Sweetgrass, 83
Swing Shift, 173
Switchboard, 16, 60

T

Tabora, Lito, 527
Tadda, Don, 517
Takilma, Oregon, 88, 283, 298
Tarver, "Planet" Janet, 13, 291, **296**, 301, 490, 514
Tarver, Steve, 490
Tattoo, 151
Taylor, Jennifern, 377
Teddy Bears' Picnic (fair volunteer event), 174, 311-312, 329, **390, 399,** 399, 417, 490
"Teddy Bears' Picnic, The," (song), 151, 216, 266, 445
Teen Crew, 134, 288, 357-358, 421. *See also* Youth Job Services
Terrarium, 387-388
Theios, Joyce, 40-41, 495
Thomas, Rhys, 173, 218, 287
Thompson, Ann, 176
Thompson, "Sir" Kenneth, 308, **312**
Thompson, Robert, 155, 159, 165, 166, 235, 294, 327
  photo credits, 171, 189, 267
Thornbury, James, 250
Throbbing Gems, The, 336
Ti, David, 181, 272-275, 277, 278, 284
Tilth, 266, 351, 388
Tiranoff, Michael (aka Toes), 25, 49, 78, 105, 366
Toby's Family Foods, 250
Toby's Tofu Palace, 144, 245-252, **248, 251,** 288. *See also* Alves, Toby
Todd, Dennis, **133,** 358, 360, 369, 370, 399, 401-402, 412-413, 414-415, 417-418
Toes Tiranoff. *See* Tiranoff, Michael (aka Toes)
Tofu Palace Products, 250
Togawa, Paula, 341
Toilets at the fair, 38, 40, 164, 240, 297, 370, 397
Tooinsky, Izzy, 218, 331
Toymil, Rich, 291
Traffic Camp, 174
Traffic Crew, 149, 261, 360-361, 381, 410, 418, 421, 422, 432, 460
  coordinators, 75, 137, 150, 152, 159, 161, 174, 391, 408, 491, 499, 517
Traffic Equestrian Crew (aka Traffic Horse Crew) 269, 274
Tree Crew, 122, 490
Tremayne, Charlene, 375, 514, 520
Trickle Down Reforestation, 324
Trillian Green, 218
Troll de Bogen, 280
Troll de Mor, 280
Troupe Rhajjahan, 185
Turner, David, 510

U

Ulrich, Robin. *See* Kinkley, Robin Richardson Ulrich)
Ulrich, Ron, 16, 18
unicorn, **80,** 80-81, 82, 84, 86-87, 100, 105, 109, 111-113
U.S. Department of Health, Education, and Welfare, 317
U.S. Environmental Protection Agency, 440
Unity School, 351
University of Oregon, 16, 64, 122, 123, 124-125, 150, 166, 289, 291, 318, 364, 371, 380, 394, 433, 481
  Committee for Protection of Human Subjects, 314
  Department of Geography, 205
  Drug Information Center, 313-321, 516
  and Fair Thee Well, 486, 487, 488, 490
  Landscape Architecture Department, 440
  Law Library, 490
  Museum of Natural & Cultural History, 204, 205, 508
  School of Law, 114-115, 292-293
  School of Music, 250
Unstuck in Time, 473, 474
Up for Grabs, 218
Urban, Mel, 516

V

Vaden, Paula Jo, 66-70, **67**
Vancouver Folk Festival, 105, 110, 112-113, 179
Vaudeville. *See* New Vaudeville

Vaudeville Crew. *See* Entertainment Crew
VegManECs, 297, 385-387, 389, 392-393, 400, 413, 415, 423, 430, 434
  Fair Thee Well, 483, 484, 492
Veneta City Council, 434, 436, 439,
Veneta, Oregon, 11, 21, 149, 188, 191, 193, 226, 284, 289, 339, 349, 473
  and fair neighbors, 12, 120, 357, 405, 434, 436-437, 439-440, 441, 461, 462-463, 469
  and Highway 126 reroute, 198-199, 205, 206, 360
Veneta Skate Park, 436
Venezia, Bob, 264, 331-332
  and Laughing Moon Theater, 57, 263, 266, 331, 337, 366
Verner, Bill, 393, 400, 425, 430, 434
Vietnam War, 16, 54, 73, 125, 320, 338, 350, 484, 490
Village Restaurant, 82, 223-224, 230, **231**
Village Vision newsletter, 285, 299-300, 366
Village Yurt, 232, 291
Vils-Small, Paloma, **331**
Vils, Tove, 324, 331
Vitasek, Barbara, 514
Vortex I, 18-20

W

Wadsworth, Lois, 371
Wagner, Mary, **149,** 150, 159, 199, 235, 248, 262, 292, 415, 416-417, 516, 517
Walker, Paul (aka Ensign Paul), 309-310, **312**
Walker, Rainbow, 370
Wally's Way, 487
Walton, Keith, 192
Warden, Crow, 325, 359
Warden, Laura. *See* Stuart, Laura Warden
Ware Barn, 378, 381
Ware, Malcolm, **133**
Warren, Barbara J., 491
Warren, Mark, 527
Water Crew, 37, 150, 159, 352-353, 359-360, 369-370, 401, 421, 492, 517
Watershed Enhancement Board, 440
Wavy Gravy, 244, 303

W.C. Fields (Memorial) Stage, **36,** 38, 402, 443
Weihl, Heather, 444, 449-452, 453, 454, 475, *photo credit, 475,* 527
Weinman, Richie, 404
Weinstein, Archie, 114, 119-120
Welsh, Jim, state representative, 461, 463
Wemple, Betsy. *See* Hartzell, Betsy Vaughn Wemple
Wemple, Edd, 149, 491
Wemple, Noah, 491
Wendel, Peggy (aka Spike Wilder aka Carmina Burana), 49, 57
Wenk, Tom, 517, 520
West End Co-op, 191
Western Aerial Contractors, 120
West Lane News, 462, 469
Westphal, Jerry, 514
Westwind Travelin' Vaudeville, 34-35, 57-58, 59
White Bird Clinic (Sociomedical Aid Station), 16, 81, 110, 150, 152, 163, 299, 313, 314
  Crisis Intervention Training (aka Human Intervention aka HI Training), 163, 241, 262, 465
  and electricity controversy at fair, 349, 410-411
  at fair, 73, 159, 161, 163-164, 172, 189, 239, 262, 322, 328, 423, 468, 517
Whiteaker neighborhood in Eugene, 63, 247, 249, 488, 489
Wieselman, Doug, 445-446, 450, 527
Wilcoxon, CiCi (aka CiCi Dawn, aka Dusty Rhodes), 145, 485, 523
Wilder, Spike. *See* Wendel, Peggy
Wildlife Safari, 78-80, 84, 85
Willamette People's Co-op, 62
Willamette Valley, 201, 205-207, 209-210
Willamette Valley Observer, 80, 324, 325, 372
Willamette Valley Solar Energy Association, 39, 41, 42, 435
Williams, Alice, 225, 233
Williams, Andrea, 527
Williams, Harold, 21
Williams, Joshua, 491
Williams, Jules, 225, 233
Williams, Karl, 145
Williams, Kate, 225, 228, 233

Williams, Robin, 54, 350
Williams, Sam (aka Samwise aka Smerdyakov Karamazov), 49, 56, 109, 151, 337, 367, **447**, 454, 491, 527. *See also* Flying Karamazov Brothers, Laughing Moon Theater
Williams, Zachary, 491
Wind Arts Kites, 492
Winfree-Andrews, Robin
Winship, Shelley, 527
Winslow, John, 386, 388, **399**, 399, 415-416, 492, 516
  as fair caretaker, 348, **348**, 354, 355, 369, 389, **401**, 411, 412-413
Winslow, Seth, 492
Wintergreen Farm, 192
Wise, Adrienne, 479, **481**
Wise, Marge, 266, 276, 476, 479, 508
Wisnovsky, Steve, 421, 470
Wolden, Anna, 359
Wolden, Tim, 352-353, 359, 360, 369-370, **370**, *photo credit*, 370
Wolf Creek, 173
Women's Action for Nuclear Disarmament, 293
Women's Grounding Circle, 133, 172, 230, 243, 333, 366. *See also* Community Village
women's movement, 33, 60-71, 114-115, 228-229, 286, 288, 373, 384
WomenSpace, 299
Wooden Nickel, the, 113
Wood, Chris, 125
Wood, Roger, **376**
Woodstock, 30, 177, 418
Wooten, Bill Wooten, 20, 39, 72, 74, 116, 157, 246, 471, 492
  and the fair, 11, 22, 23, 24, 25, 40, 49, 75, 117, 261
  and the fair's twentieth anniversary, 361-363, **363**
  Memorial Endowment, 436, 471, 491
Wooten, Cynthia "Cindy" Ernst (later Cohen), 20-21, 25, 75, 114, 115, 116, 121, 157, 166, 246, 402, 408, 436, 471, 492
  and the fair, 11, 22, 23, 24, 49, 261
  and the fair's twentieth anniversary, 361-363, **363**
Wooten, Eileen, 361, 492

WOW Hall, 23, 181, 190, 235, 241, 330, 373, 384. *See also* Community Center for the Performing Arts)
Wright, Moz, 29, 33, 81, 105, 239, **239,** 330, 327-328, 499-501, 512
  as board member, 159, 201, 235-237, 262, 330, 408, 418-419, 498-500
  Entertainment coordinator, 49, 80, 82, 138, 158, 159, 175-176, 275, 365, 377, 499, 516
  and Westwind Travelin' Vaudeville, 34-35, 57
WYMPROV!, 71

Xavanadu, 471

Yanok, Ulee, 369
Yarrow, Peter, **470,** 471
Yazzolino, Brad, *photo credit*, 38
Youth Craft booth, 472
Youth Job Services, 134, 288, 357, 517
Youth Stage, 36, 381, 443, 472

Zell–Ravenheart, Morning Glory (aka Diana Moore), **80,** 80-81, 82, 84, 86-87, 99-100, 492
  and Old Time New Age Chautauqua, 102, 105, 106, 109, 113
Zell, Oberon (aka Tim aka Otter), 80, **80,** 84, 86-87, 99, 492
  and Old Time New Age Chautauqua, 102, 105, 106-107, 109, 113
Zenger, John Peter, 32
Zoo Zoo's restaurant collective, 82, 223, 230, 513
Zulu Spear, 333
Zumwalt Park Campground, 437-439, 440, 484

www.ingramcontent.com/pod-product-compliance
Lightning Source LLC
Chambersburg PA
CBHW052051110526
44591CB00013B/2170